ISLAM INSTRUMENTALIZED

Religion and Politics in Historical Perspective

Does Islam bear some responsibility for a lack of development in the countries in which it dominates?

In this book, economist Jean-Philippe Platteau challenges several specific claims seeking to connect Islam with a lack of development. Through a nuanced analysis, he disputes the widespread view that the doctrine of Islam is fundamentally reactionary, defending tradition against modernity and individual freedom, and the related view that Islam is an obstacle to modern development because of a fusion between the spiritual and political domains. At the same time, his analysis identifies how Islam's decentralized organization, in the context of autocratic regimes, may cause political instability and postpone reforms. Ultimately, he emphasizes how secular authoritarian leaders in Muslim countries have tended to instrumentalize religion at the cost of widespread corruption and regressive measures, creating an unfortunate association between secularism and self-serving cynicism.

Jean-Philippe Platteau is Emeritus Professor of Economics at the University of Namur, in Belgium. He has devoted his research career to studying the role of institutions in economic development and the processes of institutional change. He is the author of several books, including (with R. Peccoud) *Culture, Institutions, and Development: New Insights into an Old Debate* (2011), *Institutions, Social Norms, and Economic Development* (2000), and (with J. M. Baland) *Halting Degradation of Natural Resources: Is There a Role for Rural Communities?* (1996).

CAMBRIDGE STUDIES IN ECONOMICS, CHOICE, AND SOCIETY

Founding Editors

Timur Kuran, *Duke University*
Peter J. Boettke, *George Mason University*

This interdisciplinary series promotes original theoretical and empirical research as well as integrative syntheses involving links between individual choice, institutions, and social outcomes. Contributions are welcome from across the social sciences, particularly in the areas where economic analysis is joined with other disciplines, such as comparative political economy, new institutional economics, and behavioral economics.

Books in the Series:

Islam Instrumentalized

Religion and Politics in Historical Perspective

JEAN-PHILIPPE PLATTEAU

University of Namur, Belgium

CAMBRIDGE
UNIVERSITY PRESS

One Liberty Plaza, 20th Floor, New York, NY 10006, USA

Cambridge University Press is part of the University of Cambridge.

It furthers the University's mission by disseminating knowledge in the pursuit of
education, learning, and research at the highest international levels of excellence.

www.cambridge.org
Information on this title: www.cambridge.org/9781316609002
DOI: 10.1017/9781316658727

© Jean-Philippe Platteau 2017

First published 2017

Printed in the United States of America by Sheridan Books, Inc.

A catalogue record for this publication is available from the British Library

Library of Congress Cataloging-in-Publication Data
Names: Platteau, J. P. (Jean-Philippe), 1947– author.
Title: Islam instrumentalized : religion and politics in historical
perspective / Jean-Philippe Platteau, Universite de Namur, Belgium.
Description: New York, NY : Cambridge University Press, 2018. |
Includes bibliographical references and index.
Identifiers: LCCN 2017003165 | ISBN 9781107155442 (hardback : alk. paper) |
ISBN 9781316609002 (paperback : alk. paper)
Subjects: LCSH: Islamic countries – Economic conditions. | Islam – Economic
aspects – Developing countries. | Religion and politics – Islamic countries. |
Economic development – Religious aspects – Islam. | Economic
development – Islamic countries.
Classification: LCC HC499.P53   2018 | DDC 320.917/67 – dc23
LC record available at https://lccn.loc.gov/2017003165

ISBN 978-1-107-15544-2 Hardback
ISBN 978-1-316-60900-2 Paperback

To Nicole Moguilevsky, for her patience and intellectual curiosity

Contents

vii

Preface

This book has a long history. It started about twelve years ago when I was teaching a course on the Institutional Foundations of the Market for students of the economics master's degree at the University of Namur. One of my lectures was devoted to a discussion of the role of religion in development, and the starting point was, of course, the work of Max Weber on Protestantism. I then discovered the book *What Went Wrong* (2002) by Bernard Lewis, which provided me with a direct application of Weber's analysis: Unlike Protestantism whose doctrine is conducive to growth, Islam is antagonistic to modernity because it is intrinsically unable to separate religion from politics. Here was therefore a neat thesis, enunciated by an historian, which might not fail to appeal to economists who are used to thinking in terms of elegant models articulated around a well-delineated argument. However, as I expounded Lewis's thesis to my students, I felt increasing unease with its underlying argument. I then began to reflect on the reasons behind my doubts by taking account of major works addressing the relationship between state and religion in the history of Islam, both historical studies and studies dealing with contemporaneous regimes.

As my lecture on religion and development evolved, I wrote two journal articles where I formulated my thinking (Platteau, 2008, 2011). This gave me a first opportunity to receive detailed written reactions to my critique of Lewis's Huntingtonian thesis. At about the same time, I also had several opportunities to present my ideas in Belgium and in Arab countries in front of audiences that included Arab intellectuals and scholars. It was during a conference held in Cairo in 2008 that I made the decision to embark on a book venture following the explicit advice of James Robinson, who attended the event. This decision was reinforced by the strong encouragement I received from Arab intellectuals who found my central argument convincing: Bad politics and the instrumentalization of Islam by cynical autocrats are responsible for the problems confronted by their countries, rather than Islam per se.

I then looked at my 2008 journal article, dividing arguments amounting to three to four pages each into several future chapters. All of my subsequent work consisted of the elaboration of these chapters and the addition of new ones that appeared essential to completing the argument.

The question remains as to why another book on Islam is needed considering the flurry of such books during the last decades. Of course, the subject is immensely topical given the threatening rise of Islamist movements and their insertion in the heart of advanced European countries. But is an abundance of books really helping improve our understanding of the predicament of Muslim countries? And in which sense can I argue that the present book makes an original contribution that justifies all the efforts put into it?

A combination of five characteristics makes this book unique among the numerous scholarly studies available. Although the book shares certain elements with a number of other studies, no single book uses a similar perspective based on all five traits. Let me now identify each of the five key characteristics.

First, my book looks at Islam from a particular angle: the relationship between religion and politics. This approach logically follows from the puzzle that motivated my query: Is there indeed a fusion between these two domains in the case of Islam? And, more generally, is there a specific sort of relationship between Islam and politics that creates an obstacle to development and modernity? One of the great merits of Lewis's aforementioned book is precisely that it highlights the critical importance of politics. On this score, I entirely agree with him. Indeed, my investigations drove me to the conclusion that it is misleading to consider the role of Islam while ignoring the way it is positioned vis-à-vis political rulers, autocrats in particular. However, I simultaneously raise serious doubts about views that attribute the problems of Muslim countries to a clash of civilizations. There is actually scant empirical ground for arguing that Islam and politics are or have always been merged.

Second, the book adopts a comparative perspective in the sense that it makes repeated references to other religions. Since Lewis draws a contrast between Islam and Christianity, it was just natural to check whether and in which sense religion and politics are, in fact, separated in Christianity. In addition, given the importance of radical puritanical movements in Islam today and their considerable impact on international politics through the actions of al-Qaeda and ISIS, it is almost unavoidable to wonder whether these movements are a specific feature of Islam. My foray into the worlds not only of Christianity (Chapter 2) but also of Hinduism, Buddhism, and Sikhism (Chapter 8) results in a negative answer to that question.

Third, the book delves deeply into the history of Islam (and that of Christianity). Because Lewis identifies the problem of Islam as linked to an intrinsic feature that can be traced to its very foundation, this inquiry must also go all the way back to that remote period. What I propose is therefore an ambitious perspective that covers the whole history of Islam. The contemporaneous relationship between Islam and politics in a large number of Muslim countries (from the postindependence period to the present) receives a lot of attention, particularly in Chapters 6 and 9. Yet this analysis appears at the end of an historical investigation intended to place events in a long-term perspective.

Fourth, the book is grounded in a theoretical framework drawn from economics, which has helped me structure the central argument running through the book. That is why its setup and essential intuitions and results are explicitly discussed (in Chapter 4) in a language accessible to all social scientists. This framework clearly belongs to the field of political economics in the sense that it models the behavior of the state (an autocratic power). Since my interest lies in the relationship between state and religion, the behavior of the religious clerics is also featured.

Fifth, the approach of the book is decidedly multidisciplinary. Although inspired by an economics framework, it draws upon a considerable number of works written not only by economists but also by historians, political scientists, sociologists, and anthropologists. The real challenge that I confronted was precisely how to make diverse but relevant studies intelligible within a coherent framework that could be easily grasped by a wide audience of scholars and intellectuals.

By now, it should be clear that the book is the outcome of a social science research endeavor aimed at drawing a "big picture" of the interaction between religion and politics in the specific case of Islam. It took me a lot of time to write, not only because of the abundant material to cover but also because I wanted to have a clear theoretical structure to support the entire argument and to link complex facts together. I believe that my book is very useful in understanding present-day events because it places them in a long-term and comparative perspective. The advantage of such a perspective is that it compels us to take enough distance from the immediate shocks that atrocities committed by fanatics necessarily cause (I am writing this preface just a few days after the killings committed at the national airport and a metro station in Brussels on March 23, 2016) to enable comprehension of their full meaning and of the context in which they take place.

It is my great pleasure to acknowledge the intellectual support of many people from my own profession and from other disciplines. First and foremost, I wish to express my strong gratitude to four persons who played an important role at critical junctures in the elaboration of this book. By chronological order and, as it happens, reverse alphabetic order, these persons are Karim Zouaoui, James Robinson, Timur Kuran, and Emmanuelle Auriol.

Karim Zouaoui, a biophysicist from the Free University of Brussels, has engaged repeatedly with me, from the very beginning of my enterprise, in deep discussions about the problems of Islam. These discussions were a big stimulus to the thoughts germinating in my mind even before I decided to write on the subject. James Robinson, now at the University of Chicago, motivated me to upgrade my articles into a full-fledged book, as I mentioned earlier. Timur Kuran, now at Duke University, knew quite well the work I did on issues of institutions and development before I became interested in the study of Islam. I am quite thankful to him for having continuously prompted me to work in this new field in which he is an internationally reputed expert. In addition, his advice, remarks, and suggestions as my book took shape were always of very high value to me. I am also immensely indebted to him for having read and edited line by line the final version of the manuscript. In this way, I was able to benefit greatly from his long experience and professional skills in writing books. I took the time he spent to help me improve the book as a measure of his interest in the topic, and so I felt strongly encouraged to deliver a well-polished book. Lastly, Emmanuelle Auriol, from the Toulouse School of Economics, came late but at a decisive stage of the book's finalization. I was then trying to work out a coherent and pertinent theoretical framework to buttress its central argument. My sustained and repeated discussions with her, as well as our joint work on a coauthored paper (in press), proved essential to a central question of the book, namely the differences between centralized and decentralized religions.

Next, I have benefited from many thoughtful comments and suggestions made in a long series of seminars, workshops, conferences, and roundtables organised for the specific purpose of discussing this book's manuscript. The roundtables took place at the Toulouse School of Economics (2015) and the University of Torino (2016); the other events spanned a ten-year period (2006–16) and were held at Namur (twice), Barcelona, Cairo, Kuwait City, Beyruth, Brussels, Stanford, Firenze, Oxford, Torino, Moscow, and Saint Petersburg. Among the people to whom I want to express special thanks are

Jean-Paul Azam, Jean-Marie Baland, Inayatullah Baloch, Abhijit Banerjee, Pranab Bardhan, Lisa Blaydes, François Bourguignon, John Bowen, Samuel Bowles, Guilhem Cassan, Michael Castanera, Imane Chaara, Eric Chaney, Denis Cogneau, Pierluigi Conzo, Roberta Di Peri, Joan Esteban, Ahmed Galal, Günes Gökmen, Avner Greif, Saumitra Jha, Mark Koyama, Samir Makdidi, Matteo Migheli, Rinchan Mirza, Dilip Mookherjee, Tom Murphy, Mustapha Nabli, Hillel Rapoport, Debraj Ray, Roberta Ricucci, Mohammed Saleh, Paul Seabright, Rohini Somanathan, Alessandra Venturini, Thierry Verdier, and Shlomo Weber.

Introduction

1.1 The Rising Interest in Religion

To the surprise of many, religion and its role in society have recently resurfaced as major issues to be investigated by social sciences. To be fair, many social scientists have always been skeptical about the pertinence of the modernization theory, according to which the role of religion should gradually vanish as development proceeds and material levels of living are elevated (Yousfi, 2011). Two pieces of evidence justify such skepticism. First, there is the puzzling fact of religious persistence and even resurgence in highly developed countries. In the United States, in particular, religious resurgence takes on the form of born-again Christianity and charismatic sects. Second, religious movements remain vital in many developing countries, as reflected, for example, in the explosion of African-born churches in sub-Saharan Africa, the spread of Protestant sects in Central and Latin America, the revival of Islam, the increasing assertiveness of Hinduism and Buddhism in Asia, and the growing adherence to the Christian Orthodox religion in Russia. Skepticism about the validity of the modernization theory of secularization has been aptly expressed by Sudhir Kakar (1996), who questions the belief in the primacy of political and economic structures in the shaping of consciousness. According to him, cultural traditions transmitted through the family, which include religion, "can and do have a line of development separate from the political and economic systems of a society" (p. 196).

Economists have for a long time paid attention to religion, and its role was already a central concern for classical political economists writing at the end of the eighteenth and the beginning of the nineteenth century – Adam Smith, Thomas-Robert Malthus, and John Stuart Mill, in particular. Recent economic research on religion, however, has tended to focus on two distinct questions. On the one hand, we find attempts to analyze religion as a market phenomenon, with churches competing to attract adherents and satisfy demands for spirituality, mutual support and insurance, trust-based transactions, and other services. Using the industrial organization approach, this analysis treats the content (as well as the number) of religious denominations as an endogenous instrument in this competition.[1] Empirical works along this line are largely based on U.S. data (for recent reviews, see Aldashev and Platteau, 2013; Iyer, 2016). On the other hand, economists have pursued the task of assessing quantitatively the manner in which particular religions affect long-run economic growth performance or have tried to uncover correlations between religion and economic prosperity. They have done so by adding religious measures to other determinants in conventional cross-country regression frameworks. The underlying assumption is that particular religious affiliations have stable characteristics that influence economic behavior. In this sense, this assumption echoes the thesis of the "clash of civilizations" that claims that certain religions possess more or less fixed attributes that make them more suitable for modern social, economic, and political development (Huntington, 1993). The clash is especially fractious between Islam and Christianity, whose mutual relationships are alleged to have always been "deeply conflictual" (Huntington, 1996, p. 209).

This view aligns with the work of Max Weber, who stressed the pro-growth and pro-accumulation virtues of the ethics of Protestantism. Of late, increasingly visible social tensions and political instability, as well as retrograde social and cultural movements in the Muslim world, have prompted certain scholars to tread the same route by privileging religious explanations of development. They point to the inherent difficulties that Islam raises when meeting the challenges of modernity, understood as a set of achievements including not only economic growth but also an enlarged space for personal freedoms and broad human rights, as well as increased opportunities for self-expression inside large collectivities. Some of these scholars have been highly influential, as attested by the role of Bernard Lewis as special adviser for Middle Eastern affairs to U.S. president George W. Bush. Lewis went as far as saying that Islam and democracy are antithetical and that this incompatibility can be traced to Islam's very foundational act. Because Islam was born inside a body politic rather than in opposition to it – in stark contrast to Christianity – separation between state and religion never occurred in Muslim lands (Lewis, 1993, 2002). The logical implication is that these lands would have to abandon Islam to be able to start evolving

---

[1] Since the early 1990s, rational-choice sociologists have followed the same route.

toward democracy and modernity (for an extremely pessimistic and negative view of the Muslim faith, see Harris, 2004).

Along with this growing emphasis on the barriers that Islam allegedly puts up against modern development, there has been a recent surge of literature extolling the virtues of Christianity for its support of modernization. In this literature, essentially of North American origin, the Catholic Church is often depicted as the vanguard of modernity. This theme is epitomized by the titles of some of the books written by Rodney Stark, one of the most well-known American sociologists of religion: *The Victory of Reason: How Christianity Led to Freedom, Capitalism, and Western Success* (2005) and *For the Glory of God: How Monotheism Led to Reformations, Science, Witch-Hunts, and the End of Slavery* (2003). *How the Catholic Church Built Western Civilisation*, by Thomas Woods (2005), and *The Evolution of the West: How Christianity Has Shaped our Values*, by Nick Spencer (2016), are in the same vein.

This book takes religious explanations seriously, and its central objective is to assess their relevance in the specific case of Islam. To what extent and in what sense can Islam, the religion of Muslims, be considered responsible for the problems encountered by the countries in which it dominates? Foremost among such problems are a high level of political instability and the postponement or reversal of social reforms conducive to long-term development. Political instability results from the lack of legitimacy of the prevailing (autocratic) regimes and the inability to eject incumbents peacefully.[2] Postponed reforms include changes to the family code, measures to improve women's status, modernization of school curricula, and measures to minimize rote learning of religious and other texts. The resulting social costs are significant: The comparatively low educational attainment and workforce participation rates of women in the in Muslim countries – the Middle East and North Africa (MENA) region has the lowest women's participation rate in the world – are very costly in terms of growth opportunities foregone (Norton and Tomal, 2009; World Bank, 2008). The same can be said of the high total and youth unemployment rates that exceed those oberved in other regions of the world. Especially worrying is the fact that in some countries like Egypt, unemployment rates are highest among university graduates. The inadequacy of educational systems seems to be at least partially responsible for this predicament: It is striking that higher levels of education in

---

[2] Since 1991, not one incumbent has been ejected at the ballot box in Arab countries. By contrast, at least thirty-six incumbents have lost power in sub-Saharan Africa (*Economist*, 20–26 August 2016, p. 27).

Muslim countries do not breed greater openness or more critical thinking. Governments and religious authorities use schooling as a form of indoctrination to perpetuate ideas of obedience and, often, misunderstanding or even hatred of other faiths and sects (*Economist*, August 6–12, 2016a, p. 18). Policies that lower competition and create an uneven playing field constrain private sector job creation. Access to jobs and to government licenses and subsidies typically depends on possessing the right connections ("wasta") within a deeply authoritarian and clan-based political system (Schiffbauer et al., 2015).

This book attempts to explain the simultaneous presence in many Muslim countries of political instability and lack of progressive social reforms in the context of kleptocratic and clan-based autocracies. It rests on two propositions. First, I disagree with the essentialist view according to which Islam is a major obstacle to modern development because it has always been associated with a merging of religion and the state or a fusion between the spiritual and political spheres of life. Second, I hold that Islam possesses a special feature: a highly decentralized structure. This characteristic tends to make politics comparatively unstable, even though rulers can mitigate instability at the cost of a reduced pace of institutional reforms or backpedaling on them.

In the next section, I elaborate on these two assumptions by summarizing the narrative that underpins this book's main line of argument. The narrative contains stylized facts and insights derived from the history of Islam, as well as propositions derived from a formal theory that is only sketched here. As will become evident, far from offering a monocausal explanation, I put forward a complex argument that is articulated around a central idea – the key role of autocratic politics – but at the same time allows for the influence of several important forces, including international factors.

1.2 The Central Storyline of the Book

This narrative starts with the idea that only in the times of the Prophet were religion and politics truly merged in the history of Islam. After the death of Muhammad, violent confrontations between different power-seeking factions became the order of the day, and each faction claimed legitimacy for its own version of inheritance from him. Politics thus took precedence over religion, and military men often occupied the commanding positions, whether at the center or behind the stage. The implication is that Islam is separable from politics, and religious clerics must therefore be conceptualized as actors separate from the state who must decide how to relate to it. The vision of present-day Salafists according to which the primeval caliphates of the Umayyads and the Abbasids were entirely guided by the principles of Islam is just a myth that resembles the glorified origins of nations imagined by ultranationalist movements. Both types of movements, Islamist and ultranationalist, follow the same objectives: (1) to escape the hard and painful reality of underachievement in a globalizing world where international comparisons are unavoidable and foreign influences pervasive and (2) to alleviate deep anxieties about the destiny and even survival of the cultures of the periphery that such comparisons arouse. True, some measure of self-esteem based on strong (national) ideologies is required to construct the economic and technological capacities required for modern development. However, when romantic views of past grandeur are mobilized not to project a country or a region into the future but to vindicate a return to earlier institutions and policies, they become dangerous and self-defeating.

Not only has autocracy persisted as the dominant political system in Muslim countries since the times of the Umayyads and the Abbasids but also the submission of the clerics to the autocrat quickly became a general rule of conduct. Not infrequently, it amounted to slavish obedience. This characterization also holds true in the numerous instances where Islam was used as a catalyst for national unification and as a banner waved to legitimize actions aimed at controlling rebellious territories or bringing together a fragmented political space. The idea that religion is the handmaiden of politics and that religious clerics are expected to cooperate with absolute monarchs in a subordinate position has been justified in principle, despite the professed aim of Islam to establish a righteous world order and provide guarantees against despotic rule. In this general situation, the autocrat succeeds in wielding complete control over the religious clerics, and the political regime is therefore rather stable. I characterize such a state in which the sovereign runs the territory without being contested by these clerics as the archetypal politico-religious equilibrium in which the autocratic ruler chooses an *opposition suppression strategy*. The alternative equilibrium is obtained when the ruler chooses the *opposition confrontation strategy* in which only a fraction of the religious clerics are brought into submission. A possible outcome of this second equilibrium strategy is that the popular anger mobilized by rebelling clerics leads to an upheaval that shakes up the ruling regime. Religious figures suddenly come to the forefront of politics, and the relationship between politics and religion is inverted. The political crisis then arises as the endogenous outcome of the autocrat's bad policies or his inability to confront adverse external circumstances, foreign aggression in particular. To better understand how the autocratic ruler may choose to have partial rather than complete (or near-complete) control over the clerical body, it is important to realize that the tradeoff between political stability and the autocrat's ability to pursue his own selfish interests is critically influenced by the behavior of the clerics.

Religious clerics have two special features that distinguish them from other elites: (1) They hold values regarding social justice and human rights or proper behavior that they draw from their religion, and (2) as representatives of the supernatural world and as wise men possessing deep knowledge (theological and philosophical, in particular), they have a natural prestige and influence on the population. Because of these two traits, the clerics are susceptible to playing a role as political actors or social leaders, especially in traditional societies where most people are uneducated and believe strongly in the role of supernatural forces. At the same time, however, the clerics are vulnerable to corruption, meaning that they can be "bought off" – seduced or corrupted – by the autocrat. The price of their submission increases with the distance between their values and the policies or practices of the autocrat.

Given that the preferences of the clerics are heterogeneous (they attach different weights to the values inspired by their religion than to income), the autocrat chooses the proportion of clerics whom he wants to co-opt. This he does with the knowledge that those left out may become opposition leaders, thereby representing a threat to the stability of his autocratic rule. Obviously, co-option of clerics constitutes only one arm of the autocrat's strategy. The other arm consists of the policies followed: Policies that have strong disequalizing effects and involve a great measure of elite corruption or those that hurt religious values or interests tend to arouse more opposition from the clerical body, for given levels of perquisites received from the autocrat. When choosing both the kinds of policies and the extent of co-option of religious clerics, the autocrat pursues his own interest, which is conceptualized as the expected income earned, implying that he pays attention to his income and his political survival probability. Both variables are influenced by the extent of religious co-option, the former because co-option involves costs that must be subtracted from the gross income of the autocrat (and his clique), and the latter because more extensive co-option reduces the risk of popular rebellion.

The co-option strategy may create a divide in the religious body. On one side are the official clerics, who are co-opted by the autocrat, and on the other side are the clerics who stand outside the ambit of the state and are therefore more independent. They either belong to independent institutions run by the ulama themselves, or they are self-appointed clerics and firebrands who act outside any kind of organization. Clerics of the latter type are particularly radical socially, and they are especially able to organize popular rebellions. Such a division is possible in the world of Islam, because no hierarchy exerts authority over the whole clerical profession. Because no church establishment exists, the clerics operate in a decentralized way, pronouncing their own fatwas as they deem fit. Fatwas issued by official clerics can thus be followed by counter-fatwas issued by one or several self-appointed clerics. The situation is highly unstable, especially when self-appointed clerics head well-structured and longstanding Islamist organizations.

The archetypal politico-religious equilibrium, or the dominant system of politico-religious interactions, is brought about when the autocrat's strategic choices consist of extensive co-option of religious clerics combined with moderately popular policies. An unstable autocracy prevails when the opposite choices are made: The autocrat follows policies that blatantly favor his inner circle and the surrounding elite, surrender national sovereignty to external powers, and/or antagonize traditional values cherished by religious representatives. If the bad scenario materializes – that is, if an open rebellion occurs that succeeds in overthrowing the autocrat or in severely limiting his ruling capacity – a crisis situation arises. Rebellious clerics then successfully enter the political stage to protect the common people or rescue the nation. Under these circumstances, socioeconomic and cultural grievances tend to be expressed in the language familiar to most people – a religious idiom depicting a fateful struggle between the forces of good and the forces of evil and promising to bring justice to the oppressed.

Antagonizing traditional values and reforming traditional institutions upheld by the religious elite may generate political instability in the same manner as inequitable policies. Nonetheless, pervasive corruption, cynicism, aloofness, and callous indifference of the elite around the autocrat seem to be far more damaging to political stability than progressive institutional changes ushered in by an honest, equitable, and dedicated ruler. It is when the former situation occurs that religious clerics appear to be more prone to rebellion or their opposition drive is more likely to resonate among the masses. As a matter of fact, religious dignitaries can exchange their positions in traditional religious institutions for positions in new state structures, whereas self-appointed clerics do not care much about the way the ruler treats institutions of the "high Islam," insofar as they are excluded or have excluded themselves from these. It is moreover evident that the most unstable political situation is created when the autocrat simultaneously pursues reforms antagonistic to tradition and socially unjust policies. In contrast, when the reformist autocrat is wise enough to adopt inclusive growth policies to accompany institutional change, and to introduce such change in a manner that does not openly confront the "low Islam" of the uneducated masses, he can be said to be "enlightened." This implies that he achieves the best compromise between political stability and long-term development of the country.

The situation most often observed in many Muslim countries since World War II is best depicted as unstable autocracy. It is characterized by the combination of socially inequitable policies and pervasive elite corruption with partial co-option of the religious elite, resulting in a division between official and nonofficial clerics eager to preserve their privileges and to forestall equalizing policies and corruption-preventing and democratizing reforms. In this situation Muslim autocrats mobilize Islam to buttress their legitimacy and condone their unjust policies. Because of this strategic choice, most public debates and controversies are framed in religious terms. On the one hand, by presenting progressive and secular opposition forces as apostates and enemies of Islam, the regime not only prevents any serious discussion of its policies but also justifies its harsh crackdown on these forces. On the other hand, the opposition, gradually deprived of its secular and leftist components, becomes dominated by self-appointed religious leaders who blame the autocrat and his clique for their corruption, cynical opportunism, and hypocritical behavior. Such domination is easily established because in traditional societies leftist ideas do not have a large appeal. Ordinary people are therefore not ready to come to the rescue of leftist militants when they are the victims of brutal repression.

In many countries, the political stage has thus been largely dominated by, on one side, official clerics who pronounce fatwas in support of the regime's religious legitimacy and, on the other side, rebellious clerics from the low Islam who pronounce counter-fatwas accusing the ruling clique of being miscreants who transgress Islamic values and pervert the original message of pure Islam. The former type of cleric is faithful to a deep-rooted Islamic tradition prescribing that, to avoid chaos and disorder, Muslims should obey their sovereign regardless of the despotic character of his rule. The only condition is that he be considered a pious Muslim on the superficial basis of his official gestures and postures. As for the second type, they are deviant clerics who have entered into open rebellion against the official religious establishment.

What the autocratic authority is thus sparking is a dangerous religious war in which both the regime and the opposition try to outbid each other in their claim to be the most legitimate bearer of Islamic values and principles. Intransigent discourses and a winner-take-all attitude come to invade the political space in which arguments are replaced by anathema and confrontation takes on the form of a Manichean struggle between the forces of good and evil. Some strand of religious opposition, which is typically of urban origin, may get radicalized and take on the shape of puritanical movements preaching a return to the pristine form of Islam. More moderate groups clamor for the replacement of state laws by the sharia, which they deem to be the only way to coax the despotic sovereign to end blatant corruption and oppression (the original meaning of sharia is a way of promoting the well-being of the individual and the community). An "obscurantist deadlock" is thereby created in unstable autocracies, and how it ends up is an open question. One possible outcome is the sort of chaos so much feared by official clerics, a chaos that may be triggered by the assassination of the autocrat. This may be followed either by a takeover of political power by the army acting in support of autocracy or by religious leaders coming to the frontline of politics determined to restore social order in the name of Islam. When the prevailing chaos ends in a military coup, the general result (with a few notable exceptions such as Pakistan) is the emergence of a secular regime relying on the use of coercion and repression. The corruption and cynicism of often secular despotic rulers, who are often secular, are largely to blame for this sobering association between secularism and force. It is utterly disappointing for all those who believe that secularism should promote a democratic order and an inclusive society based on tolerance, fair access to economic opportunities, and peaceful cooperation among people.

When autocrats opt to obtain wide religious support to stabilize their regime or make up for their lack of legitimacy, they may have to rely on the allegiance of religious family dynasties that lead big Sufi brotherhoods and wield considerable local political influence due to their moral authority and patronage power. In these cases, the co-option of clerics goes beyond the world of high Islam to reach out to lower rungs. The rulers are then automatically tempted to enact laws or adopt measures that reflect erstwhile tribal customs and not only the preferences and values of the high-level urban ulama. The consequence is the consolidation of tribalism and clannism.

To understand why, since their independence, many Muslim autocracies have been politically unstable, it is necessary to examine the role of the international context. One important channel of influence goes through the supply of Islamist ideologies, the propagation of which is facilitated by the abundant oil wealth of Saudi Arabia, the Iranian Islamist Revolution, unresolved problems of statehood in Pakistan and Afghanistan, and the ready availability of effective mass communication technologies. At the same time, the demand for ideologies stressing the victimhood of Muslim people and demonizing Western civilization has been stimulated by the one-sided meddling of advanced Western countries in the regional conflicts of the Middle East. Such meddling has been associated with colonial interventions, the priority given by Western countries to their own geopolitical interests in the context of the Cold War and the struggle against emerging left-wing and nationalist movements in developing countries, and the unflinching support of Israel by the United States in particular. Factors pertaining to the supply of and demand for Islamist ideologies, plus the threats and challenges arising from the pressure to catch up with the rapidly developing economies of the West, modify the tradeoff faced by Muslim autocrats. Religious clerics, at least those who are relatively sensitive to social injustice, become harder to buy off (they are more "expensive" than before), and as a result, the autocratic regime becomes more potentially unstable. Confronted with a growing threat, autocrats are not expected to remain passive, however. Their predicted response consists of moderating their controversial policies and ill-framed practices or of adopting regressive measures that accord more influence to Islam in public life. The policy shift ought to be large enough to ensure that they eventually regain the support of the clerics, even at the cost of creating new barriers to economic growth and development.

Islamist movements, which tend to appeal to educated or semi-educated people with dislocated life experiences, are born of deep-seated frustrations caused by the behavior of both political and religious elites. Their struggle tends to be especially fierce and determined when, as a result of the corruption and/or incompetence of the political autocracy, national interests are surrendered to foreign powers. The proclivity of these movements to adopt puritanical scripturalist interpretations of the Prophet's message is the result of two circumstances: (1) the association of corruption with the values of material individualism and atheism and (2) the obsequious attitude of religious dignitaries accused of being "lackeys of the prince" and hurting the "dignity of Islam." This second feature is especially important because it reinforces the idea that what matters are deeds and not talk: Speaking in the name of Islam even with the apparently highest credentials may just be a trick to conceal a devious cooperation with those who treat the state as their personal fiefdom and as a set of arrogated privileges that can be sold to foreign foes. Official Islam is thus seen as a debased version of the primeval faith, justifying the need for the latter's restoration.

Globalization of the jihad, in the sense of a redefinition of its objectives to include a declaration of total war against the West itself, is of rather recent origin. It was initiated by Osama bin Laden, the head of al-Qaeda, in response to the 1990 intervention of the United States in Kuwait and the prolonged presence of U.S. military bases on Saudi Arabia territory since that time.

In the postwar pattern of autocratic polity in the lands of Islam, the ruler instrumentalizes a portion of the clerical body that constitutes the set of so-called official clerics. Since those left out stand beyond the ruler's control, they are a potential threat to the regime. As revealed by the recent experiences of several Arab countries (e.g., Syria, Algeria, Yemen, and Egypt), things may be more complicated: Indeed, the "deep state" consisting of various forces obeying the Ministry of Interior, the intelligence services, and the top brass in the army may act behind the public stage of autocratic regimes to defeat left-wing secular movements, through thuggish groups if needed. In such situations, both the state and radical religious groups play the same vicious and fateful game of extremism, which consists of justifying all means by the ends pursued. Intelligence and police forces may thus nurture and encourage extremist Islamist organizations on the condition that they directly attack leftist or other secular opposition movements operating on university campuses, inside trade unions, and within professional associations. The autocratic authority then relies on two kinds of religious forces to buttress its regime: official clerics who serve as its "clean" partners and violent Islamist organizations that are its covert and shameful ally in the struggle against secular opposition. Political cynicism and perversion are at their highest when the autocratic regime simultaneously supports violent outfits and misrepresents moderate religious opposition forces. It does so by demonizing the latter, conflating them with the former so as to justify the harshest repression against moderate opposition in the name of the antiterror struggle.

It is a sobering fact that the Western powers – the United States and the United Kingdom in particular – have not hesitated to cynically support radical Islamist movements when it suited their own geopolitical and economic interests. This was especially manifest in their protracted struggle against Arab nationalism and in their tactic of using radical Islamists as proxy allies against communism and the Soviet Union. They thus played a "devil's game" that later proved to be disastrous when Islamism became a force that turned against its sponsors.

Under the decentralized organization of Islam, clerics unhappy about the coziness of the arrangement of their official co-religionists with political power tend to opt for independence. This leaves them the possibility of leading a popular rebellion against the despised autocratic regime. When religion is centralized, clerics dissatisfied with the compromising attitude of their church may choose to leave it and even join revolutionary movements, such as happened in Russia during the last two Romanov reigns (Obolonsky, 2003, pp. 110, 136–7) and in Latin America during the 1960s and 1970s.[3] In the process, they cease to be members of their church (they are excommunicated). Hence, unlike dissident Muslim clerics, they lose their religious credentials and their ability to claim supernatural legitimacy.

As should have become clear, the narrative of this book is inspired by a political economics approach that puts the state at the center of a deep understanding of Islam. This analysis thus aligns with the work of Daron Acemoglu and James Robinson (2008) who, in various articles and books, have stressed the primary importance of politics for development. Economic institutions are shaped by the nature of political institutions and the distribution of political power in society. And it is the political nature of an institutional equilibrium that makes it very difficult to reform economic institutions. The political economics approach can also be taken with other religions; for example, religious legitimization has been extremely important for rulers in Christianity (Greif, 2006a; Greif and Tadelis, 2010).

My focus on the relationship between autocratic politics and religion makes sense for the following reasons. Modern states tend to be nondemocratic during the crucial phase of their formation and consolidation, as attested by the importance of absolute monarchies in Western Europe before the Industrial Revolution. Because their legitimacy cannot rest on the principles of democracy, autocratic regimes need to rely on other sources. In the context of traditional societies in which literacy levels are low and religious authorities have a monopoly or quasi-monopoly on the transmission of knowledge, these authorities exert an important influence by conferring legitimacy through loyalty upon the ruling autocracy. The subjects are encouraged to believe that the ruler has the right to rule and the power to provide protection and other public goods, and thus the right to collect

---

[3] In the case of Russia, the main revolutionary movement had characteristics strongly evoking a centralized religion with its counter-church. Marxist or communist ideology actually supplanted the Orthodox faith, "which had discredited itself by means of its complete submission to crown" (Obolonsky, 2003, p. 166). It operated as a new faith antithetical to Christianity, with its temptation to turn stones into bread, to make social miracles, and to build an eternal kingdom on earth. Communist ideology had its own cult of saints, its own holy legends, and its own dogmas. Any doubt, criticism, or disrespect regarding these symbols of the new faith was sanctioned by excommunication, and even the horrors of inquisition were imposed on the people living under the new faith (pp. 166–7). For pioneering insights, the reader can refer to the writings of the philosopher N. A. Berdyaev; see, in particular, Berdyaev (1948, pp. 135–57).

taxes. In sum, given the power of religious belief, the word of the religious authorities – through sermons and speeches delivered as part of their official function – could provide "a single, coherent, and effective source of legitimacy" (Coşgel, Miceli, and Rubin, 2012, p. 362).

A major advantage of this theoretical scaffolding, as is evident from the contrast between centralized and decentralized religious organizations, is that it does not treat religions in an undifferentiated manner, but sharpens both the similarities and differences between them. Similarities originate from the fact that, like Islam, Christianity cannot be properly analyzed outside a setup featuring the state, and this applies to the periods preceding and following the rise of national churches. The central difference between the two faiths lies in their internal organization: Unlike Islam, Catholic and Eastern Orthodox Christianity are endowed with a hierarchical structure under the form of a centralized church. Something akin to a war of fatwas and the resulting disorder cannot therefore occur, yet schisms are possible. In the absence of a schism, either the church cooperates or is in conflict with political power. A key prediction of my theory is that political instability is greater with a decentralized religion than with a centralized religion. Therefore, autocratic rulers will try hard to construct a centralized national churchwhenever this proves possible, such as when a new state is formed.

During the critical period corresponding to the formation of their centralized modern states, European countries were particularly successful in building a cooperative relationship with national church establishments. By contrast, the decentralized character of Islam makes the same task much more arduous in countries with large Muslim populations, where the state tends to follow the path of increasingly unstable autocracies. A sudden shift toward democracy appears quite difficult in such conditions. But even a less radical and more realistic transition involving a shift from kleptocratic or predatory autocracy to liberal autocracy has proven to be problematic in most Muslim countries. In a kleptocratic autocracy, the despot not only ensures law and order but also provides exclusive and unjustified economic privileges to his surrounding elite. Law and order therefore appear to be aimed at defending these privileges, rather than at protecting ordinary people faced with threats against their physical security and their day-to-day livelihoods. By contrast, a liberal autocracy is a regime in which the economic space is open to genuine competition, instead of being controlled by the autocrat and his clique for their own benefit. Because a liberal autocracy provides fair access to economic opportunities for all the population groups, the authoritarian methods used to establish law and order are then considered acceptable by a large majority of people.

By treating the Left as the most dangerous threat to their political survival, predatory autocrats end up suppressing the progressive forces that could have compelled them to become gradually more accountable to their people. The pressure exerted by these forces might have brought about the discontinuation of the most blatant privileges granted to an elite exclusively concerned with its own well-being. Not only would the scope of corruption have been reduced but also, and more importantly, its form would have evolved from the noxious type of prebendiary taxation, expropriation, and racketeering for purely patronage purposes to a system of privileges conditioned upon socially useful achievements, such as has been observed in East Asia (Amsden, 1989; Wade, 1990; Khan, 2000a, 2000b).[4] A transition from patrimonial to liberal autocracy is certainly more conducive to economic and social development than running the risk of a religious takeover in order to leave unchanged a system of rent capture that exclusively benefits a narrow ruling clique. Because religions stress moral absolutes and thereby create an aversion to political compromises, a cleric-led opposition is quite unlikely to stop short of a revolution that, if successful, would reproduce autocracy rather than establish an accountable political regime. The crushing of progressive, left-leaning forces therefore appears to be a real tragedy for a large part of the Muslim world.

When considered under the specific angle of decentralization, Protestantism – North American Protestantism in particular – appears closer to Islam (and Judaism) than to the other brands of Christianity. One therefore wonders why North America has prospered while the lands of Islam have not. The answer is that in North America democracies were established and formed by immigrants coming from politically advanced countries of Europe. Within the context of North American democracy, it is clear that the decentralized character of Protestantism cannot produce the effects that it would have produced under an autocratic system. At the same time, it should not come as a surprise that, during the times of the Reformation – that is, much before the advance of democracy in Europe – fundamentalist Puritan movements flourished, leading to a state of anarchy resembling that observed in Islam today. Moreover, when Protestant leaders wielded

---

[4] As pointed out by Mushtaq Khan (2000a), the growth implications of the overall structure of transfer-based rents can be positive or negative depending on whether and "how much of the transfers goes to individuals or groups who have the incentive and opportunity to make the transition to productive capitalism." It also depends "on the configuration of political forces which determines the structure of the transfers to political intermediaries and their factions" (p. 39). In other words, rents can be associated with rapid capital accumulation and growth or result in large-scale thefts.

power and influence, most notably Calvin in Geneva and Luther in Germany, political absolutism and intolerance prevailed.

Given that, like Islam, Buddhism and Hinduism are decentralized religions, one should not be surprised that even in East Asia, autocracies may show signs of instability. This is witnessed by the political tensions plaguing countries such as Thailand, Sri Lanka, and Myanmar where autocrats find it difficult to deal with a divided religious (Buddhist) body.

To explain the impact of Islam on long-term development, Timur Kuran (2011) has proposed a well-known theory according to which the effect is indirect and operates through certain institutions derived from Islamic law or the classic Islamic system. Path-dependence mechanisms create an "institutional trap" in the lands of Islam, and although the problematic institutions of Islam were not incompatible with progress in earlier periods, they present clear obstacles to indigenous economic modernization in modern times. An interesting link can be made between Kuran's theory and the political economics approach followed in this book. Indeed, formal or official institutions have an effect on actual behavior only if the associated rules are effectively enforced by the political or administrative authority. Politics must therefore play a behind-the-stage role in Kuran's argument, and clues will be provided in this book about the way politics interacts with Islamic laws and institutions, as well as about the contexts most conducive to their effective or their poor enforcement.

1.3 Methodological Approach

Let us now turn our attention to the methodological approach used in this book to explore the relationship between religion and politics. The Islam-is-the-problem view, which is widely diffused through the press and the media (see, for example, *Economist*, January 17–23, 2015, p. 22), rests on the idea that Islam has historically determined features that have shaped the destiny and institutional trajectory of Muslim countries, even in the very long term. More specifically, the circumstances in which Islam was born and the ensuing fusion between the religious and the political spheres have prevented these countries from evolving toward democracy and from gradually developing civil societies able to confront autocratic rulers. Furthermore, Islamic law acted as a barrier precluding the transformation of all kinds of institutions required for sustained economic growth in the modern world. The implied concept is the notion of path dependence: Initial conditions influence terminal outcomes because some underlying processes, mechanisms, or institutions tend to produce lasting effects that remain observable today.

A recent trend in development and growth economics is the use of historical experiments by empirical studies to demonstrate the effect of past events or institutions on presently observable outcomes. The researcher identifies a past shock argued to be exogenous and then tries to show that present outcomes differ depending upon whether they are observed in the (treatment) area where the shock actually occurred or in the (control) area where it did not. Whenever appropriate, works based on historical experiments are mentioned in this book; already in the next section, I refer to an especially relevant study of this type. However, one key limitation of this methodology is the following: Measuring the impact of distant legacies does not elucidate the mechanism behind path dependency, whether it consists of large setup or fixed costs, learning effects, coordination effects, or adaptive expectations (see North, 1990, pp. 94–5). These mechanisms may therefore remain a black box.

What comes closest to a quantitative test of one central aspect of our theory – the negative impact of religious decentralization on the extent of political stability – is the exercise carried out by Lisa Blaydes and Eric Chaney (2013). These authors compare durations of autocratic rule for the Christian West and the Muslim world, looking at rulers assuming power on or after 700 CE and before 1500 CE. They find that, from the tenth century onward, Christian kings were increasingly long lived compared to Muslim sultans. Although before the year 1000 CE, ruler duration in Western Europe and the Islamic world were not statistically different at the 10 percent level, after this date one can reject the null hypothesis that leadership tenures were the same. Divergence in ruler duration does reflect a change in political stability. Indeed, there is an inverse relationship between ruler duration and the probability of being overthrown, suggesting that ruler duration is a reasonable proxy for political stability. Over time, rulers in Western Europe were therefore significantly less likely to be deposed than their Muslim counterparts. Because a centralized religion prevailed in the Christian lands while a decentralized one characterized the Muslim lands during the period considered, what Blaydes and Chaney have established is a positive relationship between the centralization of religion and political stability under autocratic regimes. In line with the limitation of the methodology of historical experiments, the mechanism operating behind the uncovered relationship remains speculative, and it is thus revealing that the explanation proposed by the authors differs from the one I suggest.[5]

---

[5] Blaydes and Chaney's explanation rests on the contrast between the use of mercenary (slave) armies in the lands of Islam and the use of loyal armies at the service of the autocrat

Blaydes and Platas Izama (2015) have recently reached a conclusion that seems to support another prediction of our theory, namely that progressive reforms are easier to achieve with a centralized church structure than with a decentralized one. Their study aims to identify the factors responsible for recent changes in the prevalence of female genital mutilation in Egypt, where this practice is forbidden by law. Especially relevant is the contrast observed between the perceptible decrease in the practice among the Christian Copts and the rather unchanged situation among the Muslims. The authors tentatively attribute this difference to the different religious authority structures prevailing in the two communities: Whereas a hierarchical order prevails among the Copts, the Muslims are used to a much more decentralized system. More precisely, there exists a centralized Coptic church that exerts a significant influence on its believers, and its leaders have chosen to take a clear stand against the cutting of girls. Muslims, in contrast, attend mosques that are run by different imams who have varying opinions about the practice.

Could we take the central part of our story to data pertaining to recent times? As will become clear later, there are almost insurmountable problems inherent in any exercise using national-level data. Assume that we want to compare autocracies in Muslim countries with autocracies in Christian (Catholic) countries during the period after World War II. The following difficulties immediately arise. First, do we take into account those countries of sub-Saharan Africa where the tradition of high Islam represented by official, city-based ulama has been of short duration or weak? Second, because most autocracies in Catholic countries, typically located in Latin America, ended a few decades ago while many Muslim (especially Arab) autocracies still persist to this day, we will necessarily be comparing countries over different time periods. Third, and more importantly, how can we avoid the risk of confounding effects caused by the absence or the poor measurement of key explanatory variables? And how can we ascertain that reverse causality is not at work? Ideally, one would therefore wish to compare subunits of country spaces (municipalities, districts, etc.) as in Cantoni (2015). Unfortunately, this is not a valid approach in our instance because, to make sense of our theory, the dependent variable should be measured at the national, not the local level.

---

in the lands of Christianity. Their argument is not completely clear, however: by enabling Muslim autocrats to overcome internal tribal divisions, the recruitment of military slaves may have actually contributed to political stability rather than instability (Fukuyama, 2012, pp. 196–201, 451).

Clearly, we need an alternative approach that would enable us to analyze in depth and detail the central question raised in this book. My preference is the reasoned and comparative use of historical material buttressed by a well-defined analytical argument. The study of Turkey by Kuran fits this definition. It rests upon an elaborate analysis of the adverse effects of Islamic institutions on economic incentives in a modern growth context that requires the establishment of impersonal relationships among agents. Kuran's contribution belongs to the new field of institutional economics: It discusses the efficiency of Islamic institutions considered in the light of the economic theory of contracts and argues that the lack of institutional change (the "institutional trap") stems from a path-dependence effect. It must also be stressed that Kuran's approach includes comparative analysis. As he points out in the preface to his most recent book, *The Long Divergence: How Islamic Law Held back the Middle East* (2011), "all good social science is at some level comparative, for to interpret findings and measure achievements one must have a context larger than the social unit under focus"; moreover, comparative analysis "generates intellectual puzzles by isolating the unusual" (p. xi).

My approach has the following four characteristics: (1) It is unashamedly qualitative, (2) it relies on secondary sources, (3) it has a tight analytical structure, and (4) it adopts a comparative perspective. It is qualitative because of the research question addressed – is Islam a special problem? – and its deliberate preference for historical exploration. The choice of the historical approach to the subject is justified by its comprehensive and quite ambitious scope. This study aims at formulating general conclusions about the relationship between religion and politics in the world of Islam, rather than confining its attention to one particular country and one particular time period. The historical approach is especially appropriate when elements of context and dynamic aspects are so important that missing them would deprive the analysis of much of its content. This is certainly true in the present case where the two critical variables, politics and religion, are assumed to be interrelated in complex ways.

Comparing different regions over different periods of time is necessary to dig out similarities and contrasts in the hope of drawing out a general picture that allows for variations across countries and time periods. Because of the book's huge scope, the proposed analysis is entirely based on secondary sources and a wide range of in-depth case studies by historians and political scientists. Furthermore, at critical stages of the discussion, I make comparisons between Islam and other religions because the final objective is to determine whether and how Islam constitutes a special case from the standpoint of its relation to politics.

Finally, it is evident that the aforementioned objectives are impossible to attain if facts are not articulated together within a coherent logical structure. As indicated in Section 1.2, the framework chosen to explore the relationship between religion and politics in the lands of Islam rests on two fundamental distinctions. The first is between situations of stable and unstable politico-religious equilibrium (associated with the opposition suppression strategy and opposition confrontation strategy of the autocrat, respectively), state crisis being a possible outcome of political instability. The second distinction is based on the idea that decentralized religions do not behave like centralized ones. The analytical apparatus is grounded in modern microeconomic theory – more precisely, in the political economics approach to political phenomena. One defining feature of this approach is that the state appears as an actor that interacts strategically with society; another is that the state's political power needs to be explained. This whole field covering religion, political processes, and their interaction with economic processes – the "wider scope" – is one in which there is a dearth of research by economists, both empirical and theoretical (Iyer, 2016, p. 432).

On the theoretical level, this book's contribution lies in proposing a scheme of analysis of religious seduction under autocracy, which implies that the state and the religious clerics are seen as separate actors. An autocratic ruler faces a religious class that carries social prestige and legitimacy in the eyes of the common people, but can be partly or fully co-opted, or "seduced," by the political regime. In addition to choosing the level of co-option of the religious clerics, the ruling autocrat must make policy cloices that are not neutral from the standpoint of their acceptability to clerics. Negotiations between the ruler and religious clerics are easier when the latter are regrouped into a hierarchical structure. Attention is restricted to autocracies not only because almost all Muslim countries have always been ruled by autocrats but also because even in Western Europe, modern states that instrumentalized religion were autocracies (absolute monarchies) at some point in their development.

A study that comes close to my analysis because it shares most of the aforementioned characteristics, yet not (3) – having a tight analytic structure – is *Religion and Politics in the Middle East* (2014) by Robert Lee, a social scientist. Each chapter of his book, except the introductory and concluding chapters, deals with a particular country (Egypt, Israel, Turkey, Iran, and Saudi Arabia), and the case study material is presented under the following sequence of dimensions: identity, ideology, institutions, and political culture. The discussion thus evolves within a broad conceptual canvas that nevertheless remains short of an analytical structure. Another study that has the interaction between politics and religion (Islam) at its core is William Cavanaugh's book *The Myth of Religious Violence* (2009). It is based on the idea that "there is no such thing as a transhistorical or transcultural 'religion' that is essentially separate from politics" or from secular phenomena (p. 9). Christianity is the central reference for Cavanaugh's book, which focuses on the issue of violence: It is mainly a refutation of the thesis that religion is inherently violent while the secular state is a solution to that problem (state violence being used to bring peace).

1.4 Concerns with Quantitative Studies

This section starts by discussing the endogeneity issue that plagues many empirical attempts to measure the effects of religion. Then, it presents a brief survey of the weak results that can be derived from existing cross-country studies. This provides an opportunity to discuss additional problems involved in these studies. Next it looks at an alternative methodology that is more effective in circumventing the endogeneity issue, that of historical experiments. It concludes by clarifying the purpose of the analysis conducted in this book.

The Endogeneity Problem

Although it is quite uncommon among economists, the idea of relating religion, and culture in general, to politics is not new in social sciences. It can even be said that a defining feature of contemporary sociology and political science lies in their continuous stress on the endogeneity of religion, as well as other cultural agencies, to economic and political circumstances. The main concern regarding endogeneity is the possibility of reverse causality: Rather than blocking development, a particular religion may evolve in a nasty direction as a result of weak growth, or conversely, it may evolve in a pro-growth direction as a result of sustained growth. This happens when conversion from one religion to another follows the desire to better match the needs of dynamic entrepreneurs or economically mobile social groups, or when the content of a religion is reinterpreted or its mode of organization refashioned toward the same purpose. An example of economically motivated conversion is the conversion to Protestantism of Catholic merchants from Antwerp (as further discussed in Chapter 2). It provides a vivid illustration of the possibility of the self-selection bias: Adepts of a particular religion may be comparatively dynamic not because they have been subject to its influence but because they have self-selected into that religion, which offers incentives or rules suitable to their economic ambitions (see Platteau, 2000, chs. 5–7; for numerous examples related to sub-Saharan Africa, see Platteau, 2014).

An example of reinterpreting religion to support economic development can be found in modern Japan where the Tokugawa Shogunate adopted the Chu Hsi school of Confucianism in the early seventeenth century (Hayami, 1997, pp. 275–6). Originating in the Sung dynasty in China, this school was called neo-Confucianism because it combined Confucianism with Buddhism. A central feature of the new doctrine was that it rationalized the social hierarchy in an imperial order, in which the emperor was believed to be ordained by heaven. Under the Tokugawa, neo-Confucianism served the function of legitimizing the prevailing vertical structure dominated by the tycoon in Edo and, under him, the warrior class.[6] As the market economy developed in the eighteenth century, a new school of moral philosophy emerged and received support from merchants in the commercial town of Osaka. The most important sect of this school, known as the Ishida School, was "an admixture of Confucianism, Buddhism, and Shintoism, but in substance it taught the same morals that Adam Smith considered to be the basis of the wealth of nations – frugality, industry, honesty, and fidelity" (p. 275). In this instance, rather than self-selecting into a given religion, dynamic individuals worked to transform the one they inherited so as to make it better adapted to their objectives in a changing economic environment.

Muslim long-distance trading communities or trading diasporas in West Africa illustrate the role of religious organizations and their rituals in promoting trade. Dating to the thirteenth and fourteenth centuries, these networks or sodalities were typically formed on the basis of religious ties – adherence to a common faith and observing its rituals – in order to foster trust and honest dealings when new economic opportunities arose to which merchants wanted to respond. New entrants were accepted, but only on the (obviously restrictive) condition that they shared or accepted the essential cultural requirements for participation in the moral community that separated its members from the host society: Islam and the appropriate trading language (Austin, 1993, p. 115). The adoption of Islam thus spurred the economic integration of West African regions (along the Juula and Hausa inland networks, as well as at the Sahelian entrepôts along the

---

[6] This was a twisted use of the foreign ideology, because in the Tokugawa system the emperor was deprived of any real power and was reduced to a purely symbolic figure. Recognition of this inconsistency later became the ideological basis of the Meiji Restoration under which feudal fiefs were integrated into a nation-state under the emperor's authority to counter a feared aggression of Western powers (Hayami, 1997, p. 275).

Niger bend) and their integration into the trans-Saharan trade by increasing the safety of the caravans and reducing contract enforcement costs (Cohen 1969, 1971; Hopkins, 1973, pp. 58–65; Levtzion, 1973; Brooks, 1993, p. 117; Lydon, 2009b).

In the language of economics, adherence to a common faith thus serves the function of signaling or identifying members, and the sodality works as a club, the entry into which involves a fixed cost (the initial fee) in the form, useless for outsiders and not individually portable, of learning the language as well as its doctrine and rituals. The religious network replicates a gift exchange relationship by a group of agents and is effective to the extent that any violation of the prescribed code of behavior (honest trading) within the club is punished by the termination of club membership (Aoki, 2001, pp. 64–7; see also Platteau, 2000, ch. 6; Fafchamps, 2004, chs. 15–16; Greif, 2006a, ch. 3; for a direct application to religious organizations, see Berman, 2000; Iannaccone, 1992; Carvalho, 2016, 2017 (b))).

In the example of the trading communities, there is a combination of the aforementioned two endogenous processes: self-selection through conversion for the traders who were not Muslim in the initial situation and inner transformation of the faith and its associated rules. Clearly, a fecund approach to religion must pay attention to factors that explain the demand for religious tenets or services, and it must address the question as to how religion is determined or shaped in some specific contexts.[7]

Additional Problems and Weak Results from Cross-Country Studies

To say that economists interested in religion have not been very alert to the possible endogeneity of religion to economic and political circumstances is an understatement. This weakness is especially evident in the cross-country empirical studies that attempted to assess the effect of religious beliefs and participation in religious activities on attitudes toward various aspects of economic and social life (saving, work, honesty, free-riding, time preference), as well as on economic and political performance. It is fair to say that these studies did not properly overcome the endogeneity problem. And studies probably never will be able do so, given the difficulty of finding an instrument that can explain religion without at the same time influencing economic or political achievements otherwise than through the channel of

---

[7] In economics, the conventional Beckerian approach to religion has essentially focused on supply-side factors (see, in particular, Iannaccone, 1990, 1995, 1997; Stark, Iannaccone, and Finke, 1996; see also Aldashev and Platteau, 2013, for a recent review).

religion itself. This is why the results of cross-country regressions are better considered as correlations than as causal relationships and why we need alternative methodologies to advance our knowledge of religion. An appealing advantage of case studies, in particular, is that they may shed light on the mechanisms through which religion plays its role in relation to economic and political phenomena (Aldashev and Platteau, 2013).

Reverse causality is not the only problem that arises when trying to determine the effect of religion on economic and political performances. How to measure what we understand by religion is another serious issue. It is actually linked to reverse causality to the extent that not only the content of a faith but also the meaning of identification with a particular religion are susceptible to variation depending upon the economic and political environment. Therefore subtle measures of religious affiliation are needed to elucidate the relationship between religion and economic or political phenomena. Most often, however, religious affiliation is measured in a relatively crude manner that does not allow distinguishing between various denominations. For instance, when testing for the influence of Islam, no distinction is made between Shi'ism and Sunnism, or between the four different schools of Sunni Islam, or between different strands of thought inside a particular school (there are considerable differences inside the Hanefi school, as attested by the opposition between the Barelvis and the Deobandis over many points of observance and doctrine), or again between perfunctory and deep adherence to a faith. When intensity of religious beliefs or participation in religious activities is measured, it is by means of self-reported frequencies regarding attendance at religious rituals and masses, prayers, and so forth (for Islam, see Chaara, 2015).

Still another problem stems from the bias of omitted variables. For example, a particular faith could be associated with relatively high levels of religiosity for reasons that are independent of the faith itself. If this was the case, religiosity rather than the characteristics of the faith would be the real determinant of the outcome observed. In a study on the effects of religion on creativity and innovations as measured by patents per capita, low creativity in majority-Muslim countries was thus found to be driven by relatively high religiosity rather than by Islam per se (Bénabou, Ticchi, and Vindigni, 2015). We cannot be certain, indeed, that religion is not just a proxy for some underlying force that we do not measure. In particular, when a positive effect of adherence to a (monotheistic) religion on economic achievements is discerned, it might be the case that religion stands for individual-centered values as opposed to collectivist values, or for a worldview that involves identification with "abstract others" rather than with "concrete others," which typically means people from the same extended family, clan, tribe, or ethnic group. Put another way, is adhering to a religion equivalent to forsaking norms of sharing and obedience inside a traditionally defined group (Platteau, 2000, 2014, chs. 5 and 7)? The answer to these questions would not matter if religion was the only available vehicle of pro-growth values and attitudes. Because this is not true, the question arises as to why some countries in some contexts need religious rather than other secular ideologies to propel economic growth, assuming that the causal effect runs from ideology to economic growth.

Keeping in mind all these caveats, what conclusions can be derived from cross-country exercises carried out by economists? Perhaps unsurprisingly, the findings are disappointing. Even if the null hypothesis that religious affiliation is uncorrelated with economic or political performances can frequently be rejected, implying that religion seems to matter, the regressions do not yield a robust pattern of coefficients with respect to particular religions, specific effects, and sample sizes (Durlauf, Kourtellos, and Tan, 2012; Aldashev and Platteau, 2013). This amounts to saying that there are few specific lessons to be learned from cross-country regressions taken as a whole. Religion may affect growth or growth-related performances, but the nature of the relationship is unclear.[8]

Special mention needs to be made of the work of Guiso, Sapienza, and Zingales (2003) because it has the advantage of exploring some of the

---

[8] La Porta, Lopez-de-Silanes, Shleifer, and Vishny (1997) thus found that countries with more dominant hierarchical religions (Catholicism, Orthodox Christianity, and Islam) "have less efficient judiciaries, greater corruption, lower-quality bureaucracies, higher rates of tax evasion, lower rates of participation in civic activities and professional associations, a lower level of importance of large firms in the economy, inferior infrastructures, and higher inflation" (pp. 336–7). As pointed out earlier, however, the inclusion of Islam among hierarchical religions is inappropriate, and the results obtained are therefore impossible to interpret. Another study, by Barro and McCleary (2003), shows that Hinduism, Islam, Orthodox Christianity, and Protestantism are negatively associated with per capita income growth relative to Catholicism, whereas Sala-i-Martin, Doppelhofer, and Miller (2004), who use a larger sample, find the opposite result: Islam is a positive rather than a negative correlate of growth. The latter result is confirmed by Noland (2005, 2007) for whom the notion that Islam is inimical to growth is not supported by his data. If anything, the relationship is positive rather than negative (at least when the sample consists only of developing countries). As for Pryor (2006), he reaches the conclusion that no special Islamic economic system can be isolated on the basis of a cluster analysis and data on forty-four economic institutions used to define economic systems. Moreover, the share of Muslims in the population is unrelated to the presence or absence of most particular economic institutions, and when the sample is limited to developing countries from which Muslim countries that are too small or too rich (from oil resources) are excluded, it does not explain variations in economic growth performances.

channels through which religion can influence economic behavior. They analyzed the effects of religiosity of an individual (whether one declares belonging to some religious denomination or not), the intensity of his or her religious beliefs (as measured by religious upbringing and the frequency of attendance at religious services), and the particular denomination to which he or she has professed to belong on six broad categories of attitudes related to economic behavior, growth and development. These categories include attitudes toward cooperation, government, women, legal rules, the market economy and its performance, and thriftiness.[9] The study finds a rich set of associations. On average, religious beliefs are correlated with economic attitudes conducive to higher per capita income and growth. In particular, religious individuals (as compared to atheists) have more trust in others, in their governments, and in the legal system; are less willing to break the law; and believe more strongly in the fairness of market outcomes. On the other hand, religious people tend to be less tolerant overall and less favorable toward an active economic role for women. As for the intensity of religiosity and religious upbringing, they appear to matter for attitudes, but in an asymmetric way. In particular, trust in others correlates with the intensity of religious participation, but not with religious upbringing. Finally, the effects differ substantially across religious denominations.[10]

The study suffers from two limitations, however. First, taken as a whole the obtained findings do not tell a consistent story of the manner in which religion exerts its influence on economic performances. And, second, most variables used to measure religion and the outcomes considered are self-assessments reported by respondents in the World Values Survey. As is well known, such subjective measures are subject to much noise and various types of reporting bias.

It bears emphasis that the state as actor is conspicuously absent from the conceptual approach underlying the empirical studies described here. In particular, they ignore the possibility that the instrumentalization of religion by the state affects its impact on economic or other outcomes. Also

---

[9] Note that the authors account for the possible existence of country-specific unobservable factors that correlate to both religion/religiosity and attitudes by adding as controls country-fixed effects; they account for the individual-level characteristics that can affect simultaneously religiosity and attitudes by adding a set of individual observable characteristics (health status, age, gender, education, incomes, and perceived social status).

[10] For example, participation in religious activities correlates positively with trust only among Christians (and the effect is stronger for Protestants than for Catholics), and support for private ownership is much stronger for Catholics than for Protestants, whereas Muslims and Hindus are strongly opposed to competition.

bypassed is the influence of international players and the international environment, with the noticeable exception of the work of Ibrahim Elbadawi, Samir Makdisi, and Gary Milante (2011). These authors isolate the Arab or non-Arab character of a country, rather than its Muslim or non-Muslim character, as a possible determinant of political (rather than economic) performance (see also Elbadawi and Makdisi, 2007). Their concern is therefore about the particular situation of Muslim countries of the Middle East (with the exception of Turkey), rather than about that of Muslim countries in general.

These authors reached three main conclusions. First, the "resource curse" hypothesis according to which natural resource wealth tends to make political regimes less accountable to their people (see, e.g., Robinson, Torvik, and Verdier, 2006, 2014) cannot provide a satisfactory explanation for the Arab "democracy deficit" (as it has been termed by the World Bank, 2003). The same conclusion has been reached by Rowley and Smith (2009) and Potrafke (2012). Second, the Arab identity of a country also does not explain the democracy deficit: What best explains it is the conjunction of being Arab with involvement in regional conflicts. Unlike what is observed in other parts of the world, interstate conflicts and wars tend to promote authoritarianism rather than democracy. Thus the Arab world appears to be distinct from other regions of the world, not because of its oil wealth or its religion, but because of the peculiar influence of wars on democracy in the region. In the words of the authors, "the Arab-Israeli conflict and the perceived adversarial global power interventions in the region have provided potent arguments for an authoritarian brand of Arab nationalism for most of the last 50 years or so" (Elbadawi and Makdisi, 2007, p. 55). Third, the democracy deficit contributes to the high short-term volatility of Arab growth as well as the collapse in growth following the adverse external shocks of the mid-1980s. The negative growth effects of lagging democratization in Arab countries are persistent and accumulate over time. Conclusions along the same line were reached by Noland (2008) and Tessler (2002), yet not by Fish (2002).

Historical Experiments

Because it can get around the tricky endogeneity problem, the methodology of historical experiments has gained increasing favor among economists (see Acemoglu, Johnson, and Robinson, 2001, for a benchmark paper). One privileged approach exploits the fact that the borders of contemporaneous nation-states do not coincide with those of former empires. It is then possible to infer causality through the use of variations in historical institutions for a given set of contemporaneous institutions that are implemented inside present-day nation states. The legacy of institutions belonging to a distant past can thus be firmly established.

A recent study that is particularly relevant is that of Pauline Grosjean (2011). She analyzes the impact of Ottoman financial institutions on contemporaneous financial development, using the occupation of southeastern Europe by the Ottoman Empire as a way to detect causality. She shows that, within a country, provinces that were integrated into the Ottoman Empire have a lower degree of financial development yet are not significantly poorer. (Note that when the empire is considered as a whole and compared with the rest of the region, its levels of both financial development and income are lower.) At the same time, former Ottoman rule is associated with negative outcomes on a number of institutional quality measures. When current formal institutions are controlled for through the inclusion of country-fixed effects, the coefficient measuring the impact of former Ottoman rule on financial development drops significantly, suggesting that much of the impact of past institutions runs through contemporaneous institutions (which is in keeping with Acemoglu and Johnson, 2005).

More directly relevant to the central theme of this book is Grosjean's finding that Islam does not turn out to have an influence on financial intermediation and development: Muslims in the former Ottoman Empire are no different from members of other religious denominations within this political entity in how much they rely on formal finance. In other words, the obstacle to the development of formal finance does not seem to be Islam as a religion (the impact of which is measured by the proportion of Muslims in the population), but rather the Islamic institutions implemented by the Ottoman Empire. Equivalently, the Islamic religion is not a channel of the long-term persistence of Ottoman rule's effect on financial development. What this channel is exactly cannot be determined, and here lies a major limitation of the methodology of historical experiments.[11]

A few studies overcome this limitation by harnessing historical data on the dynamics behind the causal mechanism. An apt illustration is provided by the work of Maristella Botticini and Zvi Eckstein (2005). They make the puzzling observation that, although before the eighth and ninth

---

[11] Another potential difficulty that many studies based on historical experiments struggle to overcome is the possibility that, even controlling for initial conditions, areas under study were subject to different external influences (for example, of a political nature) both during and after the treatment, which might also influence subsequent outcomes.

centuries CE, most Jews were farmers (like the rest of the population), with the establishment of Islamic empires, they entered urban occupations en masse. Because there was no restriction prohibiting Jews from remaining in agriculture, the occupational shift was undoubtedly voluntary. Moreover, it led to persistence in occupational selection. The authors argue that this transition from agriculture into crafts and trade was the outcome of the Jews' widespread literacy, prompted by a religious and educational reform in Judaism in the first and second centuries CE, which gave them a comparative advantage in urban, high-skill occupations. In subsequent works (2007, 2014), Botticini and Eckstein present convincing evidence that a Jewish religious norm requiring fathers to educate their sons had a major influence on this persistence dynamics.

Other studies of economic history in which the authors directly address the issue of causality and that are pertinent for various parts of the argument of this book are mentioned at the appropriate places in the subsequent chapters.

Final Clarifications

The outline of this book, as presented in Section 1.5, makes clear what are the successive steps of the analysis and how they help construct an answer to the question that triggered the whole exercise. That question is not concerned with the relationship between religion and economic growth per se, but with the relationship between religion and politics, with a special focus on political stability. However, because the degree of political stability also determines, or is jointly determined with, the extent of progressive government reforms, there exists a deep link between religion and long-term economic development. From the standpoint of economics, this book is unconventional. It actually attempts to bridge the gap between economics and other social sciences. By applying to Islam the idea that the role of religion is often shaped by the strategies of political and economic actors and that the international environment matters, it draws inspiration from the social sciences. And by elaborating such an idea within an analytical framework inspired by economics, it manifests its debt to that discipline.

Before embarking upon that final step of this introductory chapter, it is useful to stress that the relationship between a political regime and economic growth is far from clear. Democracy has not been shown to yield growth outcomes unambiguously superior to those produced under autocracy. Because there exist different types of democracy and different types of autocracy (bear in mind the foregoing distinction between liberal and illiberal autocracies), and because we know that enlightened or benevolent despots can outperform democratic regimes in conditions where a long-term decision horizon is important, such a conclusion is not actually surprising. Both regimes have advantages and disadvantages from the standpoint of economic growth. Whether one is superior to the other depends upon conditions that need to be carefully stated. It is appropriate to cite here the conclusion drawn by some of the best specialists on the subject: "There is little difference in favor of dictatorships in the observed rates of growth. And even that difference vanishes once the conditions under which dictatorships and democracies existed are taken into account. Albeit in omniscient retrospect, the entire controversy seems to have been much ado about nothing" (Przeworski, Alvarez, Cheibub, and Limongi, 2000, p. 178; see also Bardhan, 1993).

As a consequence, even if Islam were bad for democracy, this would not imply that it is bad for long-term economic development (as already suggested, however, it may still be bad for economic stability and resilience). This said, I made the important point in Section 1.2 that one must distinguish between two essential forms of autocracy to be able to meaningfully assess its impact on growth and development. Along the same line, it may be argued that the adverse effects of autocracy on economic development can arise from another mechanism: If the autocratic regime rests on an extensive network of patronage, it tends to develop a large public sector in which clients can be readily absorbed. The main problem, here, is that productivity in government jobs tends to be low, and the expansion of such jobs is generally accompanied by the limited development of a dynamic, competitive private sector economy into which qualified people can be productively integrated. This could explain why in the countries of the Middle East and North Africa, in particular, productivity growth was slow despite a high rate of investment in both physical and human capital in the 1970s, 1980s, and 1990s, thus leading to slow growth compared to East Asia and Latin America (World Bank, 2008, pp. 43–54).

1.5 The Outline of the Book

The Weberian view about the positive influence of the Protestant Reformation on economic incentives and individualization of European society is the mirror image of the Islam-is-the-problem view according to which Islam is inimical to democracy and modernity. In Chapter 2, the historical foray therefore begins by assessing the Weberian view in light of the latest available evidence. The discussion first leads me to dismiss that view and to emphasise reverse causality. Second, I show that, far from relegating religion to the private sphere of life, the Reformation caused a polarization of politics along confessional lines. This confessionalization involved the emergence of puritanical movements that closely resemble present-day Islamist movements. Third, I throw doubts on an alternative explanation of the industrial leadership of Western Europe, according to which it was the Early Enlightenment rather than the Reformation that brought about modernity in Western Europe. Fourth, I argue that the formation of modern states in this advanced region was accompanied by the rise of national religions whose centralized structure favored cooperation with the absolute monarchs of the times. The chapter concludes with an examination of the argument that the Catholic Church exerted a decisive influence on modern institutions in Western Europe. This discussion provides key insights to understand the early demise of tribalism in the West.

From Chapters 3–7, Islam is the central focus of attention. In Chapter 3, the Islam-is-a-problem view, according to which Islam is uniquely characterized by a fusion between religion and politics, is expounded in detail. It is subsequently qualified in a way that highlights the need to make an important distinction that will prove very useful at later stages, namely the distinction between "high Islam" and "low Islam." Moreover, I make the point that no real difference exists between Islam and Christianity in regard to the relationship between religion and politics. In both cases, the dominant principle of conduct is that religious clerics should obey the sovereign, however iniquitous, in all matters dealing with worldly affairs and protection of the nation. Chapter 4 then provides an assessment of the Islam-is-the-problem view, based on the broad sweep of history of the lands of Islam since the time of the Prophet. It proceeds by characterizing the dominant, stable politico-religious equilibrium that prevailed in these lands during ordinary times. In a nutshell, religion is the handmaiden of politics, rather than the other way round.

In Chapters 5 and 6, attention turns to situations of state crisis, seen as deviations from the dominant stable politico-religious equilibrium. Chapter 5 deals with a type of state crisis that arises when the state is weak due to internal dissolution or foreign aggression. In these conditions, the risk of a fall into anarchy and the intense pain suffered by ordinary people may prompt religious authorities or movements to play an active role in politics that they eschew in normal times. The case of post-Safavid Iran is discussed in detail, because it provides important clues to the later transformation of the Iranian state into a theocracy. In this chapter, too, a distinction is made between state-appointed and self-appointed clerics that is amply discussed in the next two chapters. Chapter 6, one of the two most critical chapters of the book, addresses situations in which the central state is not only strong but also oppressive and despotic. In this context, rulers are often tempted to instrumentalize and manipulate religion with a view to entrenching their abusive power and silencing their critics. Case studies form a large part of this chapter and include Egypt, Pakistan, Sudan, Algeria, Indonesia, Iraq, and Syria.

From there, we are naturally led to Chapter 7, which explores the conditions of the birth and rise of Islamist movements. The chapter illuminates the modernization crisis that underpins Islamism. The critical role of the international environment, and of foreign domination, is brought to center stage in the ensuing discussion. In Chapter 8, this line of inquiry is pursued by considering the cases of Hindu fundamentalism in India and Buddhist fundamentalism in Sri Lanka and Myanmar. These cases are especially interesting because they concern two non-monotheistic religions with a reputation of tolerance and peacefulness.

After Chapter 6, Chapter 9 forms the most sizable piece of the book. It aims to examine the experiences of two countries in which determined and enlightened despots have apparently succeeded in transforming their society in the direction of secular modernity. These countries are Turkey under Atatürk and Tunisia under Bourguiba. Moreover, I also focus on the less well-known but equally instructive episodes during which enlightened despots tried and failed to follow the same path in Afghanistan. The analysis based on these instances of top-down Westernization yields important lessons and insights regarding the challenges to modernity in Muslim countries. In other words, conditions for effective enlightened despotism are inferred from the only partially successful experiences of Turkey and Tunisia. To help structure the argument, I refer to a theory that frames the interactions between a central state and a local informal authority. Behaving in a strategic manner, the local authority chooses to what extent local customs evolve in response to institutional changes decided at the top. This theory is sketched at the end of Chapter 9.

Chapter 10, the last chapter of the book, offers more than a conclusion. It has three parts. In the first one, I examine the well-known theory of the institutional trap developed by Timur Kuran and set up a bridge between our two approaches to the role of Islam in development. This bridge rests on the concept of the "enforcement environment. The second part summarizes the approach and the key results of this book. It emphasizes the novelty of the approach followed and underscores that it ties together the salient findings emerging from the country case studies. I also show that the approach can throw a completely new light on the nature of the "civiliza-tional crisis" confronted by Muslim countries in present times. Finally, in the third and last part, the important issue of the persistence of tribalism in Muslim lands is addressed and linked to the discussion in Chapter 2 of its early demise in Western Europe.

Before we embark upon our investigation, a practical remark aimed at helping the reader needs to be made. The main results of each chapter are summarized in each one's concluding section. These sections are typically found at the end of each chapter, except in Chapter 4, where the conclu-sion or summary corresponds to Section 4.4. In that chapter, the theoretical framework that underpins the concept of politico-religious equilibrium is presented in a nontechnical manner in a section that follows the conclud-ing section (Section 4.5). To sum up, the hurried reader can limit his or her attention to the last sections of Chapters 2–3 and 5–9, to Section 4.4 of Chapter 4, and then proceed directly to Chapter 10.

Insights from Early Modern Europe

The question at the heart of this book is whether some religions are more conducive to development than others. The most striking contrast that comes to mind is the opposition between progressive Western Christianity and retrograde Islam. In this chapter, I evaluate the first part of this claim – whether Western Christianity is indeed progressive. Since the Protestant Reformation is often considered to be a turning point in the evolution of Western Christianity and since modern European economic growth is often seen as causally related to that key moment, I start by examining critically Max Weber's celebrated thesis about the central influence of Protestant ethics on European development (Section 2.1). The next section considers an alternative view – that it is the intellectual revolution heralded by the Early Enlightenment rather than the Protestant Reformation that put Western Europe on a different path (Section 2.2). Both views are based on the hypothesis that ideas and values determine economic forces, instead of the latter influencing the former. Taking a critical stance toward the idealist approach to development opens the door to a similarly critical assessment of the view that the doctrine of Islam is an obstacle to development. Drawing lessons from early modern European history (Section 2.3) makes that assessment possible.

2.1 A Skeptical View of the Role of the Protestant Reformation

This section provides a detailed critique of Weber's thesis. To complete the analysis, I assess the nature of the relationship between politics and religion in Western Europe both before and after the Reformation.

An Updated Critique of Weber's Approach to Protestantism

Weber's Theory of the Birth of European Capitalism

In "The Ethics of Protestantism and the Spirit of Capitalism" (1905), Max Weber put forward his celebrated thesis that the Protestant Reformation was the main factor responsible for the emergence of capitalist development in Northwest Europe. This conclusion is inferred from the observation that the countries of Europe where capitalism broke through were those that were strongly influenced by Protestantism. The causal mechanism is well known. In addition to promoting the ideal of sober and disciplined pursuit of one's profession in society, the Protestant ethic created a strong motivation for effort and risk-taking because economic success was a sign of election for those who believed in predestination for eternal salvation or damnation. More fundamentally, Protestantism (especially the Calvinist brand) helped "privatize morality," placing an ever-increasing emphasis on the individual, the individual conscience, and the realm of the private as *the* arena of religious activity (Seligman, 1997, pp. 138–41). It implied the rejection of a submissive attitude toward authority and religious hierarchy, and it aimed to ground religious life in the inner ability of the individual believer to know religious truth. This required that believers read the Bible themselves instead of listening passively to the truth as stated and interpreted by ecclesiastical authorities. The Bible was the accepted source of all true knowledge, and anyone could understand God's word if he studied it carefully enough and if the grace of God was in him (Hill, 1975, pp. 93–4). Protestant exploitation of the printing press linked the Reformation to early modern science in diverse ways; in particular, Protestant printing firms increasingly took over scientific publication (Eisenstein, 2012). Protestantism therefore helped develop the scientific spirit and the critical mind (Febvre, Martin, and Nowell-Smith, 2010; Pettegree, 2010).

Recently, the thesis of Max Weber has been energetically rekindled by David Landes (1998). On the empirical level, he notes, "Records show that Protestant merchants and manufacturers played a leading role in trade, banking, and industry" – for example in France, Switzerland, and Germany where Protestants were typically the employers and the Catholics the employed (p. 177). On the theoretical level, Protestantism helped produce "a new kind of man — rational, ordered, diligent, productive," all virtues that were generalized among its adherents "who judged one another by conformity to these standards" (p. 177). In other words, this special brand of religion "encouraged the appearance in numbers of a personality type that had been exceptional and adventitious before" (p. 178). This happened because

Protestantism changed the rules governing European societies. There, it spread by giving a boost to literacy, spawning dissents and heresies, and promoting the skepticism and refusal of authority that are at the heart of the scientific endeavor (p. 179).

Influenced by the Protestant ethic, the industrious middle classes in town and city became convinced that it was a religious duty to impose regular, disciplined labor on the lower classes – or at least to create social conditions that discouraged idleness and inculcated habits of punctuality and an orderly life. Doing so required that observance of saints' days and the traditional village festivals and sports, as well as sexual irresponsibility, had to be fought against (Hill, 1975, pp. 324, 327).

A First Set of Problems: Reverse Causality

Two strands of criticism can be directed at Weber's thesis, both of which call into question the autonomous character of ideas and beliefs. The first criticism questions the role played by the Protestant Reformation in the rise of capitalism in Northwest Europe. A central problem with Weber's thesis, indeed, is that many entrepreneurs in the Protestant Low Countries whom he singled out in support of his theory were actually of Catholic origin. Catholic cities such as Antwerp and cities in northern Italy were major centers of economic activity and trade prosperity even before Amsterdam became one, and migration provided a direct link between the presence of entrepreneurship in Catholic and Protestant cities. As a matter of fact, in the sixteenth and seventeenth centuries in the Low Countries, dynamic individuals, merchants in particular, fled from southern areas (Antwerp, most notably) to northern Calvinist-controlled areas to escape the oppressive climate of the Counter-Reformation (Szirmai, 2005, p. 490; Murray, 1970; Stark, 2005, pp. 131–47).[1]

That the residents of the prosperous cities of today's northern Belgium were disgruntled by the increasing absolutism of the Spanish emperor was evident from a series of revolts and acts of resistance or insurgency. For example, the patrician families of Ghent were outraged by the emperor's attack on their privileges, symbolized by a charter that he had forced them to accept at the time of his "Joyous Entry" into the city in 1515. Similarly, Antwerp refused to publish the anti-heresy edict of April 1550 because it

---

[1] Religious wars proved disastrous and the victories of Catholicism pyrrhic ones: In the decades of persecution, the Catholic princes of Europe expelled the Calvinists and with them their financial reserves and mercantile and manufacturing skills. The industrial heart of Europe was displaced (see, e.g., Moore, 1981).

imposed a certificate for Catholicity on anyone willing to take up residence in the city. The local patricians, artisans, and merchants feared that this edict would seriously jeopardize trade with Protestant England and the Baltic (Greengrass, 2014, pp. 374–5).

In a new development, a significant number of city dwellers who had opted for migration chose to convert to Protestantism in their new location.[2] This sequence of events strongly suggests that, rather than being the driving force of capitalism, the rise of Protestantism was stimulated by emerging capitalist entrepreneurship. Thus, dynamic individuals did not become merchants or capitalist entrepreneurs because of their (Protestant) beliefs, but instead adopted a religion that was compatible with their economic aspirations and their interests. In other words, entrepreneurial people from the middle classes valued patience and the work ethic not because they became Protestant, but rather became Protestant because the new faith promoted these two cultural values in which they, or their ancestors, had earlier decided to invest. And it is because they worked in occupations requiring skills, effort, and experience that they had chosen initially to make such a cultural investment (Doepke and Zilibotti, 2008).

Thus, Luther's initial call for reform strongly resonated in the provinces of the Low Countries, a region with "proud and prosperous urban communities eager to sponsor a renovation of religious life." In these provinces and in German-speaking areas, the articulate, highly literate population welcomed the printed literature of the Reformation, including Dutch translations of the Bible (Pettegree, 2001, p. 68). In a similar manner, after acknowledging the strong relationship between Protestantism and literacy and book consumption – Protestantism was able to explain almost all of the difference in literacy between Northwestern Europe and the rest of the subcontinent – Jan Luiten van Zanden (2009) draws attention to the endogeneity problem. Was the Reformation an external factor, an exogenous shock that caused

---

[2] Emigration was particularly important after Farnese's successful campaign of conquest: Every time Farnese compelled a city to capitulate, hundreds or even thousands fled to the rebellious North. The city of Antwerp, the most powerful and prosperous city in the entire Netherlands, saw its population shrink by roughly half in only four years (in the mid-1580s). After the sack of 1576, Protestants of Antwerp were given two years to emigrate, which caused an outflow of tens of thousands. By contrast, in the early 1600s, one-third of the inhabitants of Amsterdam (estimated at a total number of about 100,000) were foreigners recently arrived in the city (Stark, 2005, pp. 144–5; Greengrass, 2014, p. 415). The exiled south Netherlanders, whether Flemish or Walloons who did not want to live in a re-Catholicized south, were generally endowed with substantial capital and skills, and they thus contributed to the Golden Age of the Dutch Republic (Marnef, 2001, p. 103; Pettegree, 2001, p. 81; Murray, 1970).

literacy to improve dramatically, or should it be considered endogenous? For example, growing literacy at the grassroots level during the late medieval period might have created favorable conditions for the dissemination of the message of Luther and Calvin.

Studies that adequately control for this endogeneity problem are not available, with one exception. Using data for Prussia in the late nineteenth century, Sascha Becker and Ludger Woessmann (2009) show that Protestantism had a positive and significant impact on education. This conclusion is supported by Robert Woodberry (2012), who suggests that, in the process of disseminating their faith, Protestant missions fostered mass education and the dissemination printed publications, while at the same time reinforcing civil society and constraining colonial abuses and elite power. The case of Sweden also probably supports the idea of causality running from the Reformation to literacy, rather than the other way around. It was a largely rural kingdom with a greatly dispersed population where the Lutherian church, backed by the state, embarked on highly successful literacy campaigns that resulted in an overall rate of literacy that was probably higher than 80 percent by the end of the seventeenth century (Todd, 1990, p. 137).

It bears emphasis that, based on this evidence, it is through the accumulation of human capital rather than through a change in work ethic that the Protestant Reformation brought prosperity to certain areas of Europe. Two central questions remain pending, however. First, how can we account for the fact that in Switzerland, a partially Protestant country that was a leading publisher during the sixteenth century, literacy rates declined dramatically during the next two centuries (van Zanden, 2009, p. 195)? And why is it that England, despite its comparatively high degree of urbanization and commercial development, remained, outside of London, a laggard in literacy compared to Sweden, Germany, and the Low Countries (Todd, 1990, p. 138)? Second, establishing a causal link between the Protestant Reformation and education does not automatically imply that the Reformation stimulated growth. Here again, a careful study by Davide Cantoni (2015) is available that properly controls for endogeneity in estimating the potential impact of Protestantism on economic growth. Using microeconometric evidence, the author constructed a novel dataset on German cities (272 cities in the period 1300–1900), exploiting their substantial but denominationally stable religious heterogeneity. He finds no effect of Protestantism on economic growth. This finding is robust to the inclusion of several controls, and it does not appear to depend on data selection or sample size. In addition, Protestantism has no effect when interacted with other likely determinants of economic development.

Interestingly, Tawney (1926) himself was more inclined than Weber to reckon that the Reformation stimulated a movement that was already underway. Other scholars followed in Tawney's path. For example, Higgins (1968) noted that the more highly developed districts were precisely those that gave the most support to the Reformation, finding its creed more suitable to aggressive and progressive ways of life (pp. 163–4). Growing emphasis on the individual and on individual liberties thus appears to have been the result, as much as the cause, of increasing economic liberalization. Walker, a contemporary critic of Weber, was therefore right to blame him for taking the Reformation as a datum rather than inquiring into the causes that lay behind it (Walker, 1937; see also Robertson, 1933). To the extent that economic liberalization and the rise of capitalism required the intervention of path-breaking innovators, those visionaries seem to have been supplied by migrant minority groups with very different religious backgrounds and a strong spirit of dissent (see, e.g., Meier and Baldwin, 1957, p. 168; Szirmai, 2005, p. 490; Samuelsson, 1961; Gorski, 2003; and Camic, Gorski, and Trubek, 2004, for a thorough critique of Weber).[3] In short, the direction of causality seems to be the opposite of that indicated by Weber: Instead of emerging as a consequence of the spread of Protestant beliefs, capitalist entrepreneurs were inclined to adhere to them when they suited their needs (they therefore selected themselves into Protestantism). Economic conditions were ripe for the propagation of an ideology emphasizing private initiative, individual liberty, and personal autonomy. In the sharp words of John Hicks (1969), "it was practice that made the [Protestant] Ethic, not the other way round" (p. 79).

The channel through which the Protestant Reformation exerted, or did not exert, its influence is also of particular interest. A rare empirical study of relevance belongs to Arruñada (2010). Having found that Protestants form the only religious group that favors high-powered economic incentives, he puts forward two competing hypotheses regarding economically relevant values of Christian believers: the (Weberian) "work ethic" argument

---

[3] Schumpeter's critique of Weber deserves to be noted at this stage. Indeed, he finds fault with Weber for having misused the approach of ideal types. In his own words: "So soon as we realize that pure Feudalism and pure Capitalism are equally unrealistic creations of our own mind, the problem of what it was that turned the one into the other vanishes completely. The society of the feudal ages contained all the germs of the society of the capitalist age. These germs developed by slow degrees, each step teaching its lesson and producing another increment of capitalist methods and of capitalist 'spirit'. ... [Weber] set out to find an explanation for a process which sufficient attention to historical detail renders self-explanatory" (Schumpeter, 1954, pp. 80–1).

according to which Protestants are prompted by religion to work harder, and the "social ethic" argument according to which they are more motivated to monitor each other's conduct and to support growth-promoting political and legal institutions. Using data from the 1998 religion module of the International Social Survey Program (ISSP), the author conducts a horse-race test between these competing hypotheses. He finds substantial support for the "social ethic" hypothesis, but none for the "work ethic" hypothesis. Protestantism does seem conducive to capitalist economic development, but the channel is not the direct psychological route suggested by Max Weber. Rather, Protestantism promotes an alternative social ethic that facilitates impersonal trade. Nonetheless, the possibility of self-selection cannot be ruled out: Supporters of growth-friendly political and legal institutions may well have chosen to adopt Protestantism.

In support of the idea that religion tends to be adapted to economic circumstances is the following argument made by Carvalho and Koyama (2016) to explain transformation in Judaism. A powerful movement of Reform Judaism emerged at the turn of the nineteenth century in Germany, which followed the emancipation of Jews (partial or complete) in various parts of Europe and constituted a belated reaction to the Protestant Reformation (Lilla, 2007, pp. 234–50). Strikingly, this movement was first driven by practical men rather than by rabbis and intellectuals. According to Carvalho and Koyama, the attractiveness of new economic opportunities prompted religious Jewish communities to relax practices, such as dietary laws and strict observance of Jewish holidays and the Sabbath, that complicated economic and social interactions within the society in which they lived. Reform Judaism allowed urban and secularly educated Jews to maintain their religious and cultural identity while participating in social and economic spheres of activities previously reserved for Christians. As for intellectual leaders (Abraham Geiger and Hermann Cohen, for example), their role was played out later when the need was felt to rethink the religious foundations of Judaism in a way justifying the innovations that had already taken place.[4]

---

[4] Thus, Hermann Cohen wrote, "Love of our country is a necessary corollary of the idea of the messianic God .... For messianic mankind by no means implies a disintegration of all nations, but rather their unification in a spirit of morality. ... It is the duty of any Jew to help bring about the messianic age by involving himself in the national life of his country. ... Our state is our fatherland" (cited by Lilla, 2007, p. 241). Cohen was not concerned that the religious passions traditionally associated with messianism, which resulted in so many heresies, false prophecies, massacres, and self-immolations, were still alive (p. 243).

In other areas, particularly in Eastern Europe and Russia where economic opportunities remained few in number, at least for members of Jewish communities, what dominated was an ultra-Orthodox reaction that condemned innovations and imposed strict observance of religion-based prohibitions. Whereas Reform Judaism altered Jewish religious practices to keep pace with an evolving outside world, ultra-Orthodoxy modified Judaism with the purpose of isolating it from those changes. In other words, ultra-Orthodoxy was a form of cultural resistance, emphasizing features that distinguished Jews from outsiders.

In the theoretical model they use to explain these transformations, Carvalho and Koyama (2016) explicitly assume that the content of religion depends on the economic environment. They thus conceive that the level of strictness in observance of religious rituals is set by religious leaders who face a tradeoff. By imposing strict rituals and thus "taxing" outside activities, the leaders induce the members of the community to redirect effort toward production of the religious club good. But doing so implies that monetary contributions to the community are foregone. When economic development proceeds slowly and outside economic opportunities are scarce, the gains to the religious authority associated with the strategy of "taxing" participation in outside activities exceed the losses incurred as a result of reduced monetary contributions. Conversely, when economic development occurs rapidly, the increased financial contributions from a richer congregation more than compensate for the lower levels of effort applied to the production of the club good.

A Second Set of Problems: A Revolution Overdone

The second line of criticism of Weber's thesis is that it places undue emphasis on the role of Protestantism in the advent of European modernity: This critique claims that the Reformation of the sixteenth century was less a revolution than a prelude to one. As pointed out by a forceful critic of the Weber-Tawney thesis, both scholars exaggerated differences between Protestantism and Catholicism. For example, Calvin's attitude toward interest and usury was essentially the same as that of the Catholic Church (Robertson, 1933). The Reformation also gave rise to enormous confessional tensions and intense competition among rival religious denominations, reflecting Protestantism's propensity for schism and splintering. These tendencies resulted in an abrupt increase in moral standards imposed by austere moralizing creeds and an extension of the sacred into all areas of life.[5] At least, this was true

---

[5] The term "confession," it must be noted, refers to a type of document, the "confession of faith," that constitutes a declaration of the fundamental doctrines held by a church. One

for a minority of enthusiasts, but more tolerant Christians found it difficult to resist these moralizing efforts openly (Briggs, 1999, pp. 174–6, 191; Duffy, 2005; Naphy, 2007, p. 67). In the process of this evolution, religion became less and less a set of ritual practices and more and more a set of beliefs and tenets intended to define a church's identity. Under the influence of Protestantism, particularly that of Calvinism, which was a creed of the literate and therefore more prone to be uncompromising and doctrinally radical, believers of all kinds were thus asked to internalize the teachings of their church and to act according to the principles of their particular creed (Kaplan, 2007, pp. 30–1; Anderson, 1998, p. 140). In the words of Kaplan (2007), "salvation was to be sought not in habitual acts of observance but in the self-conscious adherence to prescribed (and now proscribed) religious tenets" (p. 31). A creedal religion was thus born in which secular and religious authorities were allowed to administer tests of belief and to monitor behavior (Greengrass, 2014, p. 350). Following the concept of "visitation" found in Calvin, because people have an inherent susceptibility to sin, not only their religious conformity but also their opinions and acts in the matters of everyday life were to be constantly monitored through the eyes of a genuine vice squad (Zweig, 1976).

The spread of obscurantism, the explosion of sectarianism, and an "an orgy of denominational violence" (Naphy, 2007), led to sharp divisions within Christianity at the popular level and attested that "any idea that conformity and orthodoxy can be inculcated through the Bible and the catechism could hardly withstand this practical evidence to the contrary"? (Briggs, 1999, p. 181). There were thus insurmountable problems inherent in Luther's assertion of a priesthood of all believers and in the view of Protestant humanists and radical reformers that "the Bible's meaning was plain, simple and clear, open to both learned scholars and humble ploughmen under the guidance of the Holy Spirit" (Naphy, 2007, pp. 110–11) or that "the inner light is one, and can be recognised by the children of the light" (Hill, 1975, p. 101). The religious opponents of early modern Europe came to picture the world as divided into two camps: truth and falsehood, good and evil, Christ and Antichrist. They reduced all differences to binary oppositions. As a consequence, European society was divided "by faith" in a way it had never been before, and people became passionately and emotionally involved in their religion. In this confessional religious culture, intolerance served as a

of the best-known examples is the Augsburg Confession of 1530, which came to define Lutheran orthodoxy (Kaplan, 2007, p. 29). Another example is the Calvinist Thirty-Nine Articles (1571), which served as a confession of faith for the Church of England (Naphy, 2007, p. 102).

primary way for people to assert their own faith and church affiliation and was viewed as such an essential mark of true piety that its absence could by itself bring down suspicion and punishment (Kaplan, 2007, pp. 28–38; Naphy, 2007, pp. 160–1; see also Koenigsberger, Mosse, and Bowler, 1989, pp. 222–5, 351–4).

English Puritans (who called themselves "the godly") or Dutch Protestant soldiers, in demanding a clear line of separation between the sacred and the profane, displayed extreme moral rigor and intolerance. They rejected every representation of God in their churches and reacted against cults of saints, relics, and eucharistic wafers in an attempt to purify the house of God from intrusive idols.[6] These actions were a direct consequence of the Protestants' paramount objective: to restore a model of the pristine religion "stripped of superstitions and scholastic quibbles, of ceremonies and abstruse doctrines added in later centuries" (Toynbee, 1972, pp. 475–6; Naphy, 2007, pp. 124–32; Kaplan, 2007, p. 129). Thus, in August 1566 violent rioting broke out in many towns of present-day Belgium and Holland. In Antwerp, Ghent, and other cities, "mobs invaded churches and smashed images, altars and all the trappings of 'superstition' that good Calvinists so detested." The fact that this "spectacular orgy of destruction was set off largely by economic stress" just meant that vulnerable sections of the population (unskilled workers, for example) were "responsive to Calvinist preachers attacking what they saw as idolatry" (Anderson, 1998, p. 154).[7]

---

[6] "Puritans demanded a new moral discipline, not only of themselves, but of the whole community as well. They were opposed to many folk customs as well as amusements such as Maypoles, morris dancing, ballad singing and plays. They wanted a clear line to separate the sacred from the profane, calling for an end to Sabbath breaking, elaborate funerals, and the use of churchyards as places for public gatherings and festivities ... they wanted to stamp out semi-magic rituals" (Koenigsberger et al., 1989, p. 354; see also Naphy, 2007, pp. 125–6).

[7] Iconoclasm has deep antecedents in the history of Christianity. It was during the reign of Leo III the Isaurian, in 726, that the most severe religious crisis of the Byzantium Empire broke out. This emperor, who successfully ended a period of anarchy corresponding to the late Heraclides period, contended that because the *Basileus* was the only intermediary between God and the people, he was the only human being susceptible of worship on the same footing as the Apostles. At stake was the outcome of a profound struggle between the imperial power and the influence of the monks, which had risen during the preceding troubled times. Running counter to the monks' belief in the divine power of the images representing Christ, the Virgin and the saints, the iconoclastic theory stated that the cult of images and all practices of revering saints and relics were disapproved by God, as witnessed by the curses that befell the empire (external aggressions and natural disasters). These practices amounted to idolatry and unacceptable superstition aimed at treacherously mobilizing the illiterate masses. To terminate the violent confrontations caused by the controversy around the sacred images, Empress Irène convened the second Council of

Outbreaks of image breaking, desecration of churches, and public displays of heretical religious attitudes aimed at "purifying" church rituals and beliefs through biblical supremacy clearly evoke the attitude of present-day Islamists who advocate a return to the caliphate model of pristine Islam, strict adherence to the Quran, and an end to Sufi practices of popular piety. The Puritans demonstrated "the powerlessness of previously revered sacred objects as they were cast down and humiliated" (Pettegree, 2001, p. 75), yet through such acts of iconoclasm they also antagonized moderate segments of the population that wanted religious toleration and not simply the replacement of one religious dogma by another or the continuation of religious persecution under another garb.[8] Especially hard to accept was the rebels' declared aim to establish a new radical Calvinist regime (which they actually attempted to do both in Ghent and Antwerp in 1578), under which the monopoly of the reformed church would replace that of the Catholic Church: Far from accepting the status of a tolerated minority, the rebels were intent on imposing their own religious and sociopolitical system despite the fact that most local inhabitants were Catholic (van Nierop, 2001a, p. 39).

Historians thus agree that the fanatical activities of the Calvinists, especially in the southern part of the Low Countries, played a major role in detaching the moderates from the revolt and prompting them to reconcile with the Spanish Crown (see, e.g., Marnef, 2001, pp. 93–4).[9] This critical

---

Nicée II (in 787), which eventually approved image cults. In the process, Byzantium elaborated a theology that laid the foundation of the approach of the European civilization to pictural representations of godly figures. In essence, icons are not idols because they are not of the same nature as their divine models: rather they must be seen as points of entry into the sacred universe, which the golden background of the icons symbolizes (Brubaker and Haldon, 2011).

[8] Many members of the Catholic elite, including the nobility, the town magistrates, and the jurists attached to the provincial courts of justice, opposed the anti-heretical legislation and its severe punishments. Numerous local magistrates were actually lax in implementing the "placards," so much so that they did not hesitate to sabotage them (van Nierop, 2001a, p. 36).

[9] As pointed out by Mark Greengrass (2014), the Habsburgs bore responsibility for the radicalization of the Protestant movement. This is because the thoroughness of Charles V's persecution deprived it of those who would naturally have been Protestantism's conservative leaders. The door was thus opened to the Anabaptist movement, which was less dependent on a civic leadership and developed a radicalism that was found nowhere else. In 1530, Melchior Hofman, who had a great impact among Dutch artisans, conceived an apocalyptic message calling on the followers "to separate themselves from the world through the true sign of the covenant (rebaptism) in order to be among those saved in the coming Apocalypse" (p. 376). The original vision of the Anabaptists, stated in the Schleitheim Confession (1527) and particularly appealing to country folk, described a restoration of the church as it had existed in the days of the Apostles (p. 349).

move eventually led to the split of the seventeen provinces into two distinct parts that still prevail today: Belgium in the south and Holland in the north (Darby, 2001). If the moderates in the south were more ready than their counterparts in the north to withdraw from the opposition and submit to the central government's repressive regime under the duke of Alva, it is mainly because they knew from experience how dangerous it was to grant concessions to the rebels whose Calvinist agenda had become clear during the iconoclastic riots. In the north, on the contrary, "Alva's remedies seemed worse than the disease" (van Nierop, 2001a, p. 45). This is partly because during the riots Protestants living north of the rivers had adopted less extreme behavior than their co-religionists in the south, where painful recollection of these events was still very much alive (Marnef, 2001, pp. 97–8).[10] William of Orange himself, who viewed the conflict as a national liberation struggle and dreamed of an inclusive, tolerant autonomous state free of Spanish troops, had to reluctantly give in to the rebels' demand that the Calvinist faith be the only form of worship permitted in the liberated towns (Pettegree, 2001, p. 79). As a result, wherever Calvinist rebels were successful, magistrates of the conquered cities were removed from office and replaced with Calvinists while Catholics were summarily expelled and images smashed (Greengrass, 2014, p. 414). Moreover, the state-building process was very different in the Calvinist and the Catholic areas. While the dynamic, urbanized western region, which depended on commerce and industry (in Brabant, Flanders, and Zeeland) had long felt the strong presence of the central government in Brussels (located at the heart of the Brabant province), the Walloon provinces (Hainault, Artois, Namur) were dominated by a large class of nobles that provided one of the pillars of the Burgundian state and the ties binding these provinces to the center.[11] Furthermore, the northeastern provinces from Utrecht to Groningen had only recently been added by Charles V to the hereditary lands belonging to the Spanish Habsburgs; hence, their eagerness

---

[10] It is thus revealing that in Dordrecht, Gouda, Rotterdam, and Haarlem iconoclasm had never occurred. On the contrary, Utrecht and Amsterdam, restless in 1566, remained loyal to the Spanish king until the late 1570s (Marnef, 2001, p. 98).

[11] It is interesting to note in this regard that the central government was not exclusively imposed from above and against the wishes of the subjects. Thus, most of the ordinances issued by the Privy Council were not taken on the initiative of the government, but instead flowed from petitions and requests sent by private individuals or organizations. In fact, "it was above all the merchants and entrepreneurs (but also many noblemen) in the western core regions who required uniformity in legislation, justice and administration" (van Nierop, 2001a, p. 35).

to achieve a separate status and far-reaching autonomy within the common-wealth (van Nierop, 2001a, pp. 34–5).

By attacking "the paraphernalia of Catholic worship" and by demand-ing a reform of both church and the society in a narrow, Puritan spirit, Protestant radicals alienated a large section of Catholic moderates. They also caused deep fracturing within the world of Protestantism, especially when, in the course of the seventeenth century, they started accusing mod-erate groups of leaning toward popery and acting as crypto-Catholics to subvert the reformed church from within (Kaplan, 2007, pp. 73–93). Thus, in the Netherlands, the Calvinist clergy severely condemned the moderate strand of Arminianism, which believed in a mild theory of predestination (all those who had faith retained a chance of salvation) and wanted a cer-tain amount of decoration in the austere Dutch churches (Pennington, 1970, p. 137). Whereas Lutheranism had become by the mid-seventeenth cen-tury an orthodoxy at least as rigid as Catholicism – its theologians spent considerable time expounding the arid minutiae of esoteric doctrines and attacking the errors of Calvinism – Calvinism had characteristics that were bound to cause fragmentation: "Predestination was above all the faith of sects, each believing itself to be the 'elect' minority" (pp. 135–6). Intolerant attitudes sometimes led to horrible persecution, as attested by the massacres of Anabaptists in Germany and the Netherlands.[12]

Such unity as the Protestant radicals had ever had was eventually destroyed, and all seventeenth-century sects came to jump at each other's throats. Consider what occurred in England:

After 1649 all trends of opinion disavowed the Levellers ... the Quakers all had to counter accusation of being Levellers. Ranters disrupted the Digger commu-nity ... Baptists excommunicated Ranters and Quakers; Quakers attacked Baptists and Ranters as antichristians. To judge by the surviving church books, excommu-nication was one of the principal activities of the early sects. The maintenance of internal purity disrupted unity; without internal purity survival as a sect was impos-sible. ... There was still broad agreement on political aims – opposition to tithes, to the state church and its ministry, to the law, to the existing franchise; but on theo-logical issues, on the Second Coming, they split. (Hill, 1975, pp. 377–8)

The result was aptly described by Fernand Braudel (1995): "Inaugurated under the banner of liberty and revolt, the Reformation soon lapsed into the same degree of intransigence of which it accused its enemy. It built a

---

[12] It was in Brussels in 1523 that the first martyrs of the Reformation were executed by Catholic authorities. Within a few years, Protestants also legitimized the use of violent means to attain religious ends (Kaplan, 2007, p. 128).

structure as rigid as medieval Catholicism" (p. 353). Robert Briggs (1999) writes in the same vein that, "despite its initial appeal to the laity, Protestantism rapidly evolved into a new and highly demanding form of clericalism, whose rigid doctrines and intense moralism were ill-suited to win general support" (pp. 182–3). But even more relevant to the central theme of this book is the following statement of William Naphy (2007):

> Although they strongly disapproved of any system that placed the Church under State control, they [the Puritans] did not want separation of Church and State. Rather, they believed that the State had a divine obligation to work in cooperation with the Church (in practice, guided by the Church) to maintain and promote godliness, to protect and reward virtue, including 'true religion', and to punish wrongdoers ... one of the wrongs they expected the State to punish was anyone reading the Bible and coming to a radically different interpretation from their own. (p. 130; see also Barzun, 2001, pp. 265–6)

It is not surprising then that English kings (James I, then Charles I) viewed the Puritan movement as potentially dangerous to royal control of the church, a fear exacerbated by the Puritans' shared belief in the priesthood of all believers (Naphy, 2007, pp. 126–8). Tensions between the monarchy and its subjects concerned not only the extent to which the king was to be constrained by parliaments but also over whether religion was to be dictated by the monarch or chosen by subjects (p. 131).

In this new context, the Catholic Church was to be a stronger command structure than it had been in the previous centuries. According to Benjamin Kaplan (2007), "until the reformations the Catholic church had been a rather loose institution with room, beneath its broad umbrella, for considerable diversity" (p. 42). A movement like conciliarism, which vested supreme authority in church councils rather than in the pope, was perfectly orthodox until the Council of Trent (1545–63), which was itself a reaction to the Protestant Reformation (see also Anderson, 1998, p. 141). As the Catholic Church reinforced its vertical structure, the Catholicism of the Counter-Reformation became "the religion of princely courts and bureaucratic and hierarchical societies" (Moore, 1981, p. 89).

Catholic confessionalism "entailed a suppression of internal tensions and differences, a stifling of variety, and the imposition on the entire church of a narrow new definition of orthodoxy," which was by and large completed in 1614 (Kaplan, 2007, p. 43). The new standardized beliefs and practices, as they were defined by the canons and decrees of Trent, produced a spiritual unity much tighter than that of medieval Christendom. They were also relatively easy to enforce because Catholic reformers could rely on an international institution with a single head: Uniformity was thus promoted by the centralizing authority in Rome and streamlining the chain of command from pope to bishops to priests (pp. 43–4).[13] Thus the times were over when Christianity was above all a creed emphasizing personal dispositions toward moral excellence, rather than a structure equipped with a doctrine defining a set of correct beliefs, rightful tenets, and appropriate rites to oppose against other religions. Beliefs started to supersede practice, and religion came to mean a system of doctrines that could be either true or false (Cavanaugh, 2009, pp. 66, 72–3).[14]

Protestants, Calvinists in particular, "agreed not only to teach the same doctrines, but to sing the same psalms, recite the same prayers, decorate their churches similarly, and celebrate the same few holidays. ... Not only did they suspect variety as an opportunity for deviance, they regarded it in itself as a species of disorder offensive to God. Uniformity, by contrast, they declared 'holy'" (Kaplan, 2007, p. 43). If there never was an organized and coherent Calvinist international that would have made Calvinism resemble Catholicism in regard to structured conformity, there did develop a scholarly and theological supranational network that gave the movement a strong intellectual unity. The strong Calvinist aspiration to total harmony of church order and liturgical practice was eventually recognized at the synod of Emden (1571) for Dutch Calvinism. This event established "the putative organisation of the Dutch church" articulated around colloquies and local synods that were themselves based on individual congregations (Pettegree, 2001, p. 78). Yet, in spite of the coordinating structure of synods, the focal point remained the local community (Marnef, 2001, p. 102).

Organized within the ambit of political units, Lutheran churches were governed by boards known as consistories, whose function was to discipline and, if necessary, to excommunicate wayward church members, while synods did the same for ministers.[15] Since local churches consulted regularly with each other and made collective decisions (both at the regional level through presbyteries and at higher levels through provincial and national synods), they were bound to obey decisions made by majority vote, even

---

[13] Revealingly, the principle of papal authority was one of the main hurdles that doomed to failure all subsequent attempts at reconciling Protestantism and Catholicism (Kaplan, 2007, p. 130).

[14] This proposition was most clearly stated by Hugo Grotius, the patron of Jacobius Arminius, the founder of Arminianism. It is found in his book *De Veritate Religionis Christianae* that appeared in the early seventeenth century (Cavanaugh, 2009, p. 73).

[15] According to Kaplan, "of all the confessions Lutheranism promoted the closest integration of church and state. In fact, it tended to incorporate the church into the structure of the state, turning it practically into a department of government" (Kaplan, 2007, p. 104). Bear in mind the aforementioned example of Sweden (see fn. 4).

though authority flowed upward through a pyramidal hierarchy. Between territories and countries, Protestants strived for uniformity by influencing one another and building consensus, yet Lutheranism never achieved the sort of unity and strength attained by Calvinism (Kaplan, 2007, p. 44; Anderson, 1998, p. 141).

The situation was noticeably different among the Anabaptist congregations and their descendants, the Mennonites: Because their self-governing churches were essentially autonomous, strict uniformity was impossible to implement (Kaplan, 2007, pp. 44–5). Moreover, Protestant sects thrived outside of the state church, applying the principle of individualism that rejects all mediators between people and God. In England, these sects were strongest in the towns, where they created hospitable communities for men, often immigrants, who had escaped from feudal lordship and whose bond of unity lay in their common acceptance of the sovereignty of God (Hill, 1975, p. 41). Members of such sects recognized each other as "the elect in a godless world," and they organized social services and poor relief, thus providing social insurance for their members "in this world as well as in the next" (p. 42). Here again, the parallel with present-day Islamist movements, such as the Muslim Brothers, is straightforward.

To reach common interpretations of the Bible and counter the risk of anarchic individualism, radical sects considered that any verdict lay with the congregation of believers, viewed as "a society of all-round nonspecialists helping each other to arrive at truth" thanks to the action of the spirit present in everyone (Hill, 1975, p. 372). Being dependent on the voluntary contributions of their congregations, the ministers, insofar as they were still operating, had to reflect the theological and political outlook of the members. There was thus no more room for a church acting as an organ designed to impose and maintain a single consistent outlook (p. 99).[16] As pointed out by Christopher Hill (1975), however, many Protestant sects were too demanding for ordinary people, and intense moral pressure could not be sustained beyond extraordinary periods during which the end of the world seemed imminent. Hence, all but the most dedicated believers were driven back to the state church so that "the sects became restricted to a self-selected elite, the elect" (p. 375).

A final point concerns the relationship between state and religion, which is central to this book. But before looking at how this relationship evolved after the Reformation, a few words are in order about the nature

---

[16] In the even more democratic churches of Baptists and other sectaries, the distinction between clergy and laity simply ceased to exist.

of that relationship before that turning point in the history of Western Christianity.

State and Religion in Western Europe before the Reformation

Christianity emerged within the Roman Empire, and this determined a confrontational course that prompted the first Christians to establish a church structure. What needs to be added now is that the period of opposition between church and state did not last long: The distinction between God and Caesar became blurred when Constantine converted to Christianity and the Holy Roman Empire was later established in Europe with its rulers claiming to be defenders of the faith (Goody, 2006, p. 117). The pagan Roman aristocracy converted to Catholicism on realizing that the Catholic Church was the only way to preserve the Roman civilization after the collapse of the Roman Empire in the fifth century. There followed a period of several centuries during which the ecclesiastical power of Rome was the only central effective power in the western part of Europe. Other corporate organizations that emerged during those times were decentralized, and they included guilds, cities, and religious orders.

A determining moment in the history of Roman Catholic philosophy coincided with the life of Augustine (354–430), who lived in the era of "dismay, pessimism, and confusion" corresponding to the fall of the Roman Empire. Augustine's philosophy, which embodies a remarkable social and historical vision of these times, aimed to enable the Catholic Church to survive the empire by giving it a mission and an identity distinct from the dissolving Roman world and classical culture (Cantor, 1993, p. 75). An important aspect of his philosophy, which was to become extremely influential in the development of medieval thought and of the entire course of Western civilization, lay in his doctrine of original sin and the pessimistic belief that salvation cannot be achieved through political and social change: Evil exists because people are inescapably selfish and bad, and they are unable to redeem themselves through their own efforts. Without the intervention of God, people cannot escape their nature and their grim fate. The secret of salvation therefore rests on religion (Lane-Fox, 2015). Augustine actually perpetuated the Judaic, messianic, apocalyptic idea of the world, seeing the Second Coming of Christ "as the ineffable end of history, when men would be judged and the world that we know would dissolve in glory" (Cantor, 1993, pp. 76–7). In this manner, Augustine sought to reconcile the God of ancient Israel, who appears to be inexplicably unfair, with the Christian God of love (Lane-Fox, 2015).

In Augustine's vision, the role of the state is to establish peace and security, but it cannot extend to providing happiness to human beings, who can never be made good through any political institution. Yet, the instrument of state power can and should be used to force people into the church, which must have absolute authority in this world. In spite of all its imperfections and the "sinful" behavior of those who govern it, the "earthly city" exists for the sake of protecting the "city of God," and its role is therefore vital for people's salvation. Opposing worldly rulers amounts to opposing God's plan. Therefore, Roman Catholic believers should not attempt to overthrow governments even if they turn out to be tyrannical (O'Daly, 2004). Chapter 4 reveals a striking similarity between Islam and Catholicism on this point.

After the fall of the Roman Empire in 476, far from being seen as an entity separate from the church, the state was conceived as an instrument of religion, and vice versa (Goody, 1983; Lal, 1998; Woods, 2005). Hence, it is unsurprising that a great confusion of symbols prevailed. For instance, when Charlemagne became the first Holy Roman emperor in 800, the pope, who governed his own principality, used a language evoking the lineage of imperial Rome, rather than the Sermon of the Mount (Lilla, 2007, p. 44). This was when links with the eastern empire and the eastern emperor were decisively broken while the Carolingians pledged themselves as protectors of the Catholic Church everywhere in the world (North et al., 2009).[17]

Separation between church and state in Western Christianity did not start in earnest until the Gregorian reforms of the eleventh century. Initially intended to shield the Roman papacy from the political ambitions of the German emperor posturing as the head of the Holy Roman Empire, these reforms ended up causing "a genuine separation between the clergy and the laity, between God and Caesar, between the pope and the emperor" (Le Goff, 2003, p. 86). A major cause of the dispute between secular and ecclesiastical powers during the so-called investiture controversy lay in competing claims over the right to appoint high-level religious clerics.[18] In 1075, Gregory VII

---

[17] As pointed out by North, tense relations between the pope and Byzantium, which dated to the fifth century, induced the former to seek an alliance with the Franks in the first part of the eighth century (Ullmann, 1969, p. 1).

[18] Underlying the controversy was the papacy's fear that the Holy Roman emperor would permanently reassemble Charlemagne's empire in Western Europe. In the words of Philip Hoffman (2015), "In their battles against the Holy Roman emperors, the popes gained the support of cities and aristocracies in Italy and Germany. They won over reforming monasteries in Germany and got the Normans as allies by recognizing their conquests in southern Italy. They resorted to divide and rule too, by urging powerful vassals to abandon the emperor's cause and by encouraging urban elites in Italy to drive out the bishops whom the emperor had put in charge of city governments" (p. 132).

decreed that no one was allowed to receive a bishopric or an abbey from the hands of a layman. In the Augustinian tradition, he defended a system where, in matters important for their salvation, people must obey an authority (the pope) and a law (canonical law) distinct from the political authority that controls the territory of their residence (Facchini, 2009, p. 13).

Before the Concordat of Worms (1122), conflict between the two spheres of power – political and religious – erupted whenever this frontier was trespassed, and often the outcome was the excommunication of sovereigns by the popes (for example, Robert II of France, who had insisted on his right to appoint bishops, was excommunicated and ultimately forced to back down in 998) and sovereigns setting up imperial candidates as anti-popes.[19] After the Concordat, the emperors and the kings largely gave up the right of investiture, and in turn the church recognized their authority in a range of temporal matters. It is true that the church continued to meddle in temporal affairs and sovereigns continued to manipulate the papacy and establish their own candidates, as witnessed by the Avignon popes of the fourteenth century and by the conflict about the right to appoint the archbishop of Canterbury in England, which led to the Anglican schism.[20] Nonetheless, each party came essentially to accept, as an inevitable compromise, a separation between the domains of the spiritual and the temporal. That ended the caesaropapist period in the history of the Western church (Fukuyama, 2012, pp. 266–7).

Nevertheless, the impact of the rise of nationalism, which started to be felt as early as the fourteenth century, gradually tilted the balance of power in favor of the secular state. Failed attempts by the pope in Rome to bring back to the fold the popes that the French Crown had installed in Avignon seriously damaged the prestige of the Vatican in all parts of Europe. In the Italian lands, the transition toward more assertive state power was not only gradual but also partial. In feudal times, indeed, the political leaders were either bishops, in the Episcopal see cities, or secular lords and nobles, in the non-Episcopal see cities. In the former cities, the bishops were simultaneously political leaders and the local heads of the church, whereas in the latter

---

[19] Pope Gregory VII excommunicated Emperor Henry IV and tried to depose him; Pope Alexander II excommunicated Harold II, king of England; Pope Urban II excommunicated King Philip I of France; Pope Paschal II excommunicated Henry V, Holy Roman Emperor; Pope Adrian IV excommunicated William I of Sicily; Pope Innocent III excommunicated King John of England; Pope Honorius III excommunicated King Afonso II of Portugal, etc.

[20] For Thomas Aquinas, a major philosopher of the Middle Ages, religion was not separable, even in theory, from political activity in Christendom (Cavanaugh, 2009, pp. 67–9).

cities religious authority was separated from political power (Belloc, Drago, and Galbiati, 2015).[21]

In the countries of Northwestern and Central Europe, as the next section shows, the emergence of modern nation-states from the sixteenth century onward decisively strengthened the power of political authorities at the expense of Rome. National churches rose into prominence, and they began to identify strongly with their own monarchies.

State and Religion in Western Europe after the Reformation

The division of Western Christendom into competing confessions, which was sealed with the Council of Trent, became explosive when combined with the emergence of political units resembling modern nation-states. During the sixteenth century all across Europe, religion and politics combined in such a way that "religious enemies, their hatred fanned by confessional ideology, became political enemies, and vice versa, as people at odds with one another for social or political reasons tended to choose opposing sides religiously as well. ... Competitions for power, wealth, or land became cosmic struggles between the forces of God and Satan" (Kaplan, 2007, p. 102). In such circumstances, rulers across Europe tended to chose among faiths and impose their choice on their subjects, thereby turning religious choice into an attribute of sovereignty. Modern European nations were thus "imagined communities" in which civic and sacral allegiances had to largely coincide on the national or territorial level. They were built on the principle that the cement holding states together consisted, largely if not also primarily, of a shared religion, and that religious division undermined social and political unity, if only because religious dissenters were perceived as potential traitors. As kings strove for religious unity in their lands, regarding it as the foundation of political unity, they thus came to equate orthodoxy with obedience, and religious dissent with rebellion (pp. 102–3). A natural consequence was increased persecutions of heterodox believers castigated as heretics (Johnson and Koyama, 2013).[22]

---

[21] In the same paper, the authors argue that the transition from feudal to communal institutions was more difficult in Episcopal see cities where political and religious powers were in the hands of the same person. They use the occurrence of an earthquake as the exogenous shock that could potentially trigger such a transition.

[22] It bears emphasis that castigating deviant believers as heretics worthy of persecution is a practice that started before the Reformation. In conformity with the argument made in this discussion, it developed in the context of growing state power. It is thus the emergence of a centralized state in France that enabled medieval monarchs to eradicate deviant

Politics thus became increasingly polarized along confessional lines, and by the early seventeenth century, the religious identity of most European states "had sunk roots deep enough that it could not be overturned" (Kaplan, 2007, p. 122). As concluded by Pennington (1970), "Whatever religious or material factors may have determined the original spread of the Reformation, the boundaries between Catholic and Protestant Europe were eventually drawn by political power" (p. 135). The varieties of confessional Christianity had thus succeeded in supplying governments with official ideologies and in providing large, geographically dispersed communities with common symbols and values that became a defining aspect of political identity. Those inhabitants who did not subscribe to the official creed and church of their polity could not claim all the privileges of full citizenship, and against them the harshest regimes could bring the charge of treason when they felt threatened (pp. 110, 114–15, 121–3, 136; see also Gunn, 1999). According to Kaplan (2007) again, this "fusion of religious and political identity, piety, and patriotism" was a great cause of religious intolerance in early modern Europe (p. 102). Clearly, the Augsburg principle *cuius regio, eius religio* had revealed its basic flaw: It was utterly dependent "on the whims of individual rulers and dynasties that had considerably more concerns than what denominations their subjects practiced" (Naphy, 2007, p. 119). A few illustrations prove useful at this point.

The Dutch revolt attests that a nonconfessional cause – the defense of freedom and local privileges following the medieval model of a loose federation of autonomous communities and town corporations, and the concomitant resistance against princely absolutism[23] – could end up being associated with a particular confession: Begun as a rebellion by people of all faiths, the revolt ended "as a war pitting Catholic Spain against an officially

---

religious practices as a way of enhancing their own legitimacy. Furthermore, "because of the amorphous nature of religious belief in the south of France during the thirteenth century, the centralizing state faced little incentive to secularize legal institutions. Instead, it chose to restrict tolerance and in the process created a 'persecuting society'" (Johnson and Koyama, 2013, p. 11). It is revealing that, before the crusade against them, the heretics of the Languedoc (known as the Cathars) did not necessarily reject the Catholic faith: They were often buried with orthodox Catholics and participated in the Catholic sacrament. It is the Church's Inquisition (1244–45) that actually created the image of an organized heresy, and in so doing it hardened the boundaries between orthodox Catholicism and deviant belief (p. 10).

[23] For example, during the latter quarter of the fifteenth century, Mary of Burgundy had been forced to grant the "Great Privilege." The concessions given in this constitutional document applied to the entire Burgundian Netherlands and reinforced the position of representative institutions. It is therefore not surprising that, a century later, the rebels would often refer to the Privilege in their struggle against Spanish rule (Marnef, 2001, p. 89).

Calvinist republic" (Kaplan, 2007, p. 110; see also Anderson, 1998, pp. 155–7; Darby, 2001; Marnef, 2001, p. 99).[24] It is, indeed, thanks to its association with patriotism that Calvinism became the official religion of the newly independent Dutch republic. And, conversely, it is thanks to its association with the Calvinist rebellion that the anti-Spanish war could be waged and eventually won.

As pointed out earlier, by inclination William of Orange favored an open and tolerant Dutch republic that would be free of any Spanish troops. But disastrous defeats on the battlefield soon taught him that unless he sank his own cause into that of the Calvinist rebellion his prospects of repelling the Spanish army were doomed (Pettegree, 2001, p. 78). Since at the beginning of the revolt the Calvinist congregations were more active in the southern provinces that returned to the Spanish fold than in the northern provinces that emancipated themselves from Spanish rule, the end outcome of the conflict in the Low Countries was produced by "an ironic turn of events" (Kaplan, 2007, p. 109).[25] Pressures to identify Calvinism with the revolt were all the more irresistible as Catholicism became associated with loyalty to Philip II, the devoutly Catholic king of Spain, and as Pope Gregory XIII threatened Catholics with excommunication if they supported the revolt (Anderson, 1998, pp. 158–63). Whatever the mechanisms at work, the result was that "the Netherlands was not the haven of religious liberty that it imagined itself to be later in the seventeenth century." But, thanks to the military victories won by Mauritz of Nassau, William of Orange's son, the United Provinces of the Netherlands "learned to be a state-like structure with which the rest of Europe had to deal" (Greengrass, 2014, pp. 416–7).

In Poland, where a tradition of religious tolerance had come to prevail even after many nobles converted to Calvinism beginning in the mid-sixteenth century, identification of the nation with Catholicism came only

---

[24] Thus, in the 1560s a broad coalition of noblemen and burghers, Catholics and Calvinists alike, was formed in opposition to Philip II's plan known as the "new bishoprics scheme." In this plan, the king of Spain strengthened the power of bishops, appointed inquisitors in each bishopric, and arranged the borders of the bishoprics so as to make them contiguous with those of the Habsburg territories. Catholics joined hands with their Protestant countrymen because they could not identify with the intolerant, confessional policies of Philip that resembled so little the Catholicism in which they had been raised. In fact, many Netherlanders at the time could not be easily classified as either Catholic or Protestant, "for their piety combined a variety of influences" (Kaplan, 2007, pp. 107–8).

[25] This was especially true of Antwerp and, to a lesser extent, of Bruges and Ghent (in the Flemish-speaking provinces) and Valenciennes and Lille (in the Walloon, French-speaking provinces). In all these cities, Calvinist congregations included many among the local financial and merchant elites (Pettegree, 2001, pp. 71, 76).

after the invasion of the Swedes around the midpoint of the next century. The conflict between the two countries did not begin as a religious war, yet it became one in due course. Resenting the Swedish occupation (and the ensuing attacks by Brandenburg Prussia and Transylvania), the Poles began to recast the war in religious terms, viewing the struggle against the Protestant invaders as a war against heretics in defense of Catholicism. For their part, the Swedes treated Polish Lutherans as natural allies, thus contributing to a self-fulfilling prophecy: Increasingly discriminated against, Protestants started looking to Sweden and Brandenburg for protection and support (Kaplan, 2007, pp. 111–14; Naphy, 2007, pp. 106–9). In Sweden itself (particularly under King Gustav Adolf), the Lutheran Church became a local administrative machine of the state (which assessed and collected taxes and even helped organize conscription) and was extremely rigorous in imposing its severe moral code on the population (Pennington, 1970, p. 136). As in Germany where the centralization of principalities was often achieved by Protestant princes through religious change, the Swedish Reformation turned out to be a conservative affair.[26] In fact, it "relied on top-down religious structures in which secular forces played a dominant role": In a context of obsession with "order," the appeal to religion was essentially a way to govern people's social and moral behavior (Greengrass, 2014, pp. 350–1).[27]

The case of England is especially interesting because in this country the reform was initially a conservative movement driven by a despotic king to satisfy his sexual lusts and dynastic desires. As pointed out by William Naphy (2007), "had the king Henry VIII been able to gain some measure of direct national control of the Catholic church within his realms, as had the kings of France and Spain, and the rulers of many Italian states, there would not have been a Reformation" (pp. 92–3). The passage by Parliament

[26] Charles V, although making some concessions to Protestant sensitivities, essentially achieved a re-Catholicization of the German territories. The main exception was the Protestant state of Magdeburg, an early adopter of the Reformation. According to Greengrass (2014), the siege of Magdeburg was "a manifestation of the politics of conviction, where religious identity would be coterminous with political loyalty, both couched in historically rooted salvation myths" (pp. 348–9). The failure of that attempt to bring Magdeburg into submission led to the Peace of Augsburg (1555). This treaty laid the basis for the later Reformation in German lands, "legalising Lutheranism in the hands of established authority" (p. 349).

[27] Not much was actually changed in terms of religious rituals. The Swedish Mass retained altars, crucifixes, candles, vestments, the Virgin Mary, and saints' days. Changes were mainly confined to replacing Latin with the vernacular, the communion in both kinds, and the suppression of incense and holy water. By contrast, political changes were substantial: Gustav Vasa dispossessed the Catholic Church of its lands and replaced the Danish clergy with its own (Greengrass, 2014, p. 351).

(guided by Thomas Cromwell) of the Act of Supremacy (1534), which made the king supreme head of the newly established Church of England and repudiated papal supremacy, sealed the break with Rome. Iconoclasm was almost always sanctioned if not orchestrated by the state, and the ordination of priests was replaced by a government-controlled system of appointments, thus establishing secular legal sovereignty over ecclesiastical affairs (pp. 98–9)[28].

Although it was never Henry's intention to found a Protestant church, because its aim was essentially to reverse the historic increase of papal power versus the power of secular rulers in England[29], under his son Edward "a true princely Reformation" occurred. It was to be subsequently strengthened under Elizabeth who permitted the Church of England to take a more explicitly Protestant line. The active involvement of Spain and the pope in various attempts to remove the queen from power in order to reestablish Catholicism, albeit unsuccessful, had the effect of linking Anglicanism with

---

[28] The right of the king to nominate bishops was recognized in the Ecclesiastical Appointments Act. Note that in France and Spain, also, the kings held a similar power, yet they at least accepted that, technically, the pope had the final say (Naphy, 2007, p. 96).

[29] An increase in papal power can be traced as far back as the early thirteenth century when Angevin King John, better known as Landless John, was twice humiliated by Pope Innocent III. First, there was a quarrel about the appointment of the archbishop of Canterbury: John regarded the appointment of Stephen Langton by the pope as a gross violation of the traditional royal authority over the English church. The conflict escalated to such a point that Innocent, after having placed England under an interdict that suspended church services, encouraged Philip Augustus, king of France, to prepare for the invasion of England under the papal banner (1213). Frightened at the prospect of losing England to his archenemy as he had lost most of his continental possessions, John abnegated power before the pope. As a result, he became the pope's vassal and made England the fief of the papacy. This was a complete reversal of the state of Anglo-papal relations as they had existed since the time of William the Conqueror.

In 1214, John suffered his second great humiliation. Indeed, he had to appeal to his papal overlord to absolve him from the vows he had made to the English barons under the terms of the Magna Carta. Innocent III, who did not like the erosion of his vassal's power that the charter implied, immediately complied. The barons reacted by taking up arms against the king and inviting Louis, the son of the king of France, to take the throne. The sudden death of John made possible the restoration of peace between the royal government and the magnates. John's heir, Henry III, was even more subservient to the pope, who handed Sicily over to the brother of the French king when the English Crown proved unable to pay its taxes to Rome. This failure was a result of strong disagreement with the magnates who were dissatisfied with Henry's government and refused to give their consent to the imposition of new taxes. It is only under his son, who came to the throne as Edward I in 1272, that the situation started to change: Edward I had become conscious of the corporate and national feelings of his country, and he was determined to channel these attitudes toward the reconstruction of royal authority both vis-à-vis the pope and the local magnates (Cantor, 1993: 422–3, 452–7; see also Duby, 1987).

the identity of the English nation: "Popery" soon became the imagined foe against which the country defined itself as a nation. Fear of Catholicism has, therefore, to be seen in the context of the continuous threat posed by the country's inveterate enemies, Spain or France, which were identified with that particular religion. There prevailed a constant fear, real or imagined, of a Catholic restoration, at least as long as people suspected their own king of Catholicism (and as long as there lived in the country a Catholic Stuart with a claim to the throne). Strikingly, religious violence tended to erupt in times of specific crises, including the Glorious Revolution of 1688–9, which always coincided with threats of foreign invasion (Kaplan, 2007, pp. 115–18; Naphy, 2007, pp. 102–3; Vallance, 2007; Harris, 2007; Pincus, 2009).

It would be misleading, however, to think that European kings were mainly driven by religion when making political decisions. Even Philip II of Spain, a devout Catholic, often behaved in ways that put political interests before religious aims. In fact, he would "never allow policy to be decided merely by religious emotion," and "however strong his faith he was always sensitive to any threatened clerical infringement of his authority within his own dominions" (Anderson, 1998, p. 142). The predominance of political considerations was especially visible in the sphere of foreign policy where "the necessities of the king took precedence over the feelings of the Catholic" (p. 143). Nowhere was this more evident than in his ambivalent attitude toward England. On the one hand, as pointed out earlier, he considered England as the enemy of Catholicism, but on the other hand, he was eager to use England as a countervailing force against the threatening ambitions of France. Thus, Philip did not agree when the French king Henry II proposed that they work together to strengthen Catholicism and royal power in Scotland. Putting the Catholic Mary Stuart, queen of Scots, in Elizabeth's place presented the risk of encouraging a future French invasion of England. To maintain the alliance with England, it was therefore essential to keep Elizabeth on the English throne, whatever her religious allegiance. Likewise, Philip opposed the plan of Pope Pius IV to excommunicate the English queen because this would have ignited a Catholic revolt aimed at overthrowing Elizabeth and would legitimize a French invasion. Such a reaction made Philip the objective ally of the English Reformation (pp. 143–4).

In France, likewise, Philip saw many political advantages in the survival of the Huguenots, however much he deplored it from a religious point of view. The fact of the matter is that, while he sincerely wanted France to be Catholic and the French Calvinists to be defeated, he also wanted France to be weak, and these two objectives were clearly incompatible (Anderson, 1998, p. 148). In a similar fashion, Catholic France funded Lutheran Sweden to liberate the

Calvinist palatinate from Catholic Spain.[30] And Catholic Bavaria joined the Protestant princes against the Habsburgs. Quite a few Catholic states lent their support to Protestants, and Protestant states to Catholics during the Thirty Years War (1618–48) that killed about 35 percent of the population of Central Europe (Naphy, 2007, pp. 124–5; Moore, 1981, p. 91). Almost one century before, the Catholic kings of France had been so alarmed by the Habsburgs' centralizing ambitions that, from 1521–52, they engaged in five military campaigns against the Catholic emperor, Charles, who was supported in these conflicts by many of the Protestant German princes. Henry II of France, a Catholic, did not hesitate to join the Lutheran League in an attack on the emperor's forces (Armstrong, 2014, pp. 227, 230).

The crux of the matter is that no ruler could allow policy to be shaped merely in terms of religious allegiances or preferences, and political considerations came to increasingly govern the course of events. As aptly pointed out by Sutherland (1973), "What could once have been represented as a religious struggle pursued in the political sphere, became more and more a political struggle pursued partly in the name of religion" (cited in Anderson, 1998, p. 149). The Peace of Augsburg, which signaled the defeat of Charles and shattered the Habsburgs' ambition of imperial rule, greatly enhanced the political power of the princes, Protestant and Catholic alike. Indeed, they were now able "to use the Reformation to their own advantage, taxing their clergy, appropriating Church estates, controlling education and potentially extending their authority, through the parishes, to every single one of their subjects"; that is, they were now able to subdue and control the church in their own realms (Armstrong, 2014, pp. 226–7). Compared to medieval times when the church was integral to government and religion was hard to distinguish from politics, the time had come for statesmen to clearly distinguish between the two worlds and to assert the domination of politics over religion (pp. 232–4; see also Skinner, 1978, Vol. 2, pp. 349–50). In the stark words of William Cavanaugh (2009), "Ostensibly, the holy was separated from politics for the sake of peace; in reality, the emerging state appropriated the holy to become itself a new kind of religion" (p. 11).

In England, one of the main purposes and effects of the Anglican schism was that it allowed the country to gradually construct its nationhood and to

---

[30] Cardinal Richelieu, chief minister of France, persuaded King Gustav Adolf of Sweden to invade the Habsburg Empire, and when Lutheran German peasants tried to drive the Lutheran Swedes out of their country in November 1632, they were simply massacred. Eventually, the German Catholics and Protestants fought together against the Swedes, and the rest of the Thirty Years War became essentially a struggle between Catholic France and the Catholic Habsburgs.

confront the threat posed by external enemies, France in particular. Speaking about the Glorious Revolution (to which I soon return), Steve Pincus (2009) thus writes,

The Revolution of 1688–89 was a successful act by the English political nation to replace a government that they increasingly perceived to be ruling in the French style with an English government. It was a Protestant revolution in the sense that the English national religion was explicitly defended and celebrated as one of the elements – arguably one of the most important elements – of English national identity threatened by James. It was not, however, a war of religion, a war in defense of universal religious truth. ... The English – including William's own propagandists – understood the war against France as a war to protect national integrities against an aspiring universal monarch, not as a war of religion. (pp. 338–9)

Inside France, the use of religion proved opportunistic in the sense that it aligned with political motives. Whereas in the beginning, support for the Reformation was concentrated in the towns, the situation changed rapidly after Henry II passed away (1559) and power was vested in the young Francis II. In that power vacuum, the Guise family, who were strong Catholics, tried to push their advantage. A realignment of power loyalties followed that for the first time embraced the growing religious divisions. In the words of Andrew Pettegree (2001), "Those who wished to challenge the Guise hegemony saw increasing merit in opposing their policy of uncompromising opposition to religious dissent. By doing so they could not only advance their own claims to influence; they could also tap the growing strength of the Calvinist communities and thereby create a new network of allegiance to challenge the power which accrued to the Guise by their monopoly of patronage" (p. 73). As a result, Anthony of Navarre and Henry of Condé (his brother) became increasingly identified as the champions of the new religion and the leaders of the Huguenots; their example was soon imitated by large numbers of lesser nobles who had been impoverished after the end of the Franco-Habsburg war (1559). Clearly, the French Wars of Religion (1562–98) "were more than a fight between the Calvinist Huguenots and the Catholic majority; they were also a political contest between competing aristocratic factions" (Armstrong, 2014, pp. 227–8; see El Kenz and Gantet, 2008, pp. 95–118, for a more elaborate treatment).

Influential noblemen were also in the lead of the religious rebellion in the Netherlands before the outbreak of the Dutch revolt. In this region, too, there was a sizable noble class frustrated by the erosion of its power under the centralizing policies of Margaret of Parma, regent for the absent Philip II. High nobles – William of Orange and the counts Egmont and Hornes in particular – led the struggle, and they quickly gained support from a larger body of lesser nobles. Nevertheless, in striking contrast to the situation in France, the Dutch Calvinist communities emancipated themselves at an early stage from reliance on their noble patrons, which goes a long way toward explaining why Calvinism was firmly embedded in the foundations of the free Dutch state and why the Reformed church would always remain at the heart of its life and cultural identity (van Nierop, 2001a, pp. 37–8; Van Nierop, 2001b, pp. 48–66; Pettegree, 2001, pp. 73–5, 82).

In Germany, too, the Protestant Reformation was much more than a theological revolt. It was also "a protest against internal disorder and external encroachments in the Empire" (Simms, 2013, p. 19). Brendan Simms (2013) thus explains the impact of the Reformation in certain regions of Germany in a way strikingly similar to the explanation of Islamist movements offered in Chapter 7:

> Luther, Ulrich von Hutten, Andreas Osiander and other reformers … sought to revive the German nation through spiritual transformation, a call to repentance and prayer which would purge the Empire of the impurities which had weakened it in the face of attacks from east and west. Luther's message resonated not only among educated people, but also with the inhabitants of rural areas, especially in the south and west, who saw in the Reformation a chance to emancipate themselves from the control of the lords, and an opportunity to reform the Empire and restore German national 'honour' in Europe. (p. 19)

Three final remarks on state-religion relations after the Protestant Reform are now in order. First, the role of political expediency in the choice of national religions has a wider scope of application than what has been suggested earlier. In Hungary, for example, the original choice of Catholicism rather than Eastern Christianity (Rome versus Byzantium)

> was dictated not so much by cultural and theological as by momentary political considerations. Wedged between the eastern and the western empires, and facing a papacy feuding with the German emperors, Hungary was in a relatively favourable bargaining position which she used to maximum advantage. Her rulers extracted from the pope concessions that had been granted to few occidental monarchs. Thus in the course of negotiations that preceded his conversion (in early eleventh century), the future king of Hungary and his successors were given "apostolic rights" which included, among others, the right of veto over all ecclesiastic appointments, and the right of refusing to promulgate any of the papal bulls. (Janos, 1982, pp. 11–12)

Second, a religion different from the official religion of the political regime could be used to ensure obedience and submission in newly colonized territories. An example that springs to mind is Russia, as attested by the confessional policy followed by Empress Catherine II in Kazakhstan in the second half of the eighteenth century and thereafter by several of her successors. The central idea governing this policy was that control of the Muslim elites necessitated the centralization of religious affairs and the bypassing of the decentralized, informal system of Sufi orders that was deeply rooted among the Kazakh nomads, in particular. In a first step, Catherine made her toleration of Islam an official policy enshrined in a famous edict that became a law (the "Toleration to All Faiths" edict) in 1773. She then took a series of important measures aimed at attracting Muslim military and religious elites to the empire's cause: the construction of numerous mosques along the Kazakh steppe, the sending of Tatar mullahs to propagate Islam among "wild nomads" of the region, and the establishment of a Muslim state publishing house in St Petersburg (it moved to the city of Kazan in 1802) (Bobrovnikov, 2006, pp. 205–6).

As things turned out, however, these seductive measures of religious toleration and support laid the ground for more active steps destined to impose religious discipline using Islamic affiliation as the means of domination and projecting imperial power on the empire's frontiers. Nowhere was this more evident than in the setting up of the Orenburg Assembly, also called the "muftiate," which was responsible for opening and registering mosque congregations in St Petersburg, Moscow, Inner Russia, the Volga-Ural region, Siberia, and the Kazakh steppe. Based on both the sharia and imperial laws, it worked as a kind of Muslim Supreme Court, issuing legal decisions in civilian matters as well as in appointments of imams and mosque building. The mufti at its head was appointed by governors, effectively placing the religious and legal practices of Muslims under state control (Bobrovnikov, 2006, pp. 207–8). This policy was furthered by Alexander I who created a Department of Spiritual Affairs after the consistorial pattern of Napoleonic France (1832). One of its functions was supervision of the Orenburg Assembly. Nicholas I reinforced the dependence of Muslim religious elites on the imperial administration as so-called Polizeistaat laws attempted to manage even symbolic expressions of Islam. Moreover, to reduce the importance of the Orenburg Assembly, the tsar established the Tauride Directorate, within which a more strict hierarchy of Muslim religious elites was set up: Village and town imams (the "khatibs" and "mullahs") "were put under the control of the district qadi who in his turn obeyed the orders of the directorate" (Bobrovnikov, 2006, p. 209).

Finally, it is remarkable that the Protestant Reformation did not fundamentally change the vision of the relationship between religion and politics that was embedded in the Augustinian tradition. Thus, for Martin Luther, to rebel against one's sovereign was equivalent to rebelling against God

himself. Has not God awarded to some persons the privilege to govern?
Even when the ruler appears to be unjust, God cannot have made a mistake:
If people are ruled by a cruel sovereign, this must be the outcome of a divine
punishment. It is in the name of this principle that in 1525 Luther staunchly
supported the implacable repression of German peasants who were driven
to rebellion by sheer misery and inspired by the egalitarian ideology proclaimed by Anabaptist leaders. Luther's attitude was of great portent since
the so-called war of the German peasants resulted in more than 100,000
deaths (Nichols, 2002).

2.2 A Skeptical View of the Role of the Early Enlightenment

A Dutch philosopher, Jonathan Israel, has most persuasively argued the
view that the Early Enlightenment sparked the modernization of Western
Europe. I summarize this argument in this section before embarking on a
critique that bears close resemblance to the arguments used against Weber's
approach.

The Early Enlightenment as the Decisive Breakpoint?

According to Jonathan Israel, the period from 1680–1750 was the most "dramatic and decisive period of rethinking" because it was during those years
that "the mental world of the west was revolutionized along rationalistic and
secular lines" (Israel, 2001, p. 20). Before this period, despite the profound
disarray and distress caused by the Reformation, hardly anyone shared the
view that "the individual should be free to think and believe as he or she
thought fit." Education and any expression of opinions were closely supervised and controlled "by an elaborate apparatus of royal, ecclesiastical, and
academic authority" (pp. 16–17). Toward the late seventeenth century, however, "the old hierarchy of studies, with theology supreme, and philosophy
and science her handmaidens, suddenly disintegrated" (p. 10). This dissolution was to lead to the more radical movement of the eighteenth-century
Enlightenment.

Perhaps surprisingly, the proponents of the Reformation did not question the subservient status of philosophy and science. Although it caused
a deep split in Western Christendom that resulted in a confessionalization of the European societies (see the earlier discussion), the Reformation did not pose a genuine challenge to "the essentials of Christianity or
the basic premises of what was taken to be a divinely ordained system of
aristocracy, monarchy, land ownership, and ecclesiastical authority" (Israel,

2001, p. 4; see also Lilla, 2007, p. 319). Oleg Kharkhordin (1999) perhaps expresses the limitation of the Reformation most aptly: Indeed, if the Reformation stressed the notion of individual conscience, so that conscience was no longer seen as a shared capacity, it did not separate the notion of "conscience" from that of "consciousness." The Protestant understanding of the conscience was that of "an individual, and yet undifferentiated capacity of moral and factual judgment, exercised in accordance with the Holy Word." It was only later, with the advent of modernity, that consciousness "became the site of the cognitive capacities and judgments of fact, while conscience became a purely moral faculty, robbed of any pretensions of giving objective information on the external world" (p. 57).

For Israel, the advent of modernity coincided with the intellectual upheaval of the Early Enlightenment in the late seventeenth century (spawned by Baruch Spinoza, Pierre Bayle, John Locke, and Gottfried Leibniz), a movement that reflected a deep crisis among the elites but also quickly had an impact on ordinary men's attitudes. In its most radical version, it combined "immense reverence for science, and for mathematical logic, with some form of non-providential deism, if not outright materialism and atheism along with unmistakably republican, even democratic tendencies" (Israel, 2001, pp. 4–5, 12). Based on the idea that nature is self-moving (motion is inherent in matter), it led to the rejection of a providential God governing the destinies of humans, while emphasizing the existence of a rational principle inherent in the physical and social universe, which then started to appear as intelligible concepts for the reasoning individual (p. 160).[31] The process of rational inquiry could be applied to the scriptures themselves, and Richard Simon advanced the idea that biblical writers or their sources could be subject to human fallibility (Pennington, 1970, pp. 153–4).

Although the overthrow of the traditional social order and hierarchy was no goal of the mainstream Enlightenment thinkers, given that their ideal was mainly to spread enlightenment, tolerance, and humanity among the educated, changes caused by the gradual diffusion of the ideas of the new philosophes across all strata of European societies, including the elites, proved to be of a much more radical nature than anything they had ever imagined. Even though they could envision a political revolution of the

---

[31] For Spinoza, the leading philosopher behind the whole movement, "nothing is based on God's Word or commandment so that no institutions are God-ordained and no laws divinely sanctioned: hence the only legitimacy in politics is the self-interest of the individual" (Israel, 2001: 5; see also Chap. 8).

kind occurring in England (the so-called Glorious Revolution), they did not anticipate the far-reaching social and economic consequences that their teachings were to entail (Hampson, 1968, pp. 155–61).

Back to the Reverse Causality Problem

Political Emancipation and the Gradual Rise of the Rule of the Law
Israel's account of the emergence of modern Europe suffers from the same flaw as that of Weber: It suggests that the intellectual revolution of the Early Enlightenment was autonomous, in the sense of having arisen independently of material forces or determinants. To see why such a view is incomplete, one just needs to bear in mind that the Glorious Revolution occurred in England in 1688; that is, right at the beginning of the period of intellectual crisis referred to by Israel. From the works of historians such as Richard Bonney (1991), Charles Tilly (1992), Philip Hoffman and Kathryn Norberg (2002), Steve Pincus (2009), and Jan Luiten Van Zanden and Maarten Prak (2009), we know that this political revolution was the outcome of a protracted struggle in the course of which the most influential segments of society (including successful merchants in large and prosperous cities such as London) gradually asserted themselves by confronting a strong state power naturally bent on further entrenching its supreme position.

Economic forces were not absent from this political revolution: The political struggles between rulers and citizens partly concerned the nature of the linkage to be established between taxation and representation. Because of his dependence on economically prosperous individuals (the landed aristocracy, the gentry, merchants, etc), particularly so in times of fiscal crisis, the British monarch was compelled to grant them the representative institutions that they required in exchange for their financial contributions. The Glorious Revolution initiated the era of parliamentary supremacy, implying that the Crown could no more claim to be above the law and "could no longer capriciously make, and break, promises" (Bates, 2001, p. 80; see also North and Weingast, 1989; Vallance, 2007; Harris, 2007; Pincus, 2009). This major concession, which went against the absolutist divine-right rule that the king had so far been claiming for himself, was won only gradually by Parliament. An important precedent was the Petition of Rights (1628), itself based on a much older document, the Magna Carta (1225).[32]

---

[32] King John originally issued the Magna Carta under intense pressure from feudal barons whom he had repeatedly fleeced. But he very soon reneged on the charter, which was nevertheless reissued by the succeeding regent, William Marshal, and later on by his own son,

Chapter 39 of the Magna Carta's original states that "no free man shall be seized or imprisoned, or stripped of his rights or possessions, or outlawed or exiled, or deprived of his standing in any other way, nor will we proceed with force against him, or send others to do so, except by the lawful judgment of his equals or by the law of the land" (cited from *Economist*, December 20, 2014–January 2, 2015, p. 46). In sum, the document provided that the king could not proceed against any freeman in the realm except by the prevailing due process of common law, thereby affording all men with property a legal protection against royal absolutism. As for the Petition of Rights, it was a genuine proto-constitution because, unlike the Magna Carta, it was approved by Parliament. It set limits to monarchical power, recognizing that even the sovereign is subject to God and the law, and it granted all Englishmen a set of rights protected by law (North, 2005, p. 145; Naphy, 2007, p. 133; Vallance, 2007, p. 176; Cantor, 1993, pp. 453–5; Pincus, 2009, p. 145; *Economist*, December 20, 2014–January 2, 2015, p. 47).

Such a basic change in perceptions of the rights of individuals – from the medieval views of status (those at the bottom of the hierarchical structure of the society were excluded from access to liberties) to the modern view of Englishmen as freeborn – can only be understood if placed in the context of incremental changes that included the development of a legal literature (beginning in the twelfth century in Anglo-Saxon England) emphasizing the idea of authority as an obligation of the sovereign to the people (Bloch, 1961, pp. 110–11; Obolonsky, 2003, p. 28; North, 2005, p. 136). The Petition of Rights was an extensive concession that King Charles had to make when he needed Parliament to furnish funds for the opening phases of the Thirty Years War. Thereafter, however, he again attempted to restore his divine rule and to reign without Parliament, a relapse that would last only until 1640 when he needed additional money to finance his campaign in the Bishops' Wars. Members of the Parliament, after an initial refusal to grant him funds, presented the king with a longer list of grievances that, in contrast to the Petition of Rights, also included complaints about religious practices. One year later, the Star Chamber, a judicial court entirely controlled by the king, was abolished, a step followed by the ruling that all cases involving property should be tried at common law courts (North and Weingast, 1989; Naphy, 2007, pp. 132–3).

Henry III, on his coming of age in 1225. The charter then largely disappeared from view for the next four centuries until it was reactivated in the form of the Petition of Rights that the English Parliament forced King Charles I to sign.

The Treaty of Westphalia in 1648, which ended the Thirty Years War, closed "the era of the unfettered prince as sovereign and ushered in a progressively more secularized system of leadership," in the sense that princes no longer acted as agents of religious authority and worship became a private matter distinct from the practice of ruling (Duffy Toft, 2007, pp. 107–8). By the end of the war, mutual exhaustion and bargaining between princes, on the one hand, and merchants and bankers, on the other hand, had "combined to make the previous century's ideal of a religiously sanctioned, all-powerful prince nearly extinct (it survived only in Russia)" (p. 108). This move toward separation of religion from politics was nevertheless partial and shaky. It was partial because the treaty did not amount to a truly European accord: England, Poland, Russia, and Turkey did not take part in the negotiations.[33] Moreover, the treaty did not end France's war with Spain, nor did it prevent the German emperor from attempting to re-Catholicize its empire (Greengrass, 2014, pp. 641, 643; El Kenz and Gantet, 2008, pp. 147–9).

Yet, emancipation from princely absolutist power and enhancement of individual rights struck even deeper roots than what has been suggested here. To see how, it must be borne in mind that the Glorious Revolution resulted from the invasion of an Anglo-Dutch force (in the autumn of 1688) led by William III of Orange and comprising British exiles acting in coordination with the Dutch States General. This force joined with English opponents to Stuart rule and chased James II from the throne where he was replaced by a member of the House of Orange, the ruling family in the United Provinces. The Dutch lost no time in transforming English political institutions in a direction shaped by their own historical experience, which implied the imposition of strong checks and balances on the ruler's power (Bates, 2001, pp. 79–80; Pincus, 2009, pp. 323–33).[34]

---

[33] Under the Peace of Westphalia, the Austrian Habsburgs remained in control of their hereditary lands, and the Swedes gained possession of Pomerania, Bremen, and the Baltic region. As for Prussia, it emerged as the leading German Protestant state, whereas France obtained a large chunk of the Alsace (Armstrong, 2014, p. 232).

[34] When James II reconciled himself to the Catholic Church in 1669, long before he acceded to the throne in 1685, he had made clear his profound ideological antipathy of the Dutch Republic. He became more and more determined to destroy the Netherlands through a military alliance with Louis XIV and the French. Among the main grudges that he held against the Dutch was his strong aversion to the Dutch model of polity. According to him, this polity was based on a set of heinous principles, particularly because the Dutch believed in popular government (Pincus, 2009, p. 327). He therefore took provocative actions that evoked a serious threat to which the Dutch felt they had to respond.

Thus, during the sixteenth century in the towns and cities of the Low Countries, the Habsburg prince had to obtain the consent of his subjects to raise revenues. This was done through the provincial assemblies to which the subjects were convoked as estates. The deep and continuous need for money caused by the costly wars that Charles V and Philip II were fighting against France made them extremely dependent on the provincial states. The latter were thus provided with a convenient lever that they did not fail to use to obtain crucial advantages for themselves: In exchange for financial support, they demanded not only far-reaching control over the collection, administration, and expenditure of tax revenues but also the right to meet as they wanted and to discuss any matter of business (apart from fiscal issues) that they deemed relevant. In this way, writes Henk van Nierop (2001a), "the States evolved from being instruments of the prince to become self-conscious representative bodies which could take responsibility for the public administration" (p. 35).[35] As always, the provinces of Brabant, Flanders and especially Holland, which together bore 80 percent of the tax burden, were in the vanguard of this movement (p. 35).

Moreover, during the rule of Charles V the provincial assemblies of Holland learned to run important affairs that affected the entire province. Summarizing the work of James Tracy (1990), van Nierop (2001a) points out that "the towns consulted with the high nobility about the defence of the province, despatched on their own initiative embassies to foreign powers and collected taxes and administered the revenues. They issued bonds and guaranteed to pay both the interest and the principal; they assembled on their own initiative and formulated their own political agenda" (p. 43). These prerogatives were so important that the states of Holland were able to exercise sovereign power effectively after 1572, and the States General (under the leadership of the towns of Brabant and Flanders) did likewise after 1576. Strong collective organizational capacity proved to be a major factor in the success of the revolt against Spanish rule, but urban particularism and intercity rivalries, by blocking the formation of a centralized national state, were sometimes a barrier (Marnef, 2001, p. 102).

Family Reforms: Unintended Effects and New Doubts about Causality
Another important strand of the literature traces the origin of economic individualism and freedom to reforms of the family brought about by Pope

---

[35] Thus, in Antwerp, the Great Council from which the collegium of magistrates was chosen comprised the representatives of the twelve quarters into which the city was divided, as well as two representatives of the twelve most important guilds (Stark, 2005, pp. 202–3).

Gregory I in the late sixth century. The central idea of this perspective is that, for self-interested motives, the Catholic Church played a crucial role in overturning the Eurasian marriage and inheritance patterns in Western Europe. Characterized by love rather than arranged marriages, the freedom of the testator rather than kin-directed inheritance rules, the employment of the unmarried outside rather than within households, and the fission of households on marriage, the new European system not only promoted personal choice and economic initiative but also emphasized contractual relationships (for example, in matters of care for the old) and allowed the couple to control its fertility (essentially through postponement of marriage) (Goody, 1983, ch. 6).

Following the rise of the nuclear family – "a small group of lineal descendants, with women and children as important members, each with their own individual rights, depending upon sex and age" (Goody, 1983, p. 155) – some economic surplus could be made available for investment instead of being eaten up by population growth. Of course, such dramatic changes would take time to yield perceptible effects, and they were not necessarily occurring in all social groups (White, 1988). For example, Lawrence Stone (1979) argues that the decline in both kinship and clientage relations among the British aristocracy and greater gentry occurred in the period 1500–1750 and not earlier (see Chapter 4). The concept of kin responsibility for individual crimes and actions also took time to get established: Before 1500, the blood feud and the vendetta were more important means of law enforcement than the royal writ and the royal law courts (p. 95). In fact, we know that there were great variations in the role of kinship in English villages, and it was typically in seigneurial regions of medieval England, where the marriage norm of village exogamy prevailed, that the incidence of kinship ties was understandably the lowest. Elsewhere, unlike what Macfarlane (1978) suggests, extensive kin relationships, mostly along cognate lines, held sway, although they were often supplemented by weaer affine contacts. To further complicate matters, in France kin density and parish endogamy were quite high in comparison with England, which seems to imply that the church's strictures against cousin marriage were repeatedly breached (Seccombe, 1992, pp. 81–2).[36] As a rule, the twin processes of individualization of rights and decay of kinship-centered customs were slower in France than in England (White, 1988, pp. 199–200). The key message that I want to

---

[36] Both household atomism and village communalism are stereotypes, writes Seccombe (1992): "Neither extreme is at all representative of the great majority of medieval villages in Western Europe" (p. 82).

emphasize is the following: Western Europe embarked on a different evolutionary trajectory than the rest of the world once the traditional patterns of marriage and inheritance were questioned in the early seventh century (see also Seccombe, 1992, ch. 2).

How did Gregory I spark off such a momentous institutional change? The answer lies in papal injunctions that owed "little to Scripture, Roman law, or the existing customs in the old or new areas colonised by the Christian church." These injunctions rejected practices of heirship, such as inheritance of familial property, the provision of an heir (possibly through adoption), and the retention of social status in an advanced agricultural society (Lal, 1998, p. 83). As pointed out by Jack Goody (1983), the prohibition of close marriage and of the levirate custom (marriage to the widows of dead relatives); the discouraging of adoption practices; and the condemnation of polygyny, concubinage, divorce, and remarriage had the effect of depriving many families of immediate male heirs (p. 45). The church's attitude was self-interested, because by defending the right of women to control or inherit a portion of their husband's property, it became "a natural candidate for their bequests." Yet the church did not only profit from widows. Indeed, by exalting virginity it also contributed to the creation of a sizable class of female faithful without any family of their own but endowed with properties inherited from their fathers and mothers (Lane-Fox, 1988, p. 311, cited in Lal, 1998, pp. 84–5).

Pope Gregory VII instigated the second papal revolution in the eleventh century to counter attacks against the enormous accumulation of property by the church. According to Goody, these reforms, which included enforcement of celibacy of the clergy and strengthening of the prohibitions on marriage[37], were aimed at securing the maximum amount of property for the church (Goody, 1983, p. 118). In the same line, Wally Seccombe (1992) writes, "While buttressing patrilineal inheritance, the Church's exogamic intervention (against cousin marriage and unions with affines) cut down the field of eligible partners, complicating mate selection and the transmission of family holdings between generations. The Church thus enhanced its opportunities for acquiring land through wills and deathbed bequests" (p. 71). The same effect was reached through rules discouraging the remarriage of widows, thereby strengthening the "happy alignment" of ecclesiastical concern for the morality of family life with the church's

---

[37] The range of degrees of kinship between which marriages were forbidden was thus widened, and the severity with which the canonical rules were applied was simultaneously increased (Goody, 1983, p. 155).

material interests "as it became Europe's greatest landlord, possessing perhaps a quarter of the wealth of Western Europe by the eleventh century" (pp. 71–2).

As pointed out earlier, Gregory's reforms were also accompanied by efforts to create modern legal institutions: It was at that time that the Roman Church transformed itself into a church-state, a law-state, and a bureaucratic apparatus that came to form the first modern Western system of government and law (Lal, 1998, p. 82). With the pope as the undisputed leader at its head, this strongly hierarchical organization was far more institutionalized than the religious establishments of any other world religion (Fukuyama, 2012, p. 267; Moore, 2012). Furthermore, as the first systematic body of law in medieval Europe, especially in such areas as marriage, property, and inheritance, canon law became the model for the various secular legal systems that would later emerge. Before the twelfth century, custom and kinship rather than statutory law regulated much of both the ecclesiastical and secular domains, implying that collective rather than individual responsibility mattered. One of the main merits of the canon law is that, in the chaotic context that resulted from the barbarian invasion of the Roman Empire, it restored the best of the Roman legal order, bringing forth the concept of free consent and the necessity to prove guilt and innocence through rational rules of evidence rather than through magical tests such as the ordeal of the fire (Woods, 2005, pp. 189–97; Berman, 1983, pp. 179–95).[38] Therefore, concludes Deepak Lal (1998), the legal institutions that arose from the Papal Revolution of Gregory VII "ultimately led to the European miracle" (p. 94).

Lal's claim is exaggerated for two reasons. First, it is hard to disentangle the role of religious reforms from the process of political emancipation undergone by Western Europe, and these two factors may have reinforced each other. Second, one may justifiably wonder why, in both Lal's and Israel's accounts of the rise of Western Europe, economic and political trajectories of different European countries diverged, in spite of their initial common belief structure inherited from the papal and the Enlightenment revolutions. To understand these divergent paths, one must conclude that the initial belief structure evolved differently in various parts of Europe as

---

[38] In the words of Thomas Woods (2005), "Scholars of Church law showed the barbarized West how to take a patchwork of custom, statutory law, and countless other sources, and produce from them a coherent legal order whose structure was internally consistent and in which previously existing contradictions were synthesized or otherwise resolved" (p. 191).

a consequence of diverse experiences on the levels of the economy and the polity.[39]

The same objection applies to the explanation that attributes the transformation of the European household system to the actions of the Catholic Church. In this view, it was by undercutting the established strategies of kin groups to arrange marriages and to keep property within the family that the Catholic Church promoted the nuclearization of the household and the emancipation of women. Yet, until recent times late marriage was primarily a feature of Northwestern Europe only. As stressed by Richard Smith (1981, 1990), for the theory to be convincing, late marriage should have come to dominate in the south as well as in the north of Europe, but it did not. It must also be noted that enforcement of the church's proscriptions should not be taken for granted. In many regions, Smith observes, these proscriptions were bypassed or defied: For example, it was often the case that betrothed couples paid no attention to the prohibited degrees of kinship and ignored ecclesiastic hostility to remarriage. Similarly, Hartman (2004) points out that, in Christian Europe, families were able to maintain "sturdy patriarchal marriage strategies, often in open defiance of ecclesiastical dictates" (p. 98; see also p. 100).

In the same vein, Seccombe (1992) highlights "the vast cultural remove between the stipulations of bishops, inscribed in Latin, and their vernacular reception amongst the 'illiterati'" (p. 77). In particular, although papal decrees refused to recognize marriage among kin to the seventh degree, at the level of the parish, the ban merely extended to cousins, and whether church prohibitions were publicly aired had more to do with prevailing community norms than with the formal strictures of canonical law (p. 110). The fact of the matter is that Christian norms were "usually blended with other forces rather than radically displacing them," and "in most cases, the indoctrination of adherents in 'popular Christianity' was selective, avoiding direct confrontation with pre-Christian customs" (p. 77; see also pp. 108–15). The existence of these enforcement problems, however, does not imply that Catholic injunctions had no influence, only that their impact was mitigated. Chapter 9 shows that sporadically followed formal rules could still

---

[39] It is odd that Goody (2006) himself stresses that claims about the uniqueness of Western Europe (and the Catholic Church, in particular) in developing individualism, humanism, and democracy "need qualifying very radically" if only because "Islam has the same roots as Judaism and Christianity as well as many of the same values" (p. 240). This is clearly off the point because, as he has explained, major reforms in Christianity brought about deep changes in European society.

change behavior by causing customs to evolve. It is noteworthy that Seccombe attributes to clerical intervention and church courts (dating back to the fourteenth century in England) a far-reaching impact on the laity's familial norms. In her words, "The installation of Christian conjugal norms and sexual repression in the Middle Ages was a formative impulse in the development of the Western European marriage pattern" (p. 74; see also p. 116).

The extent to which we must ascribe a critical role in transforming the European family system to the Gregorian reforms is especially debatable in view of an alternative explanation proposed by David Herlihy (1985) and Georges Duby (1974). According to these historians, as the slave economy of Antiquity collapsed in the late Roman Empire and as the supply of slaves dried up with the stabilization or erosion of Rome's frontiers, big landlords dealt with the shortage of agricultural labor by shifting to a system based on incentives that allowed some slaves to marry and settle on the empty lands. Although these erstwhile slaves paid some form of rent to their lords and patrons, they could hold permanent rights over the lands they cleared and the houses they built, including the rights to retain the greater part of the produce and to pass these rights on to their heirs. The same privileges were granted to freemen, called "coloni," by the institution of the Roman colonate created for the purpose of encouraging resettlement on small-scale family farms. These free cultivators were granted the right to benefit from their efforts to clear and cultivate the land. In a desperate move to stop the economic decline of the empire, the Roman government went as far as settling even barbarian contingents on the land, again on the basis of family farms endowed with permanent possession rights (Herlihy, 1985, pp. 59–61). The uniqueness of Northwestern Europe in terms of the early birth of the nuclear family system therefore lay in the fact that it was the only significant area on the Eurasian continent in which rich lands remained underpopulated and underexploited; moreover, it so happened that large chunks of land were under the control of a landed aristocracy before the demise of slavery and before the expansion of the areas under the colonate system suddenly made labor scarce for its members.

What needs to be added is that, because they refer to a roughly similar and early time frame, both explanations – that of Goody and that of Herlihy – accord with the following observation of Marc Bloch (1961): Feudalism in Europe did not break up the large family system, but rather was created on the basis of family units that were already individualized. By the thirteenth century, according to this authoritative account, European people's agnatic lineages had been fatally weakened, and nuclear families very similar to contemporary ones had already started to emerge in most parts of Europe: "The vast kindreds of not so long before were slowly being replaced by groups much more like our small families of today" (p. 139). Therefore, the entire institution of feudalism can be seen as a desperate adaptation to social isolation in a society that could not fall back on kinship ties as a source of social solidarity in the face of external aggressions that began in the late seventh century by innumerable warlords who emerged as the Carolingian Empire collapsed in the ninth century. In the words of Bloch,

Yet to the individual, threatened by the numerous dangers bred by an atmosphere of violence, the kinship group did not seem to offer adequate protection, even in the first feudal age. ... That is why men were obliged to seek or accept other ties. On this point history is decisive, for the only regions in which powerful agnatic groups survived –German lands on the shores of the North Sea, Celtic districts of the British Isles– knew nothing of vassalage, the fief and the manor. The tie of kinship was one of the essential elements of feudal society; its relative weakness explains why there was feudalism at all. (p. 142)

Since neither the state nor the family could provide proper security, weak people needed to be sheltered by more powerful individuals, and they were ready to voluntarily submit to them in exchange for protection. Under feudalism, the relationships therefore had a strong contractual element rather than (kin-based) status, even though these relationships were obviously quite asymmetrical. In this new context, blood feuds were harder to carry out if only because the circle of people bound by the obligation of vengeance was dwindling (only second cousins or even first cousins were included), and the group was unstable enough so that an individual could belong to both clashing families, one through the father and the other through the mother (pp. 138–41).

Before moving to our next topic, and using evidence related to the transformation of family systems and gender relations in Europe, let us return to the theme with which this chapter started: the role of culture and values in bringing about social changes. It appears that considerable institutional changes occurred first, followed by ideological or cultural changes in their footsteps. Or if the two types of changes occurred more or less simultaneously, the latter type (culture) had a facilitating rather than a sparking role. Institutional changes were either driven by the self-interested motives of the ruling elite or organizations and their long-term societal consequences were then largely unintended, or they consisted of individual-level adaptations to changes in the surrounding economic or political conditions.

The former of these two possibilities was earlier illustrated in the case of Gregorian family reforms and can be further documented with the help of an insightful example taken from Mary Hartman (2004). The idea is that in Northwestern Europe gender equality was promoted in the sixteenth century by the reduced incentive for a preference for male children caused by the Catholic Church's new role in the performance of ancestral rites. In agricultural societies, one important motive for the strong preference for sons was that they performed ancestral rites for their father after his death, thereby ensuring the peace of his soul. Such rites continued to be performed inside the household in most extended family systems elsewhere, implying that a man might spend a portion of every day of his life performing rituals for a deceased father. The situation was radically transformed in medieval Europe: There, the Catholic church took charge of these rituals, and if prayers and found masses remained a common practice followed by children of either sex, mourning became more restricted in length and intensity. The emergence of Protestantism helped accelerate this substitution process since all forms of exchange and communication between souls in the other world and the living had to be swept away. This done is in accordance with the predestination doctrine: The souls of the saved were present in Christ and the damned were already in hell so that there was no longer any intercessory role left for surviving kin of either sex (pp. 41–2).

In this account, a religious ideology or doctrine caused a significant change in the Northwestern European family system and, more specifically, in gender relations. It is nonetheless clear that the Catholic and Protestant Churches did not intend to modify women's position inside the family: The delaying of girls' marriage was "inadvertent" (Seccombe, 1992, p. 74). That some institutional changes were essentially stoked by shifts in the surrounding economic or political conditions, and not by measures initiated by church or state authorities, is again suggested by Hartman (2004). Her starting point is an odd family formation model, labeled by Hajnal (1965) "the late-marriage model." It became well established in Northwestern Europe from 1500–1750 and may even have been in place for centuries earlier.[40] Characterized by comparatively late marriage, especially for women, significant numbers who never marry, life-cycle domestic service, a preponderance of nuclear households, and relatively equal sex ratios at marriageable

---

[40] Hartman traces the origin of the late-marriage family system in Northwestern Europe to Late Antiquity and the formation of the seigneurial/feudal mode of production. Other scholars, such as Seccombe (1992, pp. 148–56) and Voigtlander and Voth (2013), see the Black Death (1347) as the major turning point. The critical change occurred in the demand for women's services, which conferred value on them. For Voigtlander and Voth, it was the opportunity cost of women's involvement in husbandry production rather than in grain production and children making that proved to be decisive.

ages, it differed radically from the early marriage arrangements that prevailed in almost all other agricultural societies and seem to have survived in many places, including China, for millennia (p. 82). The emergence of this late marriage system has arguably been a significant step in the individualization drive that made Northwestern Europe a pioneer in both modern economic growth and the transition to the nuclear family.

On the basis of detailed microhistorical evidence gathered by family historians, Hartman proposes that family transformation in this small region of the world was largely a bottom-up process. More precisely, the tightening of sexual discipline in Catholic and Protestant doctrines seemed to have taken place as a response to a strong demand by people and communities confronted with the challenge arising from late marriage and the increasing mobility of boys and girls, particularly the latter. Thus, "it was the family household, not the church or the state, that played the catalytic role in generating a new sexual code with the same rules for both sexes" (p. 59). In support of this interpretation of causality is the well-documented fact that "men and women alike sought out church courts of their own volition for resolution of disputes" caused by the pregnancy of a young woman (p. 63). The late medieval rise in repression of sexual activity was partly a response to the growing neeed to protect single working woman because children as young as fifteen were looking for work outside the household long before they were to marry. Unlike what happens in early-marriage societies where control of marriage and sexual behavior belongs to elders, in Northwestern Europe youngsters themselves had to become more responsible for their sexual behavior. Women became increasingly assertive in refusing sexual relations until after marriage (pp. 62–3).

The Stickiness of Religious Conventions

Just as Weber overemphasized the revolutionary nature of the changes brought by the Reformation, the aforementioned theories exaggerate the speed and initial impact of the changes brought by the papal reforms and the Early Enlightenment. Religious conventions actually proved remarkably durable, and Western European society became secularized much slower than often thought. For several centuries, religion continued to provide the framework within which everything was set, and Christian doctrine was able to easily absorb new intellectual trends . In particular, science and religion were not seen as being in direct conflict inasmuch as "knowledge of the natural world was also knowledge about the divine purpose" (Briggs, 1999, pp. 171, 204–5; see also Blom, 2010). Only in the course of the twentieth century did churches lose much of their power and authority, so that clergy ceased to play a major role in politics, education, and social welfare; people stopped explaining natural phenomena and human events with the help of religion; and religious beliefs were privatized and driven from the public sphere (Kaplan, 2007, p. 357). In the 1950s Joseph Schumpeter (1954) made the point in his typically vivid style, stressing the gradual nature of ideological and intellectual transformations in Europe: "There is little if anything to the saga of a new light that had flashed upon the world and was bitterly fought by the powers of darkness, or of a new spirit of free inquiry that the henchmen of hidebound authoritarianism vainly tried to smother ... the authority of the Church was not the absolute bar to free research that it has been made out to be" (pp. 80, 82).[41]

In particular, the idea that the Enlightenment put an end to religious intolerance and conflicts in Western Europe needs serious qualification. For Kaplan, the rise of toleration in the wake of the Enlightenment is largely a myth that perpetuates our ignorance. According to this myth, "toleration triumphed in the eighteenth century because reason triumphed over faith," which presupposes that the free exercise by individuals of their rational faculties is incompatible with faith (Kaplan, 2007, pp. 345, 356). As is evident from a careful examination of the evidence pertaining to the period between 1650 and 1789, religious warfare, persecution, and popular violence continued in many parts of Europe well into the eighteenth century. Although Christians had been finding ways to live peacefully with one another despite their religious differences, for a majority "toleration remained after 1650 what it always had been, a pragmatic arrangement for the limited accommodation of regrettable realities." On an ideological plane Catholics and Protestants remained "committed foes": "They hated one another's churches, rites, and dogmas, and this antagonism remained a force in European politics." It is therefore not surprising that accommodative arrangements frequently broke down and severe conflicts erupted. The risk of such flare-ups existed continuously throughout the first half of the eighteenth century because many Europeans continued to suspect religious dissenters of disloyalty and to persecute them in times of war when they could easily accuse them of sedition or collaboration with foreign enemies (pp. 335–43).[42]

---

[41] Galileo, after all, got into trouble precisely because he was sponsored by one part of the Vatican (*Economist*, "In the Name of God," Special Report, November 3, 2007, p. 17).

[42] The most notorious act of persecution of the eighteenth century, the expulsion of Lutherans from the archbishopric of Salzburg, was justified in this manner.

An important aspect of the gradual rise of religious toleration in early modern Europe is that it was initiated by the elites and the highest official authorities (such as magistrates), and only on the eve of the French Revolution. It is only then, indeed, that the first major toleration acts were issued; for example, England's Catholic Relief Act of 1778, which allowed Catholics to purchase land without legal subterfuge and reduced the penalties if priests and schoolmasters were apprehended, and the French Royal Edict of 1787, which restored to Protestant Huguenots some civil rights, enabling them to marry legally and own land. Those, however, were still rather mild steps that remained far away from a full granting of freedom of worship for people of all faiths and from an end to religious discrimination. Thus, the 1778 act in England did not allow Catholics to vote, hold public office, or take university degrees and refused to award them the freedom of worship. The 1787 act in France likewise failed to legalize Protestant worship.

Even then elite initiatives to increase toleration provoked a popular backlash, casting doubt on any purported "rise of toleration" among a majority of Europeans. Thus, half the regional parliaments in France opposed the 1787 royal edict, and the Crown had to force three of them to register it. In Britain, reactions to the 1778 act were violent, amounting to genuine popular furor. The government had to push the bill through Parliament late at night after allowing only minimal debate. In response, a Protestant association was formed to lobby for its repeal. In Scotland, this protest movement caused riots that frightened the government so much that it gave up its plan for an equivalent Scottish bill. In London, protesters were heartened by this success and the so-called Gordon Riots, which were severely put down by the army, soon broke out (in June 1780). Rioters "wrecked mass houses, embassy chapels, Catholic schools, and the homes and businesses of prominent Catholics" while attacking officials and members of Parliament who were believed to favor greater toleration for Catholics, Britain's ongoing war against France and Spain heightened popular fears of a Catholic conspiracy (pp. 352–3).

That the elite did eventually understand the value of greater religious tolerance for society can plausibly be ascribed to the influence of the Enlightenment ideas. Yet, the question of causality cannot be evaded; one has to ask why the elite became receptive to these ideas. In England, for example, growing prosperity, increasing population, greater mobility, both social and geographic, as well as urbanization and the emergence of new centers of social life alongside the parish church (coffeehouses, clubs, theatres, playhouses, libraries, etc.), were critical forces that started to operate in the late seventeenth century and continued in the eighteenth century. They helped create an environment congenial to the development of broader outlooks and more open attitudes toward different people among the upper and upper-middle strata of urban society (merchants, professionals, gentry, and prosperous artisans). In such a context of increasing individualism and emerging civil society, it is therefore difficult to ignore the role of material factors in explaining the rise of religious tolerance among the elite (pp. 347–50). Recall the aforementioned interpretation of Reform Judaism in early nineteenth-century Germany: The rise of attractive economic opportunities, by raising the cost of a closed Orthodoxy, induced changes in religious rules and rituals that allowed for greater integration into the broader world (Carvalho and Koyama, 2016).[43]

When analyzing the evolution of ideas, even if one detects a neat moment of rupture or discontinuity, one must recognize that such a moment cannot be the reflection of a similar abrupt transformation in the real world of human institutions. In *The Stillborn God*, Mark Lilla (2007) frames a pivotal question and provides a stark answer to it: "Can one really pinpoint a moment in Western political history when the Great Separation [between religion and politics] took place? If one is looking for a precise moment when Western institutions and customs were suddenly (miraculously) transformed, the answer is no. Political history does not work that way" (p. 312).

2.3 Central Lessons from Early Modern European History

The main criticism that can be leveled against the views of Max Weber regarding the rise of capitalism in Western Europe is that he exaggerated the influence of values on politics and the economy. As we have seen, many key institutional changes occurred first, with ideological or cultural changes

---

[43] Johnson and Koyama (2013) developed a theoretical framework to investigate the relationship between legal centralization and religious tolerance. Applied to the Reformation period, it yields the following scenario: The Reformation led to the diffusion of new beliefs concerning the relationship of individuals to God and the role of the Church, yet at the same time European monarchs were occupied with imposing greater legal centralization over the disparate regions that they nominally ruled. Although the process of legal centralization initially intensified religious persecution, the situation was reversed when the costs of enforcing religious conformity became so high that the monarchy found it more profitable to grant a measure of religious toleration. What needs to be added in the light of our own discussion is that the costs of enforcing religious conformity were decisively influenced by the extent of economic mobility and market integration. In the case of France, which Johnson and Koyama use as an illustration, these latter factors were profoundly modified by the development of extensive communication infrastructure (Weber, 1976).

coming second; when the two types of change took place in parallel, cultural change had a facilitating rather than a sparking role. Changes in rules or institutions were either driven by the self-interest of dominating groups or organizations (including the church), or they essentially consisted of individual-level adaptations to changes in the surrounding economic or political conditions. In the first instance, as witnessed by the reforms of Pope Gregory I and Pope Gregory II, the long-term consequences for society were the byproduct of decisions made on the basis of self-interest. In the second instance, ideas and values adapted to realities shaped by political events, as well as social and economic factors, the latter taking precedence when the economy was relatively unimpeded by the whims of despotic rulers.

The Protestant Reformation did not unleash a decisive drive toward individual emancipation and the type of consciousness that capitalism requires to thrive. This drive actually took place later, arguably during the Early Enlightenment; however, by then a number of key political events had happened, at least in England, in the direction of the increased recognition of individual rights. Some works suggest that, in Northwestern Europe at least, individualization got underway before the Reformation, as early as in the century following the demise of the Roman Empire; that is, before the first age of feudalism. Conditions of land abundance and/or the Gregorian Reforms helped facilitate the individualization of the family system. In the light of all the evidence available, it seems helpful to think of the mental world and the attitudes of the Europeans as changing in a gradual manner so that it is impossible to discern a neat breakpoint. In other words, there is no convincing evidence that religion under the form of the Reformation, or ideology under the form of the (Early) Enlightenment philosophy, caused a neat break that freed the latent forces of modern economic and political development in Western Europe.

Micro-evidence about Antwerp's merchants during the sixteenth and seventeenth centuries shows that religious beliefs do not determine economic behavior in the way Weber imagined. Instead, economic motives play a critical role when economic agents have to choose a religion or decide whether to abandon the religion inherited from their ancestors. The history of Islam does not teach a different lesson: Rather than religion influencing socioeconomic status, the socioeconomic position of an individual influences the choice of religion. This is particularly evident during times of conquest, as when Egyptians were confronted with a choice between remaining Christian Copts or converting to Islam when their country was conquered by the Arabs in 641. As persuasively shown by Mohammed Saleh (2015), poor Copts self-selected into conversion to avoid the (regressive) poll tax imposed by Muslim rulers on all non-Muslim people. Evidence also exists to show that the content of religion can evolve in response to changes in the environment but not necessarily so, which raises the question as to which conditions are conducive to adaptation.

It therefore seems difficult to maintain that beliefs, values, and ideologies are primary factors determining the shape of institutions and economic outcomes. At the same time, it is equally hard to deny that values influence outcomes and institutions. There are interactions between culture and development, in general, and between religion and development, in particular. Today, this more complex approach, which allows for mutual feedback effects and has the advantage of yielding multiple (dynamic) equilibria, is gaining increasing currency among economists dealing with issues of culture.[44] The remainder of this concluding section is devoted to three other important lessons of Western Europe's early modern experience. These lessons are of direct relevance for the observed patterns in Muslim-dominated countries.

First, even though papal power was always a political force to contend with because it could rely on an effective state structure located in a precise geographical area, the history of Europe shows that religion was often instrumentalized by ambitious rulers and dynasties. During the sixteenth century, the central power of Rome was replaced by national religions increasingly identified with emerging modern states. These states did not hesitate to orchestrate divisions and splintering to advance their own selfish interests and ambitions. Domination of politics over religion was typically reflected in the "one flock, one faith, one shepherd" principle. Accordingly, national churches began to resist the claims of the pope in favor of supporting their own monarchies. People with the wrong religious affiliation were presented as traitors belonging to a fifth column that threatened the unity and security of the nascent nation-states. As the experiences of England and the Netherlands testify, the religious denominations practiced by subjects in a particular area could be the outcome of purely coincidental circumstances. In Ireland, Protestantism, which was clearly English speaking, became inextricably linked with English-speaking rule and foreign invasion.[45] Moreover, when the need arose, the power game of the sovereigns could produce strange alliances that ran counter to religious predilections or affinities.

---

[44] For a recent review, see Alesina and Giuliano (2015).

[45] In Wales, by contrast, the state favored the use of Welsh, thus following the wise injunction of the Reformation to give religion to the people in the vernacular (Naphy, 2007, p. 103).

The fact that religious identity was generally defined by state authorities in the nascent nations of modern Europe must qualify the view that the distinction between religion and politics – between the religious and the secular spheres – accompanied the creation of modern European states. The underlying idea is that centralized modern states and strong bureaucracies operating on the basis of legal and rational principles treated individuals and not groups as the primary source of social rights and the main component of social organization. This meant that, unlike what happened earlier, citizens gained the ability to choose or reject their religion rather than considering it as a given source of their social identity; their participation in public life no longer rested on their religious identity, but rather on their belonging to a secularly defined entity (Kopelowitz, 2003, pp. 86–7; Cavanaugh, 2009, p. 80). This sequence of evolution of the relationship between religion and politics now appears too simple: To the extent that emerging modern states anchored their legitimacy in religion, the social identity of the individual was mainly redefined and shifted from the world of primary groups to a new, abstract entity that needed to be buttressed by a national ideology couched in a sacralized language.

Second, religious radicalism was inseparable from political and social radicalism, and Puritanism was "a religion of revolt," as attested by the impact on religious radicals of the egalitarian ideas of Christianity (Pennington, 1970, p. 141). Radicals often blamed religious establishments for having submitted to the strong hand of the state out of sheer expediency, thereby corrupting their goals: In their minds, Christianity was thus returned "to the disastrous path it had taken when it had allowed itself to become enslaved to the Roman state under Constantine" (Naphy, 2007, p. 151).

It is interesting to bear in mind that, since its inception, an important strand of Christian political theology has emphasized the "messianic and apocalyptic elements of the faith, which in the right circumstances can be shaped into an eschatological vision of political life" (Lilla, 2007, p. 48). This vision proclaimed the inevitable advent of the destruction of the world and the church and the simultaneous establishment of a new order under Jesus Christ. Guided by a simplistic political theology and driven by the "pursuit of the millennium," Christian radicals thus "promoted allegorical readings of the apocalyptic biblical verses and tried to suppress the heterodox, often mystical, literature growing out of them" (p. 49).

As for the term "fundamentalism" itself, it appeared much later, in connection with controversies raging within American Protestantism in the 1920s, particularly the fundamentalist-modernist controversy in the Presbyterian Church. It was borrowed from the title of a four-volume set of books called *The Fundamentals*, published in 1909 by the Bible Institute of Los Angeles. Its essays called on all Christians to affirm specific doctrines as fundamental. What American fundamentalists of those times advocated was a return to what they considered the founding tenets of a religion whose identity was in need of being rescued from absorption in modern Western culture. Unlike militant Islamists who do not refer to themselves as fundamentalists, Protestant groups are happy to use this term to identify themselves (Naphy, 2007, pp. 248–50). It is worth stressing that, already during the Protestant Reformation, Puritan movements blossomed and unleashed religious intolerance to the surprise of liberals, who thought Protestantism was a liberating faith.

Implied in fundamentalism is the idea that sacred texts (the Bible for Protestants) are the authentic and literal word of God. God has precisely articulated his will and intent to the prophets, and the followers have a perfectly reliable record of God's revelation. Therefore, nobody has the right to change it or even to disagree with it. The scriptures are infallible, historically accurate, and literally true. Therefore, by following the texts literally, believers are guaranteed to practice their religion as the first church adherents did, and this is how it should be. They must encounter God directly through scripture and not through church, saints, or rituals. On the basis of this definition, a dominant religious group or orthodoxy can obviously be fundamentalist. A good illustration is provided by the attitude of the Catholic Church when, on a literal reading of the Bible, it condemned Galileo and his heliocentric theory that the earth rotates on its axis and revolves around the sun (Naphy, 2007, pp. 241–2, 250–2). Because of its rigid worldview, fundamentalism is permeated by intolerance and a Manichean emphasis on the language of light and darkness, or good and evil. It is also militant in the sense that its adherents generally call for "a return to an egalitarian form of faith uncorrupted by the secular forces of the day," as witnessed, for example, by the evangelical movement that began in early eighteenth-century England and America (Griswold, 2010, p. 28).

Intolerance easily leads to extreme violence. Looking back at the regime of terror inflicted by Calvin on the city of Geneva after he disposed of the Republicans, one is struck by the similarity with the regime imposed today on conquered cities by the Islamic State in Iraq and Syria (ISIS). Especially awesome was Calvin's statement that it is preferable to see an innocent unfairly hit than a single culprit escape God's judgment. Any method, however cruel, was justified when it came to fighting the "sons of Satan," understood as those who refused to accept the immutability and infallibility of his theses (Zweig, 1976, ch. 2).[46] Similarly, Luther expressed violent opinions regarding how to deal with renegades. For instance, he wrote. "The one who thinks that there is nothing more dangerous, pernicious, or devilish than a rebel must knock him down, strangle him, and bleed him, publicly or secretly" (Zweig, 1935, p. 157; my translation).[47]

In reality, because the scriptures are "a mass of apparent inconsistencies,",they could not alone provide strong moral or spiritual guidance to the believer. Therefore, as aptly noted by Pennington (1970),

The primary function of the Bible was to be for every individual a talisman that gave him the assurance of direct contact with God irrespective of the mediation of a superior clerical caste. Of course the Puritan convinced himself and others, with massive quotation and summary, that he derived directly from the Bible the whole of his faith and his habits of thought and behaviour. But to do this he needed other parts of the Puritan system. One was the 'godly preaching ministry' whose sermons were for the most of the flock the principal means of contact with the great conflict in the rest of the world. But the minister was not the voice of priestly authority: he differed from the congregation only in his professional skill and knowledge. Puritans learned their creed as much from their fellow laymen as from the experts. (p. 139)

Third, Luther's idea that all believers can be their own priests (no intermediary is allowed to come between the individual believer and God's word), and the related idea of many reformers that the meaning of the Bible was plain, simple, and clear when read under the guidance of the Holy Spirit, led to insurmountable deadlock. Instead of the expected unity, and against the wishes of the earlier proponents of the faith (Luther, Zwingli, and Calvin), this idea produced schisms and splinterings that profoundly divided the Protestant movement. In addition to the fundamental rift between two different lineaments of the Reformation represented by Luther and Zwingli,

---

[46] By sentencing Michel Servet, a dissenting Protestant theologian, to be burnt at the stake together with his allegedly heretical works, Calvin committed an atrocity in direct contradiction with the basic principle of the Reformation – freedom of interpretation and conscience. Ominously, this act of Protestant Inquisition occurred (in Geneva) after barely two decades of the Reformation.

[47] Luther uttered these terrible words against the renowned philosopher and humanist Erasmus: "I order you in the name of God to be the enemy of Erasmus and to shirk his books. I will write against him, even if he has to die as a result; I will kill this Satan with my pen ... like I have killed Münzer, whose blood falls on me" (Zweig, 1935, pp. 158–9; my translation).

the spawning of diverse denominations, such as the Anabaptists, Socinians, Unitarians, anti-Trinitarians, and Presbyterians (and, in the United States in later centuries, Jehovah's Witnesses, Social Gospellers, Christian Scientists, Mormons, etc.), bears witness to the sort of religious anarchy that could easily result from strict adherence to the principle of the priesthood of all believers. As vividly remarked by Jacques Barzun (2001), "Singly or by sects, the Puritans were ready to devour one another" (p. 271). Diversity and splintering were particularly evident in Eastern and Central Europe, most notably in Poland and Lithuania, where sovereigns were relatively tolerant (Naphy, 2007, pp. 106–10; Greengrass, 2014, p. 351). By contrast, in countries where national identity was linked to the more structured churches of Lutheranism, Calvinism, or Anglicanism, a considerable measure of unity in religious beliefs and practices was noticeable.

The case of the United States clearly falls into the first category. There, indeed, because of its connection to the English Crown and the loyalist sympathies of most of its clergy, the Anglican Church did not attract popular support. Moreover, early Puritan immigrants – deeply religious people who had faced political persecutions in Europe – tended to see religion as "mainly a source of opposition to oppressive political authority" (Kuru, 2009, p. 79). Consequently, religious groups in America "accepted the lack of an established church at the federal level and disestablishments at the state level without nostalgia for an ancient regime" (p. 75). Because of the great diversity of religious groups and movements (mainline Protestants, Quakers, Baptists, Evangelicals, Catholics, Jews, etc.), the principle of church-state separation enshrined in the Constitution was widely regarded as a strong guarantee of religious freedom: No denomination or affiliation was in a position to dominate and threaten the others. Also, given the absence of an alliance between an old monarchy and hegemonic religion, rationalist liberals (including Thomas Jefferson, one of America's founding fathers) did not become antireligious or anticlerical, thus promoting a sort of "passive secularism" in Ameican society (pp. 29, 82–3).

Finally, even when compared to the second category of countries where Protestantism could rely on a structured church, Catholicism was always better able to ensure unified thinking and action because it possessed a central, overarching structure. However, it was not until the Council of Trent that, in reaction to the Protestant Reformation, a narrow concept of orthodoxy came to prevail inside the Catholic Church.

We are now ready to start exploring interactions between religion and politics in the case of Islam. As we see, especially in Chapters 6, 7, and 9, the earlier observations about the history of Western Christianity evoke many striking similarities with the history of Islam. It nonetheless bears emphasis that the decentralized organization of the Islamic faith makes it closer to Protestantism than to Catholicism and Eastern Christianity. This is manifested in the characteristics of the fundamentalist and puritan movements that they both have spawned.

Conflation between Religion and Politics

The Case of Islam

This chapter first outlines the widespread view according to which Islamic doctrine constitutes an obstacle to modernization and democratization because it is based on the conflation between religion and politics. Then, it highlights key aspects of this doctrine that add considerably to its complexity. In the absence of a full knowledge of these varied aspects, a sound assessment of the influence of Islamic thought cannot be reached.

3.1 Conflation between Religion and Politics in Islam: Statement of the View

In the light of the lessons from the Western European experience presented in Chapter 2, the thesis expounded by Bernard Lewis in *What Went Wrong?* (2002) seems all the more problematic He contends that Islam is a genuine obstacle to development and that it differs radically from Christianity. In other words, religion is not necessarily an obstacle to development, but in the case of Islam, it seems to be so. Much the same position is espoused by Deepak Lal (1998) when he writes, "It is difficult to avoid the conclusion that the Islamic legal system was not conducive to development" (p. 63).

Lewis's argument rests on the contention that, unlike in Christian Europe, the separation between politics and religion, God and Caesar, church and state, spiritual and temporal authority, never occurred in the Islamic world. As a consequence, individual freedom, social pluralism, civil society, and representative government were prevented from developing in Muslim societies. The lack of separation between the religious and the political spheres in the Muslim world is argued to be a result of history: The Prophet Muhammad became the political leader of his own city, Medina, resulting in a complete merging of religion and politics and suppressing moves toward building an independent religious establishment (Lewis, 2002, ch. 5). In the

words of Ali Shari'ati, "the Prophet of Islam was the only one who simultaneously carried the sword of Caesar in his hand and the heart of Jesus in his
chest" (Shari'ati, 1986, p. 23; cited by Hassan and Kivimäki, 2005, p. 125).
Naturally, the succeeding caliphs held both temporal and spiritual powers.

Unlike the first Christians who built up a church structure to defend
themselves against a state that oppressed them and who adhered to the principle, "render unto God that which is God's and unto Caesar that which is
Caesar's" (Matthew 22:21), the Muslims had no need to isolate the religious
sphere from the political one: Muhammad was born in a context where he
had to construct a political, economic, and social order. Avner Greif (2006)
establishes an interesting parallel between Islam and Judaism in this regard:

Because the Roman Empire had a unified code of law and a rather effective legal
system, Christianity did not have to provide a code of law governing everyday life
in creating communities of believers. Christianity developed as a religion of orthodoxy and proper beliefs; in earthly matters, Christians followed Roman law and later
other secular laws. ... Islam rose through a very different process, in which Muhammad established both a religion and a political, economic, and social unit. Islam
therefore had to provide, and emphasize the obligation of adherents to follow, the
Islamic code of law, the Sharia. Like Judaism, therefore, Islam, is a religion that reg-
ulates its adherents' behaviour in their everyday, economic, political, and social life.
(Greif, 2006a, p. 206; see also Lal, 1998, pp. 62–64; Kuran, 2004b; Kepel, 2005, p. 237;
Lilla, 2007, pp. 56–8, 318; Berkey, 2010, p. 41)

In Islam, no ecclesiastical body has ever existed nor has there been any vertical chain of command to direct believers: Muslim believers directly refer
to God and his law on earth, the sharia. Revealingly, the values of the sharia
privilege individual rights and responsibilities (Berkey, 2003, p. 214). It is
because the state was Islamic, and was indeed created as an instrument of
Islam by its founder, that there was no need for any separate religious institution: "The state was the church, the church was the state, and God was head
of both, with the Prophet as his representative on earth. ... From the beginning, Christians were taught, both by precept and practice, to distinguish
between God and Caesar and between the different duties owed to each of
the two. Muslims received no such instruction" (Lewis, 2002, pp. 113, 115).
The only exception is found in Iran where the Shi'a tradition prevails and
a clerical establishment exists, which has expanded since Khomeini's revolution. Yet, as explained in Chapter 5, the Shi'a religious hierarchy emerged
rather late (early seventeenth century) when the Safavids decided to build
a strong religion to buttress their regime. Going back to the time of its origin, we find that Shi'ism actually began "as a rather vague and undefined
movement of support for the leadership of someone from the family of the

Prophet" (Berkey, 2003, p. 136). This was a normal occurrence because there were many individuals who claimed that role during the period of formation of Islam. We return to this point in Chapter 4.

The fusion between state and religion in the lands of Islam implies that there is no room for a laity:

> The idea that any group of persons, any kind of activities, any part of human life is in any sense outside the scope of religious law and jurisdiction is alien to Muslim thought. There is, for example, no distinction between canon law and civil law, between the law of the church and the law of the state, crucial in Christian history. There is only a single law, the sharia, accepted by Muslims as of divine origin and regulating all aspects of human life: civil, commercial, criminal, constitutional, as well as matters more specifically concerned with religion in the limited, Christian sense of the word. ... One may even say that there is no orthodoxy and heresy, if one understands these terms in the Christian sense, as correct or incorrect belief defined as such by duly constituted religious authority. ... Even the major division within Islam, between Sunnis and Shi'a, arose over an historical conflict about the political leadership of the community, not over any question of doctrine. (Lewis, 2002, pp. 111–12)

The only vital division in Islam is between sectarian and apostate: "Apostasy was a crime as well as a sin, and the apostate was damned both in this world and the next. His crime was treason –desertion and betrayal of the community to which he belonged, and to which he owed loyalty. His life and property were forfeit. He was a dead limb to be excised" (Lewis, 1995, p. 229). As for the rest, "the absence of a single, imposed, dogmatic orthodoxy in Islam was due not to an omission but to a rejection – the rejection of something that was felt by Sunni Muslims to be alien to the genius of their faith and dangerous to the interests of their community. ... The profession of Islam ... is that God is one and Muhammad is his Prophet. The rest is detail" (pp. 229–30).

A direct implication of this simplicity is that, in Islam, tolerance must be extended to all those who "reach the required minimum of belief," while intolerance is required toward all those who deny the unity or existence of God – the atheists and polytheists (Lewis, 1995, pp. 229–30). "Minimal Islam," as Fazlur Rahman (1982) describes it, consists of five pillars: the profession of the faith, prayer, fasting, charitable donations (the "zakat"), and pilgrimage to Mecca (p. 31). As pointed out by David Landes (1998), of the great monotheistic faiths, Islam makes the least demands on new adherents (p. 394). The Quran reflects this approach because it does not put forward any philosophical arguments for monotheism, but is essentially practical: Human behavior had gone astray, and it needed to be radically changed to end spiritual malaise, destructive warfare, and rampant injustice (Crooke, 2009, p. 236). Set against the doctrines of Christianity – Jesus as the son of God, Christ as the preexisting Logos, the doctrine of the Trinity – which required complex theological explanation and justification, Islamic faith thus appears to be remarkably simple (Berkey, 2010, p. 41).[1]

Finally, there is no concept of nation in the Islamic world, only that of a community of believers (the "umma"), which transcends physical boundaries. This is best expressed by Hassan al-Banna, whom we discuss again later, when he states, "Islam is a comprehensive system that deals with all spheres of life. It is a country and a home or a country and a nation" (al-Banna, 1996, p. 7, as cited by Hassan and Kivimäki, 2005: 127).[2] Or, as Bernard Lewis put it, Muslims do not consider themselves as "a nation subdivided into religious groups but rather as a religion subdivided into nations" (Lewis, 2001, cited by Beloucif, 2003, p. 152).

To sum up, according to this account, the difference between Christianity and Islam is so radical that it reflects a clash of cultures and civilizations: To the Western conception of a separation of religion from political life and the assertion of individual rights, the Muslims oppose an all-encompassing view of the divine law that implies the amalgamation of religion and politics and the recognition of collective rights for all the Muslim faithful. From there, it is just a short step to contend that "Islam and democracy are antithetical," because obedience to religious tenets is inherent in Islamic religious doctrine (Lewis, 1993, p. 91). In the same vein, Samuel Huntington (1996) believes that "Islamic culture explains in large part the failure of democracy to emerge in much of the Muslim world" (p. 29). The specific element of the Islamic culture that is mainly responsible for this situation is "the Muslim concept of Islam as a way of life transcending and uniting religion and politics" (p. 210).

Along the same lines, François Facchini (2009) argues that monotheism in Islam "favoured a return to community salvation, holism and fatalism which was not favourable for the emergence of the notion of individual

---

[1] Eventually Muslims developed a more sophisticated theology, but its central issues grew out of specifically Muslim concerns, most of them raised by a thoughtful reading of the Quran. It was typically elaborated by theologians eager to defend the doctrines of Muslim faith when confronted by arguments based on rational skepticism that challenged beliefs grounded in simple faith (Berkey, 2010, pp. 41–3).

[2] It is thus revealing that the Palestinian Islamist movement, Hamas, was strongly blamed by Osama bin Laden and his al-Qaeda movement for having agreed to run in a national election (January 2006). After its victory, Hamas has ruled over a national territory instead of fighting on behalf of the global Muslim community.

rights. ... In the Muslim world there is no difference between religion and state. ... If the state and religion are one, one cannot instrumentalise the other. This unity of state and religion explains why the Muslim world did not discover the values of free democracy," or the virtues of political freedom and the secularization of law, and why Muslim law could not adapt to social and economic evolution (pp. 13, 15, 17). As attested by numerous writings, this argument has gained increasing support (see Badie, 1986; Maila, 1991; Huntington, 1993; Miller, 1993, pp. 45–51; Kepel, 1994, p. 194; Pipes, 1995, p. 192; Hudson, 1995; Duffy Toft, 2007, p. 109). It is particularly characteristic of contemporary liberalism that "has found its definitive enemy in the Muslim who refuses to distinguish between religion and politics" (Cavanaugh, 2009, p. 5). It is also echoed in books that make the point that Christianity and the Catholic Church, in particular, have played a critical role in the rise of Western civilization, helping shape its ideas and values, its scientific achievements, its laws, and institutions (Lal, 1998: ch. 5; Stark, 2003, 2005; Woods, 2005)

As underlined by Karl Marx, a modern market economy cannot develop in the absence of a civil society, understood as an autonomous sphere of economic activity, unimpeded by political and religious restrictions (see Avineri, 1968, pp. 154–5). For Lewis and others, it is precisely this sort of emancipation or separation that is prevented from occurring in the lands of Islam because of its specific historical legacy. As a consequence, identification with a nation-state or a social class and the advent of a truly secular and morally legitimate regime are "unthinkable to all denominations and sects in the Middle East," where religion is "the raw material of politics" (Makiya, 1998, pp. 210–11; see also Crooke, 2009, chs. 4, 8).

In some crucial respects, and not unsurprisingly, the view espoused by present-day Islamists closely matches this characterization of Islam. Thus, for example, Sayyid Qutb (1906–66), the spiritual leader of Egypt's Muslim Brotherhood, made clear that Islam is not merely a religion to be consigned to the realm of individual conscience and belief, but is rather a total system meant to govern human life in every aspect and concerned with all minor or major affairs of humankind. Moreover, because its only criterion is belief in one God, Islam is able to create "a community of belief" and transcend all barriers created by race, ethnicity, and nationality (Cook, 2012, pp. 86–7).

In the following section, I show that in practice the expansion of Islam has resulted in accommodations to reality that caused the Islamic faith to depart from the simple vision embodied in the message of the Prophet. The implication is that, even if the stated thesis of the fusion of religion and politics in Islam were correct, it is not clear what this would mean in terms of the content of its religious doctrine and the way it would influence society.

3.2 Varied Aspects of the Islamic Doctrine

The Islamic doctrine is much more varied and complex than it may appear when only the Quran is considered as its foundation. There exist several sources of Islamic law and several schools of interpretation of these sources, and to make matters still more complicated, local customs have always played an important role. These customs have contributed to shape a "low Islam" that must be carefully distinguished from the "high Islam" of the official Islamic jurists, the ulama. This distinction plays a central role in subsequent chapters that expound the core of this book's thesis.

Plurality of Sources of the Islamic Law

Clearly, Christianity and Islam were born in quite different historical circumstances, and certain contrasts between the two faiths must be traced to the critical moments of their foundation. Islam emerged in a world dominated by Bedouin tribal culture, a culture permeated by values of great generosity and an obsession with honor, as well as "a fiercely independent and ardently anti-state attitude" (Ayubi, 1991, p. 166). The latter two characteristics implied that carrying arms was a normal attribute of manhood and violence was readily resorted to, whether in vendettas or in acts of rebellion against the authorities. It soon became evident that the behavior of Muslims could not be governed only by reference to texts, however sacred, elaborated during the times of the founder of the faith. The idea that the sharia could not be reduced to the Quran, and that the words it contained were not a sufficient guide for Muslim believers, rapidly gained ground well before the Islamic Empire became so vast as to stretch from Spain to Central Asia. As a matter of fact, one of the strengths of Islam during the times of conquest, when it came into contact with peoples of diverse local cultures and religions, was the recognition that different manifestations of popular piety would have to be tolerated within the umma.[3]

---

[3] For example, when the Arabs conquered Egypt (639–41), the local inhabitants were offered a choice between adopting Islam as their religion or retaining their (Christian Copt) religion and paying a poll tax. Because the majority of the population remained Christian and retained their own language, the process of Arabization and Islamization in Egypt took several centuries to accomplish. Unfortunately, the people of Egypt were not governed with

During the period from the eighth to the tenth centuries, it became increasingly recognized that a uniform code of conduct defining what is absolutely true and eternal could be devised and enforced only by complementing the Quran with three other sources of law that would come to form the sharia: the tradition of the Prophet (known as the "sunnah"), which comprises his sayings and actions (the "hadith"); analogical reasoning based on precedents (the "qiyas"), which is used to extend the principles inherent in the divine revelation to cover new cases; and the consensus of the community ("ijma"), which represents the collective expression of a common religious conviction. The ijma leads to the "ijtihad," understood as the whole process of appreciation of the sharia. It is determined by the decisions of the ulama, who are the jurists-cum-theologians in charge of interpreting the intent of God's revelations and assessing the legality of the actions of individuals on the basis of their compliance with God's commands (Coulson, 1964, pp. 76–78; Berkey, 2003, ch. 15; 2010; Cleveland, 2004, p. 27; Saint-Prot, 2008, pp. 134–42). The ulama establishment comprises the individuals trained in Islamic law: the scholars who compiled the sharia, the judges who applied it in the Islamic courts (the "qadis"), the legal experts who advised the judges (the "muftis"), and the teachers who educated the Muslim community (the "mudarris") (Cleveland, 2004, pp. 27–8; Gleave and Kermeli, 1997). Interpretation and judgment were all the more needed because many reported hadiths seem to contradict each other, and their reliability is not always well established (Lee, 2014, p. 57).

At least in theory, the normative power of the prophetic sunnah – the idea that believers should conform to the attitudes and recommendations of the Prophet – casts a cloud over the idea of innovation. In practice, however, many jurists recognized that forbidding all innovations was impractical and absurd. One of the principal mechanisms used to justify innovations that were deemed useful and consonant with general principles of the faith was the "fatwa," a legal opinion issued by a legal scholar in response to some question. Since fatwas had no binding authority and their force depended simply on the reputation of the jurist issuing the ruling, there was plenty of room for disagreement among jurists. As a result, evolution in the practical application of legal principles was hampered, and "it was one of the hallmarks of classical Islamic law that it was never codified" (Berkey, 2010, p. 40).

as much equanimity under some Umayyad and Abbasid rulers, which is one of the reasons why they increasingly converted to Islam in the hope of escaping future oppression (Marsot, 2007, pp. 1–6).

Where no consensus is in fact achieved, differing opinions are recognized as equally valid attempts to define God's will, meaning that varying solutions are ratified as equally probable interpretations of God's intent (Coulson, 1964, pp. 78–9; for a comprehensive account, see Daftary, 2010). Such an approach legitimated the official recognition of four schools of (Sunnite) Islam – Hanefite, Malekite, Shafeite, and Hanbalite – whose divergences are often deeper than "mere variations of substantive doctrine" and strike "to the very roots of their juristic method and outlook" (p. 98; see also Saint-Prot, 2008, pp. 113–24).[4] This divergence is not surprising insofar as their individual characteristics were fashioned by their circumstances and places of origin, which explains why particular regions and populations of the empire tended to adhere to different schools. The most conservative societies, including the Bedouin tribes of Saudi Arabia, adhered to the most literal interpretation of the Quran as predicated by the Hanbalite school. The most progressive societies – Ottoman Turkey, for example – opted for the relatively liberal Hanefi school, which left much room for free interpretation of the sacred texts.

Competitive hostility between those schools gradually gave way to a mutual tolerance eventually sanctioned by the classical doctrine of ijma. Traditional Islamic doctrine allows a believer to change schools at will, and courts owing allegiance to one school may apply the principles of another school (e.g., the personal law of the litigants involved). For example, in the Ottoman Empire where the Hanefi school of Islamic jurisprudence was dominant, a judge operating within that jurisdiction always had the option of adopting views from other schools and of sending a case to a judge from another school. By the same token, acceptance of diverging interpretations of God's will had the effect of legitimating the equal validity not only of the four canonical schools but also of different solutions applied within particular schools. Within each school, doctrines were actually graded the relative authority of conflicting views, classifying them as either "dominant," "preferable in certain circumstances," or "weak" opinions (Coulson, 1964, pp. 89, 101, 145, 183; An-Na'im, 2008, pp. 188–9).

---

[4] An important distinctive feature of the Maleki and Hanefi legal schools, as opposed to that of the Shafi'i and Hanbali schools, is their recognition of supplementary sources of law (Coulson, 1964, p. 91). The Hanbali school, which has adopted an extremely moralistic approach to law and considers the "traditions" as the supreme guide to conduct (it initially rejected the method of analogical reasoning), never succeeded in gaining real territorial ascendancy until its tenets were eventually adopted by the Wahhabi movement in the eighteenth century (pp. 89, 99–100).

The doctrine known as "the closing of the door of ijtihad" replaces the right of ijtihad by the duty of "taqlid" (imitation). It implies that, once fully formed around the early tenth century, the ijma was infallible. In other words, further discussion was precluded once the consensus had been established not only on matters of uniform agreement but also on those matters where the ulama had agreed to differ. From then on, Islamic jurisprudence was confined to the elaboration and detailed analysis of established rules, involving itself in essentially scholastic works and exhaustive commentaries. At the same time, because of its idealistic and moralistic perspective, it produced an attitude of "doctrinaire isolationism" and "an introspective science" in which the law "was studied and elaborated for its own sake" (Coulson, 1964, pp. 80–2). In the words of N. J. Coulson, "the elaboration of the law is seen by Islamic orthodoxy as a process of scholastic endeavour completely independent of historical or sociological influences. Once discovered, therefore, the law could not be subject to historical exegesis, in the sense that its terms could be regarded as applicable only to the particular circumstances of society at a given point in time" (p. 85).

Providing a similar appraisal, Rahman (1979) observes that the Islamic consensus gave primary importance to "certain dead or purely formal and extrinsic formulae," as though they were meant to be literally eternal (p. 256). This was a regrettable move since the only meaningful approach to the Quran is to uncover the rationales behind the concrete treatments of actual issues and then to deduce the general principles of social justice underlying them (pp. 19–20).[5] With the "closing of the door of the ijtihad," the clock was thus set backward, since the early jurists had granted themselves the freedom to interpret the Quran in the light of prevailing social conditions during the formative period of Islamic jurisprudence (p. 39; see also Coulson, 1964, p. 216). However, this ossification of legal thinking in Islam mainly concerned the intellectual sphere of official ulama. As pointed out by Coulson, changes continued to occur in practical life, but they happened "more by a pragmatic and instinctive adjustment than through intellectually considered opinion, which seems to have little direct relationship with practical issues and appears to be undertaken for its own sake and

---

[5] Rationalist theologians were opposed to this literal and timeless approach to the sacred texts, but they did not prevail. "It is one of the remarkable phenomena in Islam that all rationalist groups, like the Mutazila and the philosophical Shi'a, who have exercised their intellectualism with astonishing freedom, have fallen in line with tradition on practical matters, keeping intellectual and practical aspects of life somehow in watertight compartments: the ijma, or past consensus, has effectively prevented legal ijtihad, or new thinking on legal matters" (Rahman, 1982), p. 107).

purely for the enjoyment of the abstract" (p. 107). A major consequence, which is amply illustrated later, follows from this feature of classical Islamic law:

> The classical sharia texts were always accorded a supreme respect and veneration as the portrayal of a pure religious ideal, which is why developments in the doctrine often assumed the aspect of reluctant concessions to the practice by way of *exceptio utilitatis*; but from a realistic standpoint the classical doctrine never formed a complete or exclusively authoritative expression of Islamic law. (Coulson, 1964, p. 148)

The idealistic-academic outlook of Islamic law and its freezing toward the early tenth century explain why there is so much confusion about the constraining nature of Islam compared to other religions, Christianity in particular. In Islam, precise legal injunctions, when they exist, tend to be particularly rigid, yet they are not necessarily uniform. There are not many such injunctions anyway. These few legal enunciations essentially concern private matters – family relationships (e.g., law of inheritance, polygamy, and divorce by repudiation) and civil transactions (e.g., prohibition of usury, and inalienability of landed property constituted as a religious endowment). Clearly, Islamic teachings cannot be regarded "as a long catalogue of 'off-the-shelf' rules that could be consulted on every occasion" (El-Affendi, 2011 p. 19).

In fact, many of them are not legal injunctions at all. Rather, they consist of moral principles "requiring and offering a wide area of discretion and initiative." The idea that Islamic teachings cover every facet of life and offer ready guidance to the faithful in most circumstances of their life, writes Abdelwahab El-Affendi, "is contradicted by unequivocal Quranic verses demanding that believers should not ask too many questions of the Prophet" (El-Affendi, 2011, p. 19; see also Bowen, 2003). Rahman (1982) writes in the same vein that Islamic law "is not, strictly speaking law, since much of it embodies moral and quasi-moral precepts not enforceable in any court. ... Islamic law ... is on closer examination a body of legal opinions or an endless discussion of the duties of a Muslim, rather than a neatly formulated code or codes ... this body ... presents a bewildering richness of legal opinions and hence a great range and flexibility in the interpretation and actual formulation of the sharia" (p. 32).

Not only may there be several statements, not necessarily compatible, regarding the duties of a Muslim on a particular subject but the statements themselves may also be ambiguous, leaving ample space for free interpretation. Consider, for example, the advice from the Prophet to the faithful on whether married women ought to be encouraged to go to the mosque to pray: "Do not prevent your wives from going to the mosque even though they are better off in their homes" (reported by Muslim, N° 442 and certified by Al Albani, N° 530). This is a remarkable manifestation of the prudence of the Prophet when he wanted to introduce a progressive change in the mobility of married women in the context of the strongly traditional patriarchal societies of the Arabian desert.

Role of the Islamic Jurists

The question then arises as to whether the ulama fulfill a function more or less equivalent to the ecclesiastical body in a large part of the Christian community that has the authority to enforce a uniform interpretation of God's message. Admitting such an equivalence would obviously undermine Lewis's argument that, unlike what is observed among Christians, Muslim believers directly relate to God and just a "minimum of belief" (to recognize the unity or existence of God) is required of them. The crucial importance of this point becomes more evident later. Leaving aside the particular case of Iran, Lewis is essentially correct that no priesthood exists in the Islamic world. Indeed, there are no human intermediaries between the individual believer and God. As stated by Malise Ruthven (1997), there is no church in Islam in the sense of "a formally instituted body empowered to supervise or dictate the religious agenda, to articulate an 'official' Islamic view comparable to that of the Papacy or the appointed or elected leadership of Protestant denominations" (p. 9). At the same time, and although their opinions were purely advisory and their role was purely consultative, the ulama were able to provide a measure of unity to law and doctrine by codifying and transmitting religious knowledge. As such, they have always exercised substantial control and influence over how Muslims interpret Islam within the ambit of their particular school. Moreover, the madrasas, those schools of instruction created in Baghdad in the eleventh century, helped a great deal to maintain a certain unity in the Islamic scholarly tradition (Makdisi, 1981; Rahman, 1982, p. 46; Berkey, 1992, 2007; Kuran, 1997, p. 52; Goffman, 2002, p. 72; Cleveland, 2004, pp. 28–9).

Bearing this qualification in mind, a significant difference exists between Islam (and Judaism) and Christianity: In spite of the presence of the ulama (or the rabbis), Islam (or Judaism) leaves an ample margin of freedom for interpretation of the sacred texts. Rahman (1982) goes so far as saying that the proliferation of hadiths "resulted in the cessation of an orderly growth in legal thought in particular and in religious thought in general" (p. 26). The main reason for that is, in addition to there being four different schools of Islamic law, rules tend to be scattered throughout the works of the ulama who, moreover, do not form a religious establishment that can declare by fiat which is the correct interpretation of the Quran. No central power structure resembling the Vatican has ever existed to lead the Muslim world community, except for the first caliphate. Thus, Muslim believers are both more and less constrained than their Christian counterparts. They are more constrained in that all aspects of their lives fall under the purview of the sharia, which is "a composite science of law and morality" and has therefore a much wider scope and purpose than a simple legal system as conceived in the West (Coulson, 1964, p. 83). And they are less constrained because, in strictly religious matters, they are generally not subject to precise and rigid rules. In the words of El-Affendi (2011), "not only did Islam *not* have a rule for every conceivable situation, but it is moreover *a fundamental rule of Islam not to have such rules*. This leaves the widest possible margin for initiative and fresh thinking on the most appropriate ethical conduct in all areas" (p. 20).

The latter statement about ethical conduct must again be understood in light of the circumstances that surrounded the birth of Islam and of the Quran in particular. As emphasized by Rahman (1982), the Quran does not enunciate many general principles. For the most part, it provides solutions to and rulings on specific and concrete historical issues, and there are actually few such rulings. Inevitably this means that, in addition to these rulings' general goal of promoting social justice, the sociocultural conditions prevailing during the time of the Prophet played a major role in determining their precise content (p. 20). For example, the Quran's prescription that daughters should inherit half the share received by their brothers reflects both the Prophet's ideal of bringing more social justice (in this case, more gender equality) to his society and his realistic concern with remaining within the bounds deemed acceptable by its dominant (male) groups. Given that the society of his time was deeply patriarchal and women were therefore not entitled to inherit any property, the Quran inheritance law was indeed progressive.

It is striking that, in the lands of Islam, religious luminaries may preach to and teach the faithful in the numerous existing madrasas and mosques. Typically this means that the messages conveyed can vary considerably from one place to another. As mentioned earlier, fatwas are opinions that carry only the legitimacy of the ulama or the group of ulamas issuing them (Beloucif, 2003: 150; Filiu, 2008). Revealing in this regard is the story reporting the reaction of the father of Averroes in Andalus when he realized that his son's inclination for art and poetry would not go away. Completely disappointed, he told his son something like this: "If this is what you want to do in your life, then try to find for yourself a mosque where you will be able to preach your own truth ... " The message is clear: Mosques vary a lot in the content of what is taught to the faithful, and it should always be possible to find a mosque to one's own liking. Turning to present-day realities, we are told that in Pakistan the content of syllabi differs according to the madrasa, and the militant and sectarian teaching is transmitted orally and depends very much on the political affiliation and personality of the preacher (Piquard, 1999, p. 76). In Egypt, even though the ulama belong to institutions designed to control access to religious status, room for expression has always existed for Muslim thinkers whose initial training was not controlled by the institutions officially in charge of dispensing religious knowledge. These institutions have tended to react either by co-opting the deviant thinkers or by stigmatizing them as heretics (Kepel, 2005, pp. 57–8).

While in the Catholic Church, the Vatican has the monopoly on excommunication, in the lands of Islam any learned person can issue a fatwa (a juridical opinion based on the Quran and presented as a ruling) against an individual, group, or regime considered impious or an infidel. This difference provides an important link to the main argument developed later in this book. Since Muslims can turn to preachers of their own choice, and these preachers are not subject to the rigid ruling of a priestly caste acting as the representative of God, could religion not be manipulated by politics? Such a possibility is all the more likely because preachers can always accuse imams of interposing themselves between God and the believers. Yet it is normally precluded in Lewis's scheme of analysis where states and political authorities appear to be largely subsumed or merged into the religious realm.[6]

Role of Local Customs: Islam as a Cultural Hybrid

The Sharia Law and the Custom

Before investigating this important question, we need to stress the importance of custom in Islamic jurisprudence. The jurists immediately

---

[6] Oddly enough, Lewis points out that, in Islam, religious agents never really succeeded in imposing ecclesiastical constraints on political and military rulers. He also describes as rare the attempts made by Muslim sovereigns to bring religion under control (Lewis, 2002, pp. 135–6). One wonders how the first statement can be reconciled with his central thesis about the lack of separation between religion and politics. As for the second statement, it is questionable in light of the evidence adduced later that political rulers often succeeded in instrumentalizing religion in the lands of Islam. Whether this amounts to saying that they succeeded in bringing it under control is an open question that is largely semantic.

recognized its important role, for example in the domain of commercial life. They thus went to some lengths to ensure that their legal rulings were consonant with the custom of the marketplace. As a result, commercial law, which deals with sales, loans, business partnerships, and contracts, allows for a great deal of flexibility and adaptability to the demands of business life (Berkey, 2010, p. 41). Yet, such adaptability was the outcome of the amalgamation of the customs of those regions where the law originated, mainly Western Arabia and Iraq, and the teachings of the Prophet; the same applied to other domains of law, especially the sensitive area of family matters. This amalgamation was bound to arouse serious resistance in parts of the Arab Empire where different customs prevailed. As illustrated later, many communities rejected the influence of the sharia in religious rituals and the regulation of their family relationships, for example. As pointed out by N. J. Coulson (1964), "they accepted Islam as a religion, but not as a way of life, and consequently remained, from the standpoint of strict orthodoxy, superficially Islamicised" (pp. 135–6). The Berber populations of North Africa provide a perfect illustration of this reality (Lugan, 2011, 2013).

Thus, the sharia had to make important concessions to custom, even though custom per se had no binding force in Islamic legal theory. Custom actually operated as a principle of subsidiary value: Customary law is implicitly endorsed by the Quran unless it is expressly rejected (Coulson, 1964, pp. 117, 143). Flexibility in regard to customs is even greater in the Maleki school, because of its adherence to the maxim that "necessity makes prohibited things permissible" (p. 144). In general, local customary laws were called on when the sharia or the other classic sources of Islamic jurisprudence failed to provide answers to recurring problems or simply when the "law of the land" prevailed. Hence, by its very nature, Islamic legal practice was "a cultural hybrid," and legal service providers had to know local cultural norms in addition to Islamic codes (Lydon, 2009a, p. 653). The "fiqh" principle, which is human knowledge of a divine law and is therefore fallible (it is not law in the sense of sacred rules), recognizes the possibility of reciprocal acculturation between Islam and local culture as a basic tenet of religious jurisprudence: A society's customary practices are a source of law in Islam (Bowen, 2003, pp. 15, 158). This is especially evident in the case of the Ottoman state, which drew on all four schools of Islamic law in its lawmaking (even though the Hanefi school was the official and dominant school of the empire), institutionalized various systems of Sufism (Islamic mysticism) within its urban communities and military organizations, and did not hesitate to use customary law to placate its disparate population of Christians, Jews, and followers of different schools within

Sunni Islam (Goffman, 2002, p. 73; Finkel, 2005, pp. 10–11; An-Na'im, 2008, pp. 188–91).

The hybridization of Islam does not cause problems in the absence of possible contradictions or tensions between the sharia and the custom. In any case, these contradictions can be denied and subsumed under a broad religious reference. As aptly pointed out by Lawrence Rosen (1995) with reference to North Africa, "custom does not stand apart from the sacred law but is seen by its adherents as itself Islamic and hence indissolubly linked to Islamic law. Local practice and universalising principles of the sharia thus merge in popular conceptualisation" (p. 194). This blending of the two sources of law is facilitated by the aforementioned fact that any local custom or practice that is not strictly forbidden by the sharia is considered consistent with Islam and may therefore be brought within the ambit of the Islamic. People then tend to attribute to Islam what are actually principles derived from their traditional patriarchal culture.[7] And if the state has adopted Islam as its official ideology, as in Saudi Arabia, many tribal customs may be embalmed as Islamic by the religious establishment itself (*Economist*, May 17–23, 2014, p. 32).[8] Such reconciliation need not occur, however. As we see when we turn to concrete examples from non-Arab countries, there may exist genuine contradictions between what religion prescribes and what custom prescribes, and the people may perceive them as such. Ways to justify dissonant practices must therefore be found.

The Pervasive Influence of Sufism

Often manifested in spiritualist and syncretic forms, Sufism represents an important strand of Islam, and its role in the amalgamation process is hard to overestimate (for a detailed account, see Knysh, 2010). Born among the Muslims whose response to the troubled times of the eighth century took the form of concentrated piety, Sufi mysticism slowly moved from the fringes of the Islamic intellectual world to its center. By the twelfth century, the Sufis had succeeded in creating a vivid form of spirituality that grasped the imagination of both Muslims and non-Muslims. Like Christian mystics, Sufi spiritual leaders indulged in acts of self-denial and displayed ascetic behavior involving continual fasting and the wearing of coarse garments (Sufi means "wearer of wool"). However, they did not fully embrace the

---

[7] See, for example, Chaara (2014) on the basis of fieldwork in Morocco.

[8] Rosen (1995) tells the following story. In the 1930s, when the French tried to divide Moroccans by placing Arabs under Islamic law and Berbers under customary Berber law, the Berbers were deeply offended. This is because they strongly felt that, because their practices were permissible within Islamic law, they amounted to Islamic law (p. 207).

other-worldliness of Christian monks who lived in remote places behind monastic walls. Instead, they generally mingled with ordinary people (Berkey, 2003, p. 154). Revealingly, conversion to Islam during the centuries of Islamic expansion took place more often through their efforts than through those of any other representatives of Islam. In particular, the conversion by Sufis of the Turks of Central Asia came just in time to save the Islamic world from disaster. Indeed, by the time hordes of Turkish-speaking nomads moved from Central Asia into the Muslim Middle East in the middle of the eleventh century, the Turkish conquerors had recently converted to Islam, largely thanks to the missionary activities of the Sufis. They did not, therefore, try to change the religion of this region (Mottahedeh, 2000, pp. 145–6).

In Central Asia, Adeeb Khalid (2007) reminds us that the Quran was not central to the everyday conduct of Muslims, and learned people were not expected to master given passages of the holy text. Rather, local communities "asserted their Muslim identities through elaborate myths of origin that assimilated elements of the Islamic ethical tradition with local norms and vice versa" (p. 21). Although Islam does not have officially canonized saints, Muslims came early on to accept that certain individuals have an intimate relationship to God and may intercede with him on behalf of ordinary Muslims. This cult of sacred persons was actually a replication of patronage networks that existed in society. After the death of the friends of God, their mausoleums became shrines, places of pilgrimage, and foci of communal identity, and their disciples provided a living link to sacred origins (p. 22). In the thirteenth to fifteenth centuries, the Sufi movements of Central Asia became gradually institutionalized in "tariqats," which were seen as sources of authority complementary to the sharia. In fact, all the ulama had Sufi affiliations. Hence, one may speak of the ulama and the Sufis as a single group (pp. 27, 31).

The predominance of Sufism also characterized the history of Islamic South Asia. Mingling classical Islamic mysticism with Hinduism and folk beliefs, popular Sufism has been, and still is, an emotional faith mainly expressed in the veneration of saints, living and dead, with associated ceremonies of remembrance, mourning, and ritual marriages and funerals; in pilgrimages to shrines and burial sites; or in festivals full of superstitions and magical representations or rituals.[9] For orthodox Sufis, such practices

---

[9] The distinctive feature of the various Sufi orders was the organization of a brotherhood built around the total devotion and obedience of the disciples to the master. In addition to believing in the miraculous powers of their saints, the Sufis thought that the order of the

are absurd because they believe that it is through self-knowledge that the devout mystic strives to attain knowledge of God. Yet, this belief also sets them apart from scripturalist Islam, which is committed to the beliefs and laws set out in the Quran, the hadith of the Prophet, and the sharia. Whereas Islam's classical functionaries demand obedience and discipline, Sufis tend to stress tolerance and the cult of pleasure through poetry and physical love. It is largely thanks to them that "the diversity of South Asian Islam is a staggering multicultural achievement" (Lapidus, 1988, p. 458; *Economist*, December 20, 2008, p. 70).

For example, under the Chistis, a powerful Sufi order that began in the thirteenth century soon after the conquest of Delhi by an army of Persian-speaking Afghans, a remarkably harmonious cohabitation came to prevail between Hindus and Muslims in India. This was made possible by the great amount of tolerance displayed by adherents to both Hindu and Sufi Muslim beliefs. In particular, the Chistis preached a nonpolitical and nonviolent philosophy based on the central idea that one's spiritual attitude was more important than specific religious laws or practices. In accordance with this idea, they have always shown a lot of laxity with regard to enforcement of Islamic law. In addition, they had no problem accepting recalcitrant non-Muslims as Sufi initiates, and they understood that Islam and Hinduism shared spiritual insights, which facilitated the assimilation of Sufi and Hindu beliefs. Popular saint worship blurred the religious distinctions between Muslims and Hindus, and certain Sufi theories and cosmologies blended Hindu and Muslim concepts (Lapidus, 1988, pp. 447, 449, 458–9).[10] Shared practices among Hindus and Muslims thus "reflected highly syncretised understandings and expressions of religious-cultural affiliation and close ties between communities" (An-Na'im, 2008, p. 152).

Rather astonishingly, not only did Sufi orders adopt Hindu ceremonies, devotional songs, and yoga techniques but they also did not wholly exclude the worship of local gods within and alongside Islam. The veneration of Sufi graves and their annual festivals even coincided in some cases with the Hindu calendar. Thus, "in Bengal and the Punjab Muslims celebrated

---

universe was upheld by a hierarchy of Sufi masters. For them, the sharia was only a preliminary step toward "haqiqa," the realization of God that is attained only through ascetic exercises and emotional insights (Lapidus, 1988, pp. 448, 460).

[10] For example, in orthodox Islam and Sufism, dead Muslim saints cannot intercede with God or perform miracles. This would be a form of idolatry. Therefore, if Muslims pray at their shrines, it can only be for the dead man's own salvation. In practice, however, the Sufi orders have not insisted on the strict observance of such a principle (*Economist*, December 20, 2008, p. 68).

Hindu festivals, worshipped at Hindu shrines, offered gifts to Hindu gods and goddesses, and celebrated marriages in Hindu fashion." If Hindus who converted to Islam retained many of their past beliefs and practices, it is also true that many Hindus venerated Muslim saints without changing their religious identity (Lapidus, 1988, pp. 446, 449). The end result was that "popular religious culture became a mixture of Muslim and Hindu practices", and "despite the formal Muslim establishment, the influence of the ulama on the general society was very limited" (pp. 447, 449). The fact of the matter is that, for the majority of Muslims, the sharia was "only an object of reverence, not a body of law that was, or could be, enforced" (Mujeeb, 1967, p. 213).

It was the Sufi orders that played the critical role in the creation of a Muslim community in India, giving rise to communal-religious structures pervaded by a syncretic and pluralistic tradition. Originating in the period of the Delhi sultanates (1206–1526), these structures were passed on to the Mughal Empire, at least until the reign of Aurangzeb (1658–1707), who reversed the policy of conciliation of Hindus in favor of Islamic supremacy.[11] Indian Muslims thus came to form numerous religious bodies divided by allegiance to schools of law, Sufi orders, and the teaching of individual masters, scholars, and saints (Lapidus, 1988, pp. 458, 463).

The lesson from Muslim India has been aptly summarized by Ira Lapidus:

Thus in India the pursuit of a cosmopolitan state identity led to a distinctive civilisation. Similarly, Muslim religious life both resembled and departed from Middle Eastern norms. Islam in India replicated the basic forms of ulama and Sufi Islam ... the various forms of ulama scholarship, Sufi contemplation, worship of saints, and reformist tendencies remained in open competition with each other. ... The formation of a popular Muslim subculture in India was not, however, a departure from Muslim norms, but an example of a process that was universal in the formation of Muslim societies. In the Middle East, Islam had been formed as a syncretism of popular Christian and Jewish religious practices with Muslim teachings, though the passage of time has concealed the syncretic nature of Middle Eastern Islam. Thus the Mughal era bequeathed to modern India a distinctive variant of Muslim institutions and culture. (Lapidus, 1988, p. 466)

---

[11] The Mughals, indeed, intended to create a cosmopolitan Indian-Islamic order based on a synthesis between Hinduism and Islam. The famous emperor Akbar (1556–1605) actually supported the Chisti order and considered himself to be a Sufi master and a philosopher-king in charge of protecting all his subjects, regardless of their religious beliefs. During the Mughal period, however, the order of importance of Sufi orders shifted: The influence of the Naqshbandis and the Qadiris gradually replaced that of the Chistis and the Suhrawardis (Lapidus, 1988, pp. 456, 459). We return to this significant shift later, when we consider the role and nature of Islamist movements in Chapter 7.

To India and the Middle East, Lapidus could have added the Caucasus as another instance of a region where reciprocal religious acculturation took place. In that region, indeed, certain sacred places were jointly honored by members of different religions, Islam and Christianity in particular. In the city of Movka, for example,

common shrines revered by followers of both religions [Christians and Muslims] are by no means rare. The tomb of St. George in the Church of Mokus-Su and the Christian shrine of Dzivar are honoured by both Georgians and Armenians on the one hand and by Azerbaidzhan and Moslem Kurds on the other. According to a local tradition the former was built by a Christian and a Moslem shepherd. Similarly the Moslem shrine of Pir-Dovgan (or Saint Dovgan) was revered as earnestly by the Armenians as by the followers of Mahomet. (De Waal, 2010, pp. 13–14)

Examination of the case of Afghanistan broadly confirms these observations. Throughout this country, indeed, customs and superstitions of pre-Islamic origin persist everywhere. In the tribal areas, in particular, the tribal law and the sharia are clearly opposed, and the former supersedes the latter. Thus, in the tribes, following the principle of strict patrilineage, women are not allowed to inherit property, even though the Quran prescribes that they should inherit half of the male share; the dowry frequently exceeds the limits set by the sharia; the repudiation of a wife by her husband, which is not opposed by the Quran, is practically impossible, since it would be an insulting gesture toward the wife's family; and vengeance is allowed by the tribal code to defend the family's honor, although the sharia attempts to limit the occasions on which it can be used. At a deeper level, the ulama, who do not recognize ethnic entities in accordance with the universalistic approach of the Quran, are seen as a threat to the identity of the tribe, to the extent that they appear willing to replace the tribal code (the "Pashtunwali") by Islamic law and to minimize the role of the khan, whose power rests entirely on secular foundations.

Revealingly, the village mullahs, whose status is low (placed in the same social category as the artisans, they are not consecrated as clerics), are typically closer to the tribal communities than the ulama, and their influence and moral prestige are generally considerable and proportional to their piety. They are typically careful not to interfere in delicate matters where tradition and Islam may clash (Roy, 1990, pp. 35–6; Magnus and Naby, 2002, p. 75). Similar situations have been observed in the tribal societies of the Middle East (e.g., in Iran and Yemen) and North Africa (e.g., among the Berbers in Morocco, and in Algeria's Kabylia) (Coulson, 1964, pp. 136–7; Keddie, 2003, pp. 31–2).

It is not only in South Asia but also in sub-Saharan Africa that the traditional forms of ulama and law school organizations play no significant role and Sufi brotherhoods are the principal form of Muslim association. In East Africa, for example, a dominant role for the ulama is found only in Sudan. Elsewhere, Muslim life is mostly organized around brotherhoods, fraternities, Sufi families and lineages, individual holy men, and revered local shrines. Until today, Muslim communities in Africa remain mainly associations for worship, education, and welfare:

Whereas Islam is in principle a religion which shatters all lesser loyalties, in Africa it is an integral part of Hausa, Berber-Somali, Arab, Mossi, Dyula, and other linguistic and ethnic affiliations. Whereas in principle Islam is a universal religion based on a revealed scripture, in Africa it takes on an infinite variety of local forms. Islam, then, is a symbol of identity adaptable to various economic, social, and political circumstances. Its principles of religious belief, communal organisation, and state power can be combined and recombined in different ways. (Lapidus, 1988, pp. 877–8)

Interactions between Islam and local African customs have often been highly syncretic, allowing for both an "Africanization of Islam" and an Islamization of certain customary rules, a tolerance of animist and spirit worship practices, and even some changes in the dogma and legal principles (I. M. Lewis, 1966, pp. 58–75; Brenner, 2000, p. 347; Robinson, 2004, ch. 4; Ntampaka, 2004, p. 158; Soares, 2005, p. 35). For example, the value of talismans was generally accepted, provided that they contained Quranic verses (Robinson, 2004, pp. 148–9). The fact of the matter is that Muslim religious leaders tend to recognize the necessity of balancing strict religious principles with the practical needs of the common people for magical sustenance and adherence to local customs (Lapidus, 1988, p. 876). Owing to the many continuities in belief and practices that were thus preserved between the old rituals and the new creeds, there was actually "a great deal more osmosis and cross-over, more *convergence* than *conversion* in the sense of radical change," when Africans converted to Islam or to Christianity, for that matter (Sarro, 2009, p. 145).[12]

Conciliatory Gestures and Stratagems
Deserving special emphasis is the flexibility regarding some of the most explicit Islamic rules, such as the law of commercial partnerships and inheritance prescriptions (contained in the Quran). Thus, among the Juula and

---

[12] Sarro (2009) also makes the point that religion is a technique "to make a synthesis between what is inherited and what is received from outside" (p. 147).

the Hausa (in present-day Northern Nigeria), descent rules can be manipulated so as to circumvent the prescription that all children ought to inherit from their parents, thus avoiding dispersion of business assets. This is done by selecting one unique successor among slaves/clients (rather than relatives), who is recruited into the trading organization as a junior partner. In effect, specific solutions "depended almost entirely upon arrangements made within a modified version of the secular kinship idiom" (Austen, 1987, pp. 43–4).

That mergers of the sharia and customary law could take place at the most official level is attested by the concessions that the former had to make to the latter in Northern Nigeria after the Fulani conquests of the early nineteenth century. There the courts of the qadis came to recognize the custom whereby a wife may obtain dissolution of her marriage by returning to the husband the brideprice she received from him. This custom differs from the form of divorce known as "khul" in Islamic law (release of the wife in consideration of a payment made by her); khul can never be enforced by the wife unilaterally, but is a normal contract for which the free consent of the husband is absolutely necessary. Likewise, the rule according to which male children must be removed from the custody of their divorced mother as soon as they reach the age of two is drawn from the customary practice and not from the sharia.

In Java, to take an example from Asia, the customary regime of common ownership by husband and wife (a doctrine known as "adat") gained recognition in the Islamic courts thanks to the fiction that a commercial partnership existed between the spouses. This fiction thus allowed the Islamization of customary Javanese law through an idiom that could be justified in terms of Islamic jurisprudence. In this manner, the sharia courts were entitled to apply, inter alia, the customary rule that a wife was entitled on divorce to receive one-third of the couple's joint earnings (Coulson, 1964, pp. 137–8; Cammack and Feener, 2008). Moreover, the 2:1 ratio prescribed by the Quran in matters of inheritance was circumvented on the grounds that such a rule is justified only in conditions where the man bears most economic burdens and responsibilities within the household. When women put in considerable effort and even manage small-scale businesses, equal division between the genders is the only fair rule. And the move is legitimate because the Quran also says that we must be just and good (Bowen, 2003, pp. 162–3).

Another striking illustration from Indonesia concerns Minangkabau society in West Sumatra. Here is a society with a matrilineal tradition prescribing that ancestral lands are passed down from mothers' brothers to sisters' sons. By the late eighteenth century, some groups in the region began to clamor for a change of custom in the name of Islam. Unsurprisingly, those groups included dynamic coastal traders and highlands cash-crop farmers who had acquired new wealth. They wanted the right to transmit their assets directly to their own children, thus availing themselves of a powerful incentive to create that wealth. It was therefore natural for them to ask for the application of the Islamic law in the place of the (matrilineal) custom. In due time, such a claim gave rise to a heated debate between reformist and traditional Islamic jurists. The latter defended the customary system by resorting to the following argument: Ancestral ricelands formed a type of endowment (waqf), held in trust by the sub-lineage heads in each generation, and therefore, they were not to be divided according to the "science of shares," which the reformists viewed as the correct Islamic rule (Bowen, 2003, pp. 142–3). Conservative clerics argued that the custom-based rule of transmission applied not only to ancestral lands but also to other forms of property.

Around the same time as that controversy raged, a practice developed on the ground whereby the new elite increasingly resorted to premortem donations rather than to the division of wealth into shares after death as recommended by Islam (for a similar process in matrilineal societies of Ghana, see Quisumbing et al., 2001; La Ferrara, 2007; Aldashev et al., 2012b; Platteau and Wahhaj, 2013, pp. 666–9). The perceived advantages of such donations were that they allowed the parents to designate the persons to receive the property and the gift could be taken back if the children failed to take good care of the parents. This second rationale has been labeled the "strategic bequest motive" by economic theorists (see Bernheim, Shleifer, and Summers, 1985). It bears noticing that no objections seemed to have been made to these inter vivo transfers on Islamic law grounds, while strong resistance came from advocates of adat (custom).

A formal compromise was eventually reached in 1952. According to the agreement, landowners must give one-third of their nonancestral lands to their sisters' children and divide the remainder on the basis of the Islamic rule of shares. At about the same time, court decisions also recognized the right of parents to donate non-ancestral lands to children, provided that this is done with the knowledge of the sisters' children. By the late 1960s, this formal consensus of jurists "coexisted with a wide array of social and legal practices in West Sumatra": Many Minangkabau people actually donated all their nonancestral property to their children. They "were supported in the courts in the rare instances when such donations were challenged" (Bowen, 2003, p. 144). It is therefore unsurprising that Bowen strongly disagreed with "all ideas that Islam (or any other collection of norms) consists of a fixed set of rules – as if a codebook called sharia contained a timeless and repressive plan for abolishing rights and diversity" (p. 19).

Encounters between High and Low Islams

From time to time, urban reformers from the "high Islam," who stood for Islamic orthodoxy, have tried to reestablish a purified order among the rural self-governing communities practicing a "low Islam." In particular, they have asked for a strict enforcement of tIslamic family law that is regarded as a vital and integral part of the scheme of religious duties (Coulson, 1964, p. 147). Historical evidence attests that in most instances when reformers of the high Islam attempted to make the beliefs and practices of the popular masses more consonant with the injunctions of Islam, they prevailed for only a limited period of time. Afterward, things slowly returned to normality (Gellner, 1992, p. 14). For example, toward the beginning of the twentieth century, the reformist ulama Ibnou Zakri rose against the archaism of rural Islam in Kabylia, denouncing, in particular, the people's ignorance of the Islamic law of inheritance. Yet, although he succeeded in persuading the French colonial administration to abrogate the customary Berber law according to which women are not entitled to inherit parental wealth, his struggle did not produce tangible effects on the ground (Chachoua, 2001, pp. 185–7). The central Saharan Berbers, despite Islamization, clung to their language and many of their customs. They even succeeded in absorbing the Arab groups as tributaries into their own tribal system (Fage and Tordoff, 1995, p. 189).

In Senegal and Mali, as my own fieldwork has revealed, local customs regarding inheritance (girls do not inherit) remain very much alive in spite of long centuries of Islamization. When my team brought to the notice of the men that they were thus violating a precise prescription of the Quran (Verse 4:12, stating that daughters should inherit half the share of their brothers), they did not deny the fact. Instead, they started smiling and looking at each other, perfectly aware of the blatant contradiction between their behavior and Islamic law in this regard. Recognizing the question as important, however, they did not try to eschew it. The type of answer elicited from several village communities in the regions of Koutiala and Sikasso (Mali, February 2008) is remarkably identical. Essentially, inhabitants advance the somewhat contradictory claim that Quranic prescriptions ought to be taken literally, yet a difference exists between theory and practice. Actual practice should take account of local customs bequeathed by their ancestors, which implies that they persist in parallel with Islamic tenets. Schematically, their customary ways are pertinent because of two reasons. The villagers' sheer poverty prevents them from abiding by the Quran as they would like. This is particularly evident in the case of inheritance. Indeed, land is their only wealth, and if they would divide it among sons and daughters, the parcels bequeathed would fall below a viable size. Had they possessed other forms of wealth, they would readily share it equally among all their children, girls included. Moreover, under the patriarchal tribal system women obtain access to land through their husband. On marriage, their daughters join another family, and it is the duty of that family to provide for the needs of women and children. Therefore, parents must keep enough land to give to their own sons who, when they become husbands, must be able to ensure a decent livelihood for the daughters-in-law, which often implies that the latter are granted use rights over particular parcels.

In the whole discussion, emphasis is thus placed on poverty and local customs. Because they are poor, they cannot afford to abide by all the Quranic prescriptions. They just try to follow as many as possible, which is why they cannot be accused of being bad Muslims. Islamic law, says one villager, provides that we should be clean while praying, but this is a luxury that we cannot afford because we are so poor that we have only one set of clothes. Interestingly, in the village of Samogossoni (near the town of Sikasso), a local mullah (called "imam" in local parlance), was listening to the whole discussion, and by nodding, he discreetly indicated his approval of what the villagers were saying. Although he had been quite talkative until that stage of the focus-group discussion (in fact, he nearly monopolized the floor when the subjects addressed did not have a religious character), he suddenly stopped intervening as soon as I brought to light the contradiction between the villagers' behavior and Islamic law. In another village (Ouahibera, again in the Sikasso region, but closer to the Mali-Côte d'Ivoire border), a middle-aged villager who plays an active role in local committees told me in private that their mullah tends to defend a strict observance of the sharia, but in actual practice he is the first to violate it whenever it suits his interests. This causes the villagers to laugh quite a bit when the mullah blames them for their bad behavior. Some practices are forbidden by Islam, but are done in a concealed manner by everybody, including the imam. In still other villages, there are several mullahs, and they differ in how they interpret Islamic law.

In the Senegal River valley (region of Podor), the reactions of the household heads when they were confronted with the contradiction between their inheritance practices and the Quran was similar to that encountered in Mali. Nevertheless, they were eager to stress that the contradiction is more apparent than real because, in compensation for their inability to inherit land, women receive gifts from their brothers (e.g., harvest shares). Unfortunately, it proved difficult to make out from the interviews the size or regularity of such transfers. In Niger, likewise, Barbara Cooper (1997) reports an arrangement known as "aro" whereby women, in recognition of their ownership rights, receive part of the crop harvested on some portion of the family land by their brothers. Yet, women's access to land remains fragile and difficult to secure: Owing to their absence from the native village following marriage, they find it typically hard to exercise whichever rights over land might have been granted to them, especially if their male relatives are ready to exploit the situation (pp. 78–81). Bedoucha (1987) offers yet another illustration of the flexible interpretation of Quranic inheritance law among the Tuaregs. Such flexibility obtains, he says, because practice is based on a subtle blending of written tenets, oral tradition, and tacit understanding.

If a marriage breaks up, the custom in many African countriess provides that the separated or divorced woman has a right to return to the parental household and make a living there until she becomes remarried. Typically, the woman is awarded temporary use rights over a parcel of family land. This social protection mechanism is especially strong when the husband is deemed responsible for the marriage's failure (Gaspart and Platteau, 2010). Problems arise, however, when land becomes scarce. Brothers then tend to get nervous about applying the custom, and they pressure their father to deny their sisters the right to return to or stay on a portion of the family land. In such circumstances, a separated woman can be forced to go back to her husband (in the event she took the initiative of leaving him) or to accept quickly a new one so as to free up the land. Hence separated women can fall into a precarious position and have little bargaining power vis-à-vis their husband in the event of an unhappy marriage. Under conditions of increasing land scarcity, customary norms become less pertinent, and the granting of inheritance rights to women, such as prescribed by the Quran and, in a still more equitable measure, by modern statutory law based on the Napoleonic code, is increasingly justified. Therefore, uneasiness about the persistence of the custom in the face of these evolving economic conditions and in the presence of alternative prescriptions, especially those drawn from religious texts, is bound to rise as time passes. What deserves to be emphasized, however, is that if the inheritance system eventually evolves (as it has started to do gradually in densely populated regions of sub-Saharan Africa, such as Malawi, Rwanda, Burundi, and parts of Kenya and the Senegal River valley), the evolution is ultimately caused not by religion, but by profound

changes in the surrounding economic, ecological and demographic environment.

This discusison shows that, in large parts of the Islamic world, customs
remain strongly resistant to Islamic law when the two stand in clear contradiction. In matters of inheritance, in particular, the strength of custom is
observed in many regions, particularly in countries of sub-Saharan Africa
and South Asia where the traditional ulama and law schools are weakest,
being almost nonexistent or without much influence.[13] There Sufi brotherhoods and orders are the principal form of Muslim association, and Muslim identity is often superimposed on one's preexisting village identity. The
influence of Islam has been manifest mostly in the spheres of trade and politics, as well as in the blending of faith in the miraculous power of Islamic
holy men with pre-Islamic beliefs. Social usages, by contrast, remain very
much guided by erstwhile customs. In the words of Lapidus (1988), again,
Islamic belief "did not necessarily lead to the formation of an organised body
of believers, but could serve as a shared identity among diverse people who
preserved their own kinship, territorial, linguistic, ethnic, and other bases
of non-Islamic culture in group organisation and social relations" (p. 262).[14]
The acceptance of Islamic rules was always easier in merchant circles, both
in Africa and South Asia. For these people, indeed, conversion to Islam
made sense because it integrated them into intra- and interregional trade
networks using effective contract enforcement mechanisms based on the
sharing of Islamic beliefs and culture (Platteau, 2009).

In Indonesia, for example, traders adopted Islam quickly simply because
it gave them something in common with their South Asian and Middle
Eastern trading partners (by the thirteenth and fourteenth centuries, most
of the traders exporting Indonesian spices west to Europe were Muslims
from these two regions) who preferred to deal with fellow co-religionists.
Moreover, they had no particularly strong religious beliefs of their own, or

[13] An anthropological study of a small village in Upper Egypt has concluded that "both Christian and Muslim families follow inheritance rules where a daughter inherits half the share
of a son and where part of the property will go to other male members, such as the father,
brothers, or brothers' sons, if a man does not leave a son at his death" (Bach, 2004, p. 187).

[14] The long persistence of pagan social usages and beliefs in spite of conversions to monotheistic religions has been observed in numerous contexts. Thus, most of the Abkhaz people
in the Caucasus converted to Islam in the nineteenth century after having been Orthodox
Christians, a religion to which many returned later in the same century. The important
feature of their religious practices, however, is the persistence of pre-Christian rituals and
customs. This led the Abkhaz historian and politician Stanislav Lakoba to describe his
people as "80 percent Christian, 20 percent (Sunni) Muslim and 100 percent Pagan" (cited
from De Waal, 2010, p. 148).

they found those that they had increasingly at odds with the changing world within which they lived. Conversion to Islam, therefore, offered them spiritual benefits in addition to commercial ones (Brown, 2003, p. 31).

Before concluding this chapter, it is worth saying a few words about Shi'ism because this strand of Islam has some peculiar characteristics that make it relatively flexible in doctrinal matters.

Shi'ism as a Mixture of Doctrinal Flexibility and Charismatic Leadership

An important difference between the Sunnite and the Shi'a strands in Islam lies in the greater doctrinal flexibility found in the latter. As a matter of fact, the tradition of law in the world of Shi'ism emphasizes the ongoing work of Islamic jurists to reinterpret the Quran and the sunnah of the Prophet in the light of contemporary circumstances. In the late eighteenth century, this tradition was best represented by the Usulis, who insisted that wisdom must be reinterpreted in every generation (Lee, 2014, pp. 182–3, 195; Buchan, 2012, p. 96).[15] Likewise, Hasan Yousefi Eshkevari, a dissident voice under Khomeini's regime, was close to the tradition when he asserted that religious rulings fall into two categories: rulings about worship, which are unchanging, and rulings that must be adapted to social circumstances. Women's rights are a good example of the latter because those stated in the Quran reflect conditions prevailing in pre-Islamic Arabia (Lee, 2014, pp. 190–1).

The Shi'a approach to Islamic rulings does not necessarily lead to a consensus at any given point of time because a plurality of interpretations is considered to be normal. This is because a long tradition among the Shi'a insisted that all hadith must be transmitted through individuals closely associated with the cause of Ali, rather than those who came to be recognized by the Sunni tradition as authoritative transmitters. Much more than among Sunni Muslims, the locus of authority was shifted from the community as a whole to the imams, thereby attesting that the central issue was one of religious authority rather than of original content of the doctrine. According to a radical interpretation, hadith carry authority if they can be traced back not only to the Prophet but also to imams among his descendants (Berkey, 2003, p. 136). Charismatic leadership thus came to play a significant role in Shi'ism, with the prestige of the religious leader being more important than the relationship of his rulings to the Quran or the sunnah. This has been particularly in evidence in Iran after the establishment of the Islamic

---

[15] We return to this in Chapter 5, with regard to the role of religious clerics in modern Iran.

Republic where the charisma of Khomeini and his position in the religious hierarchy conferred an indisputable authority on him. This authority was much more important than the question of the consonance or lack of it between his decisions and some preestablished template of Islamic ideology (Lee, 2014, p. 186). Islam was made "a matter of convention rather than faith," with convention decided by legitimate authorities. Therefore, a good Muslim is one who "behaves in approved, conventional ways, whatever he or she believes" (pp. 179–80).

Once the leader passes away, and perhaps even before, volatile and plural opinions are quick to return. In the Islamic Republic of Iran, Lee (2014) writes: "The government first opposed birth control in the name of Islam. Then it changed its mind and endorsed birth control as permitted by Islam. Some legislators have championed public enterprise and expansion of the welfare state in the name of an egalitarian Islam. Others have championed privatization in the name of Islamic commitment to private property" (p. 186). That positions, even when antagonistic, were rationalized in religious terms was a clear result of the nature of the regime, state Shi'ism.

3.3 Conclusion

The picture offered in the preceding discussion is complex, and two central lessons may be drawn from it. First, if the Islamic doctrine appears to be all encompassing in scope, it contains few precise injunctions as to how a good Muslim ought to behave. Second, official Islam needs to be carefully distinguished from the Islam of the masses, and the high Islam of the learned urban classes from the low Islam of popular rural groups. These two points are obviously interrelated.

The complexity of the Islamic doctrine arises from the existence of multiple sources of Islamic law, different schools of thought representing varying approaches to the way these fundamental sources ought to be interpreted, and variations even within particular schools. Although interpretive discussions (ijtihad) have been officially closed since the tenth century, leading to an impoverishment of the intellectual/theological debate in Islam, considerable differences in the interpretation of the Sharia were not suppressed but frozen. These differences, it must be emphasized, occur in high spheres of the faith, among the jurists of Islam (the ulama). Many more variations and idiosyncrasies nevertheless appear when we descend to the world of ordinary people who live mostly in rural areas, small towns, or the peripheries of cities. These are the domains of low Islam, where customary norms and practices remain very influential. Since Islam has explicitly accepted the influence of local customs, a process of hybridization of the faith has taken place. This is especially manifest in the Sufi rituals.

What such a picture reveals is therefore the immense variety and flexibility of Islam rather than rigidity and orthodoxy. This situation is no doubt the result of the decentralized organization of a religion that does not grant to its official representatives the power to offer a unique and authorized interpretation of the Prophet's legacy. As a rule, they do not have the right to interpose between God and the believers because Muslims are expected to relate to God directly.

The hybridization of Islam raises important questions, however. Amalgamation of local customs does not create serious problems when two conditions are fulfilled, one on the level of high Islam and the other on the level of low Islam. On the former level, the ulama and law school organizations are weak, or their influence does not extend much beyond the walls of the cities where they are established. On the latter level, the Islamic faith and local customs complement each other (say, because the customs address issues that Islam does not deal with), or they are at odds with each other but there is strong agreement that the customary practice is better adapted to local conditions than the relevant Islamic injunctions. The situation becomes less manageable, even explosive, when this agreement ceases to exist and the forces of high Islam are active. This typically happens when some customs, such as those involving inheritance, evolve in a way that blatantly harms the interests of marginalized groups such as women, and when dynamic agents such as merchants, market-oriented farmers, and businesspeople want to be emancipated from constraining customary rules. If the interests of such categories of people are better served by some Islamic injunctions, they may openly express support for a stricter enforcement of the religious law. Two important examples illustrate this logic.

In Islam, women are not on an equal footing with men in matters of inheritance, yet they receive better treatment under the Islamic law than under patriarchal customs. This advantage may prove especially attractive when land pressure undermines some elements of the custom that traditionally compensated women for their lack of inheritance rights. In these circumstances, indeed, reference to Islamic law may act as a safeguard against a regressive evolution of the custom from the standpoint of women. Men, too, may have an interest in clamoring for respect for Islamic law. For example, to pursue economic activities and accumulation strategies unhampered by obstructive customs, entrepreneurial people may choose to join religious networks inside which Islamic law is better applied and actually serves as a trust-building and commitment device. Temptation to overtly oppose the

custom by escaping to an alternative universe of meanings and social interactions is particularly strong when powerful redistributive pressures act as
a brake on the motivations and activities of dynamic elements of the society (Platteau, 2014). In some other instances, as documented in Chapter 7,
prosperous merchants may refer to extreme, puritanical interpretations of
Islam as a way to counter monopolists who adhere to official Islam (e.g., the
maraboutic class in the Senegalese Sine-Saloum). The implication is that
variations in the type of Islam sought or upheld by the people often need to
be understood in the context of ongoing class struggles or confrontations
between opposing economic interests.

In view of the complexity and heterogeneity of Islam, reformist or Islamist
movements appear as forceful attempts to unify and centralize currents and
strands of thought that are by nature almost irreconcilable. In a manner
strongly reminiscent of Europe's Protestant Reformation, these movements
have striven, or continue to strive, toward purifying the religion from all its
superstitious, magical, and ritual corrupting influences so as to allegedly
return to a model of the pristine religion. Yet, they also differ from the
Protestant reaction because, unlike in Christianity, Islam features no centralized church organization that claims to speak in the name of all the
faithful. As seen in the next chapter, reference to an allegedly unified Islam
embodied in the caliphate period stems from a complete distortion of reality. As is always true of radical fundamentalist movements, whether they
extol a primeval religion, nation, or ethnic group, they paint with excessively broad brushes and nostalgic fervor an ideal world of the origins that
stands in stark contrast with the present reality. The defects of the latter are
amplified while those of the period of the founding myth are obliterated.

After having thus looked carefully into the various aspects of the Islamic
doctrine and described a key feature of its organization (the absence of hierarchy), we are now ready to examine the manner in which high Islam has
related to the world of politics from the birth of the Islamic civilization up to
present times. Chapters 4–6, which form the heart of the book, are devoted
to this task. Subsequently, we return to Islamism, a movement that essentially refuses submission to political authority that is accused of being corrupt and oblivious of Islam's fundamental principles. By this logic, it is also
at war with representatives of official Islam, which condones the policies and
behavior of autocratic rulers.

The Dominant System of Politico-Religious Relations in Islam

A Historical Perspective

This chapter critically examines the thesis of the fusion between religion and politics in the lands of Islam that was introduced in the preceding chapter. In Section 4.1, our investigation begins with an exploration of the early history of Islam, whereas Section 4.2 describes the dominant relation between religion and politics, illustrating it by examples taken from the Mughal and the Ottoman Empires, as well as from the Maghreb and Afghanistan. Section 4.3 presents a special circumstance in which ambitious rulers use the banner of Islam to serve political ends, such as controlling rebellious territories or unifying a fragmented political space. Section 4.4 summarizes the results of our foray into history. Finally, Section 4.5 provides the theoretical framework underpinning our approach to politico-religious interactions. It will allow us to better understand the difference between the archetypal politico-religious equilibrium documented in this chapter and the more unstable situations described in the following two chapters.

4.1 First Insights from the Early History of Islam

A good starting point from which to explore the relationship between religion and politics in the lands of Islam is the history of the first centuries of Islamic rule (see Hourani, 1991, pp. 14–26; Armstrong, 2001, pp. 3–31; Marsot, 2007, p. 5). As attested from the very beginning by the murders of three of the four caliphs who succeeded Muhammad, the history of Islam is full of violent confrontations between various factions vying for power and adhering to different interpretations of the Quran, each claiming legitimacy for its own version of inheritance from the Prophet. During the times of Muhammad, there was already continuous competition and warfare not only between the merchant dynasties of the cities (Medina and Mecca, in particular) and the Bedouins coming from a rugged desert terrain but also within each of these groups. It is revealing that, after his decisive military victory over his opponents, which ended in an alliance between Meccan merchants and the Bedouins, Muhammad urged all people to respect each others' properties and to abandon the practice of vendettas and plunder so as to establish peace and harmony in the chronically violent society of Arabia.[1] The advice was not heeded, however, (Hodgson, 1974a, pp. 187–230; Donner, 1981).

For one thing, because the Bedouins looked at Muhammad in the same way as they looked at clan patriarchs, they owed loyalty to him, not to the new religion (they were those who "submit," not those who really "believe"). As a consequence, the "religion-based clan" formed by Muhammad was extremely fragile in the absence of a strong and prestigious authority (Polk, 2005, pp. 38–40). In addition, debate quickly erupted over the rule governing succession of the founder of the faith. On Muhammed's death, because he had no male descendant, a conflict broke out between the Meccans and the Medinese. Those who advocated a family succession line proposed that politico-religious power be bequeathed to Ali ibn Abi Talib, the Prophet's cousin and son-in-law. Others opposed the view that power should accrue to a relative of Muhammad, arguing instead that an assembly of notables should select the successor from among distinguished believers. The latter position predominated, and Abu Bakr (632–4), the father of Muhammad's youngest wife, became the first caliph.

Under his rule, conflict nevertheless persisted. The converts from Medina now claimed that political power should be made accessible to all Muslims. For his part, Abu Bakr argued that it should remain the exclusive preserve of the original group of believers, meaning members of the Quraysh clan and Hashemite lineage, to which Muhammad belonged.[2] The first caliph's

---

[1] It is worth noting that the first resistance to Muhammad's monotheist message came from the Meccan establishment, dominated by the Umayyad lineage, which feared that it would threaten their business interests. The spread of monotheism, indeed, was to cause the rejection of local deities, alienating the tribes that kept their totems round the Kabah and came specifically to visit them during the hajj. As a result, Muhammad's followers, still a small segment of the Quraysh, were economically and socially ostracized, and they were soon compelled to leave Mecca for a safer place (Armstrong, 2014, p. 163).

[2] This requirement – that the office of the caliphate belongs to a member of the tribe of Quraysh on election by the qualified representatives of the community – was to be reasserted in the most famous theoretical exposition and defense of the caliphate, that of al-Mawardi (d. 1058) (Hourani, 1991, p. 142). The Kharijites opposed that requirement and held that the sole requisites were piety in the faith of Islam and personal capability (Coulson, 1964, p. 103). They were thus closest to the Prophet's teachings, going as far as saying that it did not matter whether the successor to Muhammad was Arab or non-Arab, or what tribe he came from, as long as he was a Muslim (Fukuyama, 2012, pp. 194–5).

decision to appoint elite members of the Meccan aristocracy (from the rival Umayyad lineage) as commanders in the military campaigns, although they had only just recently converted to Islam after years of fierce and adamant opposition to the Prophet, proved to be highly controversial. Under Umar, the second caliph, the ruling elite was riven by personal and factional differences. The early companions of the Prophet continued to look askance at converts who had obtained power. They asserted privileges based on early conversion and close links with Muhammad, clashing with claims to the nobility of ancient and honorable ancestry. Powerful tribal loyalties thus continued to trump purely ideological considerations, undermining the formation of a Muslim state and fueling chronic kinship quarrels (for a comprehensive account, see Berkey, 2003).

Such tensions came again to the surface during the reign of the third caliph, Uthman (644–56), who acceded to power after a personal enemy assassinated Umar, the second caliph, in an act of private vengeance. Because he belonged to the inner core of Quraysh and had also been an early convert, Uthman could have worked toward reconciling the contending factions.[3] However, he earmarked the best state positions for his own clan, thus arousing fierce opposition from factions in Medina, Kufa, and Fustat. He was eventually murdered by a contingent of Arabs stationed in Egypt seeking a more equitable share of political appointments. This assassination unleashed Islam's first civil war. And it is because he wanted to take revenge for the murder of Uthman, his close kinsman, that Muawiya, a general whom Umar had appointed governor of the new province of Syria, laid claim to the caliphate. He eventually ordered the murder at Karbala of Hussein ibn Ali, the Prophet's son-in-law and also a Qurayshi, after he became the fourth caliph of the Arabs.[4] One result of this impious act was a complete dissociation between politics and religion, and the function of the caliphate became emptied of all its sacred content. Nonetheless, the newly born Umayyad state, which moved the capital city from Mecca to Damas in 657, sought to maintain the fiction that the authority of the caliphs was an extension of the authority of the Prophet. It established a hereditary dynasty

---

[3] Note that it is under his rule that the Quran was established and finalized.

[4] At the head of an army recruited in Syria, Muawiya marched into Iraq to oppose Ali and the force he had recruited in Arabia. From then on, a series of events led to Ali's defeat. The resentment and feeling of political alienation of the followers of Ali deepened when his second son, Hussein, marched heroically into a battle he knew he would lose against the Umayyad caliph Yazid in 680. The massacre of Hussein and his small army gave rise to an annual ritual of mourning and self-flagellation in the Shi'a community performed to this day (Lee, 2014, p. 174; see also Berkey, 2003, pp. 133–5).

akin to the Sassanian and Byzantine monarchies (Lapidus, 1988, ch. 4; An-Na'im, 2008, pp. 61–2).

Rather than originating in a doctrinal conflict, Shi'ism, the movement supporting Ali's descendants, thus began "as a movement of support for the leadership of certain Arab candidates in the caliphate, in opposition to the hegemony of Syrian Arab tribes ruling from Damas" (Makiya, 1998, p. 213). The Khurasani tribes from the Iranian northeastern highlands allied with Iraqi Shi'ism and the underground Abbasid movement – whose claim to rule also originated in the House of Hashim, Muhammad's broader tribal family – to overthrow the Umayyads. The ensuing destruction of Syrian tribal power erased distinctions between the original conquering tribes and the new Muslims who came from the conquered populations of the Fertile Crescent. The hitherto Arab character of the caliphate was thus transformed (p. 213).

It did not take much time, however, before the Baghdad-based Abbasids got rid of their allies and established their preeminence over the Islamic world. The destitution of the Umayyads was presented as necessary because they were unrighteous and had turned their authority into secular kingship. Founding their claim to rule on a shared lineage with the Prophet, the early Abbasid caliphs attempted to revitalize the sacred function of the caliphate, thereby restoring the unity of religious and political leadership. Yet, the inherent contradictions of their claims to this dual leadership were soon exposed by the theological inquisition (known as "al-Mihna") started in 833 by the caliph al-Mamun. Intervening in the long-standing debate between the Mutazilites, who favored a more allegorical and rational approach to Islamic sources, and the Asharites, who adhered to a strictly textual approach, al-Mamum and his successors tried to force the latter doctrine on the whole ulama community. The ensuing confrontation over religious authority shattered the notion of a unified religious and state authority. In a manner heralding future political regimes of the Middle East, opponents who dared defy the caliph's authority were tried for their alleged religious views instead of sedition. Rather than enhancing the caliphate's Islamic authority, al-Mihna thus contributed to undermining it fatally: Both the aura of piety associated with the caliph and his temporal power gradually eroded, and his religious legitimacy became more symbolic than real (Hourani, 1991, p. 142; Magnus and Naby, 2002, p. 89; An-Na'im, 2008, pp. 62–5). By the middle of the tenth century, the institution of the caliphate had lost its religious legitimacy (Meddeb, 2002, pp. 96–9).

The institutional separation of state and religion became the norm for the late Abbasid caliphate; the Seljuq and Mamluk sultanates; the Ottoman,

Safavid, Mughal, and Uzbek Empires; and other Muslim regimes. It became a landmark of premodern Islamic societies that, contrary to the Muslim ideal, the caliphate was transformed into "a largely military and imperial institution legitimated in neo-Byzantine and neo-Sassanian terms," while the religious elites developed "a more complete authority over the communal, personal, religious, and doctrinal aspects of Islam" (Lapidus, 1996, p. 12; see also 1988, p. 881). To consolidate their rule under the threat of continuous rebellions that often arose from intertribal conflicts, the Abbasid caliphs employed non-Arab mercenary/slave soldiers (called Mamluks in Egypt), who felt little allegiance to the Islamic ideal. They thus initiated a tradition of military slavery that reinforced the division between political and religious authorities (An-Na'im, 2008, p. 65; Fukuyama, 2012, pp. 196–201). Like the Ayyubids and the Seljuks, the Mamluks of Egypt had no other justification for rule than their superior military capability, which was amply demonstrated by their victory over the Mongols in 1260, at Ayn Jalut, south of Damas. Hence, "their legitimacy rested on their self-assertion as guardians of Islam" (An-Na'im, 2008, p. 74). Their religious credentials were limited to rather perfunctory claims of protecting Muslim lands and the endowments of religious institutions (training institutions, in particular), of displaying their presence in the holy cities of Mecca and Medina, of bearing religious titles, and of indulging in other similar activities or public gestures.

Saïd Amir Arjomand (2010) perhaps provides the most apt characterization of the change of political system that occurred in the late Abbasid era; he labels the distinctive type of regime that emerged then as "Islamic royalism." In this type of regime, the fundamental distinction between the political and the religious orders "did not disappear but was accommodated within the framework of the post-caliphal sultanism." The key feature was that the ruler maintained both orders and "was therefore the shadow of God on earth and the 'king of Islam.'" His role as "God's immediate deputy" was particularly important during the expansion of Islam among the infidels in Central Asia when the "king of Islam" led the "army of Islam" to victory. Arjomand concludes that "the Abbasid caliphate was thus made redundant even before its overthrow" and that "after its extinction, the king's claim to being God's deputy gained universal acceptance, and the kings added caliph as well as sultan to their titles" (pp. 245–6).[5]

---

[5] The Ottomans followed that tradition closely. Thus, Mehmed II was the "king of Islam" and added "God's caliph" to his titles in accordance with Muslim royalism long before becoming "the Conqueror" with the overthrow of the Byzantine Empire (Arjomand, 2010, p. 258–9).

The assuming of religious grand titles is actually a legacy of the Umayyad caliphs, who used titles such as deputy of God ("na'ib Allah"), vice regent of God ("khalifat Allah"), and guardian of God ("amin Allah") to assert their supreme religious authority (An-Na'im, 2008, p. 61). In keeping with this tradition in which political power is exercised by military figures who dress themselves as emirs, the Mamluk sultan al-Zahir Baybars used the prestigious title of caliph to sanctify his own worldly glory, in the same way that Friedrich II (1194–1250), a Hohenstaufen, obtained the title of king of Jerusalem to enhance his power in Europe (Meddeb, 2002, chs. 16–17).[6] The Cairo caliphs actually lacked power, which facilitated the task of the Mamluks, who exploited them and appropriated their titles as instruments to establish their legitimacy (Finkel, 2005, p. 111).[7]

When, toward the end of the tenth century, al-Muizz, an Ismaili Shi'a missionary, came from Baghdad to North Africa to found the Fatimid kingdom, he succeeded in rousing the people to eject their last (Aghlabi) ruler by proclaiming himself a descendant of the Prophet. Whether the new ruler was a genuine descendant of the Prophet or not "was really of no consequence" (Marsot, 2007, p. 14). What mattered most were the military strength and financial wealth of the willing ruler.[8] In the case of the Fatimid state, the demonstration of physical strength was especially important because, to restore the unity of religious and political authority, it effectively imposed Shi'a orthodoxy on a majority of Sunni Muslims. The latter resisted from the start, making it clear that though they accepted the military rule of the Fatimids as the de facto authority, as the Sunni ulama commonly did, they rejected their religious authority. Clearly, the whole approach of the Fatimids was primarily political (An-Na'im, 2008, pp. 70–3).

The central implication of this cursory account is hard to reconcile with the view that "at no time in history did Muhammad or his successors separate their religion from the state" or depart from "the fusion of the religious and political rules" (Facchini, 2009, p. 16). The essentially political nature

---

[6] To assert and to maintain their monopoly over the right to rule, the Ottomans also laid claim to several honorary titles that had spiritual significance among their subjects.

[7] An-Na'im (2008) writes that the Mamluk sultans "generally kept the caliph under strict watch, reserving him mostly for public ceremonial displays" (p. 75).

[8] When al-Muizz arrived in Egypt in 973, and the ulama asked him to present his credentials and his genealogy so that he could be accepted as a descendant of the Prophet, al-Muizz is reported to have shown his sword and said, "Here is my genealogy .... Then he showered the floor with gold coins and said: 'here is my lineage.' The ulama had nothing further to say" (Marsot, 2007, pp. 16–17). One of Muizz's successors, Hakim (al-Hakim Bi-Amr Allah), who was obviously an eccentric man, went so far as pretending to be the incarnation of the godhead (p. 19).

of the whole process of consolidation of power throughout the Arabian Peninsula is clear: What appear at first glance as conflicts between various religious factions or interpretations of the faith often conceal more down-to-earth struggles between different clans or tribes over access to political power and the economic privileges that go with it. It is commonly accepted that during the first centuries of Islam the core conflict was betweent the group of Muslims who migrated with the Prophet from Mecca and those who welcomed and supported him in Medina (An-Na'im, 2008, p. 56). In fact, all major controversies were deeply political. Thus, when Abu Bakr decided to fight his wars of apostasy against the ostensibly infidel Arab tribes that refused to pay zakat to the caliph and insisted on spending it on their own tribes, the most prominent companions of the Prophet strongly disagreed with this brutal approach. Had not Muhammad actually refrained from using force in the collection of zakat? Such an attitude would have been inconceivable had the caliph been considered the supreme religious authority. Also, the fact that Abu Bakr invoked religious justifications for his position does not mean that the decision to fight the rebel Arab tribes was religious and not political. By the same token, the dissenters, who refrained from implementing what they considered the correct view, did so presumably out of respect for Abu Bakr's political authority as caliph (An-Na'im, 2008, pp. 58–9, 78–9). It is worth quoting here the conclusion that An-Na'im draws from these events:

Thus, whatever justification is considered, it is difficult to separate the religious aspects from the political ones …. Religious reasoning includes political consider-ations and vice versa. … Abu Bakr was able to enforce his view over the objections of the leading Companions because he was the caliph, not because he was "right" or "correct" from an Islamic point of view … there was no possibility of an inde-pendent authority that could have adjudicated or arbitrated his disagreement with the other Companions … if Umar or Ali, for instance, had been the caliph instead of Abu Bakr, the wars of apostasy would not have occurred … it may [therefore] be helpful to distinguish between Abu Bakr's religious views and his political deci-sions and actions as the caliph. Similarly, some leading Companions disagreed with Abu Bakr, probably on religious grounds as well as political ones. (An-Na'im, 2008, pp. 60–1)

As noted earlier, the history of Islam generally followed a pattern in which real power remained in the hands of the military oligarchy, and the Islamic states never succeeded in transcending their tribal divisions. In the words of Francis Fukuyama (2012),

Powerful tribal loyalties trumped purely ideological considerations, and the Mus-lim state continued to be undermined by kinship quarrels and animosities. … The

Prophet Muhammad bound together the Medinan tribes by force of his own charismatic personality during his lifetime, but he left behind no system for succession to the caliphate. The young religion barely surviced the power struggles over leadership in the generation following, and in may respects is still living with that failed early institutionalisation in the form of the Sunni-Shiite split. (Fukuyama, 2012, pp. 195, 451)

In reality, caliphs often became prisoners of the palace guards recruited from the tribes; in the worst circumstances, such as the late Abbasid era, they were mistreated by their praetorian guards, who did not hesitate to depose, maim, and blind them at will (Ruthven, 1997, pp. 13–14; Marsot, 2007, p. 11). In more benign circumstances, such as under the Ottoman Empire, which based its power on the systematic recruitment of military slaves, the title of caliph was used "in a rhetorical sense rather than as a straightforward political-legal assertion of sovereignty over the Muslim community" (Finkel, 2005, p. 111). It is only during the eighteenth century that stories about an official transfer of the caliphate to Selim began to circulate. This was not coincidental. By then Ottoman rulers felt it necessary to counter Russian claims to protect Ottoman Christians with claims to Ottoman spiritual authority over Russian Muslims. Until that time, the most important source of legitimacy for Ottoman rulers after Selim I conquered Egypt and Syria was the possession of the Holy Places of Mecca and Medina. The Ottoman sultans then became the guarantors of the pilgrimage routes by which the Muslim faithful traveled to sites associated with the life of the Prophet (pp. 110–11). As for the institution of "Shaykh ul-Islam," it was essentially an attempt to impose a hierarchical structure inside Sunni society to control and rally the populace to accept the sultan's rule and support his policies (Magnus and Naby, 2002, p. 89).

This account fits well with what we know about both Arab countries and other lands of Islam. The example of Mali is instructive in this regard. An ambitious warlord, Askiya Muhammad Ture (1493–1528), became one of the most renowned rulers of the Songhaï Empire. Trying to rally the support of Muslim religious leaders, he made Islam the official religion, built mosques, and brought Muslim scholars to Gao. Furthermore, to increase the chances of success in his military campaigns, he went to Mecca in 1496 and, on his return, took the title of "Caliph of the Soudan." Using his new Islamic credentials, he embarked on a jihad and quickly displaced political contenders (Lapidus, 1988, p. 494; Davidson, 1991, p. 106; Milet, 2005, pp. 41–2). In fact, the whole history of the Songhai Empire of Gao (1528–91) was one of continuous struggle between two political groups, "one with colours that were Songhai, pagan and nationalist, and the other proclaiming a Mali-type Muslim universalism" (Fage and Tordoff, 1995, p. 79).[9]

In the early seventeenth century, the Massassi, a people of mixed Soninke and Fulani descent, "had Muslim clerics in their entourages and, when it suited their interests, acted in Islamic ways." Yet, "their political actions were in no way Islamic; they were concerned with converting the clan and age-grade structures of traditional Bambara society into associations of serfs and clients subordinate to their will as war-leaders" (Fage and Tordoff, 1995, p. 189).[10]

About two centuries later, al-Hajji Umar (c. 1795–1864), went on pilgrimage to Mecca at the age of twenty-three and returned with the title, "Caliph of the brotherhood Tijâniyya for the Sudan." In the Fouta-Djalon (in today's Guinea) where he took temporary refuge, he founded a "zaouïa," a Sufi brotherhood, which was successful in attracting numerous young Tukolor (in French, Toucouleurs) willing to learn the new religious doctrine and to embark on a jihad that ended with the destruction of the Muslim kingdoms of the Khasso and the Masina, as well as the Bambara kingdom around Segu (in today's Mali). His regime, in which local forces interacted with international reformist (Wahhabi) influences introduced by the Tijâni order, stretched from the Niger to Senegal.[11] After his army occupied Timbuctu, he was murdered by a coalition of shaykhs, Fulani and Bambara, and Qadiri and Kunta, themselves allied with urban ulama (Fage and Tordoff, 1995, pp. 209–11; Lapidus, 1988, p. 564; Sall, 2000, pp. 374–83; Milet, 2005, p. 50).

Still another manifestation of the political logic underlying the use of Islam is the fact that the Muslim ruling elite did not always look favorably on conversion to Islam. Thus, under the Middle East's early Arab regimes, "Islam signified the suzerainty and the solidarity of an otherwise factious ruling caste" (Lapidus, 1988, p. 444). The conversion of members of local aristocracies in conquered countries was seen as a threat because, once converted, these elites ould compete for political power. By contrast, conversion

---

[9] The renowned Sunni Ali, who initiated the Songhai's systematic conquest of their neighbors (1464), tended to rely on the support of farmers rather than city dwellers and merchants. As a result, he was "much more a potent force in Songhai traditional religion than a good Muslim" (Davidson, 1991, p. 105).

[10] This is about the same story as that of the marabouts of the Sine-Saloum (Senegal), who came to play in their Mouride sodality the dual roles of religious leaders and dynamic patrons exercising authority over highly submissive disciples-cum-clients (the "talibé") (Cruise O'Brien, 1971, 1975; Boone, 1992, pp. 106–9).

[11] The Tijâni brotherhood was originally created by a Moroccan shaykh (d. 1815), who was later accepted as its leader in Western Sudan (Fage and Tordoff, 1995, p. 210).

of dependent members of the lower classes was encouraged because it was natural for them to adopt the religion of their masters. Apparently, a similar situation obtained during the Muslim conquest of India, beginning in the early thirteenth century. There, the Turkish and Afghan warrior elites seem to have been hostile to conversions of Hindu nobles, lest they should compete for power. Hence the observation that "while the aristocracy was composed of Muslims who came from Afghanistan, Iran, and Inner Asia, Indian converts were mostly from the lower classes" (Lapidus, 1988, p. 443).

4.2 The Archetypal Model of Politico-Religious Interactions in the Lands of Islam

This section has two parts. The first characterizes the dominant system of relations between politics and religion in the Muslim world, and the second offers insightful illustrations of those relationships.

Subordination of Religious Authorities to Political Rulers

As the foregoing account suggests, and as confirmed by An-Na'im (2008), the states under which Muslims lived in the past were never Islamic: "The state was inherently political and not religious because of differences between the nature of religious authority and political authority" (p. 49). The fact that rulers often deemed it desirable to claim a measure of Islamic legitimacy to sustain their political authority over Muslims did not make the state they controlled Islamic (p. 52). As for the argument for the historical origin of the conflation/convergence of religion and politics in the lands of Islam, it may be easily overturned. Indeed, such an ideal has been impossible to achieve since the time of the Prophet, because "no other human being can enjoy the Prophet's combination of religious and political authority. ... That experience was unique and cannot be replicated, because Muslims do not accept the possibility of prophets after the Prophet Muhammad" (p. 53). Revealingly, Ibn Taymiyya (1263–1328), the leading Islamic traditionalist scholar and a foremost religious writer of the Egypt's Mamluk period (more about him later), asserted that the selection of public officers or magistrates should not be based on considerations of religious piety but only on the pragmatic requirements of the job being assigned and the ability of the candidates to comply with them ethically and professionally (cited from An-Na'im, 2008, p. 49; Hourani, 1991, p. 144).

Throughout Islamic history, beginning with Islam's original expansion, the message of social justice and the equality of men conveyed by

Muhammad's preaching and preserved in the Quran came up against the realities of tribal and dynastic power (Ruthven, 1997, p. 12). Political rulers tended to have the upper hand in their dealings with religious authorities, and the principle of detachment of the ulama from worldly affairs generally prevailed. While accepting the necessity of political order, the ulama disdained political involvement and withdrew into communal and personal religious affairs (Lapidus, 1988, p. 882; Saint-Prot, 2008, pp. 312–13). According to Albert Hourani (1991, pp. 143–5, 458), if rulers had to negotiate with the ulama, and if their authority was legitimate only if used to maintain the sharia and thus "the fabrics of virtuous and civilized life" (a caliph's main duty was to watch over the faith), a powerful tradition among the ulama (among both Sunni and Shi'a Muslims) was that "they should keep their distance from the rulers of the world" (p. 458). This implied that they should avoid linking themselves too closely with the government of the world while preserving their access to the rulers and their influence on them. Such a passive, or quietist, approach of religious authorities toward political power was legitimated by the fact that the jurists of Islam were primarily concerned with regulating the relationship of the individual Muslim with his God. As a result, the role of the ulama is to formulate standards of conduct that represented a system of private, and not of public, law (Coulson, 1964, pp. 120, 123).[12]

The Quran does not cover genuine constitutional or administrative law (Lal, 1998, p. 62; Anderson, 1979, p. 498). In addition to mentioning that it is the duty of the ruler to ratify and enforce the standards of conduct prescribed by the law, the Quran contains only two points about the proper system of government: consultation ("meshverret") and obedience to authority ("ulu'l emr"). Moreover, it does not insist on any particular form of government (An-Na'im, 2008, p. 199). Even if the ruler was unjust or impious "it was generally accepted that he should still be obeyed, for any kind of order was better than anarchy" (Hourani, 1991, p. 144).[13] As a result, the daily conduct of politics was dictated by "raison d'état," rather than by injunctions laid out in the scriptural sources of Islam (Khalid, 2007, p. 28). The conferral of Islamic legitimacy on military elites was historically linked to the legitimacy that they acquired from successful conquests (p. 30).

---

[12] For example, in fiscal law, ulama were primarily concerned with those limited aspects of public finance that were deemed to constitute a man's obligations toward God, such as the payment of the zakat tax (Coulson, 1964, p. 124).

[13] In Afghanistan, for example, the ulama advocate the implementation of the sharia "but do not care who is in charge of the state, provided that he supports the sharia and protects the religion" (Roy, 1993, p. 494).

Accommodation with the existing power was thus seen as desirable by the ulama for whom denouncing a ruler who claimed to be a good Muslim was unjustified.[14] In the words of N. J. Coulson (1964) "Might, in fact, was right, and this was eventually recognised by the scholars in their denunciation of civil disobedience even when the political authority was in no sense properly constituted. Obviously the effective enforcement of the whole system of sharia law was entirely dependent upon the whim of the de facto ruler" (p. 83). This conclusion has also been reached by Lapidus (2002) who writes, "From the Islamic point of view, the sultan's authority was derived from his role as executor of the shari'a, and in turn his subjects were responsible to him. Even a government that seized power by military force was regarded as legitimate as long as it recognized the sovereignty of the shari'a and respected the basic interests of the Muslim community. The shari'a, however, did not cover all aspects of [Ottoman] political and social life" (p. 260). This situation seemed to have been a compromise resulting from the mutual dependence of the political and the religious elites. In fact, "both groups relied upon each other, the ulama needing the financial support provided by the soldiers, the latter benefitting from the ideological legitimation which only the former could supply" (Berkey, 2003, p. 215).

This was in stark contrast to the view of the Islamists for whom no compromise can be struck with any state whose foundations are not thoroughly Islamic (Roy, 1993, p. 495). Thus, if the merger of religion and politics is a classic Islamic ideal, only recently have they actually been brought together (Lapidus, 1988, p. 889). With hindsight, this ideal appears as a imagined reality of Muslims, a "collection of images" that precludes an objective self-reflective analysis of one's culture while feeding fantasies based on romantic ahistorical visions of the past (Arkoun, 1994, pp. 6–13).

In a vivid manner, the traditionalist and very influential philosopher al-Ghazali (1058–1111) wrote, on the one hand, that "the jurisconsult serves as master and director of conscience for political authority in administrating and disciplining men that order and justice may reign in this world," and, on the other hand, that "the tyranny of a sultan for a hundred years causes less damage than one year's tyranny exercised by the subjects against one another. ... Revolt was justified only against a ruler who clearly went

---

[14] Sufism generally adopted an attitude of detachment from worldly powers, which brought Sufi masters much social prestige and spiritual authority. For example, the Chistis who played such a major role in the pattern of Islamization of India (see Chapter 3) "implicitly accepted the political cadre of the Sultanate and indirectly validated the authority of the Sultans by advocating a concept of universal hierarchy which Sultans could use to validate their claims to be the heads of a temporal world order" (Lapidus, 1988, p. 451).

against a command of God or His prophet" (cited by Kepel, 2005, p. 238; and from Hourani, 1991, p. 144). In short, communal strife ("fitna") or chaos ("fawda") is the most abhorred state, and to prevent it from emerging, despotism is justified. Religious authorities thus tolerate an oppressive or even an illegitimate political ruler as the lesser of two evils (An-Na'im, 2008, p. 52).

Gilles Kepel (2005) conveys the same idea when he writes, "The excommunication of the prince, be he the worst of despots, was pronounced only exceptionally, for it opened the prospect of considerable disorder and created dangerous jurisprudential precedents" (p. 59). Excommunication was deemed an especially dangerous weapon because "it could all too easily fall into the hands of sects beyond the control of the ulama and the clerics" (p. 56). It bears emphasis that the tradition of condoning despotic practices developed in spite of Islam's professed aim to establish a righteous world order and to provide guarantees against despotic rule. Under the Mamluks, the ulama often declared outright allegiance to whatever military commander ruled over the city of their residence (e.g., Damas), because they expected this action would restore order as quickly as possible. In times of external warfare or foreign aggression, such an attitude implied that they authorized new taxes and even the diversion of funds from religious foundations for military purposes. As we see in Chapter 5, only under conditions of acute crisis such as civil conflict would the ulama shift their loyalty in favor of the suffering masses. And when a rebel religious leader emerged from among the ulama, the sultan often rudely repressed him because his religious beliefs contradicted the consensus of the scholarly community and his fatwas disquieted the minds of the common people (An-Na'im, 2008, pp. 75–6).

The opinions voiced by the ulama were purely advisory and could be given effect only in court judgments by Islamic judges (the qadis). However, the position of these judges, who had become the central organ for the administration of law by the end of the Umayyad period, reflected the previously described preeminence of the established political power. As a matter of fact, the judges "were in no sense an independent judiciary": Their judgements were subject to review by the political superior who had appointed them, and they were entirely dependent on his support for the enforcement of their decisions (Coulson, 1964, p. 121). Although their declared policy was to implement the system of religious law elaborated by the ulama, the Abbasid rulers were never prepared to allow independence to the religious courts. Despite their self-posturing as servants of the sharia, they were used to issuing peremptory directives to the judiciary, to reversing whatever decision displeased them, and to dismissing arbitrarily those judges who dared to confront them (pp. 121–3). This is a general feature of Islamic history: Being in a subordinate position, the qadis were never able to deal effectively with claims directed against a high official of the state. Such officials would simply refuse to recognize the decision of the judge in these cases, and as a consequence, the machinery at his command would not be activated to enforce it. In short, "supreme judicial power was vested in the political sovereign," and "the jurisdiction and authority of sharia courts were subject to such limits as he saw fit to define" (p. 122).

In the hierarchy of judicial authority the so-called courts of complaints ("Mazalim") stand above the qadi courts. Their pronouncements are "the direct expression of the supreme judicial and executive powers combined in the sovereign," and their jurisdiction is "superior particularly because of their recognised competence to formulate principles of substantive law additional and supplementary to the scheme of strict sharia doctrine" (Coulson, 1964, p. 130). Moreover, the sovereign could always decide to sit himself as a Mazalim court, for example, to deal with complaints against the behavior or the judgments of the qadis themselves. Hence, in the event of severe confrontation, his own views would always prevail (p. 122).

As a matter of practice, the distinction between the Mazalim and sharia jurisdictions came very close to the notion of a division between secular and religious courts, with the former assumed to represent the ruler's law (Coulson, 1964, pp. 128–9). In general, the competence of the qadis was restricted to private law – in particular, family law, inheritance, civil transactions and injuries, and religious endowments (see infra). By contrast, the sovereign had the widest discretionary powers in the domain of criminal law: here, he could freely determine what behavior constitutes an offense and what punishment is to be applied in each case (p. 132). In all spheres of life in which so-called public order or public good considerations were involved, the way of political authority dominated. For example, land law was a matter of special concern to rulers because political allegiance was often secured through land concessions. For this reason, "the political authority himself chose to exercise jurisdiction in this sphere, on the basis of a discretionary system of procedure, and indeed of substantive law" (p. 128).

To sum up, let us again cite N. J. Coulson:

The wider and supreme duty of the sovereign was the protection of the public interests; and in pursuance of it he was afforded an overriding personal discretion to determine, according to time and circumstances, how the purposes of God for the Islamic community might best be effected …. Doctrine had granted the ruler such wide discretionary powers on the assumption that he would be ideally qualified for office. But it is precisely here that the idealistic nature of the doctrine is at its most apparent; for there existed no constitutional machinery, and in particular no independent judiciary, to guarantee that the ruler would be so qualified and that those powers would not be abused … [the doctrine] never seriously challenged the ruler's autocratic power to control the practical implementation of that law; and it finally reached the point of abject surrender and recognition of its total impotence by acknowledging the principle that obedience was due to the political power whatever its nature, and that even the most impious and tyrannical regime was preferable to civil strife … the only limits upon the de facto power of the ruler were those that he found in his own conscience. (pp. 129–30, 133–4)

The Ottoman experience essentially matches Coulson's characterization. Although during the eighth and ninth centuries the power of the courts expanded in parallel to the development of schools of Islamic jurisprudence and legal traditions, this expansion never meant that the judiciary could challenge the sovereign's authority more than occasionally. And well before the establishment of the Ottoman state in 1299, sultans gained effective control over the judiciary, assuming sole authority over the appointment and dismissal of judges, placing religious and judicial officials on the state payroll, and conditioning the judiciary's well-being on state support. The Ottoman sultans further enhanced their control by rotating and replacing judges regularly, both to weaken local loyalties and to reduce corruption (Kuran and Lustig, 2012, pp. 638–9; Coşgel, Miceli, and Ahmed, 2009; Imber, 2002, ch. 6).

Robert Lee (2014) draws an appropriate parallel between the Ottoman Empire and Europe. Although the Ottoman Empire identified with Islam when it began on the fringes of the Byzantine Empire, its rulers did not depend on a political or religious ideology any more than the French monarchy did so under Louis XIV. Indeed, political ideologies – elements of philosophy combined with recipes for action – emerged only from the French, American, and Russian Revolutions. Not until the nineteenth century did any government perceive advantages in committing itself to a programmatic objective such as liberalism, constitutionalism, or nationalism (pp. 49–50).

For the sake of completeness, it must be noted that in nomadic societies, such as those of Central Asia, where there is no tradition of book learning through madrasas, access to Islam was primarily through sacred lineages. As a result, communities paid allegiance to individuals, usually Sufi shaykhs, who belonged to lineages that had "brought Islam" to them. The important point, however, is that although members of such sacred lineages (e.g., among the Turkmens and the Kazhaks) enjoyed immense social prestige and sometimes wealth, political power remained firmly in the hands of tribal chiefdoms. Power in those societies was imagined in genealogical terms, and "to the extent that state structures existed, they derived their moral authority from adat, tribal custom and the traditions of the elders" (Khalid, 2007, p. 33).

That view is clearly at variance with the recent analysis of Noah Feldman (2008) regarding the nature of the Islamic state. According to him, the classical order of Islam is a constitutional order in which the force of the ulama offers an effective countervailing power to the political ruler. Acts of injustice were rare because the ulama kept the ruler's decisions within the bounds of the sharia through the threat of stripping his legitimacy. For example, the ruler's temptations to steal property and abuse his citizens were "blocked by the sharia acknowledgement of the sanctity of private property and its corresponding prohibition of theft" (p. 47). Moreover, important policy decisions made by the state apparatus required validation by religious scholars in the form of fatwas (pp. 51, 97). Feldman's thesis confounds principles and reality. It overlooks problems of enforcement of the ideas of justice contained in the religious law. His contention that the ulama constituted an effective countervailing force against political oppression is clearly exaggerated. There is no empirical basis to the claims that acts of injustice were rare and expropriations by the sovereign limited.

Illustrations

Under the dominant type of politico-religious equilibrium prevailing in the lands of Islam, then, political rulers had their way, and religious leaders were either enticed to cooperate with the political agenda of rulers or coerced to do so to avoid facing harsh consequences (An-Na'im, 2008, p. 56). The widespread tactic of enticement, which involved the distribution of rewards and privileges according to a patronage logic, enabled the rulers to gain Islamic legitimacy from the endorsement of the state by their client ulama. The result was a largely cooperative relationship between the religious scholars and the sultans, in the sense that the latter obtained a relatively unconstrained space to govern in exchange for granting favors to the former (Hallaq, 2010). This cooperative relationship was sufficiently strong to make the political regime quite stable; it was shielded from significant political opposition. The examples of the Ottoman and the Mughal Empires as well as that of Safavid Persia readily come to mind here. At these empires' head lay a strong and centralized state; at the same time, the moral authority of Islamic religious leaders served as a check on the authoritarianism of the political ruler and his officials.

Mughal India

Even such a progressive (Mughal) ruler as Akbar (1556–1605), who claimed legitimacy directly from God and not from any specific religion, which implied the religious equality of all his Indian subjects, felt the need to have the leading ulama sign a statement declaring him the caliph and the sultan of Islam. The first part of this political strategy enabled him to enlist the support of the Hindus; the latter part allowed him to officially sever the symbolic allegiance to the caliphate of the Middle East (An-Na'im, 2008, p. 144). In spite of their official posture of being the guardians and the enforcers of the sharia, the Mughal emperors generally followed their own political logic rather than the tenets of Islamic law. Doing so was not too difficult: "Since there were nearly as many interpretations as there were jurists, monarchs had considerable freedom in deciding what was right and wrong" (Eraly, 2007, p. 260). In fact, "whatever the theory, in practice, the royal will was the law," and "crime was what offended the emperor" (p. 259).

This held true even for the most pious and intolerant Mughal ruler, Emperor Aurangzeb. About him, a British historian would write,

> He was so great a dissembler in other matters, that he has been supposed a hypocrite in religion .... His zeal was shown in prayers and reading the Koran, in pious discourses, in abstemiousness .... But neither religion nor morality stood in his way when they interfered with his ambition; and, though full of scruples at other times, he would stick at no crime that was requisite for the gratification of his passion. (Elphinstone, 1843, pp. 379–80)

Aurangzeb's instrumentalization of Islam was most clear in his manner of seizing supreme power against the wishes of his father, Emperor Shah Jahan, who was then seriously ill. His elder brother, Dara Shikoh, was the heir apparent and was known for his religious tolerance: He openly professed the tenets of Akbar and wrote a book to reconcile the Hindu and Muslim doctrines, going as far as calling the *Upanishads* the hidden book of the Quran. When Prince Aurangzeb succeeded in defeating Dara Shikoh militarily after some deceptive maneuvers involving an alliance with his other brother, Morad, some Islamic judges refused to legitimize what they rightly saw as an usurpation of the throne. Aurangzeb then decided to obtain the support of the most conservative ulama by alleging Dara Shikoh was an adulterer: "No topic, therefore, could be selected more likely to make that prince [Dara Shikoh] unpopular than his infidelity, and in no light could the really religious Aurangzeb be so favourably opposed to him as in that of the champion of Islam. In this character he had also an advantage over [his other brother] Shuja, who was looked on with aversion by the orthodox

Mahometans from his attachment to the Persian sect of the Shi'as" (Elphinstone, 1843, p. 380).

Aurangzeb was able to persuade jurist Abdul Wahab to issue the required fatwa. Wahab declared that Dara Shikoh was physically unfit to govern so that the throne was effectively vacant when Aurangzeb stepped in. In 1658, Shikoh was declared a heretic by a group of compliant ulama convened by Aurangzeb. The accusation, grounded in trivial charges such as mixing with Hindu religious leaders and accommodating Sufi ideas of syncretism, carried the penalty of death.[15] In this manner, Aurangzeb succeeded not only in eliminating his most popular rival but also in manipulating religion to establish and consolidate his power. As a reward for his fatwa, Abdul Wahab was made the Chief Judge of the empire, a position that allowed him to acquire an unequalled reputation for corruption. As a matter of principle, crimes against the state, which were in effect crimes against the emperor, could be punished according to his own pleasure, and it was mainly those political crimes that caught his attention (Sarkar, 1912, pp. 298–302; Eraly, 2007, pp. 260–1). By sitting at the top of the Mughal judicial organization and by controlling the Chief Judge, the emperor was in control of the main lever of absolute power.

The Ottoman Empire

In the Ottoman Empire, the head of the ulama, the sheikhulislam, was appointed by royal warrant. It is true that, reciprocally, accession to the Ottoman throne was sanctioned by a fatwa from the sheikhulislam. Yet, even though the head of the ulama occasionally refused to issue such a fatwa, he was always acting as party to a palace coup, never on his own independent initiative. On the contrary, when a sultan deposed a sheikhulislam, he was always following his own will (An-Na'im, 2008, p. 186). In the stark words of Cleveland, "the entire religious establishment held office at the pleasure of the sultan" (Cleveland, 2004, p. 48; see also İnalcík, 1973; İnalcık and Quataert, 1994; Kafadar, 1995; Goffman, 2002; Imber, 2002). The Ottoman legal system also embodied the decisive superiority of political over religious power: The sultan appointed and paid all the judges, determined the scope of their jurisdiction, and enforced their judgments. Not only were state

---

[15] On this occasion, Aurangzeb displayed his usual hypocrisy. After the execution that he himself ordered, Aurangzeb asked for the head of Dara Shikoh to be cut off, placed on a platter, and wiped and washed in his presence. Then, "when he had satisfied himself that it was the real head of Dara, he began to weep, and, with many expressions of sorrow, directed it to be interred in the tomb of Humayun" (Elphinstone, 1843, p. 411).

officials thus allowed to decide the geographical and subject-matter jurisdiction of judges whom they authorized to apply the principles of the sharia
but the sultan also enacted many laws (known as "kanun") that were usually derived from custom and were therefore not bound by the methodology
of the sharia and varied from one part of the empire to another. Moreover,
a party who did not accept the ruling of a judge applying the sharia was
allowed to demand a second hearing of the case by the court of the sultan
("divan") acting as the ultimate appellate court (An-Na'im, 2008, pp. 188–
91). In many cases, such appeals were not necessary because senior religious
officials were "quite inventive in formulating legal justifications for whatever
their patron rulers wished to institute" (Zubeida, 2011, p. 15).

By subordinating themselves to the political authority, members of the
religious classes gained substantial economic and political privileges. The
sultan and his inner circle used various instruments of patronage to win
their loyalty, including the administration of religious endowments that
controlled vast tracts of land, tax exemption for Muslim scholars, and the
granting of official positions. It is not surprising that Islamic scholars, especially those coming from religious families with long-standing honorable
ancestries, competed for religious offices, titles, and tax farms and that official religious classes were actually converted into a core element of the
Ottoman nobility and a linchpin of provincial administration (Hourani,
1993). A "cozy relationship" was thus established between the sultan and
the religious clerics – not only the ulama but also the Sufi orders (Malik,
2012, p. 8).

Lapidus (2002) describes in particularly vivid terms the manner in which
the ulama played into the hands of the Ottoman political ruler, trading their
ideals for apparently irresistible economic and political privileges:

The biographies of scholars show that, with the elaboration of a bureaucratic hierarchy, interest in careers outweighed genuine piety and learning. The influence
of entrenched families enabled them to promote their children into the higher
grades of the educational and judicial hierarchies without having reached the proper
preliminary levels, while theological students who could not find patronage were
excluded. In the course of the eighteenth century the ulama became a powerful conservative pressure group. As servants of the state the ulama no longer represented
the interests of the people, nor protected them from the abuses of political power. No
longer did they represent a trancendental Islamic ideal opposed to worldly corruption. Their integration into the Ottoman empire made them simply the spokesmen
of Ottoman legitimacy. (Lapidus, 2002, p. 268; see also Hourani, 1991, pp. 224–5)

In view of the tight grip maintained by the Ottoman state on religion, the
break between it and the modern republican state of Turkey should not be

exaggerated: The modern state has actually continued many of the Ottoman practices of recognition, support, and control of religious institutions and practice (An-Na'im, 2008, p. 203).

North Africa

In many ways, the trajectory of Tunisia resembles that of Turkey. In spite of their undoubted spiritual and social influence, Muslim clerics in pre-colonial Tunisia did not come anywhere close to exercising political power. This was particularly evident in the last quarter of the nineteenth century during the reign of Khayr al-Din. Yet Muslim clerics held an important place in Tunisian society for three reasons. First, as the educated graduates of the principal mosque-affiliated madrasas, they occupied the positions of teachers and magistrates. Until the foundation of the Sadiqi college in 1875, they controlled all levels of the secondary education system. Second, until the appearance of modern newspapers, they monopolized political opinion. Finally, they could rely on strong social connections, because many of their sons worked for the government and were tied by marriage to official and merchant families, who typically pushed their children into religious scholarship. What needs to be stressed, however, is that such strong social influence and prestige were not accompanied by political power: On the contrary, "the Beys insisted on loyalty and passivity in return for appointments to office" (Lapidus, 1988, p. 698).

Precolonial Morocco supplies us with yet another insightful illustration of the dominant politico-religious equilibrium found in the lands of Islam. According to the account given by Mohamed el Mansour (1979), the whim of the prince was merely tempered by the advice of the ulama, who acted as de facto mediators between the populace and their sovereign, playing the role of a shock absorber whenever the regime's actions sparked dangerous tensions (see also Kepel, 2005, p. 238; Lugan, 2011). The rule of Moroccan sultans was generally strong, as reflected in their authoritarian and centralizing policies. To counterbalance the overwhelming powers of the sultan, there existed an institution called the "hurm." Because it was a sacred place whose residents were considered uniformly "holy," all forms of violence were prohibited within it.[16] As a shelter for people seeking God's protection, it was inviolable, implying that the sultan's men could not invade it and fugitives were immune from pursuit. In reality, that sanctuary provided only temporary protection to the fugitive, typically a political

---

[16] The idea of sanctuary is as old as religious belief itself, and it was certainly an integral feature of Semitic religious tradition (el Mansour, 1979, p. 50).

dissident. The main purpose of the institution was to afford him the opportunity to reach a negotiated arrangement with the sultan and regain his favour. In periods of heavily centralized power, the hurm was seen as an important vehicle for tempering the "strong hand" of the sultan (el Mansour, 1979, pp. 63–5, 69).

Each hurm had well-defined limits. It was the property of a religious group whose identity and continuity it symbolised, and it carried a number of economic and social privileges (tax exemptions, in particular) in addition to moral benefits. The granting by the sultans of considerable privileges to those holding the sanctuaries actually reflected the distribution of power between the temporal authorities and the religious groups. In some sense, the hurm served as a buffer institution between the central government and the various loci of religious power, because the sovereign was in no position to monopolize religious legitimacy in spite of his special relationship to God under Islam (el Mansour, 1979, pp. 69–70). Yet, cooperation between political rulers and religious authorities and groups was the dominant pattern observed in precolonial Morocco.

When the sultan's power was contested, as when the houses of the Sa'di and the Alawi, both of which originated from the southern desert fringe, replaced the prestigious Idrisis as the central power, and sheer force proved ineffective in curbing rebellious movements, the sultan co-opted local religious elites and granted them privileges in the form of donations, tax exemptions, honorific titles, land grants, and the right of sanctuary.[17] Potential opponents were thus confined to the religious field and persuaded that spiritual leadership was more important than involvement in worldly political affairs. On the contrary, when the rule of the sultan was well established and strong, he would curtail the powers of the religious groups by limiting their sanctuary privileges.

It is quite plausible that Muslim sultans in many parts of the Islamic world used the institution of the waqf in a similar manner. Established during the earliest periods in Islamic history, a waqf is a private immovable property turned into an endowment aimed at supporting any social service (schools, mosques, charitable institutions, etc.) permissible under Islamic law (Kuran, 2004b, p. 75). Except under Maleki law (which, probably for this reason, was rarely invoked for the purpose), the founder of a waqf held the right to appoint himself, or a person of his choice, as the administrator of the property, and he and his descendants were often able to benefit

---

[17] Such tactics proved to be particularly useful in the sultan's relations with the powerful urban community of Fez.

directly from the revenues generated by it. He also received regular prayers, usually performed in public, from those who benefited from the institution and soon became his loyal clients. It is therefore no surprise that political rulers, high officials, and rich merchants eagerly sought to enhance their reputations as pious leaders of their community by establishing waqfs (Kuran, 2005b, pp. 799–802; An-Na'im, 2008, pp. 79–82; Khalid, 2007, pp. 30–1). To the extent that waqfs were an important source of social patronage and, potentially, of political influence based on the mobilization of religion[18] – by being designated for a particular purpose, a waqf allowed the rise of an autonomous group – strong rulers did their best to keep them under control when they were not endowed by themselves or close political allies.

Afghanistan
The last illustration of the clear subordination of religious authorities to political rulers comes from Afghanistan. Olivier Roy (1990) observes, "Public order, which is a prerequisite of all what is socially desirable in society ('maslahat') has always seemed, to the ulama, preferable to the demand that politics should be completely open to the promptings to religion." In accordance with this principle, the Afghan ulama never opposed the power of the emir and rarely became involved in his appointment, a prerogative that was considered to belong to the tribes (pp. 49–50). It was not until the program of progressive social reforms enacted by Prime Minister Mohammad Daoud (1953–63) brought down on him the wrath of the mullahs that the ulama entered the political fray. To implement the reform program, which included the removal of the obligation to wear the veil and the purdah, Daoud allied himself with the small leftist educated elite of Kabul, thus neglecting the ulama and the tribes (Barfield, 2010, p. 214–15). When the mullahs took to preaching against the regime in their mosques, their leaders were arrested and charged with heresy and with treason for advocating the overthrow of the government .

Commenting on this event, Angelo Rasanayagam (2005) points out that "in traditional Islamic theory a de facto government rules by 'divine sanction' that can only be withdrawn or refused by his Muslim subjects if the ruler openly violates the law of Islam. In practice, however, an autocratic ruler with strong powers of coercion at his command continues to have his way in spite of such theories" (p. 35). The same conclusion, clearly

---

[18] Even private waqfs require a guardian from the community of ulama, whose salary is paid from the waqf income (Keddie, 2003, p. 15).

incompatible with the idea of a theocratic state, is also reached by Thomas Barfield (2010):

Traditional Islamic legal thought forbade popular rebellions against an established Muslim ruler by his subjects on the grounds that it created too much social disorder. This helped preserve the power of existing rulers, but also laid the ground for their replacement. The popular rebellions that characterised the two Anglo-Afghan wars were justified on the grounds that Muslims should not be ruled by infidels or the Muslim rulers, who were seen to be their clients. ... The civil war that drove Amanullah [1919–29] from power had been a product of internal rebellions. His opponents claimed that even a previously legitimate amir could be replaced if he lost his status as a Muslim ruler by implementing 'un-Islamic' policies. But since Sunni Islam lacked a hierarchical clergy, such declarations often failed to stick because they were the personal opinions of the clerics issuing them. Indeed if a rebellion failed, such clerics frequently lost their heads –a doubly useful punishment for the ruler, since the binding power of a fatwa on any issue was deemed ended on the death of the cleric who issued it. Thus, when the PDPA [the Communist party] came to power [in 1978] it was within a political milieu prone to accept even a usurper's rights if he held power firmly. (p. 227)

4.3 Islam in the Service of National Unification

An obvious circumstance favoring the concentration of religious and political powers in the hands of an ambitious ruler occurs when he uses the banner of Islam to extend his control over a rebellious territory or to unify a fragmented political space. These are times when it is especially important to obtain religious legitimacy because the stakes are high, and reference to an ideology that transcends regional, ethnic, and other divisions seems to be a key factor of success. In this section, I provide apt illustrations of such an instrumentalization of Islam in critical conditions, beginning with several historical examples of old imperial and dynastic regimes and then shifting emphasis to Afghanistan, a country that has remained in the limelight to this day. I then argue that the approach of Afghan rulers has been inspired by illustrious Islamic thinkers. Note that the next chapter presents an additional illustration of the manner in which Islam can be used for the purpose of national consolidation. This illustration is particularly important because it concerns Iran at the time of the officialization of Shi'ism.

Examples from Old Imperial and Dynastic Regimes

When Timur (1336–1405), known as Timur the Lame or Timurlenk, set out to end the chaos of feuding Mongol principalities and to reconquer the old Mongol territory, he not only claimed Mongol descent but also developed a bigoted version of Islam that bore little relation to the conservative party of the ulama: "He saw himself as the scourge of Allah, sent to punish the Muslim emirs for their unjust practices" (Armstrong, 2001, p. 91). When the Timurid Empire was displaced by the Uzbeks who came from the north to reestablish Genghisid rule in the region in the form of what became the khanate of Bukhara, the second Uzbek ruler, Ubaydullah Khan (d. 1540), again had recourse to Islamic legitimacy to counter the threat of Babur (then allied to the Safavid dynasty in Iran). He thus made a vow at the shrine of the Sufi master Ahmed Yesevi in the town of Turkistan that he would rule in full accordance with the sharia if he defeated his enemy in battle (Khalid, 2007, pp. 28–9). Finally, when the Manghits, who could not claim Genghisid descent, took over Bukhara in the late eighteenth century, they had no choice but to assert their legitimacy through Islam alone. Because they could not use the title of the khan, they called themselves "emir" to convey their Islamic credentials. The first two rulers of the Manghit dynasty formed especially strong alliances with the ulama, even intermarrying with the more august families in their ranks (p. 32).

In North Africa, the Rustamid, Idrisid, Fatimid, and Almohad dynastic regimes were successive attempts to unify Berber tribal peoples by using Islamic religious beliefs as a way to legitimize the new political elites. Islam was conceived as the basis of political solidarity among factious populations, and most of these regimes were "the ideological equivalents of the Caliphate," because the Idrisid, Fatimid, Almoravid, and Almohad rulers all claimed "an unmediated, divine authority based on their personal qualifications, and their descent in the family of the Prophet" (Lapidus, 1988, p. 376). The Almohad Empire, whose collapse marked the end of the "caliphal" phase of state formation and Islamization in North Africa, had adopted a particularly puritanical interpretation of Islam. Its founder, Muhammad Abdallah Tumart, who made a pilgrimage to Mecca, wanted to restore the Islamic community as it had existed in the Prophet's lifetime. Toward that end, he denounced the pagan Berber customs absorbed into Islamic practice as impious and proscribed wine drinking, music, and the enjoyment of luxurious clothing. A key moment in his ascent occurred when he received the support of a local chieftain, Abu Hafs Umar, and he succeeded in superimposing a religious hierarchy on a tribal society. He then declared himself Mahdi, imam, and "ma'sum," or infallible leader sent by God. Interestingly, his successor, Abd al-Mumin (1130–63), put his family in power and quickly converted a religious hierarchy into a family-based monarchy (pp. 374–5), thus repeating the experience of the original caliphate described in Section 4.1.

Afghanistan

We now turn to more recent history. The first (internationally recognized) king of Afghanistan, Emir Abdul Rahman Khan (1880–1901), who worried about the threats to his central power coming from the main tribes of the country, constantly referred to Islam as a way to establish his authority and legitimize his power. To pacify the northern opposition, to extend his authority to the east and the center, and to overcome the profound sense of tribal identity among Afghan people, he took the title of "Protector of the Nation and of the Religion" ("Zia-ul Millat wa Din"), thus claiming spiritual leadership of the Afghan millat (a subdivision of the umma). Ruling by the "grace and will of Allah," he fulfilled the dual role of leader and interpreter of Islam and Islamic law ("mujtahid"). Ushering in the theory of the divine rights of kings for the first time in Afghan history, he enlisted high-ranking ulama in defense of the country, taking various measures aimed at undermining the power of the ulama as a class.

He also decided that he was the only person qualified to declare the jihad, a necessary precaution in the face of so many rebellions from different quarters in his kingdom. Rahman wanted to guard against the possibility that fatwas for jihad would be issued by religious figures close to his enemies, such as happened when he was driven into war with Ayyub in Qandahar or, later, with Ishaq Khan in Turkistan (Magnus and Naby, 2002, pp. 89–90; Rasanayagam, 2005, pp. 11–12). In the former case, Ayyub had convinced important clerics to issue fatwas justifying the war on the grounds that Rahman was an infidel (a "farangi emir) who gave "blasphemous aid to infidels." It was in response to this move that Rahman had his own clerics issue fatwas denouncing Ayyub as a rebel. To obtain such a counter-fatwa was not easy, however, and he had to distribute material privileges to the dissenting clerics. When he eventually routed Ayyub's army, Abdur Rahman sought out one of the clerics who had issued the fatwa against him, and even though this cleric had taken refuge in the sacred Shrine of the Cloak (at Qandahar) where violence was forbidden, he confronted him with a raised sword and severed his head (Kakar, 2006, p. 61; Barfield, 2010, pp. 145–6).

In the mind of Rahman, it was the duty of all good Muslims to support their king in his efforts to unify and strengthen the country against the infidels; for example, by dutifully paying taxes to the center and delivering fighting men (a responsibility that accrued to village and clan leaders). He advocated the implementation of the sharia, instead of tribal common law, and attempted to integrate the clergy into the secular institutions of state by controlling the madrasas, the waqf, and their remuneration. In particular, he set up ministerial departments to oversee the administration of education and justice, the traditional monopolies of the clerics, and he turned the ulama into paid servants of the state. He demanded that judges pass examinations that he devised, and those clerics who made judgments that displeased him lost their positions and salaries. He also nationalized the country's Islamic endowments (waqfs), which had long supported the independence of religious institutions from the government. The central principle buttressing Rahman's rule was that, to overcome the factionalism of tribal life, the leader must appear as coming from outside the tribal world, having his legitimacy in the umma that transcends all the differences between Muslims (Roy, 1990, pp. 15–16, 59; 1993, p. 493; Magnus and Naby, 2002, pp. 36, 89; Rasanayagam, 2005, p. 12; Barfield, 2010, p. 160). In his case, appeal to a rather retrograde version of Islam (Rahman portrayed himself as "a paragon of Islamic leadership" or "the light of the nation and religion" chosen to defend the country's integrity against attacks by infidels) was accompanied by a relentless use of sheer force so that, by the end of his reign, he had created a powerful police state that instilled "fear unmediated by affection" in the population (Barfield, 2010, pp. 147, 151, 158, 174).

Reflecting on the history of Afghanistan, Roy (1990) remarks that "harping on the pan-Islamic theme has never been anything more than a means of strengthening the power of the state, and this has always been a major aim of those in power." Every time that the people's fervor for pan-Islamism rose to such a point that it endangered the Afghan state, the sovereigns always chose to play it safe and resist the pressure of the ulama, such as when Rahman opposed the religious leaders who wanted to hurl the frontier tribes into battle against the British (pp. 62–3). Creator of the modern Afghan state as currently constituted, Rahman "stressed the pure Islamic character of the Afghan state while creating a fundamentally secular government that dominated the religious establishment" so much that Islamic clerics "were reduced to being either arms of the state or apologists for it" (Barfield, 2010, pp. 155, 166). Despite his many references to Islam, he considered that his new state laws had priority over both traditional religious law (sharia) and customary law (p. 160).[19]

---

[19] Although Rahman's centralized model of government looked like the political system of Safavid Iran or the Ottoman Empire, it proved to be much less successful, and most of Rahman's achievements were ephemeral. According to Thomas Barfield (2010), the main reason for his lack of success was that his policy of eliminating the existing class of khans and community elders went against the grain of Afghan tradition: "Unlike Persia or the Ottoman empire, where the authority of shahs and sultans was buttressed by a strong

Illustrious Predecessors: Ibn Hanbal and Ibn Taymiyya

In acting as he did, Abdul Rahman essentially followed the route pointed out a long time ago by Ibn Hanbal, the first Islamist thinker and the founder of one of the four juridical schools of Sunni Islam, in his reflections on the best ways to avoid the violent upheavals and murderous tribal rivalries that Islam had witnessed during its first centuries. Unlike those who argued for a retreat from the ugly realities of world politics through some form of mysticism or theological quietism (particularly prominent among the oppressed Shi'as who took refuge in messianistic expectations, with the new messiah being supposed to reincarnate Ali)[20], Hanbal stressed the need to follow the letter rather than the spirit of the Quran (Saint-Prot, 2008, pp. 164–94); he thus initiated the scripturalist or literalist tradition in Islam. To reconcile the contending factions and reach a broad consensus among Muslims, he proposed to ban all personal opinions and to rally the whole community of believers around a unique truth. Reading of the Quran had to be literal, avoiding any allegorical exegesis. Indeed, strict adherence to the Islamic law had to replace particularized interpretations of tribal laws so that segmented ties based on kinship could give rise to harmonious relationships grounded in a religion of universal brotherhood. Ibn Taymiyya, discussed in Chapter 5, was inspired by Hanbal's vision, but he radicalized it by justifying the right to launch a holy war, the jihad, for the purpose of religious proselytism.

In developing their puritanical ideals, Hanbal and Taymiyya were probably influenced by the links between the traumatic circumstances of their times – the violent first centuries of post-Prophet times in the case of the former, and the Mongol invasion in the case of the latter – and the experience of the birth of Islam in Mecca and Medina. Indeed, a plausible theory about the rise of Islam in the seventh century contends that these two cities were advanced trading and agricultural places outside the direct sphere of the Byzantine and Sassanid Empires and were at the point of state formation. Therefore, they needed a unifying ideology to integrate the urban populace and nomadic tribes into a state (Keddie, 2003, p. 5).

It bears emphasis that the appeal to an all-encompassing Islam and umma is not a sure recipe for success. The recent history of Afghanistan offers vivid proof. After the victory of the Afghan Islamic resistance against the Soviet occupiers, tribal and ethnic affiliations penetrated the structures of

---

cultural tradition of autocracy, Afghan rulers were historically forced to work within a political system that was more federal and consultative" (pp. 161–2).

[20] This is a reaction similar to that of the Pharisees under the Roman Empire.

the supposedly modern political parties, transforming them into networks of patron/client relationships based on common traditional identities. The use of Islamic slogans, symbols, and ideology was unable to transform the population's deeply rooted social and cultural patterns to which modern fundamentalists remained ultimately captive (Roy, 1993, pp. 499–500; Magnus and Naby, 2002, pp. 94, 162). Rahman had well understood the limits of Islamic ideology: His appeals to the umma were astutely coupled with efforts to create an elite class of bureaucrats, formed by the royal family and the leading chiefs of the Mohammadzai clan from Qandahar, who would be dependent on him alone and detached from their tribal or ethnic affiliations. Moreover, he sought to cut off the khans and other dignitaries from their local power bases through a mix of strategies that included the splitting of provinces into districts and subdistricts that did not coincide with tribal and ethnic territorial divisions, and the appointment of non-indigenous governors and administrators in the regions (Rasanayagam, 2005, p. 12).

4.4 Summary: Asymmetric Cooperation and Sanctuary Rights

In this summary, I first emphasize the subordination of religion to politics in the tradition of Islam. I then highlight the moderately counterbalancing role of religion in the dominant system of interactions between politics and religion.

The Subordination of Religion to Politics

Bearing in mind the distinction between high and low Islam introduced in Chapter 3, what emerges is a two-sided picture of the influence of Islamic law. The masses follow a set of hybrid practices inspired both by Islam and local customs. By contrast, high officials and urbanites look to qadis for interpretation of law but only to the extent that it remains confined to the private sphere of life and does not interfere with the whims or the interests of the political ruler and his clique. In other words, on matters that concern the ruler directly, religious autonomy is restricted and politics holds sway.

Because the Quran does not deal with constitutional and administrative matters and the few Islamic prescriptions regarding proper political behavior are stated in rather general terms, Islamic officialdom has never constituted a real obstacle to despotism and tyranny. Even in the best cases, its countervailing power was limited to offering political opponents and dissenters the shelter of sanctuaries that the autocrat could not easily invade. The counterbalancing influence of the ulama was especially weak because they adhered to the doctrine that social and political order is what matters most and despotism is preferable to civil war and anarchy. Moreover, to the extent that they received ample material privileges from the sovereign and belonged to important families tightly intertwined with power circles, they were not simply passive attendants but active collaborators often ready to make the requested pronouncements to support and legitimate the prevailing political regime. As figures of power and influence, the ulama "acted like other politicians, participating in patronage, control of resources and factional struggles, but with the advantage of being able to invoke religious sanction" (Zubeida, 2011, p. 15).

By formulating legal justifications (in the form of fatwas) for whatever decision the ruler desired, the ulama seriously compromised the autonomy that their religious position and status could have granted them. In other words, the Islamic jurists proved to be seducible or corruptible, which tempered their quest for a righteous order. The oft-heard statement that there exists an inherent "contradiction between a secular polity and a religious community in a civilisation that lacked any distinction between church and state" (Lal, 1998, p. 62) is clearly an oversimplification. In fact, there was a separation between religion and politics in the world of Islam: The relationship between them was characterized by the domination of politics over religion in all public matters.

Regarding the political instrumentalization of religion, it is hard to detect substantial differences between Islam and Christianity. The principle, "render unto God that which is God's and unto Caesar that which is Caesar's" (Matthew 22:21), seems to apply to both civilizations equally. The strategy of seeking religious legitimacy to buttress political power, especially when reference to a transcendental system of values and precepts seems essential to national unification, was followed not only by Muslim despots but also by ambitious European rulers. Al-Ghazali and other Muslim scholars asserted that rebelling against despotic rulers only because they pursue oppressive policies is not a justifiable attitude on the part of the ulama. This is strikingly reminiscent of St. Augustine's statements discouraging Roman Catholics from taking action to overthrow even tyrannical governments.

Where Eastern and Roman Catholic Christianity radically differ from Islam is in the existence of a hierarchical structure that exerts ultimate authority over believers. Whereas in Western Christianity the head of the Catholic Church is a pope ruling from the Vatican, in Eastern Christianity, the Orthodox churches have no internationally recognized pope and their national heads interact as friendly but independent organizations, which may occasionally struggle among themselves for primacy.[21] The centralized organization of original Christianity has an important implication that is directly relevant to the theme of this book: In cases of conflicts between religion and politics, a possibility considered in Chapters 5 and 6, a head-on confrontation between two well-defined powers would arise in the world of Christianity, whereas the struggle would be much more uncertain in the lands of Islam. In Christianity, as we saw in Chapter 2, the conflict often arose from the fact that the pope claimed the right to appoint the head of the church in Catholic kingdoms (for example, the archbishop of Canterbury in England), and his choice was not necessarily to the king's liking.

The Moderately Counterbalancing Role of Islam

In many instances – for example, in precolonial Morocco, Safavid Persia, Egypt under the Mamluks, and the Ottoman and Mughal Empires – a politico-religious equilibrium prevailed under which the autocratic regime was stable and its relationship to the clerics essentially cooperative. By co-opting religious scholars who were left largely free to make decisions on matters of personal status, and by committing to pursue relatively moderate actions and policies, the ruler ensured that spiritual legitimacy was credibly conferred on the state. An institution that symbolized the moderately counterbalancing influence of the clerics in such contexts is the sanctuary. It played the role of a buffer against the ruler's potential abuses and of a mediation mechanism through which political conflicts could be resolved: Political opponents had a chance to negotiate with the sovereign rather than being crushed by him outright. It bears emphasis that this institution is quite different from the system of representative democracy in which the buffer, instead of consisting of a shelter, a refuge, or an asylum, takes on the form of a parliament endowed with genuine rights for the citizens, or at least some categories of citizens, to participate in political decisions.

An absolute monarch would think twice before deciding to invade a sacred site because doing so could cost him the legitimacy awarded by the clerics. Revealingly, the gradual erosion of the sanctuary (hurm) privileges in nineteenth-century Morocco was made possible only because reformist ulama decided to attack popular religion as practiced by the "zawiya" and

---

[21] There are two obvious contenders for Orthodox leadership: Constantinople and Moscow. The Patriarchate in Moscow considers itself to be the greatest local Orthodox Church in the world, whereas the Patriarchate in Constantinople considers itself the symbolically most important seat of the Orthodox faith since Constantinople was once the capital of the glorious Byzantine Empire (*Moscow Times*, 11–17 February 2016).

the religious brotherhoods, thus contributing significantly to delegitimizing the hurm institution considered to be the locus of traditional religious power. Only then did sultans succeed in obtaining fatwas from the ulama authorizing them to invade the territory of a sanctuary. Invasion of the sacred territory was generally permitted to arrest a mutinous governor on the grounds that he was using it as a means to transgress the divine law (el Mansour, 1979, pp. 65–7). In this instance, an internal division of the religious body allowed the autocratic ruler to dispense with the usual restraint imposed by the need for spiritual legitimacy.

Another possibility arises when a new ruler comes to power who lacks the sense of moderation of his predecessors and does not refrain from violating sanctuary rights. This happened in Afghanistan under the prime ministership of the autocratic Daoud when the government was confronted with a determined refusal of Qandahar landlords to pay taxes to the central government in Kabul. The following scenario repeated itself over the years: After hearing the governor notify them about their fiscal obligations, local landlords or their representatives marched to the compound of a neighboring mosque where they claimed sanctuary ("bast"), which by tradition protected them from government authority, until the governor gave up for the sake of peace. In December 1959, however, after the usual meeting at the governor's headquarters, the landlords found their habitual way of proceeding to the mosque blocked by armed policemen. Under these new circumstances, they no longer had recourse to bast. Although the landlords and religious leaders who had large landholdings in the form of religious endowments fomented antigovernment riots, they were quickly suppressed by the police and the army (Rasanayagam, 2005, pp. 35–6).

The prevailing politico-religious equilibrium that used to provide political stability buttressed by Islamic legitimacy is then disrupted. Typically, the autocrat invokes his dual duty as political leader and guardian of the faith to confer on himself Islamic legitimacy. In this way, he gets rid of countervailing forces and concentrates power in his own hands, yet at high risk for the stability of his rule. Less extreme options are available, however. In particular, as explained in Section 4.5 and documented in detail in Chapter 6, he may choose to co-opt a positive fraction of the clerics comprised of the less radical or most compromising elements among them.

Islam as a Banner for Political Unification and Nation-Building

There are some circumstances under which the autocratic ruler has a great need to strengthen his Islamic credentials, particularly when territorial integrity and national cohesion are under threat or not well established. In the most frequent cases, civil war rages, rebellious attacks occur on the borders of the country, interregional or interethnic tensions mount inside it, or attempts at secession flare up in some of its parts. Since the beginning of Islam, political leaders have often thought that Islam could provide the unifying force able to bring together rival factions, groups, and regions.

The final section provides the theoretical scaffolding supporting the argument presented in this and subsequent chapters. At the core of the theory lies the idea of the co-optability of the religious clerics for which persuasive evidence has been offered in Section 4.2. Characterizing in more rigorous terms the archetypal politico-religious equilibrium that has been dominant in much of Islam's history, I investigate the conditions under which it can be obtained. This allows us to better understand how different equilibria can come about and, in particular, how an autocratic ruler might prefer an opposition confrontation strategy to the opposition suppression strategy that underlies this chapter. The discussion paves the way to the next chapter.

4.5 Analytics of Politico-Religious Interactions

The analytical framework underlying the following discussion is elaborated in a separate paper written with Emmanuelle Auriol and titled "Religious Seduction under Autocracy: A Theory Inspired by History" (Auriol and Platteau, 2017a). It describes a theoretical model with clear microeconomic foundations. Here I present its key assumptions before stating some of its core results. Note that the proposed interpretation is not the same as that offered in the paper, although it is obtained analogously: In the paper, the two instruments available to the autocrat are the extent of progressive reforms that he chooses to undertake and the level of the "wage" paid to the clerics, which itself determines the proportion of the clerical body that is co-opted. In this section, by contrast, the instruments are the rate of appropriation of national wealth by the ruling elite, which measures corruption, and the clerics' wage. Because the underlying logic is the same, the two interpretations can be easily combined, as we have shown in a companion paper (Auriol and Platteau, 2017b). Illustrations of the interpretation in terms of reforms are provided both in the following discussion and in later chapters.

Of course, there are other means available to autocrats than co-option, and co-option of the clerics in particular. Repression and income redistribution directed toward the whole population are two such alternative strategies. The tradeoff between the latter two strategies has been analyzed by a number of authors: Desai et al. (2009) label it the "authoritarian bargain," whereas Bove and Rivera (2015) look at it as a balancing act between vertical repression of the population and horizontal repression of the elites (see also De Mesquita et al., 2005; Koga, 2015; Bove, Platteau, and Sekeris, 2017). By focusing on the strategy of religious seduction, I do not deny that alternative ways may allow autocrats to tame political opposition. But I implicitly assume that cooperation with the clerics or, more exactly, their subjugation plays a critical role in the sustainability of autocratic regimes in the Muslim lands or, at least, is perceived as such by the autocrats themselves. Thus this analysis departs from political economy models in which a dictator makes transfer payments directly to the population or to a subgroup (say, an ethnic group) in order to stay in power and generate personal rents (Acemoglu and Robinson, 2001; 2006; Padro i Miquel, 2007; Sekeris, 2011). It bears emphasis that the assumed primacy of co-option of the (religious) elite is consistent with the finding that the elite are generally considered to be the most serious threat to autocratic power: Evidence indeed shows that elites tend to control the fates of dictators, and statistically most dictators are overthrown by members of their inner circle rather than as a result of genuine popular uprisings (see, for example, Svolik, 2009).

The Setup

Consider a situation in which there are two intervening actors: the sovereign and his ruling clique, on the one hand, and religious clerics, on the other hand. The government is autocratic, and because of its prebendary behaviour, it faces a risk of popular rebellion. The clerics have two characteristics: They hold values regarding social justice and human rights, and as representatives of the supernatural world and as wise men who possess theological and philosophical knowledge, they have a natural prestige and influence on the mass of the people who are poorly educated and have a traditional mindset. Thanks to these two traits, the clerics may exercise political influence if the people endure too much suffering at the hands of despots. They may thus become leaders able to articulate people's grievances, express their anger, and direct their energies into effective manifestations of opposition.

To mitigate or possibly suppress the risk of popular rebellion, the autocrat can nevertheless try to seduce the religious clerics by granting them material privileges. In other words, these potential opponents are susceptible of being "bought" by the autocrat, yet at a price that must be subtracted from the rents appropriated by the ruling clique. The most convenient manner to conceptualize the behavior of the official clerics is to assume that their welfare or utility has two components: an objective component represented by their expected income or consumption and a subjective component corresponding to their taste for the equity and social justice inspired by Islam. These ideals include the idea that a political ruler ought to consult with his subjects ("meshverret") and act as a benevolent guide. While higher wages or privileges increase their utility through the income/consumption channel, they also reduce it because acquiescing to corruption amounts to a betrayal of their religious ideals. There thus exists a tradeoff: More income/consumption is bought at the expense of diminished commitment to values.

Moreover, the clerics have heterogeneous preferences, implying that they value differently the ideals of social justice and conformity to the sacred precepts. As a consequence, the price of their submission to the autocrat is not uniform; it depends partly on the strength of their adherence to Islamic ideals. This price also varies as a function of other variables, in particular the economic and social status of the families to which the clerics belong. Assuming the existence of a continuum of clerics who attach different weights to a function measuring aversion to corruption, the ruler simultaneously chooses the share of national wealth that he wants to appropriate to himself and his close supporters, and to the mass of religious clerics whom he wants to seduce or co-opt with a view to taming potential opposition against his rule. The clerics who are not co-opted form a category of "nonofficial clerics" and lie beyond his control, so that they may be tempted to openly support and guide a popular rebellion.

If the autocrat decides to co-opt the entire population of religious clerics, it is assumed that revolution cannot occur because of a lack of leadership: People are unable to solve the unavoidable collective action problems that arise in the organization of protests without the guidance and natural authority of religious leaders. This strategy of the autocratic regime is called the opposition suppression strategy (OSS). The other possible equilibrium strategy is the opposition confrontation strategy (OCS) whereby the autocrat refrains from "buying" the whole class of religious clerics because this proves too costly. As a result, violent confrontation is a possibility, and political power may be lost with a positive probability. The concept of the dominant politico-religious equilibrium used in this chapter corresponds to the opposition suppression strategy: The autocratic regime is inherently stable in the sense of being immune to the risk of rebellion. The ruler is thus in complete control of the population because his seduction/co-option strategy is so effective that his regime cannot be overthrown. This, of course, is a rather extreme situation, and the corresponding condition could be somewhat relaxed by considering that the dominant politico-religious equilibrium is obtained when the probability of rebellion is zero or close to zero; that is, when all or almost all the religious clerics are co-opted by the regime.

An important feature of the model is that it allows a clear distinction between a decentralized religion, such as Islam, and a centralized religion, such as Catholic or Eastern Orthodox Christianity. Under the latter type, there are a clear hierarchy and a chain of vertical command. The clerics belong to a church and have to be obedient to its authority, which decides in their name whether or not it supports the autocrat. If the church's head opts to support the regime, he must compensate the clerics who dislike the autocrat's policies to varying degrees. This is to ensure that in equilibrium they all get a positive utility. Fine-tuning the design of the compensatory transfer scheme is possible because each cleric is scrutinized and trained by the church's hierarchy before he joins it. During this process of religious formation, clerics live in closed communities and learn a great deal about each other so that preferences are easily revealed. In this context of close contact where obedience and confession are highly valued, the hierarchy possesses the necessary information to compensate the clerics on an individual basis. In sum, the centralized organization of the religion enables the members to overcome their collective action problem.

Yet, the fact that the clerics are duly compensated for their aversion to autocracy does not guarantee that the head will agree to legitimate the oppressive regime. Indeed, he must bargain with the autocrat over the surplus available in the economy, and they are both acting selfishly. It is assumed that the bargaining power of the head is exogenously determined and that, in the case of disagreement, he and the autocrat obtain their status quo utility (their disagreement point is zero and attention is confined to the Nash bargaining solution).

Results

The key parameters of the model are (1) the level of average aversion to social injustice, economic inequalities, and corruption among the religious clerics; (2) the shape of the distribution of the clerics in terms of this aversion or, equivalently, in terms of their income-ideology preferences; and (3) the taste of the autocrat and his clique for personal wealth; that is, the ruling elite's greediness. Before discussing the comparative statics of the model, let us look at the results derived from the equilibrium analysis under the assumption of a decentralized religion.

Suppose the clerics have polarized preferences, in the sense that a large majority are either relatively insensitive or highly sensitive to corruption (the density function is U-shaped). In this instance, there exist various possible equilibria depending on the parameter values. The ruler may refuse to seduce any cleric, thus accepting a state of maximum regime instability. Alternatively, he may choose to seduce or co-opt the whole set of clerics, thereby opting for maximum stability. Or else, there may exist two stable equilibria in which the ruler either seduces all the clerics (again a corner solution) or only a fraction of them (an interior solution). In the latter case where these two equilibria exist, it is of interest to know under which conditions the interior solution dominates the corner solution. This domination will occur if the elasticity of the clerics' disutility caused by the corruption of the regime is not too large compared to the elasticity of the utility that corruption brings to the autocrat. In other words, the intensity with which clerics are adversely affected by an additional amount of embezzlement of national wealth must not exceed by too large a margin the intensity with which the autocrat's well-being is positively influenced by the same increase in wealth appropriation. If the converse is true, the autocrat will opt for full control, through seduction, of the religious class and, concomitantly, for a moderate level of wealth appropriation or corruption. Maximum regime stability is then achieved.

The following comparative-static results are obtained when the third, most intuitively appealing situation prevails. When the greediness of the ruling elite increases or when their committment to enhancing the welfare of the nation is weaker, it is straightforward that their rate of appropriation of national wealth becomes larger in the new equilibrium. Whether the material privileges extended to the religious clerics increase or decrease depends on the way the clerics respond to corruption in the country: If they respond strongly to changes in the corruption level, the extent of privileges will be reduced (the two instruments are strategic substitutes), whereas it will be raised in the opposite case (the two instruments are strategic complements). The important point is that, even in the latter case, privileges will not be enhanced enough to prevent a decrease in the proportion of co-opted clerics. As a consequence, the probability of revolution becomes higher at the new equilibrium. If initially the regime was perfectly stable, it stops being so. Conversely, when the ruling elite's greediness decreases, the co-opted fraction of the clerical class increases and the probability of rebellion declines concomitantly. If the change of preference among the elite is significant enough, the political regime may even become perfectly stable.

The second comparative-static result relates to the effects of a change in the preferences of the religious clerics. When the men of religion become more responsive to social injustice, economic inequalities, and corruption of the elite, they are harder to seduce or more expensive to co-opt. Other things being equal, in the absence of any reaction by the autocrat, the probability of the autocrat staying in power decreases. However, the autocrat does not remain passive. His response consists of moderating the extent of wealth appropriation. As for the privileges of the clerics, they may be simultaneously reduced or increased, but in either case, the effect on the stability of the regime is the same: Support from the clerics increases, and the probability of rebellion decreases. It is even possible that the autocrat's response to the radicalization of the clerics is to co-opt the whole clerical body. Corruption is then sacrificed in the name of political stability. Conversely, when the ideological purity of the clerics is relaxed so that their venality increases, the equilibrium level of corruption increases and the regime becomes more unstable.

In Auriol and Platteau (2017b), a discrete instead of a continuous distribution of clerics is assumed: Clerics belong to either the low or the high type depending on whether they are loosely or deeply attached to moral principles derived from their religion. We find that when all the clerics become more radical, or when the proportion of low-type clerics decreases, the autocrat reduces corruption in order to enhance political stability. In contrast, if only the high-type clerics become radicalized, the opposite result is obtained: The autocrat relies more on the low-type, more easily seducible clerics. and he embezzles a larger share of the national wealth.

In sum, the autocratic regime is more likely to be (perfectly) stable, and to therefore correspond to the dominant system of politico-religious interactions (the OSS), if (1) the autocrat does not attach too much weight to personal enrichment (he is enough of the benevolent despot type), and (2) a significant number of religious functionaries have a strong enough aversion to corruption born of their beliefs regarding what constitutes a just social order. When these conditions are not satisfied, a counter-elite of self-appointed religious clerics emerge from the population to contest both the ruler and the official clerics. This was the situation observed in Egypt under the regimes of Presidents Sadat and Mubarak when they ruled in cahoots with the official clerics of al-Azhar, but were sharply critisized by the Muslim Brotherhood and by extremist groups of the religious right. This story is told in detail in Chapters 6 and 7.

If we allow for parametric changes in the shape of the distribution of the clerics, a radicalization of religious opinions may take the form of a shift of a significant number of clerics from indifference vis-a-vis corruption to an intermediate level of aversion to it. In this case, as can be directly inferred from the equilibrium analysis, it is quite possible that a perfectly stable regime will become highly unstable. From co-opting all the clerics, the ruler may move to a situation where he refuses to co-opt any. This is because the costs of buying out a critical portion of them may have become too large relative to the expected benefit. The precise form taken by religious radicalization thus matters greatly: Whereas increased aversion to corruption in the absence of any shift in the distribution of clerics may cause the regime to become more stable, changes in that distribution may generate the opposite effect.

As a final step, let us turn to the case of centralized religions. When the head of the church is hostile to the autocratic regime, the ruler has to abandon large rents to the church to win its support. The monetary transfer is large so that the clerical members are easily compensated from the fund awarded to the church. By the same token, when the head of the church is close to the autocrat, the problem of the latter is to transfer enough resources to the church so that it can buy the support of all the clerical members. The former situation corresponds to the medieval struggle that opposed secular and religious powers in Western Europe until the period of the Great Schism. The latter describes the period that marked the rise of national churches from the sixteenth century onward (see Chapter 2).

An important question that arises is whether centralized or decentralized religions are more conducive to political stability under autocracy. For the sake of comparison, it is assumed that the distribution of the clerical body along the continuum of values representing their income-ideology preferences is identical between the two types of religious organizations. It is then found that, unambiguously, centralized religions lead to more political stability than decentralized religions. The logic of this result is as follows. With a centralized religion, the autocrat negotiates directly with the head of the church. He needs to transfer enough resources not only to seduce him personally but also to compensate the church's members, on average, for the reforms to be undertaken. In exchange for these rents, he gets the support of the church's hierarchy and the full clerical body. In equilibrium, therefore, the system is fairly stable. By contrast, under a decentralized religion, the autocrat has to gain the support of each cleric individually. Because it is costly to enroll the whole clerical body (i.e., the transfer must be large enough to seduce the most extreme type), the autocrat often chooses to seduce only a fraction of them. In equilibrium, the fraction of religious clerics who support the autocrat is thus generally smaller under a ecentralized than under a centralized religion. This conclusion reflects the fact that the autocrat's decisions are driven by the *average* cleric under a centralized religious structure, whereas they are driven by the *marginal* cleric under a decentralized one.

A prediction of the theory is therefore that, everything else being equal, the tenure of autocrats in Catholic countries, for example, should be on average longer than the tenure of autocrats in Muslim countries. Blaydes and Chaney (2013) precisely show that, under conditions of autocracy, a centralized religion (Catholicism) was historically associated with greater political stability than a decentralized one (Islam). Their interpretation of this result is nevertheless different from the one proposed here: It rests on the contrast between the use of mercenary (slave) armies in the lands of Islam and the use of loyal armies at the service of the autocrat in the lands of Christianity (see Chapter 1).

The next step is to compare the level of corruption obtained under centralized and decentralized religions. If we assume that political stability is endogenously chosen by the autocrat under the two types (the entire clerical body is co-opted), we find that the optimal fraction of national wealth that he appropriates is unambiguously larger under a centralized religion. The rationale is that the clerics are easier to buy under a centralized than under a decentralized religious organization because in the latter instance, the autocrat must seduce the most radical among them to achieve political stability. As a consequence, the autocrat can better afford policies antagonistic to the clerics when the religion is centralized. Interestingly, this result holds whether the head of the church is hostile or close to the autocrat. The reason is again that the structural heterogeneity of the clerics is a more important obstacle to the autocrat's ambitions if they are unable to surmount their collective action problem because of their decentralied organization.

Three final remarks are in order. First, if we consider the case in which political instability is optimally chosen by the autocrat under a decentralized religion whereas political stability is chosen under a centralized religion, the comparison between the two systems becomes blurred. In fact, it is now possible that the amount of corruption is higher at equilibrium under the decentralized than under the centralized religion. It bears emphasis, however, that the sustainability of corruption is not guaranteed under the former system (because the regime is politically unstable), whereas it is well secured under the latter.

Second, these results can be analogously interpreted by considering that, instead of choosing a level of corruption, the autocrat chooses a level of reforms that antagonize the clerics. What the theory then shows, for example, is that under conditions of political stability, the level of reforms is always smaller under a decentralized than under a centralized religion. In support of that alternative interpretation, Blaydes and Platas Izama (2015) adduce evidence that supports the existence of a relationship between the degree of centralization of religion and the rate of abandonment of female genital mutilation in Egypt today: While the practice has receded among the Christian Copts, its prevalence remains stationary among the Muslims (see Chapter 1). Not only is this conclusion entirely consistent with the prediction of our theory but the evidence the authors provide also strongly suggests that the causal mechanism underlying it is effectively at work. Our theory can actually be considered as offering a rigorous formalization of Blaydes's and Platas Izama's argument.

Third, the two interpretations suggested in the preceding discussion are not contradictory. In addition to the "wages" of the clerics, the autocrat may choose a mix of progressive reforms and corruption, two policies that arouse the potential hostility of the clerics. This potential hostility is the highest, and political instability most likely, when the autocrat indulges in a lot of corruption and simultaneously adopts many unpopular reforms or reforms susceptible of displeasing the clerics – and vice versa (see Chapter 1). When the autocrat chooses an ambiguous mix – a high level of corruption but a small measure of reforms, or a low level of corruption and a large measure of reforms – the net effects on political stability are indeterminate.

An interesting question is whether reforms and corruption are substitutes or complements to choices made by the autocrat. For example, if the return to secular reforms strengthens, will the autocrat increase both the measure of reforms and the extent of corruption, or will he intensify reforms but simultaneously reduce corruption? In Auriol and Platteau (2017b), where we explicitly model corruption and reforms as separate decision variables available to the autocrat, we show there that there is no unambiguous answer to this question. We predict that complementarity is more likely, except when additional units of corruption (secular reforms) have the effect of strongly increasing the impact of more reforms (corruption) on the disutility of the clerics.

What about the Merchants?

In this theoretical framework, attention is clearly focused on the relation between autocratic politics and religion. As emphasized in Chapter 1, this focus is reasonable on two counts. First, most countries, including many advanced countries of Western Europe, were nondemocratic during their national formation phase. Second, given the power of religious belief in societies where literacy levels are low and religious authorities have a monopoly or quasi-monopoly in the transmission of knowledge, religion typically provides a powerful source of legitimacy for autocratic rulers. What is therefore left out of the picture is the dynamics of the transition from autocracy to democracy: When the autocrat's equilibrium strategy is the opposition confrontation strategy, there is a positive probability that he will be overthrown, yet regime collapse cannot shift the country to another political system.

It is clear that, in such a setting, the role of merchants and businessmen considered as a class acting autonomously is ignored. This does not imply that merchants are ruled out altogether because they may possibly collude with, or accept the leadership of, rebelling religious clerics if their interests are thus effectively defended. A striking illustration of this possibility is presented in Chapter 5 when we examine the interactions between religion and politics under the Qajars in Iran. But if it is the hard bargaining between commercial classes and the ruling elite that sparks political crises and forces the gradual transformation of autocracies into proto-democracies, in the manner described by Charles Tilly (1992), Douglass North and Barry Weingast (1989), Robert Bates (2001) and others, then our theory obviously fails to account for the role of merchants and other business-minded categories of the population.

This being said, some interesting insights about the triangular game between the ruler, the clerics, and the merchants can be gained from our approach, even though the behavior of the merchant class is not explicitly modeled. In the aforementioned case of Iran, autocratic power is threatened by a cleric-merchant coalition. Another scenario arises when the clerics and the merchants have opposed interests. The autocrat is now in a better position because he can play one class against another. In particular, because the clerics have a comparative advantage in the provision of legitimacy, it is more cost effective to co-opt them than the merchants, whose pleas can therefore be ignored. Reforms conducive to capital accumulation and economic development may then be forsaken. Under the first scenario, too, the situation of the merchants may be awkward; yet, an alliance with the clerics may later become hard to manage, especially if a religious autocracy succeeds a secular one.

The situation of the merchants is most favorable when they turn out to be cheaper to placate because their economic interests and those of the ruling elite are converging or because the religious class is weak and strongly divided internally. This scenario does not happen often, although it seems to have occurred in Kuwait. Even there, however, it did not survive the discovery of oil resources. Unlike what was observed in the southern Gulf states and Saudi Arabia, the rise of the Al Sabah family to the leading political position in Kuwait was neither accomplished by force nor backed by Britain. Rather, it resulted from an agreement between all the main tribes inhabiting the territory. Because it lacked any rents (from natural resources) or subsidies (from Britain), the ruling family was fiscally dependent on the sizable merchant class that was active in the pearl business and wielded strong control over debt-tied workers. As a result, the Al Sabah could not rule unchecked and had to accommodate the interests of the merchants (Atallah, 2011, pp. 183–91).[22]

After several attempts, the merchants were granted a major concession in the form of a national assembly (the "majlis"), itself preceded by the creation of municipal councils. Initially, the members of this new body managed to cancel the pearl tax, export duties, the import tax on fruits and vegetables, and monopolies. But, then, the tables were turned: Ahmad Al Sabah dissolved the assembly and arrested its members, because of his displeasure at the merchants' demand to monitor the "next oil check." Oil had entered onto the stage of Kuwaiti politics, and this was to be a curse for the merchants' cause (Crystal, 1992),[23] as described by Atallah (2011): "In pre-oil Kuwait, due to the emir's fiscal dependence on the merchants, they were successful in forcing him to grant them political rights through the creation of the assembly in 1938. But, as soon as oil became a significant source of revenue, the emir felt strong enough to break the tacit understanding between the ruling family and the merchants, by dissolving the assembly. Awash with

---

[22] This became clear when Mubarak increased taxes to finance his military adventures. The merchants immediately threatened to leave the country, and, to make their threat credible, they started to board their workforce on the ships in preparation for their move. It did not take long before the ruler lowered the taxes that infuriated the merchants. In 1921, wary of the ruler's attempt to encroach again on their interests, the merchants called for the creation of an assembly in which he would be forced to discuss any decision affecting their wealth. On becoming ruler, Ahmad Jabir promised the merchants to consult with them on all important matters, but like the Stuarts in the first half of seventeenth-century Britain, he never followed up on that promise because the assembly was never called into session.

[23] Britain initially supported the democratic movement of the merchants not so much as a way to encourage democratic participation but more to curb the power of the emir. In fact, whenever the merchants wanted to have a say in matters of oil or security, two areas of great concern for the British, Britain withheld its support. Worried that the assembly, although pro-British, would eventually turn against its interests, Britain sought to maintain a balance of power between the ruler and the merchants that would best suit its interests (Atallah, 2011, p. 185; see also Crystal, 1995, p. 51).

cash, the emir not only became autonomous but also paid off the ruling family's debt to the merchants" (p. 187).[24]

The bargaining position of commercial and entrepreneurial classes has been weak in most parts of the Muslim world. This situation persists even today, particularly in Arab countries. As a matter of fact, the support given by powerful segments of society to governments has very often been passive, partly because they did not participate actively in the making of decisions. As pointed out by Hourani (1991, p. 454),

In most regimes this was done at a high level by a small group, and the results were not communicated widely; there was a tendency for rulers, as they settled into power, to become more secretive and withdrawn – guarded by their security services and surrounded by intimates and officials who controlled access to them – and to emerge only rarely to give a formal explanation and justification of their actions to a docile audience. Beneath this reason for the distance between government and society, however, there lay another one: the weakness of the conviction which bound them to each other. (see also Marsot, 2007, pp. 145–6).

[24] It is revealing that, in many other Gulf states, no bargaining between the ruler and the merchants took place prior to the exploitation of oil on a significant scale. This is because the Ottoman Empire and, later, Great Britain for geopolitical reasons decided to support the emir directly so that the latter did not need to rely on the resources of the country's merchants to maintain his own family and to reward different tribes for their loyalty (Atallah, 2011, p. 188).

5

The Rise of Islam in Conditions of State Crisis

The Case of Weak States

We learned from Chapter 4 that, in the canonical model of politico-religious relations, the ruler opts for an opposition suppression strategy that guarantees the stability of the regime. This is not his only option, however; alternatively, he may sacrifice political stability to his greed. This happens if he follows the opposition confrontation strategy, which has the potential of instigating open rebellion. In this and the following chapters, our attention turns to the ensuing state crisis. Before describing the structure of this chapter, I make a key distinction between two types of state crisis.

5.1 Two Types of State Crisis

A situation of state crisis may be characterized by the two polar circumstances of lawlessness and unrestrained despotism. In the first instance, a political vacuum or anarchy is created by weak central power under ineffective leadership, possibly combined with foreign aggression. As seen in Chapter 4, this is the situation most abhorred and feared by religious officialdom. In the second instance, the crisis is the consequence of kleptocratic despotism resting on the deeply entrenched corruption of a despotic autocrat and the elite around him. Under both types of conditions, religious authorities and groups tend to play a more active role in politics and to reassert themselves as the most effective shield against the vicissitudes of power. In the words of Roy (1990), the ulama are better described as "reacting to events, not directing them" (p. 50).

This chapter considers state crises caused by a weak central power. When there is a power vacuum, contending political factions vie for political power, causing a state of anarchy and lawlessness under which people endure many hardships. Religious leaders are then tempted to come out of their seclusion to substitute for the missing central power or to help people

159

in distress. To return to the Moroccan example discussed in Chapter 4, it is a well-substantiated fact that in periods of political vacuum, sanctuaries become more numerous and are more frequently sought. This is unsurprising because, in an environment characterized by instability and violence, they became more useful both as islands of peace and as sites through which conflicting tribes and other social groups can work out nonviolent solutions (el Mansour, 1979, pp. 57, 69–70).

In this chapter, two examples, one from Ottoman Egypt and the other from post-Safavid Iran, illustrate the logic governing the rise of religious elites in situations of weak states. Special attention is given to post-Safavid Iran because of its great significance to understanding the present-day relationship between politics and religion in that country. After a review of these two cases in Sections 5.2 and 5.3, I present examples where religious reaction to government failures is sparked off by Sufi orders and quietist branches of Islam (Section 5.4). This provides the first opportunity to highlight the importance of the distinction between state-appointed and self-appointed clerics that occupies a central place in the analysis conducted in Chapter 6, which deals with the second type of state crisis (kleptocratic despotism), and in Chapter 7, which discusses Islamist movements. In Section 5.5, the role of Islam as a reaction to foreign domination is brought into focus and illustrated by a series of new examples. Section 5.6 concludes and discusses the puzzle of Iranian theocracy.

5.2 Ottoman Egypt

By the end of the eighteenth century, the Ottoman rule in Egypt had become extraordinarily chaotic. The French conquest (1798) had shown that the Mamluks were no longer able to defend the country against a foreign invasion, which was the only reason why the Egyptians had put up with their frequent exactions.[1] The Ottoman sultan responded to the crisis by allying himself with British forces and reoccupying the country. However, the Ottoman-appointed governors were "rapacious, incapable, and they had little authority over their own soldiers," who treated the land as though it were conquered territory to be sucked and looted at will (Marsot, 2007, p. 62;

---

[1] The first Mamluks (1250–1382) were mercenaries working for individual princes or lords and generally were of Turkic origin. During the second period of Mamluk rule (1382–1516), most Mamluks were bought as boy slaves from the Russian Urals, the Central Asian steppes, or the Caucasus Mountains. They received military training in the households of older Mamluks who became the object of their affection and loyalty (Marsot, 2007, pp. 31–2).

Yapp, 1987, pp. 145–6). Military factions and regiments, grouped by ethnicity, fought with each other for power, and one governor was assassinated after another.

The situation became particularly desperate when the Ottoman governor imported Syrian soldiers known as the "delhis," or madmen, with a view to controlling his undisciplined army. The behavior of these soldiers was even worse than anything the Egyptians had yet seen. In desperation, the ulama looked for a providential man able to restore law and order. They found him in Muhammad Ali (Mehmed Ali Pasha), who was the commander-in-chief of the Albanian regiment of the Ottoman army: "They asked him to become governor of Egypt, according to the will of the people, so long as he undertook to govern in accordance with their advice, and abide by their norms, that is, that he would agree to rule in consultation with the ulama" (Marsot, 2007, p. 63).

Muhammad Ali accepted their proposal, which was also ratified by the Ottoman sultan, and he became governor of Egypt in 1805, a position that he retained until 1848. He immediately embarked on establishing a centralized authority that brought back law and order, thereby reviving trade and commerce. Under his rule, the country was thus politically transformed "from a condition of anarchy into a strong centralised state which possessed unprecedented power over the lives of its citizens" (Yapp, 1987, p. 152). His rule was aimed at modernizing the country, including the army, so as to make it a stable, independent, and prosperous political entity. He improved irrigation; stimulated the production of cotton and other cash crops, as well as of industrial goods (military supplies in particular); created trading monopolies; and introduced important legal reforms such as the mixed courts in which Egyptian and European judges could evolve their own system of law (Marsot, 2007, pp. 65–97; Yapp, 1987, pp. 152–5; Lapidus, 1988, p. 559; Finkel, 2005, pp. 411, 427–8; Crecelius, 1972). Ironically enough, Ali's success cost the ulama dearly. Indeed, Ali starved them financially, eliminating their privileges, particularly their tax exemptions; confiscating their religious endowments; and breaking any source of their power. In the words of Karen Armstrong (2014), "for the Egyptian ulama, modernity was forever tainted by this ruthless assault and they became cowed and reactionary" (p. 288).

This was a huge setback because before they succeeded in bringing Muhammad Ali to power, the ulama had played an important political role during the tumultuous times of the Mamluk regime. Thanks to their social prestige, dissenter or rebel groups often sought the religious sanctioning of their actions. This created a competition for the support of the ulama between the ruling elite and the contenders, and it is precisely this competition that drove the Mamluks to try to recruit prominent ulama into their circle of power. In his discussion of civil wars under the Mamluk regime, Lapidus (1984) notes that "the support of the ulama, and with it massive popular backing, was often of decisive importance. Rebels and pretenders vied for recognition of the legitimacy of their claims, and sought fatwas or judicial opinions justifying rebellion" (p. 134). Such support was especially important in matters of tax collection. Thus, for example, in the later decades of Mamluk rule, the qadis were "invaluable intermediaries for the collection of taxes from a recalcitrant populace," and because many of them were officials in the bureaucracy they could lend "the prestige which inhered in them as representatives of Islam to the purposes of the state" (p. 135).

The Mamluk ruler's support from the ulama was not fully guaranteed, however. There were notable instances in which they decided to shift their loyalty to the common people because of the excessively rapacious behaviour of Mamluk functionaries (especially tax inspectors). When conflicts between the demands of the Mamluks and the common people thus strained the whole system of Mamluk-ulama cooperation to the breaking point, "outright rebellions of the town populace (in cities such as Cairo, Damas, Aleppo or Tripoli) were usually led by the ulama," who not only sanctioned but also actually led the protest or revolutionary movements (Lapidus, 1984, pp. 150–2). Ulama leadership was vital because it helped coordinate communal risings and overcome weaknesses in the organization of the popular masses. Masses, indeed, were typically fragmented and reliant on emotional appeals, strident speeches, and spontaneous demonstrations (p. 153).

Populist challenges led by the ulama ceased under the rule of Muhammad Ali – not only because he brought order and stability to the country but also because he imposed radical measures to keep the religious sphere under control. He thus confiscated the waqf lands that provided financial resources to the ulama class, making the religious institutional establishment beholden to the state. He elevated the mosque-university system of al-Azhar to a dominant position within Egyptian Islam and simultaneously subordinated it to the sovereign. At the time of the French conquest in 1798, the shaykh of al-Azhar was only one among nine or ten members of the native ulama elite. By raising him to the position of chief ulama, and putting him and the other ulama on the state payroll, Muhammad Ali made the religious elite susceptible to his pressure and his will. Another central institution of Egyptian Islam, the Dar al-Ifta, or the office of the mufti, was created in 1895. Because it could issue fatwas, this office was quite influential. The fact that the mufti was made a political appointee established another channel of control over the religious establishment (Lee, 2014, pp. 60–1).

5.3 Post-Safavid Iran

The case of Iran is equally interesting and deserves special attention in view of the comparatively large influence exerted by Iranian religious authorities in modern times and up to the present day. In addressing it, I first describe the successful cooperation between state and religion during the Safavid rule, which established the first modern centralized government in the country. This situation corresponds to the archetypal politico-religious equilibrium that was the focus of Chapter 4. With this background in mind, this chapter considers the collapse of state-religion cooperation during post-Safavid times, highlighting the conditions that brought the clerics to the front stage of Iranian politics under Qajar rule. The concluding subsection accounts for the fundamental change in state-religion relations between the Safavid and the Qajar rules in terms of the theory sketched at the end of the preceding chapter.

Successful Cooperation between State and Religion under the Safavid Rule

The Safavids largely succeeded in making religion subservient to their own ends and in building a strong and centralized state that created political stability and economic prosperity in a country where much of the population consisted of nomadic tribes equipped with powerful militia.[2] Success was epitomized by the splendors of Isfahan, designated as the new imperial capital by Shah Abbas (1598), whose reign marked the apogee of the Safavid state (Hodgson, 1974c, book 5, ch. I, pp. 16–58). One important feature of Safavid rule was the subservience of religion to the objective of building and consolidating a strong, prosperous state.

---

[2] Nomadic tribes were estimated to form as much as one-half the Iranian population in the early nineteenth century and a quarter at the end of the same century (Keddie, 2003, p. 23). Because soil aridity apparently increased over the centuries, leading to agricultural decline, the Turkish nomadic tribes that invaded Iran in the beginning of the eleventh century did not, as had earlier nomadic invaders, settle in the interstices between inhabited areas. Instead, finding arid lands suitable for nomadism, they continued their erstwhile mode of living. Tribal leaders thus remained important power figures with whom central authorities had to contend in one way or another (p. 19).

In a striking parallel with seventeenth-century Europe (see Chapter 2), Shi'ism in its present form (Twelver Shi'ism, in particular) was largely conceived by Iranian rulers as a convenient ideology of nation-building vis-à-vis the rival Ottoman Empire. From Abbasid times to 1501, when the Safavid dynasty began, Twelvers by and large cooperated politically with the Sunnis, and numerous religious movements actually combined Shi'i and Sunni ideas, expressing popular grievances and providing justification for peasant or nomadic revolts.[3] Originally a quietist Sunni order from Azerbaidzhan, the Safavids became militant warriors who followed a kind of Twelver Shi'ism in the mid-fifteenth century, after traveling among the Anatolian nomadic tribes. Their brand of Shi'ism was radical, reminiscent of Shi'as of the earliest times: Believing in divine reincarnation, they considered their leaders to be divine, and their egalitarianism was strong (Keddie, 2003, pp. 10, 13).

Yet, soon after they conquered power in Tabriz, the Safavid rulers began to moderate their views, turning their doctrine "from one suitable for popular, enthusiastic, egalitarian revolt and conquest into one suitable for stable, conservative rule" and concomitantly ignoring their tribal followers, justifiably considered to be too anarchic (Keddie, 2003, p. 10). In reality, they were keen to enlist members of the old Persian-speaking bureaucracy who had gained a great deal of experience in administration and tax collection under previous dynasties, as well as Persian landlords and merchants. They also imported some official Twelver theologians from Eastern Arabia and Syria. Having few ties with the local population and benefiting from the financial and political largesse of the ruler, these learned men quickly became a strong pillar of political support for the new regime (pp. 10–12, 15). As a consequence of such strategic choices, the egalitarianism of their early tribal followers was gradually abandoned, and extremist ideas were banned to leave room for a strictly enforced Shi'a Twelver orthodoxy. As part of this ideology, the Safavids cursed the first three caliphs considered holy by the Sunnis, and they claimed descent from the Seventh Imam, which gave them impeccable religious credentials (pp. 13–15).[4] Ismail resorted to

---

[3] Twelver Shi'ism is one of the three lines of Shi'ism that took shape under the Abbasids (749–1256), the other two lines being the Zaidis or "Fivers" (who revere the fifth imam) and the Ismailis or "Seveners." The Twelvers, who believe that the infant son of the eleventh imam went into "occultation" in the ninth century, consider that there is no infallible interpreter of the twelfth imam's will until he reappears as the Mahdi to institute the realm of perfection and justice (Keddie, 2003, p. 7; Berkey, 2003, pp. 134–7).

[4] Initially, the Safavids stressed the semi-divine powers of the ruler, one of the few elements taken over from their previous "extremist" religious ideology. However, they gradually gave

brutal methods of "vigorous persecution" to eradicate all Sunni remnants in Iran: Sufi orders were dispossessed of their endowments, and Sunni ulama were either executed or exiled (Hodgson, 1974c, p. 23).

As Keddie (2003) has pointed out, one of the main reasons why Isma'il – who proclaimed himself shah (king) in 1501 – and his followers chose to cause a split between Sunnis and Twelver Shi'is was to endow Iran with a specific ideological distinction and national identity vis-à-vis its (Sunni) military-political enemies, the Ottoman Empire, and, for a time, the Central Asian Uzbeks (p. 11).[5] In the words of Lee (2014), "political decisions and opportunities have recast a version of Islam (Twelver Shi'ism) from a passivist, minority stance into a badge of national identity, a religious establishment like no other in the Muslim world, ... and an authoritarian effort to promote religion" (p. 169). The consequences of the split between two main strands of Islam, now viewed by each other as heretics and enemies, have carried over into the present time.

Although the establishment of this state owed much to the military prowess of the Qizilbash tribesmen (from Anatolia), who were duly rewarded by Isma'il, their fractiousness and their continuous resistance to the imposition of state control posed a recurring problem for his successors. However, Shah Abbas managed to control the unruly Qizilbash leaders by building up a standing royal army that he directly financed and that was directly responsible to him. By the same token, the Safavid state, like the Ottoman state, was strongly supported by an organized ulama bureaucracy that was deeply committed to the regime and derived ample material privileges from this association. It directly organized or controlled Muslim judicial, educational, and social functions, thus transforming Muslim associations into "virtual departments of the state" (Lapidus, 1988, p. 882). As in precolonial Morocco, mosques and shrines served as refuges for individuals and groups threatened by the government (Keddie, 2003, p. 30).

The Post-Safavid Collapse of State-Religion Cooperation

After more than two centuries of stable Safavid rule, the rebellion of an Afghan chieftain in 1722 led to the sudden demise of the Safavid state. The collapse of the Safavids occurred in the context of an incipient economic

---

up this unorthodox claim (claims to divinity or incarnation are, indeed, against Islamic orthodoxy, both Sunni and Twelver Shi'i, for which God is unique).

[5] Iran would have to wait until the twentieth century to be governed by a monarch who, unlike the Safavids and the succeeding Qajars, had a true Persian origin in the sense of having always spoken Persian or a related dialect (Mottahedeh, 2000, p. 146).

decline caused by the continuing marginalization of Iran as a transit stop following the development of overseas trade by Europeans (Algar, 1969; Keddie, 1969, 1971, 1999, 2003; Abrahamian, 1982; Arjomand, 1984; Floor, 2000; Cleveland, 2004, pp. 51–5, 109–16; Martin, 2005; Gleave, 2005). But the real decline of the Safavid dynasty can be traced back to 1666, which marked the start of the disastrous reign of Safi, known as Shah Soleiman (after he changed his name on the occasion of a second coronation). Safi had little interest in running the state and preferred to spend his time drinking and debauching. He considerably weakened the central bureaucracy and army inherited from his predecessors, partly by killing military chiefs and leaders of the bureaucracy. Moreover, it was during the latter part of his reign that the persecution of religious minorities, not just Christians and Jews but equally Sunni Muslims and Sufis, was introduced.[6] This persecution worsened during the reign of his successor, resulting in growing discontent among the Sunni populations in Dagestan, Shirvan, Baluchistan, and Afghanistan. Repeated rebellions in the areas where these populations lived and the eventual assault on Isfahan by the Ghalzeh Afghan tribe proved fatal to the Safavid rulers, who could not mobilize effective resistance against them (Katouzian, 2009, pp. 129–33).[7]

There followed a long period of chaos dominated by warfare between contending tribal confederations, foreign invasions, military adventures, expropriation, and weak, short-lived states; it continued until the Qajar dynasty was eventually consolidated in 1794 and was able to retain power, at least nominally, until the 1920s (Katouzian, 2009, ch. 6). In the aftermath of the demise of the Safavids, the ulama lost their privileges and wealth mainly because their religious endowments were often confiscated or plundered. As a consequence, many emigrated to southern Iraq and India or elsewhere (Axworthy, 2013, p. 20). However, their situation dramatically improved

---

[6] This contrasted with the religious tolerance of the previous Safavid rulers. Some of these rulers, such as those in Mughal India, were cruel and brutal, yet cruelty was mostly inflicted on their immediate entourage, especially close relatives, who were seen as a threat to their power. In particular, Abbas II did not hesitate to blind his own already half-blind father when he deposed him and to kill several of his sons on suspicion of plotting against him. To guard against the danger of an overthrow, he started the tradition of immuring royal males in the harem, so they would be ignorant of the outside world and cut off from would-be plotters. This had a disastrous effect on the future Safavid shahs who emerged from the harem unprepared to rule the country (Katouzian, 2009, p. 126).

[7] Thus, Tahmap Mirza, who after his father's abdication declared himself shah and ruled from the former capital, Qazvin, "spent more time on wine and sex than on mobilizing resistance to the Afghans" (Katouzian, 2009, p. 133).

during the eighteenth century, when they were able to reassert their social authority and to restore their wealth.

From an early stage in the development of Shi'ism, reverence for the imams had been particularly great, tending to turn them into more than superhuman figures, as visible manifestations of the spirit of God (Hourani, 1991, p. 184). As noted in Chapter 3, this feature is linked to a common thread of Shi'a doctrines, charismatic leadership: The followers of Ali believe that he embodied a primary concern for the spiritual welfare of the Muslim community (Lee, 2014, p. 175). What is noteworthy in the case of Iran, however, is that even though the Shi'a religious establishment rose to prominence during the period of decadence of the Safavid rulers and, later again, during the times of the Qajars, when a modicum of order had been reestablished, the stability and legitimacy of their rule were far weake than that achieved by the Safavids at the apex of their civilization. The Qajar shahs never were able to re-create a strong centralized state epitomized by the royal absolutism and bureaucratic centralism of the Safavids (Katouzian, 2009, p. 129; Cleveland, 2004, p. 55).[8] In actuality, the Qajar shahs never could mobilize sufficient resources to bring under control the powerful centrifugal forces had taken root in Iran during almost the whole eighteenth century. Administrative instability, insecurity, and low legitimacy resulting from widespread corruption and little concern for the people's welfare were the hallmarks of most of their rule.[9] Particularly problematic were the important powers, including prerogatives in matters of foreign policy, wielded by provincial governors: Recruited from the Qajar nobility, they acted as great potentates who resisted all efforts to strengthen the central government at the expense of the provinces (Yapp, 1987, p. 170).

It is in this particular context that the ulama began to function independently of the government; backed by a population that granted them extensive authority in religious and legal matters, they constituted a powerful force either as supporters or opponents of the policies of the shahs. Popular belief held that the rulings of the mujtahid (learned individuals qualified to exercise ijtihad to give new interpretations of law and doctrine in

---

[8] To tame tribal leaders, the weak Qajars resorted to indirect rule, playing off one tribal faction against another (Keddie, 2003, p. 19).

[9] Because even elementary public work projects, such as the building and repair of roads and caravanserais, were seldom undertaken, making provinces difficult to reach, and because the central government did not think it proper to build a strong army or police, it "had to rely upon indirect means of rule, such as dividing opposing forces, encouraging factional fights, offering bribes, sometimes as gifts or annuities, and holding in Tehran hostages ('guests') from powerful tribes and families" (Keddie, 2003, pp. 27–8).

response to new questions) were more authoritative statements of the will of the Hidden Imam than the proclamations of the shahs who made no claims to divinity. Thus, "if a mujtahid denounced a royal decree as incompatible with the teachings of Islam, then believers were enjoined to accept the mujtahid's decision. In this way, the ulama gained a powerful voice in Iranian political life" (Cleveland, 2004, p. 111; Keddie, 2003, p. 28).

An intense debate took place between the Akhbari and the Usuli schools regarding their precise role in society. For adherents of the former, including some of the ulama who wanted to reduce the ulama's role, each Muslim believer could rely on, and interpret, the traditions of the Prophet and the imams. Thus, ulama were not needed to interpret religious tenets. This view is close to the traditional line of Sunni Islam, which holds that there is only a limited place, if any, for the interpretation of religious law based on reason. By contrast, for adherents of the Usuli school, ordinary believers were not competent to interpret the foundations ("usul") of the faith; hence, they needed the guidance of mujtahids, who were less fallible than any temporal ruler. Ijtihad was necessary to reinterpret religious law in each generation, in the light of prevailing circumstances and new understanding. In the course of the eighteenth century, the Usuli school won a decisive victory over the Akhbari school. A new arrangement then gradually developed whereby ordinary Muslims gave their allegiance, as well as a portion of their earnings, to the mujtahid, a class of ulama specially qualified to perform ijtihad. In each generation, among the whole body of mujtahids, one or two clerics (called "marja-e taqlid") emerged to serve on religious matters as a supreme guide to other ulama, as well as to ordinary Muslims (Axworthy, 2013, p. 21). In this way, not only did a religious hierarchy take root in Iran but the groundwork was also laid that justified awarding the mujtahid far more power than that granted to Sunni ulama in other parts of the Muslim world. Even more important, "there was now a clear doctrinal basis for appeals to the ulama over the head of a ruler, and for claims by the leading mujtahid to make political decisions, provided they touched on Islamic principles, independently of temporal rulers." These powers were increasingly used from the early nineteenth century on (Keddie, 2003, p. 20).

The special importance of the clergy in Iran cannot, then, be entirely or mainly attributed to the Shi'a character of Iranian Islam. The difference between Shi'ism and Sunnism appears to have developed over recent times, and "many points often made about Shi'ism are really only, or mainly, true during the past century or two" (Keddie, 2003, p. 4). It is thus useful to examine some key events that shaped the historical trajectory of Iran during these recent times. As hinted at earlier, the rise to prominence of the clerics in the post-Safavid era must be understood against the background of the weakness of central power, its inclination to surrender to the pressures of foreign economic exploitation, severe injustices, and the deep corruption of the royal court, the bureaucracy, and the judicial system. Although the Qajars attempted to bring about reform, these measures reached only a small elite and did not touch the mass of the population. Moreover, in many instances the reforms were simply ineffective, inadequate to enable the centralization of state power and insufficient to oppose foreign encroachment (Lapidus, 1988, p. 575). A long tradition took root in which socioeconomic and cultural grievances tended to be "expressed in the only way familiar to most people – a religious idiom arraying the forces of good against the forces of evil and promising to bring justice to the oppressed" (Keddie, 2003, p. 3).

Especially worth emphasizing is the role played by several unfortunate acts of foreign economic policy, which gave the ulama the opportunity to act as effective leaders of the opposition against an unpopular and exploitative regime. The first event came in 1872 when the reformist government of Mirza Hosain Khan granted to a British baron, Julius De Reuter, an extensive concession conferring exclusive rights for an array of economic activities. Lord Curzon called it "the most complete and extraordinary surrender of the entire industrial resources of a kingdom into foreign hands that had probably ever been dreamed of" (cited by Keddie, 2003, p. 54). This concession was granted in return for a modest royalty, but Prime Minister Khan personally profited from it. Following protests by patriotic officials, ulama, and economic agents hurt by Khan's reforms, the shah eventually annulled the Reuter concession and dismissed his prime minister. However, a new series of similar economic concessions soon followed, testifying that Iran continued to fall prey to British and Russian interests. Because these concessions brought only small returns to the government, while bribes to the shah and officials to promote them were quite large, tensions between the state and society remained high.

From 1890 onward, an important change occurred in the formation of political opposition to the shah. Before then, most secularist reformists, who were typically educated people influenced by Western ideas, had been rather hostile to the ulama, in contrast to the traditionally close ties between ulama and the bazaar classes,[10] In the last decade of the nineteenth century, however, they started to reconcile with the clerics who were willing

---

[10] The bazaar class comprised not only wealthy merchants but also the larger group of bazaar artisans and shopkeepers organized into guilds, and they typically belonged to the same families as the ulama, thanks to frequent intermarriages. Moreover, much of the ulama's

to fight against the regime's policies, particularly against the sale of Iran's resources to foreigners. The architect of this unusual alliance between religious and radical elements was Jamal al-Din "al-Afghani" (1839–97), an anti-imperialist and pan-Islamist reformer brought up in the rationalist philosophical tradition of Avicenna (Keddie, 2003, pp. 59–60; Mishra, 2012, pp. 48–123). The impetus for this alliance was again an important economic concession to foreign interests considered to be a sellout of the country's resources. In 1890, indeed, the corrupt and inefficient government of Nasser al-Din awarded G. F. Talbot, a British capitalist, the exclusive right to produce, sell, and export the country's entire tobacco crop. Because tobacco was such a vital commodity in the economy, this decision immediately aroused tumultuous mass protests (Keddie, 1966; Rodinson, 1966, p. 166; Lapidus, 1988, pp. 576–7; Cleveland, 2004; Gleave, 2005; Katouzian, 2009, pp. 163–4).

The first major protest flared up in Shiraz, and despite the exile of its religious leader to Iraq, the revolutionary movement, known as the Tobacco Protest, spread like wildfire to Tabriz, Mashhad, Isfahan, Tehran, and elsewhere. A noteworthy feature of all these popular demonstrations was that they were organized by members of the Shi'a ulama who "urged the population to join them in preserving the dignity of Islam in the face of growing foreign influences; they portrayed the shah's concession as a transgression of the laws of Islam and used their independent power base to denounce the government" (Cleveland, 2004, p. 115). In December 1891, Mirza Hussein Shirazi, a mujtahid from Shiraz who acted in concert with Afghani, issued a fatwa declaring tobacco consumption an impious act (an offense to the Hidden Imam) that would be considered as unlawful until the cancellation of the concession. The Iranian people responded by boycotting all tobacco products, forcing the government to cancel the whole concession in early 1892. Considerably weakened by this event, it completely reversed its policy and became openly hostile to contact with the West.

This was a significant moment in modern Iran's history not only because the movement was the first successful mass protest against government policy but also because it rested on the coordinated actions of ulama, secular or modernist reformers, bazaaris (especially merchants), and ordinary townspeople. Unlike what happened with the Safavids, the religious establishment was no longer co-opted by the Qajar shahs, creating a risk of

income came from levies paid mainly by bazaaris and payment for services provided during religious or partly religious ceremonies celebrated by the guilds (Keddie, 2003, p. 30; Axworthy, 2013, p. 22).

political upheaval. This risk was especially high because there was now proof that religious authorities could use their power of interpretation to confront a government's economic policy; the class of the ulama, or at least the most radical among them, was now convinced that "the Iranian people were receptive to calls for political activity based on Islamic frames of reference" (Cleveland, 2004: 115; Hodgson, 1974c). The ulama could thus provide leadership for what Nikki Keddie (2003) calls "the religious-radical alliance," an alliance that had shown its potential for changing the course of Iranian policy (pp. 61–2). It was to remain effective during the subsequent decades and even during the following century.

The power of the ulama was displayed, for example, in the reactions to the punishments ordered by the governor of Tehran against two sugar merchants from the city's bazaar in December 1905. The merchants, one of whom was a respected elder, were administered the bastinado punishment (caning of the soft soles of the feet) for not lowering their prices as ordered. In response, the bazaar, and soon the whole city of Tehran, closed down, an expression of the unrest and dissatisfaction with the Qajar government that had been growing for years. Many merchants and mullahs, led by two senior clerics (Ayatollahs Behbehani and Tabatabai), took sanctuary in nearby shrines and refused to return until the shah met their demands for some voice in the government, removed the governor who had ordered the beatings, and dismissed the Belgian, Joseph Naus, who had been given control of customs. The shah eventually gave in on most of the points after a month of stalemate. He promised to meet the main demands of the protesters, who then returned to Tehran in great triumph, thus marking the beginning of the first Iranian revolution (Hodgson, 1974c, p. 311; Mottahedeh, 2000, pp. 35–7; Axworthy, 2013, pp. 25–6).

This was not a decisive victory, however. New concessions were soon granted by the shah to the Russians, triggering new demonstrations of popular anger. In protest, a great mass of mullahs (low-ranking clergy members) and bazaar merchants left Tehran for refuge in the city of Qom (1906), bringing business to a standstill in Tehran. In an attempt to eliminate all political opposition and to restore his unlimited authority over the country, Muhammad Ali Shah then started to obstruct the normal functioning of the parliament. It did not take long before, with the help of Cossack brigades, he fomented a state coup, which resulted in the suspension of the constitution and abolition of the parliament (June 1908). To justify this move in the name of Islam, he resorted to the argument voiced by a few ulama: "Establishing a parliament and offending Islam were one and the same thing" (Luizard, 2009, p. 225). However, the majority of the religious dignitaries, and all the most important mujtahid (the marja), considered Muhammad Ali Shah as an illegitimate ruler and an infidel who allied himself with foreign enemies of Islam. They were constitutionalists who viewed the parliament as a privileged means to fight against tyranny, end corruption, and spread the law of God throughout the country. Khurâsâni, the leading figure among the constitutionalist marja, wrote from Najaf a virulent letter to the shah, in which he denounced his manipulation of Islam and the impious character of his iniquitous rule. The following are the most striking excerpts from this letter, which played a decisive role in strengthening the uprising in Iran:

Your defunct father had granted the Constitution in order to eliminate tyranny and illegal practices vis-à-vis the people who have been heavily oppressed during many centuries. ... Since the first day you seized power, you have trampled upon all promises and the Islamic faith, and you have resorted to all kinds of tricks against constitutionalism .... The proclamation which you issued against the Constitutionalists is the outcome of foreign influences. It was written by a mujtahid hostile to Islam, who sold his religion, his faith and his existence for the sake of money, a fiend who pretended to speak in the name of the Islamic religion and law .... By divine order and by the will of the people, in the name of the Shi'ites who defend their honour, we say to him: "your justifications based on the Islamic religion and law are just lies and vain words .... You are thus an enemy of our sacred religion and a traitor to the motherland ... ". You, the shah, and your traitor mujtahid profoundly ignore the religious truth, because this truth requires that justice must be considered as a duty even in minor matters. We assert the following: "in the constitutionalist doctrine, there is not a single point that contradicts the Muslim religion. Moreover, this doctrine is in agreement with the principles of the religion and the instructions of the prophets, particularly in matters concerning justice and the end of people's oppression. We therefore urge you to resist the temptations of Satan and issue another proclamation which recognises people's freedom. If you were to prevaricate in your efforts to follow our prescription, we would all leave for Iran and declare a jihad against you." (cited by Luizard, 2009, p. 227; my translation)

During the subsequent decades, the mujtahid-led rebellion remained on the lookout, always ready to flare up again in the defense of social justice and national sovereignty. A well-established tradition of political xenophobia had taken root among the country's intelligentsia and contributed to the formation of Iranian defensive nationalism. In the late 1940s and early 1950s the alliance between religious clerics, merchants, and radical reformers was reactivated, and fatwas were issued around the ownership status of the Anglo-Iranian Oil Company (Rahman, 1982, p. 105). The protest movement demanded its nationalization, and it remained on the war path until the 1978–79 revolution, which brought Ayatollah Khomeini to supreme political power. It is revealing that, in the initial clashes of this revolution initiated by a well-organized clergy, the main components of the social forces that first responded to the opposition movement were not only theology students but also bazaar merchants, and these groups were far more in touch with the population than the (small) secular parties. As before, the clergy were able to effectively mobilize the Iranian masses through their decentralized religious networks based in each locality and with centers in the mosques and shrines (Halliday, 1996, p. 56). As pointed out by Lapidus (1988), "for the first time in the modern era religious leaders have been able to successfully oppose a modernized regime, and have taken control of the state. ... Revolution has come, not primarily from the left, but from the religious establishment; not in the name of socialism, but in the name of Islam" (p. 591).

The frequent abuses committed by government agents thus largely explain why Iranian merchants continuously sought the protection of a conservative religious class and refrained from demanding serious reforms. Only at the beginning of the twentieth century did some of them dare provide open support (including financial support) to reform movements, thus entering into conflict with the ulama whose conservative positions on certain points strained internal relations inside the ulama-bazaari-secular alliance (Keddie, 1999, 2003, pp. 68–71).[11] Yet, a crucial factor enabling the independence of the religious establishment from the central government was its financial autonomy, which had grown considerably since the Safavid times.[12] This independence was partly due to the fact that in Shi'a Islam the ulama, rather than the temporal authority, are entitled to the religious tax incumbent on Muslims, zakat. In addition, the ulama received income from teaching, administering waqfs[13], registering deeds and titles, and maintaining mutually advantageous ties with urban merchants. Because these funds

---

[11] Thus, during the Iranian constitutional revolution (dated from December 1905), reformers aimed to establish a constitutional monarchy in the country. This implied not only that the approval of the parliament (the majles) was required on all important matters, including foreign loans and treaties, but also that equality before the law, as well as personal rights and freedoms, would be guaranteed to all citizens. The latter provision was opposed by some ulama on the ground that members of minority religions should not have equal status with those of the state religion, Islam. They also demanded that the compatibility of statutory laws with the sharia be verified, a provision that was eventually approved but not implemented (Keddie, 2003, p. 68).

[12] Thanks to their financial independence, emphasized Ayatollah Motahhari, the ulama are able not only to respond to the demands of the people but also "to stand up to governments and fight against their excesses and their cruelty" (Rahnema and Nomani, 1990, p. 46).

[13] Private waqfs, whose incomes were usually accrued to the donor's descendants, were often used to circumvent the strict inheritance rules prescribed by the Quran. As pointed out earlier, a guardian drawn from the community of, and whose salary is paid from the waqf income, is required even for private waqfs (Keddie, 2003, p. 15).

were largely used to provide educational services and social assistance to the needy, the influence and popularity of the ulama grew: Their image as the true protectors of the people was all the more attractive as the government became increasingly viewed as corrupt and impious (Keddie, 2003, pp. 15–16; Cleveland, 2004, p. 113).

Unsurprisingly, then, whenever the Iranian state aimed to curtail the influence of the clergy, it tried to dent the ulama's privileges. For example, the government of Emir Kabir (1848–51) under the reign of Nasser al-Din Shah tried to strengthen the state through the following measures: limiting the jurisdiction of the ulama, establishing new courts, restricting the right of sanctuary in mosques and shrines, controlling endowments, reducing allowances, and sponsoring the formation of secular schools in competition with ulama schools (Lapidus, 1988, p. 575). Such measures immediately triggered a determined reaction from the ulama, eager to defend their privileges. Nor is it surprising that in normal times many ulama supported the state authority and identified with the ruling elites, accepting state pensions, gifts, and positions at court or in government service and owning land. Those who refused to do so adopted a quietist position out of religious and doctrinal considerations, turning their backs on the corrupt affairs of the world and striving to preserve a measure of religious purity while waiting for the return of the Hidden Imam (Floor, 1983; Lapidus, 1988, p. 579).

Thus the basic conflict between the state and the religious establishment did not stem from an inherent religious opposition to state authority. It is revealing that, before the mid-nineteenth century, the ulama were rarely active in opposing government policies, and the shahs of this period used to treat them well (Keddie, 2003, p. 43). Instead, the tension resulted from a particular configuration of circumstances – foreign interventions, corruption of state agents, centralization policies intended to restrict judicial and educational prerogatives of the ulama – that impelled the ulama "to adopt the active rather than the passive side of their complex tradition" (Lapidus, 1988, p. 590). In terms of the analytical framework presented at the end of Chapter 4, political instability was generated by a series of policies antagonistic not only to the interests of the clerics but also to those of the merchants, businessmen, and lower classes. From the viewpoint of the clerics, wrong-headed public policies consisted of both self-serving measures that nurtured large-scale corruption and measures that limited their own prerogatives as religious functionaries.

The ulama were not uniformly in favor of political change. Although a significant number of high-ranking members of the clergy struggled to defend the common people and establish social justice, the religious class as a whole did not challenge the structure of Iranian society or the norms of political life (Floor, 1983, p. 117). Thus, in the realm of justice where religious courts were overwhelmingly dominant, religious judges, although they were not entitled to any fees, "often received considerable presents or just plain bribes to influence their judgements" (Floor, 1983, p. 114). In general, however, they "were seen as doing this less than government officials" (Keddie, 2003, p. 30). Hence religious courts grew in importance during the Qajar period, not only because their number increased but also because their area of competence expanded (they could deal with commercial and many other matters) under the pressure of demands from the people, who tended to prefer religious over official courts, whose judges were considered particularly corrupt and unreliable (Floor, 1980; Gleave, 2005).

The corruption of state justice actually worsened after the reform of the judicial system of April 1911, which formally subordinated the religious courts to the state (yet did not suppress them) and introduced "adliyya" courts spanning the whole array of modern courts – from the supreme court of appeals and the court of appeals to the petty court, through the court of first instance and the criminal court. The problem was that judges, prosecutors, investigators, lawyers, clerks, assistants, and registrars were all susceptible to corruption, so that "the degree of success in getting one's right depended on the length of one's purse and/or influence." It is therefore not surprising that the adliyya courts, in which, paradoxically, the mullahs played a major role,[14] became popularly known as the courts of injustice ("zulmiyya"), the "despoilers rather than upholders of justice" (Floor, 1983, pp. 130–2). Accordingly, the religious courts and other rival procedures, including arbitration, continued to dominate the Iranian judicial system, particularly in civil cases.

Linking the Change to Theory

What these malpractices indicate is that, in conformity with a key assumption of our analytical approach to the relations between religion and politics, there is significant heterogeneity among the clerics. As a result, one should

---

[14] Indeed, in spite of being formally government courts ("urf" courts), the adliyya courts had religious judges on the bench; moreover, many mullahs were normal members of the courts in their personal rather than their religious capacity (Floor, 1983, pp. 127–8). The situation gradually deteriorated as "every unemployed person with a letter of recommendation from a mujtahid or a politician could get a job as judge, the more so if they had a madrasa training. In this way, a great many people were employed who knew neither civil nor religious law. ... Because mujtahid and other high-ranking ulama considered the function of judge to be below their standing, 'every ignoramus with some metres of black or white textile on his head could become a qadi,' commented Mustawfi .... The mullahs really controlled the administration of justice" (p. 131).

not expect all of them to join an open rebellion against the political authority: Those who highly value the material benefits they can extract from the prevailing system will not oppose it. In the best case, they will keep silent.

There remains the question as to how the collapse of state-religion cooperation in post-Safavid times can be represented in terms of the same approach. This question can be reformulated as follows: Which parameters in the model described in Chapter 4 have changed, and with which expected consequences, after the demise of the Safavids? Let me suggest two parametric changes that added their effects to produce the situation of political instability that characterized Qajar rule.

The first change was a shift in the distribution of the clerics so that a great number became more suspicious of the objectives and policies pursued by the autocratic ruler. Under the Safavids, a large majority of clerics were close to the ruler, giving rise to successful cooperation between state and religion and thereby facilitating the emergence of a strong, modern centralized state in the country; in contrast, under the Qajars, most clerics were antagonistic to the state, which created acute tensions between the two agencies. This shift in the distribution of Iranian clerics was itself the consequence of a prolonged period of quasi-anarchy and state vacuum that followed the end of Safavid rule. As documented earlier, the chaotic transition between the Safavid and the Qajar dynasties profoundly affected the manner in which the clerics related to the state.

A second factor played a significant role in the transformation of the state-religion relationship: the emergence of new outside opportunities in the form of trade and foreign direct investment (under colonial conditions). In terms of our model, the influence of these opportunities can be represented as an increase in the profitability of (trade liberalization) reforms. The predicted effect is that, other things being equal, more reforms and greater political instability arising from declining support of the clerics will be obtained at the new politico-religious equilibrium. This is precisely the consequence described at length in the preceding subsection.

5.4 State-Appointed versus Self-Appointed Clerics

In the case of Egypt, the surge of religious forces clearly came from official Islam. In Iran, it also originated in the sphere of official Islam, yet in post-Safavid times this sphere remained beyond the control of the state. Under the Qajar shahs, indeed, a division emerged between two kinds of ulama: government-appointed and supported scholars who filled official religious posts, on the one hand, and those who taught, preached, and made judgments in ulama-run institutions and courts, on the other hand. Among the latter, the most learned became mujtahid, endowed with the power to give authoritative interpretations on questions of religious law. Those able to attract a large following gained considerable authority and prestige, in addition to economic strength and independence (Keddie, 2003, pp. 16–17). Whereas mujtahids were few in Safavid times, their number quickly multiplied under the Qajars, and many took the name of ayatollahs.

A third possibility, as attested by the following examples, arises when the religious reaction to government failures is sparked off by Sufi orders and quietist branches of Islam that ordinarily refrain from meddling in social, economic, and political affairs. The first example concerns Iran during the period preceding the rise of official clerics against the political regime. In the early nineteenth century, deep-seated opposition to the state and the official religious establishment in cahoots with it erupted in the form of a movement inspired by Sufism and known as Shaykhism. The government quickly suppressed it at the instigation of official clerics. In 1844, a man named Ali Mohammed Shirazi (1819–50) declared himself as the Gate (the "Bab") to the Lord of the Age (the Hidden Imam) and, a few years later, as the Mahdi himself. His doctrine was strongly anticlerical, and some of his leading supporters came from the lower ranks of the ulama. Babism, as the movement was called, spread like wildfire. Again, at the urging of the official clerics, it was brutally put down (Buchan, 2012, pp. 96–7; Lee, 2014, p. 196).

Another example comes from Ottoman Turkey, a state in which the sultan held considerable powers and succeeded in incorporating the entire religious legal community into the state bureaucracy after the fifteenth century (see Section 5.2). However, the sultan's control over the ulama and various religious orders tended to weaken during periods of state crisis. Thus, dervish orders were spawned by the chaos of crossing cultural and physical frontiers that accompanied the waves of Turkoman migrations. Some of these fraternities, which existed "in bewildering variety," had an "exceptional sensibility to political and social injustices" (Goffman, 2002, pp. 73–4; Finkel, 2005, pp. 8–9). They formed an extensive network of deviant Sufis who occasionally operated as centers of opposition to the Ottoman state and its policies. When the regime was fragile, such as under Mehmed I, they could even gather a wide range of disgruntled Ottoman subjects into a massive rebellion (1416) (p. 75).

The last example comes from present-day Yemen, where tribesmen loyal to the Houthi family, a powerful northern clan, have entered into an open conflict with the government of President Ali Abdullah Saleh. Interestingly, the Houthis style themselves mujahideen in the manner of the guerrillas who chased the Russians out of Afghanistan. Most of their adherents belong to the Zaydi sect, a quietist branch of Shi'a Islam. Yet, growing resentment against pervasive corruption in and around the government, as well as the perceived neglect of Northern Yemen by the central state, has led to Zaydi radicalization in the form of a movement known as the "Believing Youth." Launched by a charismatic member of the Houthi family, this movement has drawn abundant recruits from the ranks of dissatisfied Yemeni workers expelled from Saudi Arabia in the early 1990s, when the Saudi government wanted to punish Saleh for backing Saddam Hussein's Iraq in the first Gulf War, as well as from angry northern traders whose lucrative smuggling business was disrupted by the squabble with the Saudis (*Economist*, September 12–18, 2009).

These three examples illustrate rebellions arising from outside the religious establishment and initiated by self-appointed clerics rather than by state-appointed ones. As such, they point to the role of radical religious movements in times of trouble. We return to this theme in more detail in Chapter 7.

5.5 Reaction to Foreign Domination

As the example of Iran has shown, a weak state may be both the product and the cause of foreign aggression, domination, or colonization. It is impossible, indeed, to understand the politics of modern Iran under the Qajar dynasty, more particularly the political role of religious elites, if we leave out the context of their resistance to British and Russian domination. The case of neighboring Iraq bears close resemblance to that of Iran, as attested by the rise and strengthening of the Islamist movement under British occupation. This movement declared a jihad against the British colonial power, and it is one of its remarkable features that the ulama themselves directly participated in the fighting during World War I and later (Luizard, 2009, p. 297). The decisive role played by the Shi'i ulama in the people's struggle for independence is well documented. The "marja" actually led the religious, political, and military revolution against the British occupier, and they managed the various proto-national institutions created during the revolutionary phase. Not only was the whole body of religious authorities, from the top to the lowest rungs of the ecclesiastical hierarchy, unified behind their central leader (Muhammad Taqî Shîrâzî and his successor, Shaykh ash-Sharîa Isfahânî), but the marja could also rely on the unfailing support of various tribal and other leaders of the Middle Euphrates region (pp. 351–9). Let us now briefly turn to four additional examples to portray the variety of geographical contexts and historical periods in which resistance to foreign domination occurred.

The first example comes from Mauritania, where, in the seventeenth to eighteenth centuries, Berber tribes suffered from the oppression of the Arab Banu Maqil, against whom they eventually rose in rebellion. Their leader, Nasser al-Din, claimed to be sent by God to stop the Berbers' ill treatment. He asked his followers to act in conformity with the Quran. Calling himself "emir al-muminin," the traditional title of Muslim caliphs, he proclaimed the end of time and the coming of the "Mahdi." His army swept through southern Mauritania in 1673, and his defeat led to the lasting military dominance of the Arab tribes over the Berbers (Lapidus, 1988, pp. 509–10).

The second example concerns modern Afghanistan. After seizing power in 1919, Amanullah declared war against the British and unilaterally proclaimed his country's independence. This was a daring move because Afghanistan had become a nation-state only because it was a buffer state entirely supported by foreign imperialism. It was the financial subsidies and weaponry provided by the British between 1880 and 1919 that enabled the Afghan state to somehow control its own territory. Proclaimed under the banner of pan-Islamism and anti-imperialism, Amanullah's decision led to a military defeat but a political victory: His anti-imperialist stance, indeed, gained him the immediate sympathy of the clergy, including the fundamentalists, the tribes, and the modernists (Roy, 1990).

The Mahdist revolt in Sudan provides a third illustration. Thus, when Sudanese people suffered under the rule of Egypt, primarily from the exactions committed by rapacious and brutal Turkish officials, a pious member of a reformed Sufi order (the "Sammaniya"), Shaykh Muhammad Ahmad (1848–85) "declared himself the Mahdi, the expected savior, and called for a restoration of the true Islam" (Lapidus, 1988, p. 854). By divine inspiration he gave instructions on various matters, such as the seclusion of women and land distribution, and he attempted to suppress customary Sudanese religious practices in conflict with the sharia, such as veneration of the saints. After the seizure of Khartoum, a state was born of his military endeavor (1885), which continued the movement toward the centralization of state power. In 1898, the Mahdists suffered defeat at the hands of an Anglo-Egyptian army. Despite this defeat, however, they retained wide support in the country: "They had helped overcome tribal particularism and would later be an important base for the development of Sudanese nationalism and an independent Sudanese state" (p. 856). In fact, in 1944 the son of the Mahdi formed a political party (the Umma Party) that promoted independence. Because they could mobilize mass support, the Muslim religious leaders came to play a central role in the movement toward national independence (Lapidus, 1988, p. 857; Iliffe, 2007, p. 202).

Another Islamist rebellion against Turkish domination, this time in Yemen, provides the last illustration. Toward the end of the nineteenth century, Turkish rule was so badly resented that rival claimants to the title of imam had ceased their feuding and coalesced around a single leader, Imam al-Mansur. He soon succeeded in terrifying the Turks by conducting an effective guerilla war with the help of a powerful army of Zaydi tribesmen. When he eventually laid siege to Sanaa, the Turks tried to bribe him into submission, but all their offers were consistently rejected. Al-Mansur's struggle was actually a traditional Zaydi uprising against an unrighteous ruler, "gathering fervent support by railing against the Turks' homosexuality, their European style of dress, their trousers and their fezzes, their love of alcohol and their absence from the mosque. ... If not to the merchants of Sanaa then to many Yemenis, their Ottoman oppressors seemed to have strayed so far from the true path of Islam that they could properly be reviled as 'kuffar' [unbelievers] and still worse, as 'nasara' [Christians]" (Clark, 2010, p. 40).

Under the rule of al-Mansur's son, Imam Yahya, the jihad was renewed in 1905, ending in the worst siege that Sanaa had experienced. More than two-thirds of its population were starved to death (p. 41). Yahya always made the point that he was rebelling only against corrupt Turkish officialdom, not against the Ottoman sultan, and that he was acting on behalf of Zaydis who were allegedly the rightful rulers of Yemen since the third century CE. He was possibly willing to dispense with the titles of caliph and "Commander of the Faithful" that had hitherto placed all Zaydi imams in direct competition with the Ottoman sultans, yet only if the Turks recognized his right to retain effective control of Yemen's territory. This demand entailed the right to replace Ottoman law with sharia law and to raise taxes on behalf of local authorities. In this way, the message was clearly conveyed by Yemen's northern highland Zaydi tribes that they would not tolerate outside rule, even when imposed by fellow Muslims in the name of uniting the Muslim umma (pp. 43–4).

In line with these four examples, it is worth noting that the first genuinely Islamist thinker, Ibn Taymiyya (1263–1328), developed his radical puritanical ideas in a context of foreign invasion. Raised in Damas, Taymiyya was one of the foremost religious writers of the Mamluk period. Like Ibn Hanbal several centuries earlier, he was deeply concerned by the divisions inside the Islamic world, and he believed that the unity of the umma – a unity of belief in God and acceptance of the Prophet's message – was what mattered most, even if this principle did not imply political unity. Unity of the Muslim world was a pressing need given that it was threatened by Mongol invaders and by some Christian communities that were prepared to support the Mongols. Taymiyya believed that an important duty of the sovereign was to disseminate the Muslim faith beyond the confines of the existing Muslim community and to have recourse to the jihad, the holy war, toward that purpose. In short, every Muslim believer must be a fighter for his faith, and the holy war is as important as prayer (Hourani, 1991, pp. 179–81; Meddeb, 2002, ch. 9; Saint-Prot, 2008, pp. 211–30).[15]

As noted earlier, such a prescription must be placed in a context of impending political crisis: Taymiyya proclaimed that "to fight the Mongols who came to Syria" was a duty prescribed by the Quran and the example of the Prophet (Bonney, 2004, p. 113). Taymiyya's determination to counter the Mongol threat was especially evident when he joined a delegation of ulama to talk to Qazan, the khan of the Mongol Tatars, urging him to halt his attack on Muslims. He simply could not see the logic of an allegedly Muslim people attacking the lands of Islam. In fact, he was persuaded that "the mere act of conversion was insufficient to make a person a 'true' Muslim".[16] Moreover, he came to believe that the quality and morality of Muslims had declined and that Muslim leaders, in particular, bore much of the responsibility "for not encouraging the proper faith and attitudes among the people and thus for the political divisions which had facilitated the Mongol advance" (p. 114).

In 1303, Ibn Taymiyya issued a fatwa against the Muslims of Mardin who had surrendered to the Mongols, arguing that they were not genuine Muslims because they refrained from launching jihad against the Mongol occupiers and did not openly resist the law imposed by them. He claimed that such people were either atheists or hypocrites who did not believe in the essence of the religion of Islam, or else they belonged to the despicable class of people who believed in heretical innovations. According to Richard Bonney (2004), such a ruling "created a precedent whereby so-called apostates and their likes are worthy targets of violent revolution, even if they provide legitimate (and apparently Muslim) political leadership" (p. 115). In other

---

[15] For Taymiyya, two pitfalls had to be avoided: that of a prince who does not use his wealth, army, and power to strengthen religion (the way of Christianity) and that of a powerless religion deprived of financial and monetary resources.

[16] It is no doubt true that Mongols were not genuine Muslims in the sense meant by Taymiyya. They still relied on the "Yasa" code of law derived from their polytheistic tradition. Chinghis-Khan adhered to religious syncretism: he did not belong to any religion and did not think that one religion was more worthy than another (Bonney, 2004, p. 114).

words, the good Muslim was no longer defined by his religious attitude, but by his political actions, and one could call someone a heretic for purely political reasons (Roy, 1990, p. 78).

We return to this important issue of the role of Islam as an anticolonial ideology when discussing the rise of Islamist puritanical movements in Chapter 7.

5.6 Conclusion and Final Remarks about the Puzzle of Iranian Theocracy

The evidence reviewed in this chapter attests that the guiding principle followed by Muslim clerics – they should remain at a reasonable distance from politics – may be suspended when the state is so weak as to create chronic chaos. The fear of disorder and civil war is then justified, and clerics may feel it is their duty to assume an active role in public affairs. This holds true even of clerics who belong to a quietist tradition of Islam, if they feel that official clerics are as corrupt as the political elite.

In Ottoman Egypt and Iran, high-level ulama were the main actors involved in political change. In both cases, their intervention contributed decisively to ending a situation of weak central political power that had disastrous consequences for the middle class and ordinary people. The Iranian case is particularly well documented, revealing that the ayatollahs meddled in politics in response to a conjunction of circumstances. Their meddling increased by steps; the success of demonstrations that they instigated encouraged them to intensify their actions. In other words, it was their active engagement against the iniquitous policies of the shah and his government that enhanced their social prestige and influence among the population, including among the merchant classes; their leadership role was thus gradually confirmed and sustained by the popular will. Varied circumstances prompted the ayatollahs into action: repeated imperialist encroachments on vital economic interests, glaring corruption of state agents and the entourage of the shah, blatant acts of injustice, and centralization policies aimed at restricting judicial and educational prerogatives of religious clerics. Their motives thus resulted from a mix of selfless and selfish predispositions.

In accordance with the logic underlying the principle of keeping their distance from political power, clerics ought to withdraw from the political scene as soon as order is restored and the danger of civil war or internal strife has vanished. This is precisely what happened in Ottoman Egypt after the ulama called Muhammad Ali to exercise supreme political power. But it is not what happened in Iran. There, against a well-established tradition, the ayatollahs have continued to cling to power. It is revealing that when the time came to provide a successor to the supreme spiritual leader of the Shi'a community, Ayatollah al-Sistani, the government of Iran pushed a candidate, Ayatollah Shahroudi, who had assumed a top-level political position (head of the judiciary) and was known as one of the wealthiest men in the country. This move did not go down well with the clerics of the holy city of Najaf (in today's Iraq), who were more inspired by the austere, pious, and humble way of al-Sistani.[17]

One plausible reason for the continuing presence of ayatollahs at the highest level of power in Iran is that the perceived threat of chaos or imperialist aggression is still lingering, so that their withdrawal from politics is deemed premature. The fear of U.S. invasion enhanced by the fate of neighboring Iraq added credence to the persisting perception of an external threat. An alternative explanation is that clerics have remained in power long enough to develop a strong taste for the material advantages associated with it. This would apply to at least some of them, such as the aforementioned Ayatollah Shahroudi, who has amassed a fortune through involvement in lucrative business lines (importing auto parts and equipment for oil exploration from Eastern Europe).[18] In contrast, following measures to privatize the economy, the Revolutionary Guard (the "Pasdaran"), which is only loosely tied to the religious establishment, has succeeded in becoming enmeshed in the ownership and management of enterprises that constitute 25 percent or more of the Iranian economy (Lee, 2014, p. 204). According to the second explanation, therefore, a group of opportunistic clerics and associates are ready to fight for their privileges even though such a strategy clearly betrays the moral justification for initially seizing political power. Finally, consolidating a theocratic state (with a democratic façade) provides a third possible motive for the enduring power of the Iranian ayatollah. Insofar as the political power of the clergy is what makes the Islamic Republic of Iran Islamic, this third motive is consonant with the second one.

It is too early to say which of these three motives will eventually prevail. My theory predicts that, although a few radical clerics, for either ideological or opportunistic reasons, may want to maintain the domination of

---

[17] The process of choosing the supreme spiritual leader of the Shi'a Muslims is a complicated one that relies on both the will of the people, expressed to whom they choose to pay their religious taxes (the zakat), and validation by his clerical peers (see Nasr, 2007, for more details).

[18] See Arango, T., "Iran Backs Own Man as Heir to Iraqi Cleric," *International Herald Tribune*, Saturday–Sunday, May 12–13, 2012.

religion over politics, the majority of them will eventually oppose power entrenchment and favor a return to purely religious duties. In Iraq, Muqtada al-Sadr, a Shi'a firebrand who fought against American occupation of the country, largely abandoned his politically militant position (allegedly under the influence of al-Sistani) after it became clear that U.S. forces were not staying indefinitely. The time had come to return to Najaf whose religious academy, called the "Hawza," demands from the marja that they lead a pious and ascetic life at a measured distance from the world of power.

Returning to the case of Iran, it bears emphasis that Khomeini's doctrine according to which Iran must be governed by the leading jurist of Islam (the "velayat-e faqih"), acting as placeholder for the Hidden Imam, was rejected by a number of leading clerics from the very beginning of the Islamic Republic.[19] They believed that clerical involvement in politics would sully Islam. Their stance is actually in keeping with Twelver Shi'ism whose cardinal principle provides that no temporal authority can earn legitimacy until the Mahdi (who vanished from sight in 874) has returned to earth. Establishing and sustaining a theocratic state thus totally contradict this strand of Islam (Benraad, 2015, p. 32). The voice of dissent grew steadily during the rule of Khomeini, so much so that, at his death in 1989, all the remaining grand ayatollahs except Hussein Ali Montazeri, were opposed to the idea of velayat-e faqih. Clearly, the Supreme Leader never succeeded in bringing the clerical class under his thumb (Lee, 2014, pp. 202–3).

[19] It is clear from this doctrine that the resulting political regime is a one-man rule. In the words of Ali Khamenei, "The commandments of the ruling jurist are primary commandments and are like the commandments of God ... obedience to them is incumbent. ... The Mandate of the Jurist is like the soul in the body of the regime" (cited from Axworthy, 2013, p. 274).

The Rise of Islam in Conditions of State Crisis

The Case of Kleptocratic Despotism

If the autocrat, say because he is very greedy, chooses to follow policies that are deeply disliked by the religious clerics, he will be able to seduce or co-opt only a fraction of them (the most easily corruptible), as a result of which his regime will be unstable. This is precisely the kind of situations that have been frequently observed in Muslim countries since they have acquired their independence and that we want to take stock of in this chapter. Following general considerations (Section 6.1), Section 6.2, one of the central parts of the book, presents seven in-depth case studies that document situations of partial religious co-option. They are structured in a way that allows the reader, in each country case, to grasp the sequence of events and their underlying logic, the motivations and the behavior of the autocrats, and the positioning of the various groups of religious clerics. A comprehensive conclusion forms the object of the last section (Section 6.3) so that the hurried reader can skip the long central section or read only the case studies that deal with countries of particular interest.

6.1 Instrumentalization of Islam in Support of Despotism

Under the dominant system of politico-religious interactions – the opposition suppression strategy – the entire clerical body is tamed. Because the autocrat is efficient and is wise enough not to engage in too unpopular policies, the clerics can all be bought off at prices that he can afford. In fact, because his policies do not antagonize them too much, the clerics are seducible at reasonably low prices. Among the population, including the commercial classes, a wide acquiescence to the regime prevails to the extent that public order is successfully established. Even though there is no law that stands above the ruler because he defines the law, people willingly trade their citizens' rights for physical security and a modicum of economic and social mobility. Under the opposition confrontation strategy, by contrast, the autocratic system is more unstable: The ruler has selected policies that antagonize a fraction of the clerics whom he is unable to buy off. As a result, the clerical body is internally divided, and tensions between state-appointed clerics and self-appointed or independent clerics are almost certain to arise.

The temptation to co-opt clerics is especially strong when leftist forces are mobilized against the regime. To quash dissent coming from the secular left, a convenient tactic is to use the language of religion and the authority of religious officials: By representing leftist opponents as a bunch of godless renegades, these officials play into the hands of a manipulative dictatorship. Such curses generally find an echo in popular masses immersed in traditional cultures that attach great value to submission to God and respect for customary norms and symbols. As for the nonseduced, more radical clerics, they struggle against the regime alongside the left, but inevitably their cooperation is uneasy and unstable because of the inherent contradictions between secular and religious worldviews.

As shown in the next section, recent history offers many striking examples of cynical political rulers, often with a secular background, using Islam as a readily available ideology and instrument of legitimacy to deflect criticisms, entrench their power and privileges, or bolster their nationalist credentials. They are thus able to escape the consequences of their misrule. They are able to maintain their nefarious policies and predatory practices that cause deep-seated frustrations in the population and give rise to a permanent threat of overt or covert rebellion. To a significant extent, these recent experiences remind us of the political situation that preceded the formation of Islamic law and the establishment of the legal community. Autocratic rulers were then tyrannical and ready to use Islam for sinister political ends, such as was observed during most of the rule of the Umayyads and the early Abbasids (Coşgel, Miceli, and Ahmed, 2009).

Instrumentalizing Islam is a perilous game to play for willing despots. If they can refer to Islam as a justifying ideology, radical clerics, especially self-appointed ones, may also avail themselves of the same strategy, thus creating a situation in which religion becomes "the language of both consent and dissent" (Lee, 2014, p. 245). When both opposition groups and the state invoke Islam as the main justification for their actions, thus triggering a religious bidding war, an obscurantist deadlock is created in which all political opinions and judgments are expressed in the language of religion. Despotic rulers use religious references in self-defense or as a counterattack tactic against opposition groups frustrated by the failures of corrupt, secretive, authoritarian, and ineffective states that do not deliver on what they promised (Hourani, 1991, pp. 452–3; Marsot, 2007, pp. 166–72). The situation is particularly vicious and absurd when, in their eagerness to crush left-leaning opposition, these rulers had themselves nurtured Islamist movements much in the same way as extremist movements based on ethnic affiliation have often been used to destroy political opposition (see, e.g., Posner, 2006; Lemarchand, 2009). Clearly, rather than originating in a supposed conflation of religion and politics, the main problem is the easy manipulability of religion by the state.

Before turning to concrete examples, three central characteristics of Islamic law and jurisprudence must be addressed. Although they have already been mentioned (in Chapter 3, in particular), they need to be examined here because their conjunction is liable to spark an obscurantist deadlock.

First, the Quran does not cover constitutional law. It contains only two broad principles regarding a proper system of government: consultation and obedience to authority. This leaves religious authorities relatively free to pronounce politically significant judgments as they see fit, whether in support of or opposition to the ruling elite.

Second, Islamic jurisprudence as it crystallized in the tenth century, contains few precise legal injunctions, and those few are all concerned with personal status matters (family relationships and civil transactions, in particular). Moreover, wide variations in opinions are possible because there exist four doctrinal schools in Islam, with variations within each. Local customs are an important additional (subsidiary) source of law in Islam. As a consequence, more flexibility exists than is usually imagined for expressing differentiated views and proffering accusations in the public arena.

Flexibility is even greater because of a third characteristic of the Islamic system: lack of a centralized organization resembling the Vatican. The decentralized nature of the Islamic faith facilitates the task of autocratic rulers who are seeking the allegiance of religious authorities with a view to backing up their unpopular policies and helping silence critical voices. Fatwas are no more than opinions or judgments whose legitimacy depends on the number and prestige of the ulama backing them; they are not religious laws that can be enforced throughout the whole community of the faithful. Kleptocratic autocrats are keen to enlist the most prestigious and authoritative clerics. Yet, as argued earlier, this is a two-edged sword.

A sharp contrast obviously exists between the Catholic Church, which monopolizes the right to excommunicate, and the lands of Islam, where any judge can issue a fatwa against an individual, a group, or a political regime considered to be impious or infidel (see Chapter 3). In Islam, "the decision to oppose the state on the grounds that it is insufficiently Islamic belongs to anyone who wishes to exercise it" (Zakaria, 2003, pp. 124–5, 144; Mardin, 1993, p. 215). Because Muslims can turn to preachers of their own choice, and preachers are not subject to the rigid rulings of a priestly caste acting as the representative of God, the possibility of both anarchy and manipulation of religion by despotic rulers is very serious in Islamic countries. And if the ulama try to impose a more or less unified doctrine, preachers can always accuse imams of interposing themselves between God and the believers. This was precisely the point made by Shukri Mustafa, the Egyptian leader of the Society of Muslims, who considered the ulama as "no more than lackeys of the prince, 'pulpit parrots'" (Kepel, 2005, p. 101).

The next section examines in detail seven country experiences of politico-religious interactions. There is an obvious selection bias in the way the countries were chosen because their experience had to meet two criteria: (1) be sufficiently well documented in the English or French literature, and (2) contain rich insights about the instrumentalization of Islam by despotic rulers. This bias is unlikely to matter, however. This is because my theory does not claim that all Muslim autocrats are cynical despots ready to manipulate Islam for reasons of political expediency. I show in Chapter 9 that countries exist where this was evidently not true. My aim, therefore, is limited to convincing the reader that, if the despot is of the cynical type, political instability fed by obscurantism is likely to prevail in the conditions of a decentralized religion such as Islam. In the context of this chapter, cynical despots are autocratic rulers willing to go far toward sacrificing their people's welfare to their own selfish, kleptocratic objectives. Believing that the end justifies the means, they show no moral restraint.

6.2 Evidence

In order of presentation, the seven countries are Egypt, Sudan, Pakistan, Algeria, Indonesia, Iraq, and Syria. Two are not Arab, and three – Egypt, Pakistan, and Indonesia – are densely populated, with the first two also being influential entities in the Muslim world. All the countries, but especially Egypt, Sudan, Pakistan, and Algeria, have nurtured strong Islamist movements, and in all of them, strong army-backed dictators have ruled for significant periods of time. Finally, and most importantly, in all seven countries, ruling autocrats did not hesitate to betray their secular and modernist ideals and to instrumentalize the Islamic faith for the sake of maintaining their hold on political power. In the presentation of each country case, the focus is on the relationship between autocrats in power and Islamic clerics. The chronological order of events is scrupulously followed so as to help the reader grasp the dynamics of that relationship and the possible role of external shocks or circumstances.

Case Study 1: Egypt

Faruk and Nasser: Compromising with Islamists but Not with Liberals and Leftists

When King Faruk was instated in 1937, he perpetuated the conflict between the palace and the majority party in parliament, the Wafd, that his authoritarian father (King Fuad) had formed. To silence the liberal opposition, his entourage advised, he should get closer to the men of religion in al-Azhar, Egypt's leading mosque and university, and use them as a lever against the Wafd (Marsot, 2007, pp. 117–18); he followed this advice. More ominous still was the palace's decision to grant Hassan al Banna, the founder in 1928 of the Muslim Brotherhood, access to the soldiers in the military barracks in the hope that the Brotherhood's message would counteract the appeal of the Wafd (Cook, 2012, p. 115). Apparently, that message was deemed unthreatening as long as it concentrated on proclaiming hatred of British colonialism, contempt for local Westernized elites, and hostility to political parties. The Wafd, however, came back to power in 1942 as part of a deal that moved it closer to King Faruq and the British. This alliance brought Egypt into World War II on the British side, which proved catastrophic for the reputations of both Faruk and the Wafd (Zahid, 2010, pp. 73–6; Lee, 2014, p. 43).

Tensions subsequently rose between the palace and the Muslim Brothers, eventually leading to the assassination of Prime Minister Naqrashi by a Brother, Hassan Taleb. The latter claimed that Naqrashi had neglected the Palestinian cause, fought against Islam, and banned the Brotherhood. In retaliation, the government arrested and tortured thousands of Muslim Brothers, and it forced the issuance of religious decrees condemning the movement and calling for its dissolution. In February 1949, the regime's secret police assassinated al Banna (Zahid, 2010, p. 75).

Gamal Abdel Nasser succeeded Faruk as a result of a state coup carried out by a group of young officers of the army (1952), the so-called Free Officers. In spite of his constant trumpeting of "Arab socialism," Nasser was far from willing to embark on the "secularization" program for which some elements of the Egyptian society yearned. Instead, he sought to modernize the institutions of official Islam, particularly al-Azhar, in an effort to use them as effective means of transmission of the state ideology to the masses. The prestigious university-mosque that served as a training ground for Sunni ulama from across the Muslim world was stripped of its religious endowment and prevented from holding sharia courts. In addition, Nassar usurped the authority of the shaykh of al-Azhar, whose salary was paid by the state (in 1961). Al-Azhar's Academy for Islamic Research, which started in the 1960s and claimed the right to censor Egyptian publications according to Islamic criteria, fell under political control (Lee, 2014, p. 61). By thus transforming al-Azhar into "a ward of the Egyptian state" (Cook, 2012, p. 78), Nasser continued the tradition, initiated by Muhammad Ali, of subduing the religious establishment (see Chapter 5).

To make these subjugation measures acceptable and legitimate in the eyes of the population, Nasser decided to strengthen his religious credentials. Thus, in 1964, he declared Islam as the main source of national identity by making it the country's official religion. He also abided by religious conventions such as keeping his wife out of sight, refraining from drinking alcohol in public, and posturing as an authentic Muslim uncorrupted by European decadence (Lee, 2014, p. 43).

How did Nasser handle the Islamists, the Muslim Brotherhood in particular? At a critical moment, when they decided to assert complete control over Egyptian politics and to strip party leaders of all their political rights, the Free Officers chose to reserve special treatment for the Brotherhood. The Free Officers thus ordered about 200 members of the organization, including its supreme guide, who had been arrested a few months earlier on the occasion of mass demonstrations, to be released from prison. This measure of clemency, which resulted from astute political calculation, did not apply to leftists, especially the communists, who never fully recovered from the repression they endured in this period. This unequal treatment is not surprising insofar as the plan of the Free Officers was precisely to ally with religious forces in order to tame all secular opposition. It is noteworthy, however, that Nasser never honored his promise to lift the ban on the Muslim Brotherhood and grant it legal status (Cook, 2012, pp. 52–8).

The Islamists soon started agitating against the rule of the Revolutionary Command Council (RCC) into which the Free Officers'. A major flare-up erupted over the so-called Heads of Agreement (July 1954) signed by the Free Officers and the British and regulating the British presence around the Suez Canal. The Brothers held that the agreement amounted to a surrender to British interests. They thus confronted Nasser and the Free Officers "over the very issue on which they staked their claim to power and legitimacy in the first place – nationalism." For them, "the Heads of Agreement did little more than effectively extend the Anglo-Egyptian Treaty of 1936"

(Cook, 2012, p. 60). The Brotherhood used this opportunity to demand the reestablishment of the parliamentary system and freedom of the press. This was going too far, and Nasser could not accept having the Officers' nationalist credentials questioned. The reaction was immediate. Nasser first sought to delegitimize the prestige and moral authority of the Brothers by accusing them, paradoxically, of complicity with the communists, the Zionists, and the British. After a staged assassination attempt on Nasser, used as a convenient pretext to clamp down on the Brotherhood, its leaders and thousands of their followers were taken into custody. In the words of Steven Cook, "in the end, the Brotherhood survived the onslaught, but barely. For the remainder of the Nasser period, the Brothers were either underground or imprisoned ... the showdown between the Officers and the Muslim Brotherhood in 1954 and the subsequent consolidation of the regime would have a profound impact on Egyptian politics for decades to come" (p. 61).

Sadat: Playing Safe with the Official Ulama but Playing Fire with the Islamists

Although Anwar al-Sadat, designated as the new country's president in October 1970 after the death of Nasser, chose to replace "Arab socialism" with "economic opening" or "infitah" (a change of language rather than of substance), the authoritarian face of the regime not only remained but even grew more important over the years. Indeed, the new president ruled as autocratically as Nasser, though with much less repression, while seeking ever greater legitimacy from the official institutions of Islam. Essentially, the ulama were under control, and the ruling elite had nothing to fear from them. Making sharia the primary source of legislation in the 1971 constitution served that purpose well. As for the Muslim Brotherhood, Sadat decided to resurrect it by releasing the imprisoned Muslim Brothers gradually during the years 1971–5. The official objective was to bring them back so as "to cooperate in the service of the country." In reality, he wanted to broaden his constituency and consolidate his power in the face of a rival faction that controlled the supreme executive committee of the Arab Socialist Union (ASU) and, thanks to its privileged links to the "deep state" of Egypt (the army, the police, and the intelligence service), held seemingly unrivaled political sway.[1] Moreover, he intended to use the Brothers against two political forces that continued to threaten his rule even after he succeeded in

---

[1] On Sadat's accession to the presidency, there was actually an agreement explicitly stating that he should rule collectively, meaning that the supreme executive committee of the ASU (dominated by a faction of Ali Sabri, Sharawi Guma, and Sami Sharaf) should have

eliminating that rival faction: (1) the forces of the political left, consisting of Marxists, socialists, and Nasserites, who criticized his economic liberalization policies, and (2) those of the extreme religious right, the "Jama'at Islamiyya" (the Islamic Group) and the "Takfir wa-l Hijra" (Excommunication and Exodus). In sum, although he was a religious man, the volte face that Sadat committed by allowing the Muslim Brothers to resume their activities, resulted essentially from political calculations. These calculations were part of Sadat's desire to appear as a liberal reformer who had understood the demands of Egyptian people for a more open and representative government (Cook, 2012, p. 124–7).

Sadat allowed the Brotherhood to reestablish its press, including its flagship publication, the magazine *al-Da'wa*; to proselytize openly; and to organize freely on university campuses. He also named a lawyer with strong ties to the Muslim Brotherhood, Kamal Abu Magd, as the new head of the Socialist Youth Organization of the ASU, and a prominent Islamist, Ibrahim Shukri, as director of the Professional Associations Syndicate. These measures would have a profound influence on Egyptian politics. The Muslim Brotherhood gradually took control of the prestigious professional associations of engineers, doctors, lawyers, scientists, and pharmacists (Cook, 2012, pp. 123, 125). In Asyut province, Sadat appointed as governor Muhammad Uthman Ismail, known for his fundamentalist sympathies and anti-Christian proclivities. Because he was able to remain in this post for an unusually long term (from 1973 to 1982, until Mubarak removed him), he had ample time to manipulate the sectarian strife until it reached the brink of a civil war. It is perhaps no coincidence that two of the most famous Egyptian ideologues, Sayyid Qutb and Shukri Mustafa, as well as a very high percentage of the membership of the militant Islamist groupings, came from this province (Ayubi, 1991, p. 168; Dreyfuss, 2005, p. 153).

The so-called neo-Muslim Brothers, whose opinions were voiced in *al-Da'wa*, were in complete accordance with the official ideology of Sadat when they fought against communism, which they considered tantamount to atheism. It is unsurprising, therefore, that on several occasions the government authorized them to organize meetings to denounce Assad, the president of Syria, or to support Muslim fighters in Afghanistan. Even more strikingly, *al-Da'wa*'s demand for the gradual Islamization of the Egyptian state was taken up by the state itself when Abu Talib, president of the People's Assembly and a close ally of the regime, kept on repeating that Egypt would

a say on all issues of importance and that the National Assembly, dominated by the same triumvirate, should vote on all significant matters of policy (Cook, 2012, p. 114).

apply the sharia some day soon (Ramadan, 1993, pp. 164–78; Kepel, 2005, pp. 105–31).

In spite of his shrewd political maneuvering, Sadat was treading on a tightrope because the people of Egypt expected him to end the country's humiliation at the hands of the Israelis. In the words of Cook, "Sadat was in the unenviable position of being judged almost solely on how he handled the collective national affront that Israel's occupation of Egyptian land represented" (Cook, 2012, p. 127). His apparent stalling, despite his public commitments to retaliate against the enemy, caused an outpouring of frustration that was first expressed on university campuses in 1972. The success of the demonstrations, which were initiated by students of all hues, including Islamists, Nasserists, and leftists, made it clear that the opposition was far broader than the regime admitted and that it was difficult to disentangle demands for democratic reforms from demands for military redress (pp. 129–30). To counter these threats, the authorities did not hesitate to encourage religious militant movements and even support them, organizationally and financially (Ayubi, 1991, pp. 74–5). Reminiscent of the early days of the Muslim Brotherhood when the terrorist secret apparatus grew out of athletic youth camps, the movement called Islamic Community organized government-sponsored summer camps. These camps were held with increasing frequency during the post–1973 years, and in 1974, Sadat managed to organize Islamic Community's takeover of the Egyptian Student Union. He also issued a decree providing that the Union's chief purpose was "to deepen religious values among the students" (Dreyfuss, 2005, p. 154). Around the same time, the successful crossing of the Suez Canal by Egyptian troops in the opening phase of the 1973 war contributed in no small measure to healing the deep nationalist wounds of June 1967. Suddenly, Sadat became the "Hero of the Crossing," and the ensuing national euphoria provided him "with a reservoir of popular support for the first time since he took office" (Cook, 2012, p. 135).

Two main policies followed by Sadat were to seal his fate, however. First, his policy of economic opening and liberalization, known as the "infitah" (opening), widened the gap between the masses and an emerging class of new wealthy businessmen connected to the regime. When subsidies on basic necessities were reduced at the behest of the International Monetary Fund, causing suffering among the lower and lower middle classes, their response was swift and caught Sadat off guard. What came to be known as the "bread riots" forced him to backtrack on implementing economic meaures. Even more consequential was the second policy choice: striking peace with Israel in the aftermath of the 1973 war, through the privileged mediation of the United States. The warming of relations between Egypt and the United States went hand in hand with the development of a close personal relationship between Sadat and Henry Kissinger, then the U.S. secretary of state. These daring moves were bitterly resented by many Egyptians, all the more because they coincided with a Westernization of the society for the benefit of the few. The opposition by the Islamists and the Nasserites was particularly vocal (Cook, 2012, pp. 135–43).

After Sadat accepted to go to Jerusalem and to sign a peace treaty with Israel in March 1979, the opposition to his rule became more bold, open, and broad based than it had ever been, infiltrating even the benches of the People's Assembly. Because the treaty was too heavily weighted in favor of Israel, amounting to a separate peace treaty between Israel and Egypt instead of the comprehensive settlement of the Israeli-Arab conflict, including the Palestinian question, that Sadat had announced, Egypt became a pariah in the Arab world.[2] It must be borne in mind that "many Egyptians neither recognize the historic Jewish attachment to Palestine nor Zionism as a legitimate movement of national liberation. … In the Egyptian narrative, Britain midwifed, France fostered, and the United States nurtured Israel all in an effort to split the region and dominate its resources." It is therefore not surprising that Sadat was considered to have sacrificed "the Palestinian cause, Egyptian honour, and Cairo's power for very little" (Cook, 2012, pp. 231–2).

The ulama belonging to the official establishment came to Sadat's rescue when the shaykh of al-Azhar issued a fatwa in May 1979, called the "Islamic Opinion" and the "Religious Legal Verdict," to provide religious sanctioning of the peace treaty and the Camp David Agreement. The justification rested on carefully selected Quranic verses and on the treaties that Muhammad himself concluded with the Qurayshites and the Ghatafan tribes to establish peace in Arabia (Ramadan, 1993, p. 169; Kepel, 2005, pp. 51, 116; Marsot, 2007, pp. 163–5). Interestingly, the Religious Legal Verdict canceled a previous fatwa issued by al-Azhar to the effect of forbidding peace with Israel (1962).

In contrast to the enduring alliance between official Islam and the autocratic regime of Sadat, the climate of cooperation with the Muslim Brotherhood sharply deteriorated after the negotiation of the peace treaty with Israel. Given the nature of the agreement and the unilateral nature of Sadat's move, it became impossible for the neo-Muslim Brothers to refrain from

---

[2] Arab governments punished Egypt through economic sanctions, moved the headquarters of the Arab League from Cairo to Tunis, and suspended Egypt's membership in the organization (Cook, 2012, p. 151).

openly challenging the regime. The Brotherhood thus called for an abrogation of the treaty, a return to military options regarding Israel, and nonalignment (Cook, 2012, pp. 151–2). More radical Islamist groups, such as the Islamist student associations that rapidly developed after 1972 thanks to discreet, tactical collaboration with the regime keen on breaking the left's domination of the campuses, went much further by denouncing the Islamic illegitimacy of the "iniquitous prince" and even fanning the flames of sectarian tension between Muslims and the Christian Copts. For the Jama'at Islamiyya, indeed, making peace with Israel was "munkar," meaning absolute evil or abomination, and rescinding the peace treaty was the first commandment of Islam (Kepel, 2005, p. 163). This tension was compounded by the deteriorating economic situation, rising inequality, and the unabashed corruption of the regime. In the food riots of January 1977, bearded youths set fire to nightclubs and cabarets, considering that the belly dancing and other sinful activities around these places were a serious affront to Islam, especially during the holy month of Ramadan (Ayubi, 1991, p. 75). The religious symbolism and idiom of the Islamist movements increasingly became "the language through which the petite bourgeoisie and lower classes expressed not only their resentment of corruption, decadence and inequality, but also their hostility towards the very state machine that embodied these evils" (Gilsenan, 1982, pp. 225–6, as cited by Ayubi, 1991, p. 80).

In an attempt to pacify the Islamists, Sadat amended Article 2 of the constitution, which addressed the relationship of the sharia to Egypt's law. The new text read, "Islam is the religion of the state and Arabic its official language. Principles of Islamic law are the principal source of legislation." In addition to the constitutional changes, Sadat introduced the Law for the Protection of the Internal Front and Social Peace (known as the "Law of Shame"), which criminalized all forms of opposition to the government. According to the statute, indeed, almost any opposition could be interpreted as violating public, religious, and national morals, and these violations were considered criminal offenses (Cook, 2012, p. 153). At the same time, Sadat adopted the public posture of a pious leader, putting on a religious face and cultivating an image of a good Muslim. In the mass media, he thus appeared in his white "jallabiya," going to the mosque "with a rosary in one hand, Moses's stick in the other, and with a prayer mark on his forehead," murmuring a prayer, closing his eyes, and showing signs of humility and devotion. Moreover, he would start every speech with the words "in the name of God" and end with citations of verses from the Quran (Hanefi, 1982, p. 63; cited from Ayubi, 1991, p. 75; Esposito, 2002, p. 86). In the same hypocritical vein, Sadat responded to the Islamist objection to belly dancing by decreeing that the activity could continue during the holy month provided that each performance included some religious songs in between the usual dances (Ayubi, 1991, p. 75). It was too late, however, and even these affectations of religiosity only had the effect of evoking sarcastic comments; Sadat was derisively given the title of "Believer-President."

When, under the impulse of the Muslim Brotherhood, a coalition of Islamic groups came together to form a consolidated organizational framework, the Permanent Islamic Congress for the Propagation of Islam, it became clear that Sadat's policy of balancing the political left had created a counterforce endangering his foreign policy and threatening his regime. The regime had nurtured "the snake that would later strike it" (Kepel, 2005, p. 138). A succession of repressive measures were taken against Islamists, including shutting down Islamist camps and the private mosques under the control of Islamist groups, placing other mosques under direct government supervision, banning Islamist newspapers, and arresting many militants. Other strands of the political opposition were also hit in the massive crackdown that the regime perpetrated in September 1981.[3] During the next month, the mounting tension was ended when Sadat was assassinated by an extremist from the "al-Jihad" (Sacred Combat) group, of which many members had previously belonged to the Jama'at (Ibrahim, 1995a, pp. 53–68; Kepel, 2005, pp. 16, 51–9, 105–68; Marsot, 2007, Chaps. 6–7; Cook, 2012, pp. 147–56).[4]

Mubarak: Manipulating the Official Ulama and Demonizing the Islamists

Like Sadat, Mubarak began his term of office by releasing political prisoners, including leaders of the Muslim Brotherhood. Yet, the lull was not to last long. Mubarak, like Sadat before him, believed that the strategic partnership between Egypt and the United States was the only way to provide the resources necessary for rapid economic development. Hence, he engaged Egypt on the side of the United States in the First Gulf War, a move that was duly rewarded by the cancellation of a large portion of the Egyptian debt. Egypt was thus led to follow the American initiatives in the Middle

[3] In a preemptive move, Sadat arrested 1,500 people, most of whom were radical Islamists, though many secular opponents of all political shades were also detained. He threatened that if the Islamists did not behave themselves, he would arrest 5,000 more (Ayubi, 1991, p. 76).

[4] It is out of disillusionment with the Jama'at's hesitancy and lack of national strategy that some militants joined the al-Jihad group, "which offered the prospect of rapid and violent action" (Kepel, 2005, pp. 212–13).

East, first channelling U.S. weaponry to Iraq to support Saddam Hussein against Iran and then turning against him after the invasion of Kuwait by Iraqi troops. The political opposition, in particular the Muslim Brotherhood, the Left, and the Nasserists, deeply resented the subservient attitude of Egyptian rulers toward the United States. For them, that the United States was the privileged friend and supporter of Israel made the U.S.-Egyptian strategic relationship that Mubarak nurtured during the 1980s all the more unacceptable on grounds of national pride and sovereignty (Cook, 2012, pp. 161–2).

Opposition from Islamists, especially members of the Jama'at, turned violent, and their killing campaign was directed against representatives of the ruling elite (Mubarak himself was targeted in 1995), critics of Islamic fundamentalism (the writer Farag Foda), and foreign tourists alike. To this violence, the government responded energetically. It declared war on the extremists and their supporters, rounding up the leaders of al Jama'at and al-Jihad. Simultaneously, it used the religious establishment of the country to delegitimize Islamic extremism: both the grand shaykh of al-Azhar and the grand mufti (the highest religious authority in the country) issued fatwas condemning the violence of al Jama'at (Cook, 2012, pp. 165–6).

The government decided to portray the Muslim Brotherhood, which had not engaged in violence since the 1940s, as the "intellectual fount" of the violent wave that had crippled the country. In the words of Cook, "this was a purposeful misrepresentation that provided the government a justification – albeit a flimsy one – to go after the Brotherhood, which had begun to pose its own nonviolent challenge to the authority of the Egyptian state" (Cook, 2012, p. 165). Indeed, it was during the early 1990s that the organization manifested its social concerns by helping the poor and the victims of natural disasters (the Heliopolis earthquake in October 1992), in stark contrast to the ineffectiveness and apparently callous indifference of the Egyptian state. By demonizing the Brotherhood, Mubarak made the same mistake that Sadat did in misrepresenting the political objectives of the Permanent Islamic Congress: He conflated it with the extremist groups, thereby overlooking the fact that the Brothers attempted "to absorb the extremism which embodied the real danger to the regime" (Ramadan, 1993, p. 172). Mubarak also pursued Sadat's tactic of divide-and-rule by instructing his secret police to prop up Islamic fundamentalists, the Salafists known also as a counterforce to the Muslim Brothers. Indeed, because of their ideology of nonintervention in worldly affairs, the Salafists were perceived as unthreatening to his regime (*Economist*, September 13–19, 2008, p. 32).

The political situation continued to deteriorate. Probably the most important reason was the unpopularity of Mubarak's economic policies, which involved privatization and liberalization without concern for equity or the predicament of the masses. What emerged was a partisan regime prejudiced in favor of a small class of very wealthy people closely enmeshed in the ruling clique and insensitive to the suffering of growing numbers. It was a deeply authoritarian state – a police state in the hands of big business, the armed forces, the internal security services, and the bureaucracy. The preeminence of the intelligence barons (the ill-famed "mukhâbarât"), who also managed to occupy key positions in the import and export organizations and in the foreign service, probably constituted the strongest line of continuity between the successive regimes of Nasser, Sadat, and Mubarak (Filiu, 2015, p. 55). From 2005 to 2010, a variety of pro-democracy amendments were made to the constitution and to national legislation, such as the organization of multiparty elections. Yet, they were all phoney changes: None had the effect of opening up the political system. For example, close examination of the revised law on political parties revealed that it was as restrictive as the one it replaced; although it dropped the stipulation that political parties must adhere to principles of national unity and Islamic law, the law placed new restrictions on groups seeking recognition as a political party. Vote rigging, a plethora of legal and institutional subterfuges, and an increasingly dependent judiciary system convinced the vast majority of people that no legal ways existed for seeking redress for their grievances and changing their leaders (Cook, 2012, pp. 183–92). In a nutshell, the amendments just "sought to ensure the non-democratic status quo under the guise of reform" while "all the talks of robust checks and balances could not hide the fact that Egypt's political system was rigged in favour of a core constituency" (p. 191).

Under the cover of another political party, first the Wafd Party and later the Labour Party, the Brothers were able to enter the parliament, capturing one-fifth of parliamentary seats at the 2005 parliamentary elections. There is no doubt that blunt police intervention at the polls prevented them from earning a larger victory. However, because of their minority standing, they could not exert significant influence. Still, the government was clearly worried, given that the Brothers won every seat they contested and did much better than anyone, particularly among official circles, expected. The aforementioned constitutional amendments were designed to prevent the Islamists from deriving benefits from their political gains. In particular, Amended Article 5 of the constitution proscribed political activity and parties based on religion, with the immediate effect of banning the

Muslim Brotherhood from all political activity (Cook, 2012, pp. 188–9). After postponing the 2006 municipal elections until early 2008, the government simply disqualified all but a handful of Brotherhood candidates (*Economist*, September 13-19, 2008, p. 32). In addition, Mubara's regime mounted repeated campaigns of harassment and arrest, including confiscation of business assets, to neutralize the Brothers. Although the official reason for the crackdown was that the group's ultimate aim was the establishment of a theocratic state, a claim that was not entirely groundless, the real motivation wasa Mubarak's fear that they would steal away from his regime the members of the pious middle classes whom he coveted and were already the main supporters of the Brothers (Kepel, 2005).

In such a context of increasing socioeconomic polarization and escalating mistrust, the regime maintained tight control over al-Azhar, which continued to produce fatwas that suited the rulers. Some of these religious edicts were so explicit in their underlying political intent that they reflected an attitude of almost obsequious submissiveness. This was clearly the case when the grand shaykh of al-Azhar, Shaykh Sayyed Tantawy, cited a passage of the Quran as support for his opinion that those convicted of libel should be sentenced to eighty lashes. Indeed, several journalists received this punishment after being tried and convicted of publishing false information about members of the ruling National Democratic Party and the president in 2007. Another striking example was a fatwa issued during the same year by the grand mufti, Ali Gomaa; it provided that a driver who runs over and kills someone deliberately standing in the path of the vehicle is not to blame. This judgment was issued just a few days after a woman was killed by a minibus under the control of the police as she tried to stop them from arresting her sister-in-law (*Daily News*, Cairo, December 29–30, 2007). These fatwas have to be placed in the context of an enduring Emergency Law, renewed in 2008 and again in 2010, that "allowed Egyptian authorities to ignore protections against arbitrary arrest, warrantless searches, and violations of privacy when prosecuting terrorism cases" (Cook, 2012, p. 191). Moreover, the term "terrorism" was used in an increasingly expansive sense to refer not only to violent extremists but also to members of the Brotherhood and other opposition activists (p. 191).[5] Even more ironically and cynically, people criticizing the regime – whether journalists, bloggers, intellectuals, or political dissenters – could be arrested at any time on the ground that they were

---

[5] It was highly convenient for Egyptian authorities to justify their emergency practices by referring to the provisions contained in the U.S. Patriot Act, which passed in both houses of Congress in October 2001 by wide margins (Cook, 2012, p. 192).

members of the Muslim Brotherhood, had defamed Islam, or disrupted social harmony (pp. 195–6). Actual practices and informal rules did not leave any room for doubt: No opposition was to be tolerated, and in spite of pseudo-democratic institutions and legal provisions, any argument including the defense of Islam and Egyptian dignity could be used to buttress an official smear campaign against an opponent and send him or her to prison for years.

Soon after the advent of the so-called Arab Spring, which led to the overthrow of Mubarak (during the first months of 2011), the Muslim Brothers won the first post-regime presidential election and Muhammad Morsi became president. In accordance with their declared objectives, the Brothers immediately set to achieve their professed objective of establishing the sharia as the law governing Egypt. This move aroused angry reactions from those who did not share their views and caused a deep fracture inside Egyptian society. The army, which had in the meantime taken a backseat position, seized on this opportunity to expel Morsi from the presidency and resort to the old tactic of harassing and arresting the movement's leaders, including Morsi himself. It even succeeded in getting its new leading commander, Field Marshal Abdel Fattah al-Sisi, elected as the next president of Egypt after he formally shed his uniform. In his campaign, he explained his deep opposition to Islamism, arguing that there had never been a state based on religion in Islam and that Muslim states had always been civil. On this point, he was essentially correct, as previous chapters of this book have shown. Therefore, the religious message of the Muslim Brothers is "not suited to command a state" (*Economist*, May 10-16, 2014, p. 33). Al-Sisi himself happens to be a rather pious man, and one of his daughters wears the niqab, the full face veil, while another wears the hijab, which covers the hair but not the face (*Economist*, August 3–9, 2013, p. 29).

That the ulama of al-Azhar have continuously stood by the state elite and the authoritarian regime it had created reflects a well-established tradition in modern Egypt. As early as 1925, when Ali Abd al-Raziq advocated the separation of religion and politics, arguing that Islam, as a religion, had "no application to temporal governance," the ulama from the official establishment quickly got him dismissed as a judge in the sharia court system (Lee, 2014, p. 52). Similarly, when in the 1930s Khalid Muhammad Khalid equated religious government with tyranny and claimed that religion must not deal with questions of governance and public policy, the scholars from al-Azhar immediately objected that the state has "a continuing need for religious legitimacy in order to neutralize its political Islamist rival, the Brotherhood, and promote its essentially secular policies" (Hatina, 2000, p. 36, as cited by Lee, 2014, p. 53).

Al-Sisi: Keeping the Deep State and Depicting All Opponents as Nonbelievers

Revealingly, when al-Sisi wrenched supreme power from the Muslim Brothers, the victors of the free elections following the Arab Spring, he immediately set out to consolidate his control over religion.[6] In the course of 2014, he closed many mosques and small houses of worship that appoint their own imams and are often owned and controlled by wealthy families or groups, such as Salafists. All imams and preachers not licensed by the government were banned from preaching. To have studied at al-Azhar was now the main qualification for getting a license. As of April 2014, the government estimated that the regulations had led to the dismissal of no less than 12,000 imams, who were quickly replaced by 17,000 newly appointed imams considered to be reliable, thanks to the guarantee of political loyalty provided by al-Azhar. Moreover, throughout the country, the imams were instructed to give the same sermon on Fridays, with al-Azhar serving as the model to be followed (*Economist*, August 2-8, 2014, p. 28).[7] Of course, al-Azhar itself could receive precise instructions as to what should be featured in its sermons. For instance, on the occasion of the lavish opening of the so-called New Suez Canal on August 6, 2015 (a project that expanded the canal's capacity to ninety-seven ships per day), the Ministry of Religious Affairs instructed sermons to cite the Prophet Muhammad's digging of a trench to defend Medina from attackers. The government's scripted sermon drew "useful lessons from the Prophet's example of innovative leadership, among them the unity and continuity of command, mutual love between the commander and his soldiers, and wariness of naysayers" (*Economist*, August 8–14, 2015, p. 25).

In pursuing such a harsh line, al-Sisi went much further than any previous Egyptian president had dared to go, leading the Egyptian state into a direction similar to that taken by the Kemalist state in Turkey, which also sought to take complete control of every aspect of religion: prayer, preaching, teaching, doctrine, and places of worship. Submission to the new ruler by al-Azhar official clerics appears to be complete. Thus, after ousting Morsi in the name of tolerance, inclusiveness, and an end to religious rule, the military themselves adopted a tactic that oddly resembles that of radical Islamist militants advocating violence against political opponents depicted as nonbelievers. Toward that purpose, the army command has sent religious

---

[6] The mandate of President Morsi lasted just one year: It began on June 30, 2012, and was abruptly terminated by a military coup on July 3, 2013.

[7] The sanctions are harsh: Anyone who defies the order risks a year's imprisonment and fines of up to 50,000 Egyptian pounds ($7,000).

messages to its troops that bear the stamp of the highest authority of al-Azhar. Thus, Ali Gomaa, the former mufti appointed under Mubarak, was seen in a videotape destined for soldiers and riot police as saying the following: "When somebody comes who tries to divide you, then kill them, whoever they are. Even with the sanctity and greatness of blood, the prophet permits us to fight this." In the same video made by the military's Department of Moral Affairs, Ali Gomaa likens the opponents of the military takeover to the members of an early Islamic sect who may be considered to be infidels and thus are permissible to kill (Kirkpatrick and El Sheikh, 2013).

According to Emad Shahin from the American University in Cairo, the government of al-Sisi "is waging an all-out war, and using all the weapons at their hands, including religious fatwas, to dehumanise their opponents and justify killing them" (cited by Kirkpatrick and El Sheikh, 2013, p. 4). It is in the name of the key role played by Egypt in the global war against terror that al-Sisi and the military establishment, with the shameless support of the judicial hierarchy, have vindicated their complete hold on political power. Following their definition, the Muslim Brothers could be equated with jihadism. Indeed, they were labeled a terrorist organization, justifying the harshest repression against them (Filiu, 2015, ch. 7).[8] Al-Sisi thus ordered a fierce crackdown on the Brothers, even allowing the police and the military to shoot at unarmed demonstrators in Cairo (in August 2013). The resulting slaughter was "unprecedented in Egyptian contemporary history"; "one has to go back to the ruthless repression of the Cairo riots by the French expeditionary force, in October 1798, to find a comparable level of urban violence" (p. 251).

I concur with Lee's conclusion that "it is the neediness of the state, not the character of Islam or the contingencies of the moment, that best explains the politicization of religion in Egypt" (Lee, 2014, p. 38). More precisely,

the immixture of religion and politics has been a primary characteristic of political development in Egypt since 1800. At every moment, the state has been the driving force toward fusion. It has consistently sought to subjugate Islam to its purposes ... and in this effort at subjugation the state has empowered and politicised the religious sphere. ... Ultimately assaulted by Islamists seeking to subordinate the state to their agenda, the state found itself ever more deeply involved in seeking to manipulate religion to its own advantage. The result was a spiral in the politicization of religion

---

[8] This accusation was proferred despite the lack of evidence of any link between the Muslim Brothers and the "Ansar Beit al-Maqdis" (ABM, literally the "Champions of Jerusalem"), a violent group of jihadists responsible for the killing of Egyptian soldiers in the Sinai Peninsula (Filiu, 2015, p. 181).

and the sanctification of politics that contradicts the predictions of secularization theory. (Lee, 2014, p. 38)

The state that subjugates religion in Egypt is definitely not a "civil state" as al-Sisi claims. Instead of resting on the voice of civil society, it has the army at its command following a long tradition established by Nasser. As in Pakistan, the Egyptian Army is powerful not only in the military sense but also in political and the economic terms. Since the time of Mubarak, indeed, soldiers have been involved in civil administration, and senior officers have occupied important positions in both the state apparatus and the economy, staffing monitoring and administrative agencies as well as local governments. Their role in the economy grew appreciably through the large-scale privatization program launched by Mubarak. Firms owned by the officer corps range from defense manufacturing to consumer goods, and they have become dominant in the marketplace for water, olive oil, cement, construction, hotels and gas. The income thus generated escapes public scrutiny. Army families "inhabit a parallel universe" made of separate military cities, shops, gas stations, recreation facilities, and clubs (*Economist*, August 3, 2013, p. 30).

Case Study 2: Sudan

Nimeiri: Gaining Absolute Power through an Islamic Order
Ibrahim Abbud (1958–1964) rose to power through a military coup, just two years after independence, and established an Islamic military-political complex destined to maintain the territorial unity of Sudan at all cost. He used coercion and brutality amply to create a unified Sudanese nation on the basis of a Muslim-Arab state in a country where Islam was the faith, and Arab the identity, of the northern people only. Such a project led him to introduce Arabic as the only official language of administration and education and to pour Arab teachers, bureaucrats, traders, army, police, and security agents, as well as Muslim preachers, into non-Arab parts of the country, the south in particular.[9] Strongly resisted by the southerners, these Arabization and Islamization policies were responsible for the outbreak of the first north–south civil war (1955–72), which eventually led to the downfall of Abbud's dictatorial regime (Jok, 2007, pp. 54–62, 81–6).[10]

---

[9] Islamic proselytising included the requirement for non-Arab and non-Muslim children in some regions to replace their indigenous names with Arab and Muslim names before they could enroll in school (Jok, 2007, p. 58).

[10] It is therefore not surprising that those living in the south felt that, under these "Sudanization" pressures, they had merely moved from European to Arab colonialism. The situation

A military junta headed by Jaafar Muhammad al-Nimeiri, a thirty-nine-year-old officer, seized power in May 1969 after having overthrown a civilian caretaker government that had ruled the country since October 1964. In a promising move, a new constitution in 1973 established Sudan as a secular state, implying that in civil and criminal matters, civilians' behavior was to be governed by a secular law, whereas personal and family matters were covered by the sharia law for Muslims and customary law for tribal populations of the south. It did not take long, however, for Nimeiri to change course and reinstate Abbud's policies. At the command of a deeply corrupt patrimonial system (vast amounts of foreign funds were embezzled and never invested in the intended projects), which imposed a huge foreign debt on the country, Nimeiri aroused bitter political opposition in both the north and the south. Liberalization policies resulting in abrupt increases in the prices of oil, bread, and sugar prompted widespread riots by students and angry consumers. They also sparked political activism among parties that had always been opposed to Nimeiri, including those representing powerful Islamic sects associated with traditional Sufi orders. These included the "Umma," which was pro-Mahdist and associated with the Ansar sect, and the Democratic Unionist Party (DUP) associated with the Khatmiya sect (Jok, 2007, pp. 72–3, 279).

Confronted with such a determined opposition, Nimeiri's reaction was to engineer a rapprochement with the Islamic fundamentalists and a national reconciliation deal with the Islamic political forces (Umma, DUP, and the Muslim Brothers). In 1977, he took a decisive step toward Islamic politicization of the regime by allowing the entry into his government of two prominent Islamist politicians. One was Ahmad Abd al-Rahman, who served as minister of the interior, and the other was Hassan al-Turabi, leader of the Muslim Brotherhood and founder of the National Islamic Front (NIF), whom Nimeiri had previously imprisoned.[11] Al-Turabi was not only appointed minister of justice and chief public prosecutor but was also later made a member of the politburo of the Sudanese Socialist Union (SSU) and foreign policy adviser to the president – all positions through which he gained considerable political influence. The NIF rapidly infiltrated

---

was even worse than under the British, who had ruled the north and the south of Sudan as two separate entities, which made the handover of the apparatus of the state at the time of independence to the northerners only all the more unacceptable to the southerners (Jok, 2007, p. 79).

[11] Hassan al-Turabi, a Western-educated legal scholar with strong ties to the Muslim Brothers in Egypt, returned to Sudan in 1965 and created the Islamic Charter Front, which eventually changed its name to the National Islamic Front.

student organizations in secondary schools and universities while also making its presence felt in government and private business. As attorney general, Turabi exerted steady pressure for the Islamic reform of the legal system (Lapidus, 1988, p. 859; Ayubi, 1991, pp. 106–7; Jok, 2007, p. 74; El-Affendi, 2014).

In 1982, at the risk of losing his secular support base (except among conservative army officers), Nimeiri began to dismantle the accord of Addis-Ababa (1972) that had ended the first north-south civil war. He wanted to appease Islamist groups such as the NIF that regarded the south as a challenge to Islam and therefore believed that allowing secularism in the south was not an acceptable compromise. In September 1983, Nimeiri completely reversed his previous policy by declaring an "Islamic revolution" and transforming the Sudanese state into an Islamic republic to be governed by Islamic law, with no exemption for non-Muslim regions. Sudanese law was to be immediately reformed according to the sharia, and the so-called September Laws, which sanctioned the use of physical punishment ("hudud"), gave rise to highly publicized public executions, amputations of limbs for theft, and lashings for alcohol consumption (Jok, 2007, pp. 74–76). The autonomy of the south ended, its fiscal prerogatives and budgetary responsibilities returned to Khartoum, and its armed forces put under the control of the central government (Duffy Toft, 2007, p. 122). By establishing his new "Islamic order," Nimeiri claimed that he was fighting the religious sectarianism operating through the conventional party system and striving to establish "a more integrated, cooperative society based on true Islam" (Ayubi, 1991, p. 108).

In his quest for absolute political power, Nimeiri attempted, albeit unsuccessfully, to proclaim himself as Imam, or an Islamic spiritual leader, accountable only to Allah.[12] Moreover, he demanded an oath of unconditional allegiance from all members of the civil service and judiciary, thereby causing the departure of prominent secularists and the overtaking of the civil service, the army and the financial sector by Islamists (de Waal, 1997, p. 88). Members of the NIF and the Muslim Brotherhood were thus left free to wield influence within the civil service, intelligence agencies, and institutions of government dealing with education and welfare.

---

[12] At the same time, Nimeiri wanted, but failed, to pass the following amendments to the constitution: an open presidential term for life, the right of the president to appoint his successor, presidential immunity from any questioning or trial, unaccountability of the courts headed by the president, the entrusting of the higher judiciary council to the president, and the punishment of any move to renege on the president's appointment on the charge of high treason (Ayubi, 1991, p. 108).

More ominously still, Nimeiri let Turabi draft the Criminal Bill, which was presented to parliament in 1988. It included a provision for outlawing apostasy that was sufficiently vague to allow its application to be politically determined (de Waal, 1997, p. 91; Meredith, 2005, pp. 356–7; El-Affendi, 2014). Nimeiri's public execution in 1985 of Mahmud Muhammad Taha – the eighty-year-old founder and leader of the Republican Brothers, a renowned scholar of Islamic theology, and a human rights activist – together with four of his followers on the charge of apostasy, offers a perfect illustration of the cynical use that could be made of such a bill. The crime committed by Taha was to criticize the government's application of the sharia laws as "cruel, based blindly on tradition rather than the tolerant spirit of Islam" (*Economist*, June 7-13, 2014, p. 37). Nimeiri also imprisoned Sadiq al-Mahdi, the leader of the Ansar who had joined the SSU for only a brief period and had dared criticize the pace and the methods by which the sharia was introduced.

The fact that any opposition to an Islamic government became defined as an act of apostasy was used to persecute not only secular Muslims and other political opponents but also other Islamic sects, such as the Khatmiya, Ansar, and Ansar-Sunnah, that threatened the ruling clique (Johnson, 2003, p. 129). In the light of such events, it is not surprising that many Muslims from the northern part of the country regarded the new-found Islamic piety of Nimeiri as a hypocritical posture partaking of a sinister political game (Jok, 2007, p. 159). The game was especially shocking because punishment for violation of the sharia law and the crime of apostasy was imposed summarily, arbitrarily, and cruelly by special emergency courts, which were formed by the president or his delegates and consisted of three individuals, one or two of whom were military or police officers. Their judgments were often passed, frequently in a televised performance, on the same day as the arrest, and the accused were deprived of any legal assistance and any right of appeal (Ayubi, 1991, p. 108).

The End of the Idyll

The end of Nimeiri's regime proved catastrophic as Sudan descended into a second round of a north–south civil war (1983), ran into acute economic difficulties, and was hit by a deadly famine (1983–5). When a wave of strikes and popular uprisings broke out in Khartoum in early 1984, one of the most effective ones being organized by doctors, Nimeiri reacted by enacting emergency laws. These laws were supported by Turabi, who claimed that they had precedent in Islamic tradition. Nonetheless, the social and political situation continued to deteriorate so quickly, and the new "Islamic

Order" brought such serious dislocations in the state machinery, that things quickly got out of control. The Islamic movement eventually realized that Nimeiri's dictatorial regime, even though it had made the first attempt to codify Islamic jurisprudence and create an Islamic state, was no longer worth supporting. Not long after Turabi and other Islamist leaders were arrested and detained (January 1985), a massive popular movement started by students and rapidly joined by the lumpenproletariat, the professional unions, and a substantial proportion of all popular forces led to the removal of Nimeiri in March 1985. The Islamists' falling out with Nimeiri shortly before he was deposed and their participation in the civil rebellion against him not only "saved the movement from the fate of total popular disgrace" but also enabled the Islamists to emerge as a major political force in Sudan (Ayubi, 1991, pp. 109–10).

After a one-year interlude during which the Transitional Military Council ruled the country, elections were organized, and Sadiq al-Mahdi, leader of the Umma Party, was chosen as prime minister (1986). In these elections, the National Islamic Front, which continued to have distant relations with Sufi groups (Ansar and Khatmiya) behind the two main political parties, had won almost one-quarter of the elected seats, thus representing the third largest parliamentary party and the main opposition force. The opposition that it mounted against the coalition government was strong: It vehemently opposed any reversal of the sharia laws passed under Nimeiri and any attempt at reconciliation with the non-Muslim south. Unaddressed socioeconomic problems led to escalating riots and demonstrations throughout the country, and the ability of the NIF to launch well-organized demonstrations by students and urban forces made it a potent destabilizing force.[13] This explains why the ruling government was keen to dislodge the NIF from its critical position toward the regime by inviting it into an enlarged coalition government (May 1988). Seven Islamist ministers were thus appointed, including Turabi as the minister of justice and prosecutor general and, somewhat later, as minister of foreign affairs (Ayubi, 1991, pp. 111–12).

These efforts at greater inclusiveness were of no avail because the country's socioeconomic problems were not properly addressed and the NIF remained intransigent regarding any attempt to strike a deal with southern rebel forces (despite the more conciliatory attitude of the army itself). Especially contentious was the government's plan to appease the south by

---

[13] Many of the recruits for these demonstrations came from the new middle class, people with modern education and often some Sufi family background who studied or worked in big cities, especially Khartoum.

delaying the issuing of an Islamic penalties law that had been prepared to replace the one passed under Nimeiri. Tension on the latter score was all the greater because the NIF was encouraging the formation of militias known as "People's Defense Forces" destined to confront the rebellion in the south. In March 1989, after the DUP, which favored a settlement with the south, had already withdrawn from the coalition, the NIF decided to opt out of it as well (Ayubi, 1991, pp. 112–13; Jok, 2007, pp. 132–3).

Al-Bashir: Restoring Nimeiri's System

In June 1989, Brigadier (later General) Omer al-Bashir seized power through a bloodless military coup. A devout and ruthless soldier, al-Bashir acted as the frontline player for the NIF and its charismatic leader, al-Turabi. Bashir immediately professed his goal of creating a theocratic rather than a democratic state, and soon he re-created the apparatus of Nimeiri's police state in more extreme form and promulgated the Sudanese Penal Code of 1991, which included the aforementioned provision on the crime of apostasy.[14] He also formed his own Islamic militia, and training was made compulsory for civil servants, teachers, students, and higher education candidates. All rights of free expression and belief were outlawed, and participation in public protests in opposition to the government's policies was considered not only a treasonable offense but also an insult to Islam. The message was unambiguously conveyed to all potential opponents through the summary execution of twenty-eight senior officers of the Sudanese Armed Forces and of an unknown number of businessmen on charges of corruption, money laundering, and illegal currency trading. All the executions were carried out in the name of the sharia law. As for leaders of student groups, unions, professional associations, and political parties, many were arrested and disappeared into "ghost houses" and prisons, where they were tortured or murdered (de Waal, 1997, p. 98; Johnson, 2003, p. 128; Meredith, 2005, p. 589; Jok, 2007, p. 162; Duffy Toft, 2007, pp. 123–4).

The Arabization and Islamization policies of the previous junta were actively pursued with dreadful consequences. People in the south were forced to renounce their faith and embrace Islam in order to be eligible for food aid (a major famine occurred in 1990–1), and their churches and schools were demolished under the pretext that they were built in violation of zoning regulations. In the Darfur region, a nasty conflict between

---

[14] In addition, a presidential decree in 1991 limited women's activities and imposed on them strict dress codes to be enforced by the "Guardians of Morality and Advocates of the Good" (Meredith, 2005, p. 589).

sedentary farmers and semi-nomad herders developed as a result of the increasing scarcity of land resources. Darfur had suffered from almost continuous droughts for close to thirty years and experienced a particularly severe famine in the years 1984–5. But the government remained strangely passive when herders, both Muslim and Arab, armed themselves to force their way into the grazelands occupied by farmers, mostly Muslim but non-Arab.[15] Given al-Bashir's conception of Sudan as the possession of an Arabized elite, such passivity was interpreted as a sign that the government was siding with the Arab groups (Jok, 2007, pp. 89–90, 120–7). The government of Khartoum reacted to the bloodshed in Darfur with continued politicization of Islam and Arabism. It is revealing that, when the idea of United Nations involvement was initially proposed, the proposal was immediately presented as a "conspiracy against the Arab and Islamic world" (*Economist*, March 4–10, 2006, p. 39).

During the period from 1990 to 1999, al-Turabi was a dominant force in Sudanese politics. He became the speaker of the national assembly and acted energetically to make Sudan a base for extremists from all over the Islamic world, including Osama bin Laden (Jok, 2007, pp. 136–7). A clash eventually erupted between al-Bashir and al-Turabi, and the latter was dismissed from the post of speaker of the national assembly. From then on, his political influence declined while al-Bashir was able to consolidate his grip over power, partly as a result of his newly forged alliance with the United States following his discontinuation of hospitality toward international Islamic terrorists. The fact remains that in Sudan "the bidding process forced religion to the center of what had started as a conflict over the distribution of offices and economic resources" (Duffy Toft, 2007, p. 125). The result has been catastrophic, as manifested in lethal famines and one of the longest and most brutal civil wars in the twentieth century. Eventually, the country split after the government of Khartoum accepted the results of a referendum organized in the southern part of the country about the question of its independence (in 2011).

Case Study 3: Pakistan

Opportunist Politicians, Religious Extremists, and the Army

Jinnah, the founder of Pakistan, was a committed constitutionalist for whom religious or caste affiliations were irrelevant to the business of the state. He

---

[15] In the first category fall groups such as the Baggara and the Zaghawa, whereas in the second category we find groups such as the Fur and the Masalit.

said, "Pakistan is not going to be a theocratic state to be ruled by priests with a divine mission" (cited by Abbas, 2005, p. 19). In contrast, his successors proved to be essentially opportunistic politicians ready to ally with extremist religious leaders to increase their power and privileges or to promote national interests.[16] As a result, soon after the untimely death of Jinnah, the religious forces under the leadership of Sayyid Abul Mawdûdi, also called Maulana Mawdûdi, started to assert themselves and unite in trying to confer an Islamic character on the Pakistani state. To withstand these pressures, the army had to be called on. In 1953, Mumtaz Daultana, an ambitious minister of finance who wanted to become prime minister in Punjab province, allowed a criminal agitation by religious fanatics to take place that questioned the Muslim identity of the prosperous Ahmadi community[17], thus forcing the army to intervene and restore order. Such a scenario in which religious extremists and the army laid increasing claim to power at the expense of incompetent and corrupt politicians was to repeat itself again and again, sowing the seeds of Pakistan's tragedy. In the words of Hassan Abbas (2005),

In these circumstances the only commonly shared notion of nationhood was Islam. Thus the political leadership of the day was frequently forced to fall back on the slogan of Islam to bring order out of chaos. And here lay the central dilemma of the Pakistan Muslim League and other like-minded parties, a majority of whose leadership in these early years was either secular, or at the very least moderate enough to abhor the prospect of religion being formally inducted into politics. They wanted to appeal to the slogan of Islam to forge national unity and discipline, but they did not want it to go any further than that. But the moment this slogan was out of the bag,

---

[16] The idea of creating a separate Indian Muslim state was first put forward by Sir Mohammed Iqbal (1876–1938) in 1930. Characterization of the difference between Christianity and Islam in the thought of Iqbal is very close to the account given by Bernard Lewis. Unlike what is observed in Christianity, religion for a Muslim is not a matter of private conscience or practice. There never was a specifically Christian polity, and in Europe after Luther, the "universal ethics of Jesus" was "displaced by national systems of ethics and polity." In Islam, there cannot be a Luther because there is no Islamic church order for a Muslim to revolt against. Muslims, to be true to Islam, need a Muslim polity, a Muslim state in which to enforce their religious ideal. This ideal, indeed, is organically related to the social order that corresponds to it so that the rejection of the latter will eventually lead to the rejection of the former (Naipaul, 1982, pp. 88–9). Jinnah was driven by secular ambitions and only wanted a state where Muslims would not be swamped by non-Muslims (p. 90).

[17] The Ahmadis are a controversial sect and a peaceable school of Islam that believe in the separation of religion and state. It was created in the nineteenth century by Mirza Ghulam Ahmad, an Indian who is considered a prophet by most Ahmadis. The sect claims to be Muslim, but refuses to recognize the finality of Prophet Muhammad's message or the obligation of jihad (Haqqani, 2005, p. 106).

it was up for grabs, and none but the religious parties was better qualified to pick it up and take it to its natural conclusion, that is, the call for an Islamic state with an Islamic constitution. (p. 30)

This vicious pattern seemed to be broken when in 1958 General Ayub Khan, commander-in-chief of the Pakistani army, seized power in a palace coup. He believed that mixing politics and religion would be detrimental to both and renamed the country simply the Republic of Pakistan (thus dropping the word Islamic). He was convinced that Islam should be interpreted in a liberal manner and in the context of the modern world. He did not, therefore, hesitate to introduce the Family Law Ordinance (1961), which aimed at emancipating the lot of women in Pakistan to the great dislike of the mullahs. He also cracked down on religious hard-liners; exerted greater control over the political influence of Sufi orders (particularly, that of big shrine-related families); banned the extremist religious party founded by Mawdûdi, the Jama'at-i-Islami (JI); and considered the possibility of integrating the curriculum of religious schools into modern secular education. Nevertheless, he started to rescind nearly all progressive measures that he had previously taken so as to hold the dogmatic version of Islam at bay. A plausible explanation for this complete turnaround is that Ayub needed to protect himself against the justified accusations of corruption of his family and the courtiers around him (Abbas, 2005, pp. 37–54). Support of religious authorities, down to local-level Sufi masters, became crucial for a leader whose integrity had been dented by the prebendiary behavior of his close entourage (Malik and Mirza, 2015, p. 9; Jones, 2002, pp. 14–15).

General Yahya Khan who succeeded Ayub as president of Pakistan had only a short spell in power. It was under his tenure, indeed, that the Pakistan Army was dealt a humiliating blow at the hands of the army of the arch-enemy (India), a defeat that caused the tragic loss of the eastern part of the country (1971). This was a traumatic experience for Pakistan's people for whom the triumphant propaganda of the regime had left them completely unprepared for the partition of their newly born nation: Was not Almighty Allah siding with Pakistan? Another nasty legacy of Yahya's adventurous policies is the unhealthy alliance that he fostered between the national security establishment and the Islamists. To fight Bengali forces the army did not hesitate to encourage Islamist groups, especially the student wing of the JI, to launch paramilitary counterinsurgency units. Seeing themselves "as the sun and the crescent of Islamic revival in South Asia," these brigades allegedly operated as death squads to assassinate Bangladeshi left-wing intellectuals and doctors (Haqqani, 2005, pp. 79–86).

Bhutto: A Secular Leader Using Islam as a Political Expedient

After the demise of Yahya Khan, Zulfikar Ali Bhutto became president and the first civilian chief martial law administrator of the country. Before assuming power, he had been a modern, left-oriented politician with social democratic ideas. The 1973 constitution, which he helped institute, was not an unambiguously progressive step, however. Although it outlawed military coups as acts of high treason, it also declared Islam to be the state religion (Article 2), provided that all existing laws were to be brought into conformity with the injunctions of Islam (Article 227), and prescribed that the tenets of Islam and the Quran should be taught in schools (Article 31). A provision was also included that declared the Ahmadis to be non-Muslims, a decision soon followed by the creation of the Ministry of Religious Affairs (Abbas, 2005, pp. 81–2).

Bhutto genuinely wanted to weaken the generals' potential hold on power, implying that the government would cease to rely on them to bolster its fortunes. The circumstances were favorable since the army had been humiliated after surrendering to Indian forces and losing the territory of East Pakistan in December 1971 (Siddiqa, 2017, p. 91). Very soon, however, new circumstances arose that thwarted Bhutto's plan: A separatist insurgency in Balochistan (instigated by Marri tribe militants) led him to dismiss the government of that region and to call on men in uniform to reestablish order in the country (1972). The military's credentials as the savior of Pakistan's unity could thus be reestablished shortly after the war lost against India (Abbas, 2005, pp. 77–81; Haqqani, 2005, pp. 102–3). More ominously, still, Bhutto boosted the role of the security services, which he used for various purposes: spying on his political opponents, fabricating accusations against them, disrupting opposition meetings, harassing critics, gathering intelligence on threats to national security, and shaping events through their covert operations and their secret links to extremist religious organizations (Haqqani, 2005, pp. 109–11). During the repressive operations in Balochistan, in May 1973, Bhutto created a paramilitary force, the Federal Security Force (FSF), which was placed under his direct control and led to the killing of about six thousand Baloch people. This initiative irked the generals, who suspected Bhutto of trying to minimize the role of the military (Siddiqa, 2017, pp. 94–5). His attempt to control the growth of the army's commercial ventures was also seen as an inimical gesture destined to weaken it.[18]

---

[18] The Pakistani army had access to a large amount of capital that, unlike the money allocated to the defense industry, was not recorded in the budget and did not follow the normal accountability rules of the state. It was used for the personal benefit of the military fraternity, especially the officer cadre (Siddiqa, 2017, p. 5).

Bhutto's proclivity to appeal to Islam and advocate the Islamization of the country out of political expediency became increasingly apparent (Nomani and Rahnema, 1994, p. 121). As attested by his surrender to the JI's demands to exclude the Ahmadi sect from the Muslim community, he took over the religious parties' agenda, encouraged the expression of sectarian opinion, and tilted toward an obscurantist interpretation of Islam. Bhutto's shift toward religious conservatism was a clever move not only because he could thus overtake his political opponents and balance the influence of the military, but also because he could thus push forward his economic and national security agendas (Haqqani, 2005, pp. 107–9; Paul, 2014, pp. 137–8). On the occasion of the Arab oil embargo (1973), indeed, Bhutto wanted Pakistan to benefit from the flow of petrodollars, which required that the country's Islamic identity be emphasized. As a way to achieve that objective, the Islamic summit conference was hosted in Lahore, and Pakistan took the lead in creating permanent structures for the Organization of Islamic Cooperation (OIC). The immediate result was Pakistan's recognition as a leading power in the Muslim world. In the wake of these events, Bhutto reopened the discussion of Pakistan's national identity, and in encouraging the country's self-definition as an ideological state he echoed the views of the Islamists.

This move away from his avowed ideal of a progressive Pakistan was again confirmed when Bhutto decided to use right-wing Islamic dissidents from Afghanistan to destabilize the regime of Muhammad Daoud, who had seized power in Kabul through a state coup on July 17, 1973. That is how the government of Pakistan came to back Gulbuddin Hekhmatyar, a radical Islamist and a member of the political opposition to Daoud whose secular and nationalist outlook secured him the alliance of Afghan communists. The support, which included military training from the Pakistani army, was not ideological but strategic: Because the Afghan Islamists were opposed to a nationalist ideology and to the claim made at Kabul regarding Pashtunistan, they were objectively the best defenders of Pakistan's integrity (Roy, 1990, pp. 74–6; 1993, p. 495).[19] The Islamist faction

---

[19] The Pashtun people never really accepted Afghanistan's frontier with British India that was drawn by Sir Mortimer Durand in 1893. Laid down with a view to preventing Pashtun tribes from becoming a nuisance for the Raj, the border, known as the Durand Line, "formally divided the Pashtuns into two roughly equal parts with a total lack of consideration of their own tribal organisation, history, or geography" (Magnus and Naby, 2002, p. 36; see also Haqqani, 2005, p. 160; Rasanayagam, 2005, pp. 29–33). When the creation of Pakistan became inevitable, Afghanistan demanded the creation of a Pashtun state, Pashtunistan, that would link the Pashtun tribes living in Afghanistan with those in the North-Western Frontier Province and Balochistan (located in Pakistan). Daoud, together with the Pashtun nationalists and the communists who backed him, believed that active engagement by Afghanistan's government on behalf of Baloch and Pashtun groups in Pakistan might force

run by Hekhmatyar was to play a decisive role in subsequent events unfolding in Afghanistan.

When the opportunity arose, Bhutto placed General Zia ul-Haq at the top of the army, over the heads of a half-dozen senior and more deserving generals. An obsequious but ambitious man, Zia was also a devout Muslim closely connected to several Islamists by virtue of his social and family origins. Without any objection from Bhutto, he quickly changed the credo of the Pakistani army to "Faith, Piety, and Jihad for the Sake of God" and organized mosques and prayer halls in all army units (Abbas, 2005, p. 91; Haqqani, 2005, pp. 111–13).

Bhutto's authoritarian tendencies and unpopular policies (e.g., the nationalization of private schools and colleges, which caused a considerable decline in the standard of education) became widely criticized, so much so that all the major opposition parties, from the religious right to the left, united in an unholy election alliance under the name of the Pakistan National Alliance (PNA). To the opposition demonstrations, in which street agitation led by Islamic groups played an important role, Bhutto responded by claiming more Islamic credentials than he attributed to political rivals: He declared gambling and horseracing illegal, banned the sale and use of alcohol, and made Friday the weekly holiday (Abbas, 2005, pp. 82–5). These measures did not prevent the ground from slipping under his feet. In the end, he had no option but to fall back on the army. Zia, who worked in cahoots with the chief of the Inter-Service Intelligence Directorate (ISI), General Ghulam Jilani Khan, established martial law in 1977, allegedly to end political chaos, which was partly of their own making. Bhutto was arrested and executed the following year.

The balance sheet of Bhutto's spell in power is aptly summarized by Hussein Haqqani (2005):

Bhutto, despite his weaknesses and mistakes, had succeeded in creating a new Pakistani order in which secular civilians attained ascendancy. The military could not return to power without undermining the legitimacy of this civilian order, and

---

the Pakistani government to reopen discussions about the Durand Line. Pakistani officials, in contrast, always emphasized Islam as the unifying force to combat tribal sensitivities and nationalist tendencies among the Baloch and the Pashtun. Moreover, they always had a long-term strategic interest in the affairs of Afghanistan, which they wanted to transform into a client regime (Haqqani, 2005, pp. 165–74; Hussain, 2008, p. 30). This strategic plan received a decisive push under General Zia ul-Haq, who considered that the Afghan jihad was the core of his regime's policies and an important turning point in Pakistan's quest for an Islamic identity at home and for leadership of the Islamic world, especially among the Muslim nations of Asia and Africa (Haqqani, 2005, pp. 188–93).

the military managed to do so with the help of its Islamist allies. Bhutto failed to protect his new Pakistan against this onslaught of the mosque-military combine largely because he accommodated too much of old Pakistan in his new order. It can be argued that Bhutto's downfall was partly the result of his compromises with the forces of obscurantism and his desire for a large military beholden to him. Pakistan reverted to military rule as a result of the religious sentiment unleashed during the PNA campaign against Bhutto, and this time military rule was beholden to Islamists as never before. (p. 129)

Zia: Islamization of the State and the Nation by an Ambitious General

Zia's regime, which prevailed during the next eleven years, marked a decisive step in the Islamization of Pakistan. As noted by Abbas (2005), "it did not take him long to hijack the Islamic slogan of the anti-Bhutto agitation and make it his very own" (p. 97), knowing very well that nobody would dare challenge the legitimacy of religion. For the first time, Islamization acquired legitimacy and the backing of the state (Cohen, 2004, p. 170). Embarking on a campaign of moral rearmament, Zia declared in his first address to the nation (July 1977) that "Pakistan, which was created in the name of Islam, will continue to survive only if it sticks to Islam" (Abbas, 2005, p. 92). It was in Islamization that he saw "the realization of the raison d'être of the [Pakistani] state as well as the unity and strength of the nation" (Ziring, 1988, p. 797, as cited by Haqqani, 2005, p. 148). In fact, the Pakistani state "was created exclusively to provide its people with the opportunity to follow the Islamic way of life," and "preservation of the country's Islamic character was seen to be as important as the security of the country's geographical frontiers" (Hussain, 2008, p. 18).

Such positions, of course, ensured Zia the full support of the religious parties. Revealingly, when he banned all political activity to silence growing opposition to his regime, especially by leftist opponents and the Pakistan People's Party (PPP), the JI was allowed to carry on unhindered: "Its press was immune from censorship and its penetration of the media, the bureaucracy, and even the army was looked upon with approval by Zia" (Abbas, 2005, p. 101). Under his rule, the army perfected the practice, begun by Yahya, of using Islamic parties and radical Islamic groups "as pawns in domestic and international politics" (Cohen, 2004, p. 113). Unlike other Pakistani rulers, Zia was even ready to grant clerics, religious leaders, and parties a significant role in the civilian administration and affairs of the state, going as far as allowing Islamist journalists to operate within the government-owned media (Haqqani, 2005, pp. 132, 148–9). He was a man who combined religious zeal with a shrewd political mind, and this move was part of a clever strategy of using religious forces against his political opponents.

After proclaiming himself president of Pakistan (September 1978), Zia did not hesitate to declare "that he was not responsible to anyone except Allah," so as to defuse any possibility of criticism. He also said that he would stay in power "as long as Allah wills," a logical implication of his claim that he was entrusted by God with a special mission to be fulfilled for Pakistan with the help of "the hand of Providence." Later, in 1983, as a response to violent protests from the Movement for Restoration of Democracy (MRD), Zia made his strategy of connecting Islam with his authoritarian rule even more explicit. He claimed, indeed, that it was the duty of Pakistanis as Muslims to obey his government because it was pursuing Islamic principles. As prescribed by the Quran and a hadith, as long as the head of state followed the injunctions of Allah and his Prophet, obedience was mandatory for his subjects. Therefore, "those who opposed or demonstrated against his government could be accused of waging war against an Islamic government and therefore indulging in anti-Islamic activities" (Sayeed, 1984, p. 220, as cited by Haqqani, 2005, p. 154).

In an ominous move to consolidate his power and further restore the legitimacy of the military after the loss of Bangladesh, Zia chose to present the military as "the ideological vanguard of an Islamic state." His doctrine of an Islamic state presupposed the preeminence of the military, yet it also extolled the values of piety and religious conformity, which implied a growing role for theologians in state institutions. In short, his belief, which soon became widespread in the army, was that a Pakistani nation could be forged only by emphasizing religious identity and by placing the country under the military's stewardship. According to this logic, he vowed to bring not only the army but also the economy, the judiciary, and the education systems closer in line with the sharia (Nomani and Rahnema, 1994, pp. 126–9; Zakaria, 2003, pp. 145–6; Haqqani, 2005, pp. 132–3, 147–8; Piquard, 1999).

Let me elaborate further on his policies. Zia decided to follow a puritanical course by subscribing to the Deoband school of thought, an ultraconservative strand among Pakistan's Sunnis, that closely resembles the Wahhabi Islam practiced in Saudi Arabia. At the time, Deobandism had few followers in Pakistan.[20] Against the humanist traditions of Sufism that had prevailed in the country until then, he opted to extol values of bigotry and intolerance, thus dividing his nation not only along lines of minority and majority sects but also along mutually hostile factions within the majority.

---

[20] There are, indeed, considerable differences over observance and doctrine among Hanefi Sunni, and the most significant are those between the Barelvis and the Deobandis (Synnott, 2009, p. 19).

Zia was responsible for passing some Islamic laws, introducing Islamic punishments for certain offenses, and changing the law of evidence to bring it into conformity with Islamic law, as he interpreted it. Especially radical were his Hudood Ordinances relating to sexual offenses (which made the victim of a rape practically guilty of fornication), his Blasphemy Law (which carried a mandatory sentence of death or life imprisonment for anyone using derogatory remarks against the sacred person of the Prophet or for desecrating the Quran), and his laws against minorities (it became a criminal offense for members of the Ahmadi community to preach and propagate their faith, use Islamic terminology, or follow Muslim practices of worship). He also introduced interest-free banking and the zakat tax to be compulsorily deducted through the banks. The Sh'ia minority immediately protested against the latter measure on the ground that charity is a private matter that should involve only man and God; their members were eventually exempted from the compulsory deduction. Yet, this event laid the ground for bitter Shi'a-Sunni conflict, which led in due time to the creation of terrorist militias within both sects (Abbas, 2005, pp. 103–6, 113; Haqqani, 2005, pp. 140–5; Irfan, 2010, p. 167; Zaman, 1998, pp. 72–3; Jones, 2002, pp. 14–15).

The main purpose of establishing an Islamic economy based on an interest-free banking system was again to gain support from the religious political parties and so entrench the personal power of Zia. Under the instruction of the Federal Sharia Court, the whole financial system was to be subjected to radical changes to bring it into full conformity with the sharia, and a major prerequisite was the elimination of interest. To guarantee that this objective would be reached within a period of three years, the Council of Islamic Ideology (CII) was set up under Articles 197–8 of the new Constitution of Pakistan (1956). As could be expected, the top-down imposition of a radical change in the financial sector ended up in failure, as most banks continued to charge interest but under the guise of financial markups. The governments that came after Zia modified the approach to interest. The Commission for Islamization of the Economy (CIE) created in 1991 disputed the idea that interest was to be banned on the grounds that it represented "riba" (usury), and an optional system in which Islamic and conventional banks were to coexist was preferred (Rahman, 1997; Khan, 2008; Khan and Bhatti, 2006, 2008).

The judiciary was another institution that Zia wanted to reform profoundly to make it subservient to his own interests and power game. He decided to Islamize the courts with the aim of ensuring that all existing laws and administrative regulations were brought into conformity with Islamic injunctions. This was done through important constitutional amendments incorporating the Objectives Resolution, to the effect that the Federal Sharia Court could now examine all laws. Islamic courts thus gained the power to decide whether any law was partly or wholly un-Islamic and then forcing the government to change the law if needed, as with the prevalent laws on murder and bodily harm that were considered to be repugnant to Islamic law. They were also empowered to examine laws even if no case was brought before them. In 1981, through his Provisional Constitutional Order, Zia destroyed the entire fabric of the judicial system, rendering the Supreme Court and High Courts totally ineffective. For example, their judgments delivered against martial law decisions were annulled with retrospective effect. Moreover, all their judges, through a fresh oath of office, had to voice their loyalty to the new constitutional order, while those suspected of independent opinions were not offered the new oath. Implementation of the new Islamic laws did vary in different parts of the country. It was more strict where powerful people used them opportunistically to put down individuals and families who challenged their authority or where provincial and local authorities and individual judges had a great devotion to Islam (Abbas, 2005, pp. 106–7; Haqqani, 2005, pp. 134, 146–7; Irfan, 2010, p. 167).

The education system was not overlooked either. Whereas Bhutto had initiated the process of wrecking Pakistan's colleges and universities by nationalizing private schools, Zia pushed it further by encouraging them to become seminaries. Textbooks were rewritten with an Islamist ideological agenda, full of tendentious historic narratives and "precribed myths" aimed at supporting the military regime and its ultimately religious justification. A new field, "Pakistani Studies," was made compulsory for all degree students, including those attending engineering and medical colleges. As stated in a directive issued by the University Grants Commission (1981), the shared experience of a common religion was to be the basis of Pakistani identity, and the national education system was destined to guide students toward the ultimate goal of Pakistan – the creation of a completely Islamicized state that was to make the country "a fortress of Islam" (Cohen, 2004, p. 171; Haqqani, 2005, pp. 149–50).

To Islamize the education system, Zia's military regime promoted Islamist student groups and fomented student-faculty clashes aimed at purging Pakistani universities of secular professors (Haqqani, 2005, p. 151). Worse still, the religious seminaries, which were considerably expanded owing to large inflows of money obtained from the zakat fund and from Saudi Arabia, became entitled to deliver degrees deemed equivalent to college degrees. This implied that those holding these certificates were pronounced fit to preside over the sharia courts (the "qazi") created by Zia and to compete for government jobs. A huge network of madrasas came into being as a result of this official policy: Whereas at the time of its birth Pakistan had only 136 madrasas, it is today home to 30,000, largely as a result of the push given by Zia's regime (Abbas, 2005, p. 204; Piquard, 1999, p. 73; Zaman, 2007, p. 78). These seminaries, whose success was partly due to the state of neglect suffered by the secular school system, were "to churn out tens of thousands of radicalised young men, some of whom would fight at the tail end of the Afghan resistance against the Soviets; others would provide the core element of the Taliban; still others would go on to fight the Indian Army in Kashmir" or they would operate in Pakistan itself (Abbas, 2005, pp. 107–8). The seeds were therefore sown for violent sectarianism in a region where "many schools of Islam had flourished with tolerable accommodation through the ages" (p. 113).

Finally, Zia's decision to align the army with the conservative-Islamic forces of the political right proved to be particularly disastrous, because it amounted to destroying the established norms of the institution. Zia allowed an Islamic missionary society whose roots lay in the Deoband school of thought, the Tablighi Jama'at, to operate freely within the army and among civil servants. In a very short time, barracks were invaded by "intolerant bigots and fanatics" who promoted Islamic zealotry. Such a move was encouraged by the introduction of a new recruitment policy partly based on evaluation forms that included a box for comments on an officer's religious sincerity (Cohen, 2004, pp. 108, 113, 170–1). In the words of Zia, "the professional soldier in a Muslim army, pursuing the goal of a Muslim State, cannot become 'professional' if in all his activities he does not take on 'the colour of Allah'" (cited by Hussain, 2008, p. 19). It was quickly understood that the public display of Islamic orthodoxy and devotion was an effective method of career enhancement. Along with politics, religion became the most discussed subject inside barracks, relegating professional considerations to a minor role. Inside the army there inevitably emerged sectarian divisions and even factions around various schools of thought within the same sect. As Abbas (2005) notes,

Lip service to outward religious forms increasingly displaced professionalism as a standard of judging merit ... in selection boards for officer candidates, religious knowledge became a determinant for selection in place of secular general knowledge. ... This brought a sea change in the recruitment of the officer corps. Increasingly, the best sons of the traditional military families gave up joining the army, those who were already serving started to leave; and those who wanted to join nevertheless were increasingly rejected by the selection boards. Over a period of time the military selection boards had come to be dominated by inferior officers who culled and threw out candidates whose background suggested privilege, superior education, and moderation of religious views. (pp. 98, 101–2)

Zia's army recruitment policy, which drew many people from the impoverished and relatively backward northern districts where a fundamentalist religious ethos prevailed (Hussain, 2008, p. 20), was bound to have long-term deleterious consequences. They became evident when, in 1993–4, under the influence of a religious zealot (Sufi Iqbal), a group of officers coming from the most senior ranks of the army at the military headquarters of Rawalpindi fomented a coup aimed to transform Pakistan into a Sunni Muslim state. This eventuality was barely avoided (Cohen, 2004, p. 108; Abbas, 2005, pp. 152–3). The situation was no better in the intelligence services, particularly in the ISI, where hundreds of officers had been trained and motivated to support extremist Islamic factions in Afghanistan and Kashmir. Some of these officers, "deeply religious and vociferously anti-American, considered themselves more Taliban than the Taliban" (Rashid, 2008, p. 79). Only after the retirement of the Islamist general Aslam Beg, Zia's successor as army chief, were efforts made to limit the most overt forms of Islamic commitment inside the Pakistani army and the ISI, including the call for a dedicated corps of jihadis (Cohen, 2004, pp. 172–3).

At the same time as he Islamized the army, Zia let the higher cadres enrich themselves through a vigorous expansion of their business ventures while enjoying complete financial autonomy. He empowered the senior commanders by allowing them to operate secret "regimental" funds that they could use at their own discretion. The commanders often used these funds to enhance the comfort of their families, including renovating their homes, rather than to improve the lives of their soldiers. Zia's sacking of Prime Minister Mohammad Khan Junejo and his government in early 1988 was motivated partly by his wrath against a political leader who, although handpicked by himself, dared to question the perks and privileges of senior officers. The announced intention of Junejo's government to put generals in smaller and locally made Suzuki cars, rather than the expensive imported cars they normally, used led Zia to get rid of him on charges of corruption (Siddiqa, 2017, pp. 163–4).

Nawaz Sharif: Playing with Religious Fire to Acquire Unfettered Power

When Zia died in a mysterious plane crash (August 1988), a few months after decreeing an overarching law that required every judicial decision in the country to be based on sharia law, civilian rule was restored, and the prime ministership then oscillated between Benazir Butto, who took over the leadership of the PPP from her deceased father, and Nawaz Sharif, the heir to the Zia legacy. This was far an era of clean democratic politics, however. The military rulers of Pakistan were hoping to build "a civilian facade" behind which the army and the ISI would continue to operate, thus encouraging a transition from direct to indirect military rule. The growing popularity of Benazir Bhutto immediately aroused deep concern among the bulwarks of the previous regime, including the army and the ISI. The ISI, in particular, feared, and rightly so, that she would question the core of their foreign policy with regard to Afghanistan, India, and Kashmir. By focusing people's attention on the external enemy and on the alliance with Islamist groups, this policy was the crucial means whereby the military rulers maintained their control over the country. To counter her, the head of ISI, Hamid Gul, put together the Islamic Democratic Alliance (IJI), an electoral coalition of nine partners comprising no less than six religious parties, including the the JI and the Pakistan Muslim League (moderate). This was the first time, Abbas remarks, that the army supported and used religious parties in electoral politics (Abbas, 2005, p. 134; see also Haqqani, 2005, pp. 200–3, 210–15; Hussain, 2008, p. 23; Synnott, 2009, pp. 41, 59).

To guarantee Nawaz's victory after a brief spell of power for Benazir (1988–90), the ISI engaged in pre-poll rigging (Abbas, 2005, p. 142). Nawaz won, but was in power only for a short period of time (1990–3). And after he took power again from Benazir toward the end of 1996, he opted for policies that went dangerously down the slope of supporting religious radicalism. Already in 1995, Benazir Bhutto had given in to the demand pressed on her government by a radical, Taliban-style movement (the Movement for the Enforcement of Muhammad's Law) to introduce Islamic law in the North-West Frontier province. But whereas Benazir Bhutto ceded to the pressure of events that overwhelmed her, Nawaz Sharif decided to cynically exploit Islam with a view to enhancing his powers. In August 1998, indeed, he proposed a constitutional amendment before the National Assembly to enforce rule by Islamic law, on the understanding that his government would have ultimate authority in deciding its interpretation (Synnott, 2009, p. 49).

In the same amendment to the constitution, Nawaz Sharif proposed that "the directives of the government in this sphere would be beyond the jurisdiction of courts and judicial review," so that any impediment in the enforcement of the sharia would be removed. Clearly, the move was "a bid to acquire unfettered power" following continuing efforts to transform the judiciary, the police, the bureaucracy, and finally the army into partisan bodies infiltrated by political influence and patronage (Abbas, 2005, pp. 164–5). Declaring himself the absolute leader of the Muslims, "Emirul Mominin,"

Sharif planned to propose further amendments to the constitution (Hussain, 2008, p. 31; Synnott, 2009, p. 49). When he realized that he lacked the support needed to get his amendment passed by the Senate, however, Nawaz Sharif resorted to the kind of hooliganism and religion-based violence that had recently accompanied the besieging of the Supreme Court, encouraging the mullahs to lay siege to the Senate. It is miraculous that the Senate actually held out in such circumstances when Pakistan was teetering on the brink, within an inch of becoming a caliphate. There is little doubt that Sharif's exploitation of religion for political purposes had the effect of strengthening Islamic orthodoxy and religious militancy in a country that needed just the opposite policies.

Musharraf: A General Unable to Sort out the Mess

Before Nawaz Sharif could implement his plan to sack his army chief, Pervez Musharraf, after the disastrous actions of the army at Kargil (Kashmir), the latter anticipated the move and quickly seized power (October 1999).[21] One of Musharraf's stated objectives was to tackle religious fanatics head-on. But the legacy of the preceding regimes had conferred such clout on right-wing religious movements and parties, which had become often indistinguishable from bands of thugs and criminals, that the task proved to be far more difficult than expected. An added complication was that cracking down on them would have challenged the country's foreign policy vis-a-vis Afghanistan and Kashmir. Thus, when Musharraf proposed in April 2000 to reform the controversial Blasphemy Law passed under Zia – not to remove it but just to introduce a rather minor procedural change – he provoked an enormous uproar among the religious hard-liners. He then backed down, to the great dismay of moderates, presenting his retreat as a response to the "unanimous demand of the ulama, 'mashaikh' [elder religious scholars] and the people" (Abbas, 2005, pp. 192–3).

The truth is that by acting as "petty political intriguers" ready to orchestrate disorder in the streets with the help of "the reliable street power of Islamist political parties," the military had contributed to the rise of terrorists and religious zealots in Pakistan. When it suited their purpose, in the period following the death of Zia ul-Haq, Pakistan's generals used the

---

[21] The Kargil plan consisted of sending in a mixture of Kashmiri fighters and regular/paramilitary troops to occupy the heights above Kargil before the Indian Army moved in to reoccupy them at the end of the snowy season. This operation was badly planned, however, and it did not anticipate India's reaction. The Indian Army retaliated and launched a counteroffensive with heavy artillery and air power; it turned out that Pakistani reserves of supplies and ammunition were woefully inadequate. India won back the Kargil heights, and the Pakistani Army was humiliated (Abbas, 2005, pp. 170–5).

Islamists to undermine civilian authority, thus thwarting the prospect of democratic rule. But when the Islamists came to be seen as the arch-enemy by the international community and the United States in particular, they shifted their attitude and cited the threat posed by Islamists as the main reason why the Pakistani army should receive foreign aid to maintain its control over the country (Haqqani, 2005, pp. 255–6, 260).

The central lesson to draw from Pakistan's experience is the complete failure of the attempt to create a durable national identity on the basis of Islam in a context characterized by great diversity. Pakistan not only includes several ethnolinguistic groups inhabiting the Punjab (in addition to the Punjabi of central-north Pakistan, there are the Potohari of the north and the Seraiki of the south) and the Sindh (coexisting with the dominant Sindhi are the Muhajer who migrated from India), but also large populations from tribal areas in Balochistan, dominated by Baloch people, and from the North-West Frontier and the Federally Administered Tribal Areas, dominated by the Pashtuns (see Lieven, 2012, chs. 7–10). As Hilary Synnott (2009) points out, "From the outset, the Pakistani people have had difficulty subsuming their particular ethnic customs and identities into a single national narrative," and unable to furnish a basis for a common national identity, "religion proved insufficient to hold the state together in its original form" (pp. 17–19). Instead of cementing the various strands of the Pakistani society into a national community, the appeal to Islam turned out to be utterly divisive, largely because of the opportunistic manner in which many political leaders tried to use it as a way of differentiating Pakistan from India (Paul, 2014, pp. 127–35).

Case Study 4: Algeria

Dangerously Flirting with Islam
The case of Algeria provides a striking example of Islam being "nationalized" and cynically used by the state to legitimize repressive policies and mobilization (Layachi, 1995, p. 180; Owen, 2004, p. 41). Algeria therefore presents another story of authoritarian rulers who discreetly supported or co-opted extremist movements whose ideological platforms were based on religion or ethnicity, as a way to fight political opponents threatening them.

Ben Bella, the first president of independent Algeria, resorted to using a pan-Arabic language with Islamic overtones that was close in spirit to that used by the Baath movement in Iraq and Syria. Thus, he proclaimed that there was no future for Algeria outside Arabism, which was the very objective of the revolution. Algerian socialism was to be a Muslim socialism, inspired by the country's Islamic past (Tamzali, 2007). Accordingly, the first Algerian constitution of 1963 asserted that Islam is the state religion, that the Arabic language is the national and official language of the state, and that Arabization is the first priority of the country (Bouamama, 2000, pp. 114–16; Hadjadj, 2007). In fact, during the anticolonial struggle Arabism had been invoked as a way to effectively combat assimilation and to resist French efforts to divide Arabs and Berbers. It was meant to be the ideological cement that would unify a country whose social fabric had been ripped asunder and whose political elite was deeply fragmented. The assertion of Islamic cultural roots was "a way to oppose the past grandeur of the Maghreb to the present humiliation of Muslim people in a colonised country" (Stora, 2004). The new state sought to control the expression of Islam by controlling appointments to religious offices, absorbing independent Quranic schools, sponsoring Islamic propaganda, and supervising schools, mosques, religious endowments, and the training of clerics through a Ministry of Religious Affairs (Lapidus, 1988, pp. 694, 697). The authoritarian nature of the regime was also manifested in the imposition of single-party rule and the purging of the ruling party (the Front de Libération Nationale, or FLN) of all its opponents to Ben Bella. Personalized leadership and bureaucratic-military dictatorship resulted (Laabas and Bouhouche, 2011, p. 202).

Boumedienne: Using Islam against Secular Political Opposition

Factionalism and deep antagonism among nationalist leaders quickly resurfaced, leading to a state coup. General Houari Boumedienne seized power from Ben Bella in June 1965, and the army quickly succeeded in taking control of the Algerian state, a move supported by left-wing groups in and outside the FLN. Simultaneously, Boumedienne became the chief spokesman for a Muslim and Arab identity, and the discourse of reformist Islam infiltrated all political language. Trained in religious schools (the Zitouna in Tunis and al-Azhar in Cairo), he soon changed the name of the newspaper of the FLN from "Le Peuple" (The People) to "El Moudjahid" (Religious Fighter), which has religious resonance (Hadjadj, 2007, p. 414). More ominously, a bizarre alliance was sealed between the new socialist, anti-imperialist regime and the ulama represented by the Conseil Supérieur Islamique. The unpopular policies of Boumedienne, based on state control of the economy, as well as his strong-arm tactics and the corrupt practices that he and the clique around him systematically followed to foster a rent-consuming political clientele, soon aroused a determined opposition led by intellectuals, students, and trade unions. Represented, in particular, by the UGTA Union Générale des Travailleurs Algériens (UGTA) and the Union Nationale des Etudiants Algériens (UNEA), these oppositional forces seriously challenged Boumedienne's hold on political power throughout 1968.

To break the student movement, Boumedienne mobilized Islamist students of the El Hamel Brotherhood, inciting them to infiltrate the university in Alger and demonstrate their strength with impunity. In 1971, the UNEA was dissolved and transformed into the FLN's Student Youth wing after its leaders were arrested and exiled to a harsh prison in the south (Tamzali, 2007, pp. 199–202). More generally, Boumedienne used Islam to counteract any oppositional movement and to prevent the rise of a genuine civil society. He thus gave freer rein to the ulama and the more reactionary clerics among them. In particular, he granted them the right to lead the Arabization of the country and to manage the education system (including the right to rewrite school textbooks). In a still more ominous move, he encouraged the rise of the the Front Islamique du Salut (FIS), or Islamic Salvation Front, whose more radical strand was headed by Ali Belhadj, a puritanical cleric who called for the formation of an Islamic state, if necessary by violent means (Bouamama, 2000, ch. 3; Lapidus, 2002, pp. 599–600). Thus, he strove to reach out to extremist religious forces that had escaped the influence of the official Muslim establishment and propagated their messages of hatred through a number of unofficial mosques and schools harboring an independent Muslim community life (Lapidus, 1988, p. 697).

About Boumedienne's Islamist move, Bachir Hadjadj, a close observer of the Algerian scene and himself a victim of the regime, has the following to say:

Such decisions, populist and demagogical, bore the seal of an illegitimate regime which exploited the religious feelings and emotions of the people of Algeria. The idea was to persuade common citizens that their religion was under threat and that the new laws enacted by the state were intended to preserve it. Unable to obtain their votes at the booth, the rulers chose to flatter them by rubbing them up the right way. (Hadjadj, 2007, p. 436; my translation)

Exploiting the window of opportunity thus created by Boumedienne, the more conservative members of the religious establishment started to assert their views more aggressively and to meddle openly in matters of social policy (such as dress codes, amount of brideprices, etc.). Moreover, they exerted considerable effort to implement the Arabization program, and by the late 1970s, the curricula of all education levels were completely Arabized. It was thus with the full support of the regime that religious dignitaries spread the message of a conservative Islam through the creation of a wide network of Islamist institutes directly governed by the Ministry of Religious Affairs. Radical views inspired by the writings of Taymiyya, Qutb, and Mâwdudi were diffused broadly (Chachoua, 2001, pp. 271–2).

However, the Arabization policy proved disastrous for several reasons. First, it denied the existence of non-Arabic cultures in Algeria, particularly the amazigue language of Kabylia. This shortcoming was especially serious because the Arabic language taught at school was a classical Arab that neither the Arab-speaking nor the Berber-speaking people of Algeria could understand. Second, it allowed the interference of religion in the educational sphere, which led to the excessive moralization of school teachings. Third, as in Pakistan under Zia, it promoted an increase in underqualified teachers coming from the Quranic schools (in Algeria itself or in neighbouring Egypt) while simultaneously pushing many members of the intelligentsia to leave the country (Grandguillaume, 1995). Fourth, by imposing Arabic as the only language taught in official schools, it caused considerable frustration among the newly educated people, who quickly found that they could not effectively compete with the Francophone elites for access to the highest positions in the state system. A fertile ground for future recruitment by Muslim extremists was thereby created that established an additional indirect link between Algeria's Arabization policy and its Islamization at the behest of the FIS.

The growing expression of puritanical views was part and parcel of the conservative Islamic drift. Malek Bennabi, for example, invented the concept of "colonizability" to explain why Algeria succumbed to colonization: The perversion of the original message of pure Islam by Mediterranean, dynastic, nomadic, and other obnoxious influences had so weakened Algeria that it became easy prey for the French occupiers (Bouamama, 2000, p. 225; Hadjadj, 2007, pp. 439–41). The government explicitly adopted the idea of a "renaissance" of the country based on Islamic tradition and culture (Chachoua, 2001, pp. 271–2). The minister of information and culture, Ahmed Taleb Ibrahimi, thus declared that "a cultural revolution implies a return to the sources" and that Islam represented the central value on which to build the new Algerian society: "The other values owe their importance, their existence and their prestige only to their articulation with Islam or to the fact that they are inspired by or subordinated to Islam" (cited by Bouamama, 2000, p. 163). Such views gained the highest official recognition when the Islamic character of the Algerian state was embedded very explicitly into the National Charter, considered as the ideological and political program of revolutionary Algeria:

The Algerian people is an Arab and Muslim people. Islam is the religion of the state, and one of the fundamental components of the national Algerian personality. ... It is to Islam, the religion of militant endeavour, of rigour, justice and equality, that the Algerian people returned to in the darkest times of the Crusades and colonial domination, and it is from Islam that they drew the moral force and spiritual energy required to sustain hope and achieve eventual victory. Islam has shaped the Algerian society and made it a coherent force, attached to the same land, the same beliefs and the same Arab language that enabled Algeria to start again contributing to the works of civilisation. (cited by Bouamama, 2000, p. 161; my translation)

Chadli: Running into Plain Disaster
In a way reminiscent of Sadat's tenure in Egypt, the 1976 version of the charter was not amended until 1986, when the liberal regime of President Chadli decided to revise it, primarily to suppress all references to socialism (Bouamama, 2000, pp. 161–2). Chadli, like his predecessor, deliberately chose to use Islamist forces to defeat the leftists' opposition to his neoliberal policies. Thus, in 1986 when the students' populist anger burst into the open and quickly took on an insurrectionary character, the Islamists tried to hijack the movement by taking to the streets themselves and demanding the establishment of an Islamist Republic in Algeria.[22] Against all expectations, Chadli negotiated with their leaders as though they were the key actors behind these ominous events, therefore supplying a true "launching ramp" for the FIS. Even though the new constitution, enacted in 1989, was quite liberal in its terms, explicitly banning the creation of political parties based on religion, the FIS was officially recognized during the same year, on September 5. The fact of the matter was that the platform of the FIS included the defense of private property and recourse to the intervention of the International Monetary Fund to help rescue Algeria from its economic and financial crisis, and this Islamist ideology provided badly needed support for Chadli's unpopular policies (Bouamama, 2000, pp. 214–18). In addition, and much like in Egypt, the government relied heavily on the Algerian strand of the Muslim Brotherhood to counterbalance the influence of leftist and secular views on university campuses (p. 229).

The enactment of a reactionary Family Code in 1984 and the appointment as president of the University of Islamic Sciences (Constantine) of the Egyptian imam El Ghazali – who had belonged to the Muslim Brothers and had justified violence against miscreants – bore witness to the tacit

---

[22] This tactic was to be replicated later in Egypt when the Muslim Brothers used the Arab Spring's protests to push their own Islamist agenda while they were not at the vanguard of the rebellious movement.

condoning of the Islamists' extreme positions by the Chadli regime. This happened in conditions where the regime was considerably weakened by serious infighting among the various wings of the FLN, which literally broke the party apart (Laabas and Bouhouche, 2011, p. 203). As a result the FIS rose to prominence through the ballot box and by the increasing recourse to violent means, whether overt or covert, by its more militant factions (such as the so-called Afghans, returnees from the war in Afghanistan) and its military arm (the GIA, or Groupe Islamiste Armé). Violent and anticonstitutional acts included stuffing ballot boxes, using strong-arm tactics on people suspected of voting against the Islamists, issuing death threats against political opponents, having recourse to anticonstitutional decrees in municipalities won by the FIS during the elections of June 1990, as well as the harassment and even murder of numerous leftist intellectuals or imams who refused to let their mosques become FIS staging posts.[23]

All these excesses and the prospect of a sweeping FIS victory in the second round of the legislative elections of 1991 led the Algerian army to openly interfere with the political process and eventually stage a state coup that overthrew President Chadli in September 1992. Following street protests, a curfew was enforced, the FIS was disbanded, its main leaders were arrested, and mosques refusing to stop engaging in political activities were closed (Bouamama, 2000, pp. 218–30). The country was then dominated by a small military clique called the eradicationists. It refused any compromise with the FIS and waged a full-scale war for control of society in the name of secularism. Relying essentially on military power, the new regime turned the implementation of counterinsurgency measures over to village defenae forces and militias, causing indiscriminate violence and numerous atrocities. Algeria thus fell into a nasty civil war that was "perhaps more extreme and bitter than anything hitherto seen in the Muslim world" (Lapidus, 2002, p. 600). Nominal secularism came to be gradually reestablished, but only at the price of continued military domination exerted brutally through a shadow clique of so-called decision makers (les décideurs). War weariness and a gradual reaction against the excesses of the Islamic movements helped secure growing support for the government, beginning in 1994 under

---

[23] For example, the elected representatives of the FIS in the commune of Bouira succeeded in forbidding girls from engaging in sports and in destroying the fountain in the city center under the pretext that it was in the shape of a cross. In the commune of Dellys, wearing short pants became strictly prohibited, whereas in other communes the official motto "by the people and for the people" was replaced by the name "Islamic commune" (Bouamama, 2000, p. 220; see also Dreyfuss, 2005, pp. 313–15).

General Liamine Zeroual and then under Abdelaziz Bouteflika, who succeeded him in 2001. Not only middle-class bureaucrats and businessmen
but also moderate Muslim groups such as the Movement for an Islamic Society (HAMAS) advocated for the military to rescue the country from chaos
(Filiu, 2015, pp. 94–112).

To sum up, the rulers of Algeria chose political stability over reforms. To
deflect criticisms of the regime's social and economic policies, they allied
themselves with clerics, providing them with ample opportunities to exert
influence in critical sectors of the society. The result was retrograde social
policies. In addition, necessary economic reforms were postponed, particularly under Boumedienne, who could rely on the proceeds of large hydro-
carbon resources, especially after the 1973 oil shock, to finance his costly
"socialist" policies. It must be noted that, in their efforts to crush the opposition forces from the left, Algerian autocrats established links with the most
radical religious forces in the country, including those preaching violence.
This extreme step proved to be suicidal. Its consequences were poorly anticipated by political authorities working within a limited time horizon. This
explains why, although their predominant objective was to consolidate their
hold on power, the Algerian upper political elite eventually reached a political deadlock and imposed immense suffering on the people.

As a result, the regime became even less transparent than ever before,
being run by "a cabal of unelected power-brokers" forming a shadowy clique
known as "le pouvoir." To alleviate people's frustrations, the government
awarded subsidies, social housing, and big pay rises to state employees, a
recipe that was sustainable only as long as the prices of oil and natural gas,
which Algeria possesses in plenty, remained high (*Economist*, February 6–
12, 2016, p. 31).

Case Study 5: Indonesia

Modern Indonesia offers a quite different picture from the first four case
studies; in fact, it resembles the other two countries to be considered subsequently, Iraq and Syria. In all three countries, indeed, rulers typically were
eager to keep a tight grip on all Muslim movements and avoided toying with
the idea of Islamization. Yet, to prevent Islamists from playing any significant role in politics and society, they were ready to prop up extremist groups
claiming Islamic authenticity and to manipulate these groups using sinister
tactics. In this section, I sketch the general historical background against
which such events occurred in Indonesia before describing the main facts.

Building a Totalitarian System: First Crushing the Communists
As early as 1927, at the time of the creation of the National Party of Indonesia (PNI), Sukarno, with the example of Atatürk's Turkey in mind, explicitly addressed the question of Islam. He did so in a context in which a Muslim movement, Sarekat Islam, had turned into the main force of opposition to both Dutch rule and communism.[24] Sukarno's primary emphasis was on guaranteeing the separation between state and religion, believing that religion is a private matter and should not be allowed to influence national politics. During the Japanese occupation (1942–5), however, Muslims received tremendous support from the occupying power: The Japanese helped unify and coordinate the Muslim movement, mobilizing a coalition of middle-class merchants, rich peasants, and "village" ulama to cooperate with them (Lapidus, 1988, pp. 767–8). Such support emboldened the adherents of the Muslim movement to demand an Islamic state on the country's accession to independence. But this demand was rejected by the newly formed republican regime, which, after the rise to power of President Sukarno, adopted an ideological program (1959) known as the Pancasila. This program stressed a nonsectarian commitment to belief in one supreme god, in addition to nationalist and socialist ideals (Brown, 2003, p. 202). Its goal was to synthesize nationalism, religion, and communism under a highly centralized regime and centrally planned economy (Lapidus, 1988, p. 670).

By suppressing cultural and political expression and by giving the communists an important opportunity to consolidate their political position (and to launch important progressive reforms, a land reform in particular), Sukarno soon alienated important segments of the population. On the false pretext that the communists engineered a state coup in September 1965, and with the support of the CIA, General Suharto and the army unleashed death squads to arrest, kill, torture, and rape anyone deemed to belong to the left. This ominous move resulted in the brutal persecution and slaughtering of at least a half-million communists. What followed was the gradual construction of a totalitarian state dominated by Suharto and the military. In addition, the tactic of dealing ruthlessly with political opponents, crushing them remorselessly when they became a threat to the regime, became a hallmark of successive Indonesian regimes (Vickers, 2005, pp. 156–72; Crouch, 2007). At the end of 1965, Suharto established a new military regime based on a

---

[24] In fact, Sarekat Islam reached its apex by 1927 when it emerged as a mass political movement and the main force in Indonesian opposition to Dutch rule. It later broke up over differences in ideology and political orientation, and when the leftists were forced out, it lost the mass of its followers, causing a deep split in the movement. From that time on, it had a militant Islamic, anticommunist, and anti-Dutch orientation (Lapidus, 1988, p. 666).

coalition of army officers, Islamist community organizations, and Protestant and Catholic minorities. In March 1966, with the additional support of the professional and bureaucratic middle class and the Westernized academic intelligentsia, he assumed the presidency after edging Sukarno out of power (Lapidus, 1988, p. 671). For his horrendous slaughter of the communists, Suharto was thus rewarded by being granted complete authority over the army and parliament.

Building a Totalitarian System, Then Crushing the Islamists
A key architect of the "New Order" instituted by Suharto was Ali Murtopo, the intelligence chief, who played a major role in manipulating mergers of existing political parties. In particular, he brought together the Islamic parties under a single organization with the neutral name, the United Development Party. When that party showed signs of strength in the 1977 election, following criticisms by religious leaders of corruption and the military role in politics, the clash became inevitable. To quash this reemerging opposition, Murtopo manipulated groups dedicated to violence in the name of Islam. More precisely, he encouraged young Muslims influenced by the Iranian Revolution and the Islamic revivalism of Egypt's Muslim Brotherhood to organize into a militant group known as the "Jihad Command" (JC).

Murtopo thus used the well-known tactic of fabricating a threat that could discredit the Muslim movement and justify security crackdowns on its members. After several incidents, including the hijacking of a plane and the bombing of a bank, which were rightly or wrongly attributed to the JC or to related groups, a major event in the manipulation of Islam took place in the very poor harbor area of Tanjung Priok in Jakarta in September 1984. Outside a mosque, a riot suddenly flared up, a heavy army presence suddenly materialized, and as many as several hundred of rioters were quickly gunned down by the troops. The government then used the Tanjung Priok riot as an excuse to crack down on all forms of Islamic radicalism, and many outspoken preachers and politicians who were not necessarily hard-liners were arrested, tried, and jailed, often on flimsy charges. It then began describing Islam as the force of the "extreme right," which like the "extreme left" – communism – was a threat to the country. Muslims increasingly felt that their religion was under attack and that the regime favored the non-Muslim and particularly the Christian communities. As a consequence, Muslims who looked for a voice to resist the regime channeled their energies into religion, and religious gestures, such as the wearing of headscarves, became politicized (Vickers, 2005, pp. 177–9).

Suharto's U-Turn

A few years later, Suharto undertook a complete U-turn by appearing to reconcile himself to Islam. As a gesture in the new direction, he adopted the well-known tactic of making a pilgrimage to Mecca (1991), and on his return to Indonesia he took the name of Muhammad. Just before making the pilgrimage, he charged B. J. Habibie, who was soon to become Indonesia's third president, with the task of establishing and leading an organization called the League of Indonesian Muslim Intellectuals (ICMI). All these moves signaled that the ruling group had come to understand that it was too closed and too alienated from any support base among the population to maintain itself in power. More critically, Suharto had started to question the loyalty of top military leaders, who had so far constituted the strongest pillar of the regime. Allying with Muslim groups was deemed a necessity in this context of the fragmenting power structure at the top (Choiruzzada and Nugrohoa, 2013). Designed to appeal to influential middle-class people with a strong Muslim education, the ICMI was intended to become a kind of surrogate Islamic political party broadly supportive of the government (Brown, 2003, p. 203; Vickers, 2005, pp. 199–200). Many of its members were thus appointed to top official posts, enabling them to increase their influence. It is against this background that the precursor organization, the Prosperous Justice Party (PKS), grew into a nationwide Muslim network: Religious activism was indeed less tightly constrained than the political sort during the final period of Suharto's rule (*Economist*, April 4, 2009, p. 23). This was most evident in the actions of the top Muslim clerical body, the Indonesian Council of Religious Scholars known as "Majelis Ulama Indonesia" (MUI), which became the main source of inspiration for Muslim groups, particularly with respect to the objective of Islamizing the Indonesian economy.

The end outcome is a country that is not an Islamic republic but one that has made substantial concessions to Islamists. Thus, in 2006, the government of the then-president, Susilo Bambang Yudhoyono, issued a decree requiring any believers wanting to build a house of worship to obtain the approval of the local religious affairs office, as well as the signatures of ninety members of their faith and sixty other community members. More ominously, barely two years elapsed before the same government issued another decree forbidding Ahmadis from proselytizing and declaring that violation of the decree is punishable by five years in prison for blasphemy. In the wake of these national decrees, local governments passed similar ordinances that have been enforced not only against Ahmadis but also against Shi'a and Bahai believers. Christians were the next to suffer. Local governments on the edge of Jakarta's urban sprawl blocked construction of their churches despite Indonesia's Supreme Court's ruling, in full conformity with the constitution (which, although it forbids atheism, enshrines the right of Indonesians "to worship according to their own religion or belief" and recognizes six official religions) that such churches may be built. Not even the progressive successor of Yudhoyono, President Joko Widodo, dared to annul the decrees that obviously went against the principles of tolerance proclaimed in the Indonesian constitution (*Economist*, August 8-14, 2015, p. 39).

Moreover, when the governor of Jakarta, Basuki Tjahaja Purnama, known as Ahok, was attacked by Islamists for defaming the Quran, Widodo did not come to his support, despite the fact that Ahok was his deputy when he was himself Jakarta's governor. Worse, in December 2016, he appeared at a protest alongside Rizieq Shihab, the firebrand leader of a vigilante group called the Islam Defenders Front. By thus choosing to share a platform with a man who had twice been convicted of hate speech, Widodo seemed to espouse fundamentalist views of the worst kind. After all, the only crime of which Ahok was accused by the Islamists was that he deceitfully cited a particular verse in the Quran to counter their attempt to dissuade Muslims from voting for a Christian in the election for governor to be held in February 2017. Being a Christian of Chinese descent, Ahok was twice a minority in a country where 90 percent of the people are Muslims and 95 percent indigenous. In December 2016, under the strong pressure of the Islamists and despite the condemnation of the street protests by moderate Muslim leaders, prosecutors charged him with blasphemy, forcing him to appear in court (*Economist*, January 28, 2016, p. 43).

Baathism as Secular Religiosity in the Service of a Totalitarian State: A Prelude to the Study of Iraq and Syria

The analysis of the Indonesian situation also applies to the deceptively secular ideology of Baathism. Despite its somewhat mystical and vaguely socialistic tenets, Baathism is essentially based on an authoritarian pan-Arabist model whose spirit is Islam. The core element of this model always resided in its own past, and the consciousness of pan-Arabism has been ideologized in such a way as to borrow virtually nothing of the constellation of values associated with the European Enlightenment (Makiya, 1998, p. 212; Polk, 2005, p. 109). Especially in Iraq, Baathism stressed the exceptionalism of the Arabs whose national awakening was bound up with a religious message and obligation (Makiya, 1998, pp. 198–211; Tripp, 2000, esp. chs. 5–6; see also Hourani, 1991, pp. 452–3; Dawisha, 1999).

As Kanan Makiya (1998) has convincingly argued, the political doctrine underlying the Baath Party, which emerged in the 1940s, was based on a romantic and therefore unrealizable ideal of Arab unity resting on a moral imperative inspired by Islam (pp. 208–9). Michel Aflaq, a Maronite Christian from Damas, one of the two founders of the Baathist ideology (along with Salah al Din Bitar) and its most able theoretical exponent, held that religion represents the Arab genius and "conforms to its nature": Arab nationalism cannot possibly clash with religion because fundamentally both "spring from the heart and are issued by the will of God" (cited by Makiya, 1998, p. 201). Aflaq espoused that the force of Islam took on the new appearance of pan-Arabism manifested in Baathism: The Baath Party represented "living Arab history." Yet, the party never demanded conversion to Islam as a price of entry (pp. 192, 209, 211). Drawing its force from the glorious past through a process of renaissance ("baath"), new generations would be imbued with the spirit of Arabism, which has a deep affinity with the Islamic heritage. In this messianic vision, inchoate masses would be transformed into a united and universal society linked through comradeship and anti-imperialist solidarity "to millions of other Arabs in far-off countries, none of whom were bound to each other by concrete ties of everyday life, economic interests, or even a common fate in the face of oppression" (p. 245).

In the same vein, Amatzia Baram (2014) observes that "Baath party members lived in a state of secular religiosity and Sufi-like ecstasy." He recalls memories of disciples of Aflaq who "saw him as a god with a holy countenance," enchanted by his Sufi style and warm charisma evoking Jesus. They were particularly enticed by Aflaq's "equivocal rhetoric blurring the line between Islam and Arabism" and retaining the central message of the resurrection of the Arab nation and the renewal of its spirit "so that it will become ingenious again as it ingeniously created Islam." Under his influence and spell, they continued to consider themselves Muslims, "but of a newly inspired, young and glorious breed," called to become "the prophets of a new age and a new quasi-Islamic religion" (pp. 39–40). Not only were the young Bathists incomplete secularists or atheists but also they were quite aware of their religious environment and the religious anchorage of Arab societies, which made them ready for some compromise with the religious clerics (p. 38).

By reconciling the doctrine of Baathism with Islam, suggesting that the two were inextricably linked, Aflaq and Bitar proposed a view that seriously called into question the seemingly secular underpinnings of the idea of Arab renaissance based on an appreciation of the European Enlightenment. Their view also involved a clear denunciation of sectarianism, tribalism, and the low status of women in Arab societies (Cook, 2012, p. 73). Thus, being conscious of sectarian and other divisions that ran through Syrian society and that the French authorities had exploited to consolidate their rule, the founders of Baathism were deeply hostile to any intrusion of religion on politics and to every form of discrimination based on religion (McHugo, 2014, p. 120). According to Makiya (1998), the Baathist doctrine was truly fundamentalist because it postulated that society depends for its very existence on the presence of an unbreachable basic moral norm that is associated with the Arab-Islamic character of its inhabitants and transcends all sorts of sectarian divisions. All deviance was seen as an act of treason justifying recourse to party or state violence against the enemies of the Arab nation (pp. 206–7). Such actions would be performed by the Baath Party organization conceived as the repository of the "national will," much in the same way as Lenin conceived the Communist Party as the true representative of the interests of the Russian masses. In both instances, the party was expected "to collectivize the individual, compacting him into his comrades" (pp. 254–5). More ominously, Aflaq regarded cruelty as the most reliable instrument by which to impose radical change on the population (Dawisha, 2009, p. 215).

The founding fathers of the Baath Party denigrated Western democracy, which they considered exploitative and capitalistic (Dawisha, 2009, p. 228). The deeply totalitarian nature of Baathism became tragically evident when Baath leaders tried to enforce their idealized standard of pan-Arabism in such a diverse country as Iraq, in which the search for a modern identity was a new challenge. There, Arabism was bound to be perceived as a project of hegemony of a minority of Sunnites over the Kurds, Shiites, and non-Muslims. In reality, the Baath Party, far from representing a broad spectrum of Arab elite and population groups, was captured by one sect and even by subgroups of that sect – the Takriti clan in Iraq and the Alawite officer caste in Syria (Makiya, 1998, pp. 214–16, 249). In both Iraq and Syria, the problem of religious opposition has been compounded by blatant discrimination against the majority (the Shiites in Iraq and the Sunni Muslims in Syria) at the hands of a violent authoritarian regime. Let us now delve first into the case of Iraq and then into that of Syria.

Case Study 6: Iraq

The Avoidable Slide into Sectarianism
Sectarian politics in Iraq is especially distressing because, although Ottomans favored their Sunni co-confessionalists throughout their rule

over the three provinces (Mosul, Baghdad, and Basra), cross-ethnic coop-eration had largely prevailed before World War I (Yousif and Davis, 2011, p. 243). Sunni and Shi'a notables then cooperated to establish an educa-tion system based on the Arabic language with a view to facilitating the construction of a strong national administration. Furthermore, when the British betrayed their promise to grant Iraq independence by seeking and obtaining a mandate from the newly established League of Nations, spark-ing off an open rebellion, "Sunnis and Shi'is prayed in each other's mosques, celebrated their respective religious holidays and rituals, and urged Jews (the largest ethnic group in Baghdad in 1920) and Christians to join the revolt because they were fully equal Iraqi citizens" (p. 244). The basis was thus laid for the subsequent nationalist movement that would stress anti-sectarianism, the strengthening of civil society including students' and women's organizations, a democratic press able to challenge political authority, and values encouraging Iraqis to have pride in their multiple cul-tural heritages (Davis, 2005b, pp. 55–7).

The vigorous manner in which Great Britain suppressed this nascent movement to safeguard its own selfish interests and quash demands for independence precluded the possibility of establishing Iraq as a multiethnic polity. As a matter of fact, "British colonial rule helped enshrined sectar-ian politics at the state level by forcing into exile many of the Shi'a clerics who had demanded independence from British colonial control" (Yousif and Davis, 2011, p. 244). Following the logic of "divide ut impere," the British created the Hashemite monarchy, at the head of which a rigged referendum placed Faysal bin Hussein, the son of the sharif of Mecca (August 1921). This monarchy was buttressed by a Sunni political elite drawn from Faysal's army officers, known as the Sharifians, who controlled the country until a revolution overthrew the regime in 1958 (Dawisha, 2009, pp. 92–119).

Although during the Hashemite era the Iraqi national movement was dominated by a cross-ethnic alliance that sought to implement democratic and social reforms, it was dealt a serious blow when Nuri al-Said skillfully manipulated the Arab-Israeli crisis that followed the partition resolution passed by the United Nations in November 1947 (Davis, 2005a). The pres-ence of Iraqi Jews inside the national movement was indeed significant, and it was convenient to accuse them of sympathy with Zionism. Until then, the influence of pan-Arabism had been contained because it was largely confined to the army officer corps, which was under the tight control of the monarchy. At the behest of the British, the size of the army had been reduced, and many officers had been forced into retirement. Things had changed by the late 1940s and early 1950s as the banner of pan-Arabism shifted to the Arab Socialist Baath Party, founded in Iraq in 1952.

The 1958 revolution brought into focus the sharp cleavage between the cross-ethnic majority wing of the Iraqi nationalist movement and the pan-Arabists. General Abd al-Karim Qasim, who led the revolution, broke his alliance with the Iraqist wing of the nationalism movement, which included the powerful Iraqi Communist Party (ICP), as soon as he realized that it was becoming too powerful. He then moved to create an alliance with the pan-Arabists, which did not prevent an assassination attempt in 1959 and being overthrown by the Baathists in February 1963 (Dawisha, 2009, pp. 179–80). His removal from power proved to be a major turning point in the history of modern Iraq, because Qasim was "the only modern Iraqi leader to have eschewed sectarian criteria in the recruitment of officials to positions within the state apparatus" (Yousif and Davis, 2011, p. 246). Quite opposite was the policy pursued later by Saddam Hussein, who gradually established and consolidated a "family-party state" after seizing power from Ahmad Hasan al-Bakr in 1979. This meant, in particular, that his extensive security apparatus was staffed with family and tribal loyalists (Batatu, 1978; Baram, 1991).

Qasim's Wise Handling of Islam

Qasim was also quite consistent in his policy vis-à-vis Islam. Rather than favoring the separation of state and mosque, he imposed state control over all the Islamic institutions in the country. This meant keeping the ulama out of dissident politics and keeping Islam out of regime ideology and, as much as possible, out of state education, culture, the legal system, and state symbolism (Baram, 2014, p. 47). To persuade the religious establishment to lend legitimacy to the regime's policies as necessary, some limited and unavoidable concessions were nevertheless made. These allowed the Baath Party and the regime to avoid head-on confrontations with public religiosity. The outcome is well described by Amatzia Baram (2014):

Iraq became a land of dichotomy. On the popular level of religious festivals and general deference to Islam, the regime paid the requisite lip service. However, Islam was almost absent from the realm of high culture, and occasionally was even attacked. ... In between the demotic and the high cultural levels, however, was a vast territory of ambivalence that included lawmaking, the constitution, and education. The regime recognized certain aspects of Islamic traditions when enacting laws and issuing government regulations. At the same time, it largely steered clear of imposing sharia law. ... It demanded adherence to Islam in public but left legal safety hatches as long as the offenders did not flaunt their non-Islamic practices. This approach created a bizarre chimera in the legal sphere. (p. 48)

In choosing a middle course between secular and Islamic ways, Qasim veered closer to the former than Saddam Hussein would ever do. One of his first major legal reforms was the introduction of a Law of Personal Status in 1963 that, although based on the sharia, drew inspiration from European law on some key aspects. Article 3c thus forbade polygamy, except with the permission of a judge, whereas Article 74 stipulated complete equality between males and females in respect of inheritance. Legal dualism nonetheless prevailed because, in practice, most people turned to their community's clerics rather than to the state sharia courts. These clerics strongly objected to the statutory law because it opened the door to nonsharia prescriptions. But Qasim did not bend.

After the demise of Qasim, pressures exerted by the highest religious authority (the supreme "marja") were renewed, and after some initial hesitation, the new rulers abolished Article 74 of Qasim's law.[25] In addition, the 1963 law, which was to remain in force until 2003, stipulated that, even if bigamy was practiced illegally, once a couple was married, the marriage could not be declared null and void by a court. Still, the religious establishment was not fully satisfied because what it wanted was the repeal of the law so that all matters of personal status would be left exclusively to the ulama (Baram, 2014, p. 54). The sharia courts, which dealt with personal status issues of Muslims and with religious endowments, remained in place and were very active during the subsequent decades. In matters of personal status, people could turn either to the civil courts or to the sharia courts. Yet, although both were obliged to follow the statutory law, interpretations often differed, and the rulings issued by the civil courts were typically more generous to women than those of the sharia courts (p. 55).

Saddam Hussein's Distrust of Religion and Manipulation of Nationalistic Themes

Under Saddam Hussein, the promise of a perfectly secular law was abandoned, and the more daring parts of Qasim's legislation were never resurrected. The new leader, who seized power in the aftermath of a particularly odious coup, was too ambitious and opportunistic to follow a principled line of action as General Qasim had. Hussein's regime oscillated between progressive moves, such as new legal provisions forbidding forced marriage,

---

[25] In keeping with Shi'a legislation, the new clause gave preference to heirs from the nuclear family at the expense of the agnatic tribal heirs. Thus, for example, daughters whose father had died came before men outside the nuclear family, such as the deceased man's father or paternal uncles (Baram, 2014, pp. 54–5).

and reactionary steps, such as the lowering of the minimum age of marriage from sixteen to fifteen years, a measure aimed at placating conservative (mainly tribal) circles (Baram, 2014, p. 57).

In the sphere of politics, Saddam Hussein was adept at combining measures of control, repression, and seduction to strengthen his power in such antagonistic conditions. Thus, the contents of the ulama's sermons were strictly supervised, and all Shi'a shrines and mosques were brought under centralized control by transforming all Shi'a ulama into salaried employees of the state, as their Sunni counterparts had been for some time. Repressive measures included the harassment, imprisonment, and execution of thousands of important Shi'a leaders, especially clerics, as well as the expulsion from Iraq of tens of thousands of alleged "Iranian" Shiites and the provision of special financial incentives for Iraqi men who divorced their alleged "Iranian" wives (Tripp, 2000, pp. 208, 213, 221, 225; Polk, 2005, p. 120).[26]

More seductive tactics were based on lip service to Islamic values, the appointment to positions of responsibility of Shi'a clerics whom Saddam Hussein wanted to draw into the network of his patronage, and the simultaneous exploitation of themes of Arab identity and superiority combined with "a nationalism of blood and soil based on ancient territorial ethnocultural roots" (Baram, 2014, p. 62; see also Tripp, 2000, pp. 209–11). Charles Tripp depicts Hussein's political strategy in a particularly stark manner:

Obedience to him was to be the common cause of Iraq's heterogeneous inhabitants. Under this leadership distinct myths of Iraqi identity were promulgated, stressing not only the usual qualities of martial prowess, spiritual fulfilment and historical rootedness common to all nationalist myth-making, but also emphasising the succession of absolute rulers who had allegedly presided over the mythical forging of the Iraqi nation. A continuous line of political succession was established between the rulers of the ancient kingdoms of Mesopotamia, the Abbasid caliphs and Saddam Hussein himself ... no distinction was made between pre-Islamic and Islamic rulers and any lingering unease about the implications of this for Arab identity was met by transforming all the previous rulers of Mesopotamia into 'proto-Arabs'. The imaginative entity, 'Mesopotamia-as-Iraq', was thus Arabised. ... [Saddam Hussein] was no believer in abstract visions of pan-Arabism. Rather, he saw the Arab world as a stage on which the Iraqi state, constructed as an emanation of his will, should

---

[26] In March 1980, the prestigious ayatollah Baqir al-Sadr and his sister, Bint al-Huda, an influential scholar in her own right, were thus hastily executed. This was the first time in the history of Iraq that so senior a cleric had been killed (Tripp, 2000, p. 221). The two executions were a reaction to the growth of al-Da'wa, a Shi'a underground movement that was emboldened when the ayatollah regime in Iran started talking about the need to remove misguided and infidel rulers elsewhere in the Muslim world (Dawisha, 2009, p. 222).

play the leading role, for the benefit of himself and those who sustained his rule in Iraq. (Tripp, 2000, pp. 217, 222)

There was a glaring contradiction between extolling the ancient and glorious civilizations of Mesopotomia and the perfunctory references to Islam. Those civilizations, indeed, were pagan and regarded as "Jahiliyya" (belonging to times of barbarity and idolatry) by Islamic scholars. One interpretation holds that, by adopting them as role models, Saddam and his colleagues wanted to demonstrate their secular leanings and their disdain for Islamic codes of conduct (Baram, 2014, pp. 62–4). Whatever the exact motivation, an important turning point was reached toward the end of the 1970s and the early 1980s when the regime started to officially adopt more overtly Islamic postures under the influence of major changes in the international environment.

Saddam Hussein's Dramatic Reversal: Unambiguously Seducing the Clerics

The international events that sparked Saddam Hussein's dramatic U-turn were the rise of Ayatollah Ruhollah Khomeini to power in Iran (1979), the stirrings of a Shi'i revolt in Iraq, his catastrophic miscalculation in the war with Iran, and the invasion of Kuwait. As a result, Saddam adopted what Baram (2014) calls "a revised, 'Shi'ified' version of his earlier blood-and-soil nationalism adapted to the political necessity of the time" (p. 63). The Islamization of the regime's rhetoric gradually intensified and culminated in the period starting with the First Gulf War (1991) to reach its full expression in the so-called Campaign for the Faith, or "Al-hamla al-imaniyya" (1993–2003). As the internal and international environment continued to become less and less favorable to Bagdad's regime, Islamist opposition was increasingly vocal and started to affect the legal and educational system in a significant manner. It is difficult to escape the conclusion that Saddam's metamorphosis was a strategic and cynical calculation aimed at regaining lost legitimacy through a continuous appeal to religion. At the same time, faithful to his practice of combining intimidation with seduction, he never stopped clamping down in the fiercest manner on members of underground (Shi'a) Islamist organizations, such as al-Dawa (Tripp, 2000, p. 208).

A major step in Saddam's about-face coincided with the Ninth Congress of the Regional Command of the Baath (1982), which stressed with special vigor the significance of religion together with the primacy of Iraq (Tripp, 2000, p. 228). Worries about the allegiance of the Shi'a footsoldiers

who formed the bulk of Iraq's conscript army prompted Hussein to emphasize the Arab identity of the Iraqi Shi'ites and the Islamic credentials of
the regime. In January 1991, in an act that was clearly unconstitutional,
he requested that the words "Allah Akbar" (God is great) be imposed on
the Iraqi flag and publicly declared that it had become "the banner of jihad
and faith ... against the infidel horde" (Baram, 2014, pp. 207–8). His seductive tactics now included rebuilding Shi'a mosques and places of pilgrimage, declaring Iraqi territory as sacred because it contained the soil of Najaf
and Karbala (the two Shi'a holy cities), declaring the birthday of the fourth
caliph, the imam Ali, as a national holiday, and the extravagant proclamation that he, Saddam, was a descendant of this central figure for all Shi'a
Muslim believers (Tripp, 2000, p. 238; Polk, 2005, p. 12; Baram, 2014, p. 63;
Benraad, 2015, pp. 76–7; Gerges, 2016, pp. 60–1).

Changes in public vocabulary appeared already by the early 1980s when
expressions like "secular state" disappeared from official speeches, objections to atheism were increasingly voiced, and progressively more Islamic
terminology was used in public pronouncements. By early 1982, Saddam
started speaking of jihad and of "the message of eternal Islam" (Baram, 2014,
p. 180). When, on the occasion of the First Gulf War, the possibility of war
with the United States became manifest, he justified his invasion of Kuwait
by saying that "it was God who showed us [read me] the path," and for
the first time, he claimed a direct line to God (p. 214). In an open letter
to Mubarak, he referred to himself as "the slave of God" and as "the humble servant of God" (p. 215). Adopting the language of Islamists, he even
called for a jihad against the infidels (the "kuffar") and the hypocrites (the
"munafiqun") who were trying to "extinguish the flames of Islam" (p. 220).
The parallel with Islamic fundamentalism was not fortuitous because, in
his fight against Saudi Arabia and the Gulf countries, Saddam was seeking
the support of Egypt's Muslim Brotherhood. To make himself credible, he
went as far as espousing the view of the Brotherhood's founder, Hasan al
Banna, according to which the gates of ijtihad should be reopened with a
view to recognizing only the two original sources of Islam, the Quran and
the hadith, thus denying the role of later jurisprudence and suppressing bitter controversies related to the Sunni–Shi'a schism.

In the first stage of his faith campaign launched in June 1993, Saddam
embarked on a massive educational effort to impose the study of the Quran
and the hadith, starting from the first grade of primary school and doubling or tripling the amount of time devoted to it in all grades of Iraqi
schools. Concomitantly, separation between boys and girls at school was
imposed from the first grade as well. Saddam even forced the senior party

members, including Christians in the cabinet (such as Tarek Aziz), to take Quran classes lasting up to two years, and he exerted strong pressures on adults, especially the wealthy merchants, to the same effect. He then established the Saddam Center for the Reciting of the Quran at the Imam al-Azam Mosque in Baghdad, giving the recitation of the Quran a dominant place in the educational system, placing students (at the expense of their school holidays) for months every year in the mosques, and instructing the Ministry of Education to impose new examinations to test every teacher's knowledge of Islam. Religion teachers were offered a bonus over their ordinary salary, and knowledge of the Quran was made a required subject on the general matriculation examination. The apogee of the campaign was reached when nonpolitical prisoners who learned the whole Quran by heart were released from jail and their criminal records wiped clean, and the sentences of those who managed to memorize only parts of the Book were reduced in proportion to how much they had learned (Baram, 2014, pp. 220–1, 254–8).

Clearly, Saddam implemented the Islamization of Iraq out of political calculation: He believed that men of religion were becoming very influential and that a new approach was needed to protect his regime. This approach consisted of creating his own religious movement and pushing through his own version of Islam as the only one to be allowed (Baram, 2014, pp. 318–19). All these drastic steps, unheard of in Iraqi history, had the additional calculated advantage of pleasing senior Sunni and less senior Shi'a clerics whose prestige and material status received a major boost. In the words of Baram (2014), "By upgrading their socioeconomic status, he [Saddam] could hope to buy off the clerics, and through them gain much-needed public support. In light of his expressed dislike of any and all clerics, this policy can only be seen as a cynical step" (p. 257; see also p. 323). The regime's deep suspicion of clerics in general did not disappear, however, as witnessed by the close monitoring of all religious activities and systematic spying on religious functionaries.[27] Not only were all Friday sermons in all mosques carefully screened but also the Baath Party's security men had to approve appointments by the Ministry of Endowments to any religious institution. As usual, seduction was mixed with intimidation to tame opposition, and people deemed to be harsh opponents, particularly Islamists, were silenced, arrested, tortured, and killed (p. 319).

---

[27] Amatzia Baram (2014) thus writes, "All the functionaries were apparently to evaluate each of their colleagues according to the colleague's political and religious leanings, connections with opposition movements, family relatives who had escaped from Iraq, and, finally, whether he 'prayed for Mr. President' in his sermons" (p. 269).

In his effort to justify the annexation of Kuwait, to defeat the (mainly Shi'a) Islamist opposition and other religious activists inside Iraq, and to legitimize his increasing reliance on his cousins at the expense of the party's old-timers within his close circle of power, Saddam reinvented himself as the supreme religious authority – the only one able to interpret God's will– for all Sunni Iraqis, and later for the entire Sunni Muslim world. Calling himself "the Commander of the Congregation of the Believers," he presented himself as "the sword that would end Kuwaiti and Saudi moral corruption and as the solution to the crisis of Islam. He also felt emboldened enough to encourage the National Assembly to publicly endorse his prophetic pedigree (Baram, 2014, pp. 221, 261, 329). In this way, endowed with an immense ability to manipulate history and ideology, even his own identity, to serve political expediency or his megalomania, he believed that he could entice a new generation of young Sunni clerics.[28]

Mobilization of the Shi'ites was apparently to follow from his ecumenical posturing, which incorporated much Shi'a symbolism into the national pantheon, and from his toleration of the quietist, nonpolitical clerics and their head, Grand Ayatollah Ali al-Sistani (Baram, 2014, pp. 253–4, 329). Moreover, in 1995, in a closed-door meeting of the Pan-Arab Leadership, "he hammered the last nail into the coffin of the [Baath] party's secular ideology" when he announced that the party "was no longer against the principle of a pan-Islamic state, provided that unification began with pan-Arab unity" (p. 196). In other words, in complete contradiction to his 1977 declaration that the sharia was irrelevant to modern life and to his early commitment to the ideal of a national, secular, united Arab mega-state, he agreed that Islam, rather than Arabism and the Arab culture, would be the cement holding the future state together. To the extent that the party continued to repeat its commitment to a secular pan-Arab state, the outcome "was a chimera, a

---

[28] The question of whether the Campaign for the Faith was entirely motivated by strategic calculations is an interesting one. Some scholars indeed believe that, as disasters quickly followed each other after his most unfortunate decision to enter into war with Iran, Saddam Hussein underwent a personality change or a personal metamorphosis and that part of this metamorphosis was manifested as a growing religiosity. He became more withdrawn, his paranoia deepened, and his sense of being betrayed increased, with the effect that he lost his trust in the Iraqi people and his senior officers. He nevertheless managed to partition his psyche, part of him remaining very rational and calculating and the other part turning increasingly mystical. His very strange letter to God written in 2002 attests that, toward the end of his life, Saddam could thus lose contact with reality. The event that certainly affected him most on the personal level was the defection of Hussein Kamil, his son-in-law, and of his younger brother, Saddam, together with their wives, his own daughters. In the context of a culture where the family and the tribe matter so much, this was a crushing blow that deeply humiliated him (Baram, 2014, pp. 328–38).

confusing cross between old and new" (p. 196, pp. 322–3). Or, at least, one may conclude that, if the party did not really change its secular worldview, it Islamized its outward conduct (p. 327).

Extolling Ugly Tribalism: Another Betrayal of Baathist Ideology

This account may give the impression that Saddam Hussein embraced a universalist approach, whether pan-Arab or pan-Islamic, that transcended national boundaries and even more local and tribal boundaries. This is not true, however. As early as the late 1980s, he almost overturned his previous commitment to Arabism by stressing the importance of tribal identity; this involved giving official support to reactionary codes of conduct usually associated with Islam but that genuinely belong to local tribal cultures, Bedouin cultures in particular (Haddad, 2011). This was a strange move for a leader who had always extolled the virtues of modernity and emphasized the reactionary character of tribalism. In particular, the tribal tradition of erasing dishonor with blood ("ghasl al-'ar bil dam"), in the name of which relatives of an adulterous woman are allowed to kill her, was suddenly and surprisingly incorporated into the legal system. In 1990, indeed, Article 111, which exempts from any punishment a man who kills a woman to defend his honor, was introduced in the Criminal Code of 1969. A few years later, the situation of women was made worse by the increasing assertiveness of the bloody private militia of Saddam's son Uday. As Baram (2014) points out,

Uday demanded the killing of adulteresses (though not adulterers), as this would "reflect our age-old Iraqi family tradition, which makes us, as Iraqis, stand out among our [Arab] brethren". In other words, Uday was not ready to leave the murders to individual fathers, brothers, or cousins of the "offending" woman, as was the tribal tradition: he wanted the state to do the killings ... his private militia, "Saddam's Fida'iyyin", would round up young women, whom they would then accuse of prostitution and behead in public, often in front of the women's homes. ... The practice gained wide notoriety in Iraq, as it was meant to do, and served as a powerful deterrent against any opposition activity. Most people believed, probably correctly, that the girls were not prostitutes at all, but rather that some of their male relatives were active in the opposition. (p. 267)

The military disaster suffered by the Iraqi troops after they invaded Kuwait (February 1991) and an international coalition was formed to repel them precipitated the retrograde steps and the redefinition of identity ordered by Saddam. Feeling seriously threatened by the Shi'a revolt in the south (March 1991), he thought that the only way to suppress it was to mobilize the faithful tribes and clans from the Sunni heartland, the provinces of Anbar and Salah al-Din (Dawisha, 2009, pp. 235–6; Benraad, 2015, pp. 72–3). Saddam's U-turn went far beyond official statements to the effect that the people of Iraq had come to form "a single tribe," that loyal tribes are "the swords of the state," and that tribal values of solidarity and honor are at the core of Iraqi identity. He actually decreed that individuals pursued by the Iraqi law would not be prosecuted if they sought refuge within the tribal domain (Dawisha, 2009, p. 237). He thus implicitly recognized the existence of a dual legal system in which people could opt for the customary law of their tribe.

New laws sometimes providing for barbaric penalties were enacted for the purpose of curbing practices that epitomized the corrupt ways of modern city life in the eyes of many tribesmen and rural dwellers. For example, in March 1992, the regime cracked down on nightclubs and discothèques, imposed mandatory Ramadan fasting, outlawed prostitution and made it punishable by death, and banned public alcohol consumption, allowing only non-Muslims to sell spirits. More ominously, in June 1994, amputation of the hand at the wrist was introduced to punish theft and robbery, which had become widespread as a result of the deepening economic crisis; amputation of the left foot at the ankle was to sanction second offenses. Subsequent decrees enlarged the definition of theft and robbery to make the draconic punishments applicable to unauthorised money-changers, forgers of official documents, and profiteering merchants and bankers (Dawisha, 2009, p. 238; Baram, 2014, pp. 265–7, 321). Even worse, the crimes committed by the sentenced persons could be entirely fabricated. For instance, Uday Saddam Hussein's bodyguards arrested and hanged without any legal procedure twenty-one Baghdadi merchants from their own businesses' doors in 1992. The real motive behind this extreme punishment was that Uday wanted to deter these merchants from competing with him in selling contraband goods: Accusing them of profiteering and also of Wahhabism (a code word for any organized Sunni Islamists who were not fully supportive of the regime and of Saddam's concepts of revived Islam) was a good way of getting rid of them (Baram, 2014, pp. 265, 269).

Finally, women's status, which had improved remarkably during the first decades of the Baath revolution (especially under Qasim), suffered a frontal attack at the height of the faith campaign. They were prohibited from traveling abroad unless accompanied by a male relative from the paternal side of their immediate family.[29] Saddam Hussein also declared that women should

---

[29] By 1980, after a strong campaign to raise education levels and skills of the labor force, particularly for women, they came to constitute 70 percent of all pharmacists, almost half of all teachers and dentists, and just under a third of all physicians (Dawisha, 2009, p. 220).

give up paid employment and stay home, arguing in 2000 that "keeping women at home gives the highest meaning to humanistic values"; Baram interprets this statement as follows: "This was clearly an attempt on Saddam's part to stroke the male ego, the result of both religious and tribal values that saw men as superior" (Baram, 2014, p. 301). As Adeed Dawisha (2009) notes, "All this was done to a chorus of mounting emphasis on religious symbolism, which in itself constituted a repudiation of the modernism and secularism of city attitudes, so alien to tribal sensitivities" (p. 238). Fortunately, however, the threats to eliminate women's (public) employment were not executed; the Law of Personal Status, an achievement of the Baath revolution, was not Islamized; and the pro-women amendments of 1978 and those of the mid-1980s were not reversed. The most likely explanation is that annulling the Law of Personal Status and returning all matters of personal status to the sharia courts would have strengthened the power and prestige of the ulama to an extent considered unacceptable by Saddam (Baram, 2014, p. 301). Ironically, women's rights were most severely attacked soon after the demise of the Baathist regime in 2003 when the new "democratic" regime introduced by the Americans quickly decided to fire all female judges because, according to Islam, a judge must be a male (p. 302). As a matter of fact, the faith campaign opened the way for the growing assertion of religiosity that, among the Shi'a population in particular, became a way of expressing a political no less than a religious identity and entrenched opposition to the regime (p. 316).[30]

After Saddam's Downfall: Sectarianism and Authoritarianism Continued

Although neither the Islamization campaign nor the seduction of tribal leaders produced the intended effects of increasing the regime's legitimacy, the downfall of Saddam Hussein was not caused by an internal rebellion. Considerations of regime survival probably explain why there was no opposition to the Islamization campaign among the Baath party cadres even though it clashed head-on with its core identity and mission (Baram, 2014, p. 288). Hussein's demise came about through a foreign invasion and occupation at the hands of the United States in January 2002.

---

[30] Among the Shi'ites, the relative relaxation of security rules regarding visits to the mosques and ceremonies encouraged people to increase their participation in religious activities. Because they were well aware that the regime was far more lenient toward Sunni Salafis than it was toward themselves, and because the brutal repression of the March 1991 revolt in the south of the country had left an indelible mark on the Shi'a community, their members used their greater religious freedom to build up opposition to the regime (Baram, 2014, pp. 315–16).

The new Iraqi regime put into place by the occupying forces and dominated by the Shi'ites unfortunately pursued the authoritarian and ethnosectarian practices of the previous one. Attachment to an all-encompassing Iraqi identity continued to be undermined by particularistic loyalties, and the fragmentation of the Iraqi nation accelerated with worrying speed. This first became clear under the prime ministership of Ibrahim al-Jafari (2005), leader of the al-Dawa Party and a constituent member of the Shi'a United Iraqi Alliance (UIA), which is mainly composed of Shi'a Islamist parties. Under his rule,

each ministry became almost a separate canton, where the loyalty of the minister would be directed to the leader of his party or ethnosectarian group rather than to the hapless Premier. It was in such a milieu that militias and insurgency groups grew and became even more violent as they now could count on governmental and bureaucratic support … the government had begun to resemble a collection of autonomous fiefdoms over which the Premier had nominal authority. It became common to refer to a government ministry not by what it was supposed to do, but by who "owned it", which party or group had first claim on its loyalty, as well as to its largess. Particularly notorious … was the Ministry of Interior which became a haven for Shi'ite militia and death squads. (Dawisha, 2009, pp. 250–1, 267)[31]

The situation certainly did not improve under the government of the next prime minister, Nuri al-Maliki, who was even more susceptible to particularistic loyalties and sectarian sympathies. Revealing in this regard was the selective exclusion of 511 candidates by the so-called Justice and Accountability Commission (the government agency charged with implementing the de-Baathification process) during the period preceding the 2010 election (Dodge, 2012, pp. 152–7; Haddad, 2011; Osman, 2014). The political logic underlying this exclusionary move, which was rubber stamped by the Iraqi High Electoral Council (the organization charged with delivering a free and fair election), becomes plain once it is realized that most of the excluded candidates belonged to the Iraqi National Movement ("Iraqiyya") led by Ayad Allawi. As a matter of fact, Iraqiyya sought to build

[31] To complicate matters, rivalrous relationships arose not only between the three main ethnosectarian groups of the country (the Sunnites, the Shi'ites, and the Kurds) but also between various factions inside these groups. Thus, within the UIA coalition, tensions were always high between the spiritual guide of al-Fadhila, Ayatollah Muhammad al-Yaqoubi, and the leader of the Sadrists, Muqtada al-Sadr (whose father had been executed by Saddam Hussein). They have always been equally high between the latter and Abd al-Aziz Hakim, the leader of the Supreme Council for Islamic Revolution in Iraq (SCIRI), the main constituent of UIA. On more than one occasion, relations between the militias of the latter two organizations, SCIRI's Badr Brigade and the Sadrists' al-Mahdi army, erupted in bloody clashes (Dawisha, 2009, p. 266).

cross-sectarian support and thereby initiate a more inclusive politics in Iraq. This objective, which was in the line of a long history of peaceful coexistence and even intermarriages between the Sunni and Shi'a communities, was nonetheless perceived as a serious threat by the ruling clique. Eager to recognize only parties organized along ethnic and religious lines, it had a vested interest in preserving the earlier described system of sectarian appointment ("muhasasa," or sectarian apportionment) according to which all of Iraq's sectarian and religious communities were to receive cabinet posts as a way of achieving social harmony; hence the need to undermine a coalition that won its votes on an overtly secular platform. In the words of Toby Dodge (2012), "When faced with an increasingly cynical electorate alienated by his government's continued inability to deliver jobs and services, Maliki chose to conjure up the spectre of Baathism, playing to sectarian sentiment in order to solidify his [core Shi'a] vote" (p. 154).

Especially in portraying Iraqiyya as an exclusively Sunni political force, Maliki contributed to the fracturing of Iraqi identity while at the same time destroying nascent institutions such as the Central Bank's independence (whose widely respected head, Sinan al-Shabibi, was indicted on corruption charges) and the judiciary. The latter was made increasingly pliable to the instructions coming from the Office of the Prime Minister, itself dominated by members of Maliki's family and individuals who were tied to him personally from within the ranks of his party, Dawa (Dodge, 2012, pp. 159–63, 169–70; Osman, 2014). Sunnis, who felt disenfranchised by the sectarian-based policies of Maliki, decided to organize themselves communally, thus furthering the communalization of Iraqi society (Gerges, 2016, p. 13). The situation worsened because of Maliki's authoritarian tendencies which became more and more manifest as he showed a clear inclination to use the state's coercive power (especially the armed forces, which he had seized control of) to punish personal enemies and rivals. Sinister machinations and ruthless methods reminiscent of Saddam Hussein's rule were often used to suppress the opposition, particularly under the command of Lieutenant General Mahdi Gharawi – a close ally who was known for his brutality, the murder of hundreds of Sunnis, and repeated use of torture (Gerges, 2016, p. 127).[32] It was only in mid-2014 that Maliki was

---

[32] One particularly well-documented event may serve as an illustration. On December 15, 2011, on the day marking the final withdrawal of U.S. troops from Iraq, Maliki ordered the arrest of his vice president, Hashemi, a senior politician from Iraqiyya, with the help of troops and tanks led by his own son, Ahmed. Hashemi had dared voice an opinion in favor of political decentralization. In the same aggressive move, troops surrounded the houses of two other senior politicians from Iraqiyya, Minister of Finance Rafi al-Issawi and

eventually removed from power following the disastrous defeat of the Iraqi army at the hands of the jihadists of the Islamic State in Iraq and Shaam (ISIS), an offshoot of al-Qaeda in Iraq (AQI) bent on creating a unified Arab nation ruled by a caliphate in Iraq and Syria.[33]

The situation inherited by Prime Minister Haider Abadi was desperate: As a result of the divvying up of state ministries between rival factions and their militias, the government payroll had increased sevenfold, from one million under Saddam Hussein to seven million officers toward the end of Maliki's rule (*Economist*, April 16–22, 2016, p. 26). With the powerful support of both the United States and Iran, Abadi attempted to end the quota system that plagued Iraqi politics, but when he proposed (March 2016) to appoint ministers who were outside the factions' influence, the parliament refused to approve his decisions and the tentatively appointed persons withdrew, fearful of the reaction of militia gunmen. Abadi's main failure is that he did not succeed in breaking the hold that sectarian parties, including his own, have on Iraq's coffers, government contracts, and malpractices such as collective the pay of ghost workers in defunct factories (*Economist*, January 7–13, 2017, p. 28).

The rise of ISIS, also known as IS or Daech, should be seen not only as a response to Shi'a- (or Kurdish-) dominated factional politics but also as revenge against what was perceived as an imperialist aggression against the country. Revealingly, the top commanding structure has been controlled by a significant group of former senior officers from Saddam Hussein's army who took to violent resistance after being banned from reenlisting under the de-Baathification policies of the United States and successive Iraqi

---

Deputy Prime Minister Saleh al-Mutlaq. The latter had clearly warned against the descent of Iraq into dictatorship. Most worryingly, three of Hashemi's bodyguards were arrested. After four days in detention, the trio reappeared on national television and made dramatic confessions denouncing the vice president for paying them to carry out a series of assassinations and bomb attacks. They claimed that the vice president, the minister of finance, and senior regional members of their party had set up and run a death squad, Hamas of Iraq, in the town from 2006 onward. Soon after these startling confessions were aired, evidence emerged to shed light on the political motivation behind their extraction. As the "facts" unraveled, those involved in torturing the bodyguards gave a lengthy and detailed interview explaining how they had used extended torture to obtain the confessions, admitting that the confessions themselves were factually "absurd." It became clear that, as early as 2006, the Iraqi government was using the sustained torture of prisoners in an attempt to produce incriminating evidence against Hashemi. On March 15, 2011, credence was added to the accusations of torture when one of the bodyguards died in custody. (Dodge, 2012, pp. 165–6)

[33] For authoritative accounts of the rise of ISIS, see Atwan (2015), McCants (2015), and Gerges (2016).

governments (*Economist*, September 13–19, 2014, p. 39; Benraad, 2015, pp. 90–2). Especially prominent among these senior officers were experienced men from the disbanded intelligence services. At the very top was a former intelligence officer of Saddam's air force– Samir Abed al-Mohamed al-Khlifawi, better known as Haji Bakr. Thanks to the disclosure by the German magazine *Der Spiegel* of secret strategic documents largely written by him, we have learned two essential facts.[34] First, the methods described were directly inspired by those used under Saddam's regime. As a matter of fact, the documents appear to be a blueprint for the conquest of political power and the imposition of an authoritarian rule through brutal means and vicious mechanisms of squealing, mutual spying, infiltration, and denunciation. They also display an enormous measure of cynicism regarding the transient alliances deemed necessary to fulfill blatant power-seeking ambitions. The prescriptions, as it turned out, have been narrowly put into practice and largely account for ISIS military successes.

Second, and more relevant to our topic, religious references are conspicuously absent. This did not prevent Haji Bakr and his close associates from appointing a religious cleric, Abou Bakr al-Baghdadi, as chief (caliph) of the Islamic State. The avowed rationale behind this move was to rapidly enhance the recruitment of young militants who would be fighting unquestioningly and even fanatically for the cause of IS. It is revealing that, when the emissary of al-Qaeda's chief, Ayman al-Zawahiri, who succeeded Osama bin Laden after his death at the hands of a U.S. special commando unit in Pakistan, entered into contact with ISIS, he did not meet al-Baghdadi, but rather Haji Bakr and his group. Later, the emissary bitterly complained about the presence of "these treacherous snakes who are going to betray the jihad" (my translation).

There thus seems to exist a remarkable line of continuity between Saddam's regime and the practices of ISIS. On the face of it, a religious force appears to be trying to take over from a secular regime while, in reality, the same secular military elite is in command. This elite cynically and strategically uses Islam whenever that tactic suits their interests. The other side of the coin, however, is that Iraqi society has become increasingly religious, and even inside the Baath Party, some senior cadres have started to frequent the mosque out of apparently genuine conviction. Baram (2014) explains this phenomenon partly as a result of "religiosity out of hardships" and partly due to the soaring prestige of Khomeini and his Islamic regime in

---

[34] The account here is based on the French daily newspaper *Le Monde*, which published a lengthy article based on *Der Spiegel*'s report (April 26–27, 2015).

neighboring Iran (pp. 339–42; see also Gerges, 2016, pp. 141–2, 144–69). After the toppling of Saddam's regime by the U.S. Army in 2003, Iraqi society was characterized by a high degree of Islamic generosity and strong shows of sectarian identity, and it was politically dominated by the clerics in both the Sunni and Shi'a parts of the country. The only local leaders were the tribal shaykhs (appointed by Saddam) and the clerics who, being more independent, enjoyed the greatest popularity (Baram, 2014, p. 346). This sober situation was the result of the political and socioeconomic crises of the 1980s and 1990s, Saddam's faith campaign, and his reliance on tribal power in the last years of the regime. Such was the paradoxical outcome of a bloody dictatorship that betrayed its initial ideal and identity.

Lessons from Saddam's Miscalculations: The Rising Role of the Clerics

There is no doubt that the adverse international events that hit Iraq during the latter part of Saddam's rule severely shook his regime's foundations. It could be contended that these events and their catastrophic consequences were of Saddam's own making and were therefore endogenous to the regime's choice behavior. However, there is strong evidence that if Saddam did, indeed, take the fatal decisions that sparked them, he misinterpreted the situation and poorly anticipated the effects of his choices. He was persuaded that Iran had been considerably weakened by the revolution of the ayatollahs and that its army would therefore be easily quashed in a head-on confrontation with the well-trained and well-equipped Iraqi army. He also thought erroneously (perhaps because he was lured into a trap) that the United States would not react to an Iraqi invasion of Kuwait; he did not expect the harsh embargo that Western powers would impose in retaliation for his adventurous expansionism in the region and for the way he crushed Kurdish rebellions at home. Thus, the disastrous effects of his decisions can be regarded as largely unpredicted events or exogenous shocks.

In the successive crisis situations born of those disasters, people increasingly turned to religion, and religious clerics became more sensitive to their suffering and more willing to assert their views, including criticisms against the regime. In the absence of any organized political force or opposition movement, which had all been crushed during the regime's consolidation period, it was inevitable that religion came to fill the void and to articulate the growing popular frustrations into a coherent and emotionally appealing discourse. To this rising threat, Saddam responded by increasing his efforts to seduce the clerics and to posture himself as an absolute leader with strong religious credentials. On the policy level, he adopted regressive measures that, given his previous commitment to the Baathist ideology, with its emphasis on secularism and Arabism rather than Islam, appear almost unthinkable. As is usual in this type of context, the measures touching on education and, to a lesser extent, on women's role, were probably those that produced the most adverse effects on the long-term growth potential of the country.

Case Study 7: Syria

Hafez al-Assad: Perfunctorily Bending to Islam

In line with Baathist ideology, Hafez al-Assad, who ruled Syria for thirty years (1970–2000), always stressed that he was a Muslim. In particular, he declared that the military coup through which he seized power from another Baathist leader (Salah Jadi) was "necessary to preserve the Islamic identity of the country" against Marxist "deviances" (McHugo, 2014, p. 190). On important Muslim feasts, he made a point of being seen praying with leading Sunni religious leaders. And because he belonged to the Alawi community, which had been considered as heterodox since the thirteenth century when Ibn Taymiyya launched a fatwa declaring that Alawites are enemies of Islam, he was eager to obtain a contrary fatwa from a leading Shi'a scholar in Lebanon, Musa al-Sadr. The new fatwa stated that the Alawites were true Muslims of a Shi'a persuasion, even though the Alawite identity had traditionally been defined in tribal rather than religious terms. Hafez al-Hassad wanted a strictly secular political constitution, yet he understood the need to yield to the pressure of the Muslim Brotherhood and other Islamist forces by introducing an article providing that the president should be a Muslim and accepting that Islamic legal reasoning, or the sharia, should be the "main source" of legislation. Moreover, he completed a pilgrimage to Mecca and set up a prize in his name for the best recitation of the Quran (McHugo, 2014, pp. 117, 180, 190–1, in particular).

His strategy to appear as a defender of the Muslims worked poorly, however. Syrian Baathists continued to be seen by religious radicals as seeking to turn a Muslim society into an atheist one. Underlying the open conflict between Islamists and the state lay a deep frustration among small- and medium-scale bazaar merchants and artisans following the disruption of their trade and the expansion of a state-sponsored class of rich businessmen. It is thus no coincidence that the Islamist movement first developed in Aleppo, a large city whose traditional social and trading links with the north (now Turkey) and the east (now Iraq) were severed by the division of the Near East into modern territorial states. Aleppo was thus cut off from its natural outlet to the sea and from its traditional markets and hinterland

(Ayubi, 1991, pp. 90–1). Yet, close links persisted between clerics and tradesmen, an outcome of intermarriages and the physical proximity of shops and mosques (Batatu, 1988, pp. 115–21; Hinnebusch, 1982, pp. 165–6; Hudson, 1986; Safadi, Munro, and Ziadeh, 2011, pp. 150–1).

The conflict between Islamists and the state rapidly worsened. Assassinations of prominent Alawi figures (plus an assassination attempt on Hafez al-Assad himself) and bomb attacks were followed by major disturbances centered on Aleppo and Hama (see McHugo, 2014, ch. 7, for more details) and calls for a general uprising and jihad against a regime considered as godless, socialist, and a traitor to the Palestinian cause. The accusation of socialism arose from the regime's marked tendency to nationalize the economy and expand the state bureaucracy in which Alawites were already overrepresented. As for the accusation of betrayal, it was caused by the fact that, for reasons of sheer expediency, al-Assad chose not to support the Palestinians in Lebanon.[35] The rebellion reached its climax in Hama in February 1982, and Assad's regime ferociously put it down with the strong support of the Alawites in top positions in the army and the secret services, the ill-famed "mukhâbarât" (McHugo, 2014, chs. 3–5, pp. 194–6, in particular).

After crushing the Hama rebellion, Hafez al-Assad continued his efforts to seduce the large mass of religion-minded Sunnis. It is interesting to note that the religious revival in Syria also involved an ever-increasing number of young professionals, most of whom owed their education to the regime's efforts to raise the level of literacy and schooling. Many more people were thus able to explore their religion and to learn about Arabism and Islam and so tread the paths of piety (McHugo, 2014, pp. 192–7). In his efforts to co-opt the religious revival, especially among the Sunni merchant classes of Aleppo, al-Assad was supported by some well-respected religious scholars, including the Kurdish shaykh Ahmad Kuftaro, who praised the president's "dedication and ... steadfastness on the principle of faith." For Kuftaro, Assad's regime was a protector of Islam; the regime and Islam were thus "twin brothers." Assad was also helped by Shaykh Sa'id al-Buti, who sided with him over the regime-instigated massacre of Hama dissidents. The argument invoked by al-Buti was that the Muslim Brotherhood and the Fighting Vanguard (a militant organization backed by the Brotherhood) had brought civil strife (fitna), which was against the principles of Islam (p. 197).

---

[35] To the surprise and consternation of Arab nationalists, Hafez al-Assad decided to support the Maronite militias in 1976 to save them from the leftist forces of Kamal Jumblatt and the Palestinian revolutionaries of Yasser Arafat, with whom he was on quite bad terms. This decision resulted in the defeat of the forces "which should have been the natural allies for a Baathist" (McHugo, 2014, p. 174).

Bashar al-Assad: Manipulating Violent Islamists to Safeguard a Corrupt Regime

Bashar al-Assad succeeded his father in 2000. His attempts to democratize the regime and liberalize both the economic and political systems were quickly aborted. At the very top of the regime was a narrow clique of family members, and the president could rely on the active support of a rich and increasingly sophisticated elite living in the main cities: Damas, Aleppo, Homs, and Lattakia.[36] In response to strong pressure from the regime's inner circle, restrictions on political freedom and defensive measures aimed at protecting its economic privileges and judicial immunity were soon reinstated. Corruption remained as strong and endemic as ever, the rule of law did not exist for the inner circle of the regime, and the security apparatus continued to be omnipresent. The relationship of politics to religion was also unchanged. The message that no conflict existed between the regime and Islam continued to be conveyed through the presence of Bashar al-Assad and high-level officials (including official representatives of the Baath Party for the first time in 2006) at Muslim festivals (Hokayem, 2013, pp. 24–9; Ziadeh, 2013, p. 155; McHugo, 2014, pp. 218–19).

The way in which Syria slid into civil war provides a vivid illustration of how sectarian politics and religious extremism can be cynically used by a despotic regime. Thus, when peaceful protests took place in Deera in March 2011 in response to the arrest and likely torture of children aged between nine and fifteen who wrote rebellious graffiti on the walls of their school, the security forces reacted extremely brutally. And when demonstrations spread to other cities, the same brutality was displayed, justified on the ground that the protests were instigated by Sunni fanatics or Islamist terrorists bent on destroying the country's complex social mosaic (Filiu, 2015, pp. 200–5). Sectarian attacks often perpretrated by the regime's shadowy, Alawi-dominated militias known as "shabiha" (ghosts) were part of its ugly tactic aimed at "transforming a popular, broad-based, proletarian and peasant uprising into a sectarian civil war" (Littell, 2015, p. 7). That the accusations were entirely fabricated by the regime's propaganda machine is evident from the fact that, under the guise of a general amnesty granted during the spring and summer of 2011, the ruling clique released hundreds of jihadists from jail and instigated attacks on Christians and other minorities to make

---

[36] These relatives included his younger brother Maher, who became commander of the Republican Guard and other special forces; his brother-in-law Assef Shawqat, who was deputy defense minister and deputy chief-of-staff; and his cousin Rami Maklouf, who was alleged to control 60 percent of the economy and to act as a representative for more than 200 foreign companies operating in Syria (McHugo, 2014, p. 217).

its case look convincing. Among the prisoners released in February 2012 was Abu Mus'ab al-Suri, a former member of the Fighting Vanguard and al-Qaeda, and Mohammad Abou al-Fateh al-Joulani, a well-known jihadi leader. Many of the Islamists thus released came to form the violent rebel group, Jabhat Al-Nusra, the branch of al-Qaeda in Syria that proved to be an enemy rather than an ally of the Free Syrian Army in the fight against the regime. Like many other "volunteers" from Syria, Joulani left for Iraq to join AQI, which had earlier been rebranded as ISI, the Islamic State in Iraq (in October 2006), and finally became ISIS (Islamic State in Iraq and Syria) when it sought to establish a military base in Syria on its own (Filiu, 2015, pp. 249–50; Gerges, 2016, pp. 92–7).[37] When a violent confrontation between the two organizations, the Nusra Front and ISIS, erupted at the end of 2013, a serious split was created inside the global jihadi movement, and the leadership of al-Qaeda Central regretted having endorsed ISI at the time of its formation (Gerges, 2016, p. 162–5).

In a telling manner, ISIS seems rarely, if ever, to have fought against regime forces, and vice versa: The Syrian Army has avoided bombing the locations where ISIS or the Nusra Front is based. It is difficult to escape the conclusion that strong collaborative links were forged between ISIS fighters and mukhâbarât officers when the former were encouraged and funded by the Syrian regime to cross the border into Iraq to fight the Western coalition troops after they toppled Saddam Hussein in 2003. Another odd event is revealing of the odious collaborative tactic adopted by the Syrian government. In January 2014, a heterogeneous coalition of opposition militias launched a major attack against ISIS forces, managing, at the cost of thousands of casualties, to expel these forces from parts of the northern Aleppo and Idlib provinces that they previously held. That was the first time ISIS had been defeated and repelled. Ominously, Assad's answer was a massive bombing campaign of the jihadi-free districts of Aleppo, which eventually caused the death of some 2,000 people and a massive displacement of the civilian population (Filiu, 2015, p. 206). As pointed out by Fawaz Gerges (2016), the tragic irony is that initially the large-scale popular uprising in Syria was neither sectarian driven nor violent; the protesters just wanted to send a message to the authorities advocating political and social reforms, not regime change (p. 172).

---

[37] Another "volunteer" was Boubaker al-Hakim, a French Tunisian citizen who, after staying for several months in the Zarqawi-controlled city of Falluja, went to Tunisia to organize the armed branch of Ansar al-Sharia (AS). He claimed responsibility for several murders that nearly derailed the transition process in that country, including the Tunis museum massacre in 2015 (Filiu, 2015, p. 250).

As in Algeria, Egypt, Sudan, and Pakistan, the perverse logic followed by autocratic and cronyist regimes bent on maintaining their power and privileges brought about the abhorred reality of sectarian warfare and violence (Darke, 2014, pp. 62, 127–9; Filiu, 2015; Yazbek, 2015; *Economist*, July 5–11, 2014; McHugo, 2014, pp. 227, 231; Filiu, 2015, pp. 145–8).[38] The disastrous consequences associated with sectarianism were considered a price worth paying to maintain the exorbitant privileges of the ruler and his inner circle of venal loyalists, including the business cronies and the co-opted caste of intellectuals, lawyers, and engineers who rallied to the regime's cause.

The despicable tactic whereby a despotic regime brings into existence or strengthens a radical religious group to achieve narrow political ends can also be resorted to when separatist threats are looming. Thus, in Turkey in the 1990s, a shadowy militant group known by the name of Hizbullah (with no connection to the Lebanese namesake) was recruited by the "deep state" (senior spies, military officers, and members of the judiciary) to murder hundreds of members and supporters of the PKK, the Marxist-leaning nationalist Kurdish movement. It was only when Hizbullah carried its bloodletting beyond the Kurdish region that the government began to clamp down on it, killing its leader, Huseyin Velioğlu, in a shootout (January 2000). The movement has reemerged in the form of a conservative religious party named Huda-Par ("the party of Allah"), whose declared objective is to combat the PKK in elections (*Economist*, November 23-29, 2013).

Glimpses at Palestine and Malaysia

These seven case studies offer vivid illustrations of how politics can instrumentalize Islam under autocratic regimes. The list is not complete, however, and it is not difficult to think of other examples. Thus, in Bangladesh, the ruling Aswami League of Shaykh Hasina, which remains the country's only mainstream secular force, has recently striven to appease Islamist conservatives by caving in to pressure not to pass secular laws and by using defamation laws only to target critics of the League and of Islam. These actions discourage the devout from demonstrating against the government, but also set into motion a vicious process, as some opponents are pushed toward more extremist groups of a religious nature. The outcome is an ominous weakening of the country's secular, tolerant traditions (*Economist*, November 7–13,

---

[38] Another manipulative tactic of the regime consisted of setting up a website in the name of the Syrian Muslim Brotherhood and posting on it claims of responsibility for terrorist attacks in Damas on December 23, 2011 (McHugo, 2014, p. 227).

2015, p. 50). The cases of Palestine and Malaysia also deserve to be briefly described in the same context.

Palestine: The Betrayal of Revolutionary Secularist Ideals

Palestine is a special case insofar as it is not a full-fledged state: Part of it, the West Bank, is governed by the Palestinian Authority, which is maintained under the tight surveillance of Israel and has only limited prerogatives. The case is nevertheless interesting because the liberation movements that have been fighting for the creation of a Palestinian state for more than a half-century were clearly secular in their original approaches and ideologies. Over time, however, the leading movement – the Fatah – gradually lost its legitimacy, because of its inability to achieve its central political objective, Palestinian independence, and the pervasive corruption and creeping authoritarianism of its administration and leadership. It is in this deleterious context that Islamist governments gained ground, most notably Hamas in the Gaza Strip, and the regime started to cede to the pressures of, and compromise with, religious forces. The outcome has been the Islamization of the Palestinian educational system and increasing intrusion of the ulama into Palestinians' public life.

The experience of Waleed Al-Husseini (2015) is especially gripping. This young man from Qalqilya (Cisjordania) became an atheist and created two websites ("I am Allah" – Ana Allah, and the "Voice of Reason") questioning the scripturalist approach to the Quran and highlighting the absurdity of a straightforward application of many of its tenets to present-day circumstances. He was soon accused of "destabilising the Palestinian Authority and threatening state security," was arrested, and was brought before a military court; there he was indicted on the ground that "he incited interconfessional hatred, insulted religious officials, and hurt religious feelings" (p. 110; my translation). All these offenses are considered crimes according to the Criminal Military Code of Palestine, which was largely inspired by the Algerian constitution of 1969. In proceeding with the case, the president of the Palestinian Authority acted under the pressure of the highest authority at al-Azhar and the World Council of Muslim Ulama, which sent a report requesting him to identify and immediately arrest the author of the "Ana Allah" blog.

It was in the name of Allah that the public prosecutor swore to put Al-Husseini behind bars for the rest of his life, to take down his website and eradicate it forever (p. 78). Here was thus a sacred alliance between political power and religious elite aimed at crushing dissent and political opposition. Blogging in a free manner is viewed as a serious threat to autocratic rule, and by unleashing severe punishments against free thinkers on the pretext that they are odious miscreants, the autocratic regime of Palestine seeks to entrench its power by diverting attention from its glaring failures. Al-Husseini's struggle, as he explained to the senior investigator, is to fight oppression, dictatorship, violations of human rights, corruption, and the continuous embezzlement of public money. In his own words, "Arab laicists are the victims of two kinds of oppression: oppression of despotic power and oppression of religious officials" (p. 113; my translation).

The crime of apostasy has been cynically used by many despots in Muslim countries, as documented in the case of Sudan. Saudi Arabia, which passed a law equating atheism to terrorism in 2014, is one of the nineteen countries in the world that criminalize apostasy – the turning away from one religion to another one or to no religion. More ominously, it is among the twelve countries where apostasy is punishable by death. (Note that all but two of these twelve countries are in the Middle East and Africa). Even countries with civil laws that do not expressly outlaw apostasy still find creative ways to crack down on religious deviation. In Oman, Kuwait, and Jordan, Islamic courts can thus annul the marriages of apostates, who are considered as impostors, or prevent them from inheriting property; in Pakistan, couples who convert from Islam risk having their children taken away from them. Moreover, blasphemy laws are often invoked when laws against apostasy do not exist, generally to the same effect. In Egypt, for example, where atheism is not a legal offense, an opponent who denigrates Islam and denounces the political regime can be charged with insulting religion in precisely the same way as was used against Al-Husseini in Palestine (*Economist*, March 26–April 1, 2016).

Malaysia: Playing with Religious and Ethnic Fire

The extraordinary feature of the Palestinian West Bank is that an alleged crime of blasphemy against Islam could be judged by a military court. By contrast, Malaysia has avoided such confusion by allowing Islamic courts to operate in parallel with secular ones and to hand down rulings on civil matters to Muslims, although on the understanding that they can hand down only limited sentences: According to federal law, the sentences that Islamic courts are entitled to deliver are limited to three years in jail, a moderate fine, or six strokes of the cane. But recently, the Pan-Malaysian Islamic Party (PAS), which has run Kelantan state (in the northeast) since 1990, has claimed the right to inflict harsher Islamic punishments (or "hudud"), such as the stoning to death of adulterers, in Kelantan at least. This would not be a serious threat if the United Malays National Organization (UMNO), the party that has ruled the country since independence but whose power has been severely contested during the last two decades, had not decided to instrumentalize Islam to stay in power. PAS had become part of an effective opposition coalition, the "Pakatan Rakyat," which would have unseated UMNO had not the latter resorted to blatant forms of gerrymandering in the 2013 election.

The cynical game played by UMNO has consisted of encouraging the PAS's demands for hudud with the aim of exacerbating divisions in the opposition coalition. Weakened by large-scale defections of ethnic Chinese and ethnic Indian voters, the UMNO has chosen to follow a new tactic: "to refurbish its former identity as a fierce defender of ethnic Malays and of Islam, the religion to which all Malays are assumed to adhere" (*Economist*, April 4–10, 2015, p. 44). This strategy implied tolerance toward "Malay supremacists and Islamist firebrands incubating on its fringes" and a reversal of its position on the Sedition Act, a vaguely worded law inherited from the British colonial power (which used it against independence fighters) and aimed at harrying activists and opposition leaders. Instead of doing away with this noxious act, the UMNO leadership vowed to strengthen it with clauses prohibiting speech that denigrates Islam and other religions (p. 45). Among those arrested on the ground of sedition were opponents of hudud, corporal, and capital punishments and staff at the *Malaysian Insider*, an online newspaper (*Economist*, April 11–17, 2015, p. 49). As part of the move toward increasing repression, the Internal Security Act – another relic of colonial times that allowed indefinite detention without trial and had been scrapped in 2012 – was reintroduced in early 2015. Leakers of government secrets have recently been threatened with caning and other stiff sentences by the attorney general. These threats have evoked great concern among the liberal critics of the government, because they were issued in the context of the uncovering of a huge corruption scandal in which the prime minister, Najib Razak, was deeply involved (*Economist*, March 5–11, 2016, p. 43).

There is thus the usual picture of a regime with an autocratic bent and compromised by scandals that, pushed against the wall by a democratic opposition, resists by resorting to a variety of manipulative instruments grounded in religion. These include not only gerrymandering of districts and violent repression but also vicious instrumentaliation of reactionary religious forces and ethnic-based movements. In the case of Malaysia, this last tactic is especially dangerous because it ends up fanning racial and religious tensions in a majority Malay (and Muslim) country with large ethnic Chinese and ethnic Indian minorities.

6.3 Conclusion

This conclusion first draws central lessons from the detailed review of the country cases, focusing on the polarization of societies and the Islamization of political debates. I then link the main findings with the theory presented in Section 4.5 and examine the relationships between state power and puritanical Islamist movements. Finally, I highlight the way in which foreign policies exacerbate the problem of autocratic regimes that are confronted with the potential opposition of Islamist forces; this last part provides a natural bridge to the following chapter.

Islamization of Political Debate

In the type of situations considered in this chapter, autocratic rulers choose to follow an opposition confrontation strategy (OCS). That is, they opt for policies that are so unpopular, and indulge in levels of corruption that are so high, that buying off all the clerics to ensure political stability proves too costly. Iniquitous sovereigns treat the state as their personal fiefdom, and their blatantly unjust policies hurt the interests of the popular masses in favor of their inner circle and a narrow elite. They run kleptocratic autocracies based on favoritism, unaccountable monopolies, and malpractices ranging from expropriation and bribe taking to sheer racketeering. Hence it is unsurprising that such regimes are strongly contested from within, generally on the grounds of excessive liberalism, pervasive corruption, and subordination to foreign interests.

Political opposition is especially threatening because the clerics whom the ruler does not control, the self-appointed clerics, are actively engaged in it. It is then tempting for secular rulers with a despotic bent to use the legitimating force of official Islam more strongly for the purpose of defeating both the religious discourse of clerical opposition leaders and the secular discourse of left-wing forces. The end result has too often been the tragic eradication of progressive secular forces (including trade unions, student movements, and intellectual and professional associations) and the emergence of polarized societies in which the language of Islam becomes the only tolerated way to express political opposition. The division between official clerics who pronounce fatwas in support of the regime and self-appointed clerics who identify themselves with the suffering classes and pronounce counter-fatwas on their behalf injects a dangerous poison into a political climate dominated by anathemas rather than reasoned arguments. The natural upshot of this vicious confrontation is a sort of bidding war in which the language of religion permeates all public debates and the expression of secular views arouses immediate suspicion. Nonetheless, through the politically calculated suppression of the left, the ruler hopes to avoid a serious questioning of his corrupt policies and the privileges awarded to his close supporters, particularly among relatives and kinsmen. The final outcome of this vicious struggle is deeply uncertain, and in some cases the ruler ends up being assassinated by members of Islamist movements that he had himself promoted.

Linking Results with the Theory

In terms of our theory of religious co-option under autocracy, an opposition confrontation equilibrium is characterized by a combination of deeply unpopular policies, partial co-option of the clerics, and political instability. Because such policies are a mix of social and economic strategies, on the one hand, and measures regarding the role of Islam and the sharia, on the other hand, iniquitous socioeconomic policies can be accompanied by measures granting concessions to official clerics in terms of their role in the public sphere (in education and private mores, in particular). The latter then serve to mitigate the adverse impact of those policies on political stability. What bears emphasis is that, in the situations covered by this chapter, the policy mix selected by the autocratic regime, even when understood in this large sense, is incompatible with total co-option of the clerics and, hence, with political stability. This may be because the social and economic policies are too blatantly unjust to be compensated by measures on the religious front or because the radical clerics consider these measures as hypocritical concessions.

Saddam Hussein's rule in Iraq deserves special attention because the transformation of his politics with respect to Islam can be seen as the result of a shock that radicalized clerics (what economists call a comparative-static effect). He was indeed confronted with a sudden turn of events when a series of unexpected misfortunes considerably weakened his regime. His miscalculation in the Iraq-Iran war and the intervention of the United States in Kuwait after being militarily occupied by his army shook the foundations of his "iron fist" rule. Because of the ensuing radicalization of the clerics, they became more costly to seduce, resulting in a serious threat to political stability. In this instance, the predicted response of the autocrat is to moderate policies so as to eventually increase political stability, which necessitates that even more clerics are co-opted than was the case in the initial (pre-shock) situation. As a rule, such concessions may take the form of populist policies designed to placate ordinary people (for example, subsidies on basic consumption items, social housing schemes, and pay rises for state employees), official steps that give the impression of combating corruption, and measures intended to meet demands of the clerics, particularly for a greater recognition of the role of the Islamic law. Among the responses chosen by Saddam, concessions toward the clerics figured most prominently: He opted for a complete reversal of the secular, pan-Arabist ideology that he had previously used to legitimate his absolute power. Suddenly, he not only postured himself as the defender of Islam against the attacks of the infidels but also adopted a series of regressive measures to please conservative clerics and tribal leaders. In the country that could boast having the most advanced family code of the Arab world, such a U-turn was particularly tragic.

Relationships between State Power and Puritanical Islamists

In situations where an opposition confrontation equilibrium prevails, puritanical Islamists represent the most radical component of the clerical body. As such, they are beyond the reach of the ruling power's seductive attempts. When the autocracy is very unpopular, even moderate religious clerics may prove hard to entice, as attested by the changing position of the (neo-) Muslim Brothers toward the regime in Egypt. Things may be more complicated than what this rather neat picture suggests, however. In a good number of cases, such as in Egypt, Indonesia, Algeria, Syria, and Pakistan, the darkest side of the autocratic system, the so-called deep state, may not hesitate to secretly nurture violence-based movements that profess a puritanical version of Islam. It does so not only to counter the opposition of progressive secular forces depicted as nonbelievers or apostates – a task primarily assigned to the co-opted official ulama – but also mainly to discredit moderate religious opponents.

Extremists mostly abhor moderates. According to the famous Dostoïevskian definition, extremists are people adhering to a fundamentalist worldview and for whom the end justifies the means; thus they have no qualms about collaborating temporarily with enemies whose psychological predispositions and combat methods most resemble their own. This collusion is only temporary because despotic states hope to eliminate these hotheads in due time; that is, after they have completed the dirty work of eliminating moderate political opponents. What therefore bears emphasis is that this sort of "playing with the devil" does not amount to a genuine co-option in the way usually understood. Rather than aiming at a long-term cooperation based on a true quid pro quo – material privileges in exchange for political support – collusion with puritanical, violence-based movements is an expedient to be abandoned as soon as possible. The inherent short-term quality of this sinister approach is especially evident because religious fanatics themselves look at this collusion in the same way. They are essentially non–co-optable opponents: Their level of "purity" or intransigence is so high that no material compensation can ever succeed in prompting them to end their revolt.

Another sinister tactic that an authoritarian regime can pursue when co-option of moderate religious opposition fails is to conflate the moderates with extremist groups so as to discredit their members. In Egypt under al-Sisi, the Muslim Brothers have thus been cynically misrepresented as a violent outfit to justify the same kind of harsh repression as that applied against radical terrorist groups. In Syria, likewise, Bashar al-Assad has systematically used the same tactic by picturing any moderate opposition as a bunch of dangerous and violent terrorists.

The Exacerbating Role of Foreign Policies

As some case studies in this and the previous chapters attest, foreign policies are liable to arouse the ire of a large majority of the population, particularly when they are perceived as hurting national sovereignty, dignity, and interests. Relevant examples here include the inequitable economic deals struck with foreign colonial powers by Iran's Qajar dynasty (see Chapter 5) and the iniquitous peace agreements concluded by Egypt with Israel under Sadat. In the latter case, indeed, the partisan attitude of the United States in the Israel-Palestine conflict has been reflected not only in the open military and political support to the state of Israel but also in the pressures exerted on Egypt to conclude peace with Israel on unbalanced terms. Egyptians deeply resented this peace agreement as a direct blow to their national pride and a humiliating surrender to the law of the strongest. Sadat eventually paid with his life for his decision to accept peace with Israel, even though the terms were tilted against Egypt's most fundamental demands, in particular, the resolution of the Palestinian problem.

The inability of Palestinian leadership to obtain the attributes and prerogatives of a full-fledged sovereign state for Palestine with internationally recognized status, together with the deeply corrupt practices of the Palestinian Authority (PA), created fertile ground for the rise of an Islamist opposition. Were not Palestinian leaders secular people who failed to restore the dignity of their people and to ensure an equitable development of the territory under their partial control? The PA thus lost the credibility and legitimacy that its open resistance against Israel initially granted it in the eyes of Palestinians and other Arabs. It is a tragic outcome that, in an effort to regain its lost legitimacy, the PA turned to Islam, thus betraying its original objective of building a secular, multiconfessional state in Palestine. In the cases of both Egypt and Palestine, therefore, an autocratic regime eager to preserve political stability compensated for its unpopular foreign policy by making important concessions to conservative religious and tribal forces.

No serious analysis of the problem of Muslim countries can afford to ignore the role of international factors. These go beyond the Arab world and the Israel-Palestine conflict, as attested by the difficulties of Pakistan in resolving its problem of national identity, especially vis-à-vis the country from which it seceded, India. The problem of Afghanistan is also inseparable from Pakistan's predicament. The complex interplay of international forces receives due attention in the next chapter, which focuses on the rise of Islamist movements in the lands of Islam.

Islamism in Historical and International Perspective

The objective of this chapter is to shed light on how the international environment has impinged on the autocratic regimes of Muslim countries since the date of their formation. Generally, international forces have contributed to make these regimes potentially more vulnerable, thus explaining the sort of reactions discussed in the preceding chapter on the basis of detailed country case studies. In many cases, the reactions consisted of regressive measures aimed at increasing the influence of Islam and its representatives in public life. The intent of the autocrats has been to avoid losing the support of the clerics that they deem so critical for their survival, even if the effected policy shifts harmed economic growth and development. The international forces have had both ideological and material effects. Material conditions that threaten the stability of autocratic regimes under consideration have to do with facts of domination, which can be traced to the colonial period or to the imperial dreams of ambitious regional leaders. Ideological influences come from internationally supplied Islamist ideologies, whose rise may be seen as a response to facts of domination and the perceived threat they represent to educated groups.

The chapter consists of four sections. Section 7.1 explores the conditions under which a puritanical version of Islam was born and spread. Section 7.2 continues the analysis, examining how Islamist reformism has been reinforced by a modernization crisis compounded by military defeats in the heart of the Middle East. The next section, Section 7.3, looks into the motives behind recruitment into Islamist movements. Section 7.4 emphasizes two points: the need to consider the psychosocial implications of any civilizational challenge and the important role of foreign domination in exacerbating the problems born of such a challenge.

7.1 The Birth and Spread of Islamic Puritanism

The thinking of a few religious reformers who drew inspiration from the writings of both Hanbal and Taymiyya is guiding present-day Islamist movements. Remember that Hanbal lived in times marked by disunity and bitter internal strife, and Taymiyya in periods characterized by external aggression. Their calls for a return to pristine Islam were thus directed at rescuing their societies from destruction. As becomes clear in the following overview, either or both circumstances were often present when significant movements for the reform of Islam emerged. Note carefully that these reformist fundamentalist movements must be carefully distinguished from the fanatical puritanism that characterizes nomadic tribes attracted by the egalitarian ethos of Islam. Such unsophisticated Islamists, "who cared nothing for the great achievements of Arabic thought and who were willing to listen to the hysterical strictures of the orthodox against philosophy and science," had dominated Islam as early as the eleventh century when, at both ends of the Mediterranean Muslim world, the Seljuk Turks and the Berber tribesmen succeeded in gaining political authority (Cantor, 1993, p. 227). Other examples are the Anatolian Qizilbash tribes that helped Isma'il in his conquests leading to the takeover in Iran (end of the fifteenth century) and the Ikhwan Bedouins who helped the al Sauds establish a centralized kingdom in Arabia (more about them soon).

This section reviews the most important sources of reformist Islamist thinking in modern times. It begins with an exploration of Wahhabism, which developed in Saudi Arabia several centuries ago and gained influence gradually, thanks to movements of pilgrims to the holy cities of Mecca and Medina. It was not until the twentieth century that political and economic circumstances gave rise to a widespread adoption of this puritanical interpretation of Islam. Reformist movements of political Islam were not only born of frustrations against the corruption of political (and religious) elites but were also sparked by anticolonial feelings. The two motives were actually linked inasmuch as these movements attributed colonial penetration to the corruptibility of the dominated regimes. The doctrines that inspired these movements cannot be considered a simple upshot of Wahhabi influence, although this influence was never far away. Finally, attention is paid to the doctrines of Mawdûdi and Qutb, self-appointed clerics who have recently had a considerable impact on violent Islamist movements in postcolonial Muslim countries. These two influential thinkers lived in Pakistan and Egypt, respectively, two major predominantly Muslim countries at the center of sharp tensions and unresolved conflicts in the Islamic world (see Chapter 6).

The Influence and Spread of Wahhabism

The Islamist movement that was going to exert the most profound and lasting influence on the Muslim world in modern times was itself the outcome of several proto-reformist tendencies that were joined together in seventeenth- and eighteenth-century Mecca and Medina. In those sacred cities, scholars from various parts of the Islamic world sought to eradicate religious practices deemed incompatible with the Quran and the teachings of the Prophet (Lapidus, 1988, p. 258). The political expression of the reformist tendency was the Wahhabi movement in Arabia. Its leader, Muhammad Ibn Abd al-Wahhab (1703–92), preached strict obedience to the Quran and the hadith, as interpreted by responsible scholars in each generation, and the rejection of all that could be regarded as illegitimate innovations, including reverence to dead saints as intercessors with God and the special devotion of the Sufi orders. To preserve his creed and purify Islam from what are considered to be impure accretions of custom and culture, the Wahhabi does not hesitate to destroy the relics of the past as a way to avoid any confrontation between myth and the historical document (Hourani, 1991, pp. 257–8; Feldman, 2008, pp. 93–4; Saint-Prot, 2008, pp. 271–316).

What should be emphasized here is that the puritanical doctrine of al-Wahhab broke with the general consensus of the Muslims. By regarding as un-Islamic any concept not derivable from the Quran and the hadith, it dismissed the long tradition of Muslim jurisprudence ("fiqh") that had accepted a much larger range of sources as authoritative (see Chapter 3). Mainstream public opinion, both Sunni and Shi'a, had also long agreed on the permissibility of seeking the intercession of the Prophet or other "friends of God" in one's dealings with the deity in the form of petitionary prayer, supplication, or the visitation of shrines" – all acts that al-Wahhab denounced as "shirk," the sin of compromising God's unity (Khalid, 2007, p. 45). Not only did al-Wahhab condemn all forms of what he considered idolatry (including poetry in praise of the Prophet) and reject Sufism and Shi'ism root and branch but he also outlined a theory of the jihad against all Muslims who had deviated from the true path. Fitting the definition of deviants were all those Muslims who "carried amulets to ward off evil spirits, worshipped at the tombs of their pious ancestors in Mecca and Medina, listened to music, drank alcoholic beverages, or dressed inappropriately" (Lee, 2014, p. 226).

Given its marginal character, it is not surprising that the movement created by al-Wahhab did not attain real importance in his own time (as a philosopher, he was poorly regarded by Arab colleagues). It was to acquire greater significance later, however. The reason is that al-Wahhab was linked to the ambitious Saud tribe that, despite its rather weak support among other local tribes, was striving to take hold of sovereign power and conquer the Arabian deserts. By instrumentalizing Islam for the purpose of national integration (see Chapter 4) and choosing Wahhabism as the version of the faith that would symbolically identify the emerging new nation, the Sauds succeeded in uniting diverse tribal groups into a single movement that eventually conquered most of Arabia and established the kingdom of Saudi Arabia in 1932.

That the move was opportunistic is evident from the inside accounts provided by many scholars. According to them, indeed, the Saudi royal family is essentially a secular polity that co-opted religious elites and used an ultra-austere form of Islam to consolidate a Saudi national identity and thereby reinforce its own legitimacy (Al-Rasheed, 1996, 2002, 2006; Nevo, 1998).[1] The official puritanism of Wahhabism is in stark contrast to the reality: Following Abdelwahab Meddeb (2002), the Sauds can be described as a bunch of hard-nosed businessmen (more exactly, rentiers) who hide their unrestrained capitalist practices behind a convenient Islamic façade (p. 125). In the same vein, Robert Lee (2014) writes, "Saudi Arabia is the possession of a family, not the vanguard of a religion. The monarchy has used Islam for its purposes, ... ultimately, the religious sphere, like every other field of endeavour in Saudi Arabia, depends on the power and will of the monarchy" (pp. 220, 246). Islamic institutions such as the sharia courts, the Organization for the Enforcement of Good and Prevention of Evil (established in 1929), and the religious police (founded in 1940) also depend on the will of the monarchy. The religious police's mandate derives from the Commission for the Promotion of Virtue and the Prevention of Vice (Ayubi, 1991, p. 99). Its work is performed by vigilante police militia known as the "mutaween" who are charged with enforcing the kingdom's strict interpretation of Islamic law on the streets and in the malls. Mecca is both a sacred and a profane city, and its merchants indulge in music, dancing, courting concubines, and fleecing pilgrims behind their posture of pious Muslims (Sardar, 2014). In the context of the present discussion, the key point is that

---

[1] From the very beginning, the king of Saudi Arabia was regarded as the guardian of Islam. As such, he was supposed to maintain Islamic values in the community and throughout the world (Nomani and Rahnema, 1994, pp. 137–40; Feldman, 2008, p. 96).

the support given by the Sauds to the puritanical doctrine of al-Wahhab was to prove a decisive factor in modern Muslim history.

The alliance between the Sauds and the Wahhabis was sealed as early as 1746, when Ibn al-Wahhab and Muhammad Ibn Saud, who was a petty ruler of a town in Najd, declared a jihad against all Muslims who did not share their views on Islamic purity. They conquered Mecca and Medina for the first time in 1806. There followed violent incidents of intolerance and iconoclasm resulting in the destruction of shrines, domes, and palaces; desecration of the tombs of the wives and the companions of the Prophet and other luminaries of Islamic history; burning of books other than the Quran; forced communal prayers; and the imposition of tight control over moral conduct and the behavior of local inhabitants. The Wahhabis were eventually ousted from Hijaz by the Ottomans, who forced the Wahhabi state to retreat to its core in Najd until the weakening of Ottoman power enabled the Wahhabis to launch a second, this time successful, drive to conquer the Arabian Peninsula (Robinson, 1996, p. 108; Khalid, 2007, p. 46; Feldman, 2008, pp. 93–5).[2]

Success in war and conquest from 1912 onward owed much to the help of Wahhabi ulama in creating new (agricultural/military) communities of Bedouins collectively known as the Ikhwan (the Brothers), who soon became fierce warriors for the faith. In fact, Abd al Aziz Ibn Saud (1902–53), whose legitimacy was weak given his family's lack of a strong association with tribal confederations, found it convenient to form with the Wahhabi religious leaders (the "mutawwa") a military-religious alliance aimed at buttressing his nascent state. In return, these clerics found in Ibn Saud a symbolic imam, a politico-military figure ready to endorse their cause and grant them the right to impose on the peninsula their puritanical interpretation of Islam (Atallah, 2011, pp. 179, 183). Interestingly, it was British interests that eventually constrained the expansion of the Saudi state by preventing the Sauds from assaulting Transjordan, Iraq, and the shaykhdoms of the Persian Gulf.

---

[2] Saudi Arabia was born out of the consolidation of the western coast of the peninsula, which includes the province of Hijaz, where Mecca and Medina are located, and which belonged to the Ottoman Empire, and of two proto-states known as the Najd, which included the interior of the country and the east coast. The modern Saudi state is usually dated to 1902, when Abd el-Aziz Ibn Saud recaptured Riyadh and reestablished control over the central plateau. Yet, it was only in 1925 that he succeeded in conquering the Hijaz province by defeating King Hussein ibn Ali, who had earned British friendship through his efforts against the Ottomans in World War I. Toward the end of the 1920s the shape of the new state had virtually been settled, and in 1932 Saudi Arabia was created from the kingdoms of the Hijaz and Najd.

Ironically, the king had to muster non-Bedouin troops to defeat the Ikhwan, who revolted in 1927 because they did not want to stop conquering neighboring territories (Lee, 2014, pp. 222–3, 227, 233; Atallah, 2011, p. 182). In 1927 and again in 1928, Ibn Saud held a conference with leading ulama who eventually sanctioned the use of arms against the insubordinate Ikhwan, whom they deemed "overly zealous in proclaiming jihad without the permission of the emir" (p. 243). That political expediency was the major driver of the sovereign's attitude toward religious forces was again manifested on the occupation of the Grand Mosque in 1979, when Juhayman al-Utaibi and hundreds of armed followers denounced the Saudi monarchy for corruption and promoting Westernization, and in the 1990s, when the Saudi regime was threatened by Islamist protests and jihadi attacks. In both cases, the state sought authorization of the Council of Senior Ulama to crush the rebellions by force (Ayubi, 1991, pp. 100–3; Lee, 2014, pp. 228, 233).[3] Moreover, a committee including the grand mufti Abd al-Aziz bin Baz issued a controversial fatwa authorizing the deployment of U.S. troops on Saudi soil during the First Gulf War to force Saddam Hussein out of Kuwait in 1991. It was this decision that Osama bin Laden challenged in a frontal assault against the ruling elite to which he had belonged until then (Feldman, 2008, p. 97).

Although strongly puritanical, al-Wahhab followed a well-established Muslim tradition in defining the proper attitude of Muslims vis-à-vis political power (see Chapter 4). He indeed proclaimed that, to avoid chaos and anarchy, all Muslims should obey a secular ruler, even one who is demonstrably corrupt. In this as well as in his puritanical beliefs, he closely adhered to Ibn Taymiyya's views. Moreover, because he lived in the eighteenth century, his doctrine was not conceived as a reaction to Western modernity and to European colonial presence, as the teachings of later Muslim reformers would be (Lee, 2014, pp. 230–1). Al-Wahhab's puritanical doctrine was directly inspired by the local culture of the deeply conservative society of the Bedouins of the Najd region. Other regions of the kingdom, particularly the Hijaz region and the Eastern (Shi'a) Province, never fully accepted either the domination of a Najdi clan or Wahhabism. Since Ottoman times, the residents of Jidda, the second largest city, have regarded it as a more

---

[3] Interestingly, many leaders of the Mecca takeover movement were from Najdi nomadic tribes – Utaiba, Matir, and Yam tribes – that were traditionally opposed to the political hegemony of the Saudi family. Their grandfathers had fought against al-Aziz Ibn Saud. Two-thirds of the forty-one Saudi citizens who were executed in January 1980 came from the relatively underprivileged Najd region, with one-fourth belonging to the antagonistic Utaiba tribe alone (Ayubi, 1991, p. 103).

sophisticated, diverse, and tolerant city than Riyadh. This was a consequence of the development of the Hijaz region during the Ottoman period, when the bureaucracy, a regular army, and secondary schools were established there (p. 241). But Jidda did not prevail because Wahhabism prescribed complete submission to the sovereign, and the sovereign espoused Wahhabism as the official banner under which he would rule.

How can we explain why Wahhabism gained such a significant influence across the Islamic world in the course of the twentieth century? The answer clearly lies in a purely contingent factor, namely the considerable wealth generated by the abundant oil resources in the national soil and accumulated by Saudi Arabia's elite. Because of the windfall incomes resulting from the country's economic geography, many Muslims moved to Saudi Arabia to work as migrants and later returned to their country of origin; in this way Wahhabism was disseminated very widely, helping assert Saudi Arabia's political predominance throughout the Muslim world. International influences did not just run one way, however. At the same time as the Wahhabi creed was exported through labor migration channels, Saudi Arabia felt the impact of Egyptian immigrants who belonged to the Muslim Brotherhood and had fled Nasser's regime. These well-educated Arabic speakers gradually took over the primary and secondary school systems. From there, they propagated their own ideology and created an Islamist movement complete with informal organizations "that flew below the radar of the Saudi authorities" (Lee, 2014, p. 253). Parallel to the official creed of Wahhabism, which was tightly enmeshed in the country's politics, there thus developed a rival and much less controllable strand of Islamist thinking.

Thus, even before the emergence of Saudi Arabia as a powerful Arab nation, the Islamic reformist doctrines inspired by Wahhabism had spread to many Muslim-dominated regions in the Middle East, South Asia, and Southeast Asia. And even before al-Wahhab's influence could be felt, a reformist Islamist movement had arisen in the waning days of the Mughal Empire in India. The reformist ulama eager to achieve the universalistic Islamic ideal began to criticize the policy of religious toleration of the Sufi orders and non-Muslims initiated by Emperor Akbar (1556–1605). Ahmad al-Sirhindi (d. 1624) regarded Hinduism and Islam as mutually exclusive and claimed that Muslims had an obligation to subdue non-Muslims and to impose the sharia in every way. Much more influential, however, was his follower Shah Waliallah (1702–63), who, after having visited Mecca, stressed the importance of purging Islam of saint worship, which he deemed inconsistent with the true meaning of the Prophet's life. He believed that reform required the establishment of a Muslim Indian state, modeled on the early caliphate, so as to enforce the sharia and Islamic religious practice. Moreover, to adapt Islamic law to local conditions, he urged that independent scholarly judgment be used with a view to reducing legal divergences among Muslims (Lapidus, 1988, pp. 461–3).

What is critical here is that, in conformity with the central message of Chapter 3, the discontinuation of Akbar's policy of religious toleration only became possible in Mughal India when the supreme political authority decided so. This is why the change of policy had to wait until Aurangzeb (1658–1707), the sixth and latest of the great Mughals, acceded to the imperial throne under dubious circumstances. Driven by political motives that happened to coincide with his religious convictions, he opted for a policy of open discrimination against Hindus and the active promotion of Islamic values.[4] The reorientation took place in a context where imperial authority had been undermined in many areas by violent succession struggles between father and son and among brothers (Keay, 2000, p. 339). Aurangzeb, who did not hesitate to order the assassination of his own brothers and the imprisonment of his own father (the tolerant emperor Shah Jahan), chose to secure his power by appointing loyal servants and reliable supporters, as well as by reinstating India in the world community of Islam. Those reliable supporters were mostly orthodox ulama who had backed him against his brother, Dara Shikoh, in the struggle for supreme power. Dara Shikoh was not only a tolerant scholar and a widely popular figure but also the favorite of Shah Jahan for succession to the throne (see Chapter 4). The contest was therefore more about political power than about ideology and policy. For Aurangzeb, restoring the Muslim credentials of Mughal rule meant that the Hinduization of Muslim rituals had to be stopped and reversed and that such un-Islamic behavior as gambling, singing, dancing, blasphemy, and alcohol consumption had to be suppressed. To ensure the proper enforcement of these prohibitions, Aurangzeb appointed a "muhtasib," a censor or guardian of public morality (Keay, 2000, p. 342).[5] Needless

---

[4] The most blatant forms of anti-Hindu discrimination were the replacement of Hindu employees with Muslims in the imperial and provincial administrations, the destruction of famous Hindu temples and their replacement with mosques, the imposition of a tax on Hindu pilgrims, the rescinding of revenue endowments enjoyed by temples and Brahmans, the imposition of heavier duties on Hindu merchants, and, "the heaviest blow of all" – the reimposition of the detested "jizja" (a sort of poll tax) on non-Muslims (Keay, 2000, pp. 342–3).

[5] In the imperial palace, the places of musicians, artists, and dancers were thus taken "by bearded jurists and Quranic divines who laboured to produce a standard compilation of Hanafi jurisprudence" (Keay, 2000, p. 342). Hindu rituals, the worship of "linguam" in particular, were considered as abominable forms of idolatry to be fought against with the strongest determination.

to say, his policies proved disastrous for Hindu-Muslim collaboration on which the Mughal Empire depended and were a major contributor to the empire's undoing (pp. 344–7).

Another early puritanical movement that deserves mention is the Kadizadelis in Ottoman Turkey. Its members were young and idle students from religious schools who were led into open rebellion against the Ottoman government in the early seventeenth century under the leadership of Kadizade Mehmed, who was himself inspired by a conservative ulama (Birgili Mehmet Efendi). He was a gifted self-appointed preacher who was neither a mystic nor a member of the state religious hierarchy. His movement opposed not only the high Islam on the ground that the ulama were tainted by their association with official politics and the state apparatus but also the mysticism and ritual practices of the dervishes. The puritanical message of the Kadizadelis fell on receptive ears during the chaotic early years of Mehmed IV's reign, which were marked by bitter factionalism. They proposed a multipoint program for a return to the fundamental tenets of the faith and its uncorrupted morality, which implied denouncing the evils of innovation: "Every innovation is heresy, every heresy is error, and every error leads to hell" (Finkel, 2005, pp. 214–15, 254–5). For them, "singing, dancing, whirling, smoking tobacco, drinking coffee, shaking hands, bowing for reverence, establishing cash foundations, and accepting money for religious teaching and services" were considered completely unlawful in Islam (An-Na'im, 2008, p. 185).

Echoing a familiar theme in Islamic history, the followers of Kadizade considered the Ottoman military and high Ottoman society as inept and morally bankrupt, and they attributed the recurring debacles on the battlefield (in Europe and the Indian Ocean) and the persistent palace scandals to cultural and religious decay and to deviation from tradition and distraction from true Islam (An-Na'im, 2008, p. 185). As Daniel Goffman points out, "In important ways, they constituted a forerunner to Islamic reformers in later centuries who, whether Ottoman, Egyptian, Wahhabi, or Iranian, have consistently argued that the West has defeated Islamic states only because their ostensibly Muslim leaders forgot their religious roots. Bring back the Muhammadan state, they all argue, and Islam will again take up its leading rank in the world order" (Goffman, 2002, pp. 118–19).[6] We soon return to this theme.

---

[6] As they gathered at the Fatih mosque to plan how to put their program into effect, the Kadizadelis were arrested and eventually banished by the new grand vezir (Finkel, 2005, p. 255).

Islamic Reformism as Anticolonial Reaction

In the most typical cases, it is in the hands of religious elites eager to resist European (and Chinese) colonialism that reformism became a powerful tool.[7] We have already come across several examples that illustrate this proposition; for example, the denunciation by Egyptian Islamists of the "Heads of Agreement" conceded by the Free Officers, including Nasser, to the British over the Suez Canal, or their angry reaction to the peace treaty signed by Sadat with Israel (see Chapter 6). Also remember the key role played by Iran's ayatollahs in organizing mass protests against the iniquitous sale of national resources to British and Russian interests (see Chapter 4).

Returning to the aforementioned dramatic reversal of state-religion relations in Mughal India, it bears noticing that already under Akbar's rule (1556–1605), Shaykh Ahmad al-Sirhindi joined the Nakshibendi order, an influential brand of Sufism, and became the main Indian spokesman of the reformist point of view.[8] He taught that obedience to the sharia law was the key to unity of the Muslim world, which was to be preferred to religious syncretism, and he regarded Hinduism and Islam as mutually exclusive. In the name of Islamic purity, he opposed the insinuation into Islam of Sufi and Hindu practices such as the worship of saints, sacrifice of animals, and religious festivals. Moreover, in his unrelenting struggle to establish an Islamic state, he urged rulers and nobles to permit the slaughter of cows, to remove non-Muslims from political office, and to enforce the sharia law in every way (Lapidus, 1988, pp. 377–8).

Sirhindi's teachings gave a new revivalist direction to the Nakshibendi order, which became more militant and quite influential not only in India but also in the Ottoman Empire. The important point, however, is that Nakshibendism could gain influence and spread widely only because of special circumstances that prevailed at the time of its emergence. These were characterized by the decline of Muslim hegemony and the perceived political weakness of Islam, as exemplified by the conquest of Kazan by the emerging Russian power by the mid-sixteenth century and, later, the encroachment of the new Western states on Islamic areas such as the Crimea, Egypt,

---

[7] For a summary table synthesising the various Muslim reform ("tajdid") movements from the eighteenth to the twentieth century, see Lapidus, 1988 (pp. 464–5).

[8] In the Nakshibendi approach, knowledge is defined as the pursuit of self-purification, and it is acquired from both sacred books and privileged contact with a master/mentor. The intimate bond between the pupil and the master is only the first link in what operates as a chain of linkages producing a network of Nakshibendi influences (Mardin, 1993, pp. 211, 214).

and the Caucasus. In the words of Şerif Mardin (1993), "The traditional Nakshibendi emphasis on an 'internal mobilization of the soul' was now complemented by an increasing involvement in world history and by an external mobilization directed against Western imperialism and its cultural policy" (p. 210).

The Nakshibendi reaction was especially fierce because, during the seventeenth century, its adherents began to encounter Catholic and Protestant missionaries whose influence was perceived as threatening traditional local culture. It was therefore the stark confrontation with the West that brought about fundamental changes in the Nakshibendi approach and caused this Sufi order to emphasize a return to pristine Islam. Citing Mardin again,

The fact that the West was now perceived as an adversary culture and that this became the primary preoccupation of Islam, promoted the "ideological" use of Islam. Islam itself began to be seen as a culture. ... Thus, in the nineteenth century, the order became more clearly focused on the West as the "other" rather than on backsliders who had forgotten the orthodox Islamic emphasis on the unicity of God. ... An abstract project, the re-Islamization of the Islamic culture, took the place of a narrower identification with the order ... they gave a type of instruction to the student body which prepared them to regain a preponderant position for Muslims chafing under the impious rule of colonialists or – what was not very different – under the yoke of impious Muslim regimes. (Mardin, 1993, pp. 212–13)

Toward the end of the eighteenth century and in the early nineteenth century, the Nakshibendi exerted a particularly strong influence in the Caucasus and Inner Asia, where they acted as a vehicle of new religious inspiration and political resistance to both Russian and Chinese expansion. It is in Chechnya that they were most influential, probably because of the contiguity of Chechen tribes with Russian civilization, which had suddenly intruded into their pristine culture (Mardin, 1993, p. 213). A Chechen named Ushurma, known as Imam Mansur, was the first militant Nakshibendi Sufi Shaykh in the region. Appealing to universal Sufi and Islamic principles in an attempt to consolidate the mountaineer communities around the sharia, he defeated Russian troops in several battles (1785–90) before being eventually captured (Bobrovnikov, 2006, p. 205). In the second half of the nineteenth century, North Caucasian ulama and the rulers of Bukhara and Kokand proclaimed a "holy war" against Russian conquerors. In Dagestan and Chechnya an "imamate" state, based on sharia institutions and modified Sufi principles, emerged at the end of the 1820s. It acquired its greatest strength under its last imam, Shamil (1834–59), whose activities closely resembled those of the Emir Abdelkader in French Algeria. The

Muslim resistance of the North Caucasian mountaineers to Russia became famous under the name of Muridism. In Inner Russia, the Vaisov brotherhood, founded by a Tatar Sufi master of the same name, formed as a reaction to the muftis who did not oppose the imposition of Russian rule. Later called "Vaisov's Holy Regiment of the Old Believer Muslims," it was crushed by the Russians in 1884 (Bobrovnikov, 2006, pp. 210–11).

In Turkey, too, during the Russo-Turkish war of 1877–8, Nakshibendi shaykhs volunteered for military service. One of them, a member of the Uzbek lodge, established an intelligence service that collected information from Central Asian Muslims for the benefit of the Ottomans. Later, the Nakshibendi leaders, who were especially opposed to the shift toward secularism, would lead the resistance against Ottoman modernization campaigns. Their efforts failed, but much later, during the 1973 elections, they effectively supported the first clerical party to appear on the Turkish political scene (Mardin, 1993, pp. 213, 216–18).

Going farther east, in the North-West Frontier province of India, Sayyid Ahmad Barelwi tried to organize the Pathans and the Sikhs against the British on the basis of reformist teaching (Lapidus, 1988, p. 564; Khalid, 2007, ch. 2). In Afghanistan, the origins of Islamic reformism can be traced to the seventeenth and eighteenth centuries when Indian domination under the Mughal emperors and British incursions into Afghan territory provoked strong reactions: Following the typical pattern, these reactions were based on the idea that resisting the infidels was a religious duty and submission a sin. More precisely, the idea was advanced that "it was only the rejection of Islam that had permitted the infidel to triumph, and that the way to liberation was through a return by the whole society to its former faith" (Roy, 1990, p. 56).

Notice the striking similarity between this diagnosis and Ibn Taymiyya's reaction when Damas was threatened by the Mongols (see Chapter 5). As we have seen earlier, the rise of Islamism in Yemen toward the end of the nineteenth century occurred in quite similar circumstances, and Yahya wanted to impose the sharia as an antidote to Ottoman law, which he regarded as a component of an unacceptable foreign rule (Clark, 2010, pp. 44–5). In India itself, the reformist college of Deoband (by Maulana Nanautawi in 1867) was created by some of the ulama in response to the imposition by the colonial power of the English language and Western education. The objective of the new school was to unite Indian Muslims around the leadership of the ulama, using the Urdu vernacular to issue all sorts of legal opinions on proper Islamic practice (Lapidus, 1988, p. 725). By contrast, the Tabligh ("Propagation of the Faith"), founded near Delhi in 1927, is a pietistic group that responded to modernizing influences by preaching total cultural separation from the "infidel" society of the Hindus and the Europeans. This separation is ensured through the practice of a strictly codified Islam in all areas of daily life (Kepel, 2008, p. 186).[9]

Another instructive example comes from Indonesia. There, people were used to blending existing practices of Buddhism and Hinduism with those of Islam, which began to be adopted in the thirteenth century. As in much of Southeast Asia, there was a tradition of peaceful coexistence between different religions, and intermarriage proved to be the most important factor advancing the geographic borders of Islam in that part of the world (Muslim traders married local women when they reached by ship the islands forming the Indonesian peninsula). The arrival of Spanish and Portuguese explorers caused a dramatic change in this situation because they came to present-day Malaysia and Indonesia with a hierarchical conception of the relative worth of different religions. In their view, Christianity was superior, and Islam had to be defeated (Griswold, 2010, pp. 178–9).

Usually, the objective of Christian evangelization was inseparable from European economic interests. In the words of Anthony Reid (1993), "the crusading ideology was ideally suited to serve the key Portuguese objective in the Indian Ocean – to take from the Muslims the trade that had supplied Asian spices to Alexandria and Beirut for sale to Venice" (p. 145). To defend themselves against the violent conquests of these European invaders and their subsequent expulsion from places where they used to live and work (e.g., Malacca in 1511), Muslim traders, scholars, and teachers turned to Islam as a unifying force and source of rebellion. Thus, a diaspora of dispossessed Muslim traders from Malacca established themselves in Johor, Pahang, Patani, and, above all, Aceh, "making these cities self-consciously Muslim opponents of the infidel intruders" (Reid, 1993, p. 146). Inspired by the success of Aceh as a happy "marriage of ideology and commerce," a Sumatran known in Java as Sunan Gunung Jati returned from studying in Mecca and established Banten as an Islamic center in west Java (p. 146).

Indonesian Islam underwent a further revival during the late 1800s when the Dutch tried to supplant Islam with Protestantism (the Dutch had landed in Indonesia as early as 1596). Indeed, "many Dutch colonial officers and missionaries sought to establish a human bulwark against Islam by evangelising among non-Muslims" (Griswold, 2010, p. 180). In doing so, they

---

[9] Today, Tabligh's leadership resides in Raiwind near Lahore (Pakistan). Measured by the number of adherents, it is probably the most important Islamic movement in the world (Roy, 2008, pp. 186–7).

were very aggressive, and the colonial government went so far as referring to Islam as "evil." In response the Muslims viewed a stricter adherence to Islam as their means of liberation from foreign oppression. The Islamic militants fought alongside the nationalist Sukarno to win back their independence. After the struggle was won, they demanded the creation of an Islamic state, which Sukarno refused.

In some parts of Indonesia, the assertion of Islamists encountered the strong resistance of traditional authorities, who could call on the Dutch for help. For example, in Minangkabau (Sumatra), a militant reformist movement under the leadership of Tuanku Nan Tua insisted that traditional local religious and social practices be changed to meet the demands of Islam, particularly among the newly mobile merchant and peasant population. Among the causes provoking the anger of these militants was the discrepancy between customary rules and Islamic tenets in inheritance and family matters (Lapidus, 1988, p. 478; Bowen, 2003, pp. 142–6). As argued by leaders of the Padri movement, it was urgent to bring custom into accord with the sharia. The reform movement led to bitter civil war when, in the early nineteenth century, the reformers were joined by pilgrims returning from Mecca. Preaching in villages that had been recently integrated into the market for coffee, and determinedly opposed to all types of magical practices, these returning pilgrims "called for the purification of Islamic life, adherence to the sharia, regularity in prayer, and an end to gambling, cock fighting, opium consumption, drinking, smoking, robbery, and violence" (Lapidus, 1988, p. 479).[10] A faction soon split from the main Islamist movement to form a military wing pledged to establish a new regime headed by an imam and a qadi; it was intent on burning all symbols, including schools, of a dominant Sufi order (the "Shattariya"). Most of the customary chiefs, however, refused to accept the new doctrine, and to defend themselves, they invited the Dutch to intercede. A protracted war followed (1819–39), until the religious extremists were eventually defeated.

In Malaysia, the reformist movement owed a great deal to Shaykh Muhammad Tahir (1867–1957), who was an outstanding disciple of Shaykh Muhammad 'Abduh (d. 1905), an Egyptian who studied in Mecca and tried to awaken Muslims to the need for education. Tahir founded a newspaper, *Al-Imam*, through which he taught that Muslim renaissance is impossible

---

[10] Commercial farmers and merchants were receptive to reformist Islam probably because this ideology supplied them with a way of differentiating themselves from the old traditional elite of the "priyayi" landlords, who had cooperated with the Dutch colonizers and adopted the values of secularized modernism (Lapidus, 1988, pp. 563, 567).

if the faithful do not start respecting the divine law and submitting to the Quran and hadith. Questions such as the emancipation of women and the role of savings banks and cooperatives were debated, but the core message, as in Java and Singapore, was that popular Sufi practices such as celebrations of the death days of saints, adat marriage, and funeral and holy day ceremonies must be abandoned.

More relevant to our discussion are the efforts undertaken by various reformist groups to unify their efforts and channel them into political action after the end of World War I. Radical intellectuals often penetrated these groups and called for independence both from the feudal rule of local notables and from the colonial rule of the Dutch. Organized resistance to Dutch rule used modern forms of political action. Yet, the formation of movements that emphasized religious reform, educational modernism, and political action triggered a countermovement among the traditionalist ulama and religious notables that reaffirmed the sharia, the schools of law, and the Sufi practices that were at the core of their spirituality (Lapidus, 1988, pp. 664–5). Lapidus summarizes the antagonism between the two strands in the following manner:

The traditionalists viewed religion as a a mystical and magical disposition of mind. Traditional religion was oriented to ritual, to states of feeling, and to passive acceptance of reality. Prayer, fasting, and recitation were intended to create inner peace and bring about harmony between the believer and the truth. By contrast, the reformers stressed active mastery of the self, and defined religion in terms of individual responsibility for moral and social reform. Their religion was inner-directed, ethical, and intellectual. Whereas traditional religion maintained its commitment to a concept of the harmony of the individual with his community, the community with the state, and the state with the universe, reformist religion sought to create a Muslim utopia. To achieve these goals, the reformers adopted Western organizational and educational methods, accepted scientific ideas and the use of vernacular languages, and waged a vigorous campaign in the press. Scout movements, schools, orphanages, and hospitals were essential in making Islam an active force in society. (Lapidus, 1988, pp. 665–6)

Moving now to North Africa, and in keeping with these accounts, a series of millenarian uprisings occurred in northern Algeria in the mid-nineteenth century in the context of determined resistance to French occupation. Thus, in 1849 a local shaykh named Bu Zian of Zaatsha claimed to have had a dream in which the Prophet Muhammad elected him as the representative of the Mahdi and entrusted him with the mission of resisting taxation and openly rebelling against French control. A few years later, one of his close allies, a certain Sidi Sadok al-Haji, resumed the jihad, which led nowhere. The same failure was suffered by Bu Khentash, a member of a pious and highly regarded warrior lineage, who had promised his followers miraculous protection against French bullets. Somewhat later, in 1879, Muhammas Amzian declared himself to be the Mahdi and attacked local officials in the name of his sacred mission. In southern Algeria, too, preachers and Sufi brotherhoods played a significant role in the insurrections against the French colonizers. They "created an atmosphere of ecstatic fervour" while pretending to be forerunners of the Mahdi (Lapidus, 1988, p. 682).

In sub-Saharan Africa, the same intimate connection existed between puritanical Islamic reformers and anticolonial politics, which is well illustrated by the aforementioned conquest of al-Hajji Umar in the Fuuta Tooro in the mid-1840s (see Chapter 4). Recall that Umar was an ambitious man who belonged to the Tijâniyya (Sufi) brotherhood and launched an ambitious jihad in a large part of West Africa. What needs to be added now is that his movement was a manifestation of a permanent hostility to the French presence and attempts to liberalize trade to the benefit of French merchants. To be able to recruit members on a significant scale, Umar needed more than purely religious justifications: He had to use social and political arguments. Thanks to his numerous following of talibés coming from different regions and territories, he succeeded in building a jihad state that opposed any collaboration with the French colonial power. It was only in 1890–1 that Segu and Nyooro, the two West African capital cities of the new state, were reconquered by the French (Sall, 2000, pp. 374–83).

The Wahhabist reformers who settled in Bamako (Mali) from 1945 onward targeted their attacks on the marabouts and other religious specialists whom they accused of relying too much on indigenous non-Quranic practices and Sufi mysticism and of being too close to French authorities. The main objectives pursued by these reformers were to purify Islam according to the Wahhabi doctrine that they had learned in Egypt and to use Islam as an anticolonial discourse, which they had also learned in Nasser's Egypt. In this manner, "Maraboutism and Sufism became their strongest enemies, both for religious and for political reasons" (Sarro, 2009, p. 124). In Guinea-Conakry, the jihadists led by Asekou Sayon and Asekou Abdoulaye initiated an iconoclastic movement directed against village elders and other guardians of customary rituals. It was to be used by Sékou Touré and the Rassemblement Démocratique Africain (RDA) in their drive for independence (Sarro, 2009, ch. 6).[11]

---

[11] Similar iconoclastic upheavals occurred in the first decades of the twentieth century. Especially prominent was an iconoclastic movement started by Senegalese Tijâni shaykhs when they entered the Upper Guinea coast (Sarro, 2009, p. 137).

In the Hausaland of Nigeria, a region of city-states that had been Islamized at the start of the sixteenth century, a man named Uthman dan Fodio (1802) launched a jihad initially directed against African rulers who called themselves emirs or sultans but were highly corrupt. A Sufi teacher and Fulani herder of great charisma, Uthman also aimed his virulent criticism at Muslim clerics of the court, considered to form an exploitative class; his worst invective targeted the Muslim advisers whom he labeled "venal clerics" (Robinson, 2004, pp. 139–41). The regime was deemed guilty of encouraging pagan practices, imposing unlawful taxes on farmers and pastoralists, and twisting the law of Islam for its own purposes. Although Uthman had close contact with the ruling class, he wanted to purify Islam and promote deep reforms, which included women's education. By 1810, seventy-five years before the British would claim Nigeria as its protectorate, Uthman's followers had conquered a large swath of West Africa as their own Islamic Empire governed from Sokoto. The logic of conquest became indistinguishable from that of Islamic proselytism. His most formidable enemy, al-Kanemi (from the old West African kingdom of Bornu), thus claimed that the wars of conquest led by the Uthmanian armies were "designed to extend Fulani control, and not the Islamic faith" (p. 146). With the establishment of the colonial power, however, the holy war "morphed into battles against the infidel West" (Griswold, 2010, p. 21).

The Western threat was perceived as very serious because, as in Indonesia, non-Muslim minorities easily converted to Christianity to escape their erstwhile condition of marginalization and isolation; for example, the hill tribes of the Middle Belt were under the constant threat of being enslaved by their more powerful Muslim neighbors and so were eager to convert (Griswold, 2010, p. 25). Tensions caused by religious proselytism became particularly confrontational and openly violent with the active presence of North American evangelists, who conceived of themselves as "soldiers of the Christ." Their worldview was based on a sharp distinction between light and darkness, good and evil, and most believed that Islam was their most formidable foe. Because it put enormous emphasis on the idea of an active spirit, and some of its practices such as ecstatic worship were familiar to local Africans, Pentecostalism grafted easily onto many indigenous cosmologies and spread quickly (pp. 25, 29).

Returning to North Africa, the confrontational tactic of Christian evangelists was also at work in Sudan and Egypt, where they "fanned the flames of militant Islam" owing to their "determined evangelical zealotry" (Griswold, 2010, p. 107). As early as the 1920s, to many Muslims, "Christianity appeared to be the principal instrument of their oppression," and it was out of fear that their children would be converted to Christianity that

they started to "call Muslims back to their faith" and to collectively organize toward such a purpose (p. 106). The Young Men's Muslim Association
(YMMA), which was founded in Egypt in 1927, was built on the pattern
of the Young Men's Christian Association (YMCA) as a way to counter the
evangelization push of Christian missionaries. The YMMA's most influential member was an Egyptian schoolteacher named Hassan al Banna, who
was to become the supreme guide of the Muslim Brotherhood before being
assassinated in 1949 by King Faruk's henchmen (p. 106). In Sudan, the
Mahdist movement, which remained influential even after its defeat at the
hands of the Anglo-Egyptian army in 1898 (see Chapter 6), changed its targeted enemy from the corrupt rule of the Ottomans to the poisoned presence of the infidel West (p. 95). The central theme remained unchanged,
however (i.e., resistance to foreign domination and the associated threats to
local culture).

In a paradoxical manner, after World War II, the United States also used
Islam as a political weapon against its main enemy, the Soviet Union. In
Europe, it supported many Muslim defectors from the USSR who laid the
foundations of Islamism there. In Africa, where the struggle between the
two superpowers was particularly fierce, the United States followed a similar
tactic. In Somalia, for example, during the 1960s, "the former intelligence
director Abdiqani Dahir Haashi received American books that supported
the cause of Islam against the Soviet-backed military regime" (Griswold,
2010, p. 107). The West's approach to "winning" Africa was thus based on
religion, but this time the religion was Islam, and the common enemy was
portrayed to be the evil forces of atheistic communism (p. 108).

At the closing stage of this discussion, it is worth noting that the sort
of revivalist movement described earlier is not an exclusively Muslim phenomenon: There have also been anticolonial millenarian or reformist movements inspired by Christianity. In Uganda, for example, the Society of the
One Almighty God (the "Bamalaki"), created in 1915, drew much of its
strength and owed much of its appeal from a reading of the Bible that offered
a response to the visible catastrophes of colonial conquest (famine, Spanish
flu, plague, rinderpest, and violent conflict). By so doing, it challenged the
prevailing orthodoxies of the historic mission churches (Catholicism and
Anglicanism). Even more enduring was the movement of the Saved Ones
(the "Balokole"), which took root in the 1930s and rejected any assimilation
between the church and the world, and between Christianity and African
custom (Jones, 2009, pp. 118–19).

The next subsection further highlights the spread of Wahhabism in
the twentieth century, about two centuries after the start of the proselytic

movement of al-Wahhab in the Arabic desert. The puritanical interpretation of Islam that he promoted was indeed revived in two different regions
of the Islamic world – by Abû al-A'lâ Mawdûdi (1903–79) in Pakistan and by
his fervent disciple Sayyid Qutb (1929–66) in Egypt. These two thinkers had
a deep influence on today's Islamist movement, in particular, on Osama bin
Laden of Saudi Arabia and his lieutenant in al-Qaeda, Ayman al-Zawahiri
of Egypt. Interestingly, neither Mawdûdi nor Qutb was himself an ulama or
Sufi. Mawdûdi, for example, was a journalist and by no means accurate or
profound: He "wrote at great speed and with resultant superficiality" and
contradicted himself from time to time (Rahman, 1982, p. 116).

The Doctrines of Mawdûdi and Qutb

This subsection presents succinctly the main ideas of these two thinkers.
Whereas Mawdûdi did not call for war, even though his writings lead to
the conclusion that war is required, Qutb claimored for the reactivation of
the jihad and the use of sheer violence to achieve the aims of the movement. For Mawdûdi (see his "Four Technical Terms of the Quran," written
in 1941), there is legitimacy in God only, and the whole political realm must
be reduced to the divine realm: The religious principle must be put back at
the heart of social life, and there is no room for anything else. In his own
words, "no single individual, a family, a class, a party or any individual living in the state has the right to 'Hakimiyya' [governance], as Allah is the
true ruler and holder of real power" (cited by Gerges, 2016, p. 217). Powers should not be divided, but should all be concentrated within the prerogatives of God. According to Mawdûdi, one of the causes of the decline
of the countries of Islam was that their inhabitants no longer understood
the Quranic message as they did at the beginning of the Muslim era. It was
therefore essential that they learn to read the Quran in its proper context,
without attaching too much importance to the tradition as it evolved after
the times of the first four caliphs, which evolution Mawdûdi considered scle-
rotic. Blame for distraction from the true message of God was to be put on
both political rulers and the imams who "compel people to live according
to rules that they themselves have confected out of whole cloth, while con-
cealing the Book of God behind their backs." In fact, "over nearly all the
earth," ruling families have sought to "cast themselves as part of the supernatural" just as a "pretext for consolidating their political sovereignty" (cited
by Kepel, 2005, pp. 47–9).

For Qutb, Islamic society is one that accepted the sovereign authority of
God and regarded the Quran as the source of all guidance for human life.

The struggle should aim at creating a universal Muslim society, thus marking the end of the Western world, which cannot provide the values needed to support the new material civilization. Although Qutb considered the totalitarian state (in particular, the regime of Nasser in his own country, Egypt) as the model of "jahiliyya" (pre-Islamic barbarism), he eventually came to the view that "all the societies that now exist on earth" can be described as such. This universalization of evil originated in his idea that jahiliyya societies are not only socialist and thus atheist societies but also those that limit God's domain "to the heavens, to the exlusion of the here and now."[12]

To the moral decay of the Western civilization, Muslims must therefore oppose an ethics reconstructed on the basis of Islam's own origins. It is only after having completely submitted to God, as God required, that people will be emancipated from all the servitudes of the present century. As pointed out in *Signposts*, Qutb's last book, written in a concentration camp in which he spent ten years, the resurgence of the Muslim countries, which is required to bring the umma back to life, "will be followed, sooner or later, by their conquest of world domination" (cited by Kepel, 2005, pp. 44–6, 50–1). Qutb joined the Muslim Brethren whose followers were to live according to the sharia, purify their heart, and form the nucleus of dedicated fighters of the Islamic cause, implying their readiness for violence and martyrdom (Hourani, 1991, pp. 445–6; Meddeb, 2002, pp. 114–15, 121–2). Qutb had a decisive influence on this movement and led it into open opposition to Nasser. He was himself arrested, tried, tortured, and executed in 1966.

Given the overwheming importance of the objective they proclaimed – restoring God's rule – and the readiness to use force to achieve it (as stated most explicitly in Mawdûdi's writings), it is not surprising that Salafi jihadists show no respect for democratic values. Thus, an outfit of such jihadists based in the Sinai desert and who pledged allegiance to ISIS declared that the Muslim Brothers deserve the sufferings endured as a result of the harsh clampdown of General al-Sisi after his state coup. Did not the Muslim Brothers worship democracy over God's law, and did they not bring shame and humiliation on themselves by refusing to obey the rules of Allah and by engaging in electoral politics instead of jihad (Gerges, 2016, p. 212)?

Continuous shuttling back and forth movements of ordinary citizens from one bank of the Red Sea to the other opened the door to the first operational link between radical fundamentalism and Wahhabism, which was woven during the 1970s. Yet, a second, far more critical conjunction

---

[12] "Jahiliyya society, unlike Muslim society, confers sovereignty upon others than God and turns these sovereigns into objects of worship" (Kepel, 2005, p. 47).

of events was to happen in the early 1980s in Afghanistan and Pakistan, in the very country where Mawdûdi propagated his ideology among his own brethren and in their own language (Meddeb, 2002, p. 122). Even among the mujahiddin who fought against the Soviet troops, there existed various contending factions following different sorts of Islamic creeds. They united together to oust the Soviet troops, yet tensions among them remained serious and immediately resurfaced as soon as victory was earned. With the Russians out, Gulbuddin Hekhmatyar, a Pashtun hostile toward the traditional clergy, became the prime minister of the Afghan government. He was the leader of the most extremist faction among the mujahiddin and had been recruited by the Pakistani military intelligence.[13] Because internal confrontations between the contending factions of the victors did not end, the government soon collapsed, and a new radical movement, that of the Taliban, came to power, which was quickly joined by the extremist Islamist factions of the mujahiddin.

Like Ibn Hanbal twelve centuries earlier and like King Rahman toward the end of the nineteenth century (see Chapter 4, Section 4.3), the Taliban were convinced that a uniform, rigid interpretation of the Quran was the only way to bring unity and restore order among feuding local tribes and warlords. Initially, before their religious and social policies were fully realized, they were lauded for bringing peace and security to the regions they captured. Although their doctrine consisted of a crude mixture of Salafi Islam and Pashtunwali (the cultural code of the Pashtuns), like other Islamists they gave the Quran preeminence over other sources of law so as to bypass the complex construction of tradition, casuistry, and scholasticism that the ulama used to justify the need for a body of technical experts (Roy, 1990, p. 81; Barfield, 2010, p. 261). The same characterization can be applied to Islamist movements in Africa, such as Boko Haram in northern Nigeria, Ansar Eddine in Mali, and al-Qaeda in the Islamic Maghreb (AQMI) in northwestern Africa.

Why the reformist, puritanical interpretation of Islam produced by Wahhabism spread so deeply throughout the Muslim word is an important question that we have so far answered only partially. The query is particularly pertinent to Egypt, traditionally one of the major sources of deep Muslim philosophical thinking and where the Muslim Brotherhood played a major

---

[13] As pointed out earlier, fundamentalists were used by Pakistan as a counterweight against Afghan nationalism that had laid claim to the western part of Pakistan populated by the same Pashtun ethnic group that was dominant in Kabul. They were also supported and financed by the United States (through the CIA) and Saudi Arabia.

role in propagating Islamic reformism. After all, even under conditions of foreign domination and European colonialism, the Islamist reformist reaction initiated by conservative ulama and supported by social groups whose preeminence was threatened by Western-inspired reforms (in particular, the merchants and urban notables), was far from dominant.

The new bureaucratic, military, and landowning elite that emerged from these conditions tended to adopt Islamic modernist and even secular conceptions of national transformation. The result, at least in a number of Muslim countries, including Turkey, Egypt, Syria, Lebanon, and Tunisia, was a series of important legal, institutional, and educational reforms borrowed from Western advanced countries. In those times (from the mid-nineteenth to the mid-twentieth century), Wahhabism was a minor current of opinion whose influence was limited to the rather lawless expanses of the Arabian Peninsula; in the world beyond it served largely "as a polemical foil in sectarian arguments among Muslims" (Khalid, 2007, p. 46). The next section attempts to explain why, using the words of Lapidus (1988, p. 560), there has been a shift from "Islamic modernism" to "Islamic reformism" during the second part of the twentieth century. Before embarking on this task, however, a few remarks about political shi'ism are warranted.

Political Shi'ism

The influence of radical Sunni Islamists such as Qutb was not limited to Sunni circles. It also reached young Shi'a clerics attracted by the concept of a revolutionary Islam involving political engagement. Yet, as evidenced by the Shi'a renaissance centered around the seminaries of Najaf (Iraq), Shi'ism developed its own brand of Islamist reformism, which was generally strongly opposed by the conservative establishment, in Iran especially. It was initiated by strong intellectual personalities – Baqir and Musa Sadr, Ali Shariati, and Ruhollah Khomeini, in particular. A forerunner was the first revolutionary Shi'a movement, a clandestine organization known as "Hesb al-Da'wa" (Crooke, 2009, pp. 86–9), founded by Baqir Sadr in 1957. In essence, the doctrines of these thinkers proclaimed the need for Shi'ism to abandon its apolitical, passive, and quietist approach and the associated attitudes of resignation, fatalism, and self-pity. Shi'a Islam needed to be repositioned as a revolutionary movement to become an instrument of mobilization and change. In the words of Musa al-Sadr, this required a strategic shift from a long tradition of "lethargy and abdication" that had turned Islam from "movement, vitality and work" (cited from Crooke, 2009, p. 96). For Shariati, "the origins and ethos of Shi'a Islam were exactly those of radical activism, fighting against tyranny and a struggle for social justice" (Crooke, 2009, p. 96). Was not Shi'a Islam, by virtue of its history, a more revolutionary sect than Sunni islam? As for Khomeini, he was influenced not only by the ideas of Baqir Sadr and his followers but also by those of Mulla Sadra (1571–1640), who maintained that existence was dynamic and not static, and that political reform was inseparable from spirituality (p. 102).

The harassment, jailing, torturing, and eventual execution of Baqir Sadr in 1980 by Saddam Hussein ostensibly returned the Najaf seminaries to their former apolitical and quietist stances. However, the martyrdom of Sadr effectively diffused the Shi'a awakening to key areas of the Middle East and farther afield during the following decade – to Iran, Lebanon, Kuwait, Pakistan, India, and Sudan. Political Shi'ism gave rise not only to the Iranian Revolution but also to powerful movements such as Hezbollah in Lebanon, with their focus on political and social engagement for the benefit of the masses, their adherence to the Islamist principle of a collective experience of the attainment of ethical living, and their military organization for active resistance against Israel (pp. 92, 161, 174–91).

7.2 A Modernization Crisis Compounded by Military Defeats

The discussion in this section is based on the idea that religious fundamentalism is strongly attractive to the extent that it is both a form of suffering and a cure. The suffering aspect, examined first, is conceived as arising from a deep modernization crisis compounded by humiliating military defeats. The curing aspect, the second step, follows the penetrating analysis of Sudhir Kakar in his book, *The Colors of Violence: Cultural Identities, Religion, and Conflict* (1996), where he portrays Islamism as an attempt to reformulate the project of modernity. Finally, this section provides historical examples of similar civilizational crises experienced in Europe and Russia to show that the phenomenon is not specific to Islam, although the colors in which it is dressed are necessarily idiosyncratic.

The Hard Dilemma Born of a Modernization Crisis

What has recently caused the Islamic world to turn more reformist, and what can explain the increasing appeal of radical puritanical movements? The answer seems to be that the recent radicalization of Islamic ideology is the result of a deep economic, social, and military crisis faced by Muslim societies. This crisis has its roots in the decline of the Arab civilization and its failure to meet the challenge of modernization posed by the

Western world. Thus, according to Mohamed Chérif Ferjani, the Arabs are torn between two models of civilization: European civilization that challenges them and Arab-Muslim civilization that provides them with a response to that challenge. The choice between the two models is made especially difficult because of a "psychic tension" amplified by the acute awareness of the reality of Arab decadence. A fundamental trait of most contemporary political Arab writings, whether oriented to the left or right, is thus their "obsession with past grandeur," which prevents any strand of thought from envisaging progress, modernization, and development in terms of a rupture with the past, such as happened with the Enlightenment revolution in Europe. Instead of "progress," Arab authors prefer to think of a "renaissance" ("reviving the past grandeur"); that is, they prefer to think "in magical and mythical terms": "It is as though the present and the future cannot have legitimacy if they are not rooted in the historical and cultural patrimony" (Ferjani, 1991, pp. 133–4; my translation; see also Meddeb, 2004; Pargeter, 2008). As for the Islamists' view of the past, it is centered around a "golden age" that ended fourteen centuries ago (Kepel, 2005, pp. 234–6).

Ali Allawi (2009) has recently cast the problem in a similar fashion. According to him, many Muslims "feel that the modern West 'excludes' Islam," and this feeling "feeds on the collapse in self-confidence which Muslims have undergone over the past two centuries" (p. 145). The denial in the Western public mind of the significance of the historical interchange between Western civilization and Islam and its refusal to countenance a role for Islam on the world stage have reinforced the idea that the West sees Islam as a retrograde civilization supported by a backward faith. The response of the Muslim world oscillates between "a fawning desire to be acknowledged as worthy of joining the club of civilised peoples and nations" and "the angry rejection of those who had denied them" respect. It is the latter impulse that "drives the politics of resentment and envy, which at its edges feeds into nihilism and terrorism" (p. 146).

Adopting a psychological perspective, Kakar (1996) views Islamic fundamentalism as a response to "the loss of collective self-idealisation and the fracture in self-representation brought on by historical change"; an important characteristic of this movement is the "inability to mourn," which he depicts as "an emotional state where the natural process of grieving is blocked by undue anger" (p. 171). This anger is translated into hate and, often, violent aggression against other groups or communities imagined as a menacing Other. References to the early history of Islam and the legendary elaboration of past events serve to bring home "the fact of Muslim degeneration and distress in the modern world" (p. 173). Illustrations of this view are provided in excerpts from speeches made by mullahs in several mosques of India, which characteristically refer to the broader Arab-centered history of Islam, rather than the specific history of Indian Muslims – particularly when comparing the sorry plight of the Muslims today to the lost glories of Islam. For example, the dismal state of Iraq, "a land made sacred by the blood of the Prophet's grandsons," is lamented because it is one more form of evidence that nowhere do we see Muslims "thriving, successful, or on the ascendant." This is a sobering fact because the opposite was true in earlier times. Just think of Sultan Salah-al-din Ayubi (Saladin) who, command- ing a force of 13,000 in the battle for Jerusalem and facing Richard's army of 700,000, succeeded in killing 300,000 Christians on a single day. And remember that "once, in the battle for Mecca, ... the Prophet with a ragtag force of three 113, including women, children, and old men, defeated the 1,000 armed warriors of Abu Jahl, many of them on horseback at the battle of Badr" (p. 172).

Thus feeding the anger and the hatred of Muslim fundamentalists is the unbearable reality of continuous military and "civilizational" defeats: After having gone from defeat to defeat since the victory of the Mongols over the Abbasids in 1258, and after having been often deluded by broken promises issued by Western colonial powers, Arab people suffered from humiliating military setbacks during the second half of the twentieth century. In partic- ular, frustration and feelings of injustice have been considerably enhanced by the openly declared support of the Western superpower for a small-sized enemy embedded in the body of the Arab world. In the words of Hourani,

The events of 1967 [a crushing military defeat of the Egyptian Army at the hands of the Israelis], and the processes of change which followed them, made more intense that disturbance of spirits, that sense of a world gone wrong, which had already been expressed in the poetry of the 1950s and 1960s. The defeat of 1967 was widely regarded as being not only a military setback but a kind of moral judgement. If the Arabs had been defeated so quickly, completely and publicly, might it not be a sign that there was something rotten in their societies and in the moral system which they expressed? ... the problem of identity was expressed in terms of the relation- ship between the heritage of the past and the needs of the present. Should the Arab peoples tread a path marked out for them from outside, or could they find in their own inherited beliefs and culture those values which could give them a direction in the modern world? (Hourani, 1991, pp. 442–3; see also Kassir, 2004; Marsot, 2007, p. 164)

To the extent that the first option – treading a "path marked out for them from outside" – appears as a surrender of independence to the external world, preference tends to be given to the second option. This helps explain why after 1967 there was a sudden reversal of the commonly held opinion that the Arabs were determined to catch up with the West's material and technical progress: "Secular Arab nationalism had been proved a failure and was dead; the masses would reject Western progress and turn to fundamentalist Islam as their only hope" (Mansfield, 2003, p. 325; see also Dawisha, 2003). As Galal Amin points out, "To be healthy, their political and economic life should be derived from their own moral values, which themselves could have no basis except in religion" (cited by Hourani, 1991, p. 443). In sum, whereas in the decades following World War II, ideologies associated with Arab nationalism provided potent sources of legitimacy for many authoritarian Arab regimes (Elbadawi et al., 2011, p. 42), after the devastating defeat of Arab forces by Israel in 1967, Islamist ideologies gained ground at the expense of the waning nationalist discourse.

What characterizes these ideologies is not only their reactions to the symptoms highlighted earlier – decadence, decline, and military defeats – but also the diagnosis of the disease. In the eyes of Islamists, the poor condition of Muslims is not caused by any major change in external circumstances, but by a moral decay stemming from a loss of religious faith. As suggested earlier by Ibn Taymiyya, it is because they did not keep their pact with Mohammed that Muslims lost everything – political authority, respect, and the wealth of their faith. In India, for example, Muslims lost their power not to the British, but because the last Mughal emperors, such as Mohammed Shah Rangile and Bahadur Shah Zafar, "were sunk in the quagmire of wine, women, and poetry" (Kakar, 1996, p. 173). Therefore, a striking aspect of fundamentalist religious discourse, Islamist in this instance, is the turning of the rage inward "in a collective self-recrimination and masochistic self-hate." Tragically, "the loss of Muslim greatness is not grieved for, a process that would pave the way for an eventual acceptance of its loss and thus enable the community to face the future without a debilitating preoccupation with the past. Instead, the loss is experienced as a persisting humiliation, a narcissistic injury to the group self which keeps on generating inchoate anger rather than the sadness of mourning" (p. 175).

It is not surprising that Islamist speeches are full of sadomasochistic imagery coexisting with celebrations of the lost glories of Islam, that they inculcate guilt while at the same time offering relief for those who suffer from an inchoate sense of oppression and the looming shadow of a menacing future (Kakar, 1996, p. 176). A self-sustaining vicious process is set into motion, with the religious demagogues who propose the cure being simultaneously those who spread rumors and stoke the persecutory anxiety that signals the annihilation of group identity (p. 192). Fundamentalism is thus a theory of suffering and cure, because it provides a bulwark against collective identity fragmentation or dislocation (pp. 174–6). As stated by Kakar, fundamentalism "identifies the cause of suffering not in the individual mind but in a historical process which, however, is not fatefully deterministic, but is amenable to human will and eminently reversible. Individual and collective suffering are due to a lapse from an ideal state of religious faith, and the cure lies in an effort to restore faith in one's inner life to its original state of pristine purity" (p. 175).

Muslims are called to resist the corrupting influence of modernity that has involved them in ungodly entertainments and diverted them from their sacred duty of bowing before Allah. They must return to the fundamentals of the faith as contained in the Quran to which nothing can be added and from which nothing can be subtracted. Then only will the grandiose representation of the Muslim community projected by fundamentalist zealots become reality.

Islamism as an Attempt to Reformulate the Project of Modernity

It should have now become clear that Islamic fundamentalism, like all other revivalist or fundamentalist movements, is "an attempt to reformulate the project of modernity" (Kakar, 1996, p. 144). It is based on the idea that the religious crisis is ultimately caused by the rising influence of the Western world coupled with the inability of the faithful to retain their own cultural identity, which alone can make them strong. In the words of Roy (2008), "the defence of religion is reformulated as a defence of a cultural identity, of an 'authenticity,' that is itself cut off from the complexity of real culture. ... To give in at the level of cultural values is to give in at the level of the faith and religious identity, and vice-versa" (pp. 234–5; my translation). The framing of the Muslim problem as a cultural identity issue is especially evident in the Muslim world for the reasons that have been explained earlier. It precludes the adoption of Islamic modernism, which rests on the idea that

the defeat of Muslims at the hands of European powers revealed their vulnerability, and that the restoration of their political power requires them to borrow European military techniques, centralise state power, modernise their economies and provide a modern education for their elites. By implication, the medieval forms of Islamic civilisation must be repudiated but not Islam itself. Rather Islam ought to be reconstructed on its own inherent, but neglected, principles of rationality, ethical activism, and patriotism. (Lapidus, 1988, pp. 560–1; see also Khalid, 2007, p. 48)

Political jihadism is fundamentalism coupled with an emphasis on the need and the duty of all true Muslims to fight actively against the corrupt leaders who brought about the decline of Muslim civilization. Jihadists should not stop fighting until these leaders are overthrown through the most violent means if needed. In Egypt, for instance, radical Islamist groups proclaimed that "the fight must begin internally against jahiliyya, whose major representative is the iniquitous prince who rules in contravention of God's injunctions" (Kepel, 2005, p. 127). Revealingly, the ideologue of the al-Jihad group that assassinated Sadat, Abd al-Salam Faraj, thus wrote, "In the Islamic countries, the enemy is at home; indeed, it is he who is in command. He is represented by those governments that have seized power over the Muslims, and that is why jihad is an imperative for every individual. ... The rulers of our time are apostates of Islam, nurtured at the table of colonization. Of Islam, they have preserved no more than the name. ... To carry out God's order is to build the Islamic state" (cited by Kepel, 2005, pp. 209, 211, 237). In his book *The Hidden Imperative*, Faraj showed great contempt for those who tended to blame imperialism for all Egypt's problems. He was executed in April 1982 along with the four direct participants in the president's assassination.

FIghting against corrupt Muslim leaders was also the strategy initially advocated by Osama bin Laden, the founder of al-Qaeda. He indeed built his organization as a violent protest movement against the deeply corrupt rulers of Saudi Arabia and their likes. It was only later that, in collusion with his second-in-command, the Egyptian al-Zawahiri, he decided to dramatically widen al-Qaeda's objectives by declaring a jihad against the Western world and the United States in particular. This turning point apparently occurred after the invasion of Kuwait by Saddam Hussein's troops in 1990 when, under the strong pressure of the U.S. government, the Saudi rulers accepted the prolonged implantation of U.S. military bases on their soil. Combined with the experience of jihad in Afghanistan, the First Gulf War eventually led al-Qaeda to issue the "Declaration of War against the Americans" in 1996. He considered the decision of Saudi Arabia to accept the U.S. military presence as an act of treason, tantamount to selling the country to a foreign infidel power. At the same time, because the United States had intruded into Muslim space, a step later confirmed by the occupation of Iraq and sustained military intervention in Afghanistan, the Americans deserved to be treated like the corrupt Arab leaders who had allied with them. From now on, the civilization that had corrupted many Muslim leaders would be viewed as a direct enemy. Such a move was particularly dramatic for Saudi jihadists: Being traditionally introverted and focused on internal Muslim affairs as perceived in the "closed Saudi environment," they tended to be ready to cozy up to the West (Gerges, 2005, pp. 131–40).

Even many moderate Arab intellectuals and leaders, who find the extremist approach of the jihadists repulsive and unacceptable, have accepted that something is morally wrong with the West. In their eyes, Western powers are adept at applying double or even multiple standards, depending on their own opportunistic interests. Were they not brutal exploiters of dominated nations, although each Western country could boast of nurturing a liberal democracy at home and defending increasingly tolerant and humanitarian values or ideals (Rahman, 1982, p. 55)? In the same manner that Islamism of various hues mobilized opinion against colonial rulers, it began to be used to protest what is perceived as an iniquitous international order in which Muslim countries are discriminated against and any Israeli wrongdoing is automatically condoned.

In Egypt, where for obvious reasons frustrations ran especially high, the neo-Muslim Brethren offered their adherents "a kind of seamless suit of Islamist armour to protect them from the identity crises from which they suffer." They painted a picture of an apocalyptic situation faced by the country, under siege by the attacks of modernity. Moreover, they settled on four archetypes, equated to the four Horsemen of the Apocalypse, that are generally foreign to Egyptian society: Jewry, the Crusades, secularism, and communism. The neo-Muslim Brethren were thus relieved of the task of "analysing the internal causes of the difficulties of Islam, particularly as regards the relations between the state and civil society" (Kepel, 2005, p. 127).

Waves of religious fervor, as well as the growth of mystic (Sufi) orders and religious charitable societies, tend to sweep countries when the political regime is confronted with a deep legitimacy crisis. Such popular feelings can be exploited politically both by the ruling elite and radical opposition movements. This is precisely what happened after the debacle of the Egyptian Army in the 1967 Six Day War with Israel. Groups for the study of the Quran "mushroomed among all classes of the society, who turned to religion for consolation"; Coptic monasteries, which had been closing down for lack of candidates, now had waiting lists; and a miraculous apparition of the Virgin Mary in a remote suburb of Cairo drew considerable crowds of both Christians and Muslims, who sought solace for the sons, husbands, and fathers lost during the war. The message received by the population was clear: "In spite of the defeat, God was still on the side of the Egyptians and had sent the apparition as a consolation" (Marsot, 2007, pp. 149–50; see also Ayubi, 1991, p. 72). This interpretation suited the regime well, which is why the Socialist Union, the party of the president and the only tolerated political party in the country, actively supported the popular move by organizing seating in front of the church where the apparition took place. As argued in detail in Chapter 6, radical groups exploited the exacerbated religious sensitivities of the people in an opposite manner: raising strong criticisms of the ruling elite and their disastrous policies and preaching a return to the puritanical observation of Islamic principles.

As illustrated by the Kadizadeli rebellion in the Ottoman Empire, the resurgence of religious feelings and religious puritanism tends to be observed in periods of collective self-doubt sparked off by severe military defeats and economic crises combined with high-level corruption. Today, the scale of this movement is especially huge because Islam has been extensively globalized (Roy, 2004).

Analogies with Europe

It would be a mistake to think that the sort of modernization crisis just described is specific to the countries of Islam. Other regions of the world, including countries in Europe, have gone through similar experiences. In Chapter 2, mention was made of the role of Protestant ideology in Germany, where there was a strong demand for spiritual regeneration and structural changes that would restore the dignity and honor of the people in the face of external threats and a lack of internal cohesion. The resonance of Luther's message was strong because it was seen as capable of purging the empire of its impurities (Simms, 2013, p. 19).

Other examples that come to mind concern Eastern Europe and Russia when they were faced with the serious challenge posed by the rise of Western Europe at the time of industrialization. As pointed out by Andrew Janos (1982), "To East Europeans, and most other non-western peoples ... the reality of the West's global dominance loomed large as the most important condition of their latter-day existence. The fact of their relative powerlessness was to generate among them a sense of mutual sympathy on the one hand, and a kind of collective alienation on the other. More particularly, it created feelings of sharp ambivalence, that is, resentment and admiration, imitation and rejection, dependence and self-assertion" (p. 274).

In the case of Hungary, as in Egypt, the crisis of collective self-doubt was accentuated by the painful experiences of military defeat and the considerable loss of territory: "Defeat in World War I and the peace treaty of Trianon crystallized and politicised these sentiments by seeming to offer proof for the theory that the Magyars were an 'errant people of Turan' unwanted on the European continent" (Janos, 1982, p. 274). Among some segments of Hungarian society, the response took the form of an anti-imperialistic ideology stressing the need to put "an end to the age of servility to the West" and to "seek refuge within a larger family of Asiatic nations" (p. 274). Yet the dominant reaction was to seek a far more attractive option: to make Hungary part of a pan-European, national socialist movement that was to be led by Germany, "the most vigorous entity on the Continent, and the nation most representative of the values of occidental civilisation" (p. 275).

In Russia, a major element in the resistance to changes perceived as an attack on indigenous culture and the associated identity was the movement of the Old Believers. Led by Archpriest Avvakum, its adherents were opposed to the seventeenth-century reforms of Patriarch Nikon, which were initially supported by Tsar Alexis, on the ground that they were profaning Russia and announcing the end of the world (hence the representation of Nikon as the Antichrist). The ensuing schism, known as the "raskol," left a profound imprint on Russian society that has persisted throughout the following centuries. Old Believers were estimated to make up a full quarter of the east Slavic population of the empire. Surprisingly, the schism occurred in the absence of any doctrinal disagreement between the Orthodox church and the Old Believers (Kizenko, 2009, pp. 146–8; Heretz, 2008, pp. 14–101; Coates, 2010, pp. 174–5). According to one plausible explanation, the Old Believers' revolt was a defensive reaction of the upholders of Russian culture – the Old Believers were Great Russians; that is, Muscovite Russians – to what they perceived as an attempt to change old Russian rituals and customs to accommodate foreign influences, especially those emanating from Greece and the Ukraine, or White Russia (Riasanovsky, 1993, pp. 198–200; Kizenko, 2009, p. 149; Heretz, 2008, p. 50). The Russian church had earlier developed in the direction of religious ceremony, ritualism, and formalism, which for the believers "served as a great unifying bond and a tangible basis for their daily life" (Riasanovsky, 1993, p. 201).

Over time, the Old Belief movement consolidated its reactionary character. Under the reign of Peter the Great, it took the form of a determined resistance to Western-inspired reforms aimed at modernizing Russia. Foremost among its characteristics were a literalist view of the faith[14], a rigid attachment to tradition in its more formal aspects, the projection onto the past of a utopian ideal, "a holistic outlook which views all aspects of belief

---

[14] The Old Belief, especially the radical priestless factions, was maintained by a network of so-called "bookworms" (nachetchiki) (Heretz, 2008, p. 73).

and life as part of an all-encompassing and absolute whole," a tendency to splinter into sects and factions (hence their stress on living in small, tightly knit communities), and a stridently hostile attitude toward heretics (Heretz, 2008, pp. 70–5). It is important to stress that, like the Islamists today, the Old Believers were not opposed to economic and technical progress. Their members included a good number of well-to-do merchants.

The debate of ideas within the Russian elite during the second half of the nineteenth century attests that modernization often creates a vital threat to the cultural identity of economically backward countries. Members of the Russian high society (as opposed to the masses) had to choose whether to emulate the West or follow a truly Russian path based on the country's tradition and culture. This dilemma reflected an uncertainty about whether they were truly Russian or were strangers in their own nation. Unlike the Westerners who were convinced that Russia had to radically modernize its techniques and institutions and therefore had to go through the evolutionary stages of European Western history, the Slavophiles thought that Russian society was dangerously divided and that the only possible remedy was to re-Russify the high society (Walicki, 1975, pp. 336–455; 1979, pp. 92–114; Obolonsky, 2003, pp. 63–4). This re-Russification implied a return to the way of life of the (rural) masses considered as the bearers of Slav culture and of orthodox piety that achieved a total integration of the individual within the community and thus conferred on the people a strong sense of spiritual and psychological security (Kitching, 1982, p. 146). According to Obolonsky (2003), the Slavophile surge was "nothing more than a conservative intellectual reaction to the threat of expansion on the part of the 'corrupt' Western way of life" (p. 93). Inspired by romantic illusions characterised by back-to-nature and back-to-the roots sentiments, it had an "uncritical narcissistic flavour" and rested on an "inferiority complex." In the end, these ingredients produced a messianic and aggressive pan-Slavic ideology supporting Russian imperial claims to the Byzantine legacy (which implied claims to Constantinople and the Bosporus)and the unification of all Slavic people under Russian rule (pp. 93–7).

In an important sense, communist ideology offered a solution to the dilemma of whether to emulate the West or follow a truly Russian path. It was a new "religion" that derived its inspiration from what Tim McDaniel (1996) has called the Russian idea, which combines high moral principles of solidarity and cooperation with the pressing need to catch up with the West in economic and technological terms. This combination was actually foreshadowed by the populist movement of Herzen, Vorontsov, and Danielson. They believed that, although the drive toward technological modernization was inevitable, Russia – thanks to its specific history and protosocialist rural institutions – could play a unique historical role in modern history by skipping the capitalist stage of development and jumping straight to the socialist stage (Walicki, 1979, pp. 406–48; Kitching, 1982, pp. 147–8; Berdyaev, 1948). Interestingly, the Bolshevik Revolution that was to shatter the autocratic regime of czarism and establish socialism in Russia was heralded in the 1860s and 1870s by radical intellectuals who shared many characteristics of present-day political Islamists, including a preference for destructive violence. This is particularly evident from the following description, which provides an effective transition to the next section:

Radical ideology looked attractive, especially to the young and semieducated. It containes everything dreams are made of: the romance of conspiracy and mystery, feelings of personal involvement in "making history", opportunities for direct action, hopes from prompt results, and simplicity of the doctrine distinguishing "good" from "evil."

The way to do good was made clear, and there was the illusion of a back-to-one's roots movement intended to purify, to restore healthy principles of life freed from distortions imposed from the outside. In fact, this possibility presumed to reconstruct the original form of the Golden Age. (Obolonsky, 2003, pp. 92–3)

7.3 Motives behind Recruitment into Islamist Movements

It is now a natural step forward to delve into the personal motives that drive people into (violent) Islamist movements. In this section, three different answers are suggested that may possibly reinforce each other. A first kind of motive arises from experiences of personal dislocation leading to a need for a restored self-image. Second, Islamist movements may fulfill critical social functions that the state proves unwilling or unable to perform. And, third, individuals or groups may use radical Islam to express social and economic grievances or frustrations born of unrealized expectations in contexts where inequalities in socioeconomic status and position are reflected in religious symbols and functions. This last motive fits in well with the central thesis of the book, according to which it is often misleading to analyze religion independently of considerations of power and without bringing social, economic, and political forces into the picture. After discussing these varied motives for joining and adhering to Islamist movements, the profile and motivations of their leaders as opposed to ordinary recruits are briefly presented. Finally, to end the section, the relationship between Islamism and low Islam is elucidated.

Need to Restore a Damaged Self-Image

To people who have gone through sober experiences of personal dislocation and helplessness, radical and puritanical Islam proposes a cure that is particularly well adapted to their needs. As explained by Kakar again, the rhetoric used by Islamist preachers conveys to potential recruits a sense of participation in a collectivity with a transcendent purpose, thereby imparting a higher value or meaning to their life. This is done by conveying the feeling that they have been "chosen" to accomplish a sacred mission, that of rescuing their community from extinction. The tactic thus projects the image of a relentless attack on the Muslim community and its religious symbols by a malevolent dominant culture pervaded by corruption and debauchery. In the process, it creates a feeling of persecution with all the attendant anxiety:

Persecution anxiety signals a situation of great danger and carries with it the fear of the group's symbolic death, and annihilation of its collective identity. It is only when this particular anxiety courses through and between members of a group, making individuals feel helpless, frightened and paralyzed, that people become loosened from their traditional cognitive moorings and are prepared to give up previously held social, political, or economic explanations for their sense of aggrievement and become receptive to the religious critique. … One antidote to this paralyzing anxiety is anger, preferably in a violent assertion that is psychically mobilizing. (Kakar, 1996, pp. 179–80)

The follower is then presented with "a newly born group without memory and with but inchoate desires," but whose identity and political psyche are shaped with the help of "a series of narcissistically enhancing self-images." The group self-portrait, which emphasizes the superiority of Islam, the potential strength of the pan-Islamic community, and the chance of belonging to such a blessed and exalted entity, aims to enhance a sense of collective self-esteem that has been fractured by the workings of historical fate and at countering the deathly threat to its survival (Kakar, 1996, pp. 180, 189). To nurture the feeling of superiority and stress the sacred meaning and transcendent purpose of the mission, followers must "be zealous in the observance of religious duties, accept the priority of religion in all areas of life, and acknowledge the demands of religion as having the first call on individual loyalty" (p. 185). These duties partake of "a masochistic reparation for guilt feelings." The manipulative operation whereby Muslim identity is strengthened is instrumental in creating a vehicle for resistance to perceived domination and repression. Moreover, in defining an Other as an enemy moved by a deadly intent toward one's own group, fundamentalism provides "a focus for undue anger and unresolved hate." Fantasized violence is thus the means of overcoming the paralyzing fear engendered by the heightening of persecution anxiety (pp. 184–5).

Clearly, this new puritanical Islam is mostly attractive for individuals with a dislocated life, who experience feelings of helplessness, loss, and withdrawal owing to the disappearance of their old attachments and landmarks. Religion appears to them as a way to overcome these feelings and to provide the basis for a new social cohesiveness. They are not the poorest of the poor, for whom Westernization is magical because it means an abundance of food and medicine. Nor are they the rural dwellers who are immersed in "a kind of village Islam that had adapted itself to local cultures and to normal human desires," an Islam that is pluralistic and tolerant, allowing the worshipping of saints, the singing of religious hymns, or the cherishing of art – all activities formally disallowed in Islam (Roy, 1990, p. 32).[15] Religious and cultural syncretism is a hallmark of most rural societies in the lands of Islam (see Chapter 3). In Afghanistan, for example, the mullah "is, first and foremost, the mullah of a particular village and not of the clergy; he is not a member of an institutionalised body and has scarcely any links with his superiors (the ulama)." He is not appointed by them, and he does not depend on them for his income. He is in fact the employee of the village community in which he exercises the functions of a rite performer (p. 32; Nahavandi, 1999, p. 86).

Puritanical Islam is also attractive to rural-urban migrants, whether educated or semi-educated. Being cut off from the ties of kinship and neighborliness to which they were accustomed in their village, these migrants have found a sort of compensation in strong Muslim urban organizations that act as surrogate families. In other words, the sense of alienation or loss of identity that they experienced in their new lives "could be counterbalanced by that of belonging to a universal community of Islam, ... and this provided a language in terms of which they could express their grievances and aspirations" (Hourani, 1991, p. 452; see also Lapidus, 1988, pp. 889–90; Zakaria, 2003, pp. 143-4). Naipaul's account of Malaysia and Indonesia supports this view. He sees the problem of migrants as being caused by estrangement from their native rural communities whose customs derive from the subtle blending of pagan, archaic rites (or Hindu ones) with Islamic tenets, and reflect an

---

[15] Revealingly, a recent study has shown that in Morocco rural women are more open than more educated urban women to the new Family Code, which contains provisions calling into question the traditional interpretation of Islamic law regarding relationships between women and men (Aquil, 2006).

Islam adapted to everyday village realities. Lacking solid landmarks in their new urban, modern life, rural migrants face the threat of a loss of identity. It is in Islam, and in the life of the mosque with its rules and rituals, that "they found again, or reconstructed, something like the old feudal or rural community that for them no longer existed." After having been exposed to radical Islamic teaching, these new urban dwellers want to purify their native villages, which means cleansing them of pagan (and Hindu) customs (Naipaul, 1982, pp. 369, 387).

Precisely the same conclusion has been reached by Kepel (2005) after a careful study of the lists of militants belonging to the most radical Islamist groups in Egypt. It is worth quoting him at length:

The milieu that is the most fertile source of Islamist militants is the 20–25 age group in the sprawling neighbourhoods on the outskirts of the big cities. These people are marginal in every sense of the word, to begin with in their physical location in a middle ground that is no longer the countryside from which they came but not yet the city, whose heartland they do not penetrate. Their cultural complexion, too, is marginal: the traditional village structures no longer work for them, and can no longer provide them with the resources of material life or with any real social integration. They are the children of the rural exodus, and they arrive in the suburbs with outdated customs. Contrary to their expectations, however, education (even higher education) fails to provide them with the keys to modernity. ... Education has taught them the mannerisms of modern life but not its techniques or spirit. (Kepel, 2005, pp. 225, 244)[16]

An identical diagnosis for Egypt is proposed by Nazih Ayubi (1991), who also puts great emphasis on the appalling housing, sanitation, and transportation conditions prevailing in the shanty towns of Cairo, where most Islamist rural migrants (from Upper Egypt) are recruited. These dreadful conditions are especially hard to bear because migrants and other urban

---

[16] There appear to be two distinct problems with Egypt's higher education system. First, because of the tremendous increase in the number of students during the years 1970–7 (their number rose from about 200,000 to more than a half-million), the infrastructure became totally inadequate. Second, higher education is based on the passive acquisition of modern knowledge, meaning rote learning and memorizing, and lacks any critical spirit. It does not involve any reflection on culture, particularly the inherited religious culture (Kepel, 2005, pp. 138–42). Some authors argue that rote learning has characterized the educational systems of all countries of Islam since "the gate of ijtihad" was closed somewhere between the ninth and eleventh centuries (after the Abbasid renaissance), when the Islamic system became rigidified into a set of inflexible interpretations. They believe that this "closure of the Muslim mind" had nefarious long-term effects, eventually resulting in the economic, technological, and organizational retardation of Islamic countries in the last two centuries (see, e.g., Lal, 1998, pp. 63–6). I have strong doubts about the validity of this thesis because rote learning and memorizing have been observed in many non-Muslim societies until recently, including in advanced countries.

dwellers who are financially constrained but status-conscious lower middle class people are often forced to live in close proximity to the urban sub-proletariat from which they are eager to differentiate themselves (pp. 162–9; see also Gilsenan, 1982, pp. 255–60; Hopkins and Saad, 2004). In the same vein, it has been observed that radical Islam is appealing to educated youth from lower socioeconomic strata who confront deteriorating labor market conditions, such as happened in Egypt in the early to mid-1980s (Wickham, 2002; Bayat, 2002; Binzel and Carvalho, 2017).

Recruits of Boko Haram, a particularly violent Islamist insurgency movement in northern Nigeria (the name means "Western education is forbidden") also suffer from acute problems of uprooting, estrangement, and deprivation. An effective recruitment pool for this movement consists of children from poor rural families who have been sent away by their parents to study in traditional "almajiri" schools located in urban locations. These schools are no longer regulated by the public authorities, and their quality has declined: Rote learning (reciting verses of the Quran) is the primarily method of instruction. Therefore, well-to-do families no longer send their children to these schools, which are run by untrained religious teachers incapable of providing a decent level of religious, let alone secular, education. Instead, these teachers milk their pupils for cash by sending them begging in the streets. The poor and often illiterate boys attending the almajiri schools are easy prey for Boko Haram's recruiters who use money and religion to attract recruits. They are especially vulnerable because they have been separated from their parents at a young age and have been subject to a simplistic sort of religious indoctrination, instilling in them the idea that Western education is a threat to their traditional culture and a source of enslavement to alien values (Comolli, 2015, pp. 71–6).

Only a minority of Islamists actually become terrorists or violent jihadists. It is therefore interesting to inquire into their profiles and the recruitment mechanism involved, which may explain why they commit acts of terror. Marc Sageman (2004, 2008) suggests that there are four stages in the collective process of radicalization leading to terrorism and martyrdom. The initial trigger is a sense of moral outrage, usually over some incident of Muslim suffering (e.g., Saddam Hussein's hanging or the ordeal of Palestinians in Gaza). In the second stage, this event acquires a broader meaning, becoming part of a "morality play" in which Islam and the West are seen to be at war. In the third stage, the global and the local dimensions of reality are merged together, as grievances aroused by an international conflict resonate with the personal experience of discrimination or unemployment. Finally, in the fourth stage, the individual joins a terrorist cell, which nurtures the jihadist worldview and prepares the initiate for martyrdom (see, especially, Sageman, 2004, chs. 3–4; 2008, ch. 3).

Turning now to the first question, the profile of Islamic terrorists, there is strong suggestive evidence that youngsters recruited into violent Islamist movements tend to be people with a fragile psyche and a great amount of pent-up frustration and violent feelings stemming from difficult family backgrounds. Situations where the father is absent, brutal, or alcoholic or where he is unable to impose any authority and constraints on his children's behavior, and situations where the mother is unstable and the stepfather does not manifest tender feelings vis-à-vis his wife's children, readily come to mind here (see, for example, Nasiri, 2006; Storm, Lister, and Cruikshank, 2014). When psychological fragility leads to delinquency, the four stages of radicalization are facilitated because it is then easier for jihadist recruiters to stir guilt feelings in the targeted individual. Recruiters can present jihad as a way to redeem personal sins and not only to avenge for injustices committed against the Muslim community. Engaging in the jihad erases past personal failures and allows the jihadist to become a good Muslim again.

Social Role of Islamist Movements

Identification with Islamist groups among alienated urban people has been further strengthened by the ability of Islamic movements in many countries to capitalize on the lack of legitimacy of the state. One reason for this lack of legitimacy is the poor performance of public authorities in the delivery of basic public goods; in such situations, the state retreats from the distribution of essential services, such as health, education, and child care, when in conditions of economic crisis. Another cause of low legitimacy is the failure to enable an adequate level of political participation to the whole population. In fact, many regimes have only narrow support within particular ethnic, religious, or tribal minority groups. A gap is thus wide open for Islamist organizations to fill.

In Egypt, for example, the number of Muslim nongovernmental organizations (NGOs) increased from 600 in the early 1970s to 2,000 in the mid-1980s, and the number of private mosques grew from 14,000 to 40,000 from the early 1960s to the early 1980s (Huuhtanen, 2005, pp. 78–9; see also Harik, 2005, for a detailed review of Hezbollah's social activities in Lebanon). Typically, a privately funded Islamic charitable institution provides a range of services that are organized around a private mosque, including donated clothing for the poor, a clinic for health care, a kindergarten, and a primary school. Often, these institutions also run religious schools, orphanages, and homes for the elderly.

In Chapter 6, we saw that in Egypt, with the initial consent of President Sadat, the Muslim Brotherhood gradually took control of prestigious professional associations inside the Professional Associations Syndicate. What needs to be added now is that the Muslim Brothers won the confidence of the constituencies of these associations not only by providing a wide range of socioeconomic services and facilities but also by addressing rampant corruption in the syndicates (Zahid, 2010, pp. 109–15). On the former front, for instance, they initiated a health insurance scheme in the engineers' syndicate (which included almost 200,000 members), which met with great success. Similarly in the medical syndicate, "they worked hard to extend medical insurance to members and their families, to establish social and recreational clubs in rural as well as in large cities, to increase the stock of housing available to members at lower prices, and to assist the families of those members arrested or otherwise detained by the Egyptian regime" (p. 113). On the latter front, through their pragmatic leadership, they proved able to confront problems of internal infighting between rival political factions, financial mismanagement, lack of transparency, and corruption in a way that benefited the members of all the professional associations where they operated.

The Muslim Brothers' influence over the syndicates provided them with a unique opportunity to enhance an Islamic subculture within these powerful organizations, develop leadership skills of the professionals, and facilitate their access to the middle class (Wickham, 1996). As a matter of fact, many members of the professional class supported the Islamic Bloc, a confederation of Islamic political forces, "as their members were seen to be respectable, non-corrupt figures, possessing high moral and ethical values – characteristics lacking in their competitors and rival political factions in the syndicates" (Zahid, 2010, p. 115). As a result, the Muslim Brothers became able to mount a direct challenge to the power of the Egyptian state, which had conceived of the syndicates as corporatist bodies co-opted into its authoritarian structures.

The preceding section emphasized how radical Islamist organizations help vulnerable people form new identities by imposing strict observance of religious duties and requiring total loyalty. These demands require that the individual invest time and effort in acquiring the new identity and the associated metaphysical and moral beliefs (Iannaccone and Berman, 2006; Carvalho, 2017 (b)). This section focuses on the socially useful activities that these organizations typically perform. What needs to be added now, and elaborated a bit, is that these two functions are actually linked.

The effectiveness of the doctrine of an identity-based organization is linked both to its ability to elicit sacrifices, or commitment, from its members and to its resulting capacity to coordinate collective action. Following Carvalho (2016), an organization of this type imposes a minimum level of participation on its members. An individual who is seeking a new social identity (one that departs from the mainstream identity) wishes to communicate it to others, and this is done through group membership, which is strictly observable. Membership in the group implies that the individuals participate not only in religious collective rituals but also in social activities. The latter are performed relatively effectively because members of an organization have a mutual interest in its success.[17] Hence the superior effectiveness of identity-based organizations – religious organizations in particular – in delivering social services: In the words of Carvalho, "Identity-based organisations are successful at achieving tangible goals, because participation in their activities cultivates desired forms of identity" (p. 413).

It is actually conceivable that individuals join an organization just to cultivate a particular identity, even though the organization pursues other objectives, such as social service, political opposition, and violent rebellion. More realistically, however, individuals may care both about identity and about the material goods and services exclusively supplied by the organization to its members (they are therefore club goods). This final consideration is directly relevant to our discussion of radical Islamist movements: When religious organizations are viewed as offering identity as well as social services, it can be argued that those groups cultivating more extreme belief systems can be more extreme in terms of their practical demands of members. The ability of religious groups to sponsor terrorism is thus linked to their strict club structure (Carvalho, 2016, p. 413; see also Berman, 2009).

Radical Islam as a Weapon in Class Struggles

In certain contexts, upper- or middle-class people use Islamist doctrines to oppose social groups considered to enjoy undue privileges because of

---

[17] In the analytical setup proposed by Carvalho (2016), mutual interest is obtained when an individual's payoff is determined by the average participation of fellow group members, so that identity is analogous to a rival club good. This assumption is justified because, in this setup, the ultimate identity of an individual depends on the success of the organization, which itself hinges on participation levels across the entire group.

their close connection to the regime. In Syria, for example, the Muslim Brotherhood had a different role than in Egypt: To a great extent in Syria, it served as a vehicle for the opposition of the Sunni urban population to the domination of a regime identified with the (small) Alawite community (Hourani, 1991, pp. 457). More precisely, radical Islam served as a convenient rallying cry against the Baathist regime that had brought the traditional order of urban notables and big landowners, all Sunnis, to an abrupt end. Because nationalization and redistribution of land had deprived the great families of their power and status, it is therefore not surprising that the revolution's opponents emphasized Islamic values of private entrepreneurship and property. It was also no coincidence that the heart of the Islamic rebellion was located in Aleppo, the Orontes Valley, and the areas between them – the region where much rich farmland had been redistributed from rich landowners to poor peasants. Another constituency that suffered as a consequence of the (socialist) revolution and then provided funding to the Muslim Brotherhood to stir up opposition to the regime was the tradition-minded traders operating in the souqs (markets) of big cities such as Aleppo, the citadel of Syria's private enterprise, and Hama (McHugo, 2014, pp. 188, 192).

In the Côte d'Ivoire, the rise of Wahhabism coincided with a period of increasing disruption of traditional society under conditions of rapidly growing urbanization and migration after World War II. The Wahhabi doctrine attracted rich merchants, supplying them with an ideology that was both antiestablishment and "bourgeois." It was antiestablishment in the sense of opposing the feudal-like elite of the marabouts, who are at the heart of traditional Islam, but are viewed as impostors illegitimately interposing themselves between God and the faithful. And it was bourgeois in the sense of being emancipated from the constraints of the traditional aristocratic system (Miran 2006, p. 250). It is true that its egalitarian discourse also appealed to low-caste people wishing to liberate themselves from the yoke of the traditional system of hierarchy, but it was only in the 1980s that it started recruiting from among the urban poor. For them, Wahhabism offered a partial response to their quest for social protection and spiritual advice in a context of urban economic precariousness (p. 285).[18] It bears emphasis that behind the screen of religious antagonisms lay genuine social and political conflicts:

---

[18] Until political liberalization efforts began in 1969, Houphouët-Boigny's authoritarian rule succeeded in suppressing the Wahhabi movement rather effectively.

The battleground was less religious and doctrinal than social and political. As a matter of fact, the recourse to the religious sphere through Wahhabi sectarianism allowed dissatisfied people to express differences that could not be overtly declared in the political realm. Accusations of intolerance, dogmatism and narrowmindedness against the Wahhabis were therefore partly correct: since their separatism was grounded elsewhere, no discussion of a doctrinal nature was possible and no practical compromise could be reached with traditionalist Muslims. (Miran 2006, p. 259; my translation)

In the towns of Maradi (Niger) and Koko (Nigeria), the Wahhabi attacks on the relatively tolerant forms of Islam represented by the Sufi orders can be seen as attempts by disgruntled individuals or groups to emancipate themselves from the customs of the dominant society. The younger educated elite who espouse this puritanical version of Islam want to set their members apart from the older Islamic community by rejecting the authority of local scholarly traditions and adopting distinctive behaviors and rituals. Most interestingly, they are attracted by Wahhabism's asceticism and its avowed rejection of any ostentatious redistribution of wealth. Besieged by repeated demands for support from their kin, indeed, these young elites look for an effective means to develop their own unique sense of identity and to obtain the freedom to use their wealth as they like (Launay, 1992, pp. 104–31; Gregoire, 1993, pp. 109–10; Cooper, 1997, pp. 130–4). Recently, a detailed analysis of the rise of puritanical Islam in the Baga country (Guinea) during the colonial period led Ramon Sarro (2009) to the same conclusion: Strangers and ethnic minorities (like the Susu traders), rural youth, and residents belonging to nondominant descent groups were especially prone to follow charismatic Islamic leaders bent on cleansing rural life of fetishes and ritual objects representing the customary order.

The wearing of the Islamic veil by educated and urbanized women may be considered a defensive strategy deployed in a social context in which women's emancipation may be blocked by traditional norms that control their physical movements outside the family space. By manifesting their belief in a pure Islam, women claim the right to relate directly to God and dispense with the need to follow repressive rules enforced by men in the name of Islam thereby obtaining access to public life: The wearing of the veil then appears as "the sign of submission to God and not to men" (Boubekeur, 2004, p. 151; see also Adelkhah, 1991; Göle, 1993). Because the veil conceals their body fully, it provides an astute rebuttal of the argument according to which women's free movements in the outside space threaten the honor of the whole family. If veiling is thus conceived as a strategy for integration that allows women to seize economic opportunities outside the home while preserving their reputation within the community, Boubekeur shows, bans on veiling can be counterproductive by inhibiting social integration and increasing religiosity.[19] The same can actually be said about honor- or virtue-protecting norms, such as those requiring gender segregation at marriageable and postmarriageable ages. Meyersson (2014) has thus shown that when conservative Islamic mayors are elected in Turkey, women's secular high school educational attainment goes up, whereas the effects for men are much smaller. The underlying mechanism is that these mayors provide support for more strictly segregated dormitories, which makes it easier for conservative families to send their daughters to boarding schools. This effect for women is also persistent, influencing other decisions such as engaging in adolescent marriage.

As a final example of the importance of the socioeconomic context to understanding the precise meaning of Islamist movements, the lesson drawn from Iran is worth remembering. In that country, the responsiveness of certain powerful social classes, including businesspeople, to appeals expressed in religious language is particularly strong because throughout its history, religious leaders frequently served as a rallying point for opposition movements: Relatively independent of the government, and generally respected for their piety and learning, these leaders had always acted "as the spokesman of the collective consciousness" (Hourani, 1991, pp. 457–8).

These illustrations lend credence to Kakar's thesis that, when and where it occurs, religious revival "is less of religiosity than of cultural identities based on religious affiliation": "Where the resurgence is most visible is in the organisation of collective identities around religion, in the formation and strengthening of communities of believers" (Kakar, 1996, p. 186). Cultural-religious identities and the groups that articulate them thus provide a vehicle for the redress of economic injustices or of injuries to self-esteem and feelings of helplessness caused by obnoxious combinations of market forces and state action (or inaction). Educational expansion that is not accompanied by job expansion is one such obnoxious force: The resulting mismatch breeds a growing class of unemployed educated young people who become vulnerable to the appeals of revolutionary movements, including Islamist movements. Frustration of their aspirations is made greater when their failure in the labor market deprives them of access to the marriage market, resulting in their postponing marriage and attaining independence from the parental

---

[19] Jean-Paul Carvalho (2013) reaches a similar conclusion through a different argument. According to him, veiling can be seen as a commitment mechanism that Muslim women use to limit temptation to deviate from religious norms of behavior.

household. This connexion between labor market outcomes and marriage prospects is generally observed in Muslim societies, which continue to be guided by the patriarchal principle according to which a man is responsible for the livelihood of his household.

A vivid illustration of this predicament is provided by Egypt, which was one of the few countries where the Arab Spring took hold. As shown by Binzel and Carvalho (2017), men born between the years 1949 and 1960 were the first to benefit from the expansion of the educational system, receiving free schooling across all educational levels; in contrast, those born between 1968 and 1977 were confronted with very different conditions when they entered the labor market in the late 1980s and 1990s. Not only did opportunities in the government sector decline but also the private sector remained highly regulated. The ensuing decrease in job opportunities in the formal sector and the decline in real wages in the government sector caused distress far beyond the frustrations of failed job aspirations. Perhaps the most far-reaching social implication of the widening education–job gap in Egypt (and elsewhere in the Middle East) was a sizable increase in men's age at first marriage: The median age at first marriage for Egyptian men increased by around three years from around twenty-five for men born in the 1940s to around twenty-eight for men born in the early 1970s. This trend is worrying insofar as premarital relationships remain largely taboo in Egypt and other Muslim countries.

As pointed out by Binzen and Carvalho (2016), and by Assaad, Binzel, and Gadallah (2010), men typically work for years in order to afford the costs associated with marriage, which not only include the expense of the wedding celebration but also money for housing and purchasing electrical appliances. In addition to having sufficiently high earnings, the groom is also expected by the bride's parents to hold a "respectable" job, a requirement that is partly linked to social status but also follows from the aforementioned principle that a man must be able to adequately support a family. Moreover, women's increased educational attainment has put additional pressure on grooms. Consequently, despite the great value placed on family formation in the Middle East, only about 53 percent of men aged twenty-five to twenty-nine were married in the 1990s, the lowest percentage of all developing regions.

Islamist Leaders

What are the characteristics not of the adherents but of the leaders of Islamist movements? Although the literature is very scant on this issue,

Nielsen (2012) provides insightful and ingeniously gathered evidence that points to some clear patterns. According to his research, Muslim clerics strategically decide to adopt or reject jihadi ideology based on their career incentives. More precisely, most clerics do not support militant jihad and extreme forms of the faith because doing so would hurt their career prospects within state-run religious institutions. By contrast, a minority of clerics who have relatively few connections with the religious establishment and lack access to prestigious training or prominent teachers may be tempted to make careers outside of the state system by appealing to lay audiences directly. These clerics can credibly signal independence from state elites by openly espousing jihadi ideology, making it a risky but potentially high-payoff way to advance one's clerical career.

It is a well-established fact that many Islamist teachers are rather poor thinkers who are prone to extreme simplification: Self-proclaimed mullahs form an Islamic "lumpen-intelligentsia" made of ill-educated, ignorant people who misunderstand Islam owing to their lack of historical culture (Roy, 1990, p. 73).[20] In Afghanistan, for example, the Taliban were unable to back up their rulings with theological evidence because they had no knowledge of the Arabic language and the relevant literature (Barfield, 2010, p. 262). In some regions, important official positions are even filled by ill-trained people. Thus, General Zia ul-Haq's cooperation with religious radicals caused a situation where in Pakistan a qadi could earn a diploma considered equivalent to a master's degree in law after just a short period of training at a religious seminary (see Chapter 6).

Interestingly, the clergy's lack of education and training is found in other radical movements that mix up messianistic interpretations of religion and revolutionary politics. For example, the Brotherhood of the Scythe Cross, a Hungarian revolutionary movement that started marching on Budapest in 1936, was led by Zoltan Böszörmenyi. He was "a journalist of minor accomplishments" who contributed to a local newspaper in the regional town of Tisza. He called himself the "Prophet of the poor" on a mission from God, and like Moses, he issued ten commandments; however, his commandments called on the peasantry of the Tisza region to revolt against the "lords and communists" of Budapest (Janos, 1982, p. 246). Abimael Guzman, who led the "Sendoro Luminoso" (Shining Path) movement from the remote city of

---

[20] In Afghanistan, the young mullahs have spent sufficient time in the school system to consider themselves as educated persons and to refuse to go back to the land or work in a factory, yet they have not succeeded in going beyond the secondary school level (Roy, 1990, p. 73).

Ayacucho in the north of Peru, had a profile very similar to Böszörmenyi: he was an obscure professor of philosophy at the local university. His writings, which are full of messianistic statements using both Maoist and Christian references, were aimed at mobilizing impoverished rural masses that tended to reduce the world to simple categories derived from the narrow experience of a simple autarkic economy. As pointed out by Andrew Janos (1982), when it comes to discussing politics, peasants – whether from Hungary or other developing countries – are prone to freely mixing "present and future, fact and fancy, design and reality" (p. 241). As a consequence, "the peasants had very little faith in any system that offered piecemeal solutions through legislative bargaining and bickering. Rather, they expected their salvation from a strong leader blessed with prophetic gifts and standing above the petty squabbles of parties or the tedium of administrative minutiae" (p. 242).

Returning to radical religious movements proper, a striking feature of all of them, whichever faith they belong to, is what Roy (2008) calls "sainte ignorance" (holy ignorance). This means that their refusal of secular culture goes hand in hand with a deep distrust of religious learning itself: They believe that such knowledge is not only unnecessary to obtain salvation but that it can also distract from the true path to the faith. As attested by the role of the Holy Spirit among protestant Evangelists (duly named Pentecostalists), the word of God can be conveyed directly, without the mediation of knowledge. As a result, there is no room left for theological, linguistic, and cultural learning: What matters is to communicate emotions and to convey the sensory experience of how God's presence is felt, carefully avoiding discursive arguments that represent a waste of time. What is thereby created is "a religion without culture"; that is, a religion citing words extracted from sacred texts without any reference to their historical, literary, and cultural context and outside any interpretive framework that only learning can achieve (Roy, 2008, pp. 252–3). Culture and knowledge are actually regarded as parasitic elements that have accumulated after the pristine times of the foundation act of the faith and that contribute only to debasing and distorting its original, pure message.

By preaching a return to the way of life of the first Christians, Jews, or Muslims, the surrounding dominant culture with all its ugly traits (homosexuality, alcohol addiction, free sexuality, etc.) is thus rejected; this rejection applies with especial force to popular culture. An odd situation nevertheless emerges in which radical religious groups use the symbols and technologies provided by the dominant culture, yet condemn it as corrupt and worthless. In the words of Roy (2008), "Prevailing cultural markers are replaced by religious markers, but these religious markers themselves are used precisely as though they were cultural identity markers" (p. 243; my translation). "Instead of encompassing the cultural world, religion becomes a sub-culture in the same way as that of the workers, the gays, the feminists, or the black people" (p. 247; my translation).

Islamism and the Low Islam

It should be clear that Islamic opposition movements do not form a homogeneous category and cannot be simply reduced to the world of low Islam. Instead, Islamist movements represent an extreme form of religion-based opposition, characterized by a puritanical approach that is at odds with the magical inclinations of the popular low Islam typically found in rural areas and poor urban neighborhoods. Islamism or Islamist reformism can be described as a debased version of high Islam, born of the ideological formulations of unsophisticated thinkers. Its objective of restoring a pristine form of the religion prompts its adherents to impose a complete change of life and beliefs on simple people who are accustomed not only to implement Quranic prescriptions in a rather loose manner (see Chapter 3, Section 2) but also to honor saints and perform "impure" rituals.

It is thus revealing that, in her study of Morocco, Chaara (2015) found that opposition to pro-women reforms embedded in the new Family Code (2003) came predominantly from urban men and women who were both educated and deeply religious. Educated people with weak religious inclinations tended to support the reforms, as did uneducated and mainly rural people with stronger religious beliefs and practices. In other words, the correlation between the intensity of religious practice and support of the law was conditioned on the level of education: The lower this level, the greater the impact of religion on the support for family reforms.

In Morocco, the combination of religiosity and education that led to opposition to the reforms was exemplified by the women's association linked to the Justice and Development Party (PJD). Its members advocated that the more patriarchal family structure defended by the old Family Code had to remain in place. They were also favorable to polygamy, the guardianship of the father, and marriage for women as young as age fifteen (Ramírez, 2006; Dalmasso, 2008). Chaara (2015) also observes that, in Morocco, puritanical movements were mostly found in urban areas where they mainly attracted educated people. Active on college campuses since the 1980s, these movements have exerted an important influence on university life, imposing a very conservative Islamic view of society on the type of cultural activities allowed, the manner of dressing, diet, gender relationships, and even the content of the courses. Conservative movements have also influenced elementary and secondary levels of education. The decline in the quality of public education has led to the creation of private schools, some of them linked to religious movements, and to the delivery of extracurricular activities by teachers linked to religious groups (Tozy, 1999, pp. 180–4).

In keeping with earlier observations, the existence of radical positions among Moroccan intellectuals is not new: there is a direct line to anticolonial resistance movements. As a matter of fact, during the protectorate and at the time of independence, intellectuals in Arabized cities initiated the return to a scripturalist tradition, and nationalists who joined the scripturalist Allal el-Fassi launched the National Movement, the first mass movement for independence (Geertz, 1968, p. 95).

In the words of Clifford Geertz, "Coinciding with the rise of the intense Islamic puritanism of the Egyptian and Afghan-Parisian reformers, Abduh and Al-Afghani, among the notables of the Arabised towns, and particularly those around the ancient Qarawiyin University at Fez, the Berber policy [of the French colonial power] and its implied threat to Islam stimulated the growth of nationalism under the banner of defending the faith against European-sponsored secularization and Christianization" (Geertz, 1975, p. 25).

7.4 Conclusion and Final Reflections

This final section focuses on the need for a minimum degree of continuity with the past in societies experiencing a civilizational challenge, as well as the role of foreign domination in exacerbating the feelings of victimhood that are often a driving force for Islamist radicalism.

Summing Up

In a situation of protracted crisis such as that experienced by the Muslim world, disgruntled urban groups and, as we have seen earlier, even political rulers themselves have urged a radicalization of religious beliefs f. Recourse to puritanical beliefs is more tempting when people can associate the failure of their governments in meeting the challenges of modernity with the failures of secularism and the Western path, and when military defeats are added to disappointing economic performances, corruption, and the inefficiency of rulers. A crisis of legitimacy is the outcome. Paraphrasing Andrew Janos (1982), and transposing his analysis of Hungary's political system (from the mid-nineteenth to the mid-twentieth century) to post–World

War II Muslim autocracies, one can say that "the fatal weakness of this system was that it had been rendered illegitimate by the perversion of its own charter and identity" (p. 317). In particular, perversion of national ideals have undermined the achievements of secularism in education and legal development. For example, civil and commercial laws that were secularized early on – toward the end of the nineteenth century in countries such as Egypt and Syria – have since been gradually ignored or, worse, considered a liability. In many countries, the achievements of secular education have been called into question by the exponential increase in the number of religious schools and the growing importance of religious subjects in school curricula.

An important outcome of the perceived failure of secularism and the subjugation and even obliteration of secular, left-oriented movements and organizations at the behest of cynical and myopic autocrats is that Islam has little competition in articulating popular opposition to corrupt and inequitable governments. This is patently true under the strongly authoritarian regimes of the Middle East, where the religious idiom is the only one left that people, especially young, educated, lower-middle-class individuals, can use to communicate criticism and protest "against repression, social injustice, hardening of the political arteries, and the threat to collective identity" (Ibrahim, 1995b, p. 90; Marsot, 2007, p. 164).[21] Zakaria writes,

The Arab world is a political desert with no real political parties, no free press, and few pathways to dissent. As a result, the mosque became the place to discuss politics. As the only place that cannot be banned in Muslim societies, it is where all the hate and opposition toward the regimes collected and grew. The language of opposition became, in these lands, the language of religion. This combination of religion and politics has proven to be combustible. Religion, at least the religion of the Abrahamic traditions (Judaism, Christianity, and Islam), stresses moral absolutes. But politics is all about compromise. The result has been a ruthless, winner-take-all attitude toward political life. Fundamentalist organisations have done more than talk. From the Muslim Brotherhood to Hamas and Hizbullah, they actively provide social services, medical assistance, counseling, and temporary housing. For those who treasure civil society, it is disturbing to see that in the Middle East these illiberal groups *are* civil society. ... If there is one great cause of the rise of Islamic fundamentalism, it is the total failure of political institutions in the Arab world. (Zakaria, 2003, pp. 142–3; see also Kassir, 2004, p. 39; Hassan and Kivimäki, 2005, p. 133)

---

[21] It is interesting, here, to draw a parallel with the experience of other countries – for example, India – where "it is economic stagnation, wastage, and corruption of the old [dirigiste] policies, as seen clearly in the 1980s, that have discredited secularism" and facilitated the rise to power of the Hindu right (Desai, 2005, p. 260).

Rather paradoxically, the state has too often played with the devil by nurturing radical religious movements for the purpose of struggling against and defeating left-wing organizations, which, for decades, were considered especially threatening to the regime. Breeding extremism for reasons of political expediency is always a dangerous game, as attested by the disastrous consequences in many developing countries of the political instrumentalization of ethnic identity, which closely resembles religious identity (see, e.g., Posner, 2006; Lemarchand, 2009). Like any ethnicity-based ideology, a religious ideology is typically based on appeals to a largely constructed or imagined collective identity. When such a conjunction of events happens – that is, when the state is corrupt, iniquitous, and despotic while social and political organizations of the left have been rendered powerless – people's anger against the regime can only take the form of religious dissent or upheaval. This scenario is all the more likely when the abhorred state itself has professed adherence to secular values and principles that its own officials have betrayed.

The Challenge of Civilizational Change

A typical feature of fundamentalist movements is that they accept the technologies made globally available by the expansion of market capitalism and the many institutional forms that accompany it. What they generally reject is the threat to culture and identity that globalizing forces entail. This is a serious problem because, when cultural nationalism conflicts with economic globalism, the former takes priority and tends to have a strong appeal to the emerging middle classes and the intelligentsia. This will become particularly evident when we examine the case of modern Turkey in Chapter 9. Fundamentalist movements of all hues, as will become even more evident in Chapter 8, are a deleterious force insofar as they stoke group narcissism. When the group's imagined and extolled self is brought into serious doubt, a regression occurs, and "the group's feelings of worthlessness and its singular sense of inferiority" come to the fore. The regression "is most clearly manifested in the sphere of group aggression which takes on, overtly and covertly, the flavour of narcissistic rage" (Kakar, 1996, p. 168). The problem is all the more serious because this rage does not vanish when the offending object disappears: "The painful memory can linger on, making of the hot rage a chronic, cold resentment till it explodes in all its violent manifestations whenever historical circumstances sanction such eruptions" (p. 168).

A striking illustration of the persistence of memory and chronic resentment is found in India where, as we see in the next chapter, Hindu fundamentalists are projecting an image of Hindu oppression at the hands of the Muslims at a time when the latter have lost a great deal of their influence demographically, economically, and politically. The central lesson drawn by Kakar is that, as suggested by Emile Durkheim (1912), every society requires a minimal sense of continuity with the past, a continuity of cultural memory: "In a society in the throes of modernization, the need for continuity with the past, a sense of heritage, essential for maintaining a sense of individual and cultural identity, becomes even more pressing, sharply reducing the subversive attractions of a viewpoint which emphasizes the plasticity and discontinuities of the past" (Kakar, 1996, p. 169).

If the ruling political elite do not meet such a need for a common representation of the past in times of rapid changes, as has been the case, for example, during the modernization period of Meiji Japan, the danger exists that the void will be filled by leaders of radical puritanical movements who have a good understanding of popular feelings and the psyche. It is often too late when the political elite realize that these movements can easily lead to excesses and turmoil that could have been avoided.

Note that the aforementioned motive for radicalization – the loss of a minimal sense of continuity with the past and the need to preserve cultural identity – explains why religious movements or sects that do not follow puritanical tenets and even have a long tradition of folk syncretism, such as Sufi orders, may get radicalized. A vivid example is provided by the recent stunning expression of fundamentalist feelings among many Barelvis in Pakistan. Upholders of folk Islam, the Barelvis have traditionally shunned the austere creed of Deobandism, the school that inspired the Pakistani Taliban. However, this did not prevent them from being outraged by the attempt of a liberal governor of the state of Punjab to relax a draconian ban on blasphemy. Behind this outrage is the deep conviction that a blasphemy law is essential for protecting the honor of Muhammad (Paul, 2014, 142–3; *Economist*, April 16–22, 2016, p. 40). They reacted to a move that they perceived to be an attack on their traditional culture in which the cult of honor has pride of place. The feeling of outrage was so strong that, after a Barelvi bodyguard assassinated the governor and was later hung following a court decision, a big shrine was built up in his memory, and he was proclaimed a martyr amidst huge crowds of Barelvi Muslims attending his funerals.

The Role of Foreign Domination

A critical limitation of the analysis proposed here is that it ignores the role of the power game played by advanced countries in the West. It is as though the problems that triggered the Islamist movements were entirely of the making of the Muslim world, as if various forms of colonial and neocolonial intervention by economically advanced countries do not bear any relation to these movements. In fact, one can hardly overstate that the West contributed to creating a political environment conducive to extremist reactions in the lands of Islam, particularly during the twentieth century. After a detailed investigation, Mark Curtis (2010) goes so far as concluding that British collusion with radical Islamic actors "has contributed not only to the rise of radical Islam itself but also to that of international terrorism" (p. ix). This collusion, which took on various forms including training and financing, has a long history, and its roots go back to the imperial divide-and-rule policies whereby the British sought to cultivate Muslim groups or individuals to counter emerging nationalist forces that were challenging British hegemony.

Securing access to the colossal oil reserves of the Middle East was a key imperial objective, which required overcoming the formidable obstacle posed by popular Arab nationalism led by Nasser. When conservative pro-Western monarchies could not be propped up, covert relationships with Islamist forces, notably the Muslim Brotherhood, were fomented to destabilize and overthrow nationalist governments. Otherwise, these forces were used as "muscle" to bolster right-wing pro-British regimes and to counter the remnants of secular nationalism and communism (Curtis, 2010, pp. xiv–xv). This tactic was used not only in Arab countries of the Middle East but also in other countries where the British wanted to maintain global power and achieve their foreign policy goals, such as the assertion against the Soviet Union of British political and economic interests in Asia (in Afghanistan, for example). In India, the British colonial power showered official patronage on favored Muslim leaders in the community, seeing Muslim India partly as a counter to Hindu nationalism. The construction of knowledge it promoted in the Indian colony was thus deliberately sectarian, building up the distinctions between Muslims and Hindus (p. 3). A British secretary of state for India noted that "the division of religious feeling is greatly to our advantage," whereas Sir John Strachey observed in 1888 that "the truth plainly is that the existence side by side of these hostile creeds is one of the strong points in our political position in India" and that the political interests of the Muslims coincided with the British interests (cited by Curtis, 2010, pp. 4–5).

How can we reconcile these tactics with the fact that Islamic movements, including the Deoband Sunni revivalist movement in India and the Muslim Brotherhood in Egypt, often arose in direct response to (British) colonial rule? The answer is that pragmatism and political expediency were in force on both sides. In the same manner as Muslim autocrats could play a devil's game with Islamist movements to counter the threat from secular leftists and nationalists, Western imperial powers in general, and the British in particular, could ally with these movements in spite of the fact that they rejected colonial occupation as well as Western political and cultural influence. On their part, Islamists could accept external support from Western states because they considered them as partners with whom they could do business and who did not represent an immediate danger to their values (Gerges, 2005, p. 72). The alliance was viewed as a temporary marriage of convenience that allowed Islamists to focus on their most pressing objective, namely to overthrow iniquitous local political regimes and impose the rule of the sharia so as to usher in an era of social justice under God's command. It may also be remembered that coziness to the West was rather natural among introvert Salafists, those raised in the closed Saudi shell in particular (pp. 132–4).

In short, there was apparent duplicity on all sides. Once the common enemy – left-wing and nationalist secular parties and organizations – would be defeated, Western powers and Islamists would reassert their own ultimate interests. That the British were ready to take the gamble is evident from the testimony of Fereydoun Hoveyda, Iran's ambassador to the United Nations until the 1979 revolution. In an interview given to Robert Dreyfuss in May 2004, he reportedly said the following: "The British were playing all sides. They were dealing with the Muslim Brotherhood in Egypt and the mullahs in Iran, but at the same time they were dealing with the army and the royal families" (cited by Dreyfuss, 2005, p. 112). In Iran, the British "had financial deals with the mullahs. They would find the most important ones and they would help them. And the mullahs were smart: they knew that the British were the most important power in the world. It was also about money. The British would bring suitcases full of cash and give it to these people" (p. 112).

As for the United States, to which we now turn, there is much reason to believe that its analysts largely failed to understand that the Islamist movement was not just anticommunist but also was fundamentally opposed to the West and to its most reliable long-term partners in the Middle East, namely, the secular, democratic nationalists (Dreyfuss, 2005, p. 271). In the great strategic game that unrolled in the Middle East, U.S. analysts did not anticipate the behavior of the Islamists in the medium or long term. It would nevertheless be wrong to believe that Islamists were the complete masters of that game and that their moves were perfectly thought out following a well-planned strategy. As we have seen, the decision to internationalize jihad and target the United States and the West was taken by al-Qaeda's top leadership only after the invasion of Kuwait and the experience of jihad in Afghanistan. At this important turning point, al-Qaeda's leaders were compelled to modify their version of past events and tactical choices (Gerges, 2005, p. 77).[22]

Since the mid-twentieth century, the United States has been a major actor in the Middle East, often acting in collusion with Britain. Like the latter, it has played a sinister game justified by the struggle against Arab (and Iranian) nationalism and communism. For Robert Dreyfuss (2005), the consequences have been tragic: U.S. policy during the last six decades "is partly to blame for the emergence of Islamist terrorism as a worldwide phenomenon. ... The United States spent decades cultivating Islamists, manipulating and double-crossing them, cynically using and misusing them as Cold War allies" (p. 1). The prevailing idea, as the Cold War progressed, was that the main enemy, the USSR, and its alleged accomplice, Arab (and Iranian) nationalism, had a common enemy: Islam. In their search for tactical allies in the Middle East and Central Asia, the U.S. intelligence services naturally thought of Islam "as a better bet than secularism, since the left-wing secularists were viewed as cats' paws for Moscow, and the centrist ones were dangerously opposed to the region's monarchies and traditional elites" (p. 10; see also Gerges, 2005, pp. 70–4). It is therefore not surprising that, in the late 1970s and the 1980s, the United States looked on uncritically as key allies, Jordan and Israel, covertly aided terrorists from the Muslim Brotherhood in a civil war in Syria and as Israel encouraged the spread of Islamism among Palestinians in the occupied territories, facilitating the founding of Hamas (Dreyfuss, 2005, pp. 4, 190–213; Enderlin, 2009).[23]

The game engaged in by the United States was not confined to Arab countries, but extended to a green belt along the "arc of Islam," which included Afghanistan, Pakistan, Iran, and the Central Asian republics of the USSR. To encourage restive Muslims inside those republics, seen as the soft underbelly of the Soviet Union, was thus viewed as an appropriate tactic to stir up trouble and perhaps destabilise the enemy. The American public was completely unaware of the campaign led by CIA director William Casey, who "exhibited a messianic, religiously inspired version of anti-communism",

---

[22] Not all Islamist organizations agreed with al-Qaeda's move to globalize the jihad, however (Gerges, 2005). Gerges also offers many examples of contradictions, squabbling, and infighting inside these organizations (see, for example, p. 130 for Algeria, and pp. 151–84, 200–40 for the splitting up of jihadis after the rise of Osama bin Laden).

[23] The intelligence services of Israel (the Shin Beth) secretly supported radical Islamists coming from the Muslim Brotherhood and assembled under Hamas with a view to discrediting Fatah, the main Palestinian movement led by Yasser Arafat.

and came to see political Islam and the Catholic Church as natural allies against Soviet imperialism (Dreyfuss, 2005, pp. 281-2). [24] Initially, during the early 1980s, the operations were limited to cross-border smuggling of propaganda designed to encourage Islamic fervor (which included covertly sending thousands of copies of the Quran printed in Central Asian languages both by the CIA and the government of Saudi Arabia). Toward the middle of the decade, however, these efforts were drastically expanded to include numerous cross-border raids and sabotage missions north of the Amu River. Dreyfuss has no doubt that these actions helped to stir up trouble in the region and aided the growth of powerful Islamist groups that, to this day, still plague the governments of the former Soviet republics; in particular, the Islamic movement of Uzbekistan, the Islamic Liberation Party ("Hizb ut-Tahrir"), and various Islamist organizations in Chechnya and Dagestan (Dreyfuss, 2005, pp. 281–7).

A similar tactic was followed in Iran. At the request of the British Secret Intelligence Service (SIS), commonly known as MI6, the CIA organized and carried out a state coup that dislodged Prime Minister Mohammad Mossadegh from power in 1953. On this occasion, the United States secretly funded a fanatical Iranian ally of the Muslim Brotherhood, an ayatollah who had founded the Devotees of Islam. Later in the same decade, the notion began to form that an Islamic bloc led by Saudi Arabia could act as a countervailing force to the nationalist left (Dreyfuss, 2005, p. 3). This notion was to gain increasing currency in the late 1970s, when in the United States the Christian right movement was being transformed from a politically inchoate force into a structured Christian politicized coalition (pp. 11–12). Direct support for the most fundamentalist branches of the mujahiddin in Afghanistan, obviously intended to force a humiliating retreat of the USSR from that country; the installation of military bases in Muslim post-Soviet republics of Central Asia; and the direct military occupation of Iraq, which was conceived as a way to reassert U.S. dominance in this oil-rich region were parts of the overall imperial strategy that took shape toward the end of the twentieth century. That strategy has essentially persisted until today (see Gerges, 2012).

---

[24] A devout Catholic, Casey saw political Islam and the Catholic Church as natural allies in the struggle against Soviet imperialism, and he therefore had a good working relationship with the pope. His views on religion and politics dovetailed with those of President Reagan, and both of them "had no trouble seeing the Afghan jihad as a religious war in which Christianity and Islam were allies against the atheistic Soviet Union" (Dreyfuss, 2005, pp. 282–3; see also Gerges, 1999, p. 71).

The pernicious role of Western powers, and of the United States in particular, has not only consisted of supporting radical Islam and violent religious extremists, rather than progressive secular movements, on repeated occasions but also of encouraging victimhood feelings through policies or acts that smack of double standards.[25] An example of the latter is the partisan attitude of the West in favor of Israel and the festering sense of injustice that it has nurtured among the Arab masses.[26] The United States' inability to bring about a just settlement of the Palestinian problem early on, along with the repeated defeats of the Arab armies by Israel, often with the support of major Western countries, helped discredit secularism and complicated the task of Muslim (above all Arab) regimes confronted by a religious opposition. That opposition, indeed, was quick to portray concessions to foreign pressures as so many unacceptable encroachments on the "dignity of Islam." Such a posture, it must be noted, also made uncomfortable the situation of moderate Muslims ready to take inspiration from Western institutions and organizational patterns. Autocrats often reacted to criticisms by instrumentalizing Islam to stay in power, thus exacerbating the framing of the political debate in religious terms. The disastrous approach of the U.S. superpower to the problems of autocracy in Iraq and the rise of Iran as a new assertive power in the Middle East have further aggravated the vicious nature of the obscurantist deadlock in which many lands of Islam have been trapped. In the words of Fawaz Gerges (2005),

Something clearly went terribly wrong with the architects of the American strategy. Driven by ideology and a blind instinctual ambition to "wipe the slate clean" (in Bush's first Defense Secretary Donald H. Rumsfeld's words) and restructure Arab and Muslim societies and politics, the Bush team lost sight of ends and means and the self-limiting nature of al-Qaeda. There existed a disconnect between sweeping ideological thinking in Washington and complex socio-political conditions in the region. Political oppression, the Arab-Israeli conflict, and chronic social chaos, not al-Qaeda (dangerous as it is), pose the most pressing threat to regional and international security. Contemporary jihadism is a by-product of simmering dislocations in Arab and Muslim countries, a symptom of social and political malaise. Yet the U.S. foreign policy establishment had chosen to tackle the symptoms, not the root causes, of the Middle East crisis. (p. 291; for a similar standpoint, see Rashid, 2008; Crooke, 2009; Lynch, 2016)

---

[25] "Extremism in the defence of liberty is no vice," said presidential candidate Barry Goldwater at the 1964 convention of the Republican Party in Daly City, California (*Economist*, July 16–22, 2016).

[26] Just think of the pressures on Arab and Muslim countries to sign an unlimited nuclear nonproliferation treaty without requiring Israel to do the same.

Because he could not accept the killing of innocent civilians in the name of Islam, Omar Nasiri (a fake name) did not hesitate to work as a spy for the secret services of several Western European countries. This took him to Afghanistan where he succeeded in penetrating training camps of the mujahiddin after the retreat of Soviet troops and in meeting high-level chiefs of what later became known as al-Qaeda. Despite this anti-jihadist engagement, however, he made the following clear:

I am a Muslim. And to this day, I would go to war for my faith. I am no longer a spy, but part of me remains a mujtahid. I think the United States and all the others should get off our land, and stay off. I think they should stop interfering in the politics of Muslim nations. I think they should leave us alone. And when they don't they should be killed, because that is what happens to invading armies and occupiers. I was appalled by the way Americans reacted to 9/11. The endlessly naïve outrage: we have been attacked on American soil! Three thousand Americans killed on American soil! A tragedy, no doubt. And a crime. But what about the millions of Muslims killed on Muslim soil? In the Middle East, in Africa, in Bosnia, in Chechnya, in Afghanistan. Did time stop for them? (Nasiri, 2006, pp. 318–19)

In his courageous foreword to Nasiri's testimony, titled *Inside the Jihad*, Michael Scheuer, who served the CIA for twenty-two years and was the chief of the unit responsible for tracking Osama bin Laden from 1996 to 1999, denounces in unambiguous terms "the frantic eagerness of the U.S. governing elite to ignore the irrefutable evidence Mr. Nasiri provides in his book." This applies especially to "the genuine motivation of the mujahiddin – an intense and still-building hatred for the content and impact of interventionist U.S. foreign policies in the Islamic world" (Nasiri, 2006, p. ix). When someone dares say in the United States that the Islamists are essentially reacting "to a half-century of U.S. political, economic, and military intervention in the Muslim world," that person is immediately branded "a simpleton, a defeatist, and a traitor" (p. ix). For Scheuer, therefore, "Mr. Nasiri presents Americans with a clear choice: Grab hold of the truthful life preserver he has thrown and have a chance to prevail, or cozy up to the lies proliferated by their governing elite and see America sink toward the abyss of defeat" (p. xv).[27]

The advice actually holds for the entire Western world and also for Russia. The military intervention in Libya, which was led by France, the United Kingdom, and the United States in late 2011 and that resulted in the death of President Muammar Khaddafi and the destruction of his army, went far

---

[27] For a similar analysis on the American side, see Gerges (2012).

beyond the mandate given by the UN Security Council. The Security Council, indeed, only authorized the rescue of Bingazi from Libyan army forces. Coming after the U.S. military intervention in Iraq (end of 2006), which was also decided without the approval of the Security Council and was undertaken on the basis of false claims, the Libyan operation reinforced the idea that international law was being increasingly brushed aside. By openly backing the Syrian government in the context of a tragic civil war, and intervening directly on the battlefield (in early 2016), largely in response to the West's support for opposition groups, including radical Islamists, Russia put another nail in the coffin of international rights and obligations. In the Middle East, all these steps created the impression that powerful countries act in the region by following their own interests and calculations while the fate of local populations is of secondary concern.

Revivalist Movements in Other Religions

8.1 Introduction

We have learned two important lessons from the analysis in Chapter 7. First, fundamentalist or revivalist thinking has not been a dominant feature of Islam if one adopts a long-run historical perspective. It is only when there is a special conjunction of circumstances that deep questioning of the legitimacy of political rulers and the official clerics in cahoots with them occurs and people feel strongly exploited, dominated, and even humiliated, so that simplistic ideologies stressing the purity and respectability of one's nation or cultural patrimony have a chance to gain ground among the masses. Clearly, extremist doctrines can take on the form of exacerbated nationalism, religious fundamentalism, or both.

The second lesson bears an obvious relation to the insight that religious fundamentalism is not specific to Islam. As pointed out in Chapter 2, radical religious movements have prevailed in Western Christianity as well, and their striving for purity and moral rigor have led to attitudes of sheer intolerance, sometimes even to violent outbursts. At first sight, this observation is not surprising because both Islam and Christianity are monotheistic religions based on explicit and articulated messages thought to be issued by God. Yet, revivalist movements are also observed in nonessentialist, polytheistic religions such as Hinduism and Buddhism. It is interesting to look at those religions because they suggest that the radicalization of religious beliefs, however flexible the scriptures that lay their foundations, may be used by some actors as a social and political identifier in what are perceived as critical circumstances. The role of religion then resembles that of ethnicity and other kinship markers that serve to differentiate among people, categorizing them as insiders and outsiders.

It is also worth emphasizing that religious fundamentalism can lead to violence in all religions. As aptly pointed out by Sudhir Kakar (1996), "every religion has a vision of divinely legitimized violence"; that is, every religion condones violence as a positive and necessary force for the realization of religious goals under some circumstances (p. 193). Regarding the Semitic religions, we may think of the holy war of the Christians, the just war of the Jews, and the jihad of the Muslims. In Hinduism and Buddhism, "violence is elevated to the realm of the sacred as part of the created order": In Hinduism, there is a cycle of violence and peacefulness (the Kali Age is followed by the Golden Age), whereas in Buddhism myths talk of the Seven Days of the Sword when men will look on and kill each other as beasts, after which peace will return (pp. 193–94).

The outline of this chapter is as follows. Sections 8.2 and 8.3 explore movements of Hindu and Sikh revivalisms in modern India, respectively. Section 8.4 continues the exploration of fundamentalist non-Muslim movements by looking into manifestations of Buddhist revivalism in modern Sri Lanka and Myanmar.

8.2 The Puzzle of Hindu Fundamentalism in India

Hinduism is neither an essentialist nor a monotheistic religion: "Hindus did not traditionally inquire about their essence, and probably did not think that Hinduism had such a thing" (Nussbaum, 2007, p. 158). In fact, as particularly evident in the Mahabarata, Hinduism bears a close resemblance to Greek polytheism with its plethora of gods who behave largely like human beings driven by conflicting desires. This characteristic is naturally conducive to tolerance and openness because one can easily add new gods to the pantheon to accommodate the beliefs of any new entrant. The lack of dogma and the syncretic nature of Hinduism, which has always been "a mosaic of distinct cults, deities, sects and ideas" (Frykenberg, 1993, p. 237), are well reflected in the belief that "the worship of different sects, which are like so many small streams, move together to meet God, who is like the Ocean" (Nussbaum, 2007, p. 158, quoting from the sixteenth-century poet-saint Rajjab). It is tempting to correlate the chaotic and antinomian nature of Indian society with the pluralism and openness of traditional polytheistic Hinduism, "which allows different believers to focus on different preferred gods and offers tremendous colour and heterogeneity in myth and ritual" (pp. 182–3).

This characterization seems to preclude the possibility of Hindu fundamentalism, yet the phenomenon has occurred. In *The Clash Within* (2007), Martha Nussbaum offers us an illuminating account that solves the puzzle. She has two central points worth repeating here in some detail. The first point concerns the ideological underpinnings of Hindu fundamentalism; the second deals with the circumstances surrounding its emergence and the motives underlying it.

It is a remarkable feature that the rise of Hindu fundamentalism has coincided perfectly with the rise of the Hindu right. It was in 1925 that the Rashtriya Swayamsevak Sangh (RSS) was founded, and its most prominent leaders were strongly attracted to the European ideology of national socialism. In fact, those leaders were quite "frank about their desire to reconstruct the tradition of Hinduism along European lines" (Nussbaum, 2007, p. 158), which meant taking inspiration directly from Hitler and Stalin, two model figures for the influential leaders, Golwalkar and Savarkar. Revealingly, the founders of the Hindu right thought of the unity of their movement not in terms of religious devotion, but rather in ethnic and cultural terms. Savarkar was not a religious man, and he did not believe that traditional religious belief and practice were at the heart of Hindusthan. But he did consider the cultural traditions of Hinduism to be key markers of the new India, which was to become at one and the same time the motherland and the holy land of every Hindu (pp. 77, 159). As for Golwalkar, he professed the racist view that, in India, "the foreign races must lose their separate existence ... or [they] may stay in the country, wholly subordinated to the Hindu Nation, claiming nothing, deserving no privileges, far less any preferential treatment – not even citizen's rights" (cited by Armstrong, 2014, pp. 282–3). The vision of the Hindu right that evolved from the writings of these two key thinkers partakes of a "Kulturkampf" against the theory of secularism, posing the monist view that India is a nation because it is a Hindu country with a Hindu religious majority and a Hindu society (Desai, 2005, p. 257).

According to the ideologues of the RSS, India was weak and lacked a unified sense of its identity because of its people's divided loyalties and deep regional, linguistic, and social differences. By imparting to true Indians a sense of themselves as part of a "race determined by a common origin, possessing a common blood," the RSS hoped to build a strong, modern nation able to compete with the external world. This implied that Muslims and Christians had to give up their distinctive culture and any significant manifestations of religious difference: To obtain civil rights, they had to assimilate, which implied giving up their separate family law (Nussbaum, 2007, pp. 159, 163). That was posited as the only solution to the alleged age-old hatred between Hindus and Muslims.

The intellectuals of the Hindu right have shared an acute awareness that India is a land "where there had never existed a consciousness of anything vaguely resembling a single 'majority community' and where the entire body politic consisted of an intricately arranged mosaic of separate and separately competing minority communities," including outcast communities (e.g., the untouchables) and diverse tribal groups (Frykenberg, 1993, p. 236). However, the Hindu right has clearly ignored a central lesson from Indian history: Any violation of a delicate balance of competing interests immediately threatens the stability of the whole. As a matter of fact, no "brotherhood" of true believers built from scratch by conflating the concepts "Hindu" and "Indian" and imposing the idea that "Hindutva" alone encompasses all matters (religious or political, social or cultural) can transcend communal divisions and parochial fragmentations (Frykenberg, 1993, pp. 234–7, 251; Desai, 2005, ch. 23).

What is most interesting from our standpoint is that the Hindu fundamentalists came to view Indian traditions as "too gentle, meek, and mild," as "too pliant and unaggressive" (Nussbaum, 2007, p. 164). In other words, they did not find in these traditions any source of inspiration; hence, their decision to reconstruct Hinduism on the basis of a European extremist ideology. They would do so by "semiticizing" Hinduism, making it resemble a monotheistic religion with the god Rama at its center, so that the unity of the Indian nation could be symbolized by devotion to a single god. The choice of Rama was not accidental. Never mind that Rama was only a minor figure in the south and even in some areas of the north of the country.[1] What mattered was that, in traditional depictions, he was represented as the lord of the universe. From this image, the ideologues of the RSS proceeded to turn him into an aggressive and warlike figurehead and to transform the highly polymorphous, local, and syncretistic worship of traditional Hinduism into an exclusive devotion to a strong and unbending god presented as a model of loyalty, self-sacrifice, and discipline (p. 173). This reconstructed image of Hinduism enabled the ideologues to justify the values of self-discipline, vigor, virility, and rigor expected from all Hinduist militants, as well as the daily schedules of not only mental and spiritual (public indoctrinations, oaths, and prayers) but also physical exercises (paramilitary drills and salutes) to which they were subjected (Frykenberg, 1993, p. 241). For India to become a strong nation, it needed to assert its virility, communal discipline, and revitalization (Lal, 1993, p. 416).

---

[1] Important gods in the Hindu pantheon are Shiva, whose stories convey the idea that "desire can be controlled not by denial but only by appropriate satisfaction" (Nussbaum, 2007, p. 194); Krishna, often represented as both a hero and a god indulging in sensuous pleasure (frolicking with cowherds); and Ganesha, who is very popular in South India and whose story is full of sex, fondness of sweets, and love for his mother Parvati (p. 255).

Which circumstances and motives led to such a refashioning of the images of the Hindu gods, and to such a reconstruction of religious ideas for nationalistic purposes, is the second question that needs to be addressed. Nussbaum's answer is strikingly reminiscent of Hourani's and other diagnoses of the rise of Islamist fundamentalism in the Middle East (see Chapter 7). In short, it is the feeling of humiliation and subordination at the hands of an assertive and brutal foreign conqueror that has been the most powerful motive for the aggressive reaction sparked by the Hindu right. The violence of the reaction is explained by the emotions of shame and self-hatred, which are generated by a painful experience of subjection when the dominant power asserts its superiority with utmost self-confidence and shows contempt for the vanquished. It is then likely that the latter internalizes the moral judgment of the former[2] and eventually reacts by adopting a culture of aggressive masculinity that emulates the perceived hardness of the aggressor (Nussbaum, 2007, pp. 196–8; Gold, 1991, pp. 533–42).

In the case of India, the feeling of shame and the "wounded sense of helplessness and subjection" arose from the "internalized self-hating version of the British repudiation" during colonial times (Nussbaum, 2007, pp. 198–9). The British regarded polytheism as a degenerate and primitive belief, and the worship of gods in animal form (think of Hanumantha the monkey, or Ganesha the elephant-like child god) even more so. Moreover, "when these features were combined with the overt sexuality of the Indian gods, particularly in its sensuous, playful form, the Hindu male looked from the British viewpoint like the antonym of the respectable, and Hinduism looked like a religion that could never be compatible with national unity and national success. The British conveyed in many unsubtle ways the thought that it was because of this degeneracy and these 'inferior' morals that Hindus needed to be ruled for their own good" (p. 198).

It is not surprising, then, that an essential part of the Hindu right's discourse was articulated around the reproach of impotence that seemed to characterize India in general, and the Hindus in particular (Heuze, 1992, p. 2254). Looking back in history, the Hindu right "associated the British conqueror with the Muslim conqueror and constructed a continuous narrative of shame and wounding." According to this narrative, under the Mughal Empire, powerful Muslim aggressors tyrannized and humiliated the Hindus, destroying their temples and other symbols of their culture

---

[2] The subject male says not only "I ought to be respectable" but also "I am not a true man because I have let this happen to me, and perhaps it happened to me because I was not a true man" (Nussbaum, 2007, p. 198).

(An-Na'im, 2008, pp. 162–3). Hindu fundamentalists linked "the remembered wounds of that time closely to the evils of British rule, portraying their history as that of an ideal time of unity and peace, followed by a succession of humiliating conquests" (Nussbaum, 2007, pp. 199–200). When self-hatred is turned outward, people who feel humiliated and emasculated are inclined "to turn to thoughts of purity and a cleansing by violence to wipe away the stain" (p. 6). Symbolic acts of violence, such as the horrific onslaught on the Muslim community in Ayodhya (in the state of Gujarat) in March 2002, can then be committed with a view to making a new world, in which the once helpless will be in total control, "no longer threatened by the vicissitudes of mere human limbs and desires" (p. 189).

The Ayodhya pogrom was actually the culmination of increasingly aggressive acts directed against the Muslim community at the instigation of the Shiv Sena, a regional nationalist Hindu party in the state of Maharashtra. Demands for the destruction of the Babri Masjid mosque built under Emperor Babar in 1528, allegedly on a site previously occupied by a Hindu temple dedicated to the Hindu god Ram, eventually led a Hindu nationalist mob to carry out the onslaught on December 6, 1992. Bloody Muslim-Hindu riots, organized by the Shiv Sena, followed in Bombay and elsewhere in India (Kakar, 1996, pp. 25–142; An-Na'im, 2008, pp. 163–4).

The following excerpt from a speech delivered by Rithambra, one of the champions of the new Hindu identity, attests to the civilizational dimension of the struggle of the Hindu fundamentalists, as she extols the collective heroism of the men and women who died for the resurrection of Ayodhya temple:

As far as the construction of the Ram temple is concerned, some people say Hindus should not fight over a structure of brick and stone. They should not quarrel over a small piece of land. I want to ask these people, "If someone burns the national flag will you say Oh, it doesn't matter. It is only two meters of cloth which is not a great national loss." The question is not of two meters of cloth but of an insult to the nation. Ram's birthplace is not a quarrel about a small piece of land. It is a question of national integrity. The Hindu is not fighting for a temple of brick and stone. He is fighting for the preservation of a civilisation, for his Indianness, for national consciousness, for the recognition of his true nature. We shall build the temple! It is not the building of the temple, but the building of India's national consciousness. ... The Ram temple is our honor. It is our self-esteem. It is the image of Hindu unity. We shall raise its flag. We shall build the temple! (cited by Kakar, 1996, p. 157)

In this speech, the construction of the Ram temple is a response to the mourning of Hindu society for all that has been lost: honor, self-esteem, civilization, and identity. In the words of Kakar (1996), "The temple is the body in which Hindu identity is sought to be embodied" (p. 158). Rithambra then unwinds an argument, the logic of which was highlighted in Chapter 7. To repair the damage to Hindu-ness and to enhance group cohesion, she builds a grandiose representation of the Hindu civilization that is then shown to be threatened by an antagonistic group, in this case the Muslims. In the process, the Muslims are not only the object of scapegoating but also the subject of persecutory fantasies in the collective Hindu imagination. The Hindu group self is eulogized and euphemized by projecting the bad and the impure onto the Muslims with whom the Hindus are constantly compared. Rithambra, for example, says, "Intellectuals and scholars of the world, wherever you find ruins, wherever you come up upon broken monuments, you will find the signature of Islam. Wherever you find creation, you discover the signature of the Hindu" (cited by Kakar, 1996, p. 159). The next step is to reveal the fragility of the grandiose self of the Hindus, whose immense tolerance and sense of compassion put them at risk of being annihilated by the cruel and determined enemy. Uncovering this negative aspect of the positive self-image of the Hindu demonstrates the urgent need for forceful action (pp. 164–6).

The RSS and its political ally, the Bharatiya Janata Party (BJP), have no doubt succeeded in mobilizing masses of impoverished and frustrated workers and lower middle class young men.[3] Indeed these groups have increasingly turned to religion-based politics to vent their frustration because social organizations such as trade unions were not strong enough or did not listen to their grievances. Moreover, like Islamist organizations, the RSS and its affiliated organizations are very effective in providing a wide range of charitable services at the grassroots level, and their leaders are conspicuous for their selfless devotion and discipline, their spirituality, and their relatively ascetic lifestyle. In a country where corruption is rampant, these characteristics are a sure recipe for popular support. The language used by the Hindu right to the effect that corruption weakens and defiles the motherland and that the wealthy can buy anything, especially the law, is certain to appeal to the masses (Heuze, 1992, p. 2253; Kakar, 1996, pp. 24, 181).

If we leave aside the fact that Hindu fundamentalism emphasizes the unity and purity of the nation, rather than of a universal community of believers – which does not exist for the Hindu because they did not build an empire as the Muslims did – much of this depiction is reminiscent of how Islamic fundamentalism has proceeded. It must be added that in India,

---

[3] Originally, the BJP was named Jana Sangh (People's Family).

too, an authoritarian ruler can be tempted to play with the fire of religious extremism to quash dissent. The versatility of the communalist politics followed by the Congress Party was particularly evident under the leadership of Indira Gandhi. It is, indeed, ironic that, after this party returned to power following a brief interlude of Janata Party rule (1977–80), she chose to use the discontent of the Muslim community to gain their support. It was only during the 1984 elections that the Congress Party started to pander to the Hindu nationalists (An-Na'im, 2008, pp. 173, 176). Indira Gandhi "played the 'Hindu card' by inviting a jet-setting sadhu to be her spiritual guide; by making pilgrimages to sacred rivers, shrines, and temples across the country; and by speaking about 'Hindu hegemony' in the Hindi heartland. She fomented anti-Muslim fears in Kashmir and turned a deaf ear to Sikh pleas that the constitutional definition of them as Hindus should be corrected" (Frykenberg, 1993, p. 244). Unwittingly, by courting a Sikh extremist, Bhindranwale, whom she released from jail, she eventually caused her own destruction. She was, indeed, murdered by one of her Sikh bodyguards after the escalation of killing following the battle around the Golden Temple in Amritsar, which Bhindranwale and his fellow militants/warriors had seized (p. 245). Sikh fundamentalism is explored in depth in the next section.

The son of Indira Gandhi, Rajiv, did not apparently learn from his mother's death: He did not refrain from the temptation to politicize and communalize religious issues. Not only did he fail to condemn the discriminatory rhetoric of the militant Hindu right in the late 1980s and early 1990s but also, as prime minister, he made a campaign speech near Ayodhya, the site of the disputed mosque, where he called for "Ram Rajya" (the rule of the Hindu god Ram) in India.

Yet there is a crucial difference between India and the countries in the Middle East: India cannot become a Hinduist state in the way that nations of the Middle East such as Iran, Sudan, or Saudi Arabia have turned into Islamic states. It is telling that when acceding to political power the BJP, under Prime Minister Vajpayee, had to abandon its principal goals – the introduction of a uniform code of personal status, a federal ban on the slaughter of cattle, and the rebuilding of the Ayodhya temple – and to accept major compromises. The BJP had to do so not only because of the pluralism and syncretism that have always characterized culture and religion in India but also because postcolonial India has no established tradition of despotism, the army does not constitute an independent agency of power (like in neighboring Pakistan), and the media are quite active and have always reacted strongly to extremist behavior.

The danger of the Hindu right, however, lies in the splitting of Indian national identity and the polarization of Indian society with all the attendant consequences in terms of communal tensions and horrific riots. Riots are always possible when Hindu and Muslim identities are evoked by bringing religious symbols and sentiments to the forefront of conscious concern and when the perception is created or reinforced that these identities are threatened or under actual attack (Kakar, 1996, p. 17). Unfortunately, the risk of communal flare-ups has noticeably increased under the prime ministership of Ashok Modi, a controversial Hinduist leader who played a dubious role in Muslim-Hindu riots when he was himself prime minister of the state of Gujarat. There are many signs that the marginalization of Muslims has grown under his rule: Some laws bear a distinctly sectarian cast, Muslim political representation at the highest levels has noticeably diminished, and the BJP's handling of situations of anti-Muslim harassment or violence is disturbingly lenient (*Economist*, October 20–November 4, 2016, pp. 44–5).[4] Ominously, the increasingly free movements in the country's streets and public venues of the Hinduist militia, which resembles virtue squads, have been noted in the Indian press of a number of Indian states.

8.3 Sikh Revivalism in Modern India

The case of Sikh revivalism is especially interesting because the Sikh religion, which is of rather recent origin, initially had none of the attributes that could predispose it to fundamentalist interpretations. Sikhism was founded by Guru Nanak (1469–1539) at the end of the fifteenth century. Its approach was eclectic and nonsectarian: Nanak aimed to synthesize Hinduism and Islam, so as to reach out to both Hindus and Muslims. His religion combined diverse concepts taken from both religions with unique insights of his own. He thus had no qualms about singing Hindu "bhajans" and praising Allah. He also adopted a hybrid dress code that fused Hindu and Muslim ascetic styles.

Nanak's religion was based in Punjab. His god was formless and, like the new religion itself, had no name. The conventional rituals and obligations of Hinduism, such as fasts, pilgrimages, and penances, were abandoned, as were all references to Hindu mythology. Idol worship was abhorred, and the emphasis was put on good deeds rather than grand doctrines and beliefs.

---

[4] There are fewer Muslim ministers now in the national government – just two of seventy-five – than at any time since independence. This is in spite of the fact that the Muslim share of the total population grew to reach almost 15 percent in 2015.

Sikhism was thus a religion of practical wisdom, emphasizing good conduct in everyday life. Moreover, it was entirely egalitarian, which implied the rejection of caste distinctions, the granting of equal status to women in social and religious contexts, a nonhierarchical church structure, and the selection of the head of the religion on the basis of merit rather than blood ties. Traditional Hindu and Muslim customs, such as the "purdah" (female seclusion) and the "sati" (the immolation of a widow on her husband's funeral pyre), were treated as abhorrent. To promote equality among all men and women, men and women eating together was made mandatory practice for the followers. Spiritual liberation was another objective of Sikhism. It was to be achieved through humble attitudes, prayer, discipline, and devotion to the nameless One God (Eraly, 2007, pp. 332–3; Oberoi, 1993, p. 265).

Unfortunately, these principles did not hold for long. In clear violation of Nanak's injunction, the third guru at the head of the Sikh sect, Amar Das, appointed his son-in-law, Ram Das, to succeed him. From then on, the pontificate, like kingship, became a hereditary post. Worse still, the son of Ram Das, named Arjun Das, transformed the guru's function by behaving as a potentate. In place of voluntary offerings to the guru, he introduced the custom of levying a regular tax from Sikhs. This tax was collected by his agents stationed throughout north India, from Kabul to Dacca. Moreover, he himself pursued a lavish lifestyle purportedly to assert the grandeur of Sikhism. He decided to make Sikhism a full-fledged, integrated religion by codifying its precepts and practices and by compiling the so-called Adi Granth as the sacred scripture defining the new religion. To enshrine the Adi Granth, he then built a temple in Amritsar, which came to be known as the Golden Temple. Under his influence, the number of converts rose phenomenally. Guru Arjun became Sikhism's first martyr when he was tortured and executed in 1606 by the Mughal emperor Jahangir, with whom he was engaged in a serious power struggle. According to Sikh tradition, he was asked to alter passages of the Adi Granth that were deemed offensive to either Islam or Hinduism, but refused stoically to give in to Jahangir's request (Eraly, 2007, p. 334).

Guru Arjun's martyrdom proved to be a turning point in the history of the Sikhs. His son and successor, Har Govind, "took the next logical step in asserting the temporal sway of the guru by enlisting an army" and declaring that "in the guru's house religion and worldly enjoyment shall be combined" (Eraly, 2007, p. 335). The problem is that he overreached by defying the Mughal emperor and was eventually forced to retreat into the Kashmir hills, where he died in 1645. His dynastic succession was short-lived, and following a period of great turmoil, his youngest son, Tegh Bahadur, eventually emerged as the next guru. After Bahadur's torture and death, again at the hands of a Mughal emperor (this time, Aurangzeb), it was the turn of Govind Singh to rise to guruhood. The tenth and last guru, he took up the sword of vengeance and turned the Sikhs into a military fraternity, declaring that "the sword is God, and God is the sword" (p. 336). It was he who gave the Sikhs a new, unique identity (the Khalsa) and distinctive dress (featuring a sword); it was he who required them to be baptized and to bear the community surname, Singh (lion). His ambition was to overthrow the Mughals and to establish a Sikh state. He considered himself as a (future) head of state and he lived like a prince, decked in jewels, guarded by soldiers bearing gold-tipped arrows" (p. 336). One more time, as though lessons from the past could not be learned, he embarked on a hopeless war against the Mughals, and the outcome was calamitous for the Sikh community.

Only much later, in the early nineteenth century, with the dissolution of the Mughal Empire, did the Sikhs succeed in carving up a state of their own, albeit for a short time. The dream expressed in the following quatrain, chanted by many Sikh activists during the eighteenth century, seemed to have been fulfilled: "The army of the Guru will sit on the throne of Delhi/Over its head will be carried the umbrella of royalty, and its will shall be done/The Khalsa will rule, their enemies will be vanquished/Only those that seek refuge will be saved" (cited by Oberoi, 1993, p. 268).

Several decades after India emancipated from British colonial rule to become independent in 1947, the dominion of the Sikhs was given the name of Khalistan, and again it was claimed as their rightful kingdom. In the Declaration of Khalistan (1986), the Sikh religion was pronounced the official creed of Khalistan in direct opposition to the Constitution of India that guarantees the freedom of religious practice. The Khalistan project was brought to fruition by a fundamentalist movement led by a charismatic guru, Jarnail Singh Bhindranwale (1947–84, who played a role in the assassination of Indira Gandhi); its ideology embodies millenarianism, apocalyptic thinking, puritanism, and scriptural absolutism. The last feature invalidated all secular or rational interpretations of what is considered to be a revealed text. Critical scholarship among the Sikhs was seen as a threat to the religion and so was dutifully attacked. Those who dares to practice it were under constant pressure to relent, and those who resisted faced elimination. The editor of the Punjab's oldest literary journal was thus gunned down outside Amritsar in early 1984. Bhindranwale "repeatedly reminded his audience that they should not tolerate any form of insult toward the Sikh scriptures and that, where required, Sikhs were morally obliged to kill an individual who dared to show disrespect toward the holy book" (Oberoi, 1993, p. 258).

Bhindranwale's ideas were inspired by a fundamentalist movement known as "Damdami Taksal," which came to the fore in the early twentieth century under the leadership of Sant Sunder Singh (1883–1930). A man of great piety, he set out "to purge diversity in Sikh doctrine, ritual, and practice" in the hope of creating a uniform religious community. This implied that all polysemous interpretations of Sikh scriptures had to be abolished and that a univocal reading of religious texts had to be cultivated (Oberoi, 1993, pp. 266–7). Such a stance brought Sikh fundamentalism into direct conflict with groups like the Nirankaris, who do not strictly follow the Sikh injunctions, such as bans against image worship. The Nirankaris were considered to be false Sikhs in the same way that the Ahmadis in Pakistan and the Baha'is in Iran are considered false Muslims. The assassination of their spiritual head, Baba Gurbachan Singh, in April 1980 was followed by the mass killings of Nirankaris (pp. 272–3). Sikh fundamentalists, as do other religious fundamentalists, viewed secular public culture and capitalism as breeding corruption, moral decay, and atheism. Ambiguity, such as that found in the attitudes of the Nirankaris, was an especially pernicious poison that needed to be eradicated: A false Sikh is more dangerous than a non-Sikh.

The fundamentalist Sikh project had also a millenarian social component that echoed Nanak's dream of bringing about a social order in which oppression and mutual exploitation would cease and people would lead a life of harmony, purity, and good deeds. Thus, when the the Panthic Committee announced the formation of a Sikh homeland (Khalistan) in January 1986, the declaration emphasized the following:

No individual will be allowed to exploit others. ... Profiteering, black marketing, adulteration and all such other offences and social inequalities will not be tolerated by the Khalsa, which will also not allow mental retardation of any individual. ... The policy of Khalistan will [rest upon a policy] of promoting the sense of brotherhood of mankind and a sense of involvement. The segregation of humanity based upon caste, jati, birth, locality and colour will not be permitted, and such divisions will be abolished by the use of political power. (cited by Oberoi, 1993, p. 269)

The pluralist and egalitarian philosophy of the founder of Sikhism was thus transformed and perverted by his successors, giving rise to a religion that mixed up political with religious objectives. There remains the question as to how Sikhism gave rise to a fundamentalist deviation that completely contradicted the founder's approach to religion. For an answer, we must go back to the early twentieth century when a Sikh political party, the Akali Dal (itself an offshoot of the Central Sikh League), decided to participate actively in the anticolonial struggle, thereby gaining pan-Indian recognition. After gaining this recognition, the Sikhs, who were largely unified behind the leaders of Akali Dal, nurtured the hope of obtaining a state of their own, especially after a redefinition of territorial boundaries in the postindependence period turned the Sikhs from a minority to a majority in Punjab. When this hope went unfulfilled, and Akali Dal nevertheless retained moderate views about the coexistence of the Sikhs with other Indian citizens, a more radical party emerged, the Dal Khalsa, which accused the Indian government of duping the Sikhs in the name of secularism. For the followers of this new party, only a single solution existed to right all the wrongs done to the Sikhs: the establishment of a sovereign Sikh state, Khalistan. The ideology of Dal Khalsa bore the imprint not only of a nationalist struggle but also of a social and economic revolution. Whereas the Akali Dal was led almost exclusively by rich landowners, Dal Khalsa was sensitive to increasing inequality in the country, in particular the concentration of land in the hands of the wealthy as a result of Punjab's Green Revolution and the migration to cities of a great number of Sikh smallholders or marginal farmers (Oberoi, 1993, pp. 260–4).

In such conditions, the ideal of an egalitarian and just society proclaimed by Nanak provided a useful reference, as it had earlier, particularly during the colonial period. In the words of Harjot Oberoi,

Such an ideology becomes more attractive in periods of intense social change. During the nineteenth and early twentieth centuries under British colonial rule, there were numerous movements within the Sikh community, like the Kukas, Ghadarites, and Babbar Akalis, which sought to recover the original message of Sikhism and establish a society relatively free of human distinctions. The Sikh past endowed its constituents with a highly developed vocabulary of social justice, and the community had a long experience of social movements that fought for greater social equality. By the early 1970s, ... the egalitarian impulse within the Sikh tradition was to make the voice of redistributive justice more compelling in Punjab. ... Eventually in the late 1970s they were to shape a body – the Damdami Taksal– that was to articulate their aspirations forcefully and, by challenging the status quo, to turn the 1980s into a decade of Sikh fundamentalism. (Oberoi, 1993, p. 266)

Punjab is a state where radical Sikh clerics coexist with more moderate Sikh priests. Although in early Sikhism the church and state were figured like a pair of joined swords, a polarization between two types of clerics has evolved. Official Sikhism is represented by the high priests of the most important temples or "gurdwaras," whereas non-official clerics tend to be pro-Khalistan separatists. At present, political leadership is exerted by a father-son duo, who come from the dominant Jat Sikh caste and lead a political party known as Shiromani Akali Dal. Their achievements have been quite dismal, however, consisting mainly of personal enrichment and helping their own business ventures thrive. Threatened by the prospect of losing the 2016 elections, they increasingly manipulated the high priests of official Sikhism, requiring them to make contentious official statements regarding the activities of a popular and populist preacher, Gurmeet Ram Rahim Singh. This caused a strong reaction among Sikh radicals who called a "Sarbat Khalsa," a gathering of believers that is only summoned in times of crisis.

Held on November 10, 2015, outside Amritsar, the Sarbat Khalsa gathered 100,000 people together who protested the alleged desecration of the Sikhs' holy book and claimed that blasphemy has been committed against the faith. One of their strongest demands was to replace three high priests by a pro-Khalistan Sikh radical, who was in jail for assassinating a chief minister of Punjab in 1995 (*Economist*, November 28–December 3, 2015, p. 48).

8.4 Buddhist Revivalism in Sri Lanka and Myanmar

Sri Lanka

Like Hindu revivalism in India, Buddhist revivalism in Sri Lanka was born in the context of a reaction to colonial rule. It emerged in the middle of the nineteenth century as an anti-Christian movement led by monks (Gunananda, Sumangala, and Dharmapala) who felt that the country's identity was threatened by Christian missions favored by the colonial authority.[5] A major turning point came with the foundation, in 1880, of the Buddhist Theosophical Society by Colonel Olcott. Aimed at countering the near monopoly of Protestant missions and to a lesser extent the influence of the Catholic Church on the educational system, this organization provided an institutional and propagandist basis for the Buddhist revivalist movement, mainly through Buddhist schools. With this organizational support, the movement could act "as a major shaper of a Sinhala consciousness and of a sense of national identity" (Tambiah, 1993, p. 590). Yet, because radical Buddhist monks played such a major role in the movement, puritanical morality and chauvinistic nationalism appealing to the past glories of Buddhism and Sinhalese civilization became key ingredients of this new consciousness. In the process, the original Buddhist doctrine was seriously debased.

---

[5] Unless otherwise indicated in the text, this section relies heavily on Tambiah (1993).

After a period of waning influence during which politicians were inclined to cooperate with, rather than to confront, the British colonial power, Buddhist revivalism reasserted itself when the country's first general election was held in 1947, the year before Sri Lanka gained its independence. Instead of individual monks occasionally and informally supporting particular political candidates who sought their blessings and legitimation, a group of highly educated, vocal, and activist monks set out to influence politics in a systematic manner. Numbering many hundreds and disapproved by conservative establishment monks, as well as many members of the laity, these political monks created the radical movement known as the Lanka Eksath Bhikkhu Mandalaya (LEBM), or the Ceylon Union of Monks. In hindsight, the real significance of the LEBM was its role as "the forerunner of forceful and effective participation of monks in the elections to come" (Tambiah, 1993, p. 593). As LEBM's membership grew, its Marxist inclinations gradually gave way to an ideology based on Sinhala Buddhist nationalism, to which the major Sinhala political parties broadly converged in due time.

Sinhala Buddhist nationalism achieved political success in 1956 when its central concerns were voiced in the public arena: the rehabilitation and restoration of Buddhism to its former precolonial status; the shift from English as the official language used in the administration and the education system to indigenous mother tongues, especially Sinhalese; and the formation of a national identity and a national culture. The United Front of Monks, led by the politician-monk Mapitgama Buddharakkhita, head of the Kelanya temple near Colombo, was created just before the 1956 election to promote the Sinhalese Buddhist agenda. Strongly anti-Western and anti-Catholic, it criticized the United National Party (UNP) in power, partly because it was too wishy-washy in declaring Sinhalese as the only official language in the country. The United Front supported the other major political party, the Mahajana Eksath Peramuna (MEP), considered to be pro-Buddhist, to which it provided a countrywide Bhikkhu (monk) cadre. Mobilization of the monks was massive; around one-fourth of the total monk population worked as active campaigners during the 1956 election (Tambiah, 1993, p. 597).

The MEP won the election, and the newly formed government, under Bandaranaike, immediately proposed legislation mandating the use of Sinhalese as the sole official language. Certain concessions to the Hindu Tamils, the second largest minority ethnic group on the island, were considered, including the possibility for persons trained in English or Tamil to take examinations in those languages for entry into the public service, the right of local bodies to decide for themselves the language of commerce, and the right of persons to communicate with the government in their own language. Yet, such concessions went too far for Sinhalese nationalists, including a group of Buddhist monks connected with the United Front of Monks, and the first postindependence ethnic riots flared up. The conflict over language was interwoven with the government's policy of peasant resettlement in the less populous parts of the country, which resulted in resettling Sinhalese-speaking people in areas (in the Eastern Province) inhabited by a majority of Tamils. In 1956, the Sinhala Only Bill was passed in the parliament through the combined votes of the two Sinhalese parties (UNP and MEP). Only the Tamil Federal Party and the leftists opposed it.

Under the pressure of the Federal Party, which demanded the creation of an autonomous Tamil linguistic state within a Federal Union of Ceylon, negotiations on language and local autonomy took place. A compromise involving the use of Tamil as a minority language in the administration of the Northern and Eastern Provinces, as well as significant devolution of powers aimed at allowing the Tamils to exercise some degree of control over local affairs, was embedded in the famous Bandaranaike-Chelvanayagam Pact (Winslow and Woost, 2004, p. 6), but extremists rejected it flatly. Their pressure groups, such as the United Front and the Sri Lanka Maha Sangha Sabha, stepped up their protests against what they decried as an unacceptable "surrender" to Tamil demands. They threatened to conduct a mobilization campaign in the streets and sits-in until the government repudiated the agreement. The UNP, in opposition, made an opportunistic about-face by joining the protest against any concession to the Tamils. Bandaranaike finally capitulated to the siege that the monks had laid near his prime minister's home and announced publicly that the pact was dead. This was a milestone in the postindependence history of Sri Lanka: It showed that extremists using street tactics could prevail over a democratically elected government.

What followed were a series of violent riots that started in late May 1958, just as the Federal Party prepared to hold its annual convention and to discuss launching a campaign of nonviolent protest against the rescinding of the pact. The worst violence occurred not in Colombo and Jaffna but in the remote provinces (the North Central and Eastern Provinces), haven to the largest number of resettled peasants. It is a sobering fact that Buddhist monks, who should have preached nonviolence and tolerance, played a critical role in the events that triggered the descent of Sri Lanka into the chaos of civil war. In the words of Stanley Tambiah (1993), the radical monks lost sight of "the ethical and normative components of canonical doctrinal Buddhism," and Buddhism stopped serving "primarily as an ego-ideal and a mental discipline for personal salvation" (p. 600). This debasing of the Buddhist religion was achieved through a "selective scripturalism" that aimed at purifying the religion, placing emphasis on certain doctrinal tenets, and devaluing all sorts of so-called superstitious accretions and practices. Moreover, such purification

> involved a process of popularization whereby the Buddhist doctrine and message were carried to the people in simplified catechistic terms leavened with mythohistorical claims culled from chronicles such as the "Mahavamsa". This propagandization and popularization entailed the acquisition and use of modern communication media such as the printing press, the founding of new educational institutions (Buddhist schools for boys and girls) and organisational forms (the Buddhist Theosophical Society, the All-Ceylon Buddhist Congress, the Young Men's Buddhist Association), the deployment of effective techniques of dissemination like sermons and pamphlets in the vernacular, and the celebration on a national scale of Buddhist festivals such as the "Vesak." (Tambiah, 1993, pp. 600–1)

The Buddhist religion was thus transformed "from religion as moral practice to religion as a cultural possession." The outcome was a chauvinistic reinterpretation that was barely connected to the major tenets of Buddhist ethics (Tambiah, 1993, p. 601). In a deceptive manner, Buddhist revivalism presented a politico-religious project of a more equitable society based on a Buddhist way of life, a project in which, and this is no coincidence, monks acting as advisers and counselors would play a central role at all levels. Again in the words of Tambiah,

> It refers back to certain canonical "suttas" dealing with ideal righteous rulers ... and sees in them the attainment of glorious welfare-oriented rule. It also refers back to the regimes of great Sinhalese kings of "Mahavamsa" fame ... who allegedly constructed an egalitarian rural society focused on the triad of temple ("dagaba"), the irrigation tank ("vava"), and rice fields ("yaya"). It sounds a clarion call for Sinhalese unity and berates the contemporary Sinhalese for their divisiveness. It criticizes present-day divisive party politics, present-day hankering after West-inspired materialist, consumerist, and capitalist self-seeking goals, and proposes in their place a simpler harmonious "Buddhist way of life" in a "Buddhist democracy." (Tambiah, 1993, p. 601)

The pattern established during the tumultuous 1950s persisted in the following decades. Although the monks' support was now split between the two major Sinhalese political parties, their program remained the same as before, and their appeal to violent methods continued unabated. The language issue was settled while the restoration of the symbolic predominance of Buddhism was achieved, which would culminate in inclusion in the country's constitution in 1972 of the formal declaration that Buddhism has the "foremost place" as the religion of the country. The core issue that remained to be addressed was education. Its importance could not be underestimated because it determined access to the professions and the elite. It is therefore no surprise that it lay at the heart of the report *The Betrayal of Buddhism* (1956), which was produced by the Buddhist Committee of Inquiry set up in 1954 by virtue of a resolution passed by the All-Ceylon Buddhist Congress in December 1953. A recurring theme of the report was the need to implement systematic policies to correct the glaring inequalities inherited from the colonial period and to enable Buddhism to compete with Protestant and Catholic missions whose educational and proselytizing activities constituted a dangerous threat. The educational issue was effectively tackled in the 1960s when the majority of the private schools, which were previously run by Christian organizations, were transformed into public schools under the control of the government. When Christian groups decided to retain some of their best secondary schools, they were deprived of state financial assistance and compelled to impose tuition fees. The program of school nationalization was completed before the end of the 1960s.

The struggle for Sinhalization nevertheless continued into the 1970s and the 1980s, and riots flared again in 1977, reaching an unprecedented level. Soon thereafter, the country plunged into a prolonged civil war that was to end only several decades later (in May 2009) when the Sri Lankan army, virtually a Sinhalese monopoly, eventually crushed the Tamil Tigers, signaling total victory for the Sinhalese nationalists. The root cause of the renewed violence was the imposition of quotas and discriminatory policies in university admissions and recruitment into the state administration and the professions. These policies were designed to erase the advantage of Tamils, especially Jaffna Tamils, who had traditionally occupied a prominent place in the public life of the country (Hettige, 2004, pp. 118–22). The Tamils had been given incentives to become educated and secure employment in the administration and the professions, given the economic backwardness of their distant and poorly endowed region (in the north and the east of the island). Under these conditions, the skewing of higher education in favor of the Sinhalese majority was perceived as a blatant injustice, and because it was impossible to change the government policies through constitutional means, the Tamil youth movement for Eelam (the Tamil homeland) decided to take up arms and engage in militant confrontation (Tambiah, 1993, p. 605).

This problem was compounded by another form of anti-Tamil discrimination: the accelerated expansion of peasant resettlement schemes in the sparsely populated Dry Zone of Sri Lanka (Peebles, 1990). As already noted, although Sri Lankan (and Indian) Tamils form the majority of the population in the Northern and Eastern Provinces, with Muslims as the second largest group, the peasant resettlement scheme involved the migration and resettlement of poor and land-hungry peasants from the central, southern, and southwestern parts of the country where Sinhalese were clearly predominant. The fact that, many centuries ago, the Dry Zone was the site of a much glorified Sinhala Buddhist civilization made the return of Sinhalese peasantry to the area all the more justified in the eyes of Buddhist nationalists, monks included. That such massive inflows of internal migrants were seen by the Tamils as an illegitimate intrusion into their homeland was the natural outcome of a fraught institutional environment where the interests and needs of minority groups were systematically ignored or discriminated against (Tambiah, 1993, pp. 605–6).

The Tamil armed insurgency thus began in the late 1970s after twenty years of continued mass violence in the form of riots generally initiated by Sinhala Buddhist nationalists. This violence occurred in spite of the increasing benefits that were secured for the Sinhalese majority over the course of time. As a matter of fact, Sinhalese had been recognized as the official language, state aid had been denied to Christian schools, and the status of monastic Buddhist colleges had been upgraded so as to make Buddhism the island's foremost religion. Yet the spiral of violence soon became unstoppable. In 1979, the government of J. R. Jayawardene (UNP) passed the Prevention of Terrorism Act, which contained ominously vague provisions that criminalized the speaking or writing of words intended to cause religious, social, or communal disharmony; it also mandated draconian punishments, such as arrest without a warrant and indefinite detention. Mounting tensions resulted in the riots of 1983, whose main victims were Tamil homeowners of the middle class in Colombo. During this heated period of the late 1970s, although some monks were involved in inciting the crowds, the vast majority preferred to stand aside. However, Buddhist activist monks became seriously involved once again in the 1980s as Tamils increasingly insisted on their rights to a homeland and the Tamil insurgency took an increasing toll on both Sinhalese security forces and civilians. Not surprisingly, monks and Buddhist temples became the target of attacks by Tamil Tigers, at the same time as Hindu temples were demolished and their priests killed by the Sinhalese army. The majority of monks explicitly or privately supported, or at least condoned, the Sinhalese army's killing of Tamil guerrillas, and the main body of the sangha (monastic community) did not object to the tribulations imposed on Tamil civilians.

Under pressures from the Indian government and faced with its inability to eradicate the rebels, the government of Jayawardene eventually agreed to sign the Indo-Sri Lanka Agreement (the Peace Accord) in July 1987. The accord acknowledged that Sri Lanka is a "multiethnic and multi-lingual plural society," that each ethnic group has its "distinct cultural and linguistic identity," and that "the Northern and Eastern Provinces have been areas of historical habitation of the Sri Lankan Tamil speaking peoples" (Tambiah, 1993, p. 609). Moreover, the agreement provided that a single provincial council representing both the Northern and Eastern Provinces, and wielding the powers held by a state in the Indian Union, would be formed after peace has returned. However, as in the case of the Bandaranaike-Chelvanayagam pact, the nationalist Sinhala opposition and radical Buddhist monks could not tolerate any attempt to negotiate with the Tamil insurgents and strike a deal with them on the basis of a devolution of powers to provincial councils.

Many militant Buddhist organizations proliferated in the 1980s to oppose any concession to the Tamils on the grounds that the Sinhalese people were the true "sons of the soil" or the "sons of Budha" and that signing the accord would be "an ignominious capitulation to the designs of imperialist India and its sponsorship of the Tamil cause" (Tambiah, 1993, p. 611). One particularly active organiaation was Mavbima Surakime Vyaparaya (MSV), or Movement for the Protection of the Motherland, which was founded in July 1986. It was an umbrella group for many of the new lay-cum-clerical Buddhist organizations mobilized by the Sinhala-Tamil conflict. In demonstrations, "Buddhist ceremonial and ritual, and the preachings of monks invoking allegedly Buddhist concepts and justifications, informed, colored, and legitimated the public posture" (p. 614).[6]

It was the Janatha Vimukthi Peramuna (JVP) that most systematically and effectively set out to mobilize young monks for revolutionary, anti-Tamil violence (the JVP had an armed division, the Deshapremi Janatha Vijaya-paraya). A youth political organization banned by the government after the

---

[6] Thus, "monks recite *pirit* at the public ceremonies and rallies; they stage sermons which are given the inflated name of 'dharmadesanaya'; the 'commemoration' and recall of the Budha's enlightenment itself may precede the campaign rhetoric of fighting Tamil terrorism ... . 'Bodhipujas' were held in leading temples to seek the blessings of gods in ensuring the safety and success of military personnel. Monks officiated at military functions, and the central army cantonment at Panagoda saw the erection of an impressive 'chaitya' (pagoda). If in previous times prime ministers and ministers of state did this, now military commanders too worship at the Temple of the Tooth Relic in Kandy upon appointment, and obtain blessings from the head monks of the Asgiriya and Malwatte chapters" (Tambiah, 1993, pp. 614–15).

1983 riots and consisting primarily of university students and Sinhala Buddhist male youth of rural origins, the JVP was especially adept at articulating an anticapitalist egalitarian message emphasizing the Buddhist ideal of muting worldly desires and "the nostalgic fiction of a simple homogeneous precolonial Sinhala-Buddhist peasant society" (Tambiah, 1993, p. 615).

Repelled by the violence, prominent elder monks started to distance themselves from the political engagement of their youngest colleagues. As a result, the latter became bitter, coming to see senior monks as traitors ready to sacrifice their patriotic obligations to protect their selfish interests. Persuaded that "the religion of the Budha and the language and culture of the Sinhalese cannot flourish without a sovereign territory which is the motherland of Sri Lanka," many JVP monks reacted by condoning and even collaborating in acts of violence against senior monks (Tambiah, 1993, p. 616). Because the government saw them as dangerous troublemakers susceptible of creating mayhem among the Sinhalese, many JVP activists, including militant monks, were arrested, tortured, and killed by security forces and their paramilitary organs.

The fact remains that the nexus between Buddhism and violence in Sri Lanka, however paradoxical, has a historical continuity and played a major aggravating role in one of the longest and costliest wars in modern South Asia. The majority of Sinhala Buddhist monks consistently opposed any meaningful power-sharing agreement between the two main communities of the island, and when an opportunity arose to find a compromise, they advocated an all-out military solution. Even worse, when the war eventually ended in 2009 amid serious questions of war crimes and crimes against humanity, they defended the military and its Buddhist leadership (Raghavan, 2014).

Myanmar

That political activism among Buddhist monks is not a unique feature of Sri Lanka is attested by their militant role at certain critical times in the modern history of Burma/Myanmar. There, as in Sri Lanka, political Buddhism started as an anticolonial movement. The incident that marked the beginning of Burmese monks' involvement in the country's nationalist movement was the so-called foot-wearing controversy of 1916: By refusing to remove their shoes and socks on entering pagodas and monasteries, British officials violated the sacred space of such places (Keyes, 1993, p. 375). U Ottama, the leader of Buddhist militant nationalism, saw no contradiction between being a monk and being a political activist. He justified holding the two positions by arguing that, to attain the ultimate goal of nirvana, people must first free themselves from enslavement by an alien government. The followers of U Ottama thus became the vanguard of the nascent nationalist movement in Burma. It was at the same time a revivalist or fundamentalist movement because it called traditional religious practice into question and set as its objective the restoration of a pure Buddhist society. U Ottama was eventually arrested and jailed until his death in 1939 (p. 376).

During the 1930s and 1940s, lay Buddhist nationalist leaders adapted their vision of a Buddhist utopia to socialist ideas borrowed from the West. They advocated an ideology that combined Marxist praxis with Buddhist metaphysics, with a view to constructing a Buddhist welfare state. After independence was won in 1948, the ruler U Nu signaled as early as the mid-1950s that he was "turning away from Buddhist socialism and toward a traditional model of the Buddhist kingship with himself as the de facto monarch" (Keyes, 1993, pp. 377–8). He thus organized a council of monks to purify the Buddhist scriptures and attempted to establish Buddhism as the state religion. It was this latter move that triggered protests and eventually provided the pretext for a coup staged by general Ne Win (March 1962).

The country was now set for a long period of military rule. One of the first actions of the Revolutionary Council was to regulate the relationship between state and religion. It rescinded the laws of the previous regime that promulgated Buddhism as the state religion and banned Buddhist monks from politics. To keep the Buddhist religion pure ("sasana"), the new government said that it must be kept isolated from the mundane affairs of politics. Toward that purpose, scriptural problems had to be clarified, doctrinal disputes solved, and "bogus monks" weeded out. Words were quickly followed by deeds as monks who engaged in political action were arrested. The first to be arrested were the monks who in 1965 had protested against the controls instituted over the "sangha" by the state, as well as those who demonstrated in 1974 on the occasion of the funeral of U Thant, the former secretary-general of the United Nations (Keyes, 1993, pp. 379, 382).

It was only during the succession crisis of 1987–8 that a number of monks became involved in demonstrations again and formed the movement of Young Monks ("Yanhapyo"). This movement, which resembled that of the 1920s, was revivalist; its members were eager to distance themselves from conventional monks associated with the millennial version of cosmological Buddhism as well as from those co-opted by the government in a belated effort to create a state-controlled religion (Keyes, 1993, p. 383). Their primary goal was to force the military (organized as the State Law and Order Restoration Council [SLORC]) to transfer power to the parties that had won the elections in May 1990. As they moved to the forefront of the opposition, staging repeated protests in Mandalay and the northern region, the mons became a direct threat to the regime. In October 1990, the military moved against them, banning the movement, storming monasteries, and arresting scores of monks (p. 384).

Under the regime of General Thein Sein (prime minister from 2007–11 and president from 2011–16), the house arrest of the leading political opponent Aung San Suu Kyi was eventually lifted, signaling the beginning of what appeared as a political opening. Political monks became engaged in protests again, yet this time it was in a nasty way reminiscent of militant Buddhism in Sri Lanka. In 2012, led by a rabble-rousing monk known as Ashin Wirathu, Buddhist extremists stoked violent riots against the minority Muslim group of the Rohingyas, who have lived in Burma, Rakhine state, for hundreds of years. Their anti-Muslim prejudice, which targeted other Burmese Muslims as well, found a receptive ear at the highest echelons of political power. As a matter of fact, Thein Sein proposed that the Rohingyas be resettled abroad, a proposal immediately objected to by the United Nations, and he also supported domestic policies that labeled Rohingya as "non citizens." He saw no contradiction in saying that the Rakhine riots "have nothing to do with race or religion" while simultaneously arguing that banning Buddhist women from marrying non-Buddhists was necessary "to preserve race and religion" (*Economist*, April 5–11, 2014, p. 52; *Voice of America*, 2012).

It is evident from the cases of Sri Lanka and Myanmar that Buddhist monks were far from forming a homogeneous entity: Some were clearly more radical than others and therefore posed a more direct threat to the political regime. This is what is expected when the mode of organization of a religion is decentralized. This phenomenon also is found in Thailand where two main strands of Buddhism contend with each other. Their divergences have become particularly apparent during the 2010s on the occasion of the succession of the Supreme Patriarch, the country's chief monk and the leader of its two Theravada Buddhist orders, Maha Nikaya and Dhammayuttika Nikaya. Although the organization of Thai Buddhism resembles that of Christianity, insofar as the Sangha Council operates as its hierarchical and gerontocratic governing body, in effect there are many centrifugal tendencies that continuously threaten its unity.

The brawl around the nomination of the new patriarch is particularly problematic for the ruling junta because "it finds itself caught between two embittered factions, neither of which it can ignore" (*Economist*, April 2–8, 2016, p. 47). On the one hand, the smaller Dhammayuttika Nikaya order, which stands accused of controlling the Sangha Council, has been traditionally patronized by the Thai elite. Moreover, among the backers of the council's candidate are members of an ultranationalist group, the Buddhist Protection Center of Thailand. Yet, the council's opponents include a firebrand monk, Budha Issara, who as a former soldier played a significant role in the royalist, anti-Thaksinite protests that helped bring the junta to power (in 2014) and is now one of its most outspoken supporters. Clearly, the spat is uncomfortable for the junta, which therefore chose to decline to submit the nomination of the successor recommended by the council to the royal palace for approval. The hope is that the resulting stalemate will somehow end in a solution, perhaps thanks to the anticipated death of the council's candidate, who is ninety years old at the time of this writing (p. 47).

8.5 Conclusion and Discussion

Clearly, fundamentalist movements – which are understood as movements that exhibit puritanical and millenarian tendencies, proclaim an absolute scripturalism, indulge in apocalyptic visions, and justify political engagement for their members – are not specific to Islam. We saw earlier (in Chapter 2) that Christianity was not immune to religious fundamentalism. In this chapter, we have gone one step further by showing that even religions that look least susceptible are subject to the risk of being debased by radical followers of the faith. The question, then, is not whether religions are more or less prone to fundamentalist interpretations, but, rather, what kind of circumstances may cause such interpretations to arise.

If religious beliefs tend to be reasserted during times of convulsive change or economic crisis, the emergence of radical puritan religious movements is another matter. In particular, they are characterized not by a retreat into the religious sphere as a way of consolation or protection from changes that are perceived as overwhelming and destabilizing; on the contrary, they are informed by a political engagement aimed at modifying the prevailing social, economic, and political order. This deviation from the standard pattern in which popular religion keeps a reasonable distance from politics tends to be observed when a society goes through a deep crisis of legitimacy of its state institutions. The crisis may be caused by internal factors, external forces, or by a combination of both.

State legitimacy is typically undermined by external forces when national authorities fail to put up effective opposition to colonial domination or foreign occupation. The trigger may be that authorities accommodate the foreign rulers too willingly or even that they openly collaborate with them. As the examples of fundamentalism in Hinduism, Buddhism, and Sikhism show, puritanical reactions tend to burst out when significant segments of the population feel threatened by what they perceive as alien forces allied with their own political and economic elites. In the case of the Sikhs, their own sovereign, the Mughal emperor, was perceived as foreign because he was a Muslim and too authoritarian. The Sinhalese Buddhist monks perceived the threat as coming from an economically sucessful minority, the Tamils, who possessed a different culture and religion and were supported by external forces (first, the British colonial power and, later, India). This diagnosis is in full accordance with the evidence regarding the origins of Islamist movements with a political bent (see Chapter 7).

In all these instances, a pristine version of the religion is presented as a "national" symbol of the local culture, to be defended against what is pictured as a foreign attempt to annihilate it. This involves a myth-constructing operation whereby a religious culture is idealized and claimed to stand for a harmonious and just social order implemented some time in the past. Such myth-making, it must be noted, is essentially similar to the way leaders playing on ethnic-based identity refer to the glorious past of their ethnic group. In the case of Sri Lanka, the similarity is even more striking because Buddhist monks have espoused the Sinhalese cause and constructed a narrative of a grand Sinhala-Buddhist nation in need of protection against the evil Hindu Tamils. In today's Muslim world, the struggle of Islamists is framed in sectarian terms opposing Sunnis against Shi'a, which is akin to an interethnic or "us versus them" (or indigenous versus alien) confrontation.

There are two reasons why fundamentalist movements proclaim a purified vision of the allegedly original faith. First, doing so accentuates the contrast between the native and the foreign ideology, often to the point of caricature, thereby dramatizing the threat posed by the foreign power and arousing the anger of the masses. Second, and more importantly, fundamentalist thinkers want to represent religious officialdom as morally corrupt clerics who have debased their faith and so deserve to be considered and treated as traitors. Following the narrative of these thinkers, such acts of betrayal are responsible for the lack of resistance to the foreign power and the eventual subordination of their people to an alien culture.

State legitimacy is undermined as a result of internal forces when the political ruler is despotic and his inner circle is deeply corrupt and cynically oblivious of its duties vis-à-vis the common people. Moreover, the religious establishment is seen as explicitly or implicitly collaborating with the oppressor. Reference to a pristine religion depicted in idealized terms again serves the purpose of representing the political and religious leaders as guilty of treason: By condoning immoral behavior and themselves indulging in it, official leaders have helped pervert their faith. Returning to the founding sacred texts while claiming that they allow for only a unique, puritanical interpretation is a powerful tactic intended to bring the culprits into submission. Indeed, political power can thus be claimed by the fundamentalist rebels in the name of God and according to a divinely inspired set of instructions. These instructions are alleged to state in precise terms, and not in general allegoric terms, what it means to be a good Muslim, good Hindu, good Sikh, good Buddhist, good Christian, or good Jew. One immediate consequence of such a dogmatic and Manichean approach is that, in the ensuing process of exclusion, ostracization, and persecution, attention is primarily devoted to marginal groups of believers who have adopted idiosyncratic practices, rituals, or interpretations. They are perceived as a direct threat to the new orthodoxy on the same footing as members of the abhorred elite who pretend to be good followers of their faith, but actually betray it by their behavior.

The puritanical and absolutist approach to religion found in fundamentalist movements is particularly appealing to young educated people, as well as to lower middle-class people alienated from the prevailing social, economic, and political order. Especially prominent among the latter are rural-urban migrants whose integration in the host cities is highly unsatisfactory because of a lack of regular employment, poor housing, and little access to public utilities. As discussed in Chapter 7 in the context of recruitment into Islamist groupings, the experience of the rural migrants is especially painful because their life has been profoundly disrupted and their aspirations shattered. They may therefore find in extremist religious groups "not only a sense of psychological consolation but also a new focus of identity and an alternative network of relationships." At the same time, the fundamentalist message strikes a powerful chord with them: Not only it is expressed in "a familiar devotional and moralist language that imparts a certain sense of intimacy and assurance" but it also contains a virulent critique of the existing social order and the state system (Ayubi, 1991, p. 175).

Perhaps paradoxically, educated young persons, including young mullahs, monks, gurus, and priests, are also vulnerable to the simplistic messages of fundamentalist thinkers. This is because they tend to find grand theories attractive when (1) these theories propose clear-cut paths of action leading to allegedly predictable results and (2) the endpoint is a utopian order devoid of all the imperfections of the present world. The lack of critical social analysis in their training, which is particularly evident in the case of engineering and medical studies that are overrepresented among Islamists, explains why otherwise well-trained people may respond to perceived injustices and dysfunctional institutions by adhering to simplified visions of the causes of these ills and the required remedies.[7] The problem is that, when elements of social analysis and critique are not taught, science students tend to regard a social order as a mechanical system that obeys completely intelligible and easily actionable laws. In other words, a society, even a civilization, is thought to be transformable through social engineering.[8]

In this sense, there is no difference between religious and secular extremists, whether they belong to the right or to the left. Persuaded that they have the correct theory about the social world and that their predictions will come true, they are ready to impose huge sacrifices not only on themselves but also on others to achieve their objectives (see, for example, Elster, 1985, for Marxists). The fact that there were many engineers and doctors among the staunchly secular Young Turks (more about them in Chapter 9), and that medical students among them played a major role in the Armenian genocide, provides further confirmation that their intellectual leadership of extremist movements has to do with their training and their self-selection into it, rather than with religion as such. Causality actually works the other way: They adhere to radical movements, religious or not, that contribute to shaping their ideologies because they are attracted by the simplistic depiction of the world that they propose.

This parallel between religious and secular fundamentalisms is reflected in a common scripturalist attitude. Indeed, people prone to dogmatic beliefs are keen to have a reference book where the absolute truth is assumed to be stated. Such reference books are thus "sacralised." This is true equally of Marx's and Engels' *Manifesto*, Mao's *Red Book*, Hitler's *Mein Kampf*, and religious texts ascribed to the founder of a religion. Dating back to quite remote times, the founding texts are most obviously unable to provide guidance about concrete ways of improving the organization of complex, modern societies. Yet, in a fundamentalist perspective, the inherently

---

[7] The overrepresentation of engineering and medical studies in the Islamic Student Movement of Egypt, for example, is well documented in Zahid (2010, p. 110).

[8] Nazih Ayubi's alternative explanation, according to which these students are prone to fundamentalism because of their poor access to jobs commensurate to their expectations, is obviously unsatisfactory. As a matter of fact, social science students (business, law, etc.) are in no better position in this regard. There remains the question as to why would students in engineering and medicine be more prone to a simplistic and mechanical view of society than students in physics, biology, or mathematics, for example. A plausible hypothesis is that the former are essentially taught the technical modus operandi of systems, bodies, or devices. In engineering, problem-solving ability is given absolute prominence, whereas medical students are exposed only to the fundamentals of biological science and learning also largely consists of the acquisition of technical skills as opposed to conceptual capacity.

sacred character of the holy scriptures (they are God's revealed truths) makes them eternally valid and therefore unquestionable. This ignores the fact that, like the works written by modern radical thinkers or extremist ideologues, the holy scriptures bear the mark of their historical environment. Moreover, they have been adapted and modified subsequently to better fit the circumstances of other places and times, as with the New Testament of the Christians. In the case of the Quran, changes occurred even during the lifetime of the Prophet himself. There is indeed a manifest shift in the tone used between the parts of the Quran written when the Prophet was facing persecution in Mecca and those writen when he held political power in Medina. The tone was more moderate in the first period than in the second, when concepts such as jihad emerged (Masuma, 2009; Tarabishi, 2013).

9

Enlightened Despotism Examined

Before moving to the final chapter, a last important task awaits us. Until now, attention has focused largely on situations in which autocrats antagonize religious clerics by following iniquitous, or what Heydarian (2014) calls anti-development, policies. The case study material presented in Chapter 6 revealed that, to seduce the clerics and thereby reduce the risk of rebellion, kleptocrats often resort to regressive policies in domains to which these clerics are particularly sensitive, such as education, gender relations, and personal status. In other words, by choosing policy mixes that combine high levels of corruption with concessions on private and educational matters, the rulers are able to co-opt clerics. However, because some clerics are also highly sensitive to the suffering of ordinary people, the concessions made by the rulers remain insufficient to seduce more than a fraction of the clerical body. As a consequence, political instability is not suppressed.

This picture rests on the assumption that autocrats consider policy choices in educational and personal status matters only as possible concessions to make up for unpopular policies on the economic, social, and political fronts. An alternative scenario may play out if the autocrat perceives that the ruling elite can derive substantial gains from progressive policies in matters that have traditionally been under the responsibility of religious clerics. In this instance, the enlightened autocrat may opt for such policies even though they are bound to antagonize the men of religion. Provided that he is not too corrupt and not too unjust in the economic and social spheres, he can hope to enlist a sizable fraction of the clerical body so that political instability is limited. The strategy is more likely to succeed if the targeted clerics receive a good salary and a honorable status by being integrated into the administrative apparatus of the state.

This chapter examines the experiences of enlightened autocratic regimes and assesses them in the light of the framework emphasizing relationships between the autocrat and the clerics. Two outstanding examples are modern Turkey and Tunisia, where two highly charismatic leaders and seemingly benevolent despots, Atatürk and Bourguiba, placed their countries resolutely on the path of modernity through the adoption of wide-ranging social reforms touching on matters of personal status. They consistently refused to let Muslim conservatives block what they perceived as progress of their nation toward civilization, and they did not hesitate to silence and repress opponents inspired by the doctrines of political Islam. For a shorter period of time, Afghanistan was also run by bold reformist autocrats, first under King Amanullah and later under a Marxist-oriented regime. The Musahibans made another attempt at social reforms in Afghanistan, which was much less adversarial and authoritarian than the experiments of Amanullah and the Marxists . It merits mention because, unlike the other two attempts, it seemed to be an acceptable and effective way of changing social relations and the role of religion.

The outline of the chapter is as follows. First, it offers a historical perspective of the legal reforms undertaken by Muslim countries since the middle of the nineteenth century. This overview indicates which reforms are particularly sensitive in societies where religion is a dominant part of the local culture (Section 9.1). The chapter next discusses in detail the cases of Kemalist Turkey and modern Tunisia (Sections 9.2 and 9.3, respectively) and then turns to the case of Afghanistan (Section 9.4). In Section 9.5, I draw the main lessons from all these attempts and open the way for an alternative approach that avoids the shortcomings of top-down radicalism. The experiences of Indonesia and, to a lesser extent, Morocco serve to illustrate how a middle-of-the-road approach based on legal pluralism can be designed and made to work. As I argue, this approach can be anchored in solid economic theory featuring strategic interactions between statutory laws and customary practices. A final section (Section 9.6) weaves together the main strands of the arguments developed throughout the chapter.

9.1 Legal Reforms in the Lands of Islam

In the latter part of the nineteenth century, a group of Muslim countries embarked on the path to modern development paved by advanced Western countries. In Turkey, the modernist point of view, inspired by ideas going back to the 1830s and 1840s, was first espoused by the Young Ottomans in the 1860s and 1870s. They were soon succeeded by the Young Turks, who turned from an Islamic modernist to a secular constitutionalist position

(Lapidus, 1988, p. 561). In the early phases of national movements, and despite the resistance of ulama (or at least some of them), Western-educated elites in countries such as Egypt, Syria, and Tunisia were able to provide an impetus to a number of important reforms in the fields of education, law, and political institutions.

The Ottoman Empire was the first region of the Islamic world to adopt Western laws: the Commercial Code (1850), which was in part a translation of the French Commercial Code (and included provisions for the payment of interest); the Penal Code (1858), a translation of the French Penal Code, which abolished all the punishments defined by the sharia law, except the death penalty for the crime of apostasy; and the Code for Commercial Procedure (1861) and a Code of Maritime Commerce (1863), both of which were again essentially French laws. From 1875 onward, Egypt went even further than the Ottoman authorities in the adoption of French law: in addition to the codes adopted by Turkey, it also enacted civil codes modeled on French law (Coulson, 1964, pp. 149–52). In most Middle Eastern countries and in India, criminal law and procedure have been almost completely Westernized since the second half of the nineteenth century, whereas the law of civil transactions and obligations became increasingly Westernized later, during the twentieth century. A setback nevertheless occurred in Egypt when the last civil code was promulgated in 1949. In the words of Coulson, it "represents a definite departure from the previous practice of indiscriminate adoption of European law" and may be regarded as a compromise between the traditional Islamic and modern Western systems, even though little was borrowed from e traditional sharia law in the actual terms of the code itself (p. 153).

It is only in Saudi Arabia, Yemen, Aden, and the Emirates of the Persian Gulf that traditional Islamic law has remained the fundamental law up to the present day (Coulson, 1964, pp. 151–5). Yet, even there, commercial laws have been Westernized. Morocco, Tunisia, and northern Nigeria borrowed some Western laws, but were at the same time able to preserve their traditional systems of Islamic law until recent times. This is mainly because they were ruled under the form of a protectorate (established by France for Tunisia in 1881 and for Morocco in 1912, and by Great Britain for northern Nigeria in 1912), which tended to perpetuate the status quo (p. 156). Finally, in Central Asia Islamic modernists known as the "Jadids" destabilized the traditional order of the conservative ulama and the social groups that supported them, yet had to wait until the Bolshevik Revolution to rise into prominence before being betrayed by their Bolshevik allies (Khalid, 2007, pp. 44–77).

According to Coulson (1964), Western laws have been to a large extent successfully assimilated in the various regions of Islam, and the opposition to the introduction of secular laws voiced by the scholars of the religious law "was never strong enough to constitute a formidable obstacle" (pp. 160–1). This evolution was facilitated by the fact that Islamic legal tradition has always recognized the right of the ruler to supplement strict sharia doctrine in the fields of public law and general civil law. The situation was different for family law, which has always been the preserve of the sharia. In that domain, the introduction of Western secular laws caused a reaction marked by a growing emphasis on the religious and Islamic significance of the sharia, whose influence was strengthened as a result. Coulson nevertheless claims that, even in such a sensitive area, Western standards and institutions created an impetus for reform (p. 161). Others believe that in countries where the importation of civil codes implied the reduction in authority of the sharia courts and their ultimate abolition, it was perceived by the masses as "a whole assault on a political culture in which justice had been seen as a function of religion more than politics." Testifying to this conflict between law and morality were "the many tales of villagers ensnared by a law they did not comprehend" (Lee, 2014, pp. 73–4).

Reforms dealing with private matters, such as marriage, divorce, and inheritance, are thus especially sensitive not only because they have been traditionally settled by religious authorities on the basis of Islamic law and ustom but also because, as pointed out by Bowen (2003), a great deal is at stake in arguments and conflicts over these matters and the underlying norms: "at the very least, access to land, religious identity, a sense of local control, women's rights, respect for the ancestors, modernity, the rule of law, and the problem of holding together a nation" (p. 5). Moreover, family forms are closely related to local material and cultural forces, because rules of kinship, marriage, and inheritance determine how families are divided and reproduced, as well as how people work, feast, play, and die (p. 19). Consequently, these reforms are prone to spark protests among religious leaders and their followers, and the question as to how political rulers should address issues of personal status is a knotty one.

It is not surprising that legal codes inspired by the West were not implemented immediately after their introduction, or at least, they were were not implemented on a large scale. Hania Abou al-Shamat (2007) has examined the effects in Egypt of the legal reforms of 1883 that established native courts based on the Napoleon code of law to deal with civil, commercial, and penal disputes. All Egyptians, regardless of religion, were given equal access to and representation in the courts, and documentation requirements were incorporated into the system (written documents could be used as evidence in legal proceedings). Yet Al-Shamat finds that it took more than a third of a century after the legal changes were made before national business interests responded to them by creating large enterprises and increasing investment in the industrial and banking sectors. Among the main reasons for this delayed response were poor enforcement of the new laws by the native courts, the shortage of qualified Egyptian judges and lawyers to serve in them, low trust of Egyptians in the mixed courts competent to deal with cases involving both indigenous and foreign interests, and unfair competition from foreign countries (under the so-called Capitulations, foreigners enjoyed lower tariffs and exemption from taxes).

9.2 Kemalist Reforms in Modern Turkey

Modern Turkey is especially interesting because it has long been considered a unique case of successful modernization through secularization. Under the leadership of Kemal Atatürk, religious forces were brought under control, allegedly to prevent them from blocking development and progress. As will soon become clearer, however, the Republican People's Party (RPP) of the Kemalists never won a majority in parliament through a democratic election, and when the military stopped interfering with the political process, the RPP was voted out of office. A pro-Islamic conservative party, the Justice and Development Party (later labeled as AKP), assumed power, and Islam reentered Turkish public life. To this date, AKP remains in power, having been comfortably reelected in the course of several successive elections. Moreover, the presidency has accrued to a leader from the same party (Abdullah Gül and, later, Recep Tayyip Erdoğan).

Such a shift in the Turkish political regime came as a stunning surprise and has raised serious questions about the feasibility of the Turkish path to modernization. This section explores the factors that led to what seems to be an abrupt discontinuation of the Kemalist program. I start by characterizing the Kemalist project in two successive steps, first stressing its revolutionary and nationalist nature and then describing Atatürk's authoritarian and elitist measures. I then describe the most important events that occurred after the demise of the RPP dictatorship, with a focus on the way the army tried to suppress the rise of Islamism. This rise, as shown in the two subsequent subsections, proved unstoppable. It eventually led to a second revolution in modern Turkish politics, one marked by the accession of an Islamic party to supreme power. Concluding remarks end the analysis of the Turkish case.

Kemalism as a Revolutionary and Nationalist Project

Between the demise of the Ottoman Empire in October 1918 (when it was forced to conclude an armistice with the victorious allies) and the proclamation of Turkish independence five years later, in October 1923, a strong resistance movement took shape in Anatolia. Religion played an important role in mobilizing the Anatolian peasantry to support the emancipation of Turkey from European rule, and this feature no doubt contributed to giving an Islamic flavor to the national independence struggle (Zürcher, 2010, p. 222). Yet, it can be contended that "Islamic" was equivalent to "Muslim," understood as a homogeneous race to be held together in the face of other peoples, Greeks and Armenians in particular. Mustafa Kemal Pasha, later named Atatürk ("Father of the Turks"), thus considered that the new state should belong to the Muslims who are "brothers," although he did not hesitate to use Islamic rhetoric to strengthen his point. Thus, he declared, in March 1921, that the Greek oppressors have entered "the innermost shrine of Islam in the Western Anatolia" (p. 226). Things changed dramatically after independence was won: Kemalist leaders of the new republic then broke the bonds of solidarity forged during the preceding decade and instead opted for far-reaching secularization. In the words of Erik Zürcher (2010),

The decision was deliberate to seek a new Turkish national and secular corporate political identity in order to replace the Ottoman-Muslim one. ... In the debate about Westernization, Kemal and his circle belonged to the radical wing of the Young Turks who believed implicitly in a popularized version of nineteenth-century European positivism. In their eyes only scientific rationalism could form the basis for the modernization leap Turkey would have to make, and only a nation state could give Turkey the coherence needed to compete with the national states of Europe ... they did not find a nationality in which religion was the dominant factor a suitable basis for a nation state. (p. 232)

Mustafa Kemal wanted to achieve a genuine social and cultural revolution founded on principles entirely different from those espoused by the Ottomans, who were unable to avoid defeat at the hands of the West. Having succeeded in transforming a crumbling empire into a compact state recognized by potential allies, his next ambition was nothing less than "to sweep away a medieval social system, based for centuries on Islam, and replace it by a new one based on modern, Western civilisation" (Kinross, 2001, p. 377). The revolution would not only swap out the "high" Islamic civilization but also transform the "low" culture. European civilization was seen as indivisible (as though all its parts were complementary) and therefore impossible to adopt in any piecemeal manner. Hence, there was no need to attempt any harmonization of European with Turkish culture (Kandiyoti, 1991, p. 40; Zürcher, 2010, p. 149; Kaya, 2013, pp. 12–13). In the words of Abdullah Cevdet, "civilisation means European civilisation, and it must be imported with both its roses and its thorns" (cited by Lewis, 1968, p. 236).

It was in the 1930s that the Young Turk ideology of nationalism and secularism, borrowed from France and transmitted to the Kemalist activists (Hanioğlu, 2000), was carried to extremes. Secularism became interpreted not only as a separation of state and religion but also as the removal of religion from public life and the establishment of complete state control over religious institutions. This approach was considered the only way to prevent religious forces from dividing Turkish society (White, 2013, p. 28). Meanwhile, an extreme, arguably racist, form of nationalism was developed to create a new national identity and replace religion by historical myths extolling the grandeur of a pristine Turkish nation centered in Anatolia. The central myth was that the Turks were an ancient people descended from white (Aryan) inhabitants of Central Asia who had migrated to China, Europe, and the Near East. They created the world's great civilizations, and in the Near East, they gave rise to the Sumerian (2900 BCE) and the Hittite (1600 BCE) empires. Moreover, proto-Turks contributed significantly to the development of Greek civilization. Whereas Attila and Chinghis-Khan were seen as executing civilizing missions, the Arab conquest and influence were depicted as causing a serious regression on the path of Turkish evolution toward modernity. According to Ziya Gökalp, the leading ideologist of the Turkish Historical Society (founded in 1930 by Mustafa Kemal, after Gökalp's death), the essence of the Turkish nation consisted of an ethical and egalitarian Muslim culture cleansed of Arab and Byzantine elements. Hence, it could coexist with modern Western civilization and technology (Zürcher, 2004, p. 191; White, 2013, pp. 26–7).[1]

As for Mustafa Kemal, he considered the earth of Anatolia as sacred not only because any national territory has a supreme value for a nationalist militant but also because Anatolia was "the heartland of Islam" and embodied the holy traditions of Turkey. Greeks were oppressors of the Turks because

---

[1] Gökalp's vision of the future of Turkey was grounded in a negative assessment of the effects of diversity in Turkish society. In his words, "In this country there are three layers of people. ... The first still are not freed from the effects of Far Eastern civilisation; the second are still living in Eastern civilisation; it is only the third group which has had some benefits from Western civilisation. That means that one portion of our nation is living in an ancient, another in a medieval, and a third in a modern age. How can the life of a nation be normal with such a threefold life?" (cited by Frey, 1964, p. 209).

they had entered "the innermost shrine of Islam in the Western Anatolia," thereby attacking a state "which belongs to the Muslims." The religious flavor of such statements was meant to persuade the rural masses of Anatolia to adhere to a project that was deeply secular in nature: Muslims were "true brothers" destined to form the core of the new emerging nation (Zürcher, 2004, pp. 181–2; 2010, pp. 222–6, 278).

In fact, since the 1930s, the nation had been defined primarily through ethnicity – that is, in terms of race and language – and only secondarily through religion (White, 2013, p. 31). Based on a tactical and mystifying use of Islam and Muslim identity, this representation served to justify the forced assimilation of the 30 percent of the population who did not have Turkish as their mother tongue (Zürcher, 2010, p. 149). Non-Muslims were still regarded as outsiders, while non-Turkish Muslims, such as the Kurds and Balkan Muslims, could theoretically assimilate by learning the Turkish language and culture. In actual fact, however, although they were Muslims, the Kurds were poor candidates for assimilation because of their strong tribal loyalties (White, 2013, p. 30).[2] Moreover, because they were not Sunnites, the Alevi and Bektashi Muslims were generally excluded from the definition of a true Turk.[3] The same held true for Christians (Armenians, Greeks, Circassians, Georgians, etc.) and Jews who, by converting to Islam, would not become Turkish, thus attesting the primacy of race in the definition of Turkishness. In this regard, Kemalist policies were at complete variance with the Ottoman policies that encouraged conversion as a means of social integration and advancement. Under Kemalism, Islam remained a significant marker of national identity to the extent that Turks converting to Christianity would automatically lose their Turkish identity (White, 2013, p. 107). Modern Turkish identity was thus defined on the basis of a "holy trinity" consisting of being simultaneously Sunni-Muslim-Turk (Kaya, 2013, p. 13). In the name of this holy trinity, racial purges were allowed to take place.[4]

---

[2] Using artillery, air bombardment, and poison gas, the Kemalist forces killed tens of thousands of Alevi Kurds, including women and children, in the Dersim massacre of 1937–8. Many others were internally displaced. In the words of Jenny White (2013), "the massacres were sparked by resistance to the government's policy of mass resettlement and dispersal of the local population with the intention of assimilating them into Turkish culture" (p. 108).

[3] This did not prevent the Alevi-Bektashi communities from embracing the Turkish Republic and from perceiving Atatürk as the last saint, who had come to save them from their centuries-long suffering. Unfortunately, they remained the victims of discriminatory and racist discourses and practices on the part of the dominant classes in urban life (Kaya, 2013, pp. 139–42).

[4] The most horrifying act conducted by the new Turkey was certainly the deportation and "resettlement" of Armenian Christians ordered by the Young Turks during World War I.

Kemalism as an Authoritarian and Elitist Project

Two additional features of the Kemalist regime bear special emphasis. First, it rapidly became authoritarian and even totalitarian. Second, it decided not only to make the state the engine of change but also, in the name of the new civilizational order, to meddle in the most trivial or mundane aspects of the everyday life of Turkish citizens.

Whenever the Kemalist leaders, and the Young Turks before them, faced a choice between modernization and democracy, they always opted for the former. Revealingly, soon after the proclamation of the Republic of Turkey and the abolition of the caliphate, the state suppressed the liberal and socialist opposition. There was to be a single party, the RPP, within which Mustafa Kemal had almost unlimited power. In March 1925, under the Law on the Maintenance of Order, the government was given dictatorial powers; in particular, any voice of dissent would be subject to severe disciplinary measures. All forms of (independent) civil society organizations, such as the Turkish Women's Union, the Freemason lodges, professional associations, cultural organizations, and educational clubs, were gradually eliminated and replaced with new organizations under party control (Zürcher, 2010, pp. 214, 252–3). The government, the bureaucracy, and the army were turned into a single body with Mustafa Kemal as its indisputable head. Interestingly, the only legitimate political opposition was short-lived. Allowed to form in 1930, the Free Republican Party (FRP) was abruptly terminated because it revealed the widespread discontent in the country and the unpopularity of the RPP. The enormous support for the rival FRP showed that the RPP's project of social and cultural modernization had not been accepted by the mass of the population (pp. 255–6).

The authoritarian tendencies of the Kemalists, and of the Young Turks before them, were moored in the preeminent role given to the army in the revolutionary process. The Prussian-trained military officers were imbued with a spirit of authoritarian centralism justified in the name of a radical and secular reform program destined to create a modern Turkey modeled after Western Europe (Lewis, 1968, pp. 204–5; Gellner, 1997). The new regime perceived this modernization as implying the total eradication of the country's Ottoman and Arab legacy. Following Erik Zürcher's approach (2004,

---

Aimed at creating a purely Turkic state, the operation led to the first genocide of the twentieth century. The "Executioner Governor" in charge of its implementation, the physician Mehmet Reşid, declared, "I came into this world a Turk. Armenian traitors had found a niche for themselves in the bosom of the fatherland; they were dangerous microbes. Isn't it a duty of a doctor to destroy these microbes?" (cited by Armstrong, 2014, p. 289).

ch. 11), we may distinguish between three types of reforms, depending on whether they were concerned with (1) the secularization of state, education, and law; (2) the symbols defining Turkish identity; and (3) social life.

The first type of reforms were guided by the idea that, unlike the Tanzimat reforms of the late Ottoman Empire that resulted in the coexistence of secular and Islamic schools, courts, and laws, institutional change under Kemalism was about suppressing autonomous Islamic institutions. The reform movement began in the 1820s and 1830s under Sultan Mahmut II, continued during the succeeding decades (the French commercial code was adopted in 1850 and a new civil code based mainly on the Hanefi Law in 1867), and was nearly completed between 1913 and 1918 under the rule of the Young Turks and their Committee of Union and Progress (CUP). Thus, even before the proclamation of the Republic of Turkey in October 1923, its institutions had already been reformed. Most noticeably, in spite of strong resistance from the ulama, the role of Islam had been limited almost exclusively to the realm of family law. When the Swiss civil code and the Italian penal code were eventually adopted in 1926, even this domain of the law was taken away from the jurisdiction of the ulama, and religious associations were banned.

The educational system became completely secularis zed in 1924 when the state decided to unify education throughout the country, which implied the abolition of the madrasas, or religious colleges. Also abolished was the Ministry of Religious Affairs and Pious Foundations, which was replaced by two directorates – one for religious affairs (the Diyanet) and the other for pious foundations or waqfs (the Evkaf) – and both attached directly to the prime minister's office. All imams and muftis became civil servants, and the Diyanet was given sole responsibility for religious guidance. Thus, the contents of Friday sermons (preaching before Friday prayer and sermons during the prayer) became centrally determined, and muftis started to receive precise instructions about how to advise believers. Moreover, the state became responsible for defining the contents of mandatory religious instruction in public schools and of the İmam-Hatip schools created for the purpose of training imams. Organized prayer was also forbidden in public and private schools. These changes amounted to the greatest transformation of the state bureaucracy brought about under the Kemalist republic and resulted not merely in a separation of state and religion but also in the total control of religion by the state (Zürcher, 2004, p. 187; 2010, p. 145, 279–80; Kuru, 2009, pp. 165–7, 205–11, 220; İnalcık, 1964).

The second area of secular reforms was a direct attack on religious symbols and their replacement by the symbols of European civilization.

Among the measures taken were the prohibition of traditional headgear (such as the fez and the turban) for men and outlawing the wearing of religious attire except for prayer services in the mosques. Strong pressures were exerted to make women abandon the veil. Outward appearance was tremendously important for Atatürk, so much so that he equated civilization to costume (Kinross, 2001, p. 414; Morris, 2005, pp. 36–7). Thus, in one of his speeches, he addressed the issue in the following terms: "The people of the Turkish Republic, who claim to be civilized, must prove that they are civilized, by their ideas and their mentality, by their family life and their way of living. ... They must prove in fact that they are civilized and advanced persons in their outward aspect also." He then described the dress of the Turks as a "grotesque mixture of styles" that is "neither national nor international"; hence, the absolute need to shed those clothes overnight and replace them with a unique, precisely defined costume borrowed from the West: "A civilized, international dress is worthy and appropriate for our nation, and we will wear it. Boots or shoes on our feet, trousers on our legs, shirt and tie, jacket and waistcoat – and of course, to complete these, a cover with a brim on our heads. I want to make this clear. This head-covering is called 'hat'" (cited by Kinross, 2001, p. 415).

That traditional attire was not prescribed by religion did not really matter: for Atatürk and the Kemalists, religion and tradition confounded were seen as an obstacle to progress. Islam as a total culture was seen by Atatürk as a "putrefied corpse" (Sayyid, 1997, p. 57). Until the accession of an Islamic party to power in 2007, the Constitutional Court, whose links with the Kemalists were always strong (Belge, 2006), was able to uphold the strict position that "regardless of whether it [the dress code] is religious or not, anti-modern dresses that contradict the Laws of Revolution cannot be seen as appropriate. ... Religious dresses, in particular, constitute a deeper incongruity since they contradict the principle of secularism." The dress code was so important because it reflected the person's mentality and character, "sentiments and thoughts," whereas secularism precisely consisted of "a transformation of mentality" (Order No. 1989/12 of the Turkish Constitutional Court, March 7, 1989; cited by Kuru, 2009, p. 189).[5]

---

[5] Note that these measures and the posture supporting them were very similar to those adopted by Peter the Great in Russia: his policy of coercive Europeanization included the compulsory cutting off of beards and the imposition of "Germanic" clothes. When an open rebellion erupted in Astrakhan (1705), it was harshly put down by Sheremetev, whose police force committed many atrocities against the people (Obolonsky, 2003, p. 51).

Other Westernization measures included the replacement of the Muslim Friday as a day of rest by the Christian Sunday; the adoption of the Western clock and the Gregorian calendar, Western numerals, and Western weight and measures (1926–31); the replacement of the Arabic/Persian alphabet used to write Ottoman Turkish by the Latin alphabet (1928); the removal of all Arabic and Persian words to create a pure Turkish language (1932); and the introduction of family names to replace the habit of using the birth name and, possibly, the name of the father (1934).

Finally, the third area of secularization involved social life and the attack on popular Islam, to be distinguished from the "high Islam" of the ulama dealt with earlier (in the first type of reforms). Here, the regime's most dramatic step was the outright suppression in 1925 of the dervish (Sufi) orders, or mystical fraternities (the "tarikats"), and the widespread network of convents and shrines associated with them. It constituted a far-reaching form of interference in the daily and personal lives of the people, because these religious orders played a significant role in shaping daily life of the popular masses – providing an emotional comfort lacking in "high" religion, offering social protection and cohesion, and supplying an authority structure around the shaykhs (Zürcher, 2004, pp. 191–2; 2010, p. 136; Göle, 2004). Two characteristics of the Sufi orders made them unacceptable to the regime. First, as religious brotherhoods based on closed and secretive networks, they were perceived as the hallmark of a traditional and obscurantist culture. Second, they were loci of local power situated beyond the reach of a centralized government. The latter held especially true for the Nakshibendi order, which played a major role in the anti-constitutionalist uprising in 1909 and the Kurdish rebellion of 1925 (Kinross, 2001, pp. 397–404).

The drastic long-term consequences of the government's decision have been captured by Zürcher (2004):

By extending their secularization drive beyond the formal, institutionalized Islam, the Kemalists now touched such vital elements of popular religion as dress, amulets, soothsayers, holy sheikhs, saints' shrines, pilgrimages and festivals. The resentment these measures caused and the resistance put up against them was far greater than, for instance, in the case of the abolition of the caliphate, the position of seyhülislam, or the madrasas, which was only important to official "high" religion. While the government succeeded in suppressing most expressions of popular religion, at least in the towns, these did not, of course, disappear. To a large extent, the tarikats simply went underground. But through the simultaneous imposition of an authoritarian and – especially during the 1940s – increasingly unpopular regime and suppression of popular Islam, the Kemalists politicised Islam and turned it into a vehicle for opposition. One could say that, in turning against popular religion, they cut the ties that bound them to the mass of the population. (p. 192)

It is a particularly sobering fact that, even when Islamic leaders displayed a good deal of wisdom and openness toward modernity, they could be persecuted by the regime. A striking example is the case of Sait Nursi. He enjoined Muslims to take God's unity as the basis of their lives, but also to study modern science and technology, which he saw as necessary to preserve Islam, the only true basis of social cohesion. He was nevertheless arrested and tried several times for the alleged political use of religion, although he did not engage in direct political activity until the late 1950s. His writings were banned because he preached against secularism and nationalism (Zürcher, 2004, p. 193).

As this account makes clear, the movement of the Young Turks and the Kemalist Republic that embodied their ideals displayed a fundamentally authoritarian attitude and deep-rooted mistrust of the masses. Recruited from the higher ranks of the administration, its leaders saw themselves as an enlightened and self-confident elite charged with the mission of educating their people, removing the hold of religion on their minds, and totally transforming the Turkish legal system, even though a large part of the population was still immersed in a traditional Muslim culture (Kuru, 2009, pp. 214–15; Zürcher, 2010, pp. 136, 214). This authoritarian elitist approach to modernization produced a deep-rooted fault line inside Turkish society, a division that continues to run through its economic, social, and political spheres (Kaya, 2013, p. 15; Gellner, 1994).

Ahmet Kuru (2009) characterizes the approach of the Kemalists to religion as one of "assertive secularism" inspired by the French Jacobite model. Unlike the "passive secularism" of the United States, which allows the public visibility of religious symbols, assertive secularism is a social engineering project aimed at excluding religion from the public sphere. It is based on the idea that religious beliefs belong to, and should therefore be confined to, the private sphere. There is nonetheless one central difference between the Turkish and French approaches: Whereas in Turkey assertive secularism was largely imposed as a top-down elite project, in France it was established through a more bottom-up process. Such a difference has historical roots: In France, the Catholic Church was closely connected to the Ancient Régime. As such, it tried to reestablish the monarchy after the French Revolution, thereby losing considerable prestige among the popular masses. It was therefore as a political institution rather than as faith per se that Christianity was hated and its adherents tracked down and imprisoned in those turbulent times. It is revealing that in 1790 priests were forced to choose to be loyal to either the state or the pope. In Turkey, by contrast, secularism was born of a modernization project that was essentially inspired by

Western values and therefore did not spring from an endogenous evolution of the host society. Moreover, Islamists did not struggle for or support the restoration of the Ottoman caliphate that the Kemalists equated with the Ancient Régime (Kuru, 2009, pp. 32–4, 139–40, 246).

Kemalist writers have put forward another argument to justify assertive secularism, even in the absence of historical supportive links between Islam and the old regime (Kuru, 2009, pp. 174–5). The idea is similar to Bernard Lewis's thesis that, unlike Christianity, which confines religion to individual spirituality, Islam encompasses all areas of life and therefore offers a blueprint for a whole social and political order (see Chapter 3, as well as Lewis, 1968, which is devoted to Turkey). According to Turkey's Constitutional Court, there thus exists solid ground to apply a stricter secularism in Turkey than in Western Europe. Niyazi Berkes (1964) shares Lewis's view completely: For him, indeed, the bases of the Islamic and Western legal systems are irreconcilable, being the legal foundations of two different civilizations – medieval and modern. The political essence of Islam means that a real separation of state and religion is not possible in a Muslim society (pp. 480–1). Çetin Özek (1962), likewise, has emphasized that, because Islam is not only a religion but also a political ideology, Muslims will always resist secularism. Being based on a "centuries-old desert law," the sharia hinders progress, and only strict interventionist state policies will be able to rid Turkey of Islam so it can "become part of the universal civilisation – the modern West" (p. 520).

The outcome of the policy of assertive secularism was a deep rift between the political elite and their allied supporters in towns and cities, who were dominated by bureaucrats, military officers, teachers, doctors, lawyers, and entrepreneurs of large commercial enterprises, on the one hand, and large parts of the population and even parts of the national movement itself, on the other hand. In urban locations, craftsmen and small traders formed the backbone of the suppressed traditional culture (Zürcher, 2004, pp. 193–4). As noted earlier, tensions between the Westernized elite and the popular classes were greatly exacerbated by the outright elimination of the mystical orders and fraternities that had formed a shared value of the common people's lives.

The Aftermath of the Kemalist Republic

Kemalist dictatorship in Turkey ended in 1945 under the pressure of internal democratizing forces and external influences exerted after the military defeat of the Axis powers in World War II. After a short period of transition, multiparty democracy was established, or reestablished if one considers earlier experiments with this form of democracy (1908–13, 1923–5, and 1930). Assertive secularism, however, continued to be the hallmark of modern Turkey. It was most strenuously enforced by the Turkish army, which did not hesitate to seize power if secular values were deemed to be under threat.

The landslide victory of the Democratic Party (DP) in the 1950 elections, a victory confirmed four years later, constituted a watershed in the political history of modern Turkey. Born of a split within the Young Turk coalition, the DP was "the first political organisation in the country's modern history with a genuine mass following that had been able to express its support in a free election" (Zürcher, 2004, p. 218). The National Assembly suddenly was dominated by representatives with no background in the bureaucracy and the army: A different section of Turkey's elite, less educated and younger, had come to power. It bears noting that, in the years before 1950, the DP's leaders took great care to emphasize that they would not seek to alter Turkey's secular foundations. In actual fact, their program closely resembled that of the RPP. When the increasing authoritarianism of Prime Minister Adnan Menderes elicited the growing criticism of hostile intellectuals, members of the bureaucracy and the armed forces, and even of members of his own party, he used appeals to Islamic sentiments, yet in an ambivalent manner because he did not give Islam a greater role in either administration or legislation (Zürcher, 2004, p. 232–3). In particular, he maintained the integration of the religious establishment into the bureaucracy: Every preacher remained a civil servant. This, however, did not mitigate the Kemalists' hatred against Menderes, who was eventually executed by the military in 1961 (Zürcher, 2010, pp. 271–2).

Two changes nevertheless occurred. The first one, the relaxation of restrictions on expressions of religious feelings, represented a continuation of the policy adopted by the RPP itself in the 1940s. Its main effect was to make Islam increasingly visible in everyday life in the cities. The second, more significant change consisted of accepting the existence of autonomous religious organizations, such as the Sufi brotherhoods. This was seen as tacitly admitting that religion was not incompatible with development, which was tantamount to a betrayal of the Kemalist legacy. In the words of Zücher again,

For the majority of the educated elite (including civil servants, teachers and academics and officers) who had internalised the Kemalist dogmas and who themselves owed their position in the ruling elite to the fact that they represented the positivist, Western-orientated outlook, this admission threatened their cultural hegemony and their monopoly of the political scene and the state machinery. This explains why their reaction to expressions of even non-political Islamic feeling was little less than hysterical. Within the army, which regarded itself as the keeper of Atatürk's heritage, the feeling that the DP was betraying the Kemalist traditions was especially strong. (Zürcher, 2004, p. 234)

As hinted at earlier, religious symbols were actually conflated with the culture of the countryside, which gradually entered into the cities through steady rural-urban migration flows. Rural migrants were typically treated with contempt not only because they brought with them a resurgence of Islam in modern urban environments but also because they imported backward behaviors seen as "an affront to civility and an offensive intrusion into urban life" (White, 2013, p. 115).[6] The pejorative label "Black Turks," with its implied connotation of uncivilized, traditional, and uneducated people, was used to designate all those who displayed piety and certain bodily habits. These characteristics were associated with lower-class status regardless of the actual wealth and degree of economic success of the individual (Yumul, 2010).

Those changes were enough to alarm the armed forces, which staged a coup to dislodge the DP from power in May 1960; it led to the hanging of three top figures of the DP, including Menderes. The coup was greeted with explosions of public joy in Ankara and Istanbul, with students and intellectuals among the most enthusiastic supporters (Zürcher, 2004, p. 241). Yet, democratic forces soon reasserted themselves, and the National Unity Committee (NUC) created by the conspirators was purged as early as October 1960. New parliamentary elections were held one year later (October 1961), which were won by parties considered to be heirs to the DP. In the beginning of the Second Turkish Republic (1961–80), a new constitution was passed that was more liberal than the previous one in that it tolerated a greater measure of political activity. Strikingly, there was no return to the strict, secularist policies of the years before 1945, although efforts were made to undermine the rise of Islamist movements by building new mosques, restoring shrines, enhancing religious education in schools, modernizing the curriculum of the preachers' colleges (İmam-Hatip schools), and publishing "enlightened" sermons from the Diyanet (p. 247).

The Justice Party (JP), which emerged a clear victor from the October 1965 election, had been formed a few years earlier. It was essentially a

---

[6] Offenses ranged from women wearing headscarves and men wearing pajamas in the streets, to large families picnicking in public parks, sparking the complaint that urbanites were now unable to use the park themselves (White, 2013, p. 115).

continuation of the DP and was first headed by an army officer, General Gümüşpala. The JP neatly defeated the Kemalist RPP, with which it had failed to govern effectively under a coalition government during the preceding years. In the meantime, Süleyman Demirel became the new head of the JP, a choice very much influenced by Sunay who was both president and the chief of the general staff. The political rise of Demirel symbolized "the emergence of an entirely new elite," made up of self-made men from the countryside and from the smaller but fast-growing provincial towns (Zürcher, 2004, p. 250). The JP was nevertheless a heterogeneous body with little ideological coherence, based as it was on a coalition of industrialists, small traders and artisans, peasants and big landowners, religious conservatives, and Western-oriented liberals. To keep this coalition together, Demirel resorted to a double-edged tactic in which he emphasized the Islamic character of the JP and its defense of traditional values while struggling against communism and harassing leftist movements. That struggle against the left brought the JP into an ugly collaboration with the infamous National Intelligence Organization (MIT). Thanks to continuing support in the countryside, Demirel won the 1969 elections, even though he was seriously contested inside his own party (pp. 251–2).

At the same time as the JP was thus considerably weakened, the RPP was rejuvenated by moving to the center left under the leadership of a staunch secularist, Bülent Ecevit. After a period of political turmoil punctuated by the military ultimatum of March 1971 and its immediate consequences, the RPP won the most votes in the October 1973 elections; it then led a coalition government not with the JP but with the National Salvation Party (NSP) of Necmettin Erbakan. Previously called the National Order Party (NOP), the party formed by Erbakan positioned itself as the champion of the interests of small businessmen and did not hesitate to make references to the Islamic heritage of the Turkish nation. It was based on a so-called National Vision ("Milli Görüş") that proposed a just economic order to eliminate socioeconomic inequalities and corruption. The National Vision, which aimed at constructing a modern religio-ethnic Turkish national identity, had a strong chauvinist and even racist component because of its stress on Turkish blood and history (White, 2013, p. 39).

The "marriage of convenience" between the RPP and the NSP could not survive the rising ambitions of Ecevit, and it was succeeded by a series of weak coalitions and countercoalitions (White, 2013, pp. 256–63). Precipitating the breakdown of the political system of the Second Republic and the third military intervention in Turkish politics in twenty years were several factors, of which the government's weakness in the face of rising political violence was only one.[7] Other critical factors were Kurdish separatism, a severe economic crisis caused by misguided economic policies, and a threat of Islamic fundamentalism exacerbated by the Islamic revolution in Iran (January 1979). A demonstration organized in Konya by the NSP and Islamist groups after the Iranian revolution called for a return to the sharia and a refusal to sing the Turkish national anthem, which, oddly enough, had been written by a pan-Islamist poet (pp. 268–9).

The Gradual Reentry of Islam into Turkish Politics

The coup, which took place in September 1980, inaugurated the Third Republic in a brutal but effective manner. General Kenan Evren was appointed the new president of Turkey. People suspected of leftism or Islamism were arrested or fired from their jobs, and many were executed, tortured, or died in custody. A special organization (YÖK) was created to control the universities. It decided to expel students with headscarves based on the order of the military government (in 1982). The justification provided was that an absolute freedom of dress went against Atatürk's principles and reforms (Kuru, 2009, pp. 188–9).[8] Existing political parties were disbanded and their politicians banned from political activities. The army now closely monitored political action, and in a first phase, only three new parties were allowed to compete in elections. Among them was the Motherland Party (MP), which made great strides under the strong leadership of Turgut Özal. He was a man well connected not only with big business circles but also with the Naksibendi Sufi order.

---

[7] During the late 1970s, political violence became a major problem, with extremist youth groups on both the left and the right (the fascist "Grey Wolves" and religious fundamentalists) fighting to control the streets and the campuses. The struggle was an asymmetric one because the police and security forces clearly backed the ultranationalist party (Nationalist Action Party, or NAP) linked to the Grey Wolves. At the same time, as aptly observed by Zürcher (2004), political extremism and violence in Turkey cannot be understood outside the context of a traditional culture in which honor and shame, strong identification with one's family and clan, and vendetta played a dominant role. As a result, traditional conflicts were given political connotations as when the Grey Wolves organized a series of murderous pogroms against the Alevis (Turkish Shi'as), who generally voted for the political left (p. 263).

[8] In response, the parliament passed another law that made modern dress and appearance compulsory, but allowed covering the neck and hair with a headscarf for religious reasons. Evren immediately went to the Constitutional Court, which dutifully obliged by declaring the law unconstitutional. The judges considered that religious belief could not be considered a reason for legal exemption; hence, the law threatened the unity of the nation and destroyed the public order (Kuru, 2009, p. 189).

Many in the MP, Özal among them, were influenced by the Hearths of the Enlightened, an organization founded in 1970 by influential people from the business, academic, and political worlds. Its ideology, known as the "Turkish-Islamic synthesis," also appealed to prominent military leaders, including Evren, in spite of the secularist traditions of the Turkish officer corps. The truth is that "although the military suppressed the leftist and Islamist movements mercilessly, they also realized that an ideological alternative was needed and that traditional secularist Kemalism had too limited an appeal to be able to do the job" (Zürcher, 2010, pp. 280–1; White, 2013, p. 35). The military also wanted to use Islam as a bulwark against communism and to improve relations between Turkey and Muslim countries, such as Pakistan; hence, the defense of compulsory religious education by such a staunch secularist as Evren and the apparently inconsistent policies of the regime toward religion (Yavuz, 2003, pp. 69–74).

The central message of the new ideology, which had some links to the aforementioned National Vision, was that patriotism and love for parents, the state, and the army were religious duties. Religious education was thus enshrined in the constitution adopted by the military in 1982. A Board of Higher Education was established to strengthen the role of the state in the public realm, including regulating the mode of dressing in public places and curricular content. Wearing a headscarf for women and having a beard for men were prohibited in higher education institutes, and the regulations regarding the dress code were soon extended to personnel of public institutions (Kaya, 2013, p. 162). In school textbooks, Islam was articulated through values such as nationalism, the unity and indivisibility of the nation, respect for authority, and militarism. The Diyanet was given a constitutional role, and its functions were more than ever completely subservient to the interests of the state. Regimented teaching and learning were reinforced, and military-like drills, chanting, and parades began in the earliest grades to produce adults who physically embodied the nation's militarist ideals (White, 2013, p. 75). Students in all primary schools were required to recite every morning a strongly nationalist pledge containing these words: "My foremost principle is to defend my minors and to respect my elders, and to love my fatherland and my nation more than myself. ... O Atatürk the great! I swear that I will enduringly walk through the path you opened and to the target you showed. May my personal being be sacrificed to the being of the Turkish nation. How happy is the one who says; 'I am a Turk'" (cited by Kuru, 2009, p. 166).

In sum, the military regime followed a twofold policy: emphasizing the laicist discourse, on the one hand, and adopting a kind of state-run political Islam, on the other hand. The latter arm of the strategy aimed to indoctrinate the younger generations through compulsory courses on religious culture, civic values, and morality. Non-Muslim minorities were exempted from these courses, but not non-Sunni Muslim minorities such as the Alevis, who were regarded as practicing a deviant faith whose communion houses (the "cemevis") were not recognized as places of worship equal to mosques. The next government of the MP, under the leadership of Turgut Özal in the mid-1980s, embraced a similar approach prioritizing the teaching of a homogeneous way of life based on Sunni Islam (Kaya, 2013, pp. 142–5).[9]

Concomitantly, the influence of Islam was spreading: New mosques were built; schools for preachers, whose graduates were now allowed to enter university, were being formed; the religious content of schoolbooks and state-controlled radio and television programs, as well as religious publications, grew rapidly; and members of the cabinet increasingly took part in religious ceremonies. These religious manifestations aroused the fear of religious intolerance among the old elite – although, in hindsight, they can be regarded as proof of the success of modernization in ending the elite's monopoly on intellectual debate. In point of fact, many members of the old subject class had now been educated enough to construct social and cultural projects of their own and to use modern communication technologies to publicisz them (Göle, 1997). Citing Zürcher (2004) again,

What could make Islamic currents dangerous to the existing state and society was, and is, discontent among the have-nots, created by policies that have vastly increased the differences between the rich and poor. Just as in so many other countries in Asia and Africa, so too in Turkey *politicised Islam has taken over the role of the left as the voice of the have-nots.* That Islamic movements have been able to play this role with success is partially due to the extent to which the governments of Evren and Özal have embraced and thus legitimized them, but if the discontent among the mass of the city populations had not grown so much in the 1980s the movements would have remained fuses without any powder keg attached to them. (p. 289; my emphasis)

---

[9] The Alevis had to wait for the rise of Erdoğan's AKP to power to see a change in this situation that they perceived as one of indoctrination by the state through Sunni Islam. The state curriculum was revised to include Alevi beliefs and practices, a step toward tolerating the religious differences of the Alevi (and Bektashi) communities. Not all Alevis would celebrate this change, however. Secular Alevis indeed asked for more drastic measures – more precisely the teaching of a course based on the history and sociology of religions from an academic and comparative perspective and the restriction to the private sphere of the teaching of Alevi belief (and any religion) (Kaya, 2013, pp. 142–56).

The next significant event, beyond the local vagaries of short-term politics (marked by the temporary return of Demirel at the head of a newly branded party and as president), was undoubtedly the sudden success, in the elections of March 1994, of the Islamic Welfare Party (WP) of Erbakan, the leader of the previously named NSP. This success was due both to the strong grassroots organization of the party and to its resonating in large cities such as Istanbul and Ankara. The WP could no longer be viewed as representing the interests of small businessmen; it had also become the voice of the poorest sections of the population in the metropolitan areas. As White (2013) observes, "Islamists took over the role of champions of economic justice from the left that had been decimated in the 1980 coup, although the Islamist conception differed quite substantially from the class-based ideas of the left" (p. 42). The electoral success of the WP followed both from its emphasis on issues like social justice, unemployment, poverty, social security, and corruption in high circles and from its respect for the more conservative lifestyle of the masses. Regarding the latter aspect, its main role was to open the way for a "Muslim cultural renaissance" that dared express itself publicly and for a restored dignity of the Black Turks in the face of senior military officers and traditional republican elites entrenched in state institutions and monopolies (p. 47).

From then on, things moved quickly, with the army again reasserting its power. It presented the government of Erbakan with a long list of demands aimed at curbing the influence of the Islamists in the economy, in education, and inside the state apparatus. Concern grew about the increasing numbers of graduates of the preacher schools who could not find employment in religious establishments and were therefore seeking jobs in other branches of the "secular" state administration. In the eyes of the military and many secular Turks, this trend implied a high risk of people with an Islamist agenda infiltrating and gradually taking over the state. The unsatisfactory response of the government to the army's demands led to the ouster of Erbakan as prime minister. Moreover, in January 1998, the Constitutional Court closed down the WP on the grounds that it violated the secular nature of the state (Zürcher, 2004, p. 300; White, 2013, pp. 40, 43). In the same process, the army was purged of about nine hundred military officers because of their alleged Islamic ways of life; corporations run by conservative Muslims faced discrimination in government contracts and bids; wearing headscarves was prohibited in all education institutions; and many Quran courses and all secondary sections of the preacher schools were eliminated (Kuru, 2009, p. 162).

The Second Revolution in Modern Turkey:
An Islamic Party in Power

The Welfare Party was succeeded by the Virtue Party (VP), which was itself banned in June 2001. Parting ways with the conservative faction of VP led by Erbakan, the leader of the reformist faction – Recep Tayyip Erdoğan – then founded the Justice and Development Party (AKP). In a short time span, the AKP shed its Islamic identity and styled itself as a conservative democratic party. Moreover, it defined secularism as a principle requiring the government to keep an equal distance from all beliefs. Its success was immediate: In the 2007 elections, AKP did well in every region of the country, and it won 47 percent of the overall vote.

Supported by conservative social classes – practicing Muslim small entrepreneurs from provincial towns; believers from low social backgrounds; and, last but not least, the new aspiring elites, most of whom were professionals coming from provincial practicing Muslim families and trained in secular educational institutions – the new party thus received a stunning mandate to govern Turkey along entirely new lines. Identification with Erdoğan and the AKP was especially strong among the many migrants from small provincial towns and the countryside to big cities, where they experienced a profound cultural shock (Insel, 2015, pp. 65–6, 165–6).

A democratic revolution had occurred, and a regime had been set up that proved to be remarkably enduring. It was run by cadres (counting many engineers and doctors) who typically came from socially disadvantaged families and belonged to the first generation to win access to Western education. Its leading figure was someone with strong popular appeal: Because Erdoğan did not speak any foreign language, never lived outside his native poor quarter of Istanbul, was not educated in any prestigious institution, never worked in the state army or administration, and was a pious man adhering to traditional values, he was seen as the ideal spokesman for all those who were bypassed by Kemalist policies and ignored by the old elite made up of state or army officials and businesspeople from Istanbul.

The first successful steps taken by the new government reduced the role of the army, preventing it from meddling in politics, and that of the "deep state" by de-laicizing state institutions. The former objective was mainly achieved through the sensational Ergenekon cases, initiated in 2007, which initially aimed to remove all threats to democratic power coming from secret ultranationalist movements lodged inside the Kemalist state and army, but were quickly extended to silence figures from the wider political opposition (Insel, 2015, ch. 6). As for the latter objective, a symbolic initial step was lifting the ban on wearing the veil in universities and public buildings, a measure that affected about 63 percent of Turkish women (Kuru, 2009, p. 187). These steps were part of a genuine revolution because until then in the Turkish Republic, regardless of the party coalitions in charge of the government, state policies toward religion were predominantly decided by the presidency, and the presidency had seen to it that strict secularism continued to pervade state institutions. The president's decisive influence stemmed from key prerogatives, such as approval of the appointment of high-ranking generals and top civil bureaucrats and the direct appointment of high court judges (the judges of the Constitutional Court, in particular) and presidents of universities.

The question naturally arises as to why the parliament repeatedly elected staunch secularists as presidents (the only two exceptions were Celal Bayar from 1950–60 and Turgut Özal from 1989–93). The answer is that, owing to strong military pressure and intervention, deputies refrained from voting for conservative or liberal pro-democracy candidates. After the power of the military was reduced, this was no longer possible, and in April 2007, an estimated one million protesters in several important cities of the country failed to prevent the AKP from electing one of its own men, Abdullah Gül, as the new president. This was despite pressures from the street, the opposition of the Constitutional Court, and the threat of direct intervention by the military (Kuru, 2009, pp. 183–4).

What Erdoğan has failed to establish, however, is a political system rid of authoritarianism and an obsession with power consolidation (Insel, 2015, ch. 7; Filiu, 2015, ch. 1). His repeated electoral victories have increased his confidence in his right to repress critics and settle old political accounts, ignore the voices of the opposition, and stifle any form of dissent, even that arising from Islamic circles. A striking example is the war waged in 2013–4 against Fethullah Gülen. Gülen is the leader of a secretive Islamic movement created in the early 1990s, whose vast network of followers (the "cemaat") in the country's state sector, including the judiciary and the police, had previously helped Erdoğan stage mass trials (from 2008–13) that sent hundreds of army officers to prison on trumped-up coup charges (*Economist*, August 6–12, 2016a, p. 19). The Gülenists did not form a political movement, but one that chose to promote its ideas primarily through education. To that effect, it built a vast Islamic community network (spreading to Central Asia, the Balkans, and beyond) of primary schools, high schools, and universities with the explicit objective of furthering the adoption of Western technology coupled with Islamic morals (Zürcher, 2004, p. 291). Open to modern science and knowledge, the Gülenist movement strives toward a modernity that is not cut off from the historical past. More specifically, it holds that "the Muslim national tradition is based on a cultural Muslimhood, infused with a politico-historical Turkish/Ottoman identity, rather than a racialised or language-based Turkishness" (White, 2013, p. 97; see also Yavuz, 2013). In this sense, it resembles the Meiji movement in Japan and the populist movement in Russia on the eve of its modernization drive.

Attacks not only on the Gülenists but also on all forms of even moderate dissent and government critics have dramatically intensified following a coup attempt in July 2016 that Erdoğan immediately blamed on Gülen. Under a state of emergency that allows him to rule by decree, he has embarked on a "seemingly insatiable purge" leading to the closure of thousands of universities, news outlets, and hospitals; the sacking of 100,000 officials from state institutions; and the replacement of election of university rectors by direct government appointment (*Economist*, November 5–11, 2016, p. 23).

To help him in the task of repressing dissenters, Erdoğan has not only acquired a good measure of control over the judiciary but also has increased the size and enhanced the prerogatives of the police to the point of replacing the military with a "civilian army." Worse still, he has actively encouraged Turkish citizens themselves to report to the police any manifestation of hostility against the government. In this way, he has contributed to creating a climate of mutual defamation and suspicion, instilling fear and mistrust at the heart of the societal fabric. Finally, he has not hesitated to resort to the tactic of whipping up support among nationalists and Islamists, with a view to acquiring additional powers in a referendum scheduled for 2017.

Their unashamed display of wealth is another way in which the new AKP elite, including Erdoğan and his close associates, has departed from the party's professed ideals. Running counter to the ideal of a pious, modest, and ascetic class of professionals and business people, the elite have increasingly behaved as an assertive new bourgeoisie eager to demonstrate their economic success. The luxurious palace that Erdoğan decided to build for himself after having been elected president is a blatant illustration of such a reversal of attitudes: A fortress of stone pillars and sheet glass made of 1,150 rooms, its cost was officially $615 million (*Economist*, August 27–September 2, 2016, p. 17). The religiosity of the rising class of Anatolian businessmen in Turkey seems to have been increasingly deprived of some of its key underlying values as its members reach the highest levels of political and economic power. It remains to be seen whether the essential function of that religiosity – differentiating the "Islamic way of life" from the Westernized lifestyle of the Kemalist elite – will credibly persist under the new circumstances.

Concluding Remarks

Looking at the history of modern, post-Ottoman Turkey, Hakan Yavuz (2000) suggests that the Kemalist revolution has been "superficially Western in form while remaining rigidly authoritarian and dogmatic in substance." Its attempt "to radically recast Turkish culture, history, and identity has ensured a permanent *kulturkampf* against society," an approach that undermined the transition of Turkey to a Western-style liberal democracy (p. 34; see also Yavuz, 2003, 2006, 2009). Contending that Kemalism has been "superficially Western" is both correct and misleading. It is correct in two senses. First, it is mainly the ways of the Kemalist elite that underwent a radical change, even though one must consider that the elite was rather broad, representing 10–20 percent of the population, rather than a tiny 1–2 percent. By contrast, the mass of the Turkish population, including the new rising elite of Anatolian entrepreneurs and middle-class professionals who support the AKP, often remained religious, to one degree or another. Second, the authoritarian methods of Kemalism, its obsession with unity or homogeneity over diversity, and its predilection for a strong state produced a politically illiberal regime. This regime, which was dominated by a deep state based on tacit collusion between the presidency, the military, the national security services, and the high judiciary, did not secure a proper place for civil society, and it destroyed the tradition of relative pluralism developed in Ottoman society. Yavuz's statement is misleading, however, insofar as it conceals the important fact that the Turkish state adopted new technologies and forms of economic organization, unleashed more competitive forces, and increased exposure to the outside world with the effect of sparking economic growth and modernization.

If the AKP has succeeded in causing the demise of the assertive secularist system and the associated forces of the deep state put into place by the Kemalists, it has neither ended the domination of the state over religion nor the Kemalists' authoritarian tendencies (see, e.g., Morris, 2005). In that sense, a line of continuity exists between the two regimes in spite of a change in values and attitudes of the ruling elite. Kemalism itself was not the sort of radical rupture with Ottoman society that it pretended to be. For one thing, the Ottoman Empire was far from being the religion-dominated system represented in Kemalist ideology; the ulama were civil servants paid by the Ottoman state and under the direct control of the sultan. For another, the Turkish Republic of the Kemalists inherited the secular institutions of the Ottoman Empire, such as the schools, courts, and laws, and it followed the political tradition of central statism that prevailed during the late Ottoman era (Kuru, 2009, pp. 202–3, 214). Under both systems, temporal authority clearly superseded religious authority (İnalcık, 1964, pp. 53–63; Frey, 1964, pp. 211–17; Chambers, 1964, pp. 312–22; Bayar, 2009; Gürbey, 2009; Türkmen, 2009).[10] Zürcher (2010) thus makes a valid point when he writes that Sultan "Abdülhamit's policies of establishing far-reaching state control over the contents of religious education and instruction, his standardization of the sharia and his attempt to use the religious message to increase loyalty to the throne in a sense presage the Young Turk measures aimed at a further subjugation of Islam to the state" (p. 282).

In praising Turkey's Ottoman roots, the AKP regime aims to bridge the gap with the Ottoman past that Kemalists artificially created. There is also a similarity between the AKP's approach to modernity and that of the Young Ottomans who, unlike the Young Turks (who embraced Western civilization in toto) and the Tanzimat bureaucrats (who wanted to pragmatically imitate European institutions and schooling systems), thought that modernizing Turkey could be done while preserving its Islamic identity. Seen in this light, the reappearance of alleged religious symbols, such as the women's headscarf, in the forefront of Turkey's public life should be seen as "reflecting a process of acculturation and entry into the experience of global modernity by participating in the elaboration of an Islamic social image repertory," rather than as manifesting a deep attachment to tradition and religious orthodoxy (Göle, 2011, p. 49).

In this connection, it is interesting to note that, especially under AKP rule, secularist/Kemalist rituals have become very common in everyday life, including regular visits to Atatürk's mausoleum, excessive use of the Turkish flag and images of Atatürk, and proclaiming the slogan, "Turkey is secular and will remain secular" (Kaya, 2013, p. 161). All these acts and slogans, images, and symbols reflected a cult of the hero conceived as the warrior, statesman, and educator whose role was to mold the course of modern Turkish history (Ward and Rustow, 1964, p. 450). As pointed out by Meyda Yeğenoğlu (2012), repeated recourse to them has a religious

---

[10] It is therefore difficult to agree with the statement of Robert Ward and Dankwart Rustow (1964) that "once the traditional Ottoman concept of Faith and Dynasty proved inadequate for survival, religion became a powerful obstacle to modernizing change" in Turkey (p. 443).

connotation by producing a sacralization of the principles of laicism and secularism (p. 296). In the same manner as the strict secularism of the Kemalist state and the barriers to freedom of religion that it erected led to the emergence of Islamist symbols and identity signs, such as the headscarf, the rise of an Islamist party, however moderate, caused the laicists to reinforce their display of Kemalist fervor. Because the symbols used thus serve the function of manifesting political identities in the public sphere, they carry a political and not only a religious or quasi-religious meaning (Kaya, 2013, pp. 162, 166–9).

The growing and assertive presence of Islamist symbols has had the effect of maintaining the deep polarization of Turkish society that the Kemalists brought into being and of strengthening rather than ending the culture of intolerance initiated by them. This is in spite of notable efforts, in the first years of the AKP government, to reach out to the Kurdish and Alevi communities (Kaya, 2013, chs. 3–4). Eventually, things turned out as if Erdoğan and the AKP had overturned the social, cultural, and political system by foregrounding repressed values and attitudes while trying to relegate previously established ones into the background. Charging high taxes on alcoholic drinks, building numerous new mosques and imam hatip schools (which have nearly quadrupled between 2002 and 2014), teaching the old Ottoman language and script in these schools, constructing a madrasa (Islamic seminary) in the courtyard of the Haghia Sophia museum (breeding rumors of a project to reconvert the old church into a mosque), introducing loudspeakers diffusing the Muslim prayer in the midst of large cities, emphasizing gender differentiation and praising women's domestic responsibilities, extolling the Ottoman attributes of the Turkish nation at the expense of other aspects of its legacy – all these manifestations tend to widen rather than reduce the gap between the two parts of Turkish society, that which adheres to the secular values of the Kemalist vision and the one attracted to the values of Islam and religious piety.[11] In other words, there are worrying signs that reconciliation between the two strands is becoming ever more distant under Erdoğan's increasingly authoritarian rule: The AKP has failed to end the logic of intolerance that has characterized Turkey since the demise of the Ottoman Empire (Kaya, 2013; Genc, 2016).

---

[11] In the second half of 2016, the government went so far as proposing a law that would absolve any man found guilty of a rape if he marries his victim. In November, however, the proposal was withdrawn in the face of strong opposition within the AKP itself.

In addition to their polarizing effects on Turkish society, there are other lines of continuity between the Kemalist and the AKP regimes. I already mentioned the continuation of authoritarian tendencies, although under the AKP the meddling of the army in Turkish politics has been brought to an end. Along the same line, it bears emphasis that Erdoğan has maintained tight control over mosques and sermons, even in those European countries where large Turkish immigrant communities live, where control is exerted through the local embassies.[12] Two other important similarities are the continuation of liberal economic policies and the persistence of a strongly nationalistic ideology based on the Sunni-Muslim-Turk holy trinity. Combined with the emphasis on Islamic values and behavior patterns, nationalist fervor allows Erdoğan to project an image of Turkey as a rising power with a specific identity that makes it different from, and better than, most other countries.[13]

9.3 Radical Reforms in Modern Tunisia

There are obvious similarities between the approach to modernization followed by President Bourguiba in Tunisia and by Atatürk in Turkey. Both leaders wanted (1) to get rid of traditional institutions, customs, and symbols; (2) to place religious organizations under state control; and (3) to use largely authoritarian methods to achieve their Westernization objectives. There are some important differences too. Unlike Atatürk, Bourguiba was keen to justify the reforms on the basis of Islam instead of relying entirely on rationalist considerations.

This section first describes President Bourguiba's social reforms while emphasizing that they were enacted in the framework of a personalized dictatorship. The entry of Islamic opposition forces into the political stage is then discussed, drawing attention to the ambivalent strategy of the regime that had previously nurtured these forces to counter the opposition from the left. In the two subsequent subsections, key features of the enduring autocracy of Ben Ali are detailed: the crushing of the Islamists and the rapid expansion of crony capitalism. The section ends with a short review of the Arab Spring and the Islamists' ensuing access to power.

---

[12] In Germany, about half of Turkish mosques are financed by an arm of the Turkish government (DITIP), which sends imams from Turkey (*Economist*, August 6–12, 2016b, p. 20). A similar situation is observed in Belgium, another European country with a strong Turkish immigrant community.

[13] The building of a garish new presidential complex with 1,150 rooms at a cost of $615 million attests to the grandiose ambitions of Erdoğan (*Economist*, January 3–9, 2015, p. 22).

Bourguiba's One-Man Rule

Habib Bourguiba resorted to undemocratic methods to accede to supreme political power immediately after Tunisia gained its independence from France. He coerced Amin Bey, the monarch at the head of the state during the late protectorate period (1943–57), to enact an electoral law guaranteeing that candidates chosen by the political bureau of Bourguiba's Neo-Dustur Party would control the constituent assembly (Mohsen-Finan, 2002, pp. 113–15).[14] This worked according to plan: In the 1957 elections the Neo-Dustur list won all the seats in the assembly, despite low participation rates in some parts of the country. The partisans of Salah Ben Yusuf, Bourguiba's arch-rival and scion of a prosperous merchant family with close ties to Tunisia's traditional commercial and religious elite, were thus deprived of the possibility to express a preference. Interestingly, both men had been close associates in the Neo-Dustur Party before independence, but their relationship gradually deteriorated, largely because of personal tensions and different views regarding tactics and global orientations. Whereas Ben Yusuf thought Tunisia should strengthen its links to the Arab world and anchor its newly emerging national identity in Islam, Bourguiba wanted his country to turn unambiguously to the West. The tension between the two leaders led to a confrontation that brought the country to the brink of civil war just before independence, which was granted by France in 1956. Following the defeat of Ben Yusuf after a campaign carefully orchestrated by Bourguiba at a party congress in November 1955, some of his followers engaged to violence against Neo-Dustur. While Ben Yusuf fled to Cairo, fellagha bands took arms in the economically depressed regions in the south and the west. To tame the pro-Yusufist fellagha rebellion, Bourguiba required the cooperation of the French army and police, because Tunisia's armed forces, which consisted of only a few thousand men, were inadequate to the task. On the later order of Bourguiba, Ben Yusuf was assassinated during a trip to Frankfurt in 1961 (Toumi, 1989, pp. 18–26; Perkins, 2004, pp. 115–31; Mahjoubi, 1982; Alexander, 2010, pp. 31–4).

---

[14] Bourguiba accused Amin Bey of treason on the grounds that he consented in the early 1950s to the French-mandated reforms establishing equal rights and prerogatives between French and Tunisian residents. This accusation was quite opportunistic because Bourguiba himself had been accommodating to French interests on more than one occasion (certainly to a larger extent than his political rival, Ben Yusuf), generally on pragmatic grounds. The fact of the matter is that he wanted to get rid of the Husseinid monarchy and establish a republic of which he was to be the sole leader.

In the meantime, the High Court of Justice tried 128 rebels, among whom 123 were partisans of Ben Yusuf, on the grounds that they had plotted Bourguiba's murder. In October 1959, fifteen of the rebels were condemned to death and immediately executed (Toumi, 1989, p. 25).[15] Before imposing that sentence the High Court also sued political opponents on the grounds that they either collaborated with the French (their incomes being therefore "ill-gotten") or displayed attitudes of "national indignity." Other, softer tactics involved the creation of rival organizations to weaken an existing one that posed a threat or the coerced resignation of a dissenting leader. The latter fate was (temporarily) imposed on Ben Salah, the leader of the trade union organization associated with the Neo-Dustur Party, when he dared express disagreement with Bourguiba.

Within a few years, Bourguiba succeeded in creating a political system that, in spite of being officially a republic, was actually a "presidential monarchy." Legislative and executive powers were bestowed on the president, who served as both head of the state and head of government. The assembly was rendered toothless by being relegated to a largely advisory role. The judiciary was also placed under his control. Because Bourguiba also retained his position as the secretary-general of the Neo-Dustur Party, "he stood at the apex of a system weaving together the institutions of the party, the state, and the national organisations" (Perkins, 2004, p. 133). Moreover, to achieve maximum control over Tunisian citizens, Neo-Dustur operated a huge patronage network that showered favors on loyal followers. Access to government jobs was conditioned on Neo-Dustur membership. The key qualification for the more important posts was typically the applicant's military record rather than skills or competence-based merit.

Bourguiba was a self-confident and even arrogant person who did not tolerate opposition. He was convinced that "his ideas, judgments, and interpretations of events had inherently greater worth than those of others" (Perkins, 2004, p. 206). He was able "to act cynically in the name of his ambitious plans, and never allowed doubts to arise, especially when his destiny was concerned" (Toumi, 1989, p. 20; my translation; see also Alexander, 2010,

---

[15] The so-called Yusufist plot followed the disaster of Bizerte, when President Bourguiba decided to launch the Tunisian army, although it was totally unprepared, against French troops in July 1961. As a motivation for his action, Bourguiba then argued that the decision of the French government to enlarge its military base at Bizerte was incompatible with Tunisian sovereignty. In December 1962, a group of Tunisian army officers, shocked and humiliated by the Bizerte affair, plotted a coup against Bourguiba (Toumi, 1989, pp. 48–51). Some argue that Bourguiba's decision in Bizerte was a calculated move to get rid of much of the officer corps, dominated by Yusufists.

p. 28). He surrounded himself with a loyal coterie of sycophant followers among whom none of the first-generation leaders of Neo-Dustur was to be found. At some point and on some issue, all of those earlier leaders had fallen out with him and been considered guilty of betrayal or abandonment in moments of crisis (Cohen, 1986; Toumi, 1989, p. 21; Perkins, 2004, p. 133).

When in 1964 the Neo-Dustur party was renamed the Parti Socialiste Dusturien (Dustur Socialist Party, or PSD) after a shift in focus to economic planning and state socialism, it was the only officially recognized political party in the country (the Communist Party of Tunisia had been banned in 1963). It then held a tighter grip than ever on the state and society. After the regional governors started to represent both the state and the PSD, the subservience of the state to the PSD became complete (Perkins, 2004, p. 147). Moreover, because Bourguiba tended "to formulate policy unilaterally or in consultation only with a coterie of cronies, giving short shrift to government ministers and party officials," the party-state system of Tunisia genuinely was tantamount to a one-man rule (p. 207). Autocracy was especially strong because the ruler's erratic and vindictive behaviour prevented him from trusting even his closest associates. He thus frequently rotated his top aides, removing them from top positions and calling them back as circumstances justified.[16] Because he ignored the results of elections inside his own party and chose to place obedient stooges rather than competent and committed persons in the central committee, the PSD became a self-devouring machine that gradually lost its sense of purpose: "From a party-state, the PSD was transformed into a party of the state" and was soon deserted or opposed by the younger generations (Toumi, 1989, p. 88; my translation). The indisputability of Bourguiba's power became most manifest when in 1974 he was "offered" a lifetime appointment to the position of party president by the PSD's political bureau after his designation of its members had been quasi-institutionalized (pp. 88–9; see also Alexander, 2010, p. 45). In

---

[16] In such circumstances, Bourguiba could display an unbelievable measure of cynicism. Thus, for example, when he demoted Prime Minister Ahmed Ben Salah after a disastrous attempt to bring socialism to the country, "almost overnight, Ben Salah went from being the country's economic czar to a jailed criminal accused of mismanaging the country's economy. Bourguiba expelled him and his supporters from the government and the party. ... Through it all, Bourguiba claimed that he had been duped. The economic mess was all Ben Salah's doing. Bourguiba claimed no responsibility beyond having allowed Ben Salah to amass too much power" (Alexander, 2010, p. 43). These statements of denial of responsibility were just incredible, coming from a man "who had carefully planned and directed every aspect of Tunisia's political life for more than two decades, the man who evaluated every decision in terms of its impact on his power" (p. 43).

the words of Kenneth Perkins (2004), "Although the monarchy had been abolished soon after independence, in all but title Bourguiba became the bey, exercising his authority, working and residing in his palaces, and reveling in the pageantry and rituals once reserved for the Husseinid rulers. The elections that confirmed him in office resembled nothing so much as the *bai'a*, the oath of fealty sworn to the bey by his retainers" (p. 208).

A similar but even starker judgment was issued by Yadh Ben Achour (1987). He claimed that Bourguiba always had a particular view of the rule of law, seeing himself as the source of all legitimacy. Quoting Ben Achour, "His decisions are above the law. The rule of law exists only below the stage where he himself is standing. ... He is an order, above all orders. Even the state cannot claim the legitimacy that he has. On the contrary, state legitimacy is derived from his own person. His leadership transcends the state" (p. 157; my translation). Bourguiba's numerous public declarations to the effect that he was acting "for and through the people" were mystifying in that he never took any steps to enable popular participation in political decision making.[17] The truth is that he had a quite paternalistic approach to the people's role and a *dirigiste* sense of the management of the state (Cohen, 1986). He was a distant leader who ruled based on the idea that the people of his country owed him a great debt of gratitude. All his references to "popular legitimacy" were therefore false and designed to conceal his adept instrumentalization of the people's will (Camau, 1987, p. 30).

Bourguiba's Radical Social Reforms

Bourguiba was always convinced that he had a mission to fulfill for his country and that he knew better than anyone else what had to be done to promote its social and economic development. As the founding father of the modern Tunisian nation, he saw himself as a patriarch entitled to lead and to teach his people, and the considerable power that he quickly accumulated was therefore fully justified. In the general euphoria following Tunisia's independence, he also felt that he could ride on a wave of popular support to embark on drastic social reforms. He chose to direct his first efforts to establish state control over religion, taking steps of which Ben Yusuf would have certainly disapproved. As his first act, he confiscated the land property of

---

[17] Thus, when confronted with opposition to his agrarian reform, Bourguiba declared, "When rebellious elements refuse to be persuaded and prove immune to the appeal to reason, punishment must be meted out on them so as to prevent evil and discourage those who, following their example, might be tempted to threaten *the achievements of the people*" (cited by Toumi, 1989, p. 59; my translation and my emphasis).

the Habus Council, which was in charge of administering land earmarked for mosques, Quranic schools, and charitable Islamic institutions.

A second, double-edged measure adopted by Bourguiba in 1956 was even more drastic: the absorption of the two sharia courts (for adherents of the Maleki and the Hanefi schools, respectively) into the state judicial system and that of the al-Nahda al-Nahda Mosque-University into the state education system. In 1961, this prestigious educational institution became the faculty of theology at the University of Tunis. State control over the Islamic courts facilitated the next step, the promulgation of a Personal Status Code considered the most progressive family code adopted in an Arab country in the twentieth century. Designed to strengthen the nuclear family and reduce existing inequities between men and women, it forbade polygamy, granted women the right of divorce and to approve arranged marriages, expanded women's rights in matters of inheritance and child custody, set minimum ages for marriage, and ended the male right of repudiation (the unilateral decision to divorce). However, the code did not go as far as establishing strict equality in inheritance rights: Husbands continued to be considered the head of the household, implying that only his place of residence could serve as a conjugal residence.

Two important points should be made here. First, in line with Bourguiba's leadership style as described in the previous subsection, the Personal Status Code was enacted without any pressure from women's organizations and without any consultation with the population. The Union Nationale des Femmes Tunisiennes (National Union of Tunisian Women, or UNFT), formed within the ambit of the Neo-Dustur Party, was more concerned with obtaining civil and political equality with men – the right to vote and to stand for elected office and a greater priority placed on female education – than with an expansion of individual rights. The rural masses placed priority on literacy, health, and family planning measures, even though after the promulgation of the Personal Status Code, the UNFT agreed to make special efforts to promote it in areas where women and men alike had reservations about the reforms (Perkins, 2004, p. 138).

Second, it is noteworthy that, unlike Atatürk and his followers in Turkey, Bourguiba did not justify the new code on rationalist grounds, but rather in the name of a rejuvenated Islamic law. More precisely, he talked about a new ijtihad – a renewed attempt to freely use the power of reason with a view to elaborating legal solutions to present-day problems according to the general principles of Islam. His characteristic self-confidence enabled Bourguiba to break with the centuries-old tradition of classical Islam that held sway after the closure of the ijtihad in the eleventh century.

By "reopening the ijtihad," he tried to bring Tunisia into the modern world without having recourse to an opposition between Western-inspired legislation and religion, or between modernity and tradition.

Three essential ideas guided Bourguiba in his reform efforts. First, they emphasized the value of concrete action for the resolution of real-life problems of daily living. Second, they asserted the sacred place of reason in Islam, attributing the backwardness and decadence of Muslim societies to their refusal to grant reason its due place and their consequent entrapping in tradition and imitation. Finally, they extolled the importance of study and new interpretations of sacred texts in enabling the renaissance of the Muslim community (Camau and Geisser, 2004). The claim that Bourguiba pursued secularization is thus an exaggeration: Instead of creating a separation between state and religion, he initiated a system in which "the state head becomes a sort of pre-eminent imam vested with the role of a spiritual guide of the country while the official ulama and imams are transformed into cadres and agents of the public administration" (Toumi, 1989, p. 116; my translation). In this sense, Bouguiba followed a well-established tradition observed in earlier Muslim empires and kingdoms (see Chapter 4).

Even though Bourguiba failed to obtain a fatwa approving his new policies, the religious establishment expressed little opposition to the Personal Status Code and even to the drastic institutional reforms described earlier. This is because he engaged in a variety of measures to co-opt the clerics. Bourguiba appointed a moderately progressive person as rector of the Zaituna Mosque-University, and in reorganizing the sharia courts he was clever enough to reassign and retire some judges whom he did not trust. To other prominent members of the religious establishment, he offered various perks and material advantages. Such skilful tactics, directly inspired by the politico-religious relations of Muslim empires and kingdoms (see Chapter 4), worked reasonably well in Tunisia, at least for a while. Moreover, the lack of opposition of the official ulama to Bourguiba's reforms was facilitated by their earlier collaboration with the colonial regime, which had considerably weakened their position and influence. Not only had they failed to play a significant role in the struggle for independence but they had also inherited a privileged economic and social status (Zeghal, 2002). It is worth remembering that the ulama vigorously opposed the Neo-Destourians before independence when the party used a religious argument and language to prevent Tunisians from adopting the French nationality. The Neo-Destourians proclaimed that abandoning the Tunisian nationality in favor of the French one was an act of apostasy. The ulama of Tunis retaliated by issuing a fatwa allowing adoption of the colonial power's nationality (Toumi, 1989, p. 115).[18] Regarding the ulama's privileged status, it is useful to cite Mohsen Toumi (1989) at some length:

The ulama, in fact, constituted an oligarchy regrouping a small number of family dynasties at the heart of the Tunisian bourgeoisie. Through hereditary links and through co-option, this oligarchic group had monopolised the best positions in the sectors of education, justice, jurisprudence, and mosque management. During a long period of time, too, it expressed support for the colonial order. ... On the one hand, thanks to family relationships, its members were allied to the feudal class of big landowners in the interior of the country and, on the other hand, they hunted down and eliminated all upholders of modernity, especially if they did not belong to their social group or threatened their cultural existence. ... The targets of the Zaituna people were not so much selected on the grounds that they did not serve Islam well, or violated its law, but rather because they were guilty of denouncing the decadence caused by those who had arrogated to themselves the monopoly of Islam. ... The ulama were thus projecting a negative image of their religion, and they continuously re-invented justifications for the continuation of the colonial order, which was precisely the political service that the colonial authorities required from them. ... The stake behind such a compromising support was nothing else than the rewards received by the ulama in terms of social power, immovable assets, and substantial incomes since the Zaituna possessed considerable *Habus* (indivisible) assets the usufruct of which accrued, since centuries, to the same families of qadis (judges) and mourids (teachers). (pp. 114–15; my translation)

As for ulama who did not occupy socially enviable positions and for students from the Zaituna Mosque- University who were usually recruited from the interior provinces or from the provincial petite bourgeoisie (in contrast to their teachers who typically belonged to the grande bourgeoisie of Tunis), they did not wield sufficient power to stop reforms that they disliked (Salem, 1984, p. 176; Perkins, 2004, p. 137).

Let us now turn to the issue of dress. In this area, Bourguiba held views similar to those of Atatürk, although he did not put them into practice with the heavy-handed determination of the Turkish leader. He launched a campaign to disparage all forms of traditional attire, veiling in particular. He indeed believed, and expressed the belief, that wearing traditional dress was an old-fashioned habit encouraging retrograde modes of thinking and behavior and, consciously or not, expressing a rejection of modernity. In repeated speeches, he went as far as condemning the veil as an "odious rag" that "demeaned women, had no practical value, and was not obligatory in

---

[18] Collaborators with the French colonial power were rewarded by being given land for colonization during the protectorate, a fact that served as a rationalization for Bourguiba's right to seize these lands and redistribute them as private property among the heirs of the founder of the Habus Council (Toumi, 1989, p. 115).

order to conform to Islamic standards of modesty" (Perkins, 2004, p. 137). He made equally contemptuous remarks about male traditional garments and always appeared in public in a coat and tie. Understanding how deep-rooted these clothing habits were in Tunisian culture, he nevertheless did not enforce any ban, except the prohibition of veiling in classrooms (p. 138). He preferred to invest heavily in education, hoping that these habits would gradually vanish on their own, thus opting for persuasion rather than the use of force. Yet it was only in 1991, under the next president, that a law passed making school attendance mandatory for all children between ages six and sixteen.

Bourguiba's most serious mistake in matters of religious reforms turned out to be his disparaging remarks about the fasting ritual of Ramadan. He went so far as appearing on television eating a full plate at mid-day during the Ramadan period, which outraged believers. In a 1960 speech, he announced the beginning of a jihad against underdevelopment, noting that involvement in this jihad absolved Tunisians from the religious obligation of fasting. To sanction this personal interpretation as a product of ijtihad, he demanded a fatwa of endorsement from the mufti of Tunis. The latter did not oblige in a manner that Bourguiba deemed fully satisfactory, so he was fired. Tensions did not abate, and during the next year, as Bourguiba prepared to renew his campaign, riots occurred in Kairouan, a venerable religious center and a Yusufist stronghold since well before independence. Its influential ulama openly denigrated the president's views of Islam, and they contested his claim to act as a religious authority entitled to engage in ijtihad. Repression ensued, and Bourguiba alleged that the dissenting religious leaders were actually motivated by their resentment caused by the loss of their economic power after the confiscation of habus lands. This was eventually a lost battle for the president, who came to understand that "the vast majority of Tunisians had no intention of breaking with the fundamental religious practices that defined them as Muslims" (Perkins, 2004, p. 141).

The contemptuous attitude of President Bourguiba toward erstwhile customs and religious habits, and the antagonisms that it aroused, were in striking contrast to the more flexible and tolerant attitude that he displayed during the pre-independence period. At that time, he seemed to understand that the popular masses in Tunisia would only change their political positions when issues were presented in terms of Islam, because Islam was the source of the cultural images and modes of behavior required for recognition of the injustices inherent in the colonial situation (Salem,

1984, p. 100). For example, in the pursuit of independence, the message was spread that no sacrifice should be spared and the psychosis of martyrdom was developed by reading aloud, in public meetings, Quranic verses that eulogize those who perish for their faith (p. 110). Around the same time, Neo-Dusturian leaders did not hesitate "to use the mosques as their means for spreading their ideas under the guise of lessons in Islamic history" (p. 101). In a sense, Bourguiba's later proclivity to use ijtihad to justify modernizing reforms and to refer to Islam to vindicate particular actions was in the same vein. Thus, he invoked the concept of jihad both to justify the struggle for independence and the struggle against underdevelopment, in the name of which the obligation of fasting could be dispensed with. The only difference between the two uses of the concept is that only in the latter instance did it entail the violation of a well-established religious ritual.

The contrast between Bourguiba's actions and attitudes before and after independence is most stark in his writings about veiling. In 1929, in an article titled "The Veil" (Le voile), he saw it as part of the distinctive social customs of Islam and as a component of the Tunisian personality:

I have raised in neat and precise terms the great social problem that has always pervaded our discussions: do we want to hasten, without any transition, the disappearance of our habits and mores, whether good or bad, and of all those small things that together form our personality? My answer, given the special circumstances in which we live, has always been categorically no! (cited by Salem, 1984, p. 133; my translation)

Elsewhere, Bourguiba reasserted the same position by proclaiming, "Evolution must take place, lest we should die. It will happen, but without break, without rupture, so that we can maintain a unity of our personality that can be perceived as such by our consciences at any point of time in the continuous changes that we are experimenting" (cited by Salem, 1984, p. 135; Toumi, 1989, p. 113; my translation). In other words, the status of women, like other questions arising from tradition, had to be linked to the national question. When the central problem was to create unity and social cohesion in order to attain political independence, respect for traditional habits and customs had to prevail, because they provided a system of collective representations keeping the mass of people together in harsh circumstances that demanded many sacrifices. In a context of war against external enemies, religion was an invaluable asset supplying the justification and social cohesion necessary for momentous change. After independence, however, the situation changed. In Bourguiba's vision,

Tunisia had to be modernized and Westernized, which justified a change in the attitude toward tradition and religion.

A complication in this interpretation is that, before independence, Bourguiba was increasingly toning down his appeals to Islam, avoiding Islamic themes in his speeches to instead stress the values of "national unity." The decisive factor behind that change seems to have been his growing conflict with Ben Yusuf, from whom he wanted to differentiate himself. Since Ben Yusuf tended to emphasize references to Islam, Bourguiba chose to downplay them (Salem, 1984, p. 155). In that regard, Ben Yusuf seems to have been more consistent and less opportunistic than Bourguiba, who was determined to Westernize his country and to ally himself with Western powers rather than with other Arab countries.

The Entry of Islamic Opposition Forces onto the Stage

The experiment in planning and socialism that the regime initiated in 1962 proved to be a dismal failure (Toumi, 1989, pp. 57–70). It also aroused bitter and furious reactions from the traditional stalwarts of the PSD, the big landowners who felt threatened by the prime minister's declared intention, at the start of 1969, to bring all farmland into the cooperative system. In the face of highly vocal opposition, Bourguiba dismissed his prime minister and changed tactics by shifting to the opposite option of liberalizing the economy. That option worked much better in the sense that significant economic growth resumed, but it did not resolve the problems of wealth inequality and, especially, interregional disparities. Thus, economic prosperity continued to be concentrated along the coast and in the Tunis area; the south, center, and west regions, in which the most severe levels of unemployment were traditionally seen, remained seriously underdeveloped. Moreover, urban unemployment of young people reached intolerably high levels – almost 50 percent for young men aged between fifteen and twenty-five in the mid-1970s (Radwan, Jamil, and Ghose, 1990, pp. 25–6). Social tensions grew, and anger against the regime sharpened because of the lack of any political liberalization to accompany economic liberalization. The highly centralized, authoritarian power structure of the PSD stifled any internal criticism, and the freedom to express opposing political viewpoints remained severely curbed at all levels. In fact, Bourguiba crushed any nascent tendency toward democratization of the inner workings of both the PSD and the state apparatus. And on returning from lengthy health treatment abroad, he immediately reasserted his unquestionable authority and silenced his critics.

These economic difficulties, which created a gulf between state and society, led to two traumatic events.[19] The first occurred in January 1978, when a general strike launched by the trade union organization associated with the PSD, the General Union of Tunisian Workers (UGTT, or Union Générale des Travailleurs Tunisiens), was ruthlessly quashed by the regime's police under the orders of General Zine al-Abidine Ben Ali. The second set of disturbances occurred exactly six years later, in January 1984, when public outrage was sparked by the removal of subsidies on basic staples (Alexander, 2010, pp. 49–52). Low food prices, a safety valve introduced by the government to mitigate poverty, were discontinued under the pressure of the IMF and the World Bank, which were concerned by the country's macroeconomic imbalances, such as the deepening budget deficit and the growing foreign debt burden. The police and army brutally quelled the riots. Bourguiba, personally criticized for his role in the crisis, immediately ordered the restoration of the subsidies. By the same token, he asked Ben Ali to resume his position as director general of national security, which he had left for an ambassadorial appointment in Europe.

In the meantime, Bourguiba was forced to make an apparent concession to the opposition voices demanding political pluralism. He invited political organizations to present lists of candidates for the 1981 national elections, but on the condition that "they did not draw support from outside the country, did not advocate class struggle or sectarianism, and agreed to avoid criticisms of the 'president for life'" (Perkins, 2004, p. 167). That this measure was a farcical attempt to manage the opposition became clear after the results of the election were made public. Not one of the accepted organizations cleared the 5 percent threshold required to enter the parliament. Among the organizations whose accreditation had been refused, and would be consistently refused later, was the Mouvement de la Tendance Islamique (Islamic Tendency Movement, or MTI), a radical Islamic movement founded in 1981 and led by Rachid al-Ghannouchi and Abd al-Fattah Mourou. MTI was concerned not only with the moral and ethical aspects of people's lives but also with the need for a more representative political system and a reversal of ruinous economic policies. Its followers were primarily recruited among the disadvantaged sections of the population but also the movement was joined by many middle-class men and women "who turned to their Islamic heritage when both socialism and capitalism failed to fulfil the expectations of prosperity and security they had raised" (p. 166).

---

[19] For more details, see Toumi (1989, ch. 4) and Perkins (2004, ch. 6).

It is worth noting that, following a scenario discussed in detail in Chapter 6, before turning against the Islamists, Bourguiba and the government nurtured them as a way to counter leftist forces in the country. Islamists were thus released from jail and their publications allowed to appear again when political calculations pointed to the need to deliver "a stick to the left and a carrot to the right" (Burgat and Dowell, 1993, p. 198). Islamist demonstrations were thus encouraged with a priority target in mind: the University of Tunis where leftist student organizations were particularly active, including left-wing Destourians and communists. Violent encounters on university campuses were typically sparked by well-organized and determined Islamist movements. At the same time, in the early 1970s, the first associations were formed for the defense of the Quran, and inside the mosques of Tunis, there were the first Islamist circles. Revealingly, the former organizations were granted free use of meeting facilities located in the offices of the PSD federations themselves, not only in Tunis but also in the interior of the country. As often observed in this type of situation, the Islamist movement soon extended its activities beyond university campuses to reach practically all sectors of Tunisian society. It was these Islamists who destroyed and thus forced the closure of cafés and restaurants in Sfax in September 1977 to ensure proper respect of Ramadan (Toumi, 1989, pp. 116–17).

Popular enthusiasm for the MTI caused serious worries among those at the top of the state apparatus, and both al-Ghannouchi and al-Fattah Mourou, as well as many of its adherents, were arrested on charges of defaming the "president for life." Yet, in the 1981 elections, candidates linked to the MTI fared as well as, and often better than, their secular counterparts. A few years later, the movement called for a national referendum on the Personal Status Code, contending that its promulgation had led to a massive entry of women into the labor force, causing a significant rise in male unemployment. In this way, the code allegedly undermined social and family life based on the principle of a neat differentiation between gender roles, and it eroded the traditional role and status of men as breadwinners. In addition to these typically patriarchal concerns, the MTI advocated for limits on contact between the sexes and the revival of traditional attire as a symbol of rejection of foreign influence (Perkins, 2004, pp. 168–72).

In the 1980s the conflict between the regime and the MTI quickly escalated. The two held diametrically opposed views of Tunisia's future: one Western-oriented and secular, and the other inspired by Islamic values. Bourguiba and his closest associates were convinced, and the perception was probably correct, that the MTI intended to seize power and establish an

Islamic state. Ben Ali, acting under presidential orders, deployed the vast resources of the Interior Ministry, of which he had become the head, to crush the Islamic movement. When, in August 1987, bombs exploded at tourist hotels in Sousse and Monastir (the hometown of Bourguiba), leaders of the MTI were immediately blamed. The death penalty was pronounced against several key leaders, including Ghannouchi, and lengthy prison terms were imposed on scores of lower-level militants.

The end of Bourguiba's rule was also marked by the collapse of the multiparty experiment. Its failure became clear when all the legitimate parties, except the PSD, decided to boycott the municipal elections in 1985 and the national elections in 1986. Mutual mistrust was so complete and disarray so visible inside the PSD that "relations among the stars often resembled a wholesale slaughter in which everybody was in turn bowl and skittle" (Toumi, 1989, p. 130; my translation). Bourguiba moved against the liberal opposition, not hesitating to order the arrest of Ahmad Mestiri (a previous minister of national defense whom he had earlier expelled from the party), while at the same time appointing hard-nosed party conservatives to important ministerial positions. International financial institutions again required the government to make deep cuts in food subsidies, and the gulf between state and society continued to widen (Alexander, 2010, pp. 49–50). Popular anger was repressed under the instructions of an old and sick man who adamantly refused to relinquish the power that he had wielded for a half-century, despite more and more evident signs of disintegration of the state. In November 1987, no longer incapable of assuming his leadership functions because of his poor physical and mental health, Bourguiba was succeeded by Ben Ali, who had supported all the repressive measures under his reign and whom he had promoted to the office of prime minister one month earlier.

Crushing of the Islamists under Enduring Autocracy: The Ben Ali Era (I)

On his accession to power, to convey a message of change, Ben Ali changed the name of the PSD to Rassemblement Constitutionnel Démocratique (RCD, or Democratic Constitutional Rally) (Toumi, 1989, pp. 237–9). Yet, the fusion between the party and the state was left intact: Like his predecessor, Ben Ali was simultaneously head of state, head of government, and head of the sole effective political party. More substantial measures taken at the start of the new presidency consisted of the freeing of political prisoners, including Ghannouchi and other MTI detainees, and inviting Tunisian exiles to return to their country. Although Ben Ali had no sympathy for the MTI, he opted for a tactic other than the one chosen by Bourguiba. Believing that the Islamists represented a greater potential threat "outside the political tent than within it," he bowed to some of its more symbolic demands (Perkins, 2004, p. 187). He publicly affirmed Islam as the state religion, authorized radio and television stations to broadcast the call for prayer, made a highly publicized pilgrimage to Mecca, and legalized a MTI student organization. The National Pact (1988), however, which proclaimed the centrality of the Arab and Islamic heritages of Tunisia and called for closer ties between Tunisia and other Arab countries, coexisted with Ben Ali's publicly stated support for the Personal Status Code, deemed to be an unassailable achievement of modern Tunisia. In agreeing to sign the pact, which also contained statements promoting pluralism, basic freedoms, and human rights, the MTI therefore made a major concession.

The tactic of issuing the National Pact thus followed a well-established tradition of autocratic rulers of past Muslim empires: While making symbolic concessions, the state ensured its control over religion on more substantial matters: modernizing secular reforms that implied a considerable erosion of the power and prestige of religious authorities. That the Pact was merely a tactical move became clear when the MTI was deemed ineligible for the 1989 elections despite changing its name (from MTI to Hizb al-Nahda, or Renaissance Party) to conform to the electoral law prohibiting the use of religious terminology. Islamist leaders were thus compelled to seek votes through an independent list. They were therefore on solid ground when they accused the government of impeding the emergence of a genuinely pluralistic democracy by excluding Islamic organizations from elections. In point of fact, the regime continued to fear that, once in power al-Nahda would dismantle the secular state established by Bourguiba.

In the 1989 elections, in which token opposition was provided by six other party lists, the RCD won a landslide victory, obtaining almost 80 percent of the votes and all the available parliamentary seats, thereby displaying a marked continuity with the Bourguiba era (Perkins, 2004, p. 189; Owen, 2012, p. 76). Secular opposition parties were clearly no match for the dominant party backed by the state apparatus, but al-Nahda independents fared better by garnering more than 15 percent of the popular vote (and more than 30 percent in the Tunis suburbs). Renewed demand by al-Nahda for official recognition after the elections again led nowhere, and Ghannouchi became more confrontational as a result. A vicious cycle was thus set up: Ben Ali would respond to the inflammatory rethoric of al-Nahda's leader by casting himself in the position of the defender of the secular republic to which most Tunisians adhered. This enabled him to crack down harshly on the Islamists, especially after sympathizers of al-Nahda began to indulge in acts of indiscriminate violence (in 1990–1) and events in neighboring Algeria redoubled the fear of an Islamist takeover. The most prominent figures of the movement, including Ghannouchi, who was tried in absentia (he had fled to Algeria), received sentences of life imprisonment.

In the parliamentary elections of 1994, in keeping with the pattern of every previous election, the RCD captured more than 90 percent of the total vote in every district in the country. It is revealing that the majority of secular Tunisians turned a blind eye to the excesses committed by the authorities, which were documented by the Tunisian League of Human Rights and included numerous cases of torture by security services and legal irregularities during the course of trials. The leader of the League, Moncef Marzouki, attempted to run in the 1994 election, but his candidacy was rejected by the government, which constituted another blow to democracy in that he was the only person seriously challenging the incumbent. Worse, he was arrested afterward "on charges that his calls for greater political freedom and the legalisation of al-Nahda defamed the state." This marked a new political course in which the government directed its wrath against "outspoken secular political opponents and human rights advocates who now joined al-Nahda militants as political prisoners" (Perkins, 2004, p. 197).

Before the 1999 presidential elections, two new political movements – the Forum Démocratique pour le Travail et les Libertés, or FDTL (Democratic Forum for Work and Freedoms) and the Conseil National des Libertés en Tunisie, or CNLT (National Council for Liberties in Tunisia) – were denied legal status as parties, attesting again that the regime was not serious about political pluralism. Running against two token opponents who were deemed eligible, Ben Ali received 98 percent of the votes cast, while legislative elections had results similar to those of previous elections. A few years later, 99.5 percent of voting Tunisians supported a constitutional amendment enabling Ben Ali to extend his presidency beyond his third term. This was a sobering step in a country that had directly suffered from the folly of granting life tenure to Bourguiba (Perkins, 2004, p. 202; Owen, 2012, p. 77).

Elections were carefully managed by the Ministry of the Interior to project both a false appearance of competition and a satisfactory image to foreign donors. Opponents wishing to play by the regime's rule were guaranteed an increasing number of seats in the parliament, reaching a maximum of 53 in a chamber of 212 members in the 2009 elections. Yet the domination of Ben Ali remained complete, because the opposition was malleable and had been co-opted, and critics were quickly silenced on trumped-up charges (Owen, 2012, pp. 77, 79).

The Ministry of the Interior secretly engineered not only the elections but also all sectors of the administration and the president's party. From the early 1990s onward, it had the responsibility of making all hiring and firing decisions in the public sector. It first verified whether the applicant was affiliated with the RCD. If so, the National Security Services then checked whether he or she was personally an Islamist sympathizer or if one of his close relatives was. From the late 1990s, the state security forces checked not only whether the applicant or any close relative could be suspected of Islamism but also whether there was any suspicion that the applicant belonged to any form of opposition to the regime. Likewise, any permanently employed public servant could be fired on a simple instruction, even a verbal one, from the ministry. And if an administrative court ever ruled that the public servant had been unfairly dismissed, that reversal decision was never enforced.

The omnipresence of the ministry of interior was most strikingly reflected in the wide range of political security services under its auspices: state security, special services, general information services, orientation services, municipal police, presidential security, and the services of the national guard. In addition, agencies such as the customs services, fiscal authorities, external trade, and health departments could all be mobilized to fulfill police missions or to follow politically motivated instructions. Under the direction of the Ministry of the Interior, security services as well as those outside agencies used the tools of surveillance, control, intimidation, dissuasion, and even punishment. Thanks to the existence of this all-pervasive network of surveillance, which used even taxi drivers as police informants, the information file of an applicant could either open the door or block access to employment, to administrative services, to enrolling in a university, to receiving permission to start an independent activity, and so forth (Hibou, 2006a, pp. 96–9).

Béatrice Hibou, who has meticulously studied the repressive apparatus of Tunisia, writes about the "trivialisation of the police system" to characterize the evolution of the political system from the late 1980s:

The pervasive presence of the de facto unique party, the doubling of the state administration by a party bureaucratic apparatus, the criss-crossing of the whole country by networks of tight surveillance, or the personality cult around the president's figure have been the hallmarks of Tunisia's political system since independence. Beginning with the late 1980s, what has been added is a growing intrusion by the police into the private life of the people ... the rising influence of the ministry of interior and the multiplication of police interventions have epitomised this shift from a system of control over society to a system of control over individuals. ... The police has this special characteristic that it can merge into the whole social body and pay considerable attention to the most minute details of people's lives. (Hibou, 2006a, p. 98; my translation)

Crony Capitalism under Enduring Autocracy: The Ben Ali Era (II)

If, on the political front, liberalization remained blocked to the despair of many people, the situation was different on the economic front. From the mid-1990s onward, rapid economic growth resumed, and foreign investment increased dramatically. As a result of a major privatization program prescribed by the IMF and the World Bank, the weak private sector started to expand, and prosperity accrued to many middle-class people (Perkins, 2004, pp. 202–3). This segment of Tunisians tacitly provided a measure of legitimacy to the coercive state of Ben Ali because they were protected from the threat posed by Islamists and enjoyed the benefits of the new economic opportunities made available to secular and educated urban dwellers.

Yet, most of the benefits of this economic group were appropriated by the regime's clique, which acted increasingly as a band of cronies making a good living out of "protection racket politics" (Brumberg, 2014). This system was associated with the regime of "total autocracy" or a "bully praetorian state" (Springborg, 2014, p. 151) described earlier, in which the state and the dominant party were deeply interconnected.[20] In the terminology used in this book, Ben Ali's regime can be characterized as one of kleptocratic (or predatory) autocracy. The tightly managed police state set up by Bourguiba and reinforced by Ben Ali operated for the benefit of the president, his close relatives, and a small circle of friends and advisers. Hibou's estimates that 1 percent of the population worked for the police does not include the army

[20] Daniel Brumberg (2014) contrasts total or full autocracies with liberalized autocracies defined as "political systems in which the ruling elite uses a mix of overlapping formal and informal institutions to structure a political game in which contending groups are allowed to express themselves" (p. 47). More pointedly, the leaders of a liberalized autocracy "have sustained their power not by relying on a single-party political machine but, rather, by manipulating a dense network of formal and informal bodies that funnel various benefits to myriad constituencies organised in a diverse array of institutions, including parliaments, parties, professional associations, charitable organisations, and non governmental organisations or civil society groups" (p. 47). Here is thus a system of "state-managed quasi pluralism" that "produces a level of conflict and fragmentation in society that abets autocratic rule" (p. 48). Examples of such liberalized autocracies are Morocco, Egypt, Jordan, and Kuwait. Examples of full or total autocracies are Syria, Tunisia, Saddam Hussein's Iraq, and Muammar Gaddafi's Libya (p. 49).

of informants working for the security services. Altogether, direct and indirect employment in these services sustained about one-tenth of the population (Hibou, 2006b). To these staggeringly high figures, one must add that the RCD itself, with its thousands of local branches throughout the whole country, acted more like a security apparatus than a political party (Beau and Tuqoi, 1999; Hibou, 2006a).

Tunisia's huge repressive apparatus allowed the presidential clique, and the president's wife in particular, to amass considerable wealth for themselves. Especially attractive opportunities were provided by the economic liberalization reforms, above all the measures to privatize state companies. The crony capitalism that then developed was in marked contrast to the Bourguiba era, when the president's family was only peripherally involved in economic activities. As explained by Roger Owen (2012), under Ben Ali methods of illicit enrichment included the following: "the privatisation of state assets such as hotels and manufacturing; the transfer of public land to private ownership; the granting of licenses to operate major public services, such as cell phones, airlines, international sea transport, Tunisian cruise ships, TV and radio stations; and, on some occasions, the forced sale of private assets such as banks and newspapers" (p. 78).

As in Syria, post-Soviet Russia, and the Ukraine, the economy of Tunisia functioned as a rent economy that was run at the top by a genuine mafia of crony businessman and "buccaneering oligarchs" closely interconnected with the totalitarian state and party system.[21] These oligarchs not only prospered by building businesses behind protective walls set up by security services but also by preying on existing successful undertakings and firms either through the imposition of substantial and illicit commissions or through brutal takeovers backed up by criminal acts and threats. Not surprisingly, these maneuvers and extortions were shrouded in the greatest secrecy, and any public mention of them could result in imprisonment or exile (Owen, 2012, pp. 78–9). Hibou (2006a) describes some of the most frequently used malpractices that, it must be noted, all avoided blatant forms of embezzlement:

Rigged attributions of public bids, privatisations conceded to figureheads in obscure conditions that frequently involve pressures from ruling "clans" aimed at orienting the decision, or at compelling the new owner to associate himself with a particular

---

[21] The expression "buccaneering oligarchs" is borrowed from Karen Dawisha (2014), who has written a remarkably detailed study of the kleptocratic system put in place by Putin in postcommunist Russia. For Ukraine, see Åslund (2015), and, for Syria, the reader can refer to Chapter 6 of this book.

entrepreneur or importing agent, or to accept a particular intermediary or business partner ... such practices are considered as a normal part of the everyday life of Tunisians. The business person who is coerced into an association with a member of a "clan" to import the product that he has traditionally commercialised, is in the worst case just annoyed by this situation. He can accept it under duress for fear of fiscal reprisals or expropriation of assets but, most often, he will accept it readily, knowing quite well that the commodities will then move quickly and easily through the customs and other administrative controls. ... As for the administration, it will comply with the request to deal promptly with the matter insofar as the members of the "clans" are personal representatives of the president. If the importer were irresponsible enough to refuse the "offer" made to him by people from up there, his working conditions could rapidly deteriorate, his stocks could rot in the customs facilities, the fiscal authorities could start an investigation into his books, the national social security fund could require the immediate payment of his arrears, and the bank could deny him a last credit. Likewise, the research and development group which does not give in to a request from a clan member must expect a lot of administrative troubles that will eventually prevent it from submitting a bid within the prescribed time; and an entrepreneur who refuses to sell a portion of his shares to connections of the president incurs the risk that his business environment becomes abruptly hostile, say because the police exerts strong pressures on his suppliers or service providers to the effect that they stop working with him. (p. 337; my translation)

Finally, the president used state resources as a source of selective patronage for both members of the crony business community and individual members of the security services. A particularly useful instrument was credit that was "freely provided for many privileged members of the new middle class, allowing them to buy houses and cars but leaving them deeply in debt and so enmeshed in a system of relations that it prevented them from criticizing or opposing the regime" (Owen, 2012, pp. 78–9). The continuous threat posed by the vindictive punishment strategy of Ben Ali also had the effect of keeping oligarchs quiet and submissive.

To sum up, Ben Ali strengthened the authoritarian character of the Tunisian state to the point of establishing a genuine police state, with the Ministry of the Interior, directly answering to the president, at its core. He also transformed the state and bureaucracy into an extortion machine, thereby creating a clique of voracious plutocrats whose wealth was obtained as a result of close links to the president and his wife. At lower levels, he created an army of people of less means and status tied together and to the regime through participation in numerous acts of boycott, extortion, reprisals, racketeering, and police operations. Because economic growth accompanied political repression, the established kleptocratic system seemed to constitute a stable equilibrium that could persist over a long period of time. In fact, however, it formed a highly combustible material that would blow up in a completely unpredictable manner during the Jasmine Revolution of 2011.

The Arab Spring and the Islamists' Access to Power

By 2011, important elements of Tunisia's professional urban secular elite were increasingly alienated from the regime. When a young man set himself on fire in a provincial town remote from the capital city, a spark was set off that immediately spread throughout the whole country. The authorities not only faced a mass revolt that linked almost everyone in opposition to their rule but the army also sided with the demonstrators against the security services loyal to the president and ultimately moved against him (Springborg, 2014, p. 145). The regime and all its protection racket then collapsed without offering any resistance (Brumberg, 2014, p. 50). Ghannouchi returned from exile, and although it did not play any visible leadership role in a revolution that was largely led by labor and youth groups (which were less likely to support political Islam), the Islamic movement of al-Nahda soon came back to the political stage as the only force presenting a solid internal organization and a clear vision. This vision combined religious identity and revival with a platform of social justice, respect for pluralism, and clean government (Mecham, 2014, p. 211).

In addition to its long history of communal involvement and political activism, al-Nahda enjoyed two other advantages over its political competitors. First, Tunisian citizens were reassured by the numerous statements made by al-Nahda leaders during their campaign that they would not seek to impose Islamic prescriptions on the country in sensitive areas such as the status of women and that they were ready to share power with non-Islamist parties. Second, ideological or policy preferences may have been less important to voters than al-Nahda's long-standing opposition to Ben Ali. This was especially true because so many Islamist activists had paid a heavy price for their opposition to his regime. Together with a perception that Islamist parties were less corrupt and more sincerely committed to the welfare of ordinary citizens, the past militantism of al-Nahda probably influenced the voting behavior of a significant number of Tunisians (Tessler and Robbins, 2014, pp. 260–1).

After winning the first postrevolutionary election in October 2011, earning 37 percent of the vote, al-Nahda found itself in the difficult position of being simultaneously confronted with the harsh realities of governing a country and the need to meet the expectations of its traditional supporters

(Mecham, 2014, pp. 210–11). This difficulty was compounded by two factors. The first was the nearly total lack of governing skills of most Islamist ministers, who were suddenly elevated to positions of authority for which their previous professional and political experiences left them unprepared (pp. 214–15). The second factor was the sudden emergence of the Salafists, which forced al-Nahda's leaders to demonstrate their Islamic credentials lest they lose ground to more pure defenders of Islamic values. The first challenge was left unmet: Under circumstances that required quick and wise decisions, the incompetence of the al-Nahda government proved disastrous. To respond to the emergence of the Salafists, al-Nahda opted for their selective integration into the political process. The formula did not work, however. The difficult act of balancing not only secular and Islamist interests but also moderate and radical Islamist tendencies failed to prevent the alienation of secular groups that had played a major role in overthrowing Ben Ali.

All parties were then compelled to return to the negotiating table. A compromise was reached in March 2013, leading to a new constitution that, "while far from perfect, provides real democratic guarantees and rights" (Brumberg, 2014, p. 51). A new government was formed in which al-Nahda accepted the presence of a large number of technicians without any clear party affiliation. In the parliamentary elections of October 2014, the Tunisian citizens manifested their disappointment with al-Nahda's rule by giving the highest number of votes, but not an absolute majority, to Nidaa Tounes ("Tunisian Call"), a melting pot of former members of Ben Ali's old ruling party and nonaligned figures, (*Economist*, January 3–9, 2015, p. 32). As for al-Nahda, it came in second with a much lower tally than in 2011. The result reflected the Arab Barometer's opinion surveys that showed much greater support for secular democracy than for democracy with Islam (Tessler and Robbins, 2014, p. 260).[22] Since Nidaa Tounes did not recognize the president, who has to approve the prime minister according to the constitution, a presidential election quickly followed the parliamentary elections. In December 2014, the changeover was confirmed: The incumbent president, Moncef Marzouki, chief of the Congress for the Republic (Congrès pour la République), but known to be close to al-Nahda, was defeated in the second round by Beji Caïd Sebsi, the leader of Nidaa Tounes. Sebsi, then age ninety-four, had been a minister under Bourguiba and the president of the parliament under Ben Ali.

---

[22] A clear preference for a secular political system has also been observed in Egypt.

Note the contradiction between the preference for secular democracy expressed by the Tunisian citizens and the significant share of the vote garnered by al-Nahda in the 2011 elections. In fact, the turnout rate at these elections was only around 50 percent, which implies that barely 20 percent of Tunisians voted for al-Nahda, which is not very different from the proportion of Tunisians who expressed a preference for political Islam in the Arab Barometer survey (Tessler and Robbins, 2014, p. 262; Berman and Nugent, 2015). It must also be stressed that the two leading party coalitions are very heterogeneous. Nidaa Tounes brings together communists, liberals, and other secular forces, whereas the Congress for the Republic represents various shades of Islam, including the Yusufists. The latter are moderate Islamists who stand for the rights of the southern part of the country, which allegedly has suffered discrimination by the ruling North since the times of Bourguiba. The 2014 presidential election results exposed the gulf between the poor South and the richer North: In the five southernmost regions, 80 percent of voters voted for Marzouki (*Economist*, January 3–9, 2015, p. 32; Berman and Nugent, 2015).

9.4 Enlightened Despots in Modern Afghanistan

This section describes two interesting attempts of Afghan rulers to modernize their country: first, under King Amanullah, and, second, under a Marxist-oriented regime known as the PDPA. In discussing the former attempt, I also describe the subsequent effort, this time by the Musahibans, to reintroduce some of Amanullah's reforms. I then explore the similarity between mistakes made by the Taliban regime and those of Amanullah and the PDPA.

The Bold Reformism of King Amanullah

During his short-lived ascendancy to political power, King Amanullah (1919–29) embarked on an ambitious program of modernizing Afghan society. Although he had gained the support of a wide array of social classes, including the clergy, by opposing the British under the banner of pan-Islamism and anti-imperialism (see Chapter 5, Section 5.5), his modernizing policies met with strong opposition. Indeed, as soon as Amanullah tried to reform his country's institutions and so transform an anachronistic society into a secular state, he lost the support of the conservative ulama. For the clerics, the defense of Islam was to be achieved by the return of society to the true faith of Islam; for Amanullah, by contrast, the defense of Islam was "one strand in a policy of resistance to imperialism and was to be achieved by Westernisation": in fact, Islam meant two different things to the ulama and the king (Roy, 1990, pp. 17, 64; Rasanayagam, 2005, pp. 1–10, 17–22).

Amanullah's reforms were all encompassing: They aimed to assert the role of the central state by instituting new taxes collected directly by civil servants, making conscription compulsory and universal, and interfering in family matters. In particular, the reforms sought to emancipate women (which included ending women's seclusion and abolishing the veil), prohibit polygamy among government officials, curtail child marriage, create a court system run by secular government-trained judges (who would replace the existing qadis), make education compulsory for all, reform the mosque schools, and establish a Western-style constitutional monarchy, with an elected lower house and an appointed upper house. It is striking that, as long as Amanullah's reforms were perceived to be mainly concerned with taxation and conscription, urban ulama gave their blessing to them. They thus declared that the emir was within his rights to raise taxes and change the mode of conscription as he pleased. They even issued a fatwa labeling the mainly rural rebel clergy and their tribal supporters "traitors" and hence liable to the most severe punishment (Barfield, 2010, p. 186). But when the reforms touched on family and personal matters, they antagonized not only religious authorities but also traditional political leaders. The ulama were alarmed that the reformist program encroached on the domain where they traditionally exercised their influence and from where they derived their prestige. Politicians perceived the program as a frontal attack on the very roots of rural Afghan society and its customs.

It is therefore not surprising that the loya jirga, composed of the country's leading tribal and religious leaders, rejected most of the reforms when Amanullah convened it for the purpose of approving his program. He tried to push them through nevertheless, ready to confront what he saw as an ignorant and self-interested clerical establishment and determined to break its power and influence. He went so far as cutting his ties with them, refusing to meet with even his most dignified representatives, ending their stipends, and forbidding government officials to join Sufi orders. The opposition to the king then turned outright violent. Discontented clerics declared the emir an infidel and gave a religious turn to a tribal rebellion whose leaders resented a blatant encroachment on their erstwhile prerogatives (Barfield, 2010, pp. 181–91).

In November 1928, Shinwari Pashtun tribesmen burned down the king's winter palace in Jalalabad and marched on Kabul, while a Tajik bandit from the north, Bacha Saqqao, assembled a disparate force in the defense of Islam.

Amanullah fled to Italy, and Saqqao seized power, establishing a nine-month reign of terror that subjected Kabul's inhabitants to continuous looting, pillaging, arson, and rape. The religious and traditional leaders who opposed Amanullah and had initially supported Saqqao, acclaiming him as the "Holy Warrior, Habibullah, Servant of the Faith," turned against him and eventually succeeded in chasing him from power. Nadir Shah (1929–33) was then proclaimed king by his tribal army, and he promulgated a new but reactionary constitution that perpetuated an autocratic monarchy allied to religious conservatism. Religious leaders were co-opted into the new power structure, mosque imams were put on the government payroll, relatives of influential religious figures were appointed to lucrative posts, and a special board of ulama was established to ensure that what was taught in schools conformed to Islamic values. Moreover, the new king assembled a loya jirga (September 1931), which formally abrogated many Amanullah's reforms on the grounds that he had violated sharia law and was therefore to be considered as an illegitimate emir. Eventually, very little remained of Amanullah's efforts to modernize his country. It is evident that the pace of reform was too fast and the method too brutal for the country to absorb (Rasanayagam, 2005, pp. 20–3; Barfield, 2010, pp. 190, 197).

It is revealing in this regard that, when the Musahibans later tried to reintroduce some of Amanullah's reforms, they were far more successful because they learned from Amanullah's failure. They correctly perceived that, in accordance with the analysis proposed in Chapter 4, conservative clerics are more concerned with blocking social change than with restricting government power. When the Musahibans thus reinstituted Amanullah's state-centralizing bureaucratic reforms, these clerics made no objection. As for social reforms, they were passed without stirring widespread opposition because the Musahibans cleverly chose to avoid making big public announcements and to focus their enforcement efforts in urban areas where the need for social change was well accepted (Barfield, 2010, pp. 200–2). The contrast between the approaches followed by Amanullah and the Musahibans has been well captured by Thomas Barfield (2010):

When Amanullah proposed abolishing the veil, he had made it part of a larger project designed to transform Afghan life through the emancipation of women more broadly. ... By contrast, the list of social changes introduced under the Musahiban monarchy was small and mostly visible in Kabul. They feared making broad-based reforms lest it put their regime at risk. By making it clear that they were restricting such reforms to an urban elite that already wanted them, they reduced the veil issue to the status of a fashion statement divorced from the larger and more contentious question of women's rights in general. (p. 202)

A Renewed Attempt by the Left

Obviously the People's Democratic Party of Afghanistan (PDPA), a Marxist-oriented party that took control of the government in April 1978, did not learn from Amanullah's failure. Led by eastern, mostly Ghilzai, Pashtuns (who displaced their old Durrani rivals from power after 230 years), the PDPA aimed to use state power to transform Afghan society without the cooperation of its people. This proved to be a fatal mistake. As a matter of fact, rural folk – the majority of the population – usually accepted the rule of Kabul only as long as the policies of the country's rulers did not affect them in any significant manner and their lives continued to be dominated by local patrons, landowners, and merchants, who protected them against the government and other communities (Barfield, 2010, pp. 173, 214–23). Ignoring this reality, the PDPA moved to implement revolutionary policies of land reform, education, and changes in family law and to break down "the political structure by which rural communities had insulated themselves from the central government and its officials for generations" (p. 231).

Toward this end, PDPA leaders were willing to destroy all opposition, including traditional rural landowners, the military establishment, and Islamic clergy. Moreover, they rejected the country's traditional Islamic symbols by removing religious salutations from their speeches and decrees, and by changing the color of the flag to red in accordance with their exclusive alliance with the Soviet Union (Barfield, 2010, p. 225). Their confrontational policy relied on coercion to a large extent, such as when they launched a compulsory literacy campaign requiring the attendance of young unmarried women and men in mixed classes, thus pitting "rural notions of propriety and social honor against the goals of the revolutionary vanguard" (p. 231). Moreover, they did not refrain from harshly putting down any dissent and from insulting and even killing clerics.

As could have been expected, villagers soon rose up against the new regime, and the ulama called a jihad against it. If the causes of the peasant upheavals were not directly linked with religion, Islam provided the ideological framework that allowed the rural masses to articulate and legitimize their grievances. The ulama, who were mostly concerned about the openly secular, if not atheistic, propaganda of the regime, began preaching against it. They found a receptive audience among these masses, because they spoke the familiar language of religion based on the distinction between good and evil: They condemned the agrarian reform as "non-Islamic" and the literacy campaign as atheistic propaganda. In the words of Roy (1993), "In this insurrection, the defense of a traditional society was expressed in the garb of a defense of Islam, because Islam was inextricably bound to tradition in the world view of the Afghan peasantry" (p. 496). In the minds of rural people, indeed, the defense of land property, the Islamic faith, and the honor of their families against outsiders boiled down to the same thing (Barfield, 2010, p. 232).

A key point is, therefore, that reference to Islam was mainly symbolic in Afghan rural society. Yet, "it was precisely this symbolism which helped to resist the onward march of state institutions by the creation of a space within which real autonomy was possible" (Roy, 1990, pp. 26–7). In Afghanistan, Islam always reasserted itself in times of crisis, and its role as a countervailing power to the despotism of the state increased when the latter embarked on a process of forced secularization, accompanied by the growth of an intrusive state bureaucracy. In the eyes of the peasantry, the prestige of the ulama, who as a matter of principle do not wield much influence in the Afghan countryside, was all the greater because they had been removed to the fringes of social and political life, which isolated them from corruption and gave them an aura of integrity. Their influence and power tended to grow when the tribal society underwent upheaval and the universalist ideology of the jihad allowed contenders to transcend tribal divisions (pp. 29, 36–8).

What needs to be emphasized is that religious opposition alone will not overthrow a reformist or modernizing ruler. This outcome can be achieved only when the discourse of the religious opponents finds a strong resonance among important layers of society. It is revealing that, in accordance with what has been said earlier regarding the predominance of politics over religion, religious authorities will tolerate the temporary violation of a sacred principle only if they consider the faulty ruler to be a lesser evil. Thus, when Bacha Saqqao surrendered to General Nadir Khan, he obtained a pledge, signed on the copy of the Quran, that his life would be spared. This pledge did not prevent the victorious general from publicly hanging Saqqao and his main followers a month later. At no point did this action spark an outraged reaction from the religious authorities (Rasanayagam, 2005, p. 22).

The Taliban Regime

The Taliban regime is a unique case in the modern Muslim world, in which a fundamentalist movement succeeded, before the Arab Spring, in seizing and holding political power for several years (1998–2001). This seems at odds with what has just been said and with the fact that, before 1980, the Islamist parties did not play any significant role inside Afghanistan. Their leaders never succeeded in establishing a base of national support in the country. It was only after Pakistan gave the arms supply monopoly and other aid to the Islamist parties after the Soviet invasion that these leaders rose to prominence. Resistance groups based in Afghanistan were required to affiliate with one of these Islamist parties to obtain weapons and funding. Because groups fighting in Afghanistan had actually little interest in the political ideologies of Islamist parties, affiliation was generally based on personal relationships, regional and ethnic ties, or simple opportunism (Barfield, 2010, p. 236). Regional and ethnic ties involved a clear differentiation between the non-Pashtun groups (Hazaras, Tajiks, Uzbeks) in the north and the west and the Pashtuns in the south and the east. Private interests and past disputes rather than adherence to political or religious principles influenced the formation of factions, as well as the frequently occurring defections. These features, which do not provide a basis for compromise, were to endure under and after Soviet occupation (1979–89). In the words of Thomas Barfield (2010),

The international funders justified their support of the Afghan conflict in ways that had little relevance within Afghanistan. They portrayed the struggle in Afghanistan as a Manichaean conflict of competing ideologies (e.g., Islam versus atheism, socialism versus capitalism, freedom versus oppression, feudal reactionaries versus progressive patriots, modernists versus traditionalists). Afghans never saw the war they were fighting in such black-and-white terms because politics in Afghanistan was less ideological and more personal. It was a world where yesterday's enemy might become today's ally, meaning you should take no one for granted. (pp. 243–4)

Thus, international geopolitics propelled the Taliban to power in Afghanistan. With the support of Pakistan and its Inter-Service Intelligence (ISI) and their great ability to exploit internal rivalries among their enemies, especially the long-running conflict between the Tajiks of General Masud and the Hazaras of Mazari, as well as to bribe militia commanders with suitcases full of dollar notes, the Taliban established an Islamic emirate led by Mullah Omar. In spite of having only rudimentary religious training, Omar took the title of Emir-ul Monineen ("Commander of the Faithful"), implying that he wielded absolute authority over his subjects.

What matters here is that the Taliban repeated the mistakes of King Amanullah and the PDPA: Barfield even describes them as "a mirror image of the PDPA" (p. 262), and Mullah Omar, their leader, as "a Stalinist who believed in Islamic revolution in one country" (p. 267). By imposing radical religious doctrines of foreign origin on a reluctant Afghan people, the Taliban, inspired by Deobandism, soon became unpopular, despite being initially lauded for establishing law and order in the conquered territories. The regime collapsed after a few years, even if its rapid demise was partly caused by an external intervention.[23] On this occasion, it was people living in the more sophisticated cities, Kabul and Mazar-i-Sharif, who were most angered by Taliban social and religious policies. In fact, the Taliban religious ideology was a crude mixture of Salafi Islam and the cultural code of the Pashtuns, the Pashtunwali. Urban residents did not want to abide by Pashtun rural customs that were often concealed behind the veil of Islamic principles. They considered the Taliban to be poorly educated rural bumpkins. At the same time, rural dwellers could not accept the virulent Taliban attacks against Sufism and the veneration of the saints and shrines (Barfield, 2010, pp. 261–2).

9.5 Drawing Lessons: Radical versus Moderate Reforms

This section proceeds in several steps. First, I pinpoint the main flaws in the reform programs implemented in Turkey, Tunisia, and Afghanistan, flaws that eventually led to major disruptions of national politics. Second, I outline a more effective approach to reforms that would avoid antagonizing religious clerics and ordinary people inordinately. Third, the theoretical framework underpinning an approach based on legal pluralism is described in nonformal terms. Finally, in the last two steps, I illustrate the recommended approach to reforms by referring to the experiences of two Muslim countries, Morocco and Indonesia – one Arab and the other non-Arab.

Avoidable Flaws of the Reform Programs

The key question raised at the beginning of this chapter is whether in Muslim-dominated countries institutions (including laws) can be modernized through some form of enlightened despotism. From the experiences of modern Afghanistan, Turkey, and Tunisia, it is possible to draw rich insights that contribute to answering this question. First, reform efforts in all three

---

[23] The refusal to hand Osama bin-Laden over to the U.S. authorities after the destruction of the Twin Towers in New York on September 11, 2001, led to immediate U.S. airstrikes against Taliban positions. The Northern Alliance allies moved against these positions on the ground, and many commanders defected after having received dollar notes by the trunkload. The Taliban regime quickly unraveled, and even its retreat into the Pashtun heartland did not rescue it because "the traditional Pashtun tribal leaders used the opportunity to regain power and expel the Taliban from Qandahar" (Barfield, 2010, p. 269).

countries gave rise to acute tensions that eventually ignited major upheavals: In Afghanistan, King Amanullah was overthrown by an alliance of religious and traditional forces, and later there was an Islam-based popular rebellion against the PDPA government; in Turkey, an Islamist party earned repeated electoral victories as soon as fair elections were allowed; and in Tunisia, Ben Ali's regime ended in the course of the Arab Spring, which was soon followed by the rise of an Islamist party to power.

These catastrophic outcomes were entirely predictable. Let us return to the theory sketched in Chapter 4 and consider the version in which the autocratic ruler chooses a level of progressive reforms in addition to a rate of appropriation of the national wealth (see Auriol and Platteau, 2017b). He also chooses the level of wage and perks paid to the official clerics whom he wants to co-opt. If a new ruler has a strong taste for reforms, the prediction is that he will choose a larger amount of reforms than his predecessors. In the more general case (reforms and corruption are complementary), he will simultaneously increase the level of wealth appropriation, so that the fraction of co-opted clerics will be smaller than before and the regime's political instability will increase. This situation typically occurs when the ruler is surrounded by a clique of rapacious businessmen and sycophants closely linked to the regime, as in Tunisia. In this instance, the adverse impact of legal reforms on political stability is compounded by the effect of corruption and the lack of economic inclusiveness of the policies followed. This need not be the case, however: Reforms and corruption may be substitutes rather than complements. But even if corruption decreases when more progressive reforms are adopted by the autocratic ruler, the odds are that political stability will be impaired.

At first sight, these failures suggest that top-down approaches to Western-oriented reforms in the sensitive area of private matters do not work or at least are not sustainable in the long term. Coulson's optimism regarding the possibility of enacting secular reforms to Muslim countries would thus appear ill founded. On closer inspection, however, my detailed examination of the three country experiences does not warrant such a negative conclusion. In the two countries where the reforms have been in place for a long period of time, Turkey and Tunisia, society has experienced a deep transformation, and key legal reforms introduced by Atatürk and Bourguiba, respectively, will not be easily overturned. In these two countries, the status of women has improved considerably, and the public role of religion has been significantly reduced. Although temporary relapses cannot be excluded, the requirements of a dynamic economy in Turkey and the perceived necessity to accelerate growth in Tunisia will take precedence over religious concerns, so that the latter will not be allowed to stand in the way of the former.

The second insight is that in none of these three countries were modernizing reforms implemented wisely. Dangerous backlash effects could have been avoided if the rulers had not made serious mistakes. In other words, as our theory discussed in Chapter 4 suggests, political stability could have been preserved had the reforms been less radical or enforced in a less brutal manner. Moreover, an expansion of economic opportunities for the masses would have lessened opposition to secular reforms. This is especially evident in the case of Tunisia, where cronyism became all pervasive under Ben Ali's regime. But it is true also of Kemalist Turkey, where new opportunities were mainly limited to the Westernized elites, thereby accentuating the rift between rich and poor. In Turkey, the effect was worsened by the fact that a good number of the new income-earning opportunities – those available in the form of jobs in the state bureaucracy – were actually closed to people who practiced Islam in public.

The modernizing rulers made two other serious mistakes that deserve attention. First, at least during some stage of the reform process, they opted for an approach that directly confronted traditional culture in a needlessly brutal and condescending manner. This occurred most clearly in the reforms of Amanullah and the PDPA in Afghanistan and in the Kemalist reforms in Turkey: All proclaimed an assertive and intolerant secularism. The case of Tunisia is somewhat different, because in the first stage of reforms, Bourguiba followed a nonantagonistic approach that presented the legal reforms as compatible with the Muslim faith. Rather than purporting to rid Tunisia of the influence of religion in the name of Western modernity, Bourguiba chose to cast the reforms in the garb of Islamic principles reinterpreted with the authority of a new ijtihad. He thus acted as the guardian of the faith, a strong claim deemed extravagant by many ulama, yet not by most common believers who respected the president's authority. Later on, however, he made a strange U-turn, expressing contempt for some customary religious rituals, such as fasting; he thereby aroused angry reactions among wide Islamic circles and the pious masses. Even earlier, Bourguiba had made strongly worded derogatory remarks about traditional clothing, both female and male. As in the cases of Afghanistan and Turkey, Westernization thus appeared as a movement involving the denial and the destruction of traditional culture.

The second mistake is related to the first one, in that abrupt imposition of Western institutions and habits went hand in hand with an authoritarian political regime. In the case of Turkey, the army played a major role in supporting Kemalist reforms, and it continuously meddled in political affairs, with a view to preventing any encroachment on those reforms. In Tunisia, the secret services and the police were active in every level of the society, justifying the regime's characterization as a police state. Even though its foundations were laid under Bourguiba, this regime was consolidated and considerably extended under Ben Ali's rule. Unlike in Turkey, repression in Tunisia ended up being used to protect the racketeering practices of a cynical and self-serving ruling clique, rather than to enforce secular laws.

In Turkey, the popular masses were dominated and even colonized by a Westernized economic and social elite, which uniformly imposed their values and patterns of behavior thanks to their tight control over the political system. The single-party system established by Atatürk was succeeded by a system in which the military, acting in cahoots with the Kemalist bureaucracy, determined the registration of political movements as parties and state coups occurred whenever the army considered Kemalist values to be under threat. In Tunisia, a de facto single-party system prevailed throughout the reigns of Bourguiba and Ben Ali, but there the despotic state was instrumental in creating blatant inequalities through unfair access to the sources of wealth and patronage and through the use of all forms of extortion. In Turkey and Tunisia, Islamist movements were especially targeted by the state and its repressive forces, which contributed a great deal to enhance those movements' prestige and ability to engage in resistance. When the gradual democratization of the Turkish regime eventually led to genuinely open elections, a moderately Islamist party won the contest by a wide margin and has remained in power ever since. In Tunisia, where such a democratization process did not take place, a social and political revolution that was not sparked by the persecuted Islamists but by a spontaneous eruption of popular anger brought Ben Ali's rule to an abrupt end. Again, a moderately Islamist coalition rose to power at the first postrevolutionary election. Its victory not only reflected a resurgence of Islamic values in opposition to the corruption and cronyism of the defeated regime but also corresponded to the reassertion of the Yusufist South, which had always felt aggrieved by the economic policies of the dominating North.

The Way Forward: A Middle Road between Assertive Secularism and the Status Quo

The most important message emerging from this analysis is that reforming Islam is not only possible but also feasible at much smaller costs. Three main points deserve attention here. To begin with, it must be emphasized that modernizing and centralizing the state apparatus, or democratizing the constitution and the political system, do not generally cause significant or systematic resistance from religious circles: On the one hand, the official ulama of "high Islam" tend to accept the preeminence of political rulers in such matters, and on the other hand, the mullahs, shaykhs, and other representatives of "low Islam" are too distant from changes occurring in the higher spheres of the society to feel very much concerned about them. Hence, it is in more mundane affairs, and especially in personal matters, such as marriage, divorce, inheritance, land-related rules, and clothing, that resistance to authoritarian reformism arises.

Second, the absorption of the ulama into a modern state administration does not give rise to momentous difficulties or insuperable obstacles. The reason is that the official ulama tend to belong to a privileged social class made up of family dynasties enjoying a monopoly over lucrative religious functions. As such, they are estranged from the common people, making it unlikely for them to enter into open conflict with the rulers and the state to protest encroachment on the privileges of the religious elite.

The third point shifts attention to the situation of the masses and the representatives of the "low Islam." Village mullahs live close to the rural people, understand their day-to-day problems, and share their local culture, which mixes Islamic religious beliefs and rituals with indigenous customs. Their mutual interests tend to be equally close, and the communality of feelings is strong. To directly confront popular habits and beliefs and impose Western values and mores on ordinary people unaccustomed to them is an unwise and counterproductive strategy: It is certain to cause distress and arouse the ire of these people and the representatives of low Islam, who may then act as the organizers of (violent) protests. To put it differently, attacks on cultural symbols must be avoided. They aggravate tensions unnecessarily and complicate a problem that could have been solved gradually and more smoothly. In Turkey, because traditional attire was disparaged and prohibited, it became a political symbol used by members of traditional groups to assert their rise and cultural identity, instead of being slowly abandoned. Wearing traditional garb has come to symbolize the refusal to be colonized by the Westernized elite.

As we have learned from the Musahibans in Afghanistan, the correct approach to reform is to avoid big public announcements and to refrain from implementing drastic reforms and uniformly applying them quickly to the entire population. When Westernizing reforms concern personal matters and are enacted in a top-down manner, they are perceived as a frontal assault by the urban elite and the ruling circles on the lives and culture of the common people. These reforms are better targeted to the educated and relatively sophisticated members of these elites, who have already been exposed to Western standards, values, and manner of living and are engaged in activities that would benefit from social and institutional change. Being more able to understand the need for such changes, they may have actually called for them, and if not, they are unlikely to offer resistance against them.

With respect to the remaining segments of the population, an approach to reform that offers several alternatives is advisable, implying that people should remain free to choose among different systems, including traditional beliefs, social norms, and habits. Inspiration should therefore be sought in the culture of tolerance instituted by the Ottomans, yet ignored by the Kemalists. Under Ottoman institutions, indeed, not only did the millet system respect the boundaries between religious communities but also people could choose among different systems of law and associated courts by which to run their lives and businesses and to settle their conflicts. The only serious limitation arose from the fact that, in an odd twist of fate, Muslims could not opt for a non-Muslim system but only among the different schools prevailing in Islam, whereas Jews, Catholic Greeks, and Armenians could choose a Muslim system of whatever school, if they so wished (Kuran, 2011, ch. 11).

It could nevertheless be argued that some social groups, women in particular, suffer from existing arrangements and would be left unaided if reforms do not address them. Yet, in a context of legal pluralism, the situation of the victims of traditional social systems may improve even if modern statutory law is not invoked. It is to this argument that we now turn. Then, the final stage of this section explores two country experiences that illustrate the middle road between assertive secularism and the status quo.

The "Magnet Effect" of Progressive Reforms: Theoretical Insights

The theory of the so-called magnet effect explicitly models strategic interactions between modern, statutory law and the custom (Platteau and Wahhaj, 2013; Aldashev, Chaara, Platteau, and Wahhaj, 2012a, 2012b; Aldashev, Platteau and Wahhaj, 2011). The setup of the formal model is shortly described before the central results and its relevance to the present discussion are highlighted.

Consider a society in which the state enacts a statutory law that aims to enhane the interests of a group that is disadvantaged by the prevailing custom, say, women. The custom itself is set by a customary authority, which has an intrinsic preference for the interests of the privileged group, say, men. At the same time, this authority is sensitive to the size of its jurisdiction domain because its social prestige is a direct function of the number of cases brought to its attention. Community residents (men and women), when faced with a conflict, choose between going to the formal judge, who enforces the statutory law, or the informal judge (i.e., the customary authority), who enforces the custom. Although men always have an interest in referring to the custom, this is not necessarily the case for women, because men and women have antagonistic preferences. When contemplating the option of accepting a customary judgment, women balance the cost of a relatively unfavorable verdict against the benefit of remaining on good terms with their community. Or, put conversely, when considering the possibility of appealing to the formal judge, they balance the benefit of a relatively favorable verdict against the cost of severing ties with their community or, at least, receiving some punishment imposed by this community. Punishment is meted out on the grounds that, by appealing to an external agency, a woman "betrays" her own community because "dirty linen is better washed inside the family." Note that women may choose to migrate out of their native village in anticipation of future conflicts that would be settled in a too unfavorable manner from their point of view.

Like women, the customary authority also confronts a tradeoff. Indeed, if it chooses a customary judgment that is too unfavorable to women, the gain derived from maintaining a strong consistency with its intrinsic preference for traditional values will be outweighed by the social cost of a considerable restriction of its jurisdictional domain; the opposite will occur if it chooses a judgment too favorable to women; that is, a judgment that departs too much from the erstwhile custom.

In such a setup, when the state enacts a new law aimed at improving women's rights, for example, in matters of inheritance, the customary authority may react by moving the custom in the direction of the statutory law. In other words, it will choose a judgment that is less unfavorable to women than before, yet not as favorable to women as the statutory law. The underlying reason is that, by opening a previously nonexistent exit option, the law has conferred increased bargaining strength on women: Indeed, they can now threaten to go an alternative court to have their case judged, or more precisely, they can appeal to the modern court system if they are dissatisfied with the informal judgment pronounced by the customary authority.

What is remarkable about the mechanism of the magnet effect is the following: Even if no woman actually appeals to the formal court, thereby giving the impression that the law is toothless, women's lot has de facto improved, because they receive a more favorable judgment when accepting that their case is solely judged by the customary authority. In the event that some of them, perhaps only a few in the beginning, do refer to the formal court, a situation of legal pluralism is created: Being judged by the formal court, a fraction of the women receive the best possible treatment, whereas the other women are meted out a judgment that is better than what they would have received in the absence of the law. For several reasons, the women who seek justice from a formal court differ from those who approach the customary authority. The severity of the conflict may vary, and because stakes are higher in more serious conflicts, women facing them will opt for the formal court and accept the social cost of antagonizing their community. Women engaged in more benign conflicts will make the opposite choice. In addition, women may be heterogeneous in terms of access to outside employment opportunities. Those with the best prospects will then choose to migrate to a city where they will be judged in case a conflict arises, whereas those with less attractive prospects will remain in their community and continue to accept the verdict of the customary authority.[24]

The magnet effect theory yields two interesting side results. First, it can show that a moderate law may be more favorable to women (or other oppressed sections of the population) than a more radical law. The most evident mechanism goes through the law enforcers, such as the judges or the police officers and investigators in the formal sector of the judiciary system (see Aldashev et al., 2012b, sect. 3).[25] These officers have their own preferences relating to the law, but at the same time they attach a positive value to law abidingness. This means that if the (new) law is not too different from what they prefer it to be, they will apply it because they feel it is their duty to do so. If the law is radical, however, law-abidingness considerations may be

---

[24] This situation corresponds to de jure legal pluralism. By contrast, if the custom is suppressed by the state but if some formal judges deviate from their duty to enforce the statutory law, a situation of de facto legal pluralism is created. Based on my observations of judges' behavior in countries of sub-Saharan Africa (Senegal and Mali, in particular), provincial judges are often aware of the considerable distance that often exists between the formal law and the custom and may consequently choose verdicts that stand in between the two laws. There then arises de facto legal pluralism in the sense that the formal law is not enforced in the same manner in urban and rural locations, or in cities and provincial towns. This difference may also be attributable to the preferences of provincial judges who may originate from the region and experience sympathy with the erstwhile mores of local people.

[25] Other, less straightforward mechanisms have been proposed in Aldashev et al. (2012a), where the argument is framed as a welfare effect in the presence of a public good, and in Acemoglu and Jackson (2015), where agents meet pairwise and may denounce partners who violate the law.

outweighed by the distate of the formal judges for the law. As a consequence, a fraction of the judges (the most conservative group) may decide to stop applying the statutory law and to judge the cases brought before them on the basis of their preferred version of the law. If that is the case, the expected value of the verdict for the plaintiffs (say, the women) may turn out to be smaller with a radical than with a moderate law, defeating the purpose of the legal reform.

That this sort of self-defeating effect is a serious possibility can be argued on the basis of U.S. evidence. According to Kahan (2000), the resistance of law enforcers sometimes confounds the efforts of lawmakers to change social norms. For example, as American legislators expand liability for date rape, domestic violence, sexual harassment, drugs, and drunk driving, not only do prosecutors become more likely to charge, jurors to convict, and judges to sentence severely (our second line of argument) but also the police become less likely to arrest the culprits and enforce the legal verdicts. The conspicuous resistance of these decision makers in turn reinforces the norms that lawmakers intended to change. In the language of Kahan, this pathology of "sticky norms" can be surmounted if lawmakers apply "gentle nudges" rather than "hard shoves." When the law embodies a relatively mild degree of condemnation, the desire of most decision makers to discharge their civic duties will override their reluctance to enforce a law that attacks a widespread social norm.

If we combine this theoretical insight from the magnet effect theory with the theory of religious seduction that lies at the heart of this book, we can now see that excessively radical reforms can have two distinct perverse effects. They are liable to generate greater political instability because the aversion of religious clerics may induce them to end their support for the autocratic regime. Excessively radical reforms may also give rise to a backlash effect if judges and law enforcers become more reluctant to implement laws that they find unduly progressive.

The second interesting side result of the theory is that the magnet effect caused by the introduction of a more progressive law is exactly analogous to that caused by the emergence of new economic opportunities outside the native area. These prospects induce women to migrate and so enter into the formal jurisdictional domain while the custom evolves in a pro-women direction. The role of outside economic opportunities is especially important when not only men but also women support the custom (their preferences are homogeneous), say because women have internalized the values of the patriarchal society and/or consider the traditional judge to be the only legitimate authority. In this instance, no magnet effect can result from pro-women laws. Yet, the multiplication of economic opportunities will encourage migration and thereby increase interaction with the urban world, opening the door to urban views suggested by new life experiences. As a result, traditional community ties will gradually weaken, and old social norms and customs will gradually recede. This is precisely how Eugen Weber (1976) describes the historical process of integration of the French peasantry into the emerging French nation, which occurred during the nineteenth century. Before then, he writes,

The people of whole regions felt little identity with the state or with people of other regions. Before this changed, ... they [the French citizens] had to share significant experiences with each other. Roads, railways, schools, markets, military service, and the circulation of money, goods, and printed matter provided those experiences, swept away old commitments, instilled a national view of things in regional minds, and confirmed the power of that view by offering advancement to those who adopted it. ... French culture became truly national only in the last years of the [nineteenth] century. We are talking about the process of acculturation: the civilisation of the French by urban France, the disintegration of local cultures by modernity and their absorption into the dominant civilisation of Paris and the schools ... the unassimilated rural masses had to be integrated into the dominant culture as they had been integrated into an administrative entity. What happened was akin to colonization. (Weber, 1976, p. 486)

The masses coming from France's periphery were thus assimilated into the dominant culture radiating from Paris. What deserves emphasis is that this internal colonization took place in a largely spontaneous, gradual, and imperceptible manner. I say "largely," rather than completely, because an important feature of the French experience was the existence of a uniform school system established under the aegis of the state. There is also no doubt that the French authorities in Paris did not hesitate in earlier times to resort to brutal, top-down methods, such as the outright prohibition of local languages, to bring peripheral populations into the fold of the emerging national state.

The moderate, middle-of-the-road approach that was sketched and vindicated earlier has been implemented in a number of cases. For example, it was essentially the course followed by Ottoman Turkey and Egypt, when commerce and finance no longer were the exclusive preserve of the Islamic courts, which were then forced to coexist with modern secular courts. However, we know that the pluralist imperial regime of the Ottomans was succeeded by the much more radical regime of assertive secularism of the young Republic of Turkey. As for Egypt, it is unfortunate that, since at least Nasser, the moderate legal approach to modernity has been contaminated and even perverted by patrimonial absolutism, a political system under which the autocrat and his inner circle distribute a great many privileges to relatives and friends. Such was not the case in Morocco and especially in Indonesia.

The Moderate Road Illustrated: The Case of Morocco

Morocco offers both a striking similarity and an interesting contrast to modern Tunisia. Like President Bourguiba, Kings Hassan II and Mohammed VI proclaimed a new ijtihad, implying that they were ready to use their prestige and authority to push social reforms forward through the reinterpretation of Islam's sacred texts. Yet, unlike Bourguiba, they never indulged in disparaging remarks or contemptuous behavior likely to anger the common people. They were aware that religion and tradition are inextricably mixed in the minds of the common people and, by representing their culture, help define their deep identity. As a result, the kings' prestige and authority remained intact, with most citizens believing that their rulers were acting for the good of the nation.

King Hassan II initiated the reform process in a prudent manner. Because family issues, he argued, are of an essentially religious nature, he was entitled to drive changes in those areas in his position of "Commander of the Faithful." In proclaiming a new ijtihad, he stressed that legal prescriptions cannot prohibit what God has not prohibited and cannot allow what God has not permitted. The resulting Family Code (1993), elaborated by a committee of ulama, constituted a modest advance over the code enacted just after independence (1956). In fact, the earlier code had actually legitimized practices based on patriarchal values in a context where the nationalist movement was eager to assert national identity and culture against Western values (Geertz, 1968). Major aspects of 1993 Family Code reforms concerned polygamy and divorce, which were both made more difficult to afford women some degree of protection against men's abuses of their patriarchal power. Moreover, a woman was now required to give her consent to a marriage, and in the event of the death of her father, she would no longer be subject to matrimonial guardianship (Chaara, 2015).

Progressive social movements, including some feminist organizations, were not satisfied with such timid moves, and the heated debates between them and conservatives eventually carried over to the streets. King Mohammed VI responded by treading the same path as his father: In his royal speech of October 2003, he announced another ijtihad that, as the supreme religious authority of the country, he claimed to be within the legitimate domain of his prerogatives. This time, however, the changes in the rights and status of women were more drastic than under the 1993 reform. These more significant reforms were possible because the influence of the nationalist movement had dwindled and the new king dared include academics (including three women) on the drafting committee. The voice of the ulama was further reduced as civil society organizations were invited to submit proposals. Some religion-based movements publicly expressed their disagreement with some aspects of the new legislation. For example, the women's association of the Parti de la Justice et du Développement (the Justice and Development Party, or PJD) defended polygamy, the guardianship of the father, and marriage for girls from the age of fifteen. But the king's authority carried the day, and the new code and the supporting court system were approved by the parliament.

What bears special emphasis is that, unlike the Tunisian Code of Personal Status, the Moroccan Family Code, the "Moudawana", allows people to make their own choices in several important areas, such as matrimonial guardianship, monogamy or polygamy, and the possibility of having a written contract regulating all asset transactions between the spouses. Mandatory prescriptions include the following: a minimum age at marriage for girls (set at ieghteen years, except in some extraordinary circumstances to be assessed by the judge), limited repudiation rights of the husband (divorce is a right jointly exercised by husband and wife), and limited possibilities for polygamous marriages (authorization for polygamy will not be granted by the judge if it harms the interests of the first wife and her children, for example).

Based on a sample survey in different regions of the country, Chaara (2015) finds that almost half of the women declared a strong support for the new law by supporting at least seven of its eight clauses. Support from men was much weaker: Barely one-fifth expressed strong support. Perhaps surprisingly, there was no significant difference in expressed (strong) support between urban and rural areas and between people with high and low levels of religiosity (measured by the intensity of their religious practices). Interestingly, only two provisions of the new Family Code have proven contentious. One is the clause that removes the duty of the wife to obey her husband, and the other clause allows women to marry without the official consent of their guardian. The new code thus appears to strike a compromise between rules that can now be uniformly accepted and rules that are still quite debatable.

The Moderate Road Illustrated: The Case of Indonesia

Indonesia is known to have strong local customs that Dutch colonizers compiled in the form of so-called adat laws. Initially, the colonial authorities had assumed that Muslim natives were governed by Muslim family law and so allowed local Islamic judges or officials to handle disputes involving family law matters of marriage, divorce, and inheritance. In 1937, however, the state shifted jurisdiction over inheritance in Java from Islamic courts to civil courts. From then on, Islam came to be seen as the basis of legal rulings only as long as they could be seen as part of adat, implying that it was a locally recognized practice. There were multiple adats that varied across region (Bowen, 2003, pp. 46–51).

After independence, President Sukarno favored retaining the separate adat law system, in opposition to lawyers and intellectuals who recommended a unified legal code for the whole country. In the 1950s and the 1960s, despite mounting pressures to take better account of post-revolutionary national sensibilities, the Supreme Court addressed the changing nature of local adat laws. At issue were customary notions of women's rights, which were considered to undermine the equality of gender rights. Under adat law, women do not inherit from their father or widows from their husband, and Islamic law prescribes that a daughter inherits only half the share of her brother.[26]

To promote the bilateral inheritance of property, the Supreme Court used the concept of a "living law," suggesting that adat law was not static but was changing in the direction of the new national sensitivities. As subsequent cases attested, judges at lower level courts did not necessarily follow the Supreme Court, but some did and sided with daughters or widows when they appealed to them to obtain a share of the land estate of their fathers or (deceased) husbands. According to John Bowen on whose account the present discussion is based, what emerged was the idea that the judge's sense of justice could itself be a source of law, thus validating a "judge-made law" that broke with the logic of both adat law and the civil law tradition (Bowen, 2003, p. 55). Nevertheless, when pronouncing a judgment against the custom, the judge was typically careful to invoke the particular circumstances that in his eyes justified the nonapplication of the customary (adat) rule.[27]

---

[26] Islamic law also prescribes that, after certain fixed shares of an estate have been awarded, the remainder of the estate is divided in such a way that agnatic relatives (related through males) take priority over uterine relatives (related through females).

[27] For example, the widow had previously registered her husband's land and thus cleansed it of its ancestral status (Bowen, 2003, pp. 56–7).

Moreover, when facing a conflict between Islamic law and adat (because the plaintiff referred to one while the defendant referred to the other), judges generally tried to avoid siding explicitly with either, searching for a standard that could be reconciled with both normative systems (p. 100).

This system clearly entails legal pluralism. Cases are settled either in the customary manner, through community-based dispute settlement mechanisms or an Islamic court, or by appealing to a modern court. Under the latter option, the case may still be settled on the basis of the custom, because the judge may choose to follow traditional norms or practices rather than the sense of justice promoted by the Supreme Court. Or the judge at the civil court may strike a compromise between adat (a woman does not inherit property from her father) and the principle of strict equality between sexes, by applying the Islamic inheritance law (a daughter is entitled to one-half the share of a brother). In this latter eventuality, Islamic law becomes the "living adat," as argued by Judge Ponang for the Gayo highlands (Bowen, 2003, pp. 102–3). Note that, as in colonial times, religious courts are restricted to issuing opinions rather than enforceable decisions. In other words, a religious court still has to ask the local civil court to execute a decision. Hence, the religious court's jurisdiction can always be challenged on the ground that Islamic law was not locally "living" (pp. 177–8).

The next stage in the process of elaboration of the family law in post-independence Indonesia came with the fiqh reform in the 1980s and 1990s. The fiqh principle consists of allowing reciprocal acculturation between Islam and local culture (see Chapter 3). During those decades, efforts were made to reinterpret Islam in a way that made it relevant to present-day circumstances, which differed enormously from the patriarchal setup of Arab society in the time of the Prophet. Professor Hazairin and his followers argued that what matters is the principle of justice guiding the Quran, rather than the precise rules adopted at the time, such as the 2:1 formula governing inheritance (Bowen, 2003, pp. 157–60). Calls for reforming fiqh came not only from law specialists and progressive intellectuals but also from the New Order government. Thus, the incumbent minister of religion, Munawir Szadjali, urged jurists to support a change in Indonesian fiqh such that it would divide wealth equally among sons and daughters. A critical point in his argument was that in actual practice even the ulama were already following an egalitarian rule when dividing wealth among sons and daughters. When denied that possibility before an Islamic court or after consultation with an Islamic scholar, the ulama would go to the civil court to justify their sense of justice. To profess respect for the Islamic rule and urging others to respect the letter of the Quran was therefore sheer hypocrisy on their part. Still, the powerful argument that the Islamic law was out of step with the reality and preferences of the believers could not convince Islamic scholars of the scripturalist tradition: In the Quran the ratios of inheritance shares are explicit and certain, and there is no way they can be altered. As a consequence, the 1991 Indonesian Compilation of Islamic Law contains the 2:1 ratio (pp. 161–3).

For the same reason, the Compilation of Islamic Law also prohibits the sale of waqf properties, and it retains the distinction between biological and adopted children, even though it recognizes adopted children as having the same claims to parental wealth as other children in adat (customary) law, in Java in particular (p. 49). Thus it is hard to disagree with Bowen when he comments that "ignoring the rule is much easier than rewriting it" (Bowen, 2003, p. 163).

As stressed in Chapter 3, there are few precise injunctions in Islam. This explains why the Compilation also contains provisions that mark a definite progress over classic fiqh. For example, one rule provides that joint or marital property should be divided equally between husband and wife (or their heirs) in the event of divorce or death of one of the parties. Another innovation is the provision that even a single daughter will inherit the entire parental estate if both her parents have died, implying that brothers and sisters of the deceased are "blocked" by her from receiving any share. In this second instance, the change was motivated by the Indonesian cultural model of bilateral kinship that lies beneath the Compilation, even though the Supreme Court and supporters of the Compilation have tried to justify it in fiqh terms as an acceptable interpretation of the Quran (Bowen, 2003, pp. 189, 195–6).

Another example consists of the Compilation's official acceptance of premortem donations to children, despite Islam's stress on inheritance (division of shares) only on the death of the parents. This acceptance has been motivated by the fact that such donations were increasingly prevalent in several parts of the country (see Chapter 3). To reconcile this practice with the principle of justice underlying the Quran, the Compilation has imposed limits on the extent to which a property can be distributed premortem and parents can freely decide to whom the property is transferred. These limits are intended to preserve the rights of heirs, to ensure a fair division of land estates, and to minimize quarrels among siblings (Bowen, 2003, p. 145). Finally, the Compilation has made it more difficult for a husband to repudiate his wife, for example by requiring that any claim that the couple is continuously quarelling be proven rigorously (pp. 208–9).

The legal status of the Islamic Law Compilation, however, remains unclear. There is no consensus about whether it represents a binding code prescribing uniform rules across the whole country. Some judges choose to apply it; others come up with their own interpretations where they disagree with some of its provisions (Bowen, 2003, pp. 191, 193). In particular, the innovation allowing a single daughter to "block" other heirs from inheriting from her parents has stirred abundant controversy. Many lower level judges belonging to first-instance courts, in Aceh for instance, continue to judge cases based on older jurisprudence, meaning that brothers and sisters of the deceased are entitled to share the estate with a daughter. Although it initially claimed that the Compilation merely codifies and unifies what was already present as a popular consensus, the state later admitted that the Supreme Court and the formulators of the Compilation were motivated by considerations other than those of fiqh. Allegedly, they were guided by modern norms of justice stressing gender equality, bilateral inheritance, and the nuclear family, which implies that direct descendants, male or female, are privileged over collateral relatives (pp. 191, 198).

Judges remain free to express dissent regarding some explicit rules dealing with controversial matters, yet their decisions may be overruled on appeal. This is a feature of the system to which they have grown accustomed over the years. They have also become comfortable working in a system where the Ministry of Religion yields control over court administration and assumes a fiqh oversight role. The Ministry gradually superseded the Supreme Court on the grounds or under the pretext that it was not active enough. Many Indonesian lawyers, however, have decried the mingling of executive and judicial powers, which is particularly manifest in the control exercised over the religious courts (Bowen, 2003, pp. 188, 193).

Overall, the professed goal and avowed character of fiqh reform have remained ambiguous. Here, it is worth quoting Bowen extensively:

The state has attempted to create a schema of Islamic law that contains within it the conditions of its own legitimacy – a bootstrapped fiqh. Both the form taken by Islamic law, a unique set of rules to be applied throughout the nation, and its proclaimed basis of legitimacy, that it merely renders explicit a popular legal consciousness, parallel the form and legitimacy claims associated with the Supreme Court's idea of a "living adat law". Neither corresponds to local perceptions of adat or fiqh, which are based on independent judgments. Adat draws its legitimacy, its normativity, from the experience or memory of practices specific to a place or an ethnic group. Fiqh is legitimate only insofar as it is proclaimed by persons considered to be learned in the law, religious scholars and local ulama. The Islamic legitimacy of this bootstrapped fiqh continues to depend on the acquiescence of those scholars, but the increasingly recognized idea of international norms of 'women's rights' continues to shape their responses. (Bowen, 2003, p. 199)

The judicial system of post-independent Indonesia is complex owing not only to the convoluted justifications invoked by its proponents but also to the heterogeneity of judgments implied by the principle of "legal choice" that lies at its core. Legal pluralism was actually strengthened in the late 1990s when regional assertions of authority based on adat law (for example, by the West Sumatran Adat Assembly) increased as the state began to hold out promises of greater autonomy for districts and provinces. At the same time, as a long-term ideal, the Compilation aimed to increase uniformity and consensus centered around modern principles of justice and modern values of equality, gender equality in particular. In other words, it was expected to generate a magnet effect in the sense of the aforementioned namesake theory, and this effect was understood as being part of a gradual change undergone by the whole of Indonesian society. Things are more complicated, however, because some of the new principles of justice embodied in the Compilation or advocated by the Ministry of Religion are themselves he outcome of judicial precedents or evolving practices in some parts of the country. To put it in another way, local processes and deliberations have at least partially shaped the change in national jurisprudence and the innovations brought into the Compilation. In the language of the magnet effect theory, there thus exists a two-way interaction between the statutory law and the custom, and the magnet effect is susceptible of operating only in the regions where the law provides a new reference point because it was not born of evolving local norms and practices. When social norms and practices prevailing in some parts of the country have thus been transformed by jurists and judges into a quasi-statutory rule (in the Compilation), it is only ex post that these jurists and judges have constructed an Islamic justification (Bowen, 2003, p. 146).

9.6 Conclusion

Not all Muslim autocrats are corrupt leaders unable to perceive the advantages of modernizing reforms. If enlightened, they will adopt progressive reforms and bring Islam under state control. They will therefore refuse to forego measures that displease the clerics for the sake of rallying them to their support, and as a result, the risk of an obscurantist deadlock will be avoided. The enlightened autocrats may still co-opt a good number of the clerics, thereby ensuring a measure of stability for the regime, if they pay them stable and handsome salaries and award them an honorable status through integration into the state administration. An additional condition is that they do not indulge in too much corruption, do not adopt excessively unjust social and economic policies, and do not submit to foreign powers to blatantly protect elite interests. Even this condition may not be sufficient, however. In point of fact, the approach to modernizing reforms and the way they are enacted, announced, and implemented may also matter a great deal.

The detailed examination of some well-known experiences of enlightened autocratism or despotism in the Muslim world, those of Kemalist Turkey and Bourguiba's Tunisia, plus the more transient reform attempts of Afghan strong rulers, has revealed that, unfortunately, the last condition can be violated with disastrous consequences. In those instances, indeed, a radical top-down approach has been followed that had the effect of excessively antagonizing the clerics and the mass of ordinary people.

This radical approach frontally assaulted popular culture, which mixes religion and customary practices in its most vital components. Not only did political and administrative authorities meddle in matters of personal status, such as marriage, divorce, and inheritance, but they also cracked down on popular religious movements, associations, and secret societies that crystallized deep-rooted traditional beliefs and rituals. By intruding so forcefully into the popular sphere of private and social life, enlightened despots unnecessarily complicated their task. It is revealing that other changes, such as the introduction of Western-inspired codes of commercial, administrative, and criminal law, aroused no serious opposition, largely because these changes mainly concerned elite groups that actually demanded them or were at least ready for them. By causing tremors across society through intrusions into private life, these despots threatened political stability, which they could maintain only through systematic recourse to force and blunt repression. Political stability was even more compromised when they were surrounded by a deeply corrupted elite, as in Tunisia, under Ben Ali in particular. Being secular and being corrupt were thus seen as the same side of the coin, an association that covert religious opposition shrewdly played up.

An alternative approach – less authoritarian, intrusive, and confrontational – appears much more promising and less likely to generate tensions and splits within society. Followed in countries like Morocco and, above all, Indonesia, this approach characteristically avoids open challenges to prevailing cultural norms and clashes with the masses of ordinary people. It brings about change in a discreet, gradual, and nonuniform manner so that the reforms do not appear driven by a Westernized elite antagonistic to traditional culture. Such a moderate approach to reforms is based on several key principles.

The first principle is that of legal pluralism, understood in a double sense: the existence of multiple court systems and judicial discretion in reconciling and combining different laws or practices. The former aspect means that Islamic courts and informal mechanisms of dispute resolution are not dismantled or ignored, but instead are given official or quasi-official recognition. Together with official status comes the possibility of setting constraints on their mode of operation and area of competence. As for the latter aspect of legal pluralism, it continues a long tradition of acculturing Islamic tenets to local customary practices, thus proving Islam's ability to adapt to people's mores in ordinary circumstances.

The second principle requires that, even in sensitive matters touching on personal status, the political and judiciary authorities enact a modern code that contains progressive provisions to which judges can refer if they so wish. Such a code points the way toward modern principles of justice and equality, which can best be implemented by turning into a statutory or quasi-statutory law the practices already followed in the most developed and sophisticated sectors or regions of the country. The hope is that the national code will serve as a magnet able to pull verdicts issued by conservative judges in the desired direction of more equality (gender equality in particular), while simultaneously allowing progressive judges to strictly apply modern principles of law. In addition, the national code may establish fundamental rules whose violation will not be tolerated. A striking example is honor crimes that fall under the purview of criminal courts, lying strictly outside the jurisdiction of traditional courts.

Finally, the third principle is that sufficient attention needs to be paid to the culture of Islamic jurisprudence. Islamic jurists should continue to present a fiqh-type justification for the radical reshaping of law in the modern code. Judges inspired by Islam will be more willing to pronounce gender-equitable judgments or judgments adapted to modern life if they can rationalize or vindicate them in terms compatible with the faith.

In the light of these sound principles, it is a sobering fact that enlightened autocrats like Bourguiba and Atatürk chose to tread the radical path of assertive and exclusionary secularism. Why might they have made such a choice?

At least two plausible answers spring to mind. First, the old institutions, including religious ones, may have been narrowly associated with the abhorred absolutism of the Ancien Regime. This was true in France, the model for the Young Turks, where the French Revolution also took a strongly radical antireligious stand. There, indeed, the Catholic Church actively supported the successive royal authorities, even in the terminal period of the Bourbon dynasty (see Kuru, 2009, ch. 5). Note that the same can be said of the attitude of Bolshevik revolutionaries toward the Orthodox Church (Obolonsky, 2003, pp. 109–111). Second, the old society and institutions may be despised because aspiring modern elites consider them responsible for the backwardness of their country and its inability to compete with the advancing (Western) world. This is certainly a relevant factor for Turkey, where the Young Turks attributed the relative decline of their nation to the exasperating obstacles created by traditional local culture.

Islam, Politics, and the Challenge of Enforcement

For a religion to exert a detectable influence on individual and group behavior, it must apparently possess a doctrine containing precise injunctions as well as an authority structure able to interpret them unambiguously and to enforce them effectively. The second condition may nevertheless be sufficient if the faithful have so deep a trust in the religious temporal structure that they are willing to follow its instructions, even if based on particular interpretations of rather loose tenets or allegorical statements. The central objective of this conclusive chapter is to assess the role of Islam in regard of these two distinct dimensions, the doctrine and the organization of the faith.

The discussion proceeds in two successive steps. In Section 10.1, I examine the well-known theory of the institutional trap owed to Timur Kuran, and Section 10.2 summarizes my contribution, in which politics plays a central role. I argue that Kuran's and my approaches are deeply compatible: Politics may actually provide the bridge between them, because it affects the enforcement environment in which laws and other rules are promulgated or persist. Section 10.3, then, addresses a highly topical issue that has been touched only sporadically or obliquely in this book: the persistence of tribalism. One interesting way to look at Islam consists of viewing Muhammad's message as a guide to the building of a well-meaning state that transcends tribal fragmentation. The failure to overcome tribalism deserves to be investigated and contrasted with the different fate of Western Europe. This investigation links this chapter to Chapter 2. Section 10.4 presents final thoughts that close the book.

10.1 Institutional Change and the Enforceability Issue

This section begins with a short summary of Timur Kuran's theory of the "institutional trap" inherited from the classical Islamic system. I then stress the need to define the Islamic institutions at play in the narrow sense that Kuran himself proposed. The next stage consists of formulating the enforcement problem and confronting the questions that arise from the weak enforcement of Islamic rulings. Finally, I examine the role of politics in Kuran's analysis and conclude that his attention has been restricted to the political consequences of well-established Islamic institutions.

The Theory of the "Institutional Trap" in a Nutshell

Kuran's theory of the institutional trap is based on the idea that Muslim countries have inherited a particular set of institutions derived from classical Islam (see, in particular, Kuran, 2004a, 2004b, 2011). More precisely, a direct consequence of the historical context in which Islam was born is that the Quran contains rules prescribing the rightful behavior to follow in a number of civil matters, and in these matters that it addresses explicitly, the Quran carries an especially strong authority. Kuran focuses attention on a number of central institutions of the classical Islamic system that took shape over the religion's first three centuries.[1] These institutions, he argues, had the effect of blocking critical institutional changes. These institutions are the Islamic law of commercial partnerships, which limited enterprise continuity and intergenerational persistence; the Islamic inheritance system, which encouraged wealth fragmentation and restrained capital accumulation by creating incentives for keeping partnerships small; the waqf system, which inhibited resource pooling and stifled the development of a genuine civil society; and Islam's traditional aversion to the concept of legal personhood, which hampered the emergence of private corporate organizations. Critical among these institutions is the inheritance system, which inhibited the development of Islamic contract law. Meanwhile in Western Europe people found it relatively easy to modify inheritance practices in response to changing needs, because the Bible does not prescribe rules for transferring wealth across generations.

As a result of the influence of Islam, a whole series of organizational changes that proved essential for the development of a modern economy did not therefore take place in the Middle East. The fact that from the late eighteenth century onward, the region's indigenous Christians and Jews came

---

[1] As noted by Kuran, the central economic institutions of the Middle East evolved over the three centuries following the "age of felicity" – the period of Muhammad and his first four successors. Firmly in place around year 1000, they were to persist until the nineteenth century (Kuran, 2004b, p. 72).

increasingly to dominate the most lucrative economic sectors bears witness to the adverse role of Islamic institutions. Unlike the Muslim majority, who had to do business under Islamic law, members of these minorities were free to choose an alternative legal system (Kuran 2004c; Goffman 2002, p. 73). Consequently, at the start of the twentieth century, almost all large commercial enterprises in the Middle East were owned by either foreigners or members of local religious minorities (Kuran 2004b, pp. 72, 84–7).

The example of Turkey is particularly interesting because Islamic law was abrogated when the Young Turks seized power from the Ottomans and accelerated the country's move along the Westernizing secular path (see Chapter 9). The implication is that the lingering effect of Islamic institutions that emerged during the religion's first three centuries rather than Islamic law itself is the real obstacle to modern economic growth. Institutions that were adapted to economic conditions prevailing at the time of their emergence thus proved to be a barrier in later times, when Western societies had undergone basic transformations (Kuran, 2004b). From the perspective of modern growth, the main problem with Islamic economic institutions is that they retarded the development of impersonal, as opposed to personal, exchange relationships. The ensuing limitations were largely irrelevant in the Middle Ages, but became binding during the early modern period once opportunities for large-scale trade through impersonal relationships emerged.

On the question of why inefficient institutions have persisted for so long, thus generating an institutional path dependence in the Middle East, Kuran (2011) answers that a key characteristic is that they formed systems of mutually reinforcing interrelated elements, in a way suggested by Avner Greif (2006a, p. 35) and Samuel Bowles (2004, pp. 90–1). Thus, owing to the presence of important externalities, the reform of any single institution was likely to fail unless other institutions were also transformed. The vicious circle in question was difficult to break, especially because the underlying Islamic institutions weakened civil society. As we see shortly, a weak civil society further limits the ability to make institutional innovations.

An Important Caveat

It bears emphasis that a limited number of institutions fall into the purview of Kuran's institutional trap. Some scholars have tried to extend the list, however. For example, Ghislaine Lydon (2009a, 2009b) claims that a basic flaw in Islamic legal systems was their failure to invest paperwork with legal personality. Paradoxically, although Quranic verses placed great emphasis on the importance of writing and documenting credit transactions, written documents such as debt contracts and even fatwas had no value in and of themselves and could not therefore be used as legal evidence in a court of law. Such lack of faith in paper stemmed from the belief that documents can easily be tampered with or simply forged, whereas oral testimonies given under an oath by witnesses are quite reliable. The rejection of written evidence in court, so the argument runs, constituted a serious obstacle to the modern development of Muslim economies because it inhibited the growth of "paper companies," such as joint-stock companies or corporations, as well as the development of complex and large-scale enterprises in commerce, industry, and the key sector of banking.

The main problem with Lydon's thesis is its alleged general applicability. Detailed historical evidence shows that the legal status of documents and written pieces of evidence has not been low at all times and places in the Middle East. In Egypt, for example, during the late Mamluk period, deeds regarding loans, credit, partnerships, deposits, and transactions for goods of various kinds were regularly recorded in court registers, implying that merchants could afford guarantees and did not have to simply depend on the other party's good faith. Moreover, the court documents issued in one city were recognized in the other cities so that a person in Cairo, for instance, could record a sale for a house he owned in Damas, Jerusalem, or Jedda (Hanna, 1998, pp. 50–1, 67–9).

In Ottoman Turkey, written documents could influence the judge's decisions. Using evidence from the courts of Galata and central Istanbul in the seventeenth century, Kuran and Lustig (2012) show that Ottoman subjects could register agreements in court in order to have a record in writing as insurance against misunderstandings. Moreover, the probability of winning a case in court was "massively" increased when the plaintiff had a written contract, whereas when only the defendant presented a document, the chances of the plaintiff winning the case were almost nil (pp. 652–3). In spite of this advantage, written contracts and settlements remained few. However, this may not be so surprising inasmuch as people continued to operate in a world characterized by highly personalized relationships where interpersonal trust was important and not easily called into doubt by the requirement of written statements. In the words of Kuran and Lustig: "Perhaps the most important reason for the low rate of documentation observed in our registers is not the cost of documentation but that in the seventeenth century the Ottoman economy had not yet begun the transition from personal to impersonal exchange" (p. 654).

This structural explanation, according to the authors of the study, is more convincing than the fact that in Islamic jurisprudence documents per se lacked evidentiary value in the absence of corroboration by witnesses to their preparation. Witnesses could indeed be hired to provide the necessary services. As one might expect, the practice of hiring witnesses was commonest among non-Muslims who had to produce Muslim witnesses for their contracts to carry weight against a Muslim (Kuran and Lustig, 2012, pp. 653–4). The main lesson to draw from the available evidence is therefore that Islam itself does not hinder written contracts and testimonies, although it raises the cost of using them. By the same token, recourse to documentary evidence, with the necessary witnesses, was comparatively frequent among the victims of institutionalized judicial biases, such as non-Muslims when facing Muslims, and ordinary people, whether Muslims or not, when facing state agents.

Another institution that is sometimes viewed as specifically Islamic is the prescription regarding interest rates. As emphasized by Maxime Rodinson and pointed out by Kuran himself, Islamic law does not prescribe a penalty for dealing in interest, and its main aim has been to curb excessive interest rates, rather than prohibiting the practice altogether (Rodinson, 1966, p. 189). In fact, the claim that Islam categorically prohibits all interest, regardless of form, purpose, or magnitude, on the ground that it violates a sacred Islamic command has encountered strong resistance from the earliest days of Islam, and no large Muslim community has avoided dealing in interest.[2] Muslims desiring interest-based transactions were aided by the jurists of Islam, who devised stratagems allowing people to circumvent Islam's presumed interest ban, without violating the letter of the law (Kuran, 2004b, p. 73).[3] For instance, interest was commonly buried within

---

[2] In Iran, for instance, around 1850 interest rates averaged 12.50 percent, but could range from 18 to 30 percent, depending on the availability of money (Issawi, 1971). Under the Safavids, the ulama themselves developed various subterfuges to make commercial habits compatible with Islamic precepts, particularly in the matter of interest rates (Floor, 2000). In the Ottoman Empire, interest was concealed behind the practice of double sales. Accompanying a statement according to which the principal of a loan ought to be exactly repaid at a fixed date in the future, the sale of a fictitious object took place that represented the interest of the loan.

[3] Revealingly, it is only with the present-day radicalization of Islam that we observe an energetic campaign against conventional banking in countries formally committed to Islamization (Kuran, 2004a, p. 122). In these countries, indeed, Islamic banks have emerged through efforts aiming to differentiate the "Islamic way of life" from other lifestyles, particularly from those identified with the West. Muslim piety is thus increasingly regarded as involving the shunning of interest (p. 123).

payments considered legitimate, such as commissions or salaries (Rodinson, 1966, pp. 179–200). In this respect, there is no difference between Islam and Christianity. Indeed, what the Catholic Church condemned was usurious interest rather than interest as such. Moreover, in European territories under Christian rule, stratagems were used to condone interest practices arising from economic pressures (Koyama, 2010a, 2010b; Rubin, 2011).

The Enforcement Problem

Bearing in mind this discussion, there is one important issue that cannot be avoided when considering Kuran's thesis of the institutional trap: that of enforcement. Often neglected in the literature, the enforcement problem has been recently emphasized by Mahoney and Thelen (2010) in their attempt to build a sociological theory of institutional change. There are two possible forms of underenforcement of Islamic rulings: Either the prescriptions are simply ignored, or they are circumvented or tampered with. Although in the former instance violation of the rules is presumably costless, this is probably not true in the latter because the necessary subterfuges – surreptitious modifications, lengthy negotiations and casuistry, legal fictions, exploitation of ambiguities, and corruption of rule enforcers – entail both costs and risks for the violators. The fundamental distinction is that in the latter situation incentives exist to behave in ways that alter the substantive effects of the formal rule, but without directly violating it. In other words, the actual informal rule contradicts the spirit but not the letter of the formal one, thus reflecting a process of what Helmke and Levitsky (2004) call accommodation between the two rules. This happens when the salience or effectiveness of the formal rule is strong enough to impede its outright modification or open violation, so that the need exists for a reconciliation between conflicting dimensions within the existing formal institutional arrangement.

Some situations documented in Chapter 3 illustrate the first possibility of underenforcement in which rules are simply bypassed. In rural areas of Muslim West Africa, but also in Asian countries such as Afghanistan, for instance, such precise injunctions of Islam as the inheritance rules were not and are still not followed: The prevailing rules and practices reflect a blending of local customs with Islamic principles, and in sensitive matters such as inheritance, patriarchal customs trump Islamic prescriptions.

Chapter 3 also hinted at the second possibility of rule underenforcement by noting that innovations are permissible provided that they are backed by an appropriate fatwa issued by a prestigious enough scholar. In fact, since the early times of Islam jurists were able to develop tricks ("hiyal") that, in the manner indicated by Helmke and Levistsky, allow Muslims to conform to the letter of Islamic law while accommodating the demands of business life. Moreover, the jurists "appear to have been swayed not only by custom and business necessity, but also by other legal systems" (Berkey, 2010, p. 41). Examples of rule adjustment or perversion are plentiful, and the aforementioned case of interest prohibition is only one of them.

What needs to be added is that the ulama themselves may display amazing ingenuity in circumventing Islamic rulings. The regulations affecting the waqf (pious foundations) and inheritance under the Ottoman Empire were sometimes the object of such inventiveness on the part of high religious authorities. One particular problem arose from the absence of a concept for recognizing human groups as legal entities, along with the Hanefi law of inheritance, according to which claimants to an estate are not confined to direct descendants and each legal heir has a canonical right to a fixed share of the deceased's property. By redefining the monks of a monastery as a family, Ebu's Su'ud, chief mufti of the Ottoman Empire in the mid-sixteenth century, recognized their collectivity, thus enabling them to receive the property belonging to a deceased monk. Technically, the surviving monks were considered the deceased monk's offspring. However, Ebu's Su'ud ordered the monks to make waqfs in their own names, and not in the name of the monastery, because monastic waqfs were not permitted under Islamic law. Realizing the pitfalls of this legal fiction used for the benefit of the monks of Mount Athos, he quickly issued a fatwa restricting similar claims from other monasteries (for other examples in the same vein, see Kuran, 2001).

In Saudi Arabia, on the request of King Abdul Aziz, ulama close to him managed to find a proper scriptural justification for an innovation as fundamental as photography. As a solution, these ulama argued that photography brings together light and shadow, which are both divine creations. In this way, the objection that any pictorial art is idolatrous could be rebuffed (Nomani and Rahnema, 1994, p. 139). They had to stretch themselves to analogously justify the introduction of radio or the practice of interest into the kingdom (Feldman, 2008, p. 97; Owen, 2004, p. 51).

In the light of this evidence, the question arises as to why institutions partaking of the classical Islamic system are or were effectively enforced in some countries or areas and not in others. To stick to the Saudi Arabian example, it is striking that in certain places such as Jedda, the capital, women test the law regulating proper conduct for men and women by wearing their cloak (the "abaya") rather loosely and mingling with men rather freely. By contrast, enforcement of the law is much more strict in the conservative Nejd region to which the holy cities of Mecca and Medina belong (*Economist,*

January 31–February 5, 2015, p. 27). Variations in the degree of enforcement of formal Islamic rulings are not only observable across space when circumstances spatially differ but also over time as circumstances evolve. The Islamic prohibition of innovations ("bid'a") offers a particularly apt illustration. The systematic prohibition of all techniques and practices differing from those prevailing in the times of the Prophet was quickly abandoned, and the distinction, introduced in the Middle Ages, between what constitute "good" and "bad" innovations served as a convenient compromise enabling rulers and scholars to escape absurd situations (Rodinson, 1966, pp. 180–1).

Nevertheless, the notion of harmful innovations persisted and remained available to conservative ulama wishing to block useful changes. One of the best-known examples is the rejection of the printing press in Ottoman Turkey on the ground that "neither the Prophet's words nor his language should be reproduced by mechanical means" (Goody, 2006, p. 236). For David Landes (1998), this refusal of the printing press, "which was seen as a potential instrument of sacrilege and heresy," was "Islam's greatest mistake" and the major factor contributing to cutting Muslims off from the mainstream of knowledge (pp. 401–2). However, once it is realized that the severity of enforcement of an Islamic ruling is susceptible of variations, the question about which circumstances tend to favor a strict application of the Islamic principles and which have the opposite effect of encouraging lax enforcement or outright evasion cannot be avoided.

That the question is highly pertinent can be illustrated through the printing press itself. Why, when they quickly adopted new military technologies, did Ottoman rulers wait almost three centuries to sanction printing? This is in stark contrast to Europe (not only Germany but also France, Italy, the Low Countries, Spain, England, and Switzerland) where printing spread relatively rapidly after the invention of the press in 1450, despite resistance by interest groups and temporary restrictions in some countries (van Zanden, 2009, pp. 178–87). Coşgel, Miceli, and Rubin (2012) have recently proposed an explanation based on the legitimizing relationships between rulers and their agents. Allowing for the role of religion but in a way that brings politics into the picture, their explanation can be regarded as a direct application of the theory at the core of this book. According to them, the Ottomans regulated the printing press heavily to prevent the loss it would have caused to the ruler's net revenue by undermining the legitimacy provided by religious authorities. This is because accepting the press would have antagonized the Islamic clerics, whose support was essential to keeping the cost of tax collection to a minimum.

Mass printing would have altered the technology of transmitting knowledge, providing knowledge directly from books or from literate individuals not necessarily affiliated with religious authorities; hence, those authorities' opposition to the printing press. If this innovation had been introduced, the loss of support from these authorities could have damaged the ruler substantially. That is because they conferred legitimacy to him through their loyalty, which encouraged citizens to believe that the Ottoman sultan had the right to rule as well as the power to provide protection and other public goods and services (Coşgel, Miceli, and Rubin, 2012, pp. 362–4). Why did the situation differ in Europe? In European states, so the authors of the study argue, the legitimizing function of religious authorities was dented more than a century before the invention of the press. Accordingly, European rulers had little reason to stop its diffusion. It is revealing that the Ottoman rulers eventually sanctioned printing in the Arabic script in the eighteenth century after alternative sources of legitimacy had emerged.

That a political economics approach can offer useful insights to explain enforcement variations is evident from the analysis proposed by Coşgel, Miceli, and Rubin. It is also evident from a careful examination of the intriguing case of Saudi Arabia. Here is a country whose rulers have deliberately chosen to adopt an austere, puritanical version of Islam known as Wahhabism and to enforce it rather rigidly. In making such a choice, the Saudi rulers have implicitly agreed to sacrifice economic efficiency or to impose avoidable costs on society in order to achieve political objectives of paramount importance. Wahhabism has offered, and still offers, a privileged way to construct a national identity and to acquire legitimacy that the rulers' lack of a strong association with tribal confederations failed to confer. The alliance with Wahhabism also serves their ambition to project Saudi Arabia as a major regional player, which requires a doctrine that appears more true to the original message of Islam than the versions prevailing among rival neighbors and also one that could supply a concept, jihadism, susceptible of justifying expansionist moves inside the Arab world itself (in the same vein, see Paul, 2014, p. 144).

To convey the economic costs of the politics-first strategy espoused by the al Saud family, it is sufficient to consider the closing of shops during each of the day's five prayers, which limits working time; the ban on mingling of the sexes, which compels male and female employees of a same firm to travel to meetings in separate cars; and the prohibition of driving for women, which forces their husbands to spend hours every day ferrying wives to and from work.[4] Among the efficiency losses involved, one must also count (1) the

---

[4] Regarding the latter rule, it is only very recently (February 2012) that a royal order stipulated that women who drive should not be prosecuted by the courts (*Economist*, March 3–9, 2012, p. 56).

waste of human capital caused by the stuffing of young heads with rote religious learning and the consequent neglect of more practical subjects, such as math and science, that the market demands; and (2) the transaction costs caused by complex negotiations and frequent changes in laws and decrees dealing with highly contentious issues such as interest rates. It is evident that the country's immense oil wealth affords the Saudi elite the luxury of disregarding such costs; in the absence of that wealth, they would have to limit them in one way or another.

Clearly the political economics approach offers a useful tool to detect the main barriers to institutional change and long-term economic development. It enables us to better understand the real power struggle that unfolds in a society and how and why key actors succeed in blocking changes that would reduce their power or influence and threaten their wealth. Invoking tradition or religious tenets and injunctions may be an effective way of justifying existing practices and institutions that suit their interests and strengthen their status and power (see Pamuk, 2012, for an attempted application to commercial and financial institutions in the Middle East). When religious principles prove to be harmful to their interests, however, the elites generally find ways to circumvent them while preserving appearances so that the religious law is not openly violated and the clerics can be kept happy. Here, a striking example is the Islamic ban on (usurious) interest. If it has never been seriously enforced, it is because the economic damage that its strict enforcement would cause is quite large.

In general, an approach in which the political game played by central actors is brought into the forefront is likely to provide more convincing explanations for institutional stagnation than an approach privileging cultural and religious factors and silent on the mechanisms behind path-dependent trajectories. For example, in their attempt to account for the paucity of exchanges between Europe and the Middle East and the absence of cross-regional institutional borrowing from the former by the latter region during the last centuries, Bosker, Buringh, and van Zanden (2013) refer to doctrinal differences between Islam and Christianity while other explanations are available and more plausible.

Politics in Kuran's Work

Kuran has not ignored politics but his attention is focused on the political consequences of well-established Islamic institutions. There are several channels through which Islam exerted a negative influence on political freedom and democracy. First, the institution of the waqf promoted a culture of nepotism and discouraged the elite from demanding the constitutional enforcement of private property rights. Second, by preventing the emergence of large commercial enterprises, Islam made potential opposition to autocratic rule more fragmented and less effective. And, third, the deep-rooted habit of personalizing exchanges and attributing responsibility for an adverse externality to a natural person or group rather than to a legal person has hindered the establishment of the rule of law in the modern Middle East (Kuran, 2004b, pp. 80–3, 86–7; 2005b, pp. 819–23).

Kuran's argument is most elaborate in relation to the political effects of the Islamic waqf, a charitable endowment that was the only organizational form available for the private provision of public goods. In a recent paper (Kuran, 2016), he observes that, although their huge asset base made waqfs potentially powerful political players and thus potential forerunners of a vibrant civil society capable of constraining rulers and majorities, in fact they did not sow the seeds of democratization. On the contrary, they helped perpetuate political centralization by preventing subversive communities from becoming organized. This is because they were devised as rigid and undemocratic organizations: In particular, the rules governing the waqf promoted neither broad political participation nor transparency in governance; their assets were inalienable and entirely dedicated to financing the waqf's activities forever through steady rental income; the founder had to be an individual property owner; and resource-pooling opportunities were severely restricted. As a consequence, the caretaker of a waqf faced the state alone, and the possibility of concerted actions by several waqfs (for example, those satisfying similar needs or catering to the needs of the same communities) was precluded.

Kuran also makes three other important observations. First, a waqf enjoyed considerable immunity against confiscation because of the belief that its assets were sacred. The possibility of sheltering wealth from unpredictable rulers offered a critical advantage in the absence of well-established private property rights, and the sultans usually respected the inalienability of endowed assets, except during periods of regime changes or major internal challenges.[5] Second, because a waqf's capital had to be illiquid and because high officials whose wealth was concentrated in real estate were at relatively high risk of being fired, expropriated, and even executed, the benefits of forming a waqf were expected to accrue primarily to them and their families. As for religious officials, they also gained access to rents generated by waqfs through their supervisory authority. Reality differed from the

---

[5] An asset was much less likely to be confiscated if it belonged to a waqf than if it was privately owned.

widespread depiction of the waqf as an expression of pious charity: In the eighteenth century, almost 60 percent of all Anatolian waqfs were founded by state officials (43%) and by clerics generally allied with the sultan (16%).[6] Third, the Umayyad (661–750) and Abbasid (750–1258) rulers who enacted the law of the waqf (the waqf was not among Islam's original institutions) and were themselves inspired by pre-Muslim traditions dating to the Sassanid and Byzantine Empires, knew that this institution might be used by powerful officials to threaten central power. They therefore minimized this threat by restricting the uses of waqf's assets and keeping them strictly out of politics. In short, the precise characteristics of the waqf represented the outcome of "an implicit bargain between rulers and their wealthy subjects" (Kuran, 2005b, pp. 799–802).

In view of these observations, it is unsurprising that the waqf was never a vehicle of democratization, that it contributed to generating vast constituencies with a vested interest in the status quo, and that it bred a culture of corruption and nepotism (Kuran, 2003, pp. 428–31; 2004b, p. 81). Used by the elite as a stratagem to protect their interests in the guise of pursuing Islamic ideals, the waqf mitigated the risk of potentially rebellious coalitions (assuming that the law was reasonably well enforced). In other words, the adverse effects of the waqf seem to have been at least partly intended so that analysis of these effects cannot be disentangled from the question of the emergence of the institution, which has an obvious political economics dimension. Note also that this question is closely linked to the one of enforcement discussed earlier. As a matter of fact, the waqf was probably not invented during the lifetime of the Prophet (it is not mentioned in the Quran), and accounts provided in the hadith (remembrances about early Islam), according to which Muhammad's companions formed waqfs, were probably concocted to legitimize an addition to the Islamic institutional complex. As a consequence, flexibility available to rulers to craft waqfs was even greater than on matters covered in the Quran, as with inheritance, for example – and even on such matters, as we know, Quranic prescriptions could be loosely enforced. Clearly, the political economics approach is warranted regardless of the status of Islamic rulings or institutions; that is, whether or not they are or result from precise instructions attributable to the Prophet.

The central message is the following: It is not sufficient to examine the economic, social, and political consequences of Islamic institutions once

---

[6] For a statement of the conventional view about the waqf, see, for example, Berkey (2003, p. 214).

they have been established. It is equally important, as Kuran's analysis of the waqf itself suggests, to look into the motives behind their formation and into those determining whether, and to what extent, they are actually enforced in specific times and circumstances. It is important to determine whether the Islamic rules and institutions inherited from the classical system constitute an ultimate or a proximate barrier to economic development: Do they constitute the key binding constraint on development, or is their real weight influenced by the enforcement environment, which itself is critically shaped by political forces? The contribution of this book can thus be seen as complementary to the pioneering contribution of Kuran on the role of Islamic institutions in development. Because of the enforcement issue, politics plays a role not only downstream but also upstream, and the divergence between the Middle East and Europe that drives Kuran's investigation cannot be properly understood unless the role of political authorities in the design and enforcement of institutions is elucidated (see also Malik, 2012, and Koyama, 2013, for similar claims). The role of the merchant classes and their standing vis-à-vis the landowning elites and the sovereign must also be included in the research agenda. Thus, the question as to why Ottoman merchants were "too weak to reshape the dominant ideology in their own interests" (Kuran, 2011, p. 94), for example, is an important aspect of the divergence with which Kuran is concerned.[7]

10.2 Islam in a Comparative Perspective

This section summarizes the approach and key results of the preceding chapters. I start by emphasizing the novelty of the approach and then use it to systematize the salient findings of the country case studies. Next, I argue that the same approach throws new light on the type of civilizational crisis confronted by Muslim countries in the present. Finally, I highlight the impact of the international environment on interactions between politics and religion in Muslim lands.

A Novel Approach to State-Religion Interactions

The present study is based on one core idea: The specificity of Islam must be sought less in characteristics of its doctrine than in its decentralized mode

---

[7] In fact, this is the central question raised by Obolonsky (2003, chs. 6–8) with regard to Russia: Why were the merchants and businessmen unable to constitute a powerful countervailing force able to contain czarist authoritarianism and later counter the Bolshevik plot?

of organization. Unlike in Christianity, there is no vertical command structure that can impose uniformity of belief and behavior on the faithful. At the same time, beyond a few precise injunctions contained in the Quran, there are few requirements that Muslims must meet, and it is easier to enter Islam than the other two great monotheistic faiths, Judaism and Christianity. The originality of my work is that it develops this core idea by unfolding its consequences in a systematic and articulated manner. Doing so required special emphasis on the way politics is affected by religion, and vice versa, on the basis of a tight analytical framework. Although grounded in the organizational mode particular to Islam, the analysis is able to account for substantial variations in outcomes achieved in terms of both political stability and state policies, including institutional choices.

The starting point runs counter to a widespread view generally associated with the "clash of civilizations" thesis, which holds, that unlike in Christianity, religion and politics are merged in Islam. As a result, it is commonly said that the risk of theocracy is intrinsic to the Muslim faith, and the ayatollah-dominated regime established in Iran by the 1978–9 revolution is taken as vivid testimony to that danger. My claim to the contrary, which is well substantiated by deep historical evidence, is that in the lands of Islam religion is generally subservient to politics. It is required of rulers only that they publicly profess the faith: A ruler is called an infidel if he does not fast in Ramadan, but not if he is corrupt, authoritarian, cruel, a womanizer, or even a drunkard.[8] It is only in times of state crisis, when there is a power vacuum or when despotism has degenerated into tyranny, that men of religion advance to the forefront of politics.

If I investigate the interactions between religion and politics in the specific context of autocracy, it is because many premodern countries in which religion governs the masses were ruled by autocrats. Thus, European countries that became developed during the nineteenth andtwentieth centuries had themselves been autocratically ruled in the earlier period of their formation as modern states. Although Islam is far from being the only religion possessing a decentralized mode of organization (Hinduism, Buddhism, Judaism, and American Protestantism are other examples), it constitutes the best-documented example of a religion combining religious decentralization with autocracy. This political regime is indeed the hallmark of most Muslim states from the time of the foundation of Islam until the present day.

---

[8] For example, the ulama never made a fuss about the fact that Ottoman rulers were often heavy drinkers and persons who easily abandoned themselves to a life of pleasure.

To understand why the difference between centralized and decentralized religions matters, let me first clarify key stylized facts on which the theory of state-religion interactions proposed in this book is predicated. To begin with, the autocrat must obtain the legitimacy and support of religious authorities if he wants to rule over a society whose cultural identity depends substantially on religion. This is particularly true when Islam (or Christianity) is the dominant religion, because its tenets do not forbid the involvement of clerics in politics. In fact, Islamic rulings or fatwas "represented a formality that was obtained without difficulty from accommodating theologians, in order to put in the clear religious opinion leaders who had already decided to adopt a certain measure for reasons that were strictly economic and political" (Rodinson, 1966, p. 193).

Second, because clerics are corruptible, in that they can be lured through the distribution of material privileges, the autocrat is able to seduce a fraction of them, depending on the resources that he is willing to devote to the task. Third, the co-option decision is taken in parallel with another decision that concerns the policies to be followed. The less antagonistic these policies are to clerics, the easier it is to seduce them. Antagonistic policies include not only measures that go against religious rules of conduct and encroach on religious prerogatives and institutions but also predatory policies involving cronyism, corruption, and extortion that violate the Islamic ideals of equality and fairness. Progressive institutional reforms and bad governance thus have similarly adverse effects on clerical support, although they have different effects on development. Finally, lower and more radical clerics, who are also the most costly to seduce, are relatively insensitive to progressive institutional reforms that mainly affect the high clerics. At the same time, they are relatively reactive to iniquitous policies and practices that severely affect the popular masses to whom they are close. The converse is true for high clerics.

When a religion is centralized, implying that it is organized as a church with a head at the top, political instability is less likely than under a decentralized religion deprived of any strong authority structure. The reason is that in the former case, the head of the church can bargain with the autocrat on behalf of all the clerics; however, in the latter case the autocrat faces the clerics individually, knowing that they have heterogeneous preferences. In other words they differ in their tradeoffs between values and income. When circumstances are such that the autocratic ruler can co-opt the whole clerical body even under a decentralized religious structure, the difference between the two types of religious organizations vanishes in regard to political stability, but not to development outcomes. As a matter of fact, political stability under decentralization may be obtained at the price of foregone institutional reforms, which is bad for development.

Alternatively, for the same purpose of achieving political stability, the autocrat may moderate the extent of rent-seeking and extortion, and this is is good for development from the standpoint of efficiency and equity. Institutional reforms conducive to long-term development and rent-seeking policies geared toward the exclusive benefit of a privileged elite are thus strategic substitutes available to an autocrat concerned with the stability of his rule: The more he indulges in reforms, the less he can extract rents, if he wants to keep his regime stable. The extent to which an autocrat chooses progressive reforms rather than self-seeking policies is crucially influenced by his traits and preferences. If he has a long-term view of the development potentialities of his country, from which he himself and his close circle will be able to benefit, he will be eager to carry out institutional (and other) reforms. If, contrariwise, he is myopic, he will shun away from such reforms and try to exploit any possibility of abusing his superior position to increase his short-term gains.[9]

It is possible to link a good number of the cases described in Chapters 6 and 9 to various predictions of this analytical framework. To this task I now turn.

A Reasoned Typology of Country Case Studies

Let us start by considering again the case of Saudi Arabia discussed in Section 10.1. Here is a country blessed with huge oil resources where, as a result, the potential gains from modernizing reforms are modest. Eschewing any substantial institutional reform that could antagonize the clerics did not therefore entail perceptible costs for the Saudi rulers. Moreover, their political acumen alerted them to the dangers of excessive wealth concentration in their own hands. They thus opted for some significant redistribution of oil rents to the indigenous population, yet not toward the millions of immigrants who are exploited and deprived of any political voice. The double-edged tactic consisting of moderate rent-seeking and absence of reforms enabled the al-Sauds to co-opt the whole body of clerics, achieving

---

[9] Auriol and Platteau (2017b) nevertheless show that progressive reforms and corruption are more likely to be complements than substitutes. This is because in their model more reforms lead to higher growth, and a given rate of embezzlement of national wealth now produces a higher rent for the autocratic ruler. This said, the possibility of substituting institutional reforms for corruption exists for a more reform-oriented ruler even in their tight framework.

political stability despite Islam's decentralized organization. Saudi Arabia is thus characterized by a combination of oil wealth (and the associated windfall incomes) with social conservatism and political stability. Revealingly, as a consequence of unanticipated events that shook the country (jihadist attacks in 1979 and in the 1990s), the Saudi regime became more conservative. Cooperation with religious authorities intensified, and they were allowed to stiffen religious prohibitions as well as to enhance the powers of the morality police. Hence the odd observation that in recent decades women's behavior has been more tightly controlled than in the 1930s, when they could ride on horseback to bring their wares to market (*Economist*, March 12–18, 2016, p. 31).[10]

Kemalist Turkey offers a striking contrast to Saudi Arabia. There, a dynamic autocrat eager to reform the country's institutions and promote modern economic growth achieved absolute power. According to my analytical framework, undertaking reforms results a diminished ability to co-opt clerics and reduced political stability. The reforms undertaken by the Young Turks and Atatürk, which included the outright suppression of autonomous Islamic institutions, the secularization of education, and the introduction of Western-inspired civil and penal codes, marked a major turning point in the modern history of Turkey, ending its relative stagnation vis-à-vis the Western world and laying the basis for long-term development (Kuran, 2011).[11] The other side of the coin is that, though officially suppressed, religion was not dead and popular Islam turned into a vehicle for opposition. When the regime started to democratize, the opposition came into the open; In gradual steps, Islamists began to compete in elections, and in 2002 they won a landslide victory.[12] The leader of the victorious party (the Justice and Development Party), Recep Tayyip Erdoğan, gradually revealed himself as another autocrat bent on undoing many reforms implemented under secular governments stretching back a century. The case of Bourguiba's Tunisia resembles that of Kemalist Turkey, although corruption and cronyism were much more widespread, particularly under Ben Ali, his successor. There, too, major reforms were undertaken, yet the instability of the regime became manifest in the Arab Spring of 2010–11.

---

[10] In 2016, under King Salman, the incremental and quite modest reforms of his predecessor, King Abdullah, seem to have been reversed. That this regression occurred when the king ✔ has engaged his country in a costly war with neighboring Yemen and when Iran's influence in the region has greatly increased is no coincidence.

[11] In the late 1920s, even judicial responsibility in family matters was taken away from the clerics.

[12] In 1994, they won the local elections in Istanbul for the first time.

In both Turkey and Tunisia, unnecessary tensions were created within the social fabric as a consequence of the antagonistic, even contemptuous, stand adopted by an autocratic ruler toward the culture of the masses. This was reflected in policies of exclusionary secularism that generally arise when aspiring modern elites consider the old society and institutions responsible for the backwardness of the country and its inability to compete globally. Unnecessary tensions also arose because new economic opportunities went disproportionately to Westernized elites, thereby accentuating the societal rift between the masses and elites. In Turkey, the effect was made even worse by the fact that a good number of new income-earning opportunities, those available in the form of jobs in the state bureaucracy, were actually closed to people who practiced Islam openly.

Iraq offers an intermediate case. In many respects, the Baathist rulers of Iraq resembled the reformists of modern Turkey and Tunisia. This was especially evident under Abd al-Karim Qasim. However, around the year 1980, the country suffered from a series of dramatic shocks that increased people's frustrations and dissatisfaction with the regime: the rise of Khomeini to power in Iran (1979), the stirrings of a Shi'i revolt in Iraq, Saddam Hussein's catastrophic miscalculation in attacking Iran, and the ill-fated invasion of Kuwait. The first two events radicalized the clerics, whereas the latter two undermined the effectiveness of the reforms. In accordance with the predictions of my theory of state-religion interactions, Saddam's response to the mounting criticism by influential religious clerics was to adopt regressive policies intended to placate the growing opposition. These regressive steps culminated in the ominous "Campaign for the Faith" (1993–2003), which de-secularized the legal and educational system, cracked down on manifestations of modern life, and set barbaric penalties for thefts and speculative behavior. In complete contradiction with his 1977 declaration that the sharia is irrelevant to modern life and his early commitment to the ideal of a national, secular, united Arab mega-state, Saddam claimed that Islam, rather than Arabism and Arab culture, could be the cement of the Iraqi nation.

Next, we consider country cases where a strong but effective state undertook important reforms, avoided large-scale corruption, and successfully co-opted the religious clerics. Such a combination of characteristics was found in Safavid Iran. It bears emphasis that when they built the modern Iranian state in early sixteenth century, the Safavids relied on Shi'a clerics who formed a rather homogeneous body of loyal supporters and provided a viable alternative to less controllable tribal groups. Although no church structure existed to facilitate cooperation between clerics and the Safavid dynasty, the alliance proved solid because an overwhelming majority of the new clerics (old Sunni clerics had been eliminated) were close to the new regime. Because they were foreign, their loyalty to the regime was more easily secured. The collapse of the Safavids initiated a power vacuum and a period of social disorder that broke the existing politico-religious equilibrium and eventually prompted Iranian clerics to lead the long-lasting opposition to the deeply corrupt and largely ineffective regime of the Qajar shahs. Their gradual rise to prominence in the course of the nineteenth century was strongly supported by various population groups, including merchants and bazaar people who rallied behind them after realizing the effectiveness of religious leadership. Although the clerics were in agreement with regard to the Qajar regime's abuses, they were far from unanimous in their conception of a new political and social order. This was especially evident during the constitutional crisis and the revolutions of 1905–17. Such disagreements, which reflected the absence of a unique command structure even among the Shiites, persisted until and after the revolution of 1978–9 that toppled the Pahlavi dynasty.

To complete this summary survey, we shift our attention to the most common situation encountered in the inquiry into post-independent states of the Muslim world. It concerns countries where the autocrat's policy mix consisted of moderate institutional reforms and blatant forms of favoritism, corruption, and even extortion. In these conditions, it was impossible for the ruler to co-opt all the clerics. As a result, the clerical body became divided into two groups. The high and generally urban clerics more easily agreed to trade their support to the regime against various privileges, because they were not antagonized by drastic institutional reforms affecting their role and status. Being relatively sensitive to corruption and empathetic toward the masses, the low clerics entered into political opposition. In Egypt, Sudan, Algeria, Pakistan, and other countries, corrupt autocrats and their cliques tried to fend off criticisms against their iniquitous regime not by meeting the most important objections and amending the prevailing system, but by allying themselves with religious authorities for the purpose of putting down leftist movements. By employing such tactics, they have not only miscalculated but also betrayed their mission. This last statement deserves further explanation.

Regarding miscalculation, it bears emphasis that in Muslim countries the left has never succeeded in mobilizing the support of more than a modest fraction of the population. As a matter of fact, although the urban elites, intellectuals, and trade unionists in particular may be attracted by Marxist and socialist ideas and ideals, the masses of ordinary people are generally rebuffed by irreligious doctrines of foreign origin. Targeting the left as the main enemy thus reflects an erroneous assessment of the balance of political forces. The consequences of such an ill-advised judgment are made even more serious because identifying with religious clerics is dangerous in a context where only a fraction of them can be brought under the regime's control. A bidding war between the regime and its allies in the high clergy and the masses led by members of the low clergy is thereby unleashed, which leads to a religious radicalization of the political debate. Every term of the debate becomes framed in the religious idiom, fatwas pronounced by religious officials are succeeded by counter-fatwas issued by lower or self-appointed clerics, anathema is substituted for reasoned controversies, and violent confrontation risks replacing peaceful discussion. Placing the political debate in religious territory becomes even more risky when the regime's dark forces embedded into the deep state give discreet support to violent movements of the religious right. Egypt, Pakistan, Algeria, and Syria provide sad examples of this ominous possibility.

It is perhaps the starkest and most discouraging finding of our whole study that at the root of the present predicament of many Muslim countries is a betrayal of their secular ideals by political leaders who rapidly turned into autocrats. To protect their personal interests and satisfy their quest for power, they have often mixed nationalism with Islam in a highly combustible manner.[13] The real tragedy behind the dominant political regime found in post-independent Muslim countries can be formulated as follows. Although the minimum benefit that people can expect from autocracy involves physical security and political stability, hopes for even that basic promise have been dashed in these countries. Where political stability cannot be achieved, instability might be seen as the necessary price to pay for modernizing reforms. In those cases, unfortunately, instability goes to waste. It is fueled not by reforms but by prebendiary policies that benefit a narrow elite around the autocratic power.

From the foregoing discussion, it is easy to conceive the optimum policy mix that minimizes the risk of regime demise and simultaneously pursues modernization: It combines a flexible reformism with economically inclusive policies. Flexible reformism entails institutional reforms that avoid head-on confrontation with the masses through legal and cultural

---

[13] This explains, but only partly as we see in the next section, why regimes that in the immediate postcolonial period were generally pro-Western in their political and economic ideologies and policies later lost this orientation. They became less identified with the West or squarely antagonistic to it (Huntington, 1996, p. 214).

pluralism. Under a system of pluralism, multiple court systems coexist, and judges are allowed to draw on multiple legal systems. Even on the most sensitive matters of personal status, however, political and judiciary authorities must enact a national code that promotes modern principles of equality and respect of individual autonomy. This is best done by turning into statutory or quasi-statutory law the practices already followed in the most developed and sophisticated sectors or regions of the country. The hope is that the new national code will serve as a magnet that pulls the verdicts of conservative judges in the desired direction.

Combining the magnet effect theory with the theory of religious seduction that lies at the heart of this book, it becomes evident that excessively radical reforms can yield two distinct perverse effects. They may generate greater political instability by antagonising religious clerics, and they may create a backlash by making judges and law enforcers more reluctant to implement progressive laws.

Modernity can be reached more easily if two other principles are followed. First, a national code must be promulgated that lays down fundamental rules applying strictly to all citizens. This requirement is especially important in matters of criminal justice. Second, the culture of Islamic jurisprudence must be recognized, so that judges are able to rationalize or vindicate judgments adapted to modern life in terms compatible with the faith. Several Muslim countries have adopted legal pluralism; in them, reforms tend to proceed in a calm and gradual manner. Indonesia provides the most inspiring example.

By expanding economic opportunities to the masses, the adoption of inclusive policies lessens opposition to secular reforms. This objective cannot be achieved where nepotism and cronyism are pervasive. Furthermore, there must not be strong barriers that prevent ordinary people from accessing modern education and jobs because of their traditional culture and religious beliefs. These barriers can either be imposed by the state as a result of discriminatory policies or be the outcome of internalized constraints and social norms. In the latter instance, the promotion of cultural pluralism would facilitate the integration of traditional groups into the modern economic system. Members of those groups should not fear a loss of cultural identity when they accept work in a modernized sector.

The Ingredients of a Severe Modernization Crisis

So far, state-religion interactions in Muslim countries have been analyzed as though they are autonomous entities that operate independently of the

international environment. This analytic simplification can now be reme-
died. Powerful global forces have modified, and continue to modify, the
terms of the tradeoff that Muslim autocrats face between policies antagonistic to clerics and political stability. These forces are themselves varied
and interrelated in complex ways.

A good starting point is the idea of a "clash of civilizations" that has
gained currency since it was developed by Bernard Lewis (1956, 1964, 1993),
to be later taken up and popularized by Samuel Huntington (1993, 1996).
Its essence is that a deep-rooted conflict exists between Islam and modernity, which stands in stark contrast with the intrinsic compatibility between
modernity and Eurasian civilization. The key ingredients of the conflict are
religion and the civilization built on it. For Huntington, the Muslims have
developed a superiority complex rooted in a glorious past: Islam is "a different civilisation whose people are convinced of the superiority of their
culture and are obsessed with the inferiority of their power"; reciprocally,
the problem of Islam "is the West, a different civilisation whose people are
convinced of the universality of their culture and believe that their superior,
if declining, power imposes on them the obligation to extend that culture
throughout the world. These are the basic ingredients that fuel the conflict
between Islam and the West" (Huntington, 1996, pp. 217–18). That conflict
has epic dimensions, being defined as no less than a "civilisational cold war"
born of the collapse of communism: communism was the common enemy
of the West and Islam, and its demise "left each the perceived major threat
to the other" (pp. 207, 211). The duty of the West is to defeat Islam, which
"has from the start been a religion of the sword" glorifying military virtues
(p. 263). This requires that the West assess correctly the challenge it faces:
The present discontents of the Middle East should not be interpreted as the
manifestations of a conflict between states or nations, but as a clash of civilizations resulting from the Arab world's rejection of Western civilization as
a whole (Lewis, 1956, pp. 130–1; 1964, p. 135).

Even if we are ready to ignore some ludicrous statements made in support of this thesis (the depiction of Islam as "the religion of the sword,"
for example), it has one key idea that cannot be dismissed: By intervening in Muslim lands, the West is only acting with a sense of its civilizing mission, as though selfish economic and political motives were absent
from the West's foreign enterprises.[14] In the words of Dreyfuss (2005), "By

[14] It is not surprising that Bernard Lewis officially joined the neoconservative camp in 1998
and signed a letter demanding regime change in Iraq drafted by the ad hoc Committee for Peace and Security in the Gulf. The letter was co-signed by reactionary figures in
U.S. politics, including Richard Perle and future Bush administration officials such as Paul

blaming anti-Western feeling in the Arab world on vast historical forces, Lewis absolved the West of its neocolonial post-World War II oil grab, its support for the creation of a Zionist state on Arab territory, and its ruthless backing of corrupt monarchies in Egypt, Iraq, Libya, Jordan, Saudi Arabia, and the Gulf" (p. 333).[15]

Rather than speaking about a clash of civilizations with all the West-centric ideological overtones that this notion carries, it is more sensible to claim that the Muslim world, and the Arab world in particular, is experiencing a severe modernization crisis centered on identity. Yet, many "civilizations" have experienced an analogous modernization crisis; the problem is not specific to the Arab or the Muslim world. As always in such cases, a deep identity crisis occurs, and attitudes of almost masochistic self-deprecation coexist with statements stressing national exceptionalism.

There is no intrinsic feature of the Islamic doctrine or message to which we can trace the present crisis of the Muslim world. What makes the crisis so profound and drawn out is the organizational mode of Islam, combined not only with bad political leadership but also with complicating international events and legacies from the colonial past. This is particularly evident in the case of Egypt where every big flare-up of opposing Islamic movements occurred when the ruler made what was perceived as an important pro-Western move that hurt the country's interests. This was true under King Faruk (when he engaged in World War II on the British side), under Nasser (in 1954 when he tolerated the British presence in the Suez Canal's zone), under Sadat (in 1979 when he went to Jerusalem to sign a peace treaty with Israel that completely ignored the predicament of the Palestinians), and under Mubarak (during the 1980s when he engaged Egypt on the side of the United States in the war against Iran and later in the Gulf War).

A major reason why the modernization crisis is particularly severe in the Arab world is that present troubles cast a shadow on a glorious past. The decline of the Arab civilization and its apparent failure to meet the challenges of modernization laid down by Western powers cause an immense sense of loss and helplessness. Obsession with past grandeur and an acute

---

Wolfowitz, David Wurmser, and Dov Zakheim. Lewis later exerted significant influence on top officials such as Vice President Dick Cheney and Secretary of Defense Donald Rumsfeld (Dreyfuss, 2005, pp. 334–5). He thus gave strong intellectual support to the military invasion of Iraq by the U.S. Army.

[15] Even the idea that rather than a clash of religions there exists a clash of civilizations (Sid-Ahmed, 1994, cited by Huntington, 1996, p. 213) is problematic. Indeed, to speak of preindustrial civilizations without including seems to empty the concept of part of its meaning.

awareness of the decadence of their own culture in the present have triggered enormous psychic tension. This prevents the Arabs from espousing Western values and adopting Western institutions. The idea of a renaissance of the Muslim civilization as a cure to the ills of modern Western culture is generally set in magical and mythical terms that refer to a supposed golden age. The hope for a renaissance, present in both moderate and fundamentalist Islamist movements, is reinforced by the perception that the West denies the past contributions of Arab civilization to the world's achievements and regards Islam as a retrograde civilization supported by a backward faith.

It is noteworthy that Turkey, a non-Arab country with a large Muslim majority, faced the same challenge of responding to modernity from an inferior position. The Ottoman Empire was gradually dissolved, and the reality of the West's economic and technological superiority became unmistakable in the twentieth century. No less than a revolution, that of the Turks, succeeded in overcoming the deep frustrations rooted in a destroyed "self-image" that shook country's elites. Other countries with a glorious past, such as India, China, and Russia, confronted the same challenge. None has completed the reconstruction process expected to restore self-respect and national dignity. Their contining efforts to define a national identity anchored in their own culture and distinct from Western civilization testify to the deeply felt need to have their own development trajectory. Although in China, communism still supplies the required official ideology, in Russia under Putin it has been replaced by a sort of Eurasianism detached from Western rationalism, allegedly superior to degraded Western culture and more preoccupied with spiritual goals (Dawisha, 2014, p. 318; Clover, 2016).[16] In India, the response has been provided by the Hinduist right, which claims to fight for the preservation of Hindu civilization, Indianness, and national consciousness based on self-esteem (Nussbaum, 2007).

A modernization crisis is especially hard to surmount when military defeats compound the perception of economic and technological backwardness. This obviously applies to the Muslim lands where occupation and interference by Western powers (and Russia) outlasted colonial rule. The successive defeats suffered by Arab armies at the hands of Israel, itself openly backed by the United States; the repeated interventions of the same country in Afghanistan; the entry of U.S. troops in Kuwait; the occupation of

---

[16] Interestingly, Russia experiences the same kind of victimization as the Muslim world, and the Arab world in particular. The collapse of the Soviet Union and the reduced international role of Russia have been perceived as an ordeal largely inflicted by the West. As for the Arabs, this perception is not pure fantasy, but based on facts with which the West finds it hard to reckon.

Iraq; and the crushing of Muammar Gaddafi's regime by France, England and again the United States in Libya constitute an almost continuous series of postcolonial external encroachments on Arab lands. Such external meddling breeds a strong sense of victimhood, which exacerbates the dilemma created by differences in economic performance: How, indeed, to embrace Western civilization or, at least, to acknowledge its techno-economic and organizational superiority when the West is perceived as an aggressor and an enemy of Muslim countries?

It is easy to understand how these circumstances encourage deep polarization of Muslim societies. While members of the elite are expected to cling to Western values and aspirations, and may therefore be ready to compromise with advanced countries of the West, ordinary people tend to stiffen their opposition to anything that looks Western inspired. This is especially true because, in the name of individualistic and secular ideals associated with the West, the former have evinced an impressive ability to pursue their own selfish interests and an almost autistic ability to ignore or underplay the pleas of the people living around them. Hence, it is unsurprising that ordinary people are quite receptive to messages formulated in a language familiar to them, the idiom of religion. In the case of Islamist movements, the messages of Islamic resurgence stoke a persecutory anxiety and inculcate an inchoate sense of oppression. They generally picture local elites as impious individuals who have no qualms about betraying their own culture for the sake of pleasing foreign powers and deriving personal advantages from such unhealthy collaboration.

Islamist movements share the claim that the only solution to the present-day sufferings of the Muslim world consists of placing Islamic law at the center of Muslim life. That requires a political revolution to establish a government that rules by the sharia. It is because Muslims have stopped following the dictates of their religion, Islamists hold, that they have lost their capacity to resist the aggressive moves of the Christian West. To regain their dignity, they must admit that secular nationalism failed miserably as a guiding ideology toward the future. They must also get rid of their impious and corrupt rulers. Only then will they be able to retrieve their inner soul and return to the pristine purity of the faith.

Islamist counterideologies that propose both a diagnosis and a cure for the ills of ordinary people have been supplied both endogenously and exogenously. Egypt's Muslim Brotherhood offers a clear instance in which supply was induced by the demand for a religion-based ideology of contest. The writings of Sayyid Qutb (1929–66) were inspired by the troubles prevailing in his country, and this also holds true for his master, Maulana Mawdûdi

(1903–79), who was a journalist, rather than a cleric or Sufi master, living in Pakistan.

On the other hand, the supply of Islamist ideologies was largely exogenous in the case of the oldest such doctrine, that of Wahhabism. Born in the Arabic desert more than two centuries before Qutb and Mawdûdi, al-Wahhab (1703–17) called for a strict, scripturalist interpretation of the Quran in order to impose a uniform interpretation of the faith on all Muslims. However, as we have already pointed out, it is only in the twentieth century that the Wahhabi doctrine was effectively used by the al-Saud family to build the nation of Saudi Arabia. Because of their immense wealth combined with their strong determination to dominate the Arab world, Saudi rulers were able to spread Wahhabism throughout many Muslim countries. This was done not only by financing Wahhabi mosques and other cultural institutions in foreign lands but also by importing huge numbers of Muslim workers to participate in the economic development of Saudi Arabia and its fellow oil kingdoms in the Arab world. Many of these workers were indoctrinated during their stay in Saudi Arabia. They thus helped to diffuse al-Wahhab's message on return to their native countries.

Such international exchanges show that even the doctrines of Qutb and Mawdûdi were not developed in a completely autonomous manner. One cannot escape the conclusion that a special coincidence of several historical events was a major supply-side factor behind the growing influence of Islamic fundamentalism or puritanism: the birth of al-Wahhab on Saudi soil, his close friendship with the al-Saud family, the discovery of huge oil reserves inside Saudi Arabia, and the imperialist ambitions of the Saudi rulers. We can thus enrich the analysis of the case of Saudi Arabia: The coexistence of oil wealth and a puritanical religion has given rise to conservative policies not only in Saudi Arabia but also in numerous other countries where that religion has extended its influence. The first, internal effect results from the abundance of oil resources, which prompted Saudi rulers to privilege political stability and forge a strong alliance with the Wahhabi clerics. The second, external effect appears as another consequence of Saudi oil wealth: The Saudi regime has financed the active diffusion of the Wahhabi doctrine to spread Saudi geopolitical influence. In turn, the spread of Wahhabism has caused a radicalization of some clerics in the receiving countries, making them harder to seduce. Local autocrats have responded to such a change by adopting regressive measures or backtracking on reforms.

In addition to the pernicious role of Saudi Arabia's geopolitics, two other events have significantly contributed to clerical radicalization in Muslim countries. The first is the destabilization of Afghanistan and its transformation into a battlefield where the mujahiddin and later the Taliban successively confronted the military powers of the Soviet Union and the United States. Ironically, the United States backed the mujahiddin against the USSR before turning against the Taliban, which are their offshoot, thus playing a myopic geopolitical game that paid no attention to long-term consequences for local populations. The second event is Iran's Islamic revolution in Iran, which had an enormous impact on Muslim populations throughout the region and on Shi'a populations in particular. For the first time, Islamic militants could witness the successful emergence of a truly Islamic state. The new Iranian leaders not only succeeded in removing from power the deeply hated dynasty of the Pahlavis but they also did so by openly defying the American superpower that backed it. In a context of an unequal international balance of forces and perceived Western bias against Muslims, the rise of the ayatollahs to supreme power was regarded as a just revenge for the West's unjustified use of brutal force in other Muslim lands. If, today, admiration for Iran's regime has abated and become increasingly confined to Shi'a populations, it is mainly the consequence of the accelerated sectarianization of the Middle East that has resulted from the disastrous and continuous interventions of powers external to the region and regional powers with imperial ambitions.

10.3 Persistence of Tribalism

A major obstacle to building effective centralized states and accelerating economic development is tribalism. This concept encompasses various forms of corporate, blood-based entities designed to capture and keep power for the sake of advancing their own particularistic interests. Usurprisingly, political reformers often try to overcome clannish fragmentation with a view to establishing a unified political order in their territories. The founder of Islam, who was also a political leader, can be counted as such a reformer. As Alastair Crooke (2009) reminds us, in pre-Islamic Arabia "the tribe was a sacred value," and "to turn your back on your blood group and join another was unheard of" (p. 237). Thus, by creating a community bound together by a shared ideology rather than blood, and by replacing the wider social unit of the tribe by the unit of the individual family in his legal reforms, the Prophet ushered in "an astonishing innovation."

However, things did not turn out the way Muhammad anticipated. Already in his lifetime, the purpose of his legal reform was partly defeated by traditional tribal law, in inheritance matters in particular (Coulson, 1964,

p. 220). Western Europe, by contrast, succeeded in suppressing the forces of kinship groups at an early stage of its history. It is of the greatest interest to understand why Europe stands out as almost unique in this respect.

Islam's Failure to End Tribalism

Islam was born in a region decimated by tribal warfare and pervaded by all forms of destructive clannism ("asabiyya"). That is why the Prophet and his successors wanted to build a state based on a unifying ideology. Because it emphasized universal human equality before God, the new faith was apparently well designed to transcend tribal affiliations and particularistic loyalties. This theme has been recurrent in the history of Islam. Repeatedly, great hopes were placed in the capacity of Islam's central concept of umma (the universal community of the Muslims) to end internal splintering and social fragmentation.

After Muhammad, the first group to preach that ideal were the Kharijites, around the seventh century. For them, a political leader should not be designated on the basis of ethnic or tribal criteria, but only because he is a good Muslim. Their radicalism frightened the ruling elite, and they were quickly defeated. This situation has remained essentially unchanged to this date, implying that the abstract egalitarian ideals propounded by Muhammad were abandoned almost as soon as he died.

During the Umayyad period, tribal divisions and animosities precluded the formation of a strong centralized state. Before long, the new Muslim elite "realised that the tribal identification was too well rooted in Arabian society simply to be abolished by decree or swept aside by a few measures that tended to transcend the exclusiveness of the tribal bond. The success of their integration of the tribesmen into a state, then, depended as much upon their ability to use tribal ties for their own ends as it did upon their ability to override those ties" (Donner, 1981, p. 258; also cited in Fukuyama, 2012, pp. 195–6). Under the Abbasid rulers who succeeded the Umayyads, power continued to rest less in abstractions such as the state than in the extended households of leading military elites (Berkey, 2003, p. 214). Both the Ummayad and the Abbasid Empires thus bore the imprint of the feudal/hierarchical models of the Byzantine (for the Ummayads) and the Persian/Sassanid (for the Abbasids) Empires. Fearful of the threat to their power that tribal or kinship divisions represented, Abbasid rulers resorted to a system known as military slavery: They recruited slaves of foreign origin to form the core of their army and thus hoped to create a more reliably loyal military. Becuse they were kidnapped as children and then raised in alien households, these slaves were expected to be entirely loyal to their master, the only person with whom they could identify. In the complete absence of kinship ties, their loyalty was owed to the caliph, who was presented as the superior embodiment of the state and the public interest.

The Mamluks emerged as a military institution too late in the Abbasid dynasty to prevent its decline: The central government increasingly disinte-grated under the impact of unstable patronage policies (the leading factions were rotated in office) whereby the ruler divested himself of his duties for the purpose of pure rent-seeking (Lapidus, 1988, pp. 103–8). As a conse-quence, most Abbasid territories were gradually lost and became indepen-dent sovereignties, reducing Abbasid control to parts of Iraq. Nevertheless, the institution of military slavery survived, becoming critical for the survival of Islam itself in subsequent centuries (Fukuyama, 2012, p. 200). First, the Ghaznavid Empire, a Turkic successor state centered in Afghanistan, which united parts of Eastern Persia and Central Asia, expanded throughout the Indian subcontinent. Second, the Mamluk sultanate of Egypt succeeded in stopping Christian Crusaders and the Mongols, thereby saving Islam as a world religion (Hodgson, 1974b, pp. 39–57; 267–8; 415–22). And, third, like no other state since the collapse of the Abbasid rule, the Ottoman Empire unified a large territory inhabited by Muslims and Arabs, becoming a world power (Hodgson, 1974c, pp. 99–133).

In each case, however, the success of military slavery in defeating the centrifugal forces of tribal fragmentation proved ephemeral. In the Ghaz-navid and Egyptian Mamluk cases, the decline of the state was essentially caused by the reappearance of kinship and patrimonialism within the Mam-luk institution itself. Thus, by virtue of their investment strategies, the mainly Turkish, Georgian and Circassian slave soldiers of Egypt's Mam-luk Sultanate (1250-1517) gradually gained political power. They put great weight on investing in urban waqfs so that their wealth and privileges could be passed on to their descendants (Kuran, 2017). Their complete immu-nity from civilian control enabled them to turn the country into a military dictatorship.

The Ottomans were clearly more successful. For nearly three centuries, they kept the military under firm civilian control while banishing patri-monialism and tribal-based cronyism from their state machinery. Yet, in Turkey too, patrimonialism eventually returned. The hereditary principle was reasserted in the late seventeenth century onward, sealing the grad-ual decline of the empire. This is because, even as they protected the sta-tus quo, the Christian-born Janissaries amassed economic privileges and urban wealth, enlarging their corps through the inclusion of rich freeborn

Muslims who played no military roles. In the seventeenth and eighteenth centuries, they transformed themselves from an elite fighting corps into a commercial cartel and a political pressure group with the capacity to pursue agendas of their own and influence economic policies and imperial organization. Over time the Janissary corps turned into a formidable political machine which could work autonomously against the sultan's interests and depose him if necessary (Tezcan, 2010, chs. 5 and 6). In particular, they were able to delay or block military reforms till 1826, the year when Sultan Mahmud II succeeded in annihilating them (Kuran, 2017). It is moreover noticeable that, even during the era of stability and prosperity, the Ottoman state was much more successful in reducing the influence of tribal organizations in the Anatolian and Balkan heartland than in the Arab provinces. In peripheral Bedouin communities, the structure of society hardly changed at all (Fukuyama, 2012, pp. 201, 230).

Interestingly, the baneful process of what Fukuyama labeled the "repatrimonialization" of the state – the successful efforts of kin groups to reinsert themselves into politics– was observed not only in the Middle East but also in China, as witnessed by the decay and eventual demise of the Han dynasty. There, too, state institutions had been created to overcome the limitations imposed by clan-based societies and to make individuals loyal to the state rather than to their specific kin group (Fukuyama, 2012, ch. 9, and p. 229). In fact, the whole history of unified China can be seen as an endless struggle between the Confucian and the Legalist traditions, the former serving to justify a family-based sociopolitical structure and the latter to advocate a strong centralized state (pp. 119–27). In both China and the Middle East, repatrimonialization was possible because clans and tribes continued to exist in the world outside the state, and at some point, the official classes (Eunuchs, Mamluks) wanted to emulate this dominant type of social organization. In addition, efforts to remove the clans were always conceived as top-down projects by a dictatorial state, whereas in Western Europe the clans were undermined by Christianity "both on a doctrinal level and through the power that the church commanded over family matters and inheritance" (p. 127). In both cases, therefore, a political system relying heavily on a tight alliance between central power and clan heads proved sustainable (see Greif and Tabellini, 2010, 2011, for comparison between China and Western Europe).

Observations of the present and recent past in Muslim lands confirm that tribal and sectarian affiliations have remained omnipresent and practically untouched in many places, especially throughout the Arab Middle East. Tribalism is particularly evident in Iraq, Lebanon, Libya, Syria, and Yemen,

but also in Afghanistan, Pakistan, and the Caucasus countries, where Western powers and Russia learned of its power through bitter experiences of
failed interventionism. In Saudi Arabia, too, tribalism has persisted down to
the present. In that country, however, a single family, the al-Sauds, have succeeded in appropriating power and establishing a strong monarchical rule
resulting in political stability. Whether the al-Sauds will be able to maintain their rule in the way other heads of dominant lineages did, such as
the French, Spanish, English, and Russian sovereigns, is an open question.
Then, there is the case of Iran, which appears rather exceptional. Benefiting
from the legacy of the old Persian Empire and, later, from the early modern Safavid state, Iran has largely eliminated tribal influences and loyalties.
Whereas the al-Sauds remain as well known today as they were in the seventeenth century, the Qizilbash have vanished from the Iranian scene. Divisions still exist within Iranian society, of course, but they tend to be based on
social classes rather than tribal affiliations. Turkey resembles Iran because it
is only in Kurdish provinces that tribal structures have persisted. In the rest
of the country, these structures have disappeared. For example, the Seljuks
do not exist any more as an ethnic group, and no Turkish citizen claims
Seljuk identity.

Tribalism is often hard to disentangle from religion, particularly where
local chiefs and tribal leaders, who are simultaneously religious figures, have
penetrated the high spheres of politics. A striking illustration is Pakistan,
where politics is impossible to understand unless the critical role of large
religious families linked to Sufi shrines is brought to light. The heads of these
family dynasties of important shrine guardians (the "pîrs") have thrived
since colonial times when the British considered them as natural candidates for power because they were both feudal lords and spiritual leaders.
They have attracted whole local tribes as adherents and defenders, intermarrying with other big families to form powerful networks of kinship and
patronage: in Pakistan, "it is not wealth alone, but wealth plus either kinship or spiritual prestige, or both, that gives political power" (Lieven, 2012,
p. 137). The pîr families have thus combined land wealth with a large following of "murids" who owe unquestioned submission to the authority of
their Sufi master and therefore constitute a reliable political clientele. This
situation, in which "shrines offer a domain of both allegiance and obedience" and serve as a crucial link between the rural populace and the state,
has persisted to this day in the form of incorporation of shrine-related families into officialdom through appointments to provincial bodies, legislative
councils, district boards and assemblies (Malik and Mirza, 2015, pp. 2–3, 6).
In the words of Adeel Malik and Rinchan Mirza, "They are an omnipresent

reality in every political dispensation, whether a political party is ideologi-
cally on the left or right or whether a military ruler supported 'Islamization'
or 'enlightened moderation.' ... The pîrs truly transcend traditional party
lines. They are adept at shifting political loyalties, which partly explains the
persistence of priestly power in politics" (p. 9).

Overlaps between spiritual and traditional chiefly dynasties exist in other
parts of the Muslim world. In Senegal, for instance, heads of Sufi brotherhoods such as the Tijâniyya, who are called marabouts, often exert considerable political influence both at local and higher levels (Boone, 1992;
Villalon, 2000). Clearly, religious families who head local orders or shrines
are liable to be cajoled and co-opted by national-level politicians. In such
instances, co-option goes beyond the world of high Islam to reach out to
lower rungs of Islam. In this way, rural masses that are under the influence
of local Sufi masters-cum-politicians are effectively enlisted in support of
national autocrats. When autocrats thus opt for such wide religious support, they are automatically tempted to enact laws or adopt measures that
reflect erstwhile tribal customs and not only the preferences and values of
the high-level urban ulama. The consequence is that tribalism and clannism
are consolidated. The examples of Pakistan, Afghanistan, Sudan, and Iraq
(the last period of Saddam Hussein's rule) come to mind here.

Back to Western Europe

In light of this evidence, it is remarkable that local communities organized
around tightly bonded kinship groups claiming descent from a common
ancestor disappeared from Western Europe long ago, before the advent of
feudalism. This is an important way that Europe differed from the rest of
the world, because no centralized state can be effective as long as large and
incorporated kinship groups interfere with politics and impose particularistic criteria as the basis for major political decisions. The question as to
how, so early in its history, Western Europe overcame resistance from such
groups and established a nontribalized state is therefore critical. How did a
small part of the world discard extended families and their communal logic
even before the forces of modern global markets and industrialization set
in? In the words of Fukuyama (2012),

Rather than being the outcome of these great modernising shifts, change in the family was more likely a facilitative condition for modernisation to happen in the first
place .... European society was, in other words, individualistic at a very early point,
in the sense that individuals and not their families or kin groups could make important decisions about marriage, property, and other personal issues. Individualism

in the family is the foundation of all other individualisms. Individualism did not wait for the emergence of a state declaring the legal rights of the individuals and using the weight of its coercive power to enforce those rights. Rather, states were formed on top of societies in which individuals already enjoyed substantial freedom from social obligations to kindreds. In Europe, *social development preceded political development*. (pp. 239, 231)

Fukuyama proposes an explanation based on salient findings from historical studies discussed in Chapter 2 and expanded by Guirkinger and Platteau (2016). It makes for an elegant argument that roughly accords with the central thesis of this book. This argument can be synthesized as follows.

A first step in the individualization process is the ability of individuals to dispose of land and chattels as they see fit, without necessitating the approval of many kinsmen. Even more important is the emergence of women's rights to hold, bequeath, and dispose of property, which marks a rupture with agnatic societies where women achieve legal personhood only by virtue of marriage and giving birth to a male in the lineage. In this regard, it is a noteworthy feat that, from at least the thirteenth century, English women could not only own land and chattels but they could also sue and be sued, and make wills and contracts without permission of a male guardian. Such rights are inconceivable in a patrilineal society in which property is under the control of the lineage (Fukuyama, 2012, p. 233). A further and decisive advance occurred in England when during the second half of the nineteenth century women acquired the right to hold and own movable capital following the abolition of the laws of coverture based on the common law system (Hazan, Weiss, and Zoabi, 2016).

Second, as demonstrated by Marc Bloch (1961), large agnatic lineages tracing descent to a single ancestor had practically disappeared from Western Europe by the twelfth century: "The Roman gens had owed the exceptional firmness of its pattern to the absolute primacy of descent in the male line. Nothing like this was known in the feudal epoch" (p. 137). Because Medieval Europeans did not trace their descent unilineally through the father, the boundaries between lineage segments could not be maintained, and "the group was too unstable to serve as the basis of the whole social structure" (p. 138). The system in which the ties of relationship through women were nearly as important as those of paternal consanguinity prevailed in Europe, as illustrated by the fact that there was no fixed rule regarding name giving: Children took their names either from the father or the mother (p. 137). As a consequence, there was often no feeling of belonging to one family to the exclusion of the other, and blood feuds became confusing enterprises.

The central message is that in Europe, feudalism did not break large kin networks as is sometimes believed. Instead, individualized families formed the basis on which feudalism was erected. Indeed, it is because the protection of individuals against the security threats caused by the disintegration of the Carolingian Empire could no more be properly guaranteed by kin networks that many people sought or accepted ties of personal dependence on strongmen. True, physical insecurity and the disruption of trade also pushed urban dwellers to retreat into self-sufficient villages that, combined with the collapse of larger political structures, rekindled kinship groups to some extent. Yet, Europe's agnatic lineages were too weak by then to be a source of effective support for their members during these times of troubles. Thus, the need arose for an alternative.

Third, following an argument made by Jack Goody (1983), the transition to a new family system departing from the strongly agnatic or patrilineal pattern of the Mediterranean region can be attributed to the actions and institutional interests of the Catholic Church. Reforms initiated by Pope Gregory I (in the late sixth century), later strengthened by those of Gregory VII (in the eleventh century), had the effect of dramatically transforming family structure and gender relations. They consisted of a number of prohibitions of practices, called "strategies of heirship" by Goody (1983, p. 42), that allowed kinship groups to maintain control over property across generations: These practices involved marriages between close kin, levirate marriage, adoption of children, concubinage, divorce, and remarriage. The church also curtailed parents' ability to retain kinship ties through arranged marriage by requiring the bride to give her explicit consent to the union. Bear in mind that, at the time, the likelihood of a couple producing a surviving male able to carry on the ancestral line was quite low. By severely restricting the avenues available to families for bequeathing property to descendants in the absence of a biological male heir, and by simultaneously encouraging donations to the church, the Gregorian reforms created a situation in which this institution benefited materially from a growing pool of Christians who died heirless. These effects were hardly unintended: "It does not seem accidental that the Church appears to have condemned the very practices that would have deprived it of property" (p. 95).

Women occupied a pivotal position in the church's strategy because, once they were given the right to own property and dispose of it at will, they became a large source of potential donations, mainly as childless widows and spinsters. Thus, if a widow is not compelled to remarry, she can enter a nunnery. and her property would then escape her kin group and accrue to the church. By undermining the principle of unilineal descent, the awarding of property rights to women thus "spelled the death knell for agnatic lineages," ushering in a new family system in Western Europe (Fukuyama, 2012, p. 238). Revealingly, the kinship structures of the German, Norse, Magyar, and Slavic tribes dissolved within two or three generations of their conversion to Christianity. There is thus a large and significant correlation between the spread of Christianity (for at least 500 years) and the demise of clans and lineages (Korotayev, 2003).[17] Fukuyama characterizes this massive change in a particularly vivid manner:

Europe (and its colonial offshoots) was exceptional insofar as the transition out of complex kinship occurred first on a social and cultural level rather than on a political one. By changing marriage and inheritance rules, the church in a sense acted politically and for economic motives. But the church was not the sovereign ruler of the territories where it operated; rather, it was a social actor whose influence lay in its ability to set cultural rules. As a result, a far more individualistic European society was already in place during the Middle Ages, before the process of state building began, and centuries before the Reformation, Enlightenment, and Industrial Revolution. (p. 239)

Fourth, feudalism, which substituted for weak kinship groups in times of trouble, resulted in the rise of an entrenched blood nobility that accumulated considerable wealth, military power, and legal prerogative. That social institutions were based on feudalistic rather than kin relations, proved critical to Europe's subsequent political development. Indeed, although feudalism formalized a highly unequal and hierarchical society, it had the advantage of resting on contractual obligations and broadening the undertanding of legal personhood. It is no coincidence, therefore, that peasant revolts were framed in a language stressing breach of contract on the part of landlords. Moreover, once the rights of a feudal lord were legally established, they could not be constantly renegotiated in the same way that authority within a lineage was (Fukuyama, 2012, p. 240).

Also supporting the idea that the disappearance of clan-based organizations in Western Europe worked in favor of that region is an argument developed by Avner Greif (2006a, 2006b). According to him, the decline of large kinship groups during a period of state disintegration and diminishing secular authority on the part of the church created the need for a new solution to collective action problems. That solution turned out to consist of corporations: voluntary, interest-based, self-governed, and

---

[17] Even among the Germanic tribes, as early as the eighth century, the term "family" denoted one's immediate family. It did not take long for the tribes to become institutionally irrelevant. In England, court rolls testify that in the thirteenth century even cousins were as likely to be in the presence of non-kin as with each other (Greif, 2006b, p. 309).

intentionally created permanent associations possessing legal personality. Guilds, fraternities, universities, communes, and city-states are some of the corporations that have historically dominated Western Europe and were to play a critical role in its long-term development. It is thus remarkable that Europe had more than 4,000 self-governing cities by the twelfth century in contrast to the Middle East where until the nineteenth century cities were typically ruled from the capital (Kuran, 2017).

An apt illustration of the role of corporate organizations in Europe's long-term economic development is provided by David de la Croix, Matthias Doepke, and Joel Mokyr (2016). The starting point is the following: It is mainly because of superior institutions for the creation and dissemination of productive knowledge that Europe pulled ahead of other world regions at the time of the Industrial Revolution. Worth singling out are the apprenticeship institutions developed during the Middle Ages and based on the person-to-person transmission of tacit knowledge, the young learning as apprentices from the old (Mokyr, 2002). Institutions such as the family, the guild, and the market organized who was going to learn from whom. The original contribution of de la Croix and colleagues lies in a formal argument according to which medieval European institutions, such as guilds, and specific features, such as journeymanship, offered Europe a decisive advantage over regions that relied on the transmission of knowledge within extended families or clans.

One reason why guilds appeared in Europe is that the dominance of the nuclear family in this region created a need early on for organizations that cut across family lines. Moreover, because guilds had many antecedents with a similar legal status, such as monasteries, universities, or independent cities, earlier institutional developments may have made the adoption of guilds in Europe much cheaper than in clan-based societies. Other regions of the world had less to gain from adopting new institutions, because the clan-based system performed well for most purposes. China, for example, whose society was built on strong clan structures inherited from long ago, did not adopt the guild system, presumably because the clan provided a number of advantages – mutural insurance, provision of public goods and intra-group cooperation, and effective enforcement of contracts through kin-based "limited morality" – that would have made its abandonment quite costly (Platteau, 2000, chs. 6–7; Greif and Tabellini, 2010, 2011, 2015; Greif, Iyigun, and Sasson, 2012; Greif and Iyigun, 2013). The same argument also seems to apply to India (Kumar and Matsusaka, 2009). Regarding the Islamic world, the absence of corporate forms of organization has been extensively documented and attributed to the role of Islamic institutions that rendered them superfluous (Kuran, 2005a, 2005b, 2011, 2016).

This evidence casts doubt on the simple view that, as it proceeds, market development crowds out clan-based institutions. What it suggests is, rather, that these institutions, when they exist, shape market development in a particular manner.

10.4 Final Thoughts

The conclusion drawn by Fukuyama (2012) emphasizes the unique nature of the Catholic Church that allowed it to play a central role in the economic and political development of Western Europe. In contrast to the world of Sunni Islam and India, where "religious authority never coalesced into a single, centralized bureaucratic institution outside the state," the church "is intimately bound up with the development of the modern European state, and with the emergence of what we today call the rule of law" (p. 241).

The core argument developed in this book holds that a centralized organization of religion is more conducive to political stability than a decentralized one. In addition, it is more likely to facilitate modernizing reforms undertaken by an autocratic power. In a sense, Fukuyama's account adds strength to ours: Not only does a centralized church allow an autocratic state to carry out more reform but it also may itself take the initiative for progressive moves. And inasmuch as its prestige is great, its ability to influence social norms and culture makes it an even more powerful engine of change than the state.

Yet, there is an unresolved problem with this view of Christianity's historical role: Why is it that, until recently, some areas located in the heart of Western Europe and were parts of the Roman Empire, such as Italy and Southern France, have maintained comparatively large patriarchal families and associated practices (see Guirkinger and Platteau, 2016)? Apparently, the religious law was not equally enforced throughout Western Europe. The reasons underlying variations have not been properly investigated.

Moreover, as Goody was well aware, the motives behind the Gregorian reforms were self-interested, and unlike their immediate and narrow effects, their long-term beneficial effects were unintended and unanticipated.[18] The defense of women's rights, for example, did not stem directly from Christian doctrine. Instead, it was opportunistically adopted as a means to

---

[18] There are other examples attesting that the Catholic Church followed narrowly selfish interests. Thus, an important reason for the persistence during the Middle Ages of the religious ban on lending money at interest was that it created a barrier to entry that enabled the church, and also secular rulers and a small number of merchant-bankers, to earn monopoly rents in credit markets (Koyama, 2010a).

fulfill a selfish objective of the Catholic Church acting as a collective agent. The immediate implication is that contingent circumstances may well have driven Gregorian reforms and that another centralized church adhering to the same religious tenets may have behaved differently. Tellingly, the Eastern Orthodox Church did not undertake similar reforms, and kin-based communities survived in most of the lands ruled by Byzantium (Fukuyama, 2012, p. 241). Even today, in Albania, Kosovo, Serbia, Montenegro, Romania, and Bulgaria, large family units and kin-based networks remain a strikingly important source of cultural identity. They yield a pervasive influence on the way the economy, the society, and the polity function. Equally impressive is that these networks have survived despite almost a half-century of centralized communism. The same observation can be made about Central Asian countries that belonged to the Soviet Union, where not only Muslim but also non-Muslim populations retained their traditional family-centered features.

A last difficulty with the view stressing the role of the Catholic Church in Western European development concerns property rights, and those afforded by women in particular. Indeed, Islam also recognized all the individualized rights mentioned by Fukuyama, including women's rights to hold, bequeath, and dispose of property. Western Europe was therefore not unique in this respect.

This said, the generally overlooked lesson from the foregoing discussion is that the family system may greatly impede the ability of a society to endow itself with an effective centralized state. Whether such a state is bent on improving the welfare of its people or to pursue self-aggrandizement is another matter that only shows that appropriate family structures are a necessary but not sufficient condition for long-term development. Because family patterns themselves embed deep-rooted cultural values, modernization typically requires or involves deep cultural change. In Western Europe, it appears that, in a rather inadvertent manner, the Catholic Church helped spark and sustain such a change. In the lands of Islam, absent a hierarchical religious structure, a reform process similar to that observed in Europe could not be initiated and the state had to take charge.

Two conditions are needed for state-directed reforms to be successful. First, the state must be development-oriented. And, second, because personal status matters are hypersensitive in traditional societies dominated by tribal-cum-religious values, the state must tread carefully. It must adopt a nonconfrontational approach based, at least partly, on legal pluralism: The statutory, modern law can then act as a magnet that drives customs to evolve gradually in the direction of modernity, understood as individual emancipation from group-based organizations. In all likelihood, a magnet effect was at work when the reforms of Gregory I were enacted: Christian subjects did not immediately and entirely comply with the new rules (for example, the prohibition of cross-cousin marriages), yet over time they increasingly aligned themselves with them.

What bears emphasis is that the two conditions are interrelated in the following sense: When the state is developmentally oriented and effectively pursues an inclusive growth strategy aimed at increasing the living standards of the greatest numbers of its people, reforms regarding personal matters are much more likely to achieve popular acceptance than when the state is deeply corrupt and self-serving. In many Muslim countries, unfortunately, political leaders have displayed callous indifference toward the welfare of their people, and they have utterly failed to grasp the importance of the interlinkage between modernizing reforms and the expansion of income-earning opportunities for all. They have betrayed the hopes placed in them. Moreover, their cynical use of Islam to retain power in spite of growing discontent has caused not only political instability but also considerable confusion about the relationship between religion and politics.

More ominously, they have discredited secularism by causing its identification with state corruption, and at the same time, they failed to arrest the mounting influence of Islamist movements that are cut off from religious establishments under their control. By colluding with reactionary religious figures whenever public expressions of social discontent became menacing and left-oriented organizations became assertive, autocrats in the Muslim lands have also thwarted the crystallization of class consciousness and the emergence of a civil society. They have stifled the forces most liable to articulate the contradictions and tensions that unavoidably accompany economic growth and organizational or technological change. Because these forces coax autocratic rulers to engage in the sort of social and political bargaining that generates societal transformation, their suppression has been a major setback in the long-term development of Muslim societies.

Bibliography

Scientific Publications

Abbas, H., 2005. *Pakistan's Drift into Extremism: Allah, the Army, and America's War on Terror*. M. E. Sharpe, New York.

Abrahamian, E., 1982. *Iran between Two Revolutions*. Princeton University Press, Princeton.

Acemoglu, D., and T. Jackson, 2015. *Social Norms and the Enforcement of Laws*, Technical Report. National Bureau of Economic Research, Washington, DC.

Acemoglu, D., and S. Johnson, 2005. "Unbundling Institutions." *Journal of Political Economy*, vol. 113, no. 5, pp. 949–95.

Acemoglu, D., S. Johnson, and J. Robinson, 2001. "The Colonial Origins of Comparative Development: An Empirical Investigation." *American Economic Review*, vol. 91, no. 5, pp. 1369–1401.

Acemoglu, D., and J. A. Robinson, 2001. "A Theory of Political Transitions." *American Economic Review*, vol. 91, no. 4, pp. 938–63.

Acemoglu, D., and J. Robinson 2006. *Economic Origins of Dictatorship and Democracy*. Cambridge University Press, Cambridge.

Acemoglu, D., and J. Robinson, 2008. "The Role of Institutions in Growth and Development." *Commission on Growth and Development*, Working Paper no. 10. World Bank, Washington, DC.

Adelkhah, F., 1991. *La révolution sous le voile*. Karthala, Paris.

Adler, A., 2005. *Rendez-vous avec l'Islam*. Grasset, Paris.

Ahmad, E., 2000. *Confronting Empire*. South End Press, Cambridge, MA.

Aldashev, G., I. Chaara, J. P. Platteau, and Z. Wahhaj, 2012a. "Using the Law to Change the Custom." *Journal of Development Economics*, vol. 97, no 1, pp. 182–200.

Aldashev, G., I. Chaara, J. P. Platteau, and Z. Wahhaj, 2012b. "Formal Law as a Magnet to Reform the Custom." *Economic Development and Cultural Change*, vol. 60, no 4, pp. 795–828.

Aldashev, G., and J. P. Platteau, 2013. "Religion, Culture and Development." In V. Ginsburgh and D. Throsby (eds.), *Handbook of the Economics of Art and Culture*, vol. 2, pp. 587–631. Elsevier and North-Holland, New York.

Aldashev, G., J. P. Platteau, and Z. Wahhaj, 2011. "Legal Reform in the Presence of a Living Custom: An Economic Approach." *Proceedings of the National Academy of Sciences (PNAS)*, vol. 108, suppl. 4, December 27, pp. 21320–5.

Alesina, A., and P. Giuliano, 2015. "Culture and Institutions." *Journal of Economic Literature*, vol. 53, no. 4, pp. 898–944.

Alexander, C., 2010. *Tunisia – Stability and Reform in the Modern Maghreb*. Routledge, London.

Algar, H., 1969. *Religion and State in Iran, 1785–1906: The Role of the Ulama in the Qajar Period*. University of California Press, Berkeley.

Al Banna, H., 1996. *The Message of the Teachings*. International Islamic Forum, London.

Al-Husseini, W., 2015. *Blasphémateur! Les prisons d'Allah*. Bernard Grasset, Paris.

Allawi, A. A. 2009. *The Crisis of Islamic Civilization*. Yale University Press, New Haven.

Al-Rasheed, M., 1996. "God, the King and the Nation: Political Rhetoric in Saudi Arabia in the 1900s." *Middle East Journal*, vol. 50, pp. 359–71.

Al-Rasheed, M., 2002. *A History of Saudi Arabia*. Cambridge University Press, Cambridge.

Al-Rasheed, M., 2006. *Contesting the Saudi State: Islamic Voices from a New Generation*. Cambridge University Press, Cambridge.

Al-Shamat, H. A., 2007. "The Effect of Legal Reform on Muslims' Commercial and Financial Performance in Egypt, 1883–1920." Paper presented to the eleventh annual Conference of the International Society for New Institutional Economics, Reykyavik, June 21–23.

Amsden, A. H., 1989. *Asia's Next Giant – South Korea and Late Industrialization*. Oxford University Press, Oxford.

Anderson, M. S., 1998. *The Origins of the Modern European State System 1494–1618*. Longman, London.

Anderson, M. S., 2003. *The Ascendancy of Europe 1815–1914*. Pearson Longman, Harlow, Essex.

Anderson, P., 1979. *Lineages of the Absolutist State*. Verso, London.

An-Na'im, A. A. 2008. *Islam and the Secular State: Negotiating the Future of Shari'a*. Harvard University Press, Cambridge, MA.

Aoki, M., 2001. *Toward a Comparative Institutional Analysis*. MIT Press, Cambridge, MA.

Armstrong, K., 2014. *Fields of Blood: Religion and the History of Violence*. Bodley Head, London.

Aquil, F., 2006. *Etude sur l'identification de l'état des connaissances du Code de la Famille par les bénéficiaires du micro-crédit au Maroc*. Planète Finance, Maroc.

Arjomand, S. A., 1984. *The Shadow of God and the Hidden Imam*. University of Chicago Press, Chicago.

Arjomand, S. A., 2010. "Legitimacy and Political Organisation: Caliphs, Kings and Regimes." In R. Irwin (ed.), *The New Cambridge History of Islam*, vol. 4, pp. 225–73. Cambridge University Press, Cambridge.

Arkoun, M., 1994. *Rethinking Islam: Common Questions, Uncommon Answers*, edited by R. D. Lee. Westview Press, Boulder, CO.

Armstrong, K., 2001. *Islam. A Short History*. Phoenix Press, London.

Arrunada, B. 2010. "Protestants and Catholics: Similar Work Ethic, Different Social Ethic." *Economic Journal*, vol. 120, pp. 890–918.

Åslund, A., 2015. *Ukraine: What Went Wrong and How to Fix It*. Peterson Institute for International Economics, Washington, DC.

Assaad, R., C. Binzel, and M. Gadallah, 2010. "Transitions to Employment and Marriage among Young Men in Egypt." *Middle East Development Journal*, vol. 2, no. 1, pp. 39–88.

Atallah, S., 2011. "The Gulf Region: Beyond Oil and Wars – The Role of History and Geopolitics in Explaining Autocracy." In I. Elbadawi and S. Makdisi (eds.), *Democracy in the Arab World –Explaining the Deficit*, pp. 166–95. Routledge, London.

Atwan, A. B., 2015. *Islamic State: The Digital Caliphate*. Saqi Books, London.

Auriol, E., and J. P. Platteau, 2017a. "Religious Seduction under Autocracy: A Theory Inspired by Theory." *Journal of Development Economics*.

Auriol, E., and J. P. Platteau, 2017b. "The Explosive Combination of Religious Decentralisation and Autocracy: The Case of Islam." *Transition Economics*.

Austen R., 1987. *African Economic History*. James Currey and Heinemann, London.

Austin, G., 1993. "Indigenous Credit Institutions in West Africa, c.1750–c.1960." In G. Austin and K. Sugihara (eds.), *Local Suppliers of Credit in the Third World, 1750–1960*, pp. 93–159. St. Martin's Press, New York.

Avineri, S., 1968. *The Social and Political Thought of Karl Marx*. Cambridge University Press, Cambridge.

Axworthy, M., 2013. *Revolutionary Iran: A History of the Islamic Republic*. Allen Lane, London.

Ayubi, N., 1991. *Political Islam: Religion and Politics in the Arab World*, Routledge, London.

Bach, K. H., 2004. "Changing Family and Marriage Patterns in an Aswan Village." In N. Hopkins and R. Saad (eds.), *Upper Egypt: Identity and Change*, pp. 169–89. American University in Cairo Press, Cairo.

Badie, B., 1986. *Culture et politique*. Economica, Paris.

Bano, M., 2012. *The Rational Believer: Choices and Decisions in the Madrasas of Pakistan*. Cornell University Press, Ithaca, NY.

Baram, A., 1991. *Culture, History and Ideology in the Formation of Ba'athist Iraq, 1968–1989*. Oxford University Press, Oxford.

Baram, A., 2014. *Saddam Hussein and Islam, 1968-2003: Ba'thi Iraq from Secularism to Faith*. Johns Hopkins University Press, Baltimore.

Bardhan, P. K., 1993. "Symposium on Democracy and Development." *Journal of Economic Perspectives*, vol. 7, no. 3, pp. 45–9.

Barfield, T., 2010. *Afghanistan: A Cultural and Political History*. Princeton University Press, Princeton.

Barro, R. J., and R. M. McCleary, 2003. "Religion and Economic Growth across Countries." *American Sociological Review*, vol. 68, pp. 760–81.

Barzun, J., 2001. *From Dawn to Decadence: 500 Years of Western Cultural Life*. Perennial, New York.

Batatu, H., 1988. "Syria's Muslim Brethren." In F. Halliday and H. Alavi (eds.), *State and Ideology in the Middle East and Pakistan*. Macmillan, London.

Bates, R. H., 2001. *Prosperity and Violence*. W. W. Norton & Co., New York.

Bayar, Y., 2009. "The Dynamic Nature of Educational Policies and Turkish Nation Building: Where Does Religion Fit In?" *Comparative Studies of South Asia, Africa, and the Middle East*, vol. 29, no. 3, pp. 360–70.

Bayat, A., 2002. "Activism and Social Development in the Middle East." *International Journal of Middle East Studies*, vol. 34, pp. 1–28.

Beau, N., and J. P. Tuqoi, 1999. *Notre ami ben Ali: l'envers du 'miracle' tunisien*. La Découverte, Paris.

Becker, S. O., and L. Woessmann, 2009. "Was Weber Wrong? A Human Capital Theory of Protestant Economic History." *Quarterly Journal of Economics*, vol. 124, no. 2, pp. 531–96.

Bedoucha, G., 1987. "Transmission des patrimoines en terroir oasien. Idéal lignager et pratiques sociales à El Mansoura (Tunisie)." In M. Gast (ed.), *Hériter en pays musulman. Habus, lait vivant, Manyahuli*. Centre National de la Recherche Scientifique (CNRS), Paris.

Belge, C., 2006. "Friends of the Court: The Republican Alliance and Selective Activism on the Constitutional Court of Turkey." *Law and Society Review*, vol. 40, no. 3, pp. 653–92.

Belloc, M., F. Drago, and R. Galbiati, 2015. *Earthquakes, Religion, and Transition to Self-Government in Italian Cities*. CESifo Working Paper no. 5566. Center for Economic Studies & Ifo Institute, Munich.

Beloucif, S., 2003. "L'Islam entre l'individu et le citoyen." In T. Ferenczi (ed.), *Religion et politique: Une liaison dangereuse?*, pp. 145–55. Editions Complexe, Le Mans.

Bénabou, R., D. Ticchi, and A. Vindigni, 2015. *Forbidden Fruits: The Political Economy of Science, Religion and Growth*. Working Paper, Princeton University, Princeton.

Ben Achour, Y., 1987. "La réforme des mentalités, Bourguiba et le redressement moral." In M. Camau (ed), *La Tunisie au présent*. Editions du CNRS, Paris.

Benraad, M., 2015. *Irak: de Babylone à l'Etat Islamique*. Editions La Cavalier Bleu, Paris.

Berdyaev, N., 1948. *The Origin of Russian Communism*. University of Michigan Press, Ann Arbor.

Berkes, F., 1964. *The Development of Secularism in Turkey*. McGill University Press, Montreal.

Berkey, J. P., 1992. *The Transmission of Knowledge in Medieval Cairo: A Social History of Islamic Education*. Princeton University Press, Princeton.

Berkey, J. P., 2003. *The Formation of Islam: Religion and Society in the Near East, 600–1800*. Cambridge University Press, Cambridge.

Berkey, J. P., 2007. "Madrasas Medieval and Modern: Politics, Education, and the Problem of Muslim Identity." In R. W. Hefner and M. Q. Zaman (eds.), *Schooling in Islam: The Culture and Politics of Modern Muslim Education*, pp. 40–60. Princeton University Press, Princeton.

Berkey, J. P., 2010. "Islam." In R. Irwin (ed.), *The New Cambridge History of Islam*, vol. 4, pp. 19–59. Cambridge University Press, Cambridge.

Berman, C. E., and E. R. Nugent, 2015. *Regionalism in New Democracies: Sub-National Variation in Tunisia's 2014 Parliamentary Elections*, Working Paper. Princeton University, Princeton.

Berman, E., 2000. "Sect, Subsidy, and Sacrifice: An Economist's View of Ultra-Orthodox Jews." *Quarterly Journal of Economics*, vol. 115, no. 3, pp. 905–53.

Berman, E., 2009. *Radical, Religious, and Violent: The New Economics of Terrorism*. MIT Press, Cambridge, MA.

Berman, H. J., 1983. *Law and Revolution: The Formation of the Western Legal Tradition*. Harvard University Press, Cambridge, MA.

Bernheim, D. B., A. Shleifer, and L. H. Summers, 1985. "The Strategic Bequest Motive." *Journal of Political Economy*, vol. 93, no. 6, pp. 1045–76.

Binzel, C., and J. -P. Carvalho, 2017. "Education, Social Mobility, and Religious Movements: The Islamic Revival in Egypt." *Economic Journal.* doi: 10.1111/ecoj .12416.

Blaydes, L., and E. Chaney, 2013. "The Feudal Revolution and Europe's Rise: Political Divergence of the Christian and Muslim Worlds before 1500 CE." *American Political Science Review*, vol. 107, no. 1, pp. 16–34.

Blaydes, L., and M. Platas Izama, 2015. "Religion, Patriarchy and the Perpetuation of Harmful Social Conventions: The Case of Female Genital Cutting in Egypt." Mimeo, Stanford University, Stanford.

Bloch, M., 1961. *Feudal Society. I: The Growth of Ties of Dependence*, 2nd ed. Routledge & Kegan Paul, London.

Blom, P., 2010. *A Wicked Company: The Forgotten Radicalism of the European Enlightenment.* Basic Books, New York.

Bobrovnikov, V., 2006. "Islam in the Russian Empire." In D. Lieven (ed.), *The Cambridge History of Russia, Vol. II: Imperial Russia, 1689–1917*, pp. 202–23. Cambridge University Press, Cambridge.

Bonney, R., 1991. *The European Dynastic States 1494–1660*. Oxford University Press, Oxford.

Bonney, R., 2004. *Jihad. From Quran to bin Laden.* Palgrave Macmillan, New York.

Boone, C., 1992. *Merchant Capital and the Roots of State Power in Senegal 1930–1985.* Cambridge University Press, Cambridge.

Bosker, M, E. Buringh, and J. L. van Zanden, 2013. "From Baghdad to London: Unraveling Urban Development in Europe, the Middle East, and North Africa, 800–1800." *Review of Economics and Statistics*, vol. 95 (October), pp. 1418–37.

Botticini, M., and Z. Eckstein, 2005. "Jewish Occupational Selection: Education, Restrictions, or Minorities?" *Journal of Economic History*, vol. 65, no. 4, pp. 922–48.

Botticini, M., and Z. Eckstein, 2007. "From Farmers to Merchants, Conversions, and Diaspora: Human Capital and Jewish History." *Journal of the European Economic Association*, vol. 5, no. 5, pp. 885–926.

Botticini, M., and Z. Eckstein, 2014. *The Chosen Few: How Education Shaped Jewish History, 70–1492*, Princeton University Press, Princeton.

Bouamama, S., 2000. *Algérie: Les racines de l'intégrisme*. Editions EPO, Bruxelles.

Boubekeur, A., 2004. "Nouvelles stratégies matrimoniales d'étudiantes voilées en France." In I. Taboada Leonetti (ed.). *Les femmes et l'Islam – Entre modernité et intégrisme*, pp. 145–54. L'Harmattan, Paris.

Bove, V., J. P. Platteau, and P. Sekeris, 2017. "Political Repression in Autocratic Regimes." *Journal of Comparative Economics.*

Bove, V., and M. Rivera, 2015. "Elite Co-option, Repression, and Coups in Autocracies." *International Interactions: Empirical and Theoretical Research in International Relations*, vol. 41, no. 3, pp. 453–79.

Bowen, J. R., 2003. *Islam, Law and Equality in Indonesia: An Anthropology of Public Reasoning.* Cambridge University Press, Cambridge.

Bowles, S., 2004. *Microeconomics: Behavior, Institutions, and Evolution.* Russell Sage Foundation, New York.

Braudel, F., 1995. *A History of Civilisations*, Penguin Books, London.

Brenner, R., 1976. "Agrarian Class Structure and Economic Development in Pre-Industrial Europe." *Past and Present*, no. 70, pp. 30–75. Reprinted in T. H. Aston and C. H. E. Philpin (eds.), 1985, *The Brenner Debate*, Cambridge University Press, Cambridge.

Brenner, R., 1982. "The Agrarian Roots of European Capitalism." *Past and Present*, no. 97, pp. 16–113. Reprinted in T. H. Aston and C. H. E. Philpin (eds.), 1985. *The Brenner Debate*, Cambridge University Press, Cambridge.

Brenner, L., 2000. "Sufism in Africa." In J. K. Olupona (ed.), *African Spirituality: Forms, Meanings and Expressions*. Crossroads Publishing Company, New York.

Briggs, R., 1999. "Embattled Faiths: Religion and Natural Philosophy in the Seventeenth Century." In E. Cameron (ed.), *Early Modern Europe: An Oxford History*, pp. 171–205. Oxford University Press, Oxford.

Brooks, G., 1993. *Landlords and Strangers: Ecology, Society and Trade in Western Africa 1000–1630*. Westview Press, Boulder, CO.

Brown, C., 2003. *A Short History of Indonesia: The Unlikely Nation?*, Allen & Unwin, Crows Nest, Australia.

Brubaker, L., and J. Haldon, 2011. *Byzantium in the Iconoclast Era, c. 680–850: A History*. Cambridge University Press, Cambridge.

Brumberg, D., 2014. "Theories of Transition." In M. Lynch (ed.), *The Arab Uprisings Explained: New Contentious Politics in the Middle East*, pp. 29–54. Columbia University Press, New York.

Buchan, J., 2012. *Days of God: The Revolution in Iran and its Consequences*. John Murray, London.

Burgat, F., and W. Dowell, 1993. *The Islamic Movement in North Africa*. University of Texas Press, Austin.

Camau, M. (ed.), 1987. *La Tunisie au présent*. Editions du CNRS, Paris.

Camau, M., and Geisser, V., 2004. *Habib Bourguiba: la trace et l'héritage*. Karthala, Paris.

Camic, C., P. S. Gorski, and D. M. Trubek, 2004. *Max Weber's "Economy and Society": A Critical Companion*. Stanford University Press, Stanford.

Cammack, M. E., and R. M. Feener, 2008. "Joint Marital Property in Indonesian Customary, Islamic, and National Law." In P. Bearman, W. Heinrichs, and B. G. Weiss (eds.), *The Law Applied – Contextualizing the Islamic Sharia*, pp. 92–115. I. B. Tauris, London.

Cantoni, D., 2015. "The Economic Effects of the Protestant Reformation: Testing the Weber Hypothesis in the German Lands." *Journal of the European Economic Association*, vol. 3, no. 4, pp. 561–98.

Cantor, N. F., 1993. *The Civilization of the Middle Ages*. Harper Perennial, New York.

Carvalho, J. P., 2013. "Veiling." *Quarterly Journal of Economics*, vol. 128, no. 1, pp. 337–70.

Carvalho, J. P., 2016. "Identity-Based Organizations." *American Economic Review, Papers and Proceedings*, vol. 106, no. 5, pp. 410–14.

Carvalho, J. P., 2017 (a). "Coordination and Culture," *Economic Theory*.

Carvalho, J. P., 2017 (b). "Sacrifice and Sorting in Clubs." *Forum for Social Economics*, Special Issue on the Economics of Religion.

Carvalho, J. P., and M. Koyama, 2016. "Jewish Emancipation and Schism: Economic Development and Religious Change." *Journal of Comparative Economics*, vol. 44, no. 3, pp. 562–84.

Cavanaugh, W. T., 2009. *The Myth of Religious Violence*. Oxford University Press, Oxford.

Chaara, I., 2015. *Pro-Women Legal Reform in Morocco: Is Religion an Obstacle?* Working Paper, Centre for Research in the Economics of Development (CRED), University of Namur.

Chachoua, K., 2001. *L'islam kabyle. Religion, Etat et société en Algérie.* Maisonneuve & Larose, Paris.

Chambers, R. L., 1964. "Turkey: The Civil Bureaucracy." In R. E. Ward and D. A. Rustow (eds), *Political Modernization in Japan and Turkey*, pp. 301–27. Princeton University Press, Princeton.

Chaney, E., 2011. *Revolt on the Nile: Economic Shocks, Religion and Political Power.* Department of Economics, Harvard University, Cambridge, MA.

Chaney, E., 2012. *Democratic Change in the Arab World, Past and Present.* Department of Economics, Harvard University, Cambridge, MA.

Chen, D., 2010. "Club Goods and Group Identity: Evidence from Islamic Resurgence during the Indonesian Financial Crisis." *Journal of Political Economy*, vol. 118, pp. 300–54.

Choiruzzada, S. A., and E. B. Nugrohoa, 2013. "Indonesia's Islamic Economy Project and the Islamic Scholars." *Procedia Environmental Sciences*, vol. 17, pp. 957–66.

Clark, V., 2010. *Yemen – Dancing on the Heads of Snakes.* Yale University Press, New Haven.

Cleveland, W. L., 2004. *A History of the Modern Middle East*, Westview Press, Oxford.

Clover, C., 2016. *Black Wind, White Snow: The Rise of Russia's New Nationalism.* Yale University Press, New Haven.

Coates, R., 2010. "Religious Renaissance in the Silver Age." In W. Leatherbarrow and D. Offord (eds.), *A History of Russian Thought*, pp. 169–93. Cambridge University Press, Cambridge.

Cohen, A., 1969. *Custom and Politics in Urban Africa: A Study of Hausa Migrants in Yoruba Towns.* University of California Press, Berkeley.

Cohen, A., 1971. "Cultural Strategies in the Organisation of Trading Diasporas." In C. Meillassoux (ed.), *The Development of Indigenous Trade and Markets in West Africa*, pp. 266–81. Oxford University Press, London.

Cohen, B., 1986. *Bourguiba, le pouvoir d'un seul.* Flammarion, Paris.

Cohen, S. P., 2004. *The Idea of Pakistan.* Brookings Institution Press, Washington, DC.

Collins, J. B., and K. L. Taylor, 2006. *Early Modern Europe – Issues and Interpretations.* Blackwell Publishing, Oxford.

Comolli, V., 2015. *Boko Haram: Nigeria's Islamist Insurgency*, Hurst & Company, London.

Cook, S. A., 2012. *The Struggle for Egypt: From Nasser to Tahrir Square.* Oxford University Press, Oxford.

Cooper, B. M., 1997. *Marriage in Maradi: Gender and Culture in a Hausa Society in Niger, 1900–1989.* James Currey, Oxford.

Coşgel, M., T. Miceli, and R. Ahmed, 2009. "Law, State Power, and Taxation in Islamic History." *Journal of Economic Behavior and Organization*, vol. 71, no. 3, pp. 704–17.

Coşgel, M. M., T. J. Miceli, and J. Rubin, 2012. "The Political Economy of Mass Printing: Legitimacy and Technological Change in the Ottoman Empire." *Journal of Comparative Economics*, vol. 40, pp. 357–71.

Coulson, N. J., 1964. *A History of Islamic Law.* Edinburgh University Press, Edinburgh.

Crecelius, D., 1972. "Non-Ideological Responses of the Ulama to Modernization." In N. R. Keddie (ed.), *Scholars, Saints and Sufis: Muslim Religious Institutions in the Middle East since 1500*. University of California Press, Berkeley.

Crooke, A., 2009. *Resistance: The Essence of the Islamist Revolution*. Pluto Press, London.

Crouch, H., 2007. *The Army and Politics in Indonesia*. Equinox Publishing, Jakarta.

Cruise O'Brien, D. B., 1971. *The Mourides of Senegal: Political and Economic Organisation of an Islamic Brotherhood*. Oxford University Press, Oxford.

Cruise O'Brien, D. B., 1975. *Saints and Politicians: Essays in the Organisation of a Senegalese Peasant Society*. Cambridge University Press, Cambridge.

Curtis, M., 2010. *Secret Affairs: Britain's Collusion with Radical Islam*. Serpent's Tail, London.

Crystal, J., 1992. *Kuwait: The Transformation of an Oil State*. Westview Press, Boulder, CO.

Crystal, J., 1995. *Oil and Politics in the Gulf: Rulers and Merchants in Kuwait and Qatar*. Cambridge University Press, Cambridge.

Daftary, F., 2010. "Varieties of Islam." In R. Irwin (ed.), *The New Cambridge History of Islam*, vol. 4, pp. 105–41. Cambridge University Press, Cambridge.

Dale, S. F., 2010. *The Muslim Empires of the Ottomans, Safavids, and Mughals*. Cambridge University Press, Cambridge.

Dalmasso, E., 2008. "Family Code in Morocco: State Feminism or Democracy?" Mimeo.

Darby, G. (ed.), *The Origins and Development of the Dutch Revolt*. Routledge, London.

Darke, D., 2014. *My House in Damas: An Inside View of the Syrian Revolution*. Haus Publishing Ltd., London.

Davidson, B., 1991. *Africa in History*. Simon and Schuster (Touchstone Books), New York.

Davis, E., 2005a. *Memories of State: Politics, History, and Collective Identity in Modern Iraq*. University of California Press, Berkeley.

Davis, E., 2005b. "The New Iraq: The Uses of Memory." *Journal of Democracy*, vol. 16, no. 3, pp. 54–68.

Dawisha, A., 1999. "Identity and Political Survival in Saddam's Iraq." *Middle East Journal*, vol. 53, pp. 553–67.

Dawisha, A., 2003. *Arab Nationalism in the Twentieth Century: From Triumph to Despair*. Princeton University Press, Princeton.

Dawisha, A., 2009. *Iraq: A Political History*. Princeton University Press, Princeton.

Dawisha, K., 2014. *Putin's Kleptocracy: Who Owns Russia?* Simon and Schuster, New York.

De La Croix, D., M. Doepke, and J. Mokyr, 2016. "Clans, Guilds, and Markets: Apprenticeship Institutions and Growth in the Pre-Industrial Economy." Unpublished manuscript, Northwestern University and Catholic University of Louvain.

De Mesquita, B. B., A. Smith, R. M. Siverson, and J. D. Morrow, 2005. *The Logic of Political Survival*, MIT Press, Cambridge, MA.

Desai, M., 2005. *Development and Nationhood: Essays in the Political Economy of South Asia*. Oxford University Press, Oxford.

Desai, R. M., A. Olofsgard, and T. M. Yousef, 2009. "The Logic of Authoritarian Bargains." *Economics and Politics*, vol. 21, no. 1, pp. 93–125.

De Waal, A., 1997. *Famine Crimes Politics and the Disaster Relief Industry in Africa*. James Currey, Oxford.

De Waal, T., 2010. *The Caucasus: An Introduction*. Oxford University Press, Oxford.

Dodge, T., 2012. *Iraq: From War to a New Authoritarianism*. Routledge, London.

Doepke, M., and F. Zilibotti, 2008. "Occupational Choice and the Spirit of Capitalism." *Quarterly Journal of Economics*, vol. 123, no. 2, pp. 747–93.

Donner, F. M., 1981. *The Early Islamic Conquests*. Princeton University Press, Princeton.

Dreyfuss, R., 2005. *Devil's Game: How the United States Helped Unleash Fundamentalist Islam*. Holt Paperbacks, New York.

Duby, G., 1974. *The Early Growth of the European Economy*. Cornell University Press, Ithaca, NY.

Duby, G., 1987. *Le Moyen-Age*. Hachette, Paris.

Duffy, E., 2005. *The Stripping of the Altars*, 2nd ed. Cambridge University Press, Cambridge.

Duffy Toft, M., 2007. "Getting Religious? The Puzzling Case of Islam and Civil War." *International Security*, vol. 31, no. 4, pp. 97–131.

Durkheim, E., 1912. *The Elementary Form of Religious Life*. Free Press, New York (reprinted 1965).

Durlauf, S. M., A. Kourtellos, and C. M. Tan, 2012. "Is God in the Details? A Reexamination of the Role of Religion in Economic Growth." *Journal of Applied Econometrics*, vol. 27, no 7, pp. 1059–75.

El-Affendi, A., 2011. "Political Culture and the Crisis of Democracy in the Arab World." In I. Elbadawi and S. Makdisi (eds.), *Democracy in the Arab World – Explaining the Deficit*, pp. 11–40. Routledge, London.

El-Affendi, A., 2014. *Turabi's Revolution: Islam and Power in Sudan*. Grey Seal Books.

Elbadawi, I., and S. Makdisi, 2007. "Explaining the Democracy Deficit in the Arab World."*Quarterly Review of Economics and Finance*, vol. 46, no. 5, pp. 813–31.

Elbadawi, I., S. Makdisi, and G. Galante, 2011. "Explaining the Arab Democracy Deficit: The Role of Oil and Conflicts." In I. Elbadawi and S. Makdisi (eds.), *Democracy in the Arab World –Explaining the Deficit*, pp. 41–82. Routledge, London.

El Kenz, D., and C. Gantet, 2008. *Guerres et Paix de Religion en Europe, XVI-XVIIèmes siècles*, 2nd ed. Armand Colin, Paris.

Ellis, S., 1999. *The Mask of Anarchy: The Destruction of Liberia and the Religious Dimension of an African Civil War*. New York University Press, New York.

El Mansour, M., 1979. "The Sanctuary (hurm) in Pre-colonial Morocco." In R. Bourqia and S. Gilson Miller (eds.), *In the Shadow of the Sultan: Culture, Power, and Politics in Morocco*, pp. 49–73. Harvard University Press, Cambridge, MA.

Elphinstone, M., 1843. *The History of India*, vol. 2. John Murray, London.

Elster, J., 1985. *Making Sense of Marx*. Cambridge University Press, Cambridge.

Enderlin, C., 2009. *Le grand aveuglement: Israël et l'irrésistible ascension de l'Islam radical*. Albin Michel, Paris.

Ensminger, J., 1992. *Making a Market: The Institutional Transformation of an African Society*. Cambridge University Press, Cambridge.

Eraly, A., 2007. *The Mughal World: India's Tainted Paradise: Life in India's Last Golden Age*. Penguin, Delhi.

Erlihy, D., 1985. *Medieval Households*, Harvard University Press, Cambridge, MA.

Esposito, J., 2002. *Unholy War: Terror in the Name of Islam*. Oxford University Press, New York.

Facchini, F., 2009. "Religion, Law and Development: Islam and Christianity – Why Is It in Occident and Not in the Orient that Man Invented the Institutions of Freedom?" *European Journal of Law and Economics* (published online).

Fafchamps, M., 2004. *Market Institutions in Sub-Saharan Africa: Theory and Evidence*. MIT Press, Cambridge, MA.

Fage, J. D., and W. Tordoff, 1995. *A History of Africa*. Routledge, London.

Fancelli, S., 2006. *Les aventuriers du pentecôtisme ghanéen*. Karthala, Paris.

Febvre, L., H. -J. Martin, and G. Nowell-Smith, 2010. *The Coming of the Book: The Impact of Printing, 1450–1800*. Verso, London.

Feldman, N., 2008. *The Fall and Rise of the Islamic State*. Princeton University Press, Princeton.

Ferjani, M. C., 1991. *Islamisme, laïcité, et droits de l'homme*. L'Harmattan, Paris.

Filiu, J. -P., 2008. *L'apocalypse dans l'Islam*. Fayard, Paris.

Filiu, J.-P., 2015. *From Deep State to Islamic State: The Arab Counter-Revolution and its Jihadi Legacy*. Hurst and Company, London.

Finkel, C., 2005. *The History of the Ottoman Empire: Osman's Dream*. Basic Books, New York.

Fish, S., 2002. "Islam and Authoritarianism." *World Politics*, vol. 55, pp. 4–37.

Floor, W., 1980. "The Revolutionary Character of the Iranian Ulama: Wishful Thinking or Reality?" *International Journal of Middle East Studies*, vol. 12, pp. 501–24.

Floor, W., 1983. "Change and Development in the Judicial System of Qajar Iran (1800–1925)." In E. Bosworth and C. Hillenbrand (eds.), *Qajar Iran —Political, Social, and Cultural Change 1800–1925*. Mazda Publishers, Costa Mesa, CA.

Floor, W., 2000. *The Economy of Safavid Persia*. Reichert, Wiesbaden.

Franklin, S., 2006. "Kievan Rus' (1015–1125)." In M. Perrie (ed.), *The Cambridge History of Russia, Vol. I: From Early Rus' to 1689*, pp. 73–97. Cambridge University Press, Cambridge.

Frey, F. W., 1964. "Education: Turkey." In R. E. Ward and D. A. Rustow (eds.), *Political Modernization in Japan and Turkey*, pp. 205–35 Princeton University Press, Princeton.

Frykenberg, R. E., 1993. "Hindu Fundamentalism and the Structural Stability of India." In M. E. Marty and R. S. Appleby (eds.). *Fundamentalisms and the State – Remaking Polities, Economies, and Militance*, pp. 233–55. University of Chicago Press, Chicago.

Fukuyama, F., 1992. *The End of History and the Last Man*, Free Press, New York.

Fukuyama, F., 2012. *The Origins of Political Order: From Prehuman Times to the French Revolution*. Profile Books, London.

Gaspart, F., and J. P. Platteau, 2010. "Strategic Behaviour and Marriage Payments: Theory and Evidence from Senegal." *Economic Development and Cultural Change*, vol. 59, no. 1, pp. 149–85.

Geertz, C. 1968. *Observer l'Islam: changements religieux au Maroc et en Indonésie*. Editions La Découverte, Paris.

Geertz, C. 1975. *The Interpretation of Cultures*. Basic Books, New York.

Gellner, E., 1997. "The Turkish Option in Comparative Perspective." In S. Bozdogan and R. Kasaba (eds.), *Rethinking Modernity and National Identity in Turkey*, University of Washington Press, Seattle.

Gellner, E., 1992. *Postmodernism, Reason and Religion*. Routledge, London.

Gellner, E., 1994. "Kemalism." In E. Gellner (ed.), *Encounters with Nationalism*, pp. 81–91. Blackwell, Oxford.

Genc, K. 2016. *Under the Shadow: Rage and Revolution in Modern Turkey*. I. B. Tauris, New York.

Gerges, F., 1999. *America and Political Islam*. Cambridge University Press, Cambridge.

Gerges, F., 2005. *The Far Enemy: Why Jihad Went Global*. Cambridge University Press, Cambridge.

Gerges, F. A., 2012. *The End of America's Moment? Obama and the Middle East*. Palgrave Macmillan, New York.

Gerges, F. A., 2016. *A History of ISIS*. Princeton University Press, Princeton.

Gilsenan, M., 1982. *Recognizing Islam: Religion and Society in the Modern Arab World*. Pantheon Books, New York.

Gleave, R., (ed.), 2005. *Religion and society in Qajar Iran*. Routledge Curzon, New York.

Gleave, R., and E. Kermeli (eds.), 1997. *Islamic Law: Theory and Practice*, I. B. Tauris, London.

Goffman, D., 2002. *The Ottoman Empire and Early Modern Europe*. Cambridge University Press, Cambridge.

Gold, D., 1991. "Organized Hinduisms: From Vedic Truth to Hindu Nation." In M. E. Marty and R. S. Appleby (eds.), *Fundamentalisms Observed*, pp. 533–42. University of Chicago Press, Chicago.

Göle, N., 2011. *Islam in Europe: The Lure of Fundamentalism and the Allure of Cosmopolitanism*. Markus Wiener Publishers, Princeton.

Göle, N., 2004. "Islam as Ideology." In A. B. Seligman (ed.), *Modest Claims: Dialogues and Essays on Tolerance and Tradition*. University of Notre Dame Press, Notre Dame, IN.

Göle, N., 1997. "Secularism and Islamism in Turkey: The Making of Elites and Counter-Elites." *Middle East Journal*, vol. 51, no. 1, pp. 46–58.

Göle, N., 1993. *Musulmanes et Modernes*. La Découverte, Paris.

Goody, J., 1976. *Production and Reproduction: A Comparative Study of the Domestic Domain*. Cambridge University Press, Cambridge.

Goody, J., 1983. *The Development of the Family and Marriage in Europe*. Cambridge University Press, Cambridge.

Goody, J., 2006. *The Theft of History*. Cambridge University Press, Cambridge.

Gorski, P. S., 2003. *The Disciplinary Revolution: Calvinism and the Rise of the State in Early Modern Europe*. University of Chicago Press, Chicago.

Grandguillaume, G., 1995. *Arabisation et politique linguistique au Maghreb*. Maisonneuve & Larose, Paris.

Greengrass, M., 2014. *Christendom Destroyed: Europe 1517–1648*. Allen Lane, London.

Grégoire, E., 1992. *The Alhazai of Maradi: Traditional Hausa Merchants in a Changing Sahelian City*. Lynne Rienner, Boulder, CO.

Grégoire, E., 1993. "Islam and the Identity of Merchants in Maradi (Niger)." In L. Brenner (ed.), *Muslim Identity and Social Change in Sub-Saharan Africa*, pp. 106–15. Indiana University Press, Bloomington.

Greif, A., 2006a. *Institutions and the Path to the Modern Economy*. Cambridge University Press, Cambridge.

Greif, A., 2006b. "Family Structure, Institutions, and Growth: The Origins and Implications of Western Corporations." *American Economic Review – Papers and Proceedings*, vol. 96, pp. 308–12.

Greif, A., and M. Iyigun, 2013. "Social Organizations, Violence, and Modern Growth." *American Economic Review*, vol. 103, no. 3, pp. 534–38.

Greif, A., M. Iyigun, and D. Sasson, 2012. "Social Institutions and Economic Growth: Why England and Not China Became the First Modern Economy." Unpublished Working Paper, University of Colorado, Boulder.

Greif, A., and G. Tabellini, 2010. "Cultural and Institutional Bifurcation: China and Europe Compared." *American Economic Review – Papers and Proceedings*, vol. 100, no. 2, pp. 135–40.

Greif, A., and G. Tabellini, 2011. "The Clan and the City: Sustaining Cooperation in China and Europe." Mimeo, Stanford University.

Greif, A., and G. Tabellini, 2015. "The Clan and the Corporation: Sustaining Cooperation in China and Europe." Unpublished manuscript, Bocconi University.

Greif, A., and S. Tadelis, 2010. "A Theory of Moral Persistence: Crypto-Morality and Political Legitimacy." *Journal of Comparative Economics*, vol. 38, no. 3, pp. 229–44.

Griswold, E., 2010. *The Tenth Parallel: Dispatches from the Faultline between Christianity and Islam*. Allen Lane, London.

Grosjean, P., 2011. "The Institutional Legacy of the Ottoman Empire: Islamic Rule and Financial Development in South Eastern Europe." *Journal of Comparative Economics*, vol. 39, pp. 1–16.

Gürbey, S., 2009. "Islam, Nation-State and the Military: A Discussion of Secularism in Turkey." *Comparative Studies of South Asia, Africa, and the Middle East*, vol. 29, no. 3, pp. 371–80.

Guirkinger, C., and J. P. Platteau, 2016. *The Dynamics of Family Systems: Lessons from Past and Present Times*. Working Paper, Economic Development and Institutions (EDI) Project, University of Namur and Paris School of Economics.

Guiso, L., P. Sapienza, and L. Zingales, 2003. "People's Opium? Religion and Economic Activities." *Journal of Monetary Economics*, vol. 50, pp. 225–82.

Gunn, S., 1999. "War, Religion, and the State." In E. Cameron (ed.), *Early Modern Europe: An Oxford History*, pp. 102–33. Oxford University Press, Oxford.

Haddad, F., 2011. *Sectarianism in Iraq: Antagonistic Visions of Unity*. Oxford University Press, Oxford.

Hadjadj, B., 2007. *Les voleurs de rêves: Cent cinquante ans d'histoire d'une famille algérienne*. Albin Michel, Paris.

Haenni, P., 2005. *L'Islam de marché*. Editions du Seuil, Paris.

Hagen, E. E., 1975. *The Economics of Development*. Richard D. Irwin, Homewood, IL.

Hajnal, J., 1965. "European Marriage Patterns in Perspective." In D. V. Glass and D. E. C. Eversley (eds.), *Population in History: Essays in Historical Demography* Edward Arnold, London.

Hallaq, W. B., 2010. "Islamic Law: History and Transformation." In R. Irwin (ed.), *The New Cambridge History of Islam*, vol. 4, pp. 142–83. Cambridge University Press, Cambridge.

Halliday, F., 1996. *Islam and the Myth of Confrontation: Religion and Politics in the Middle East*. I. B. Tauris, London.

Hampson, N., 1968. *The Enlightenment*. Penguin Press, Harmondsworth, UK.

Hanefi, H., 1982. "The Relevance of the Islamic Alternative in Egypt." *Arab Studies Quarterly*, vol. 4, no. 1–2.

Hanioğlu, M. S., 2000. *Preparation for a Revolution: The Young Turks, 1902–1908*. Oxford University Press, Oxford.

Hanna, N., 1998. *Making Big Money in 1600: The Life and Times of Isma'il Abu Taqiyya, Egyptian Merchant*. Syracuse University Press, Syracuse, NY.

Haqqani, H., 2005. *Pakistan: Between Mosque and Military*. Carnegie Endowment for International Peace, Washington, DC.

Harik, J. P., 2005. *Hezbollah: The Changing Face of Terrorism*. I. B. Tauris, London.

Harris, S., 2004. *The End of Faith: Religion, Terror, and the Future of Reason*. W. W. Norton and Co., New York.

Harris, T., 2007. *Revolution: The Great Crisis of the British Monarchy, 1685–1720*. Penguin Books, London.

Hart, K., 1975. "Swindler or Public Benefactor? The Entrepreneur in His Community." In J. Goody (ed.), *Changing Social Structure in Ghana: Essays in Comparative Sociology of a New State and an Old Tradition*. International African Institute, London.

Hartman, M. S., 2004. *The Household and the Making of History: A Subversive View of the Western Past*. Cambridge University Press, Cambridge.

Hassan, G. S., and T. Kivimäki, 2005. "Relations between Islam and the West as a Context and Catalyst of Terrorism." In T. Kivimäki (ed.), *Islam, the West, and Violence*, pp. 116–45. Hakapaino Oy, Helsinki.

Hatina, M., 2000. "On the Margins of Consensus: The Call to Separate Religion and State in Modern Egypt." *Middle Eastern Studies*, vol. 36, no. 1, pp. 35–67.

Hayami, Y., 1997. *Development Economics: From the Poverty to the Wealth of Nations*. Clarendon Press, Oxford.

Hazan, M., A. Weiss, and H. Zoabi (2016). "Women's Liberation as a Financial Innovation." Mimeo, Tel-Aviv University and New School of Economics, Moscow.

Helmke G., and S. Levitsky, 2004. "Informal Institutions and Comparative Politics: A Research Agenda." *Perspectives on Politics*, vol. 2, no. 4, pp. 725–40.

Henry, C. M., 2014. "States and Bankers." In M. Lynch (ed.), *The Arab Uprisings Explained – New Contentious Politics in the Middle East*, pp. 127–41. Columbia University Press, New York.

Heretz, L., 2008. *Russia on the Eve of Modernity: Popular Religion and Traditional Culture under the Last Tsars*. Cambridge University Press, Cambridge.

Hettige, S. T., 2004. "Economic Policy, Changing Opportunities for Youth, and the Ethnic Conflict in Sri Lanka." In D. Winslow and M. D. Woost (eds.), *Economy, Culture, and Civil War in Sri Lanka*, pp. 115–30. Indiana University Press, Bloomington.

Heuze, G., 1992. "Shiv Sena and 'National' Hinduism." *Economic and Political Weekly*, vol. XXVII, no. 41, pp. 2253–63.

Heydarian, R. J., 2014. *How Capitalism Failed the Arab World: The Economic Roots and Precarious Future of the Middle East Uprisings*. Zed Books, London.

Hibou, B., 2006a. *La force de l'obéissance: économie politique de la répression en Tunisie*. Editions La Découverte, Paris.

Hibou, B., 2006b. "Domination and Control in Tunisia: Economic Levers for the Exercise of Authoritarian Power." *Review of African Political Economy*, vol. 108, pp. 185–206.

Hicks, J. R., 1969. *The Theory of Economic History*. Oxford University Press, Oxford.

Higgins, B., 1968. *Economic Development: Problems, Principles and Policies*. W. W. Norton & Company, New York.

Hill, C., 1975. *The World Turned Upside Down: Radical Ideas during the English Revolution*. Penguin Books, London.

Hinnebusch, R. A., 1982. "The Islamic Movement in Syria." In A. Dessouki (ed.), *Islamic Resurgence in the Arab World*. Praeger, New York.

Hodgson, M. G. S., 1974a. *The Venture of Islam: Conscience and History in a World Civilization, Vol. 1: The Classical Age of Islam*. University of Chicago Press, Chicago.

Hodgson, M. G. S., 1974b. *The Venture of Islam: Conscience and History in a World Civilization, Vol. 2: The Expansion of Islam in the Middle Periods*. University of Chicago Press, Chicago.

Hodgson, M. G. S., 1974c. *The Venture of Islam: Conscience and History in a World Civilization, Vol. 3: The Gunpowder Empires and Modern Times*. University of Chicago Press, Chicago.

Hoffman, P. T., 2015. *Why Did Europe Conquer the World?* Princeton University Press, Princeton & Oxford.

Hoffman, P. T., and K. Norberg, 2002. *Fiscal Crises, Liberty and Representative Government, 1450–1789*. Stanford University Press, Stanford.

Hokayem, E., 2013. *Syria's Uprising and the Fracturing of the Levant*. Routledge, London.

Hopkins, A. G., 1973. *An Economic History of West Africa*. Longman, London.

Hopkins, N., and R. Saad (eds.), 2004. *Upper Egypt: Identity and Change*. American University in Cairo Press, Cairo.

Horowitz, D., 1985. *Ethnic Groups in Conflict*. University of California Press, Berkeley.

Hourani, A., 1991. *A History of the Arab Peoples*. Belknap Press of the Harvard University Press, Cambridge, MA.

Hourani, A., 1993. "Ottoman Reform and the Politics of Notables." In A. Hourani, P. S. Khoury, and M. C. Wilson (eds.), *The Modern Middle East: A Reader*, University of California Press, Berkeley.

Hudson, M. C., 1986. "The Islamic Factor in Syrian and Iraqi Politics." In J. P. Piscatori (ed.), *Islam in the Political Process*, Cambridge University Press, Cambridge.

Hudson, M. C., 1995. "Arab Regimes and Democratization: Responses to the Challenge of Political Islam." In L. Guazzone (ed.), *The Islamist Dilemma. The Political Role of Islamist Movements in the Contemporary Arab World*. Ithaca Press, London.

Huntington, S., 1993. "The Clash of Civilizations?" *Foreign Affairs*, Summer, pp. 22–49.

Huntington, S., 1996. *The Clash of Civilisations and the Remaking of World Order*. Simon & Schuster, London.

Hussain, Z., 2008. *Frontline Pakistan: The Path to Catastrophe and the Killing of Benazir Bhutto*. I. B. Tauris, London.

Huuhtanen, H., 2005. "Weak States and Terrorism in the Arab World." In T. Kivimäki (ed.), *Islam, the West, and Violence*. pp. 73–89. Hakapaino Oy, Helsinki.

Iannaccone, L. R. 1990. "Religious Practice: A Human Capital Approach." *Journal for the Scientific Study of Religion*, vol. 29, no. 3, pp. 297–314.

Iannaccone, L. R., 1992. "Sacrifice and Stigma: Reducing Free-Riding in Cults, Communes, and Other Collectives." *Journal of Political Economy*, vol. 100, no. 2, pp. 271–91.

Iannaccone, L. R., 1995. "Household Production, Human Capital, and the Economics of Religion." In M. Tommasi (ed.), *The New Economics of Human Behavior*, pp. 172–87. Cambridge University Press, Cambridge.

Iannaccone, L. R., 1997. "Rational Choice: Framework for the Social Scientific Study of Religion." In L. Young (ed.), *Rational Choice Theory and Religion: Summary and Assessment*, pp. 25–44. Routledge, New York.

Iannaccone, L. R., and E. Berman, 2006. "Religious Extremism: The Good, the Bad, and the Deadly." *Public Choice*, vol. 128, pp. 109–29.

Ibrahim, S. E., 1995a. "Islamic Activism and Political Opposition in Egypt." In S. E. Ibrahim (ed.), *Egypt. Islam and Democracy: Critical Essay*, pp. 53–68. American University in Cairo Press, Cairo.

Ibrahim, S. E., 1995b. "Islamic Activism and the Western Search for a New Enemy. In S. E. Ibrahim (ed.), *Egypt. Islam and Democracy: Critical Essays*, pp. 81–91. American University in Cairo Press, Cairo.

Iliffe, J., 2007. *Africans: The History of a Continent*, 2nd ed. Cambridge University Press, Cambridge.

Imber, C., 2002. *The Ottoman Empire, 1300–1650: The Structure of Power*. Palgrave Macmillan, New York.

İnalcık, H., 1964. "The Nature of Traditional Society: Turkey." In R. E. Ward and D. A. Rustow (eds.), *Political Modernization in Japan and Turkey*, pp. 42–63. Princeton University Press, Princeton.

İnalcık, H., 1973. *The Ottoman Empire: The Classical Age, 1300–1600*. Phoenix Press, London.

İnalcık, H., and D. Quataert, 1994. *An Economic and Social History of the Ottoman Empire, 1300–1914*. Cambridge University Press, Cambridge.

Insel, A., 2015. *La nouvelle Turquie d'Erdoğan: Du rêve démocratique à la dérive autoritaire*. La Découverte, Paris.

Irfan, H., 2010. "Honor and Violence against Women in Pakistan." In Y. Ghai and J. Cottrell (eds.), *Marginalized Communities and Access to Justice*, pp. 162–84. Routledge, London.

Israel, J. I., 2001. *Radical Enlightenment: Philosophy and the Making of Modernity 1650–1750*. Oxford University Press, Oxford.

Issawi, C., 1971. *The Economic History of Iran, 1800–1914*. University of Chicago Press, Chicago.

Iyer, S., 2016. "The New Economics of Religion." *Journal of Economic Literature*, vol. 54, no. 2, pp. 395–441.

Janos, A. C., 1982. *The Politics of Backwardness in Hungary, 1825–1945*. Princeton University Press, Princeton.

Johnson, D. H., 2003. *The Root Causes of Sudan's Civil Wars*. James Currey, Oxford.

Johnson, N., and M. Koyama, 2013. "Legal Centralization and the Birth of the Secular State." *Journal of Comparative Economics*, vol. 41, no. 4, pp. 959–78.

Jok, M. J., 2007. *Sudan Race, Religion, and Violence*. Oneworld, Oxford.

Jones, B., 2009. *Beyond the State in Rural Uganda*. Edinburgh University Press, Edinburgh.

Jones, E., 1981. *The European Miracle*. Cambridge University Press, Cambridge.

Jones, O. B., 2002. *Pakistan: Eye of the Storm*. Yale University Press, New Haven, CT.

Kafadar, C., 1995. *Between Two Worlds: The Construction of the Ottoman State*. University of California Press, Berkeley.

Kahan, D. M., 2000. "Gentle Nudges vs. Hard Shoves: Solving the Sticky Norms Problem." *University of Chicago Law Review*, vol. 67, pp. 607–45.

Kakar, H., 2006. *A Political and Diplomatic History of Afghanistan, 1863–1901*. Brill, Leiden.

Kakar, S., 1996. *The Colors of Violence: Cultural Identities, Religion, and Conflict*. University of Chicago Press, Chicago.

Kandiyoti, D., 1991. "End of Empire: Islam, Nationalism, and Women in Turkey." In D. Kandiyoti (ed.), *Women, Islam and the State*, Macmillan, London.

Kaplan, B. J., 2007. *Divided by Faith: Religious Conflict and the Practice of Toleration in Early Modern Europe*. Belknap Press of Harvard University Press, Cambridge, MA.

Kassir, S., 2004. *Considérations sur le malheur arabe*. Actes Sud/Sindbad, Paris.

Katouzian, H., 2009. *The Persians: Ancient, Mediaeval and Modern Iran*. Yale University Press, New Haven.

Kaya, A., 2013. *Europeanization and Tolerance in Turkey: The Myth of Toleration*. Palgrave Macmillan, Basingstoke.

Keay, J., 2000. *A History of India*. Harper Perennial, London.

Keddie, N., 1966. *Religion and Rebellion in Iran: The Tobacco Protest of 1891–1892*. Frank Cass, London.

Keddie, N., 1969. "The Roots of the Ulama's Power in Modern Iran." *Studia Islamica*, vol. 29, pp. 31–53.

Keddie, N., 1971. "The Iranian Power Structure and Social Change, 1800–1969." *International Journal of Middle East Studies*, vol. 2, pp. 3–20.

Keddie, N., 1999. *Qajar Iran and the Rise of Reza Khan, 1796–1925*. Mazda Publishers, Costa Mesa, CA.

Keddie, N., 2003. *Modern Iran: Roots and Results of Revolution*. Yale University Press, New Haven.

Kennedy, P., 1988. *African Capitalism: The Struggle for Ascendancy*. Cambridge University Press, Cambridge.

Kermeli, E., 1997. "Ebu Su'ud Definitions of Church Waqfs: Theory and Practice in Ottoman Law." In R. Gleave and E. Kermeli (eds.), 1997. *Islamic law. Theory and Practice*, pp. 141–56. I. B. Tauris, London.

Kepel, G., 1994. *The Revenge of God: The Resurgence of Islam, Christianity and Judaism in the Modern World*. Pennsylvania University Press, University Park.

Kepel, G., 2005. *The Roots of Radical Islam*. Saqi Books, London (Originally published as *Le prophète et le pharaon*. Editions La Découverte, Paris, 1984).

Kepel, G., 2008. *Beyond Terror and Martyrdom: The Future of the Middle East*. Belknap Press of Harvard University Press, Cambridge, MA.

Keyes, C. F., 1993. "Buddhist Economics and Buddhist Fundamentalism." In M. E. Marty and R. S. Appleby (eds.), *Fundamentalisms and the State: Remaking Polities, Economies, and Militance*, pp. 367–409. University of Chicago Press, Chicago.

Khalid, A., 2007. *Islam after Communism: Religion and Politics in Central Asia*. University of California Press, Berkeley.

Khan, M. H., 2000a. "Rents, Efficiency and Growth." In M. H. Khan and K. S. Jomo (eds), *Rents, Rent-Seeking and Economic Development*, pp. 21–69. Cambridge University Press, Cambridge.

Khan, M. H., 2000b. "Rent-Seeking as Process." In M. H. Khan and K. S. Jomo (eds), *Rents, Rent-Seeking and Economic Development*, pp. 70–144. Cambridge University Press, Cambridge.

Khan, M. H., 2008. "Main Features of the Interest-Free Banking Movement in Pakistan (1980–2006)." *Managerial Finance*, vol. 34, no. 9, pp. 660–74.

Khan, M. H., and Bhatti, I., 2006. "Why Interest-Free Banking and Finance Movement Failed in Pakistan." *Humanomics*, vol. 22, no. 3, pp. 145–61.

Khan, M. H., and Bhatti, I., 2008. "Islamic Banking and Finance: On its Way to Globalization." *Managerial Finance*, vol. 34, no. 10, pp. 708–25.

Kinross, P., 2001. *Atatürk – The Rebirth of a Nation*. Phoenix, London.

Kirkpatrick, D. D., and M. El Sheikh, 2013. "Egypt's Leaders Invoke God against Dissent." *International Herald Tribune*, August 27, p. 4.

Kitching, G., 1982. *Development and Underdevelopment in Historical Perspective: Populism, Nationalism and Industrialization*. Methuen, London.

Kizenko, N., 2009. "The Church Schism and Old Belief." In A. Gleason (ed.), *A Companion to Russian History*, pp. 145–62. Wiley-Blackwell, Malden, MA.

Knysh, A., 2010. "Sufism." In R. Irwin (ed.), *The New Cambridge History of Islam*, vol. 4, pp. 60–104. Cambridge University Press, Cambridge.

Koenigsberger, H. G., G. L. Mosse, and G. Q. Bowler, 1989. *Europe in the Sixteenth Century*. Longman, Harlow.

Koga, J., 2015. "Strategic Logic of Elite Purges in Dictatorships." Unpublished manuscript, University of Strathclyde.

Kopelowitz, E., 2003. "Negotiating with the Secular: Forms of Religious Authority and Their Political Consequences." In A. L. Greil and D. G. Bromley (eds.), *Defining Religion: Investigating the Boundaries between the Sacred and the Secular*, pp. 85–108. JAI Press, Oxford.

Korotayev, A. V., 2003. "Unilineal Descent Organization and Deep Christianization: A Cross-Cultural Comparison." *Cross-Cultural Research*, vol. 37, no. 1, pp. 133–57.

Koyama, M., 2010a. "Evading the Taint of 'Usury': The Usury Prohibition as a Barrier to Entry." *Explorations in Economic History*, vol. 47, no. 4, pp. 420–42.

Koyama, M., 2010b. "The Political Economy of Expulsion: The Regulation of Jewish Moneylending in Medieval England." *Constitutional Political Economy*, vol. 32, no. 4, pp. 374–406.

Koyama, M., 2013. "Timur Kuran: The Long Divergence: How Islamic Law Held Back the Middle East?" *Public Choice*, no. 154, pp. 341–43.

Kumar, K. B., and J. G. Matsusaka, 2009. "From Families to Formal Contracts: An Approach to Development." *Journal of Development Economics*, vol. 90, no. 1, pp. 106–19.

Kuran, T., 1997. "Islam and Underdevelopment: An Old Puzzle Revisited." *Journal of Institutional and Theoretical Economics*, vol. 153, pp. 41–71.

Kuran, T., 1998. "The Genesis of Islamic Economics: A Chapter in the Politics of Muslim Identity." *Social Research*, vol. 64, pp. 301–38.

Kuran, T., 2001. "The Provision of Public Goods under Islamic Law: Origins, Impact, and Limitations of the Waqf System." *Law and Society Review*, vol. 35, pp. 841–97.

Kuran, T., 2003. "The Islamic Commercial Crisis: Institutional Roots of Economic Underdevelopment in the Middle East." *Journal of Economic History*, vol. 63, pp. 414–46.

Kuran, T., 2004a. "Cultural Obstacles to Economic Development: Often Overstated, Usually Transitory." In V. Rao and M. Walton (eds.), *Culture and Public Action*, pp. 115–37. Stanford University Press, Stanford.

Kuran, T., 2004b. "Why the Middle East Is Economically Underdeveloped: Historical Mechanisms of Institutional Stagnation." *Journal of Economic Perspectives*, vol. 18, pp. 71–90.

Kuran, T., 2004c. "The Economic Ascent of the Middle East's Religious Minorities: The Role of Islamic Legal Pluralism." *Journal of Legal Studies*, vol. 33, pp. 475–515.

Kuran, T., 2004d. *Islam and Mammon: The Economic Predicaments of Islamism.* Princeton University Press, Princeton.

Kuran, T., 2005a. "The Logic of Financial Westernization in the Middle East." *Journal of Economic Behavior and Organization*, vol. 56, pp. 593–615.

Kuran, T., 2005b. "The Absence of the Corporation in Islamic Law: Origins and Persistence." *American Journal of Comparative Law*, vol. 53, pp. 785–834.

Kuran, T., 2011. *The Long Divergence: How Islamic Law Held Back the Middle East.* Princeton University Press, Princeton.

Kuran, T., 2016. "Legal Roots of Authoritarian Rule in the Middle East: Civic Legacies of the Islamic Waqf." *American Journal of Comparative Law*, vol. 64, pp. 412–54.

Kuran, T., 2017. "Islam and Economic Performance: Historical and Contemporary Links." *Journal of Economic Literature.*

Kuran, T., and S. Lustig, 2012. "Judicial Biases in Ottoman Istanbul: Islamic Justice and Its Compatibility with Modern Economic Life." *Journal of Law and Economics*, vol. 55, no. 3, pp. 631–66.

Kuru, A., 2009. *Secularism and State Policies toward Religion: The United States, France, and Turkey.* Cambridge University Press, Cambridge.

Laabas, B., and A. Bouhouche, 2011. "Algeria: Democracy and Development under the Aegis of the 'Authoritarian Bargain.'" In I. Elbadawi and S. Makdisi (eds.), *Democracy in the Arab World –Explaining the Deficit*, pp. 196–226. Routledge, London.

La Ferrara, E. 2007. "Descent Rules and Strategic Transfers: Evidence from Matrilineal Groups in Ghana." *Journal of Development Economics*, vol. 83, no. 2, pp. 280–301.

Laitin, D., 1986. *Hegemony and Culture: Politics and Religious Change among the Yoruba.* University of Chicago Press, Chicago.

Lal, D., 1993. "The Economic Impact of Hindu Revivalism." In M. E. Marty and R. S. Appleby (eds.), *Fundamentalisms and the State: Remaking Polities, Economies, and Militance*, pp. 410–26. University of Chicago Press, Chicago.

Lal, D., 1998. *Unintended Consequences: The Impact of Factor Endowments, Culture and Politics on Long-Run Economic Performances.* MIT Press, Cambridge, MA.

Lambton, A., 1988. *Qajar Persia: Eleven Studies.* University of Texas Press, Austin.

Landes, D., 1998. *The Wealth and Poverty of Nations.* Little, Brown and Co., London.

Lane-Fox, R., 1988. *Pagans and Christians.* Penguin, London.

Lane-Fox, R., 2015. *Augustine: Conversions and Confessions.* Allen Lane, London.

Lapidus, I., 1984. *Muslim Cities in the Later Middle Age*, 2nd ed. Cambridge University Press, Cambridge.

Lapidus, I., 1988. *A History of Islamic Societies*, Cambridge University Press, Cambridge.

Lapidus, I., 1996. "State and Religion in Islamic Societies." *Past and Present*, no. 151, pp. 3–27.

Lapidus, I., 2002. *A History of Islamic Societies*, 2nd ed. Cambridge University Press, Cambridge.

La Porta, R., F. Lopez-de-Silanes, A. Shleifer, and R. W. Vishny, 1997. "Trust in Large Organisations." *American Economic Review*, vol. 87, pp. 333–8.

Laslett, P., 1971. *The World We Have Lost*, 2nd ed. Methuen, London.

Laslett, P., 1972. "Introduction: The History of the Family." In P. Laslett (ed.), *Household and Family in Past Time*. Cambridge University Press, Cambridge.

Launay, R., 1992. *Beyond the Stream: Islam and Society in a West African Town*. University of California Press, Berkeley.

Laurent, J. P., 1998. *Une association de développement en pays Mossi: le don comme ruse*. Karthala, Paris.

Layachi, A., 1995. "Algeria: Reinstating the State or Instating a Civil Society?" In I. W. Zartman (ed.), *Collapsed States: The Disintegration and Restoration of Legitimate Authority*, pp. 171–89. Lynne Rienner, Boulder, CO.

Lee, R. D., 2014. *Religion and Politics in the Middle East: Identity, Ideology, Institutions, and Attitudes*, 2nd ed. Westview Press, Boulder, CO.

Le Goff, J., 2003. *L'Europe est-elle née au Moyen-Âge?* Editions du Seuil, Paris.

Lemarchand, R., 2009. *The Dynamics of Violence in Central Africa*. University of Pennsylvania Press, Philadelphia.

Leonetti, I., (ed.), 2004. *Les femmes et l'Islam: entre modernité et intégrisme*. L'Harmattan, Paris.

Levtzion, N., 1973. *Ancient Ghana and Mali*. Africana Publishing Press, New York.

Lewis, B., 1956. "The Middle Eastern Reaction to Soviet Pressures." *Middle East Journal*, vol. 10, Spring.

Lewis, B., 1964. *The Middle East and the West*. Harper & Row, New York.

Lewis, B., 1968. *The Emergence of Modern Turkey*. Oxford University Press, Oxford.

Lewis, B., 1993. "Islam and Liberal Democracy." *Atlantic Monthly*.

Lewis, B., 1995. *The Middle East: 2000 Years of History from the Rise of Christianity to the Present Day*. Phoenix, London.

Lewis, B. 1996. "Islam and Liberal Democracy: A Historical Overview." *Journal of Democracy*, vol. 7, no. 2, pp. 52–63.

Lewis, B., 2001. "The Revolt of Islam." *The New Yorker*, November 19.

Lewis, B., 2002. *What Went Wrong? Western Impact and Middle Eastern Response*. Phoenix, London.

Lewis, I. M., 1966. "Introduction." In I. M. Lewis (ed.). *Islam in Tropical Africa*, Oxford University Press, Oxford.

Lieven, A., 2012. *Pakistan: A Hard Country*. Penguin Books, London.

Lilla, M., 2007. *The Stillborn God: Religion, Politics, and the Modern West*. Vintage Books, New York.

Littell, J., 2015. *Syrian Notebooks: Inside the Homs Uprising*. Verso, London.

Long, N., 1977. *An Introduction to the Sociology of Rural Development*. Tavistock Publications, London.

Lugan, B., 2011. *Histoire du Maroc: Des origines à nos jours*. Ellipses, Paris.

Lugan, B., 2013. *Histoire des Berbères*. Editions Bernard Lugan, Paris.

Luizard, P. J., 2009. *Comment est né l'Irak moderne*. CNRS Editions, Paris.

Lydon, G., 2009a. "A 'Paper Economy of Faith' without Faith in Paper: A Contribution to Understanding the Roots of Islamic Institutional Stagnation." *Journal of Economic Behavior and Organisation*, vol. 71, no. 3, pp. 647–59.

Lydon, G., 2009b. *On Trans-Saharan Trails: Islamic Law, Trade Networks, and Cross-Cultural Exchange in Nineteenth-Century Western Africa*. Cambridge University Press, Cambridge.

Lynch, M. (ed.), 2014. *The Arab Uprisings Explained: New Contentious Politics in the Middle East*. Columbia University Press, New York.

Lynch, M., 2016. *The New Arab Wars: Uprisings and Anarchy in the Middle East*. Public Affairs, New York.

Macfarlane, A., 1978. *The Origins of English Individualism*, Basil Blackwell, Oxford.

Macrides, R. J., 1999. "Nomos and Kanon in Paper and in Court." In *Kinship and Justice in Byzantium, 11th–15th Centuries*, Variorum Collected Studies Series. Routledge, London.

Magnus, R. H., and E. Naby, 2002. *Afghanistan: Mullah, Marx, and Mujahid*. Westview Press, Boulder, CO.

Mahjoubi, A., 1982. *Les origines du mouvement nationaliste en Tunisie 1904–1934*. Publications de l'Université de Tunis, Tunis.

Mahoney, J., and K. Thelen, 2010. "A Theory of Gradual Institutional Change." In J. Mahoney and K. Thelen (eds.), *Explaining Institutional Change: Ambiguity, Agency, and Power*, pp. 1–37. Cambridge University Press, Cambridge.

Maila, J., 1991. "Les droits de l'homme sont-ils impensables dans le monde arabe?" *Les Cahiers de l'Orient*, pp. 176–97.

Makiya, K., 1998. *Republic of Fear: The Politics of Modern Iraq*. University of California Press, Berkeley.

Makdisi, G., 1981. *The Rise of Colleges: Institutions of Learning in Islam and the West*. Edinburgh University Press, Edinburgh.

Malik, A., 2012. *Was the Middle East's Economic Descent a Legal or Political Failure? Debating the Islamic Law Matters Thesis*, CSAE Working Paper WPS/2012-08. Centre for the Study of African Economies, University of Oxford.

Malik, A., and R. A. Mirza, 2015. "Religion, Land and Politics: Shrines and Literacy in Punjab." Mimeo, Department of International Development and Oxford Centre for Islamic Studies, University of Oxford.

Mansfield, P., 2003. *A History of the Middle East*. Penguin Books, London.

Mardin, S., 1993. "The Nakshibendi Order of Turkey." In M. E. Marty and R. S. Appleby (eds.), *Fundamentalisms and the State: Remaking Polities, Economies, and Militance*, pp. 204–32. University of Chicago Press, Chicago.

Marnef, G., 2001. "The Towns and the Revolt." In G. Darby (ed.), *The Origins and Development of the Dutch Revolt*, pp. 84–106. Routledge, London.

Marsot, A. L., 2007. *A History of Egypt: From the Arab Conquest to the Present*, 2nd ed. Cambridge University Press, Cambridge.

Martin, V., 2005. *The Qajar Pact: Bargaining, Protest and the State in Nineteenth-Century Persia*. I. B. Tauris, London.

Masuma, J., 2009. *Quranic Sciences*. Islamic College for Advanced Studies Publications.

Matthew, S., 1990. *Fishing Legislation and Gear Conflicts in Asian Countries*. Samudra Publications, Brussels.

McCants, W., 2015. *The ISIS Apocalypse: The History, Strategy, and Doomsday Vision of the Islamic State*. St. Martin's Press, New York.

McDaniel, T., 1996. *The Agony of the Russian Idea*. Princeton University Press, Princeton.

McHugo, J., 2014. *Syria: From the Great War to Civil War*. Saqi Books, London.

Mecham, Q., 2014. "Islamists Movements." In M. Lynch (ed.), *The Arab Uprisings Explained: New Contentious Politics in the Middle East*, pp. 201–17. Columbia University Press, New York.

Meddeb, A., 2002. *La maladie de l'Islam*. Editions du Seuil, Paris.

Meddeb, A., 2004. "L'intégrisme, maladie de l'Islam." In I. Taboada Leonetti (ed.), *Les femmes et l'Islam: entre modernité et intégrisme*, pp. 165–79. L'Harmattan, Paris.

Meier, G., and R. Baldwin, 1957. *Economic Development: Theory, History, Policy*. John Wiley & Sons, New York.

Meredith, Martin, 2005. *The State of Africa: A History of Fifty Years of Independence*. Free Press, London.

Meyersson, E., 2014. "Islamic Rule and the Empowerment of the Poor and Pious." *Econometrica*, vol. 82, no. 1, pp. 229–69.

Milet, E., 2005. *Mali*. Olizane, Geneva.

Miller, C., 2004. "Between Myth and Reality: The Construction of a Sa'idi Identity in Cairo." In N. Hopkins and R. Saad (eds.), *Upper Egypt: Identity and Change*, pp. 25–54. American University in Cairo Press, Cairo.

Miller, David B., 2010. *Saint Sergius of Radonezh, His Trinity Monastery and the Formation of Russian Identity*. Northern Illinois University Press, DeKalb.

Miller, J., 1993. "The Challenge of Radical Islam." *Foreign Affairs*, Spring.

Minvielle, J. P., 1977. *La structure foncière du waalo fuutanké – Les terres inondables de la moyenne vallée du Sénégal, région de Matam*. Centre ORSTOM (Office de la Recherche Scientifique et Technique d'Outre-Mer), Paris.

Miran, M., 2006. *Islam, histoire et modernité en Côte d'Ivoire*. Karthala, Paris.

Mishra, P., 2012. *From the Ruins of Empire: The Revolt against the West and the Remaking of Asia*. Allen Lane, London.

Mitchell, R., 1997. "Family Law in Algeria before and after the 1404/1984 Family Code." In R. Gleave and E. Kermeli (eds.), *Islamic Law: Theory and Practice*, pp. 194–204. I. B. Tauris, London.

Mitterauer, M., and R. Sieder, 1982. *The European Family: Patriarchy to Partnership from the Middle Ages to the Present*. Basil Blackwell, Oxford.

Mohsen-Finan, K., 2002. "Tunisie: le rôle de Bourguiba sans l'abolition du beylicat." In R. Leveau and A. Hammoudi (eds.), *Monarchies arabes: transitions et dérives dynastiques*, pp. 111–19. Institut des Etudes Transrégionales, Université de Princeton, et Institut Français des Relations Internationales (IFRI), Paris.

Mokyr, J., 2002. *The Gift of Athena: Historical Origins of the Knowledge Economy*. Princeton University Press, Princeton.

Moore, R. I. (ed.), 1981. *The Hamlyn Historical Atlas*. Hamlyn, London.

Moore, R. I., 2012. *The War on Heresy*. Profile Books Ltd, London.

Morris, C., 2005. *The New Turkey: The Quiet Revolution on the Edge of Europe*. Granta Books, London.

Moscow Times, 2016. "Holy Meeting in Havana," February 11–17, p. 5.

Mottahedeh, R., 2000. *The Mantle of the Prophet: Religion and Politics in Iran*. Oneworld, Oxford.

Mujeeb, M., 1967. *The Indian Muslims*. McGill University Press, Montreal.

Murray, J. J., 1970. *Antwerp in the Age of Plantin and Brueghel*. University of Oklahoma Press, Norman.

Nahavandi, F., 1999. "L'instrumentalisation de la religion dans les pays musulmans 'convertis.'" In F. Nahavandi and P. Claeys (eds.), *Civilisations*, vol. 48 (Special Issue: La question de l'Islam et de l'Etat à l'aube du XXIe siècle), pp. 85–97.

Naipaul, V. S., 1982. *Among the Believers: An Islamic Journey*. Vintage Books, New York.

Naphy, W. G., 2007. *The Protestant Revolution: From Martin Luther to Martin Luther King Jr.* BBC Books, London.

Nasiri, O., 2006. *Inside the Jihad: My Life with Al Qaeda: A Spy's Story.* Basic Books, New York.

Nasr, V., 2007. *The Shi'a Revival.* W.W. Norton and Co., New York.

Nevo, J., 1998. "Religion and National Identity in Saudi Arabia." *Middle Eastern Studies*, vol. 34, pp. 34–53.

Nichols, S. J., 2002. *Martin Luther: A Guided Tour of his Life and Thought.* P & R Publishing, Phillipsburg, NJ.

Nielsen, R., 2012. "Adoption of Jihadi Ideology by Islamic Clerics." Department of Government, Harvard University, Cambridge, MA.

Noland, M., 2005. "Religion and Economic Performance." *World Development*, vol. 33, pp. 1215–32.

Noland, M., 2007. "Religion, Islam et croissance économique. L'apport des analyses empiriques." *Revue Française de Gestion*, vol. 171, pp. 97–118.

Noland, M., 2008. "Explaining Middle Eastern Authoritarianism." *Review of Middle East Economics and Finance*, vol. 4, no. 1, pp. 1–30.

Nomani, F., and A. Rahnema, 1994. *Islamic Economic Systems.* Zed Books, London.

North, D. C., 1990. *Institutions, Institutional Change and Economic Performance.* Cambridge University Press, Cambridge.

North, D. C., 2005. *Understanding the Process of Economic Change.* Princeton University Press, Princeton.

North, D. C., J. J. Wallis, and B. R. Weingast, 2009. *Violence and Social Orders: A Conceptual Framework for Interpreting Recorded Human History.* Cambridge University Press, Cambridge.

North, D. C., and B. R. Weingast, 1989. "Constitutions and Commitment: The Evolution of Institutions Governing Public Choice in Seventeenth-Century England." *Journal of Economic History*, vol. 44, pp. 803–32.

Norton, S. W., and A. Tomal, 2009. "Religion and Female Educational Attainment." *Journal of Money, Credit and Banking*, vol. 41, no. 5, pp. 961–86.

Ntampaka, C., 2004. *Introduction aux systèmes juridiques africains.* Presses Universitaires de Namur, Namur.

Nussbaum, M. 2007. *The Clash within Democracy: Religious Violence, and India's Future.* Belknap Press of Harvard University Press, Cambridge, MA.

Oberoi, H., 1993. "Sikh Fundamentalism: Translating History into Theory." In M. E. Marty and R. S. Appleby (eds.). *Fundamentalisms and the State: Remaking Polities, Economies, and Militance*, pp. 256–85. University of Chicago Press, Chicago.

Obolonsky, A. V., 2003. *The Drama of Russian Political History: System against Individuality.* Texas A & M University Press, Austin.

O'Daly, G., 2004. *Augustine's City of God: A Reader's Guide.* Oxford University Press, Oxford.

Osman, K., 2014. *Sectarianism in Iraq: The Making of State and Nation since 1920.* Routledge, London.

Owen, R., 2004. *State, Power and Politics in the Making of Modern Middle East*, 3rd ed. Routledge, New York.

Owen, R., 2012. *The Rise and Fall of Arab Presidents for Life.* Harvard University Press, Cambridge, MA.

Özek, C., 1962. *Türkiye'de Laiklik: Gelisim ve Koruyucu Ceza Hükümleri*. I.Ü. Hukuk Fakültesi, Istanbul.

Padro i Miquel, G., 2007. "The Control of Politicians in Divided Societies: The Politics of Fear." *Review of Economic Studies*, vol. 74, no. 4, pp. 1259–74.

Pamuk, S., 2012. "Political Power and Institutional Change: Lessons from the Middle East." *Economic History of Developing Regions*, vol. 27 (suppl. 1), pp. S41–S46.

Pargeter, A., 2008. *The New Frontiers of Jihad: Radical Islam in Europe*. University of Pennsylvania Press, Philadelphia.

Parkin, D. J., 1972. *Palm, Wine and Witnesses*. Intertext Books, London.

Paul, T. V., 2014. *The Warrior State: Pakistan in the Contemporary World*. Oxford University Press, Oxford.

Peebles, P., 1990. "Colonization and Ethnic Conflict in the Dry Zone of Sri Lanka." *Journal of Asian Studies*, vol. 49, no. 1, pp. 30–55.

Pennington, D. H., 1970. *Europe in the Seventeenth Century*. Pearson Education, Longman, Harlow, Essex.

Perkins, K. J., 2004. *A History of Modern Tunisia*. Cambridge University Press, Cambridge.

Pettegree, A., 2001. "Religion and the Revolt." In G. Darby (ed.), *The Origins and Development of the Dutch Revolt*, pp. 67–83. Routledge, London.

Pettegree, A., 2010. *The Book in the Renaissance*. Yale University Press, New Haven.

Pincus, S., 2009. *1688: The First Modern Revolution*. Yale University Press, New Haven.

Pipes, R., 1995. *Russia under the Old Regime*. Penguin Books, London.

Piquard, B., 1999. "Mobilisation politique et mouvements politico-religieux au Pakistan." In F. Nahavandi and P. Claeys (eds.), *Civilisations* (Special Issue: *La question de l'Islam et de l'état à l'aube du XXIe siècle*), vol. 48 pp. 69–83.

Platteau, J. P., 2000. *Institutions, Social Norms, and Economic Development*. Routledge, London.

Platteau, J. P., 2006. "Solidarity Norms and Institutions in Village Societies: Static and Dynamic Considerations." In S. C. Kolm and J. Mercier Ythier (eds.), *Handbook of the Economics of Giving, Altruism and Reciprocity*, vol. 1, pp. 819–86. North-Holland, Amsterdam.

Platteau, J. P., 2008, "Religion, Politics, and Development: Lessons from the Lands of Islam." *Journal of Economic Behavior and Organization*, vol. 68, no. 2, pp. 329–51.

Platteau, J. P., 2009. "Institutional Obstacles to African Economic Development: State, Ethnicity, and Custom." *Journal of Economic Behavior and Organization*, vol. 71, no. 3, pp. 669–89.

Platteau, J. P., 2011. "Political Instrumentalization of Islam and the Risk of Obscurantist Deadlock." *World Development*, vol. 39, no. 2, pp. 243–60.

Platteau, J. P., 2014. "Redistributive Pressures in Sub-Saharan Africa: Causes, Consequences, and Coping Strategies." In E. Akyeampong, R. Bates, N. Nunn, and J. Robinson (eds.), *African Development in Historical Perspective*, pp. 153–207. Cambridge University Press, Cambridge.

Platteau, J. P., and J. M. Baland, 2001. "Impartible Inheritance versus Equal Division: A Comparative Perspective Centered on Europe and Sun-Saharan Africa." In A. de Janvry, G. Gordillo, J. P. Platteau, and E. Sadoulet (eds.), *Access to Land, Rural Poverty, and Public Action*, pp. 27–67. Oxford University Press, Oxford.

Platteau, J. P., and Z. Wahhaj, 2013. "Interactions between Modern Law and Custom." In V. Ginsburgh and D. Throsby (eds.), *Handbook of the Economics of Art and Culture*, vol. 2, pp. 633–78. Elsevier and North-Holland, New York.

Plokhy, S., 2006. *The Origins of the Slavic Nations: Premodern Identities in Russia, Ukraine, and Belarus*. Cambridge University Press, Cambridge.

Poewe, K., 1989. *Religion, Kinship, and Economy in Luapula, Zambia*. Edwin Mellen Press, Lewinston.

Polk, W. R., 2005. *Understanding Iraq*. Harper Perennial, New York.

Posner, D. N., 2006. *Institutions and Ethnic Politics in Africa*. Cambridge University Press, Cambridge.

Potrafke, N., 2012. "Islam and Democracy." *Public Choice*, vol. 151, nos. 1–2, pp. 185–92.

Pryor, F., 2006. *The Economic Impact of Islam on Developing Nations*, Working Paper. Swarthmore College, Swarthmore, PA.

Przeworski, A., M. E. Alvarez, J. A. Cheibub, and F. Limongi, 2000. *Democracy and Development: Political Institutions and Well-Being in the World, 1950–1990*. Cambridge University Press, Cambridge.

Quisumbling, A., E. Payongayong, J. Aidoo, and K. Otsuka, 2001. "Women's Land Rights in the Transition to Individualized Ownership: Implications for the Management of Tree Resources in Western Ghana." *Economic Development and Cultural Change*, vol. 50, no. 1, pp. 157–82.

Radwan, S., V. Jamil, and A. Ghose, 1990. *Tunisia: Rural Labor and Structural Transformation*. Routledge, London.

Raeff, M., 1984. *Understanding Imperial Russia*. Columbia University Press, New York.

Raghavan, S., 2014. *Buddhist Monks and the Politics of Lanka's Civil War: Ethnoreligious Nationalism of the Sinhala Sangha and Peacemaking in Sri Lanka, 1995–2010*. Oxford Centre for Buddhist Studies Monographs, Oxford.

Rahman, F., 1979. *Islam*, 2nd ed., University of Chicago Press, Chicago.

Rahman, F., 1982. *Islam and Modernity: Transformation of an Intellectual Tradition*. University of Chicago Press, Chicago.

Rahman, T., 1997. "Interest-free Banking in Pakistan: An Appraisal." *Journal of Islamic Banking and Finance*, vol. 12, no. 4, pp. 6–10.

Rahnema, A., and F. Nomani, 1990. *The Secular Miracle: Religion, Politics and Economic Policy in Iran*. Zed Books, London.

Ramadan, A. A., 1993. "Fundamentalist Influence in Egypt: The Strategies of the Muslim Brotherhood and the Takfir Groups." In M. E. Marty and R. S. Appleby (eds.), *Fundamentalisms and the State: Remaking Polities, Economies, and Militance*, pp. 152–83. University of Chicago Press, Chicago.

Ramirez, A., 2006. "Other Feminisms? Muslim Associations and Women's Participation in Morocco." *Etnografica*, vol. 10, no. 1, pp. 107–19.

Rasanayagam, A., 2005. *Afghanistan: A Modern History*. I. B. Tauris, London.

Rashid, A., 2008. *Descent into Chaos: The United States and the Failure of Nation Building in Pakistan, Afghanistan, and Central Asia*. Viking, New York.

Reid, A., 1993. *Southeast Asia in the Age of Commerce 1450–1680*. Yale University Press, New Haven.

Resnick, J., 1999. "Particularistic vs. Universalistic Content in the Israeli Educational System." *Curriculum Inquiry*, vol. 29, no. 4.

Riasanovsky, N. V., 1993. *A History of Russia*, 5th ed. Oxford University Press, New York.

Robertson, H. M., 1933. *Aspects of the Rise of Economic Individualism: A Criticism of Max Weber and His School*. Cambridge University Press, Cambridge.

Robinson, D., 2004. *Muslim Societies in African History*. Cambridge University Press, Cambridge.

Robinson, F., 1996. *The Cambridge Illustrated History of the Islamic World*. Cambridge University Press, Cambridge.

Robinson, J. A., R. Torvik, and T. Verdier, 2006. "The Political Foundations of the Resource Curse." *Journal of Development Economics*, vol. 79, pp. 447–68.

Robinson, J. A., R. Torvik, and T. Verdier, 2014. "The Political Foundations of the Resource Curse: A Simplification and a Comment." *Journal of Development Economics*, vol. 106, pp. 194–98.

Rodinson, M., 1966. *Islam et capitalisme*. Editions du Seuil, Paris (English translation: *Islam and Capitalism*, Saqi Essentials, London, 2007).

Rosen, L., 1995. "Law and Custom in the Popular Legal Culture of North Africa." *Islamic Law and Society*, vol. 2, no. 2, pp. 194–208.

Rowley, C. K., and N. Smith, 2009. "Islam's Democracy Paradox: Muslims Claim to Like Democracy, So Why Do They Have So Little?" *Public Choice*, vol. 139, nos. 3–4, pp. 273–99.

Roy, O., 1990. "De l'Islam révolutionnaire au néo-fondamentalisme." *Esprit*, July-August.

Roy, O., 1993. "Afghanistan: An Islamic War of Resistance." In M. E. Marty and R. S. Appleby (eds.), *Fundamentalisms and the State: Remaking Polities, Economies, and Militance*, pp. 491–510. University of Chicago Press, Chicago.

Roy, O., 2004. *Globalized Islam: The Search for a New Ummah*. Columbia University Press, New York.

Roy, O., 2008. *La Sainte Ignorance: le temps de la religion sans cuture*. Editions du Seuil, Paris.

Rubin, J., 2011. "Institutions, the Rise of Commerce and the Persistence of Laws: Interest Restrictions in Islam and Christianity." *Economic Journal*, vol. 121, pp. 1310–39.

Ruthven, M., 1997. *Islam: A Very Short Introduction*. Oxford University Press, Oxford.

Safadi, R., L. Munro, and R. Ziadeh, 2011. "Syria: The Underpinnings of Autocracy – Conflict, Oil and the Curtailment of Economic Freedom." In I. Elbadawi and S. Makdisi (eds.), *Democracy in the Arab World – Explaining the Deficit*, pp. 142–64. Routledge, London.

Sageman, M., 2004. *Understanding Terror Networks*. University of Pennsylvania Press, Philadelphia.

Sageman, M., 2008. *Leaderless Jihad: Terrorist Networks in the Twenty-First Century*. University of Pennsylvania Press, Philadelphia.

Saint-Prot, C., 2008. *Islam: l'avenir de la tradition entre révolution et occidentalisation*. Editions du Rocher, Paris.

Sala-i-Martin, X., G. Doppelhofer, and R. I. Miller, 2004. "Determinants of Long-Run Growth: A Bayesian Averaging of Classical Estimates (BACE) Approach." *American Economic Review*, vol. 94, pp. 813–35.

Saleh, M., 2015. *On the Roads to Heaven: Self-Selection, Religion, and Socioeconomic Status*, Working Paper, Toulouse School of Economics.

Salem, N., 1984. *Habib Bourguiba, Islam and the Creation of Tunisia*. Croom Helm, London.

Sall, I. A., 2000. "La diffusion de la Tijâniyya au Fuuta Tooro." In J. -L. Triaul and D. Robinson (eds.), *La Tijâniyya – Une confrérie musulmane à la conquête de l'Afrique*, pp. 367–92. Karthala, Paris.

Samuelsson, K., 1961. *Religion and Economic Action*. Basic Books, New York.

Sardar, Z., 2014. *Mecca: The Sacred City*. Bloomsbury, London.

Sarkar, J., 1912. *A History of Aurangzeb*, vol. 1. M. C. Sarkar & Sons, Calcutta.

Sarro, R., 2009. *The Politics of Religious Change on the Upper Guinea Coast: Iconoclasm Done and Undone*. Edinburgh University Press, Edinburgh.

Sayeed, K. bin, 1984. "Pakistan in 1983: Internal Stresses More Serious than External Problems." *Asian Survey*, vol. 24, no. 2.

Sayyid, B., 1997. *A Fundamental Fear: Ethnocentrism and the Emergence of Islamism*. Zed Books, London.

Schiffbauer, M., A. Sy, S. Hussain, H. Sahnoun, and P. Keefer, 2015. *Jobs or Privileges: Unleashing the Employment Potential of the Middle East and North Africa*. MENA Development Report, World Bank, Washington, DC.

Schmemann, A., 2003. *The Historical Road of Eastern Orthodoxy*, St. Vladimir's Seminary Press, Crestwood, NY.

Schumpeter, J., 1954. *History of Economic Analysis*. Oxford University Press, New York.

Seccombe, W., 1992. *A Millenium of Family Change: Feudalism to Capitalism in Northwestern Europe*. Verso, London.

Seddik, Y., 2007. *L'arrivant du soir: cet Islam de lumière qui peine à devenir*. Editions de l'Aube, La Tour d'Aigues.

Seligman, A. B., 1997. *The Problem of Trust*. Princeton University Press, Princeton.

Sekeris, P. G., 2011. "Endogenous Elites: Power Structure and Patron-Client Relationships." *Economics of Governance*, vol. 12, pp. 237–58.

Shari'ati, A., 1986. *What Is to Be Done: The Enlightened Thinkers and an Islamic Renaissance*. IRIS, Houston.

Shaw, S. J., 1976. *History of the Ottoman Empire and Modern Turkey, Vol. 1: Empire of the Gazis: The Rise and Decline of the Ottoman Empire 1280–1808*. Cambridge University Press, Cambridge.

Shillington, K., 1989. *History of Africa*. St. Martin's Press, New York.

Sid-Ahmed, M., 1994. "Cybernetic Colonialism and the Moral Search." *New Perspectives Quarterly*, vol. 11, Spring, p. 19.

Siddiqa, A., 2017. *Military Inc. Inside Pakistan's Military Economy*. 2nd ed. Pluto Press, London.

Simms, B., 2013. *Europe: The Struggle for Supremacy, 1453 to the Present*. Allen Lane, London.

Skinner, Q., 1978. *The Foundations of Modern Political Thought*, 2 vols. Cambridge University Press, Cambridge.

Smith, R. M., 1981. "Fertility, Economy, and Household Formation in England over Three Centuries." *Population and Development Review*, vol. 7, no. 4, pp. 595–622.

Smith, R. M., 1990. "Monogamy, Landed Property and Demographic Regimes in Pre-Industrial Europe." In J. Landers and V. Reynolds (eds.), *Fertility and Resources*, Cambridge University Press, Cambridge.

Soares, B. F., 2005. *Islam and the Prayer Economy: History and Authority in a Malian Town*. Edinburgh University Press, Edinburgh.

Spencer, N., 2016. *The Evolution of the West: How Christianity Has Shaped our Values*. Society for Promoting Christian Knowledge (SPCK), London.

Springborg, R., 2014. "Arab Militaries." In M. Lynch (ed.), *The Arab Uprisings Explained: New Contentious Politics in the Middle East*, pp. 142–59. Columbia University Press, New York.

Stark, R., 2003. *For the Glory of God: How Monotheism Led to Reformations, Science, Witch-Hunts, and the End of Slavery*. Princeton University Press, Princeton.

Stark, R., 2005. *The Victory of Reason: How Christianity Led to Freedom, Capitalism and Western Success*. Random House, New York.

Stark, R., L. Iannaccone, and R. Finke, 1996. "Religion, Science and Rationality." *American Economic Review*, vol. 86, no. 2, pp. 433–37.

Stone, L., 1979. *The Family, Sex and Marriage in England 1500–1800*. Penguin Books, London.

Stora, B., 2004. *Histoire de l'Algérie coloniale (1830–1954)*. La découverte, Paris.

Storm, M., T. Lister, and P. Cruikshank, 2014. *Agent Storm: My Life inside Al-Qaeda*. Penguin Books, Harmondsworth.

Sutherland, N. M., 1973. *The Massacre of St Bartholomew and the European Conflict, 1559–1572*, London, Barnes & Noble.

Svolik, M. W., 2009. "Power Sharing and Leadership Dynamics in Authoritarian Regimes." *American Journal of Political Science*, vol. 53, no. 2, pp. 477–94.

Synnott, H., 2009. *Transforming Pakistan: Ways out of Instability*. International Institute for Strategic Studies (IISS). Routledge, London.

Szirmai, A., 2005. *The Dynamics of Socioeconomic Development: An Introduction*. Cambridge University Press, Cambridge.

Tambiah, S. J., 1993. "Buddhism, Politics, and Violence in Sri Lanka." In M. E. Marty and R. S. Appleby (eds.), *Fundamentalisms and the State: Remaking Polities, Economies, and Militance*, pp. 589–619. University of Chicago Press, Chicago.

Tamzali, W., 2007. *Une education algérienne: de la révolution à la décennie noire*. Gallimard, Paris.

Tarabishi, G., 2013. *Min Islam al Quran ela Islam al Haddeth* (From Islam of Quran to Islam of Hadith), Dar al Saqi.

Tawney, R. H., 1926. *Religion and the Rise of Capitalism: A Historical Study*, reprinted at Penguin Books, London (1987).

Tessler, M., 2002. "Islam and Democracy in the Middle East." *Comparative Politics*, vol. 34, no. 3, pp. 337–54.

Tessler, M., and M. Robbins, 2014. "Political System Preferences of Arab Publics." In M. Lynch (ed.), *The Arab Uprisings Explained: New Contentious Politics in the Middle East*, pp. 249–72. Columbia University Press, New York.

Tezcan, B., 2010. *The Second Ottoman Empire: Political and Social Transformation in the Early Modern World*. Cambridge University Press, Cambridge.

Tilly, C. 1992 *Coercion, Capital, and European States*. Blackwell, Oxford.

Todd, E., 1990. *L'invention de l'Europe*. Editions du Seuil, Paris.

Toumi, M., 1989. *La Tunisie de Bourguiba à Ben Ali*. Presses Universitaires de France, Paris.

Toynbee, A., 1972. *A Study of History: The One-Volume Edition Illustrated*. Thames and Hudson, London.

Tozy, M., 1999. *Monarchie et Islam Politique au Maroc*. Presses de Sciences Po, Paris.

Tracy, J. D., 1990. *Holland under Habsburg Rule, 1506–1566: The Formation of a Body Politic.* University of California Press, Berkeley.

Tripp, C., 2000. *A History of Iraq.* Cambridge University Press, Cambridge.

Tripp, C., 2006. *Islam and the Moral Economy: The Challenge of Capitalism.* Cambridge University Press, Cambridge.

Türkmen, B., 2009. "A Transformed Kemalist Islam or a New Islamic Civic Morality?" *Comparative Studies of South Asia, Africa, and the Middle East,* vol. 29, no. 3, pp. 381–97.

Vallance, E., 2007. *The Glorious Revolution, 1688: Britain's Fight for Liberty.* Abacus, London.

van Nierop, H., 2001a. "Alva's Throne: Making Sense of the Revolt of the Netherlands." In G. Darby (ed.), *The Origins and Development of the Dutch Revolt,* pp. 29–47. Routledge, London.

van Nierop, H., 2001b. "The Nobles and the Revolt." In G. Darby (ed.), *The Origins and Development of the Dutch Revolt,* pp. 48–66. Routledge, London.

van Zanden, J. L. (ed.), 2009. *The Long Road to the Industrial Revolution: The European Economy in a Global Perspective, 1000–1800.* Brill, Leiden.

van Zanden, J. L., and M. Prak, 2009. "State Formation and Citizenship: The Dutch Republic between Medieval Communes and Modern Nation States." In J. L. van Zanden (ed.), *The Long Road to the Industrial Revolution: The European Economy in a Global Perspective, 1000–1800,* pp. 205–32. Brill, Leiden.

Vickers, A., 2005. *A History of Modern Indonesia.* Cambridge University Press, Cambridge.

Villalon, L. A., 2000. "The Moustarchidine of Senegal: The Family Politics of a Contemporary Tijan Movement." In J. -L. Triaud and D. Robinson (eds.), *La Tijâniyya: Une confrérie musulmane à la conquête de l'Afrique,* pp. 469–97. Karthala, Paris.

Voigtländer, N., and H. J. Voth, 2013. "How the West 'Invented' Fertility Restriction." *American Economic Review,* vol. 103, no. 6, pp. 2227–64.

Wade, R., 1990. "Employment, Water Control and Water Supply Institutions: India and South Korea." In W. Gooneratne and S. Hirashima (eds.), *Irrigation and Water Management in Asia.* Sterling Publishers, New Delhi.

Walicki, A., 1975. *The Slavophile Controversy: History of a Conservative Utopia in Nineteenth-Century Russian Thought.* Clarendon Press, Oxford.

Walicki, A., 1979. *A History of Russian Thought fom the Enlightenment to Marxism.* Stanford University Press, Stanford.

Walker, P. C. G., 1937. "Capitalism and the Reformation." *Economic History Review,* November.

Ward, R. E., and D. A. Rustow, 1964. *Political Modernization in Japan and Turkey.* Princeton University Press, Princeton.

Weber, E., 1976. *Peasants into Frenchmen: The Modernization of Rural France, 1870–1914.* Stanford University Press, Stanford.

Weber, M., 1930. *The Protestant Ethic and Spirit of Capitalism.* Charles Scribner's Sons, New York (German original, 1904–5).

White, J., 2013. *Muslim Nationalism and the New Turks.* Princeton University Press, Princeton.

White, S. D., 1988. *Custom, Kinship, and Gifts to Saints: The Laudatio Parentum in Western France, 1050–1150.* University of North Carolina Press, Chapel Hill.

Wickham, C. R., 1996. "Islamic Mobilisation and Political Change: The Islamist Trend in Egypt's Professional Associations." In J. Beinin and J. Storck (eds.), *Political Islam: Essays from the Middle East Report*, pp. 120–36. University of California Press, Berkeley.

Wickham, C. R., 2002. *Mobilizing Islam: Religion, Activism and Social Change in Egypt.* Columbia University Press, New York.

Winslow, D., and M. D. Woost, 2004. "Articulations of Economy and Ethnic Conflict in Sri Lanka." In D. Winslow and M. D. Woost (eds.), *Economy, Culture, and Civil War in Sri Lanka*, pp. 1–27. Indiana University Press, Bloomington.

Woodberry, R. D., 2012. "The Missionary Roots of Liberal Democracy." *American Political Science Review*, vol. 106, no. 2, pp. 244–74.

Woods, T., 2005. *How the Catholic Church Built Western Civilisation.* Regner Publishing, Washington, DC.

World Bank, 2003. *Better Governance for Development in the Middle East and North Africa: Enhancing Inclusiveness and Accountability*, MENA Development Report. World Bank, Washington, DC.

World Bank, 2008. *The Road Not Traveled: Education Reform in the Middle East and North Africa*, MENA Development Report. World Bank, Washington, DC.

Yapp, M. E., 1987. *The Making of the Modern Near East, 1792–1923.* Longman, Harlow, Essex.

Yavuz, M. H., 2000. "Turkey's Fault Lines and the Crisis of Kemalism." *Current History*, vol. 99, no. 633, pp. 33–8.

Yavuz, M. H., 2003. *Islamic Political Identity in Turkey.* Oxford University Press, Oxford.

Yavuz, M. H. (ed.), 2006. *The Emergence of a New Turkey: Democracy and the AK Party.* University of Utah Press, Salt Lake City.

Yavuz, M. H., 2009. *Secularism and Muslim Democracy in Turkey,* Cambridge University Press, Cambridge.

Yavuz, M. H., 2013. *Toward an Islamic Enlightenment: The Gülen Movement.* Oxford University Press, Oxford.

Yazbek, S., 2015. *The Crossing: My Journey to the Shattered Heart of Syria.* Rider, London.

Yeğenoğlu, M., 2012. *Islam, Migrancy and Hospitality in Europe.* Palgrave, London.

Yousfi, H., 2011. "Culture and Development: The Continuing Tension between Modern Standards and Local Contexts." In J. P. Platteau and R. Peccoud (eds.), *Culture, Institutions, and Development: New Insights into an Old Debate*, pp. 20–84. Routledge, London.

Yousif, B., and E. Davis, 2011. "Iraq: Understanding Autocracy: Oil and Conflict in a Historical and Socio-Political Context." In I. Elbadawi and S. Makdisi (eds.), *Democracy in the Arab World - Explaining the Deficit*, pp. 227–53. Routledge, London.

Yumul, A., 2010. "Fashioning the Turkish Body Politic." In C. Kerslake, K. Öktem, and P. Robins (eds.), *Turkey's Engagement with Modernity*, pp. 349–69. Palgrave Macmillan, Basingstoke.

Zahid, M., 2010. *The Muslim Brotherhood and Egypt's Succession Crisis: The Politics of Liberalisation and Reform in the Middle East.* I. B. Tauris, London.

Zakaria, F., 2003. *The Future of Freedom.* W. W. Norton & Co., New York.

Zaman, M. Q., 1998. "Sectarianism in Pakistan: The Radicalization of Shi'i and Sunni Identities." *Modern Asian Studies*, vol. 32, no. 3, pp. 689–716.

Zaman, M. Q., 2007. "Tradition and Authority in Deobandi Madrasas of South Asia." In R. W. Hefner and M. Q. Zaman (eds.), *Schooling in Islam: The Culture and Politics of Modern Muslim Education*, pp. 61–86. Princeton University Press, Princeton.

Zeghal, M., 2002. "S'éloigner, se rapprocher: la gestion et le contrôle de l'Islam dans la république de Bourguiba et la monarchie de Hassan II." In R. Leveau and A. Hammoudi (eds.), *Monarchies arabes: transitions et dérives dynastiques*, pp. 59–80. Institut des Etudes Transrégionales, Université de Princeton, et Institut Français des Relations Internationales (IFRI), Paris.

Ziadeh, R., 2013. *Power and Policy in Syria*. I. B. Tauris, London.

Ziring, L., 1988, "Public Policy Dilemmas and Pakistan's Nationality Problem: The Legacy of Zia ul-Haq." *Asian Survey*, vol. 28, no. 8.

Zisenwine, D., 2015. *The History of an Authoritarian Regime, 1987–2011*. I. B. Tauris, London.

Zubeida, S., 2011. *Beyond Islam: A New Understanding of the Middle East*. I. B. Tauris, London.

Zürcher, E., 2004. *Turkey: A Modern History*, 2nd ed. I. B. Tauris, London.

Zürcher, E., 2010. *The Young Turk Legacy and Nation Building: From the Ottoman Empire to Atatürk's Turkey*. I. B. Tauris, London.

Zweig, S., 1935. *Erasme: Grandeur et décadence d'une idée*. Bernard Grasset, Paris.

Zweig, S., 1976. *Conscience against Violence: Castellion against Calvin*. Atrium Press, London.

Weekly Magazines

Economist, 2006, February 11–17; November 19–25.

Economist, 2006, March 4–10, "Sunnis and Shi'as," p. 39.

Economist, 2007, "In the Name of God," Special Report, November 3, p. 17.

Economist, 2008, April 26–May 2, "Our Women Must Be Protected," pp. 52–3.

Economist, 2008, July 19–25, "Flags, Veils and Sharia," pp. 29–32.

Economist, 2008, September 13–19, "Will the Dam Burst?" pp. 31–3.

Economist, 2008, December 20–26, "Of Saints and Sinners."

Economist, 2009, April 4–10, "Beyond the Crossroads," pp. 22–4.

Economist, 2009, September 12–18, "Strife in Yemen – The World's Next Failed State?" pp. 47–8.

Economist, 2012, March 3–9, "Out of the Comfort Zone," pp. 55–6.

Economist, 2013, August 3–9, "Ambitious Men in Uniform," pp. 29–30.

Economist, 2013, November 23–29, "Huda-Par's Emergence," p. 31.

Economist, 2014, April 5–11, "Myanmar's Course Is Leading in the Wrong Direction," p. 52.

Economist, 2014, May 17–23, "Women in Saudi Arabia – Unshackling Themselves," pp. 31–3.

Economist, 2014, June 7–13, "Show Who's Boss," pp. 37–8.

Economist, 2014, July 5–11, "Tethered by History," pp. 21–3.

Economist, 2014, July 26–August 1, "Mixing the Modern and the Traditional," p. 30.

Economist, 2014, August 2–8, "Manipulating the Minarets," p. 28.

Economist, 2014, September 13–19, "The Next War against Global Jihadism," pp. 38–40.

Economist, 2014–2015, December 20–January 2, "The Uses of History: How Did a Failed Treaty between Medieval Combatants Come to Be Seen as the Foundation of Liberty in the Anglo-Saxon World?" pp. 46–7.

Economist, 2015, January 3–9, "Forward to the Past," p. 22.

Economist, 2015, January 3–9, "Tunisia's New President: Don't Be Ageist," p. 32.

Economist, 2015, January 17–23, "A Struggle that Shames," p. 22.

Economist, 2015, January 31–February 5, "Keeping It in the Family," pp. 26–7.

Economist, 2015, August 8–14, "A Bigger, Better Suez Canal," p. 25.

Economist, 2015, November 7–13, "Bangladesh: Fear in the Shadows," p. 50.

Economist, 2015, August 8–14, "Religion in Indonesia: With God on Whose Side?" p. 39.

Economist, 2015, November 28–December 4, "Sikhism in India: Seeking Justice," p. 48.

Economist, 2016, February 6–12, "Algeria: Who Is In Charge?" p. 31.

Economist, 2016, March 5–11, "Malaysia's Scandals: The Art of Survival," pp. 43–4.

Economist, 2016, March 12–18, "Women in Saudi Arabia: One Step Forward, One Step Backward," pp. 30–1.

Economist, 2016, March 26–April 1, "Apostasy and Islam," p. 35.

Economist, 2016, April 2–8, "The Politics of Thai Buddhism," p. 47.

Economist, 2016, April 16–22, "Iraq's Politics: Abadi Agonises," p. 26; "Religion and Politics in Pakistan – Bad Moon Rising," p. 40.

Economist, 2016, July 16–22, "Past and Future Trumps," pp. 17–19.

Economist, 2016, August 6–12 (a), "Arab Youth –Looking Forward in Anger", pp. 15–18.

Economist, 2016, August 6–12 (b), "Sultanic Verses: Media Freedom in Turkey," pp. 19–20.

Economist, 2016, August 6–12 (c), "Old Faultlines: Turks in Germany," p. 20.

Economist, 2016, August 20–26, "African Democracy: The March of Democracy Slows," pp. 26–8.

Economist, 2016, August 27–September 2, "Al-Malarkey: Turkey's Anger at the West," pp. 17–18.

Economist, 2016, October 29–November 4, "India's Muslims: An Uncertain Community," pp. 44–5.

Economist, 2016, November 5–11, "Goodbye Republic," pp. 23–4.

Economist, 2017, January 7–13, "Iraq's Long War", pp. 27–8.

Economist, 2017, January 28-February 3, "The Race for Governor in Jakarta", p. 43.

Le Monde, April 18, 2015, "L'art russe face au péril patriote," Section Cultures et Idées, p. 3.

Le Monde, April 26–27, 2015, "Haji Bakr, le cerveau de la terreur, " pp. 9–11.

Voice of America, Burma, August 10, 2012. "Sectarian Violence Not about Race or Religion."

Index

Margaret of Parma, 59
marja, 168, 172, 178, 184, 238
marja-e taqlid, 168
Marnef, G., 36, 43, 44, 47, 53, 54, 67, 484
Maronite militias, 253
Marri tribe, 212
marriage, 67–71, 74, 106, 108–10, 135, 238,
    277, 279, 307, 308, 311, 354, 367, 383, 401,
    410, 416–18, 423, 457, 458, 459, 460
  adolescent, 307
  age at first, 308
  age of, 239
  forced, 238
  late, 71, 75
Marsot, A. L., 92, 116, 121, 123, 158, 160, 161,
    187, 189, 194, 196, 289, 293, 313, 484
Martin, H.-J., 34
Martin, V., 34, 61, 166, 467, 474, 484, 485, 490
Marx, Karl, 90, 349
Marxism, 12, 252, 337, 344, 352, 400, 403, 444
Marxists, 192, 349
Mary of Burgundy, 53
Mary Stuart, 57
Marzouki, Moncef, 393, 399, 400
Masalit people, 209
mashaikh, 222
Masina, 124
maslahat, 137
Massassi people, 124
Masud, 405
Masuma, J., 350, 484
Matsusaka, J. G., 461, 481
Matthew, S., 484
Mauritania, 179
  Southern, 179
Mauritz of Nassau, 54
Mavbima Surakime Vyaparaya (MSV), 342
Mawdûdi, Maulana, ix, 210, 211, 266, 283, 284,
    285, 450, 451
Mazalim court, 129
Mazari, 405
Mazar-i-Sharif, 406
McCants, W., 249, 484
McCleary, R. M., 24, 467
McDaniel, T., 296, 484
McHugo, J., 235, 252, 253, 254, 256, 305, 484
Mecca, 88, 116, 117, 118, 120, 121–4, 139, 142,
    232, 236, 252, 266–70, 271, 277, 278, 289,
    350, 392, 432
Meccan
  aristocracy, 118

establishment, 117
  merchants, 117
Meccans, 117
Mecham, Q., 398, 399, 484
Meddeb, A., 119, 121, 181, 268, 284, 285, 288,
    485
Medina, 86, 116–18, 120, 122, 123, 142, 201,
    266, 267, 269, 350, 432
Medinan tribes, 123
Medinese, 117
Mehmed I, 177
Mehmed II, 120
Mehmed IV, 273
Mehmed Ali Pasha, 161
Meier, G., 38, 485
Meiji
  Japan, 315
  movement, 374
  Restoration, 21
Menderes, Adnan, 365, 366
Mercier Ythier, J., 487
Meredith, M., 206, 208, 485
meshverret, 126, 149
Mesopotomia, 239, 240
Mestiri, Ahmad, 391
Meyersson, E., 307, 485
Miceli, T., 13, 130, 186, 433, 434, 471
Middle Ages, 51, 72, 433, 458, 460, 461, 462
Middle East crisis, 320
Milante, G., 26
Milet, E., 123, 124, 485
Mill, J. S., 1
Miller, R. I., 24, 90, 485, 489
millet system, 411
Minangkabau, 106, 107, 278
Ministry of Education of Iraq, 242
Ministry of Endowments of Iraq, 242
Ministry of Interior of Iraq, 247
Ministry of Religion of Indonesia, 421
Ministry of Religious Affairs and Pious
    Foundations, 360
Ministry of Religious Affairs of Algeria, 224,
    226
Ministry of Religious Affairs of Sudan, 212
Minvielle, J. P., 485
Miran, M., 305, 306, 485
Mirza Hosain Khan, 169
Mirza Hussein Shirazi, 170
Mirza, R. A., 211, 456, 484
Mishra, P., 485
Mitchell, R., 485